Longman
COMPLETE COURSE
FOR THE TOEFL® TEST

Preparation for the Computer and Paper Tests

Deborah Phillips

 LONGMAN

Longman Complete Course for the TOEFL® Test:
Preparation for the Computer and Paper Tests

Pearson Education, 10 Bank Street, White Plains, N.Y. 10606

Vice president, director of publishing: Allen Ascher
Editorial director: Louisa Hellegers
Development editor: Angela Castro
Vice president, director of design and production: Rhea Banker
Associate director of electronic production: Aliza Greenblatt
Executive managing editor: Linda Moser
Project editor: Helen B. Ambrosio
Production manager: Alana Zdinak
Production supervisor: Liza Pleva
Director of manufacturing: Patrice Fraccio
Senior manufacturing manager: Edie Pullman
Text design adaptation: Page Designs International, Inc.
Composition: Page Designs International, Inc.
Text art: Jill C. Wood
Text photography: Hutchings Photography; additional photographs: bat on page 19
    ©*Bettmann/CORBIS,* Three-Mile Island on page 20 ©*Leif Skoogfors/CORBIS,* Lewis and
    Clark statue on page 159 ©*CORBIS,* Liliuokalani on page 181 ©*CORBIS,* James Cook on
    page 181 ©*CORBIS.*

Library of Congress Cataloging-in-Publication Data

Phillips, Deborah
        Longman complete course for the TOEFL test: preparation for the
        computer and paper tests / Deborah Phillips.
            p.   cm.
        Includes bibliographical references and index.
        ISBN 0-13-040895-6 (with Answer Key)
        ISBN 0-13-040902-2 (without Answer Key)
        1. English language—Textbooks for foreign speakers.   2. Test of
English as a foreign lauguage—Study guides.   3. English language—
Examinations—Study guides.   I. Title: Complete course for the TOEFL
test   II. Title.

PE1128.P435 2000
428'.0076—dc21
                                                    00-063242

7 8 9 10—CRS—05   04

CONTENTS

THE WRITTEN EXPRESSION QUESTIONS
(Paper and Computer)

Problems with Subject/Verb Agreement

Problems with Parallel Structure

SECTION FOUR: WRITING

INTRODUCTION

ABOUT THIS BOOK

PURPOSE OF THE BOOK

This book is intended to prepare students for the TOEFL® (Test of English as a Foreign Language) test in both its *paper* and *computer* formats. It is based on the paper format first introduced in July 1995 and the computer format first introduced in July 1998.

Longman Complete Course for the TOEFL® Test: Preparation for the Computer and Paper Tests can be used in a variety of ways, depending on the needs of the reader:

- It can be used as the *primary classroom text* in a course emphasizing TOEFL test preparation.
- It can be used as a *supplementary text* in a more general English language course.
- It can be used as a tool for *individualized study* by students preparing for the TOEFL test outside of the ESL classroom.

WHAT IS IN THE BOOK

This book contains a variety of materials which together provide a comprehensive preparation program:

- **Diagnostic Pre-Tests** for each section, in both paper and computer formats, measure students' level of performance on each section of the TOEFL test and allow students to determine specific areas of weakness.
- **Skills and Strategies** for each of the sections of the TOEFL test provide students with clearly defined steps to improve performance on the test.
- **Exercises** provide practice of one or more skills in a non-TOEFL format.
- **TOEFL Exercises** provide practice of one or more skills in a TOEFL format.
- **TOEFL Review Exercises** provide practice of all of the skills taught up to that point in a TOEFL format.
- **TOEFL Post-Tests** for each section, in both paper and computer formats, measure the progress that students have made after working through the skills and strategies in the text.
- **Complete Tests**, in both paper and computer formats, allow the students to simulate the experience of taking actual TOEFL tests with all of the sections together in one complete test.
- **Scoring Information** allows students to determine their approximate TOEFL scores on the paper version of the Pre-Tests, Post-Tests, and Complete Practice Tests.
- **Charts** allow students to record their progress on the Pre-Tests, Post-Tests, and Complete Practice Tests.
- **Recording Scripts** allow the students to see the text of all the listening exercises and tests included on the audio cassettes/CDs.

WHAT IS ON THE STUDENT CD-ROM

The Student CD-ROM, with 1,475 TOEFL-format questions and 200 additional writing practice questions, includes a variety of materials that contribute to an effective preparation program for the computer TOEFL test:

- **A Tutorial** demonstrates how to answer each type of question found on the computer TOEFL test.
- **Practice Questions** for each of the sections on the computer TOEFL test provide students with the opportunity to master each of the language skills and types of questions on the test.
- **Test Sections** for each section of the computer TOEFL test allow students to simulate the actual testing conditions of the computer TOEFL test and to measure their progress. Writing tests can be printed for feedback and review.
- **Explanations** for all test items allow students to understand their errors and learn from their mistakes.
- **Diagnostic Information** relates the test items on the CD-ROM to the language skills presented in this text.
- **Scoring and Record-Keeping** enable students to record and print out charts that monitor their progress on all the practice and test exercises.
- **Screens, Buttons, and Clicking Sequences** similar to those on the computer TOEFL test provide students with practice that simulates the actual computer TOEFL test.

WHAT IS NEW IN THE COMPLETE COURSE

Longman Complete Course for the TOEFL Test has been written to include both the computer format and the paper format of the TOEFL test.

- **Diagnostic Pre-Tests** are included in both paper and computer formats.
- **The Listening Section** includes a presentation of the Listening section of the computer TOEFL test with its new types of passages and questions, plus the presentation of the Listening Comprehension section of the paper TOEFL test. For each of the new types of listening passages on the computer test (Casual Conversations, Academic Discussions, Academic Lectures), a description, language skills, question types, practice exercises, and TOEFL exercises are presented.
- **The Structure Section** includes a presentation of the Structure section of the computer TOEFL test in addition to the presentation of the Structure and Written Expression section of the paper TOEFL test.
- **The Reading Section** includes a presentation of the Reading section of the computer TOEFL test, in addition to the presentation of the Reading Comprehension section of the paper TOEFL test. The new types of questions used to test some of the language skills on the computer TOEFL test have been included, along with the presentation of a language skill on Inserting Information.
- **The Writing Section** includes an expanded writing skills section in addition to sample essays, writing strategies, and scoring information.
- **Post-Tests** are included in both paper and computer formats.
- **Complete Tests** in both paper and computer formats are also included.

OTHER AVAILABLE MATERIALS

Additional materials are available to supplement the materials included in the text:

- **Longman Complete Course for the TOEFL® Test: — Audio Cassettes /CDs** contain recordings of the listening comprehension exercises and tests in the text.

- **Longman Complete Course for the TOEFL® Test — User's Guide** includes an answer key with answers to all questions and a recording script with a transcription of all listening comprehension exercises and tests included on the audio cassette tapes or CDs accompanying the text.
- **Longman Preparation Course for the TOEFL® Test: Volume A — Skills and Strategies, Second Edition** provides comprehensive coverage of the language skills and test-taking strategies for the paper-format TOEFL test, including sample exercises, procedures, pre-tests, post-tests, a complete practice test, scoring information, and charts to record progress.
- **Longman Preparation Course for the TOEFL® Test: Volume A — Audio Cassettes, Second Edition** contain recordings of the listening comprehension exercises and tests in this text.
- **Longman Preparation Course for the TOEFL® Test: Volume A — User's Guide, Second Edition** includes an answer key with answers to all questions, a recording script with a transcription of all listening comprehension exercises and tests included on the audio cassette tapes or CDs accompanying the text, and teaching tips for each section of the test.
- **Longman Preparation Course for the TOEFL® Test: Volume B — Practice Tests, Second Edition** contains five paper-format TOEFL tests, tapescripts, answer keys, scoring information, and a chart to record progress.
- **Longman Preparation Course for the TOEFL® Test: Volume B — Audio Cassettes, Second Edition** contain recordings of the listening comprehension sections of the tests in Volume B.
- **Longman Preparation Course for the TOEFL® Test: CBT Volume** contains examples and practice for each of the types of passages and questions that appear on the computer version of the TOEFL test, a description of the test-taking strategies for the computer test, an expanded writing skills section, and computer-format test sections.
- **Longman Preparation Course for the TOEFL® Test: CBT Volume Audio Cassettes/CDs** contain the recordings of all the listening comprehension exercises and tests in the CBT Volume.
- **Longman Preparation Course for the TOEFL® Test: Bonus Test Disk** contains an additional test-bank of 860 questions not found on the Student CD-ROM, which can be used by schools to give contolled tests.
- **Longman Introductory Course for the TOEFL® Test, Second Edition** presents language skills and test-taking strategies for both the paper and the computer versions of the test, at a low-intermediate or intermediate level. This text starts below the level of the TOEFL test and continues up to the level of the easier questions on the test. It includes strategies and skills that are appropriate for students at this level. It also includes diagnostic pre-tests, post-tests, and complete practice tests in both paper and computer formats.
- **Longman Introductory Course for the TOEFL® Test: Audio Cassettes/CDs, Second Edition** contain recordings of the listening comprehension exercises and tests in the Introductory Course.
- **Longman Introductory Course for the TOEFL® Test: User's Guide, Second Edition** includes a recording script with a transcription of all listening comprehension exercises and tests included on the recordings accompanying the text, and an answer key with answers to all the questions in the text.

ABOUT THE TOEFL® TEST

OVERVIEW OF THE TEST

The TOEFL test is a test to measure the level of English proficiency of nonnative speakers of English. It is required primarily by English-language colleges and universities. Additionally, institutions such as government agencies, businesses, or scholarship programs may require this test. The TOEFL test currently exists in both a paper format and a computer format.

THE PAPER VERSION

The paper version of the TOEFL test has the following sections:

- **Listening Comprehension:** To demonstrate their ability to understand spoken English, examinees must listen to various types of passages on a tape recording and respond to multiple choice questions about the passages.
- **Structure and Written Expression:** To demonstrate their ability to recognize grammatically correct English, examinees must either choose the correct way to complete sentences or find errors in sentences.
- **Reading Comprehension:** To demonstrate their ability to understand written English, examinees must answer multiple choice questions about the ideas and the meanings of words in reading passages.
- **Test of Written English (TWE):** To demonstrate their ability to produce correct, organized, and meaningful English, examinees must write an essay on a given topic in thirty minutes. The Test of Written English (TWE) is not given with every administration of the paper TOEFL test.

The following chart outlines the probable format of a paper TOEFL test. (It should be noted that on certain occasions a longer version of the paper TOEFL test is given.)

Listening Comprehension	50 questions	35 minutes
Structure and Written Expression	40 questions	25 minutes
Reading Comprehension	50 questions	55 minutes
Test of Written English (TWE)	1 essay question	30 minutes

THE COMPUTER VERSION

The computer version of the TOEFL test has the following sections:

- **Listening:** To demonstrate their ability to understand spoken English, examinees must first listen to passages on headphones as they see pictures on a computer screen and then answer various types of questions about the passages that they just heard.
- **Structure:** To demonstrate their ability to recognize grammatically correct English, examinees must look at sentences on a computer screen and either choose the correct way to complete the sentences or identify errors in the sentences.
- **Reading:** To demonstrate their ability to understand written English, examinees must read passages on a computer screen and answer various types of questions about the ideas and meanings of words in the passages.
- **Writing:** To demonstrate their ability to produce meaningful, organized, and correct English, examinees must write an essay on a given topic in thirty minutes, either on the computer or by hand.

The following chart outlines the probable format of a computer TOEFL test:

Listening	30–50 questions	40–60 minutes
Structure	20–25 questions	15–20 minutes
Reading	44–60 questions	70–90 minutes
Writing	1 essay question	30 minutes

WHAT YOUR TOEFL® SCORE MEANS

The paper TOEFL test is scored on a scale of 217 to 677 points, while the computer TOEFL test is scored on a scale of 0 to 300 points. There is no passing score on the TOEFL test, but various institutions have their own TOEFL score requirements. You must find out from each institution what TOEFL score is required. The following chart shows how the scores on the computer TOEFL test and the paper TOEFL test are related:

PAPER TOEFL TEST	COMPUTER TOEFL TEST
677	300
650	280
600	250
550	213
500	173
450	133
400	97
350	63
300	40

When you take the paper TOEFL Pre-Tests, Post-Tests, and Complete Test in this book, it is possible for you to estimate your TOEFL score. A description of how to estimate your score on the paper TOEFL test has been provided at the back of this book on pages 601–603.

Writing is scored on a scale of 1 to 6 on both the paper TOEFL test and the computer TOEFL test. However, the score of the writing test is handled differently on the paper test and on the computer test. On the paper test, the writing is not included in the overall TOEFL score. On the computer test, the writing score is included in the overall TOEFL score.

WHERE TO GET ADDITIONAL INFORMATION

Additional information is available in the TOEFL® Information Bulletin. This bulletin can be ordered free of charge by sending a request to the following address:

TOEFL Services
Educational Testing Service
P.O. Box 6151
Princeton, NJ 08541-6151 USA

Information about the TOEFL test can also be obtained at the TOEFL® website at http://www.toefl.org.

TO THE STUDENT

HOW TO PREPARE FOR THE TOEFL® TEST

The TOEFL test is a standardized test of English. To do well on this test, you should therefore work in these areas to improve your score:

- You must work on improving your knowledge of the *English language skills* that are covered on the TOEFL test.
- You must understand the *test-taking strategies* specific to the version of the TOEFL test that you are taking.
- You must take *practice tests* with a focus on applying the appropriate language skills and test-taking strategies.
- You must work on *computer skills* if you are taking the computer version of the TOEFL test.

This book can familiarize you with English language skills and test-taking strategies, provide some practice of each of the versions of the test, and introduce the computer skills you will need for the computer version of the test. Additional practice for the paper test is provided in Volume B, while additional practice of the computer version of the test and the computer skills needed for this version are included in the CBT Volume and on the Student CD-ROM.

HOW TO USE THIS BOOK

This book provides a variety of materials to help you to prepare for the TOEFL test. Following these steps can help you to get the most out of this book:

- Determine which version of the TOEFL test (paper or computer) you will be taking.
- Take the appropriate Diagnostic Pre-Test at the beginning of a section. When you take the Pre-Test, try to reproduce the conditions and time pressure of a real TOEFL test: (1) Take each section of the test without interruption. (2) Work on only one section at a time. (3) Time yourself for the section to experience the time pressure that exists on the actual TOEFL test. (4) Play the listening material one time only during the test.
- After you finish a paper-format Pre-Test, you can determine your TOEFL score for that section using the table on pages 601–602. Then record the results on the chart on page 603. After you finish a computer-format Pre-Test, record the number correct on the chart on page 603.
- Complete the Diagnostic Exercise at the end of the Pre-Test. Note which skills cause you the most trouble.
- Work through the explanations and exercises for each section. Pay particular attention to the skills you had problems with in the Pre-Test.
- Each time you complete a TOEFL-format exercise, try to simulate the conditions and time pressure of a real TOEFL test. (1) For listening questions, play the listening material one time only. (2) For structure questions, allow yourself one minute for two questions. For example, you should take five minutes for an exercise with ten questions. (3) For reading passages, allow yourself one minute for one question. For example, if a reading passage has ten questions, you should allow yourself ten minutes to read the passage and answer the ten questions.
- When further practice on a specific point is included in an Appendix, a note in the text directs you to this practice. Complete those Appendix exercises on a specific point when the text directs you to these exercises and it is an area that you need to improve.
- For additional practice of the language skills in Volume A, work through the *Practice* exercises for each section on the Student CD-ROM.

- When you have completed all the skills exercises for a section, take the appropriate Post-Test (paper or computer) for that section. For the paper-format Post-Tests, determine your TOEFL score using the table on pages 601–602 and record your results on the chart on page 603. For the computer-format Post-Tests, record the number correct on the chart on page 603.
- When you have completed the Post-Tests for each of the sections, take the appropriate Complete Test (paper or computer). For the paper-format test, determine your TOEFL score using the table on pages 601–602 and record your results on the chart on page 603. For the computer-format test, record the number correct on the chart on page 603.
- For additional test-taking practice, see Volume B for paper-format tests and the Student CD-ROM *Test* section for computer-format tests.

TO THE TEACHER

HOW TO GET THE MOST OUT OF THE EXERCISES

The exercises are a vital part of the TOEFL preparation process presented in this text. Maximum benefit can be obtained from the exercises if the students are properly prepared for the exercises and if the exercises are carefully reviewed after completion:

- Be sure that the students have a clear idea of the appropriate skills and strategies involved in each exercise. Before beginning each exercise, review the skills and strategies that are used in that exercise. Then when you review the exercises, reinforce the skills and strategies that can be used to determine the correct answers.
- As you review the exercises, be sure to discuss each answer, the incorrect answers as well as the correct answers. Discuss how students can determine that each correct answer is correct and each incorrect answer is incorrect.
- Two different methods are possible to review the listening exercises. One good way to review these exercises is to play back the listening material, pausing after each question to discuss the skills and strategies involved in determining which answer is correct and which answers are incorrect. Another method is to have the students refer to the recording script to discuss each question.
- The structure exercises in the correct/incorrect format present a challenge for the teacher. In exercises in which the students are asked to indicate which sentences are correct and which are incorrect, it is extremely helpful for the students to correct the incorrect sentences. An indication of the type of error and/or one possible correction for each incorrect sentence is included in the User's Guide. It should be noted, however, that many of the incorrect sentences can be corrected in several ways. The role of the teacher is to assist the students in finding the various ways that the sentences can be corrected.
- The exercises are designed to be completed in class rather than assigned as homework. The exercises are short and take very little time to complete, particularly since it is important to keep the students under time pressure while they are working on the exercises. Considerably more time should be spent in reviewing the exercises than in actually doing them.

HOW TO GET THE MOST OUT OF THE PRE-TESTS, POST-TESTS, AND COMPLETE TESTS

It is essential for the Pre-Tests, Post-Tests, and Complete Tests to be taken under conditions as similar as possible to actual TOEFL conditions. You should give each section of the test without interruption and under the time pressure of the actual test.

After you have given a Pre-Test, Post-Test, or Complete Test, it is important to review the test thoroughly. The various types of tests serve different functions, so a review of these types of tests should have different emphases. While reviewing the Pre-Tests, you should encourage students to determine in which areas they are weak and need more practice. While reviewing the Post-Tests, you should emphasize the skills and strategies involved in determining the correct answer to each question. While reviewing the Complete Tests, you should emphasize overall strategies for the complete test and, of course, take this one final opportunity to review the variety of individual skills and strategies taught throughout the course.

HOW TO INCORPORATE ADDITIONAL PRACTICE INTO THE COURSE

For the most effective preparation for the TOEFL test, additional practice can be incorporated throughout a course with the **Longman Complete Course for the TOEFL Test** as its main text. This additional practice can take the form of practice of specific skills or of complete test sections or tests. The Longman TOEFL series provides ample opportunities for various types of TOEFL practice:

- Five additional paper-format tests are available in Volume B. These tests can be given periodically throughout a course that is focused on the paper version of the TOEFL test. The additional tests can be given either as complete tests or as individual test sections in listening, structure, and reading.
- Additional practice of each of the types of passages and questions on the computer version of the test are found in the CBT Volume. The exercises in the CBT Volume can be used with the entire class or can be assigned to individual students who require additional work on the passages and questions-types on the computer test (i.e., additional practice on Academic Discussions in listening, or additional practice on Insertion questions in reading).
- Considerable practice of each of the skills presented in **Longman Complete Course for the TOEFL Test** is provided in the *Practice* section of the Student CD-ROM. The practice exercises on the CD-ROM can be assigned periodically throughout a course that uses **Longman Complete Course for the TOEFL Test** as its primary text (i.e., after teaching Structure Skills 1-5 in the text, the practice exercises for Structure Skills 1-5 on the CD-ROM can be assigned.) Using the *Check Score* and *Print* functions found with the Student CD-ROM practice exercises, you can assign the Practice exercises for out-of-class assignments and have the students print out the report that shows that a particular exercise was completed, which language skills were involved, and which questions were answered correctly.
- Practice with computer-format tests is available in the *Test* section of the Student CD-ROM. The tests in this portion of the CD-ROM can be taken either as individual test sections or as complete tests. After students have taken listening, structure, or reading sections, they can use the *Check Score* and *Print* functions to produce charts showing how many questions were answered, which language skills were involved, and which questions were answered correctly and incorrectly; after they have taken a writing section, they can print out their essays for feedback and review using the *Print* function. Tests should be scheduled periodically throughout a course that is focused on the computer version of the test, either during classroom time in the school computer lab or as individual out-of-class assignments for students.
- Further practice with computer-format tests is available on the Bonus Test Disk, which contains an additional test bank of 860 questions that are found only on the disk. The additional test bank of questions on the Bonus Test Disk provides schools with a set of computer TOEFL test questions which students have not seen on the Student CD-ROM and which can therefore be used for controlled tests.

HOW TO USE THE STUDENT CD-ROM

The Student CD-ROM contains *practice exercises, section tests,* and *complete tests* for the students to complete. The results of these exercises and tests are recorded within the computer program, or they may be printed out to hand in or to be kept in a notebook.

The *practice exercises* can be assigned throughout the course <u>after</u> the related sections in the book have been completed.

CD-ROM PRACTICE EXERCISES	ASSIGN **AFTER** BOOK SECTIONS	NUMBER OF QUESTIONS
LISTENING PRACTICE		
Short Dialogues		
• *Skills 1–3*	Listening *Skills 1–3*	10 questions
• *Skills 4–6*	Listening *Skills 4–6*	10 questions
• *Skills 7–10*	Listening *Skills 7–10*	10 questions
• *Skills 11–13*	Listening *Skills 11–13*	10 questions
• *Skills 14–15*	Listening *Skills 14–15*	10 questions
• *Skills 16–17*	Listening *Skills 16–17*	10 questions
Casual Conversations		
• *Conversations 1*	Listening *Skill 28*	8 questions
• *Conversations 2*	Listening *Skill 28*	8 questions
• *Conversations 3*	Listening *Skill 28*	8 questions
• *Conversations 4*	Listening *Skill 28*	8 questions
• *Conversations 5*	Listening *Skill 28*	8 questions
Academic Discussions		
• *Discussion 1*	Listening *Skills 29–31*	5 questions
• *Discussion 2*	Listening *Skills 29–31*	5 questions
• *Discussion 3*	Listening *Skills 29–31*	5 questions
• *Discussion 4*	Listening *Skills 29–31*	6 questions
Academic Lectures		
• *Lecture 1*	Listening *Skills 32–34*	5 questions
• *Lecture 2*	Listening *Skills 32–34*	5 questions
• *Lecture 3*	Listening *Skills 32–34*	6 questions
• *Lecture 4*	Listening *Skills 32–34*	6 questions
• *Lecture 5*	Listening *Skills 32–34*	6 questions
STRUCTURE PRACTICE		
Structure		
• *Skills 1–5*	Structure *Skills 1–5*	20 questions
• *Skills 6–8*	Structure *Skills 6–8*	20 questions
• *Skills 9–12*	Structure *Skills 9–12*	20 questions
• *Skills 13–14*	Structure *Skills 13–14*	20 questions
• *Skills 15–19*	Structure *Skills 15–19*	20 questions
Written Expression		
• *Skills 20–23*	Structure *Skills 20–23*	20 questions
• *Skills 24–26*	Structure *Skills 24–26*	20 questions
• *Skills 27–29*	Structure *Skills 27–29*	20 questions
• *Skills 30–32*	Structure *Skills 30–32*	20 questions
• *Skills 33–36*	Structure *Skills 33–36*	20 questions
• *Skills 37–38*	Structure *Skills 37–38*	20 questions
• *Skills 39–42*	Structure *Skills 39–42*	20 questions
• *Skills 43–45*	Structure *Skills 43–45*	20 questions
• *Skills 46–48*	Structure *Skills 46–48*	20 questions
• *Skills 49–51*	Structure *Skills 49–51*	20 questions
• *Skills 52–55*	Structure *Skills 52–55*	20 questions
• *Skills 56–57*	Structure *Skills 56–57*	20 questions
• *Skills 58–60*	Structure *Skills 58–60*	20 questions

CD-ROM PRACTICE EXERCISES	ASSIGN **AFTER** BOOK SECTIONS	NUMBER OF QUESTIONS
READING PRACTICE		
Easy Passages		
• *Passage 1*	Reading *Skills 1–5*	11 questions
• *Passage 2*	Reading *Skills 1–5*	11 questions
• *Passage 3*	Reading *Skills 1–5*	12 questions
Medium Passages		
• *Passage 1*	Reading *Skills 1–11*	12 questions
• *Passage 2*	Reading *Skills 1–11*	11 questions
• *Passage 3*	Reading *Skills 1–11*	11 questions
Difficult Passages		
• *Passage 1*	Reading *Skills 1–14*	11 questions
• *Passage 2*	Reading *Skills 1–14*	12 questions
• *Passage 3*	Reading *Skills 1–14*	11 questions
WRITING PRACTICE		
Before and While Writing		
• *Before and While Writing 1*	Writing *Skills 1–6*	25 questions
• *Before and While Writing 2*	Writing *Skills 1–6*	25 questions
• *Before and While Writing 3*	Writing *Skills 1–6*	25 questions
After Writing		
• *Editing Sentence Structure*	Writing *Skill 7*	20 questions
• *Inversions and Agreement*	Writing *Skill 8A*	20 questions
• *Parallel, Comparative and Superlative Structures*	Writing *Skill 8B*	20 questions
• *Verbs*	Writing *Skill 8C*	20 questions
• *Nouns and Pronouns*	Writing *Skill 8D*	20 questions
• *Adjectives and Adverbs*	Writing *Skill 8E*	20 questions
• *Prepositions and Usage*	Writing *Skill 8F*	20 questions

The *section tests* and *complete tests* can be assigned periodically throughout the course. They can be used as diagnostic pre-tests before material is introduced in the book, they can be used midway through the course to assess progress, or they can be used as post-tests at the end of the course.

CD-ROM TESTS	ASSIGN THROUGHOUT THE COURSE	NUMBER OF QUESTIONS
INDIVIDUAL SECTION TESTS		
Listening Test		
• *Listening Test One*	As a beginning pre-test	30 questions
• *Listening Test Two*	As a midway progress test	30 questions
• *Listening Test Three*	As an ending post-test	50 questions
Structure Test		
• *(tests in adaptive base)*	Throughout the course	200 questions
Reading Test		
• *Reading Test One*	As a beginning pre-test	44 questions
• *Reading Test Two*	As a midway progress test	44 questions
• *Reading Test Three*	As an ending post-test	60 questions
Writing Test		
• *(questions in a base)*	Throughout the course	18 questions
COMPLETE TESTS		
• *Complete TOEFL Test One*	As a midway progress test	100 questions*
• *Complete TOEFL Test Two*	As an ending post-test	130 questions*

*The Complete Test Structure questions come from a separate adaptive base of 200 questions.

SECTION ONE

LISTENING

LISTENING DIAGNOSTIC PRE-TEST
(Paper) 📖

SECTION 1
LISTENING COMPREHENSION
Time—approximately 35 minutes
(including the reading of the directions for each part)

In this section of the test, you will have an opportunity to demonstrate your ability to understand conversations and talks in English. There are three parts to this section. Answer all the questions on the basis of what is <u>stated</u> or <u>implied</u> by the speakers you hear. Do <u>not</u> take notes or write in your test book at any time. Do not turn the pages until you are told to do so.

Part A

<u>Directions:</u> In Part A you will hear short conversations between two people. After each conversation, you will hear a question about the conversation. The conversations and questions will not be repeated. After you hear a question, read the four possible answers in your test book and choose the best answer. Then on your answer sheet, find the number of the question and fill in the space that corresponds to the letter of the answer you have chosen.

Listen to an example.

On the recording, you hear:

Sample Answer
Ⓐ Ⓑ Ⓒ ●

(man)	*That exam was just awful.*
(woman)	*Oh, it could have been worse.*
(narrator)	*What does the woman mean?*

In your test book, you read:
- (A) The exam was really awful.
- (B) It was the worst exam she had ever seen.
- (C) It couldn't have been more difficult.
- (D) It wasn't that hard.

You learn from the conversation that the man thought the exam was very difficult and that the woman disagreed with the man. The best answer to the question, "What does the woman mean?" is (D), "It wasn't that hard." Therefore, the correct choice is (D).

Wait

1. (A) The coffee is much better this morning.
   (B) The coffee tastes extremely good.
   (C) The coffee isn't very good.
   (D) This morning he definitely wants some coffee.

2. (A) The two classes meet in an hour and a half.
   (B) The class meets three hours per week.
   (C) Each half of the class is an hour long.
   (D) Two times a week the class meets for an hour.

3. (A) A few minutes ago, the flight departed.
   (B) The fight will start in a while.
   (C) They are frightened about the departure.
   (D) The plane is going to take off soon.

4. (A) He hasn't yet begun his project.
   (B) He's supposed to do his science project next week.
   (C) He needs to start working on changing the due date.
   (D) He's been working steadily on his science project.

5. (A) At the post office
   (B) In a florist shop
   (C) In a restaurant
   (D) In a hospital delivery room

6. (A) The professor drowned the cells in a lab.
   (B) The lecture was long and boring.
   (C) The professor divided the lecture into parts.
   (D) The biologist tried to sell the results of the experiment.

7. (A) She needs to get a driver's license.
   (B) Two pieces of identification are necessary.
   (C) The man should check to see if he needs credit.
   (D) A credit card can be used to get a driver's license.

8. (A) Housing within his budget is hard to locate.
   (B) It's hard to find his house in New York.
   (C) He can't afford to move his house to New York.
   (D) Housing in New York is unavailable.

9. (A) The boss was working on the reports.
   (B) He would have to finish the reports before the end of next month.
   (C) He was directed to stay late and finish some work.
   (D) He could finish the reports at home.

10. (A) The boisterous students made the teacher mad.
    (B) The teacher angered the students with the exam results.
    (C) The students were angry that the teacher was around.
    (D) The angered students complained to the teacher.

11. (A) The prices are reasonable.
    (B) The store is too far out of town.
    (C) He would like the woman to repeat what she said.
    (D) He agrees with the woman.

12. (A) It's rained unusually hard this year.
    (B) There hasn't been any rain for many years.
    (C) It's been many years since it rained.
    (D) He doesn't like rain.

13. (A) He needs to do a better job writing questions.
    (B) He certainly must make his writing better.
    (C) Without the questions, he cannot write the answers.
    (D) He needs to understand the written questions better.

GO ON TO THE NEXT PAGE

14. (A) The agent was standing in line with his passport.
    (B) The line to get new passports is very long.
    (C) The woman must wait her turn to get her passport checked.
    (D) He can check her passport instead of the agent.

15. (A) He couldn't finish closing the library book.
    (B) He hadn't finished the library assignment, but he was close.
    (C) He was working on the assignment when the library closed.
    (D) His homework was incomplete because the library wasn't open.

16. (A) All the lawyer's preparation did no good.
    (B) The lawyer prepared nothing for the case.
    (C) It wasn't work for the lawyer to prepare for the case.
    (D) The lawyer didn't work to prepare for the case.

17. (A) The history class begins next week.
    (B) He thinks the papers should be turned in next week.
    (C) He has already done the paper for next week.
    (D) The papers are not due next week.

18. (A) He's not really happy.
    (B) The contractor's work was satisfactory.
    (C) He would rather work with the contractor himself.
    (D) He was already contacted about the work.

19. (A) The man should try another type of paper.
    (B) The man should locate a typist tomorrow morning.
    (C) The man should make a tape in the morning.
    (D) The man should complete the paper without help.

20. (A) She'd like some pie.
    (B) It's easy to buy it.
    (C) The task the man's working on isn't difficult.
    (D) It's easier to prepare pie than do what the man is doing.

21. (A) He reported that the time for the budget meeting had been set.
    (B) He is always late in submitting his accounting figures.
    (C) He never manages to budget his time well.
    (D) He is never too late in turning in his reports.

22. (A) The repairs that the mechanic had indicated were already made.
    (B) The car is going to need a lot of repairs.
    (C) Buying a new car would be quite expensive.
    (D) The mechanic extended the repair warranty.

23. (A) Betty wrote the letter as directed.
    (B) The directions were given to Betty in a letter.
    (C) Betty will follow the instructions later.
    (D) Betty worked exactly as instructed.

24. (A) Walter had a lack of success with his business.
    (B) Walter failed in business.
    (C) Walter's new company is doing rather well.
    (D) Walter hoped to succeed in business.

25. (A) He should put the organ in the closet.
    (B) The closet has already been organized.
    (C) He needs to rearrange the closet.
    (D) He wishes the closet were closer.

26. (A) She didn't do the work.
    (B) She gave the assignment her best effort.
    (C) She finished the assignment even though it was difficult.
    (D) She gave the man a signal.

GO ON TO THE NEXT PAGE

27. (A) She said some terrible things.
    (B) She didn't say anything nice.
    (C) She didn't have any nice things.
    (D) She said really wonderful things.

28. (A) New employees are rarely initiated into the company.
    (B) New workers don't generally undertake actions on their own.
    (C) New employees are initially rated.
    (D) It's rare for employees to make new suggestions.

29. (A) The woman is more than a week late.
    (B) The children would have wrecked the house later.
    (C) The woman was so late that she was a wreck.
    (D) He's glad that she was not any later.

30. (A) He had not gone to the store.
    (B) He was still at the market.
    (C) He was going to take care of the shopping.
    (D) He always went to the market.

GO ON TO THE NEXT PAGE

Part B

Directions: In this part of the test, you will hear longer conversations. After each conversation, you will hear several questions. The conversations and questions will not be repeated.

After you hear a question, read the four possible answers in your test book and choose the best answer. Then, on your answer sheet, find the number of the question and fill in the space that corresponds to the letter of the answer you have chosen.

Remember, you are <u>not</u> allowed to take notes or write in your test book.

31. (A) She's a senior.
    (B) She's a junior.
    (C) She's a transfer student.
    (D) She's a graduate student.

32. (A) How to transfer to a junior college
    (B) How to find his way around campus
    (C) What courses are required for a
        literature major
    (D) Who won the campus election

33. (A) Three
    (B) Five
    (C) Eight
    (D) Ten

34. (A) American literature
    (B) World literature
    (C) Literary analysis
    (D) Surveying

35. (A) In a book
    (B) From a television program
    (C) During a trip that she took
    (D) From a lecture

36. (A) To communicate with other dolphins
    (B) To recognize objects in the water
    (C) To learn human language
    (D) To express fear

37. (A) Five
    (B) Fifteen
    (C) Fifty
    (D) Five hundred

38. (A) It is limited.
    (B) It is greater than human intelligence.
    (C) It is less than previously thought.
    (D) We are beginning to learn how much
        they have.

GO ON TO THE NEXT PAGE

Part C

Directions: In this part of the test, you will hear several talks. After each talk, you will hear some questions. The talks and questions will not be repeated.

After you hear a question, read the four possible answers in your test book and choose the best answer. Then, on your answer sheet, find the number of the question and fill in the space that corresponds to the letter of the answer you have chosen.

Here is an example.

On the recording, you hear:

(narrator)   *Listen to an instructor talk to his class about painting.*
(man)   *Artist Grant Wood was a guiding force in the school of painting known as American regionalist, a style reflecting the distinctive characteristics of art from rural areas of the United States. Wood began drawing animals on the family farm at the age of three, and when he was thirty-eight one of his paintings received a remarkable amount of public notice and acclaim. This painting, called "American Gothic," is a starkly simple depiction of a serious couple staring directly out at the viewer.*

Now listen to a sample question.   **Sample Answer**

(narrator)   *What style of painting is known as American regionalist?*

In your test book, you read: (A) Art from America's inner cities
                                (B) Art from the central region of the
                                     United States
                                (C) Art from various urban areas in the
                                     United States
                                (D) Art from rural sections of America

The best answer to the question, "What style of painting is known as American regionalist?" is (D), "Art from rural sections of America." Therefore, the correct choice is (D).

Now listen to another sample question.   **Sample Answer**

(narrator)   *What is the name of Wood's most successful painting?*

In your test book, you read: (A) "American Regionalist"
                                (B) "The Family Farm in Iowa"
                                (C) "American Gothic"
                                (D) "A Serious Couple"

The best answer to the question, "What is the name of Wood's most successful painting?" is (C), "American Gothic." Therefore, the correct choice is (C).

Remember, you are <u>not</u> allowed to take notes or write in your test book.

1 □ 1 □ 1 □ 1 □ 1 □ 1 □ 1 □ 1

39. (A) To protect its members
    (B) To save the natural environment
    (C) To honor the memory of John Muir
    (D) To improve San Francisco's natural beauty

40. (A) For less than a year
    (B) Only for a decade
    (C) For more than a century
    (D) For at least two centuries

41. (A) San Francisco
    (B) All fifty states
    (C) The Sierra Nevadas
    (D) The eastern United States

42. (A) All over the world
    (B) In the entire United States
    (C) Only in California
    (D) Only in the Sierra Nevadas

43. (A) Students signing up for athletic teams
    (B) Students going on a tour of a university campus
    (C) Students playing various sports
    (D) Students attending a university dedication ceremony

44. (A) Membership on an athletic team
    (B) Enrollment in an exercise class
    (C) A valid student identification card
    (D) Permission from a faculty member

45. (A) To the tennis courts
    (B) To the arena
    (C) To the gymnasium
    (D) To the Athletic Department office

46. (A) Go to the Art Center
    (B) Sign up for sports classes
    (C) Visit the exercise room
    (D) Watch a football game

47. (A) Science
    (B) Art
    (C) Literature
    (D) Music

48. (A) They are completely different.
    (B) They are somewhat similar but have an essential difference.
    (C) They are exactly the same in all respects.
    (D) They are unrelated.

49. (A) Objective
    (B) Idealistic
    (C) Philosophical
    (D) Environmental

50. (A) Heredity
    (B) Environment
    (C) Idealism
    (D) Natural laws

This is the end of the Listening Diagnostic Pre-Test.

Circle the number of each of the questions that you answered incorrectly or were not sure of in Part A. Then, you will see which skills you should be sure to review.

1. SKILLS 2 and 3
2. SKILL 2
3. SKILLS 2 and 3
4. SKILL 2
5. SKILL 4
6. SKILLS 2 and 3
7. SKILL 2
8. SKILLS 2 and 3
9. SKILL 6
10. SKILLS 2 and 5

11. SKILL 11
12. SKILL 7
13. SKILL 2
14. SKILL 6
15. SKILLS 2 and 7
16. SKILL 2
17. SKILL 12
18. SKILL 7
19. SKILL 12
20. SKILL 17

21. SKILLS 7 and 16
22. SKILLS 2 and 3
23. SKILLS 2 and 17
24. SKILL 8
25. SKILLS 2, 3, and 14
26. SKILL 16
27. SKILL 10
28. SKILLS 3 and 9
29. SKILL 15
30. SKILL 13

LISTENING DIAGNOSTIC PRE-TEST
(Computer) 🖥️

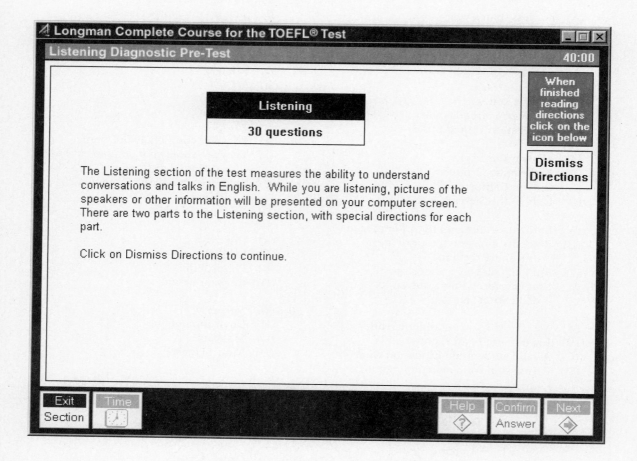

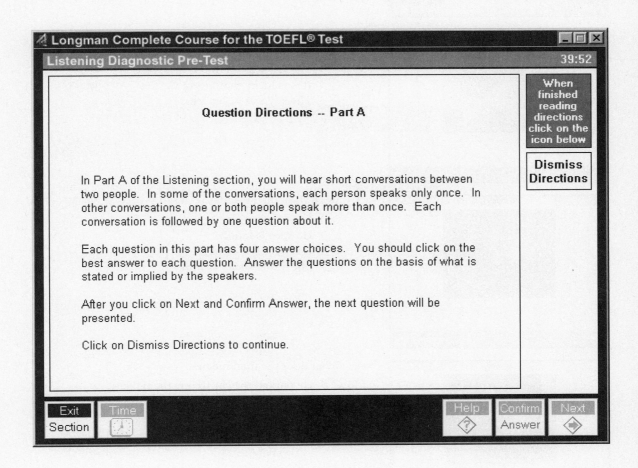

1. What does the woman mean?
   - ◯ She is too scared to try it.
   - ◯ She would like another opportunity.
   - ◯ Her time is very scarce.
   - ◯ She has gone skiing for the last time.

2. What does the man mean?
   - ◯ He was given the wrong key.
   - ◯ The key was on top of the clock.
   - ◯ It was lucky that he got the key.
   - ◯ The key was at his feet.

3. What does the woman say about Professor Nash?
   - ◯ She can see him very clearly.
   - ◯ He speaks loudly.
   - ◯ He's very soft-spoken.
   - ◯ She didn't speak to him.

4. What does the man mean?
   - ◯ He parked the car to buy the tickets.
   - ◯ He left the car where he shouldn't have.
   - ◯ He got a speeding ticket.
   - ◯ He didn't park the car.

5. What does the man say about Sally?
   - ◯ She prepared him for what he was going to do.
   - ◯ She was unprepared for what she had to do.
   - ◯ She probably didn't spend much time on her presentation.
   - ◯ She was really ready for her presentation.

6. What does the woman mean?
   - ⟨ ⟩ The tuition increase was unexpected.
   - ⟨ ⟩ She was prepared for the tuition increase.
   - ⟨ ⟩ She doesn't believe that fees were increased.
   - ⟨ ⟩ She believes that tuition will not go up.

7. What does the man mean?
   - ⟨ ⟩ He'd like the woman to repeat herself.
   - ⟨ ⟩ The woman should talk to a physician.
   - ⟨ ⟩ He shares the woman's opinion.
   - ⟨ ⟩ What the woman said was unimportant.

8. What does the woman say about the employees?
   - ⟨ ⟩ Some of them are lying down.
   - ⟨ ⟩ Some of them will lose their positions.
   - ⟨ ⟩ Some of them are choosing part-time jobs.
   - ⟨ ⟩ Some of them laid their newspapers down.

9. What did the woman believe?
   - ⟨ ⟩ That the man had been in class
   - ⟨ ⟩ That the man didn't have the notes
   - ⟨ ⟩ That she didn't need the notes
   - ⟨ ⟩ That the lecture had been canceled

10. What does the man mean?
   - ⟨ ⟩ He really enjoyed the conference.
   - ⟨ ⟩ He'll be able to go to the conference.
   - ⟨ ⟩ He couldn't attend the conference.
   - ⟨ ⟩ He heard everything at the conference.

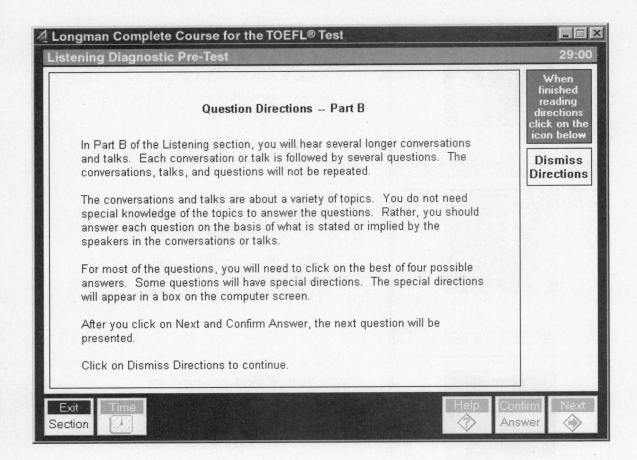

When finished reading directions click on the icon below

Dismiss Directions

Question Directions -- Part B

In Part B of the Listening section, you will hear several longer conversations and talks. Each conversation or talk is followed by several questions. The conversations, talks, and questions will not be repeated.

The conversations and talks are about a variety of topics. You do not need special knowledge of the topics to answer the questions. Rather, you should answer each question on the basis of what is stated or implied by the speakers in the conversations or talks.

For most of the questions, you will need to click on the best of four possible answers. Some questions will have special directions. The special directions will appear in a box on the computer screen.

After you click on Next and Confirm Answer, the next question will be presented.

Click on Dismiss Directions to continue.

Exit Section

Time

Help

Confirm Answer

Next

Questions 11–12

11. What happened to Carl?
    - ○ He made the football team.
    - ○ His arm was in a cast.
    - ○ He got lost in the stadium.
    - ○ He hurt his leg.

12. How did Carl break his leg?
    - ○ He was playing football.
    - ○ He was on a ski trip.
    - ○ He had an accident at a sporting event.
    - ○ He tripped over some crutches.

Questions 13–15

13. What do the students have to prepare?
    - ○ A series of questions
    - ○ A psychological self-evaluation
    - ○ A theoretical model
    - ○ A psychology exam

14. How many people must respond to the questionnaire?
    - ○ 5
    - ○ 15
    - ○ 50
    - ○ 150

15. What does the man NOT want to do?
    - ○ Prepare the questionnaire
    - ○ Get the questionnaire answered
    - ○ Analyze the data
    - ○ Write the report

Questions 16–20

Listen to a discussion about a history course. The discussion is on the Outer Banks.

History
The Outer Banks

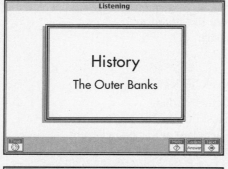

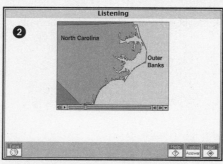

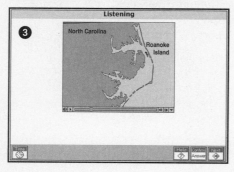

16. What are the students doing?

- ◯ Preparing for a presentation
- ◯ Reviewing a list of study questions
- ◯ Drawing maps for a project
- ◯ Planning a trip to the Outer Banks

17. With what places are these people associated?

Click on a word or phrase. Then click on the empty box in the correct column. Use each word or phrase only once.

Blackbeard	Wright Brothers	Lost Colonists
Roanoke Island	Ocracoke Island	Kitty Hawk

18. When did these people live?

Click on a word or phrase. Then click on the empty box in the correct column. Use each word or phrase only once.

Blackbeard	Wright Brothers	Lost Colonists
sixteenth century	eighteenth century	twentieth century

19. What is stated about the inhabitants of the Lost Colony?

Click on 2 answers.

- ☐ They came from England.
- ☐ They disappeared a decade after their arrival.
- ☐ They were never found.
- ☐ They were eventually found.

20. How long was the longest flight that the Wright Brothers took on December 3, 1903?

- ◯ 12 seconds
- ◯ 59 seconds
- ◯ 12 minutes
- ◯ 59 minutes

Questions 21–25

Listen to a lecture in a zoology class. The professor is talking about hibernation.

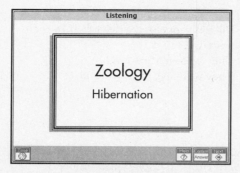

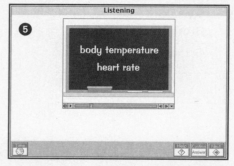

21. What is NOT mentioned by the professor as a way that various types of animals prepare for the cold weather?

⭕ Some head to southern climates.
⭕ Some increase their activity.
⭕ Some hibernate, at least partially.
⭕ Some build warmer dens or nests.

22. What is NOT stated in the lecture about Groundhog Day?

⭕ It is based on folklore about the groundhog.
⭕ It is in March.
⭕ It determines whether or not winter is over.
⭕ It requires observation of whether or not a groundhog returns to its burrow.

23. Which of the following is NOT a good hibernator?

Click on a drawing.

24. What happens to body temperature and heart rate during hibernation?

Click on 2 answers.

☐ Body temperature increases.
☐ Body temperature decreases.
☐ Heart rate increases.
☐ Heart rate decreases.

25. What part of the bear wakes up first from hibernation?

Click on the correct letter.

Questions 26–30

Listen to a lecture in a science class. The professor is talking about Three-Mile Island.

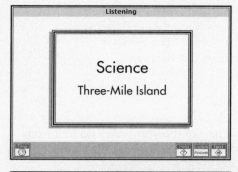

26. What do the initials PWR stand for?

○ Potential water resource
○ Potential water reactor
○ Pressurized water resource
○ Pressurized water reactor

27. How many PWRs are there on Three-Mile Island?

○ One
○ Two
○ Three
○ Four

28. What does the lecturer say about the PWRs during the accident?

○ There were no problems with the PWRs.
○ There was a problem with only one of the PWRs.
○ There were problems with one PWR after another.
○ There were problems in more than one PWR at the same time.

29. What errors did the operators make?

○ They thought that there was too much water.
○ They thought that the water was too cold.
○ They thought that there was too little water.
○ They thought that the water was too hot.

30. The professor explains a series of events. Put the events in the order in which they occurred.

> Click on a sentence. Then click on the space where it belongs. Use each sentence one time only.

The cooling water was shut off.
A partial meltdown occurred.
Instruments were misread.
The cooling valve stuck open.

1	
2	
3	
4	

Circle the number of each of the questions on the test that you answered incorrectly or were unsure of. Then you will see which skills you should be sure to focus on.

1. SKILL 2
2. SKILL 3
3. SKILL 7
4. SKILL 5
5. SKILL 10
6. SKILL 8
7. SKILL 11
8. SKILL 16
9. SKILL 13
10. SKILL 14

11. SKILL 28
12. SKILL 28
13. SKILL 28
14. SKILL 28
15. SKILL 28
16. SKILL 30
17. SKILL 29
18. SKILL 29
19. SKILL 30
20. SKILL 30

21. SKILL 33
22. SKILL 33
23. SKILL 34
24. SKILL 33
25. SKILL 34
26. SKILL 33
27. SKILL 33
28. SKILL 33
29. SKILL 33
30. SKILL 32

LISTENING

Listening is tested in the first section on both the paper TOEFL test and the computer TOEFL test. This section consists of a number of different types of listening passages, each followed by one or more questions. The paper and the computer listening sections are **similar** in the following ways:

- *some of the passages*
- *some of the language skills*

The paper and the computer listening sections are **different** in the following ways:

- *some of the passages*
- *some of the language skills*
- *the use of visuals*
- *the number of questions*
- *the amount of time*
- *the control of time between questions*
- *the procedures and strategies*

LISTENING ON THE PAPER TOEFL® TEST

On the paper TOEFL test, the first section is called Listening Comprehension. This section consists of fifty questions (though some tests may be longer). You will listen to recorded materials and respond to multiple-choice questions about the material. You must listen carefully because you will hear the recording one time only and the material on the recording is not written in your test book.

1. **Short Dialogues** are two-line dialogues between two speakers, each followed by a multiple-choice question. You will listen to each short dialogue and question on the recording and then choose the best answer to each question from the four choices in your test book. The 30 short dialogues and 30 questions about them make up Part A of the paper TOEFL test.
2. **Long Conversations** are 60–90 second conversations on casual topics between students, each followed by a number of multiple-choice questions. You will listen to each long conversation and each of the questions that accompany it on the recording and then choose the best answer to each question from the four choices in your test book. The two conversations and the seven to nine questions that accompany them make up Part B of the paper TOEFL test.
3. **Talks** are 60–90 second talks about school life or on academic subjects, each followed by a number of multiple-choice questions. You will listen to each lecture and each of the questions that accompany it on the recording and then choose the best answer to each question from the four choices in your test book. The three lectures and the 11–13 questions that accompany them make up Part C of the paper TOEFL test.

GENERAL STRATEGIES FOR LISTENING COMPREHENSION
(Paper TOEFL® Test) 📖

1. **Be familiar with the directions.** The directions on every paper TOEFL test are the same, so it is not necessary to spend time reading the directions carefully when you take the test. You should be completely familiar with the directions before the day of the test.

2. **Listen carefully to the passages.** You should concentrate fully on what the speakers are saying on the recording because you will hear the recording one time only.

3. **Know where the easier and the more difficult questions are generally found.** Within each part of the Listening Comprehension section on the paper test, the questions generally progress from easy to difficult.

4. **Be familiar with the pacing of the test.** You have 12 seconds between each question on the recording, so you must answer each question within 12 seconds and then be prepared for the next question on the recording.

5. **Never leave any answers blank on your answer sheet.** Even if you are not sure of the correct response, you should answer each question. There is no penalty for guessing.

6. **Use any remaining time to look ahead at the answers to the questions that follow.** When you finish with one question, you may have time to look ahead at the answers to the next question.

LISTENING ON THE COMPUTER TOEFL® TEST

On the computer TOEFL test, the first section is called the Listening section. This section consists of 30–50 questions. In this section, you will listen to recorded material, look at visual cues, and respond to various types of questions about the material. You must listen carefully because you will hear the recorded material one time only and the recorded material does not appear on the computer screen.

Four types of passages may appear in the Listening section of the computer TOEFL test:

1. **Short Dialogues** consist of two- to four-line dialogues between two speakers. Each dialogue is accompanied by a context-setting visual and is followed by one multiple-choice question. You will listen to each short dialogue as you see a context-setting visual on the screen. Then you will listen to a question as you see the question and four answer choices on the screen. The 11–17 short dialogues and questions about them make up Part A on the computer TOEFL test.

2. **Casual Conversations** consist of five- to seven-line conversations on casual topics between students. Each conversation is accompanied by a context-setting visual and is followed by two or three multiple-choice questions. You will listen to each casual conversation as you see a context-setting visual on the screen. Then you will listen to each question as you see the question and the four answer choices on the screen. The two to four conversations and the questions that accompany them are found in Part B on the computer TOEFL test.

3. **Academic Discussions** consist of 120–150 second discussions on academic topics by two to five speakers. Each discussion is accompanied by a number of context-setting and content visuals and is followed by three to six questions of varying types. You will listen to each academic discussion as you see a series of context-setting and content visuals on the screen. Then you will listen to each question as you see the various types of questions and answers on the screen. The one or two academic discussions and the questions that accompany them are found in Part B on the computer TOEFL test.

4. **Academic Lectures** consist of 120–150 second lectures on academic topics by university professors. Each lecture is accompanied by a number of context-setting and content visuals and is followed by three to six questions of varying types. You will listen to each academic lecture as you see a series of context-setting and content visuals on the screen. Then you will listen to each question as you see the various types of questions and answers on the screen. The two to four academic lectures and the questions that accompany them are found in Part B on the computer TOEFL test.

Part A on the computer TOEFL test consists of only short dialogues, while Part B consists of a mixture of casual conversations, academic discussions, and academic lectures.

The Listening section of the computer TOEFL test is *computer adaptive*. This means that the difficulty of the questions that you see is determined by how well you answer the questions. The section begins with a medium-level question, and the questions that follow will get easier or harder depending on whether or not you answer the questions correctly.

GENERAL STRATEGIES FOR THE LISTENING SECTION
(Computer TOEFL® Test) 💻

1. **Be familiar with the directions.** The directions on every computer TOEFL test are the same, so it is not necessary to spend time reading the directions carefully when you take the test. You should be completely familiar with the directions before the day of the test.

2. **Be familiar with computer adaptivity.** This section of the computer TOEFL test is adaptive. This means that you will start with a medium-level question, and the difficulty of the questions will increase or decrease depending on whether or not your answers are correct.

3. **Set the volume carefully before you start the Listening section.** You have the opportunity to choose the volume that you would like before you start the section.

4. **Dismiss the directions as soon as they come up.** The time starts when the directions come up. You should already be familiar with the directions, so you can click on `Dismiss Directions` as soon as it appears and save all your time for the questions.

5. **Listen carefully to the spoken material.** You will hear the spoken material one time only. You may not repeat the spoken material during the test.

6. **Use the visuals to help you focus on the context.** As you listen to the spoken material, you will see visual materials on the screen. The visual information may help you to understand the context for the spoken material as well as the content of the spoken material as you listen.

7. **Pace yourself between questions.** You control when the spoken material is played. You may take as much time as you need between questions.

8. **Think carefully about a question before you answer it.** You may not return to a question later in the test. You only have one opportunity to answer a given question.

9. **Click on an answer on the computer screen when you have selected an answer.** You may still change your mind at this point and click on a different answer.

10. **Click on** `Next` **and then click on** `Confirm Answer` **to record your answer.** After you click on the Confirm Answer button, you cannot go back and change your answer. A new question will appear, and you may not return to a previous question.

11. **Do not spend too much time on a question you are unsure of.** If you truly do not know the answer to a question, simply guess and go on. The computer will automatically move you into a level of questions that you can answer.

12. **Be very careful not to make careless mistakes.** If you carelessly choose an incorrect answer, the computer will move you to an easier level of questions. You will have to waste time working your way back to the appropriate level of questions.

13. **Monitor the time carefully on the title bar of the computer screen.** The title bar indicates the time remaining in the Listening section, the total number of questions in the section, and the current number.

14. **Do not randomly guess at the end of the section to complete all the questions in the section before time is up.** In a computer adaptive section such as the Listening section, random guessing to complete the section will only lower your score.

SHORT DIALOGUES

(PAPER TOEFL® TEST AND COMPUTER TOEFL® TEST)

Short dialogues appear on both the paper TOEFL test and the computer TOEFL test. Though short dialogues are slightly different in format on the two tests, they both test the same language skills. The paper and computer short dialogues are **similar** in the following ways:

- *the language skills tested*
- *the type of question used*
- *the number of people talking*

The paper and computer short dialogues are **different** in the following ways:

- *the possible number of lines of dialogue*
- *the use of context-setting visuals to accompany the dialogues*
- *the control of the timing between questions*
- *the presentation of the question*

SHORT DIALOGUES ON THE PAPER TOEFL® TEST

Short dialogues are found in Part A in the Listening Comprehension section of the paper TOEFL test. For each of the 30 short dialogues in this part of the test, you will hear a two-line dialogue between two speakers followed by a multiple-choice question. After you listen to the dialogue and the question, you must choose the best answer to the question from your test book. Look at an example of a short dialogue from the paper TOEFL test.

Example from the Paper TOEFL Test

On the recording, you hear:

    (man)   *This physics course couldn't be any harder.*
    (woman) *I'll say!*
    (narrator) *What does the woman mean?*

In your test book, you read:

    (A)   She has something to say to the man.
    (B)   She doesn't think the physics course is hard.
    (C)   She agrees with the man.
    (D)   She'd like to discuss the physics course.

In the dialogue, when the woman says *I'll say*, she is showing that she *agrees* with what the man just said. Answer (C) is therefore the best answer to this question.

PROCEDURES FOR THE SHORT DIALOGUES
(Paper TOEFL® Test)

1. **As you listen to each short dialogue, focus on the second line of the conversation.** The answer to the question is generally found in the second line.

2. **Keep in mind that the correct answer is probably a restatement of a key word or idea in the second line of the dialogue.** Think of possible restatements.

3. **Keep in mind that certain structures and expressions are tested regularly in the short dialogues.** Listen for these structures and expressions:
   - structures *(passives, negatives, wishes, conditions)*
   - functional expressions *(agreement, uncertainty, suggestion, surprise)*
   - idiomatic expressions *(two-part verbs, three-part verbs, idioms)*

4. **Keep in mind that these questions generally progress from easy to difficult.** This means that questions 1 through 5 will be the easiest and questions 26 through 30 will be the hardest.

5. **Read the answers and choose the best answer to each question.** Remember to answer each question even if you are not sure of the correct response. Never leave any answers blank.

---

6. **Even if you do not understand the complete dialogue, you can still find the correct answer.**
   - If you only understand a few words or ideas in the second line, choose the answer that contains a restatement of those words or ideas.
   - If you do not understand anything at all in the second line of the conversation, choose the answer that sounds the most different from what you heard.
   - Never choose an answer because it sounds like what you heard in the dialogue.

7. **Be prepared for the next question.** You have only 12 seconds between questions.

SHORT DIALOGUES ON THE COMPUTER TOEFL® TEST

Short dialogues appear in Part A of the Listening section of the computer TOEFL test. For each of the short dialogues in this part of the test, you will see a context-setting visual as you listen to a two- to four-line dialogue between two speakers. After you see the visual and listen to the dialogue, you will see the question and the four answer choices on the computer screen. You must click on the best answer choice on the computer screen. Now look at an example of a short dialogue from the computer TOEFL test.

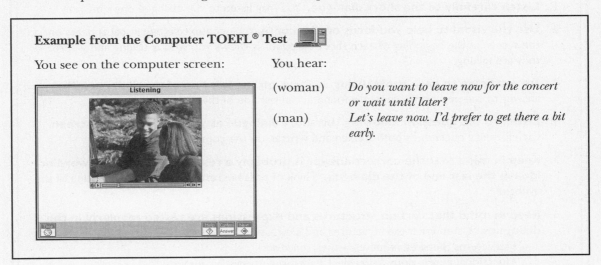

Example from the Computer TOEFL® Test

You see on the computer screen:

Listening

You hear:

(woman)   *Do you want to leave now for the concert or wait until later?*

(man)   *Let's leave now. I'd prefer to get there a bit early.*

After the dialogue is complete, the question and answer choices appear on the computer screen as the narrator states the question. This question is a regular multiple-choice question that asks what the man means.

You see on the computer screen:

You hear:

(narrator)   *What does the man mean?*

> **Listening**
>
> What does the man mean?
> - ◯ He doesn't want to go to the concert.
> - ◯ He would prefer to leave later.
> - ◯ He wants to leave the concert early.
> - ◯ He wants to go immediately.

In the dialogue, the man says *Let's leave now.* This means that *he wants to go immediately.* The last answer is the best answer to this question, so you should click on the last answer.

PROCEDURES FOR THE SHORT DIALOGUES
(Computer TOEFL® Test)

1. **Listen carefully to the short dialogue.** You may listen to the dialogue one time only.

2. **Use the visual to help you focus on the context.** A context-setting visual appears on the screen at the beginning of each short dialogue. It shows you who is talking and where they are talking.

3. **As you listen to each short dialogue, focus on the last line of the dialogue.** The answer to the question is generally found in the last line of the dialogue.

4. **Listen to the question following the short dialogue as you read it on the screen.** Each listening question is both spoken and written on the computer screen.

5. **Keep in mind that the correct answer is probably a restatement of a key word or idea in the last line of the dialogue.** Think of possible restatements of the last line of the dialogue.

6. **Keep in mind that certain structures and expressions are tested regularly in the dialogues.** Listen for these structures and expressions:
   - structures *(passives, negatives, wishes, conditions)*
   - functional expressions *(agreement, uncertainty, suggestion, surprise)*
   - idiomatic expressions *(two-part verbs, three-part verbs, idioms)*

7. **Even if you do not understand the complete dialogue, you can still find the correct answer.**
   - If you only understand a few words or ideas in the last line, choose the answer that contains a restatement of those words or ideas.
   - If you do not understand anything at all in the last line of the conversation, choose the answer that sounds the most different from what you heard.
   - Never choose an answer because it *sounds like* what you heard in the dialogue.

8. **Click on an answer on the computer screen when you have selected an answer.** You may still change your mind at this point and click on a different answer.

9. **Click on** Next . **Then click on** Confirm Answer **to record your answer.** After you click on this button, you cannot go back and change your answer.

10. **Be prepared for the next question.** After you click on Confirm Answer , the next question begins automatically.

Next, you should move on to the language skills. The following language skills will help you to implement these strategies and procedures with the short dialogues on both the paper TOEFL test and the computer TOEFL test.

STRATEGIES

SKILL 1:   FOCUS ON THE LAST LINE

The short dialogues involve conversations between two people, each followed by a question. It is important to understand that the answer to this type of question is most often (but not always!) found in the last line of the conversation.

Example from the Paper and Computer TOEFL® Tests

On the recording, you hear:

(man)	*Billy really made a big mistake this time.*
(woman)	*Yes, he forgot to turn in his research paper.*
(narrator)	*What does the woman say about Billy?*

In your test book or on the computer screen, you read:

(A)   It was the first time he made a mistake.
(B)   He forgot to write his paper.
(C)   He turned in the paper in the wrong place.
(D)   He didn't remember to submit his assignment.

The last line of this dialogue indicates that Billy *forgot to turn in his research paper,* and this means that he *didn't remember to submit* it. The best answer is therefore answer (D).

The following chart outlines the most important strategy for the short dialogues:

STRATEGY #1: FOCUS ON THE LAST LINE
1.   The last line of the dialogue probably contains the answer to the question.
2.   Listen to the first line of the dialogue. If you understand it, that's good. If you don't understand it, don't worry because it probably does not contain the answer.
3.   Be ready to focus on the last line of the dialogue because it probably contains the answer. Repeat the last line in your mind as you read through the answers in the text.

EXERCISE 1: In this exercise, you should focus on the last line of the dialogue, read the question, and then choose the best answer to that question. Remember that you can probably answer the question easily with only the last line.

1. (man)   *Can you tell me if today's matinee is a comedy, romance, or western?*
   (woman)   *I have no idea.*
   (narrator) *What does the woman mean?*

   (A) She has strong ideas about movies.
   (B) She prefers comedies over westerns and romances.
   (C) She doesn't like today's matinee.
   (D) She does not know.

2. (woman)   *Was anyone at home at Barb's house when you went there to deliver the package?*
   (man)   *I rang the bell, but no one answered.*
   (narrator) *What does the man imply?*

   (A) Barb answered the bell.
   (B) The house was probably empty.
   (C) The bell wasn't in the house.
   (D) The house doesn't have a bell.

3. (woman)   *You just got back from the interview for the internship. How do you think it went?*
   (man)   *I think it's highly unlikely that I got the job.*
   (narrator) *What does the man suggest?*

   (A) It's unlikely that he'll go to the interview.
   (B) He thinks he'll be recommended for a high-level job.
   (C) The interview was apparently quite unsuccessful.
   (D) He had an excellent interview.

TOEFL EXERCISE 1: In this exercise, listen carefully to each short dialogue and question on the recording, and then choose the best answer to the question. You should focus carefully on the last line.

 NOW BEGIN THE RECORDING AT TOEFL EXERCISE 1.

1. (A) He is leaving now.
   (B) He has to go out of his way.
   (C) He will not be leaving soon.
   (D) He will do it his own way.

2. (A) He locked the door.
   (B) He tried unsuccessfully to get into the house.
   (C) He was able to open the door.
   (D) He left the house without locking the door.

3. (A) She doesn't like to listen to turkeys.
   (B) She thinks the dinner sounds special.
   (C) She especially likes the roast turkey.
   (D) She'd prefer a different dinner.

4. (A) He'll be busy with her homework tonight.
   (B) He can't help her tonight.
   (C) He's sorry he can't ever help her.
   (D) He'll help her with her physics.

5. (A) Her eyes hurt.
   (B) She thought the lecture was great.
   (C) The class was boring.
   (D) She didn't want to watch Professor Martin.

6. (A) Not all the bills have been paid.
   (B) They don't have enough credit to pay the bills.
   (C) What she said on the phone was not credible.
   (D) He used a credit card to pay some of the bills.

7. (A) She'll call back quickly.
   (B) She'll definitely be back by 4:00.
   (C) She'll give it back by 4:00.
   (D) She'll try to return fast.

8. (A) She hasn't seen Tim.
   (B) Tim was there only for a moment.
   (C) Tim was around a short time ago.
   (D) Tim will return in a minute.

9. (A)   She doesn't like the place he chose.
    (B)   She doesn't want to get into the car.
    (C)   She's glad the spot is reserved.
    (D)   They can't park the car there.

10. (A)   There's plenty to eat.
     (B)   The refrigerator's broken.
     (C)   The food isn't in the refrigerator.
     (D)   He's not sure if there's enough.

SKILL 2:   CHOOSE ANSWERS WITH SYNONYMS

Often the correct answer in a short dialogue is an answer that contains synonyms (words with similar meanings but different sounds) for key words in the conversation.

Example from the Paper and Computer TOEFL® Tests

On the recording, you hear:

(woman)   *Why is Barbara feeling so happy?*
(man)   *She just started working in a real estate agency.*
(narrator) *What does the man say about Barbara?*

In your test book or on the computer screen, you read:

(A)   She always liked her work in real estate.
(B)   She began a new job.
(C)   She just bought some real estate.
(D)   She bought a real estate agency.

In this dialogue, the key word *started* means *began*, and the key word *working* refers to *job*. The best answer to this question is therefore answer (B).

The following chart outlines a very important strategy for short dialogues:

STRATEGY #2: CHOOSE ANSWERS WITH SYNONYMS
1. As you listen to the last line of the dialogue, focus on key words in that line.
2. If you see any synonyms for key words in a particular answer, then you have probably found the correct answer.

EXERCISE 2: In this exercise, underline key words in the last line of each short dialogue. Then underline synonyms for these key words in the answers, and choose the best answer to each question. Remember that the best answer is probably the answer that contains synonyms for the key words in the last line of the dialogue.

1. (woman)   *Did you see the manager about the job in the bookstore?*
    (man)   *Yes, and I also had to fill out an application.*
    (narrator) *What does the man mean?*

    (A)   He got a job as bookstore manager.
    (B)   The bookstore was not accepting applications.
    (C)   He saw a book about how to apply for jobs.
    (D)   It was necessary to complete a form.

2. (man)   *We're planning to leave for the*   (A) If they could leave at noon
                 trip at about 2:00.   (B) If it is possible to go by 12:00
    (woman)   *Couldn't we leave before noon?*   (C) Why they can't leave at noon
    (narrator)   *What does the woman ask?*   (D) If they could leave the room

3. (man)   *Was the concert well-received?*   (A) The performance went on for a long
    (woman)   *The audience applauded for a*   time.
                 long time after the performance.   (B) There was applause throughout the
    (narrator)   *What does the woman say about*   performance.
                 the concert?   (C) The people clapped on and on after the
                                                                  concert.
                                                             (D) The audience waited for a long time for
                                                                  the concert to begin.

TOEFL EXERCISE 2: In this exercise, listen carefully to each short dialogue and question on the recording, and then choose the best answer to the question. You should look for synonyms for key words in the last line.

 NOW BEGIN THE RECORDING AT TOEFL EXERCISE 2.

1. (A) The final exam was harder than the
         others.
    (B) There were two exams rather than
         one.
    (C) He thought the exam would be
         easier.
    (D) The exam was not very difficult.

2. (A) He's not feeling very well.
    (B) He's rather sick of working.
    (C) He's feeling better today than
         yesterday.
    (D) He'd really rather not answer the
         question.

3. (A) The company was founded about a
         year ago.
    (B) It was just established that he could
         go into business.
    (C) The family is well-established.
    (D) The business only lasted a year.

4. (A) He did not look at the right
         schedule.
    (B) The plane landed in the right place.
    (C) The plane arrived on time.
    (D) He had to wait for the plane to land.

5. (A) She'd rather go running.
    (B) She doesn't want to go into the
         pool.
    (C) She'll change clothes quickly and
         go swimming.
    (D) She needs a sweatsuit to go
         running.

6. (A) The firefighters saved the homes
         for last.
    (B) A firefighter saved the hillside last
         night.
    (C) The homes on the hillside were
         burned.
    (D) The houses weren't destroyed.

7. (A) There's enough soup.
    (B) The spices are adequate.
    (C) She thinks the soup's too salty.
    (D) The man should add more salt and
         pepper.

8. (A) He was lucky to receive a grant for
         his studies.
    (B) He used his fortune to pay his fees.
    (C) He is a scholar at a college with low
         fees.
    (D) He paid to get a scholarship.

9. (A) It profited from previous mistakes.
    (B) It earned a lot of money.
    (C) This was the last year that it would
         make a profit.
    (D) It was not so successful.

10. (A) Chuck's bank account has too
         much money in it.
    (B) He thinks Chuck has the wrong
         kind of bank account.
    (C) He thinks that Chuck is on his way
         home from the bank.
    (D) There isn't enough money in
         Chuck's account.

SKILL 3:   AVOID SIMILAR SOUNDS

Often the incorrect answers in the short dialogues are answers that contain words with similar sounds but very different meanings from what you hear on the recording. You should definitely avoid these answers.

Example from the Paper and Computer TOEFL® Tests

On the recording, you hear:

(man)   *Why couldn't Mark come with us?*
(woman)   *He was searching for a new apartment.*
(narrator) *What does the woman say about Mark?*

In your test book or on the computer screen, you read:

(A)   He was in the <u>department</u> office.
(B)   He was looking for a place to live.
(C)   He was working on his <u>research</u> project.
(D)   He had an <u>appointment</u> at <u>church</u>.

The key words in the last line of the dialogue are *searching* and *apartment*. In answers (C) and (D), the words *research* and *church* sound like *search*, so these answers are incorrect. In answers (A) and (D), the words *department* and *appointment* sound like *apartment*, so these answers are incorrect. The best answer is therefore answer (B).

The following chart outlines a very important strategy for the short dialogues:

STRATEGY #3: AVOID SIMILAR SOUNDS
1. Identify key words in the last line of the dialogue.
2. Identify words in the answers that contain similar sounds, and do not choose these answers.

NOTE: In Appendix A there are drills to practice distinguishing similar sounds. You may want to complete these practice drills before trying the following exercises.

EXERCISE 3: In this exercise, underline key words in the last line of each short dialogue. Then underline words with sounds similar to these key words in the answers, and choose the best answer to each question. Remember that the best answer is probably the answer that does not contain words with sounds that are similar to the sounds of the key words in the last line of the dialogue.

1. (woman)   *I heard that Sally just moved into a new, big house near the beach.*
    (man)   *But Sally doesn't have a cent!*
    (narrator) *What does the man mean?*

    (A)   Sally has no sense of responsibility.
    (B)   Sally sent her friend to the house.
    (C)   Sally has no money.
    (D)   Sally is on the set with her.

2. (woman)   *Did they get the new car they wanted?*
    (man)   *No, they lacked the money.*
    (narrator) *What does the man mean?*

    (A) They locked the map in a car.
    (B) They looked many times in the car.
    (C) It cost a lot of money when the car leaked oil.
    (D) They didn't have enough money to buy another car.

3. (man)   *Have you finished packing yet?*
    (woman)   *You should call the porter to get the suitcases.*
    (narrator) *What does the woman mean?*

    (A) It's important to pack the suitcases.
    (B) They need help carrying their bags.
    (C) The man should pack his suit in case he needs it.
    (D) The suitcases are quite portable.

TOEFL EXERCISE 3: In this exercise, listen carefully to each short dialogue and question on the recording, and then choose the best answer to the question. You should be careful to avoid answers with similar sounds.

   NOW BEGIN THE RECORDING AT TOEFL EXERCISE 3.

1. (A) She has to wait for some cash.
    (B) The waiter is bringing a glass of water.
    (C) The lawn is too dry.
    (D) She needs to watch out for a crash.

2. (A) The sweater's the wrong size.
    (B) The man's feet aren't sweating.
    (C) The sweater makes the man seem fat.
    (D) The sweet girl doesn't feel right.

3. (A) He has been regularly using a computer.
    (B) He communicates with a Boston company.
    (C) He regularly goes to communities around Boston.
    (D) He has been traveling back and forth to Boston.

4. (A) He thought the lesson didn't matter.
    (B) He couldn't learn the lesson.
    (C) He learned a massive number of details.
    (D) He didn't like most of the lesson.

5. (A) Some animals started the first fire.
    (B) Animals are killed by forest fires.
    (C) In the first frost, animals die.
    (D) Frost can kill animals.

6. (A) Twenty pairs of shoes are on sale.
    (B) The shoe salesclerk spent twenty dollars on pears.
    (C) The shoes cost twenty dollars.
    (D) The shoes could be repaired for twenty dollars.

7. (A) Tom tended to dislike biology lab.
    (B) Attendance wasn't necessary at biology lab.
    (C) Tom went to biology lab.
    (D) There was a tendency to require biology lab.

8. (A) The meal will be served at noon.
    (B) The males should be driven there by noon.
    (C) He's expecting the ice to melt before noon.
    (D) The letters ought to be delivered at 12:00.

9. (A) The weather will probably get worse later.
    (B) The newspaper headlines described a bad storm.
    (C) There was news about a headstrong man.
    (D) He had a new bed.

10. (A) If she could do the grocery shopping
    (B) If she prefers cooked vegetables or salad
    (C) If she could help prepare the salad
    (D) If she minds shopping for vegetables

TOEFL EXERCISE (Skills 1–3): In this exercise, listen carefully to each short dialogue and question on the recording, and then choose the best answer to the question.

 NOW BEGIN THE RECORDING AT TOEFL EXERCISE (SKILLS 1–3).

1. (A) He would like some iced coffee.
    (B) He wants to stop drinking coffee.
    (C) A drink seems like a good idea.
    (D) He needs to drink something to stop his coughing.

2. (A) She would prefer a sunny day.
    (B) The park is too crowded.
    (C) She would like a place that is not so loud.
    (D) She cannot walk because she's too old.

3. (A) He should open an account.
    (B) He should take a ride on a ship.
    (C) He should try to keep the cost cheap.
    (D) He should try something monotonous to get to sleep.

4. (A) The department is not changing the requirements.
    (B) He hasn't heard anything about the change.
    (C) The changes are believable.
    (D) What has happened is incredible to him.

5. (A) The wait has taken close to an hour.
    (B) They were stranded in their car.
    (C) Most of the people have been in line for hours.
    (D) They made a line in the sand.

6. (A) The instructor is selecting several passages.
    (B) The conductor is fair to the passengers.
    (C) The stamp collector is conducting his business.
    (D) The riders are paying for the train trip.

7. (A) The managers will take the train to the program.
    (B) A program to develop new managers will commence soon.
    (C) The new management program is very weak.
    (D) The program will be maintained to the letter.

8. (A) The fire started to attack the building.
    (B) The firefighter stared at the attacker.
    (C) The fire probably began at the top of the building.
    (D) The firefighter started to attack the fire.

9. (A) He assured the woman that he knew the truth.
    (B) He is sure that it isn't new.
    (C) He thought that the woman was aware of what happened.
    (D) He soon will know the truth.

10. (A) The art professor is not one of his fans.
    (B) His drawings were amazing.
    (C) The catches that he made were fantastic.
    (D) His sketches showed a fantasy world.

WHO, WHAT, WHERE

SKILL 4:   DRAW CONCLUSIONS ABOUT *WHO, WHAT, WHERE*

It is common in the short dialogues to ask you to draw some kind of conclusion. In this type of question the answer is not clearly stated; instead you must draw a conclusion based on clues given in the dialogue. One kind of conclusion that is common in this part of the test is to ask you to determine *who* the speaker is, based on clues given in the dialogue.

Example from the Paper and Computer TOEFL® Tests

On the recording, you hear:

(woman)	*Can you tell me what assignments I missed when I was absent from your class?*
(man)	*You missed one homework assignment and a quiz.*
(narrator)	*Who is the man?*

In your test book or on the computer screen, you read:

(A)   A newspaper editor
(B)   A police officer
(C)   A teacher
(D)   A student

The clues *class, homework,* and *quiz* in the dialogue tell you that the man is probably a *teacher.* Answer (C) is therefore the correct answer.

Another type of conclusion that is common in the short dialogues is to determine *what* will probably happen next, based on clues given in the dialogue.

Example from the Paper and Computer TOEFL® Tests

On the recording, you hear:

(woman)	*Are you going to read those books here in the library?*
(man)	*I think I'd rather check them out now and take them home.*
(narrator)	*What will the man probably do next?*

In your test book or on the computer screen, you read:

(A)   Sit down in the library
(B)   Look for some more books
(C)   Return the books to the shelves
(D)   Go to the circulation desk

The man mentions *books* and says that he would like to *check them out now.* Since the *circulation desk* is where you go to check books out from a library, the man will probably go to the circulation desk next. The correct answer is therefore answer (D).

A final type of conclusion that is common in the short dialogues is to determine *where* the conversation probably takes place, based on clues given in the conversation.

Example from the Paper and Computer TOEFL® Tests 📖 🖥️

On the recording, you hear:

(woman)	*Are you going into the <u>water</u>, or are you just going to lie there on the <u>sand</u>?*
(man)	*I think I need to put on some <u>suntan lotion</u>.*
(narrator)	*Where does this conversation probably take place?*

In your test book or on the computer screen, you read:

(A) At a beauty salon
(B) At the <u>beach</u>
(C) In a <u>sandbox</u>
(D) At an outdoor restaurant

The clues *water*, *sand*, and *suntan lotion* in the dialogue tell you that this dialogue probably takes place at the *beach*. Answer (B) is therefore the correct answer.

The following chart outlines the key point that you should remember about this type of question:

CONCLUSIONS ABOUT *WHO, WHAT, WHERE*

It is common for you to be asked to draw one of the following conclusions in the short dialogues:

1. *WHO is probably talking?*

2. *WHAT will s/he probably do next?*

3. *WHERE does the dialogue probably take place?*

EXERCISE 4: In this exercise, read each short dialogue and question, underline the clues that help you answer the question, and then choose the best answer. You will have to draw conclusions about *who, what,* and *where.*

1. (man)   *I'd like to deposit this check in my account, please.*
   (woman)   *Would you like any cash back?*
   (narrator) *Who is the woman?*

   (A) A store clerk
   (B) A bank teller
   (C) An accountant
   (D) A waitress

2. (woman)   *Have you deposited your paycheck yet?*
   (man)   *No, but that's next on my list of errands.*
   (narrator) *What will the man probably do next?*

   (A) Earn his paycheck
   (B) Write a check for a deposit on an apartment
   (C) Go to a bank
   (D) Make a list of errands to run

3. (man)   *Did you get the bread, eggs,*   (A) In a restaurant
               and milk?   (B) At a bakery
    (woman)   *Now we need to stand in line at*   (C) On a farm
               the checkout counter.   (D) In a market
    (narrator) *Where does this conversation*
               probably take place?

TOEFL EXERCISE 4: In this exercise, listen carefully to each short dialogue and question on the recording and then choose the best answer to the question. You will have to draw conclusions about *who*, *what*, and *where*.

 NOW BEGIN THE RECORDING AT TOEFL EXERCISE 4.

1. (A) In a photography studio
    (B) In a biology laboratory
    (C) In an office
    (D) In the library

2. (A) He's a pilot.
    (B) He's a flight attendant.
    (C) He's a member of the ground crew.
    (D) He works clearing land.

3. (A) Wash the dishes immediately
    (B) Use as many dishes as possible
    (C) Wash the dishes for as long as
         possible
    (D) Wait until later to clean up

4. (A) In a bank
    (B) In a restaurant
    (C) At a service station
    (D) In a beauty salon

5. (A) A salesclerk in a shoe store
    (B) A shoe repairperson
    (C) A party caterer
    (D) A salesclerk in a fixtures
         department

6. (A) On a playground
    (B) In a parking lot
    (C) At a zoo
    (D) In a photo studio

7. (A) Respond to the mail
    (B) Put the letters in a file
    (C) Create a pending file
    (D) File the answers she received to the
         letters

8. (A) In an airplane
    (B) In a police car
    (C) In a theater
    (D) At a fireworks exhibit

9. (A) Take care of Bob
    (B) Invite Bob to dinner
    (C) Let Bob know that they accept his
         invitation
    (D) Respond to the woman's question

10. (A) A pharmacist
    (B) A dentist
    (C) A teacher
    (D) A business manager

SKILL 5:   LISTEN FOR *WHO* AND *WHAT* IN PASSIVES

It is sometimes difficult to understand *who* or *what* is doing the action in a passive sentence. This problem is often tested in the short dialogues.

Example from the Paper and Computer TOEFL® Tests

On the recording, you hear:

    (man)   *Did Sally go to the bank this morning?*
    (woman)   *Yes, she did. She got a new checking account.*
    (narrator) *What does the woman imply?*

In your test book or on the computer screen, you read:

    (A)   Sally wrote several checks.
    (B)   Sally wanted to check up on the bank.
    (C)   A new checking account was opened.
    (D)   Sally checked on the balance in her account.

In this dialogue, the woman uses the active statement *She got a new checking account,* which means that *Sally opened a checking account.* The correct answer uses the passive structure that *a new checking account was opened* to express the same idea. Therefore, the best answer to the question above is answer (C).

You should note the following about passive sentences in the short dialogues:

PASSIVE STATEMENTS
1. If the dialogue contains a *passive* statement, the answer to the question is often an *active* statement.
2. If the dialogue contains an *active* statement, the answer to the question is often a *passive* statement.
NOTE: Check carefully *who* or *what* is doing the action in these questions.

EXERCISE 5: In this exercise each of the correct answers is either a passive restatement of an active sentence or an active restatement of a passive sentence. Read each short dialogue and underline the key active or passive statement. Then read the question and choose the best answer to the question. Be careful about *who* and *what* with these passives.

1. (woman)   *Alice needs to pay her tuition today.*
      (man)   *But her tuition has already been paid.*
      (narrator) *What does the man imply?*

    (A)   Alice's education has paid off.
    (B)   Alice's tuition needs to be paid.
    (C)   Alice has already paid her fees.
    (D)   Alice has already received the money.

2. (man)   *Have you been taking good*
                 care of the lawn?
    (woman)   *I watered it only this morning.*
    (narrator)   *What does the woman mean?*

    (A) She drank some water on the lawn this
         morning.
    (B) She waited for him on the lawn this
         morning.
    (C) The lawn has already been watered
         today.
    (D) She wanted a new lawn this morning.

3. (man)   *Did you hear the news about the*
                 child who was lost in the park?
    (woman)   *Yes, and I heard that she was*
                 just found!
    (narrator)   *What does the woman mean?*

    (A) Someone located the girl.
    (B) She heard about the new park from the
         child.
    (C) The child found her lost pet.
    (D) The child was the last one in the park.

TOEFL EXERCISE 5: In this exercise, listen carefully to each short dialogue and question on the recording, and then choose the best answer to the question. You should be particularly careful of passives.

 NOW BEGIN THE RECORDING AT TOEFL EXERCISE 5.

1. (A) If the restaurant is on the corner
    (B) If the man would like to go to the
         restaurant
    (C) If the vegetables are fresh
    (D) If vegetarian food can be obtained

2. (A) He admitted that he wanted to go
         to law school in the fall.
    (B) The law school accepted him as a
         student.
    (C) The law professor admitted that he
         would be a student in the fall
         semester.
    (D) He would be admitted to law
         school after the fall semester.

3. (A) Mark's plants were cared for in his
         absence.
    (B) Mark's plan was to be out of town.
    (C) Mark was careful about his plans
         for the out-of-town trip.
    (D) She was careful while Mark was
         gone.

4. (A) The lights in the trees were
         destroyed in the storm.
    (B) The storm damaged the trees.
    (C) The falling trees destroyed a store.
    (D) In the light the destruction of the
         storm could be seen.

5. (A) She was broke from skiing.
    (B) She went skiing in spite of her
         accident.
    (C) Her leg was hurt on a skiing trip.
    (D) Her skis were broken in the
         mountains.

6. (A) The road the horses took was long
         and hard.
    (B) It was hard to find the hidden
         houses.
    (C) The riders worked the horses too
         much.
    (D) It was hard for people to ride the
         horses for long.

7. (A) He didn't want the coffee that the
         woman ordered.
    (B) He wasn't sure if the woman
         wanted coffee.
    (C) He assumed the woman had
         ordered coffee.
    (D) He was unaware that coffee had
         already been ordered.

8. (A) The car was in the left parking lot
         at the airport.
    (B) The friends parked their car at the
         airport.
    (C) The airport couldn't hold a lot of
         cars.
    (D) There were a lot of cars to the left
         of the parking lot.

9. (A) The students pointed at Mac.
    (B) Mac was present when the other
         students made the appointment.
    (C) The class representative suggested
         Mac to the other students.
    (D) Mac was chosen by his classmates to
         represent them.

10. (A) After the earthquake, the
          insurance company came out to
          inspect the damage.
     (B) The insurance company insisted
          that the building be repaired to
          meet earthquake safety standards.
     (C) The inhabitants paid their
          premiums after the earthquake.
     (D) The insurance company paid for
          the earthquake damage.

SKILL 6:   LISTEN FOR *WHO* AND *WHAT* WITH MULTIPLE NOUNS

When there is more than one noun in a sentence in the short dialogues, it is common for
the answers to confuse which noun does what.

Example from the Paper and Computer TOEFL® Tests

On the recording, you hear:

(man)   *Do you know who is in the band now?*
(woman)   *I heard that Mara replaced Robert in the band.*
(narrator) *What does the woman say about the band?*

In your test book or on the computer screen, you read:

(A) Robert became a new member of the band.
(B) Robert took Mara's place in the band.
(C) Mara didn't have a place in the band.
(D) Mara took Robert's place in the band.

In the woman's response to the man's question, she talks about two people (*Mara* and
Robert), and these two people are confused in the answers. Because *Mara replaced Robert*, this
means that *Mara took Robert's place* in the band. The best answer is therefore answer (D).

The following chart outlines the key point that you should remember about questions
with multiple nouns:

WHO AND *WHAT* WITH MULTIPLE NOUNS
When there are multiple nouns in a sentence, it is common for the answers to confuse which noun does what.

EXERCISE 6: In this exercise, underline the confusing nouns in each short dialogue. Then, read the question and choose the best answer to that question. Remember to think very carefully about who is doing what.

1. (man)   *Why is Bill not at work this week?*
   (woman)   *His doctor made him take a week off.*
   (narrator) *What does the woman mean?*

   (A) The doctor decided to take some time off from work.
   (B) The doctor told Bill he wasn't too weak to work.
   (C) Bill was mad when the doctor took some time off.
   (D) Bill took a vacation on his doctor's orders.

2. (man)   *Why is Paul going back home this summer?*
   (woman)   *He's returning to Vermont for his sister's wedding.*
   (narrator) *What does the woman mean?*

   (A) Paul is getting married this summer.
   (B) Paul's sister is returning from Vermont to get married.
   (C) Paul will be there when his sister gets married this summer.
   (D) Paul's sister is coming to his wedding in Vermont.

3. (man)   *Did you hear that John's uncle died?*
   (woman)   *Yes, and John was named beneficiary in his uncle's will.*
   (narrator) *What does the woman mean?*

   (A) John received an inheritance when his uncle died.
   (B) It's a benefit that John's name is the same as his uncle's.
   (C) John knows that his uncle will come to the benefit.
   (D) John's uncle gave him a beneficial name.

TOEFL EXERCISE 6: In this exercise, listen carefully to each short dialogue and question on the recording, and then choose the best answer to the question. You should be particularly careful of who is doing what.

 NOW BEGIN THE RECORDING AT TOEFL EXERCISE 6.

1. (A) The passenger waited at the corner.
   (B) The passenger looked for a taxi at the corner.
   (C) The cab driver waited for the passenger.
   (D) The passenger cornered the waiting taxi driver.

2. (A) It was hard for her to hear Jane last night.
   (B) Jane gave a harp recital last night.
   (C) Jane was playing hard while she was hurt.
   (D) She played the harp last night for Jane.

3. (A) The baby sister went to bed quite early.
   (B) The children were forced to go to bed early.
   (C) The baby-sitter made the bed after the children got up.
   (D) The baby-sitter did not stay up late.

4. (A) The man taught his son about football.
   (B) The boy is receiving the ball from his dad.
   (C) The ball is being tossed into the air by the boy.
   (D) The man is playing with the ball in the sun.

5. (A) The students were told to go listen to the speaker.
    (B) The professor attended that evening's lecture.
    (C) The students were given directions to the lecture.
    (D) The professor was directed to the lecture hall.

6. (A) The manager went to the supply room.
    (B) The clerk set supplies on the floor.
    (C) The clerk went to the supply room at the manager's request.
    (D) The clerk backed into the manager in the supply room.

7. (A) The librarian was quite reserved with the students for two days.
    (B) Within two days the librarian had the books for the students.
    (C) The librarian reserved the books for the students.
    (D) The students put the books on hold for two days.

8. (A) The chairman decided that Tony would serve on the board for another year.
    (B) The chairman elected the board.
    (C) The board decided Tony could be chairman after one year.
    (D) Tony became chairman for one more year.

9. (A) The judge defended the murderer.
    (B) The judge tried to protect the defendant from the murderer.
    (C) The judge said that the defendant was a criminal.
    (D) The defense couldn't make a judgment about the criminal.

10. (A) The woman should announce the names of the committee members.
    (B) He is thankful to be appointed to the committee.
    (C) He is sure about the time of the appointment with the committee.
    (D) The woman will serve on the committee.

TOEFL EXERCISE (Skills 4–6): In this exercise, listen carefully to each short dialogue and question on the recording, and then choose the best answer to the question.

 NOW BEGIN THE RECORDING AT TOEFL EXERCISE (SKILLS 4–6).

1. (A) In a department store
    (B) In a stationery store
    (C) At the post office
    (D) At the airport

2. (A) The teacher gave the students a hand.
    (B) The term papers were turned in.
    (C) The students got the papers from the office.
    (D) The teacher handed the papers to the students.

3. (A) The attendant checked the oil in Mark's car.
    (B) Mark checked to see if he had enough oil in his car.
    (C) Mark checked with the service station attendant.
    (D) Mark wrote a check to pay for the oil.

4. (A) A delivery man
    (B) A famous chef
    (C) A clerk in a fast-food restaurant
    (D) An airline steward

5. (A) They need new print for the additional copies.
    (B) They can make extra copies if necessary.
    (C) Printers are needed for the additional copies.
    (D) Additional copies are needed immediately.

6. (A) The professor bought two books.
    (B) The students had to purchase two books.
    (C) The students sold two books to the professor.
    (D) The students were required to read two books by the professor.

7. (A) The doctor returned to the office.
   (B) Jim asked the doctor to come to the office.
   (C) The doctor will not return until next week.
   (D) Jim was told to come back.

8. (A) Go to work in the lab
   (B) Sample the work from the lab
   (C) Have the samples delivered
   (D) Send a note to the lab

9. (A) Mary became the new class president.
   (B) Sue took her place as class president.
   (C) In place of Mary, Sue became senior class president.
   (D) The senior class president replaced Sue and Mary.

10. (A) The panel was analyzed on the television program.
    (B) A committee evaluated recent political events.
    (C) The program featured a psychoanalyst.
    (D) The panel discussed the television program.

TOEFL REVIEW EXERCISE (Skills 1–6): In this exercise, listen carefully to each short dialogue and question on the recording, and then choose the best answer to the question.

 NOW BEGIN THE RECORDING AT TOEFL REVIEW EXERCISE (SKILLS 1–6).

1. (A) He seemed to be rather hungry.
   (B) She was quite angry at him.
   (C) He was trying to hang the posters.
   (D) She believes he was mad.

2. (A) The parents are going to stay up late.
   (B) The parents have given Hannah her allowance.
   (C) Lately, the parents have not been so loud.
   (D) Hannah does not have to go to bed early.

3. (A) At a department store
   (B) At a service station
   (C) At a collection agency
   (D) In a delivery room

4. (A) She just broke some eggs.
   (B) They need to eat fast.
   (C) She is serious about the boat.
   (D) He has a choice to make.

5. (A) It was urgent that Ellen do her best.
   (B) He really urged Ellen to do more.
   (C) He was encouraged by Ellen to try harder.
   (D) Ellen told him that she was trying to do better.

6. (A) The car stalled on the road.
   (B) Someone took the car.
   (C) Rob sold his car.
   (D) Rob heard someone steal his car.

7. (A) Buying the bigger container
   (B) Putting the milk in the cart
   (C) Taking a carton that is smaller
   (D) Getting the milk tomorrow instead

8. (A) The receptionist welcomed the businesspeople.
   (B) The man created a shipping and receiving business.
   (C) The businesspeople were rather greedy.
   (D) The businesspeople greeted the receptionist.

9. (A) The police officer was stationed near the tourist.
   (B) The tourist was forced to accompany the police officer.
   (C) The tourist became mad at the police station.
   (D) The tourist stated that the police officer never came.

10. (A) He hasn't seen her ideas.
    (B) It was a terrible deal.
    (C) He doesn't like the idea.
    (D) It sounds magnificent to him.

NEGATIVES

SKILL 7: LISTEN FOR NEGATIVE EXPRESSIONS

Negative expressions are very common in the short dialogues, and the most common kind of correct response to a negative statement is a positive statement containing a word with an opposite meaning.

Example from the Paper and Computer TOEFL® Tests

On the recording, you hear:

(man)   *How did they get to their grandmother's house in Maine in only five hours?*
(woman)   *They <u>didn't drive slowly</u> on the trip to Maine.*
(narrator) *What does the woman say about the trip?*

In your test book or on the computer screen, you read:

(A)   They drove rather <u>quickly</u>.
(B)   They couldn't have driven more slowly.
(C)   They wanted to travel slowly to Maine.
(D)   They didn't drive to Maine.

The correct answer is answer (A). If they *didn't* drive *slowly* to Maine, this means that they drove rather *quickly*. Notice that the correct answer uses *quickly*, the opposite of *slowly*. The answers that use *slowly* are not correct.

The following chart outlines the types of negative expressions that you should be careful of:

TYPES OF NEGATIVE EXPRESSIONS		
Expression	Example	Correct Answer
Regular negative: *not* or *n't*	Tom is *not sad* about the results.	*not sad = happy*
Other negatives: *nobody, none, nothing, never*	*Nobody* arrived *on time.* Sal *never works hard.*	*nobody ... on time = late* *never works hard = lazy*
Negative prefixes: *un-, in-, dis-*	The patient was *insane.*	*insane = not sane = crazy*

EXERCISE 7: In this exercise, underline the negative in the last line of each short dialogue. Then read the question and choose the best answer to that question. Remember that the best answer is one that uses an opposite meaning.

1. (man)   *I can't seem to get the door unlocked.*
    (woman)   *That isn't the right key for the door.*
    (narrator) *What does the woman mean?*

    (A)   The key in the drawer is on the right.
    (B)   The man should write the message on the door.
    (C)   The man has the wrong key.
    (D)   The right key isn't in the drawer.

2. (man)   *Were you pleased with last*   (A) The convention was disorganized.
                week's convention?   (B) She didn't plan to attend the
    (woman)   *Nothing went as planned.*   convention.
    (narrator) *What does the woman mean?*   (C) She planned the convention last week.
                                                  (D) She wasn't pleased with the last week of
                                                       the convention.

3. (woman)   *Are you planning to go to college* (A) He definitely wants to go to college.
                next year?   (B) He is certain about his plans.
    (man)   *I'm really unsure about the idea.* (C) He's hesitant about attending college.
    (narrator) *What does the man mean?*   (D) His idea is to go to college.

TOEFL EXERCISE 7: In this exercise, listen carefully to each short dialogue and question
on the recording, and then choose the best answer to the question. You should be particularly careful of negative expressions.

 NOW BEGIN THE RECORDING AT TOEFL EXERCISE 7.

1. (A) She is very busy.   6. (A) The service satisfied her.
    (B) She has lots of free time.   (B) The food was worse than the
    (C) It is not necessary to take out the   service.
         trash.   (C) She thought the service was bad.
    (D) She will do it if she has time.   (D) Neither the food nor the service
                                                      was satisfying.
2. (A) The interview is very important.
    (B) He is worried about the interview. 7. (A) He told his kids to leave.
    (C) What he's wearing to the interview   (B) He seriously wanted the woman to
         is important.   go.
    (D) He is not concerned about the   (C) He was joking when he told the
         interview.   woman to leave.
                                                 (D) He left with the woman.
3. (A) He has almost all the notes.
    (B) His attendance was perfect.   8. (A) The project will take all their effort.
    (C) He went to all the lectures but one.   (B) They have no other work to do.
    (D) He missed more than one   (C) It's impossible to finish.
         psychology class.   (D) They aren't even close to finishing
                                                      the project.
4. (A) They passed the library at
         6:00.   9. (A) She doesn't mind an hour more.
    (B) The library opens at 6:00 in the   (B) She'd rather stay more than an
         summer.   hour.
    (C) The library closes at 6:00.   (C) It's better to stay than go.
    (D) You can't check out more than six   (D) She prefers to leave.
         books in the summer.
                                             10. (A) The service at the hotel wasn't too
5. (A) Water the plants once a day.   good.
    (B) Give the plants no more water.   (B) This hotel gave excellent service.
    (C) Water the plants often while the   (C) The service at the hotel could have
         man is gone.   been improved.
    (D) Give the plants a limited amount of   (D) This hotel's service was the same as
         water.   the service at other hotels.

SKILL 8:   LISTEN FOR DOUBLE NEGATIVE EXPRESSIONS

It is possible for two negative ideas to appear in one sentence, and the result can be quite confusing.

Example from the Paper and Computer TOEFL® Tests

On the recording, you hear:

(man)   *I can't believe the news that I heard about the concert.*
(woman)   *Well, it isn't impossible for the concert to take place.*
(narrator) *What does the woman say about the concert?*

In your test book or on the computer screen, you read:

(A)   There's no possibility that the concert will take place.
(B)   The concert will definitely not take place.
(C)   The concert <u>might</u> take place.
(D)   The concert can't take place.

The correct answer to this question is answer (C). If it *isn't impossible* for the concert to take place, then it is possible, and the modal *might* indicates possibility.

The following chart outlines the situations where double negatives can occur:

DOUBLE NEGATIVES		
Situation	Example	Meaning
negative word (e.g., *not*, *no*, *none*) and a negative prefix (e.g., *in-*, *un-*, *dis-*)	He didn't like the *un*clean office.	did *not* like *un*clean office = liked clean office
two negative verbs	It *isn't snowing*, so they *aren't going* to the mountains.	implies that they would go if it were snowing
neither or *not . . . either*	Sue *didn't like* the movie, and *neither did* Mark.	both did not like the movie

EXERCISE 8:   In this exercise, underline the two negatives in the last line of each short dialogue. Then read the question and choose the best answer to that question. Remember that two negatives can make the sentence positive.

1. (man)   *Paula, you worked so hard setting up the field trip.*
    (woman)   *I hope no one's unhappy with the arrangements.*
    (narrator) *What does Paula mean?*

(A)   She hopes everyone will be pleased.
(B)   She knows no one is happy with what she has done.
(C)   She's arranged to take a trip because she's unhappy.
(D)   Everyone's happy with the condition of the field.

2. (woman)   *How was your history exam?*
    (man)   *I didn't study enough, so I didn't do well.*
    (narrator) *What does the man mean?*

    (A) He studied a lot and passed.
    (B) He failed in spite of his effort.
    (C) He got a good grade even though he didn't study.
    (D) His grade was poor because of inadequate preparation.

3. (man)   *Were your friends able to get tickets for the concert?*
    (woman)   *Mark couldn't get tickets for the concert, and neither could Paul.*
    (narrator) *What does the woman mean?*

    (A) Although Mark couldn't get both tickets, Paul did.
    (B) Both were unable to obtain tickets.
    (C) Neither Mark nor Paul wanted to go to the concert.
    (D) Mark tried to get tickets, but Paul didn't.

TOEFL EXERCISE 8: In this exercise, listen carefully to each short dialogue and question on the recording, and then choose the best answer to the question. You should be particularly careful of double negatives.

  NOW BEGIN THE RECORDING AT TOEFL EXERCISE 8.

1. (A) He'll definitely be elected.
    (B) The election is now complete.
    (C) She has high hopes for his chances.
    (D) It may happen.

2. (A) Both parts of his game were bad.
    (B) He served better than he volleyed.
    (C) Some parts of his game were better than others.
    (D) He played rather well.

3. (A) It is a surprise that he was prepared.
    (B) He was not ready, as usual.
    (C) He prepared a really big surprise.
    (D) His strong preparation came as no surprise.

4. (A) She felt good enough to go out.
    (B) She went out to get some medicine.
    (C) She felt like dancing, so she went out with everyone.
    (D) She stayed home because she was sick.

5. (A) She has problems that others aren't aware of.
    (B) Others aren't aware of her problems.
    (C) She knows she's been a problem.
    (D) She doesn't have a care in the world.

6. (A) Steve wanted to finish his paper, and so did Paul.
    (B) Both Steve's and Paul's papers were incomplete.
    (C) Steve and Paul were busy doing their term papers.
    (D) When Steve wasn't able to finish his paper, Paul couldn't help.

7. (A) It wasn't George's responsibility to pay the bill.
    (B) Bill was irresponsible about paying George's rent.
    (C) George acted carelessly by not taking care of the bill.
    (D) George took responsibility for the unpaid bill.

8. (A) It's fortunate that he was accepted.
    (B) It's good that he wasn't admitted.
    (C) Fortunately, the university didn't admit him.
    (D) It's too bad he was rejected.

9. (A) The first essay was better than the
        second.
   (B) The first and second drafts
        couldn't be better.
   (C) The second draft of the essay was
        much better than the first.
   (D) Both versions were poorly written.

10. (A) Roger has been bothered.
    (B) Roger wasn't the least bit
         disturbed.
    (C) The problems have had little effect
         on Roger.
    (D) Roger hasn't been disturbed.

SKILL 9: LISTEN FOR "ALMOST NEGATIVE" EXPRESSIONS

Certain expressions in English have "almost negative" meanings. These expressions are common in the short dialogues.

Example from the Paper and Computer TOEFL® Tests

On the recording, you hear:

(woman)   *Were you able to pay the electric bill?*
(man)   *I had barely enough money.*
(narrator) *What does the man imply?*

In your test book or on the computer screen, you read:

(A) He had plenty of money for the bill.
(B) He did not have enough money for the bill.
(C) He paid the bill but has no money left.
(D) He was unable to pay the bill.

In the man's statement, the word *enough* indicates that there was *enough,* so he *paid the bill.* However, it was *barely* enough, so he almost did not have enough and certainly *has no money left.* The correct answer is therefore answer (C).

The following chart outlines common "almost negative" expressions:

COMMON ALMOST NEGATIVE EXPRESSIONS		
Meaning	Expression	Example
almost none	*hardly, barely, scarcely, only*	There is *hardly* any food in the refrigerator.
almost never	*rarely, seldom*	He *rarely* drives to work.

EXERCISE 9: In this exercise, underline the "almost negative" expression in the last line of each short dialogue. Then read the question and choose the best answer. Remember that the best answer is one that means that it *is true* but it is *almost not* true.

1. (man)   *I hear that Mona's been offered
             the manager's job.*
   (woman) *But she has hardly any work
             experience!*
   (narrator) *What does the woman say about
               Mona?*

   (A) Mona hasn't worked hard.
   (B) Mona's experience has been hard.
   (C) Mona's job as manager is hard.
   (D) Mona hasn't worked for very long.

2. (woman)   *How much time did Sam spend on his paper for economics class?*

    (man)   *Sam has seldom taken so much time on a research paper.*

    (narrator) *What does the man mean?*

    (A) Sam usually spends this much time on his schoolwork.
    (B) Sam has rarely worked so hard.
    (C) Sam took too much time on this paper.
    (D) Sam should've worked harder on this paper.

3. (woman)   *Does Steve usually park his car there?*

    (man)   *Only once has he parked his car in that lot.*

    (narrator) *What does the man mean?*

    (A) He parks his car there once in a while.
    (B) He's parked his car there a lot.
    (C) He only leaves his car there for short periods of time.
    (D) He left his car there on just one occasion.

TOEFL EXERCISE 9: In this exercise, listen carefully to each short dialogue and question on the recording, and then choose the best answer to the question. You should be particularly careful of "almost negative" expressions.

  NOW BEGIN THE RECORDING AT TOEFL EXERCISE 9.

1. (A) There's little rain in July.
    (B) In July it never rains.
    (C) It rains hard in July.
    (D) When it rains in July, it rains hard.

2. (A) The university accepted three students.
    (B) None of the students is going to the university.
    (C) John was not accepted.
    (D) Two were not admitted.

3. (A) Although he did pass, Mark's exam grade wasn't too good.
    (B) Mark failed his history exam.
    (C) The highest grade on the history exam went to Mark.
    (D) Professor Franks didn't pass Mark on the history exam.

4. (A) He often has long waits in Dr. Roberts's office.
    (B) He must wait patiently for Robert.
    (C) Dr. Roberts is generally punctual.
    (D) He doesn't mind waiting for Dr. Roberts.

5. (A) Betty often takes vacations in winter.
    (B) Betty prefers to take vacations in winter.
    (C) Occasionally Betty works one week during vacation.
    (D) A winter vacation is unusual for Betty.

6. (A) He rarely spends time on his courses.
    (B) He's an excellent student.
    (C) He never studies.
    (D) His books are always open.

7. (A) He finished the exam in plenty of time.
    (B) He was scared he wouldn't finish.
    (C) He used every possible minute to finish.
    (D) He was unable to complete the exam.

8. (A) This was a very long staff meeting.
    (B) This was the only staff meeting in a long time.
    (C) The meeting lasted only until one o'clock.
    (D) The one staff meeting should've lasted longer.

9. (A) Meat tastes delicious to him when
         it's cooked rare.
    (B) He isn't sure if the meal is
         delicious.
    (C) This meat is the best he's tasted in
         a long time.
    (D) He'd like to eat some meat from
         this delicatessen.

10. (A) He broke his arm trying to move it.
    (B) He only hurt the broken arm.
    (C) He only tries to move the broken
         arm.
    (D) There's no pain if he rests quietly.

SKILL 10: LISTEN FOR NEGATIVES WITH COMPARATIVES

Negatives can be used with comparatives in the short dialogues of the TOEFL test. A sentence with a negative and a comparative has a superlative, or very strong, meaning.

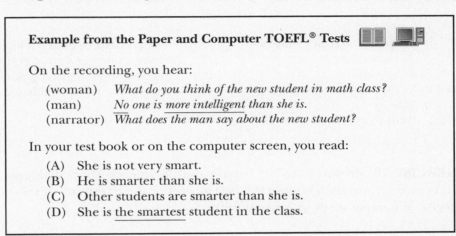

Example from the Paper and Computer TOEFL® Tests

On the recording, you hear:

  (woman)   *What do you think of the new student in math class?*
  (man)   *No one is more intelligent than she is.*
  (narrator) *What does the man say about the new student?*

In your test book or on the computer screen, you read:

  (A) She is not very smart.
  (B) He is smarter than she is.
  (C) Other students are smarter than she is.
  (D) She is the smartest student in the class.

The man responds to the woman's question with the negative *No* and the comparative *more intelligent*, and this combination has a superlative meaning, *the smartest*. The best answer is therefore answer (D).

   The following chart outlines comparisons that you should be careful of when they are used with negatives:

COMPARATIVES WITH NEGATIVES		
Comparative	Example	Meaning
more	*No* one is *more* beautiful than she is.	She is *the most* beautiful.
-er	He could*n't* be happi*er*.	He is *extremely* happy.

EXERCISE 10: In this exercise, underline the negative and the comparative in the second line of each short dialogue. Then read the question and choose the best answer to that question. Remember that the best answer is one that expresses a superlative, or very strong, idea.

1. (woman)   *Have you gotten over your cold yet?*
   (man)   *I couldn't be feeling any better today.*
   (narrator)   *What does the man mean?*

   (A) He's feeling terrific.
   (B) He felt a lot worse today.
   (C) He's not feeling too well today.
   (D) He's a bit better today.

2. (woman)   *What did you think of Mike when you first met him?*
   (man)   *He couldn't have been more unfriendly.*
   (narrator)   *What does the man mean?*

   (A) Mike was extremely friendly when he met him.
   (B) Mike could have met him sooner.
   (C) Mike didn't seem to like him at all.
   (D) When he met Mike, he didn't have a friend.

3. (man)   *Did you see Theresa's grade on the math exam? It was unbelievable!*
   (woman)   *No one else could have done better.*
   (narrator)   *What does the woman mean?*

   (A) Theresa could've gotten a higher grade.
   (B) Anyone could get a good grade.
   (C) Theresa got the highest grade.
   (D) A high grade is impossible for anyone.

TOEFL EXERCISE 10: In this exercise, listen carefully to each short dialogue and question on the recording, and then choose the best answer to the question. You should be particularly careful of comparatives with negatives.

 NOW BEGIN THE RECORDING AT TOEFL EXERCISE 10.

1. (A) She's not very happy.
   (B) She didn't do very well on the exam.
   (C) She could be somewhat happier.
   (D) She's delighted with the results.

2. (A) Paula is always lazy.
   (B) Paula didn't work very hard this semester.
   (C) Paula made a strong effort.
   (D) Paula could have worked harder.

3. (A) The prices were great!
   (B) The prices were too high.
   (C) She didn't buy much because of the prices.
   (D) The prices could have been lower.

4. (A) She is not very smart.
   (B) She always tells him everything.
   (C) He doesn't know her very well.
   (D) She's extremely intelligent.

5. (A) The patient absolutely didn't need the surgery.
   (B) The necessity for the surgery was unquestionable.
   (C) The surgeon felt that the operation was necessary.
   (D) It was essential that the surgery be performed immediately.

6. (A) They were not very lucky.
   (B) No one was hurt.
   (C) The accident was unfortunate.
   (D) She wanted to have better luck.

7. (A) Nothing was very difficult.
   (B) The exam wasn't at all easy.
   (C) The exam couldn't have been easier.
   (D) The exam had nothing difficult on it.

8. (A) She wants that job very much.
   (B) No one is going to get the job.
   (C) Everybody else wants that job as much as she does.
   (D) She is not sure about taking the job.

9. (A) She was second in the race.
   (B) She was almost the slowest person in the race.
   (C) She won the race.
   (D) She was not faster than anyone else.

10. (A) This math project was extremely complex.
    (B) This math project was less complicated than the last.
    (C) They seldom complete their math projects.
    (D) Complicated math projects are often assigned.

TOEFL EXERCISE (Skills 7–10): In this exercise, listen carefully to each short dialogue and question on the recording, and then choose the best answer to the question.

 NOW BEGIN THE RECORDING AT TOEFL EXERCISE (SKILLS 7–10).

1. (A) She can try a little harder.
   (B) There is a lot more that she can do.
   (C) She's doing the best that she can.
   (D) It is impossible for her to do anything.

2. (A) She's always been late for the bus.
   (B) The bus has always been late.
   (C) The bus only left on time once.
   (D) Only on this trip has the bus been on time.

3. (A) There wasn't enough soup to go around.
   (B) We had so much soup that we couldn't finish it.
   (C) Everyone got one serving of soup, but there wasn't enough for seconds.
   (D) Everyone around the table had a lot of soup.

4. (A) She does want to see the movie.
   (B) It's extremely important to her to go.
   (C) She doesn't want to go there anymore.
   (D) She really couldn't move there.

5. (A) She handed the paper in on time.
   (B) She was able to complete the paper, but she didn't turn it in.
   (C) The paper was a complete mess, so she didn't turn it in.
   (D) The paper was unfinished.

6. (A) Neither Tim nor Sylvia is taking care of Art.
   (B) Sylvia likes modern art even less than Tim does.
   (C) Sylvia doesn't care for anything Tim does.
   (D) Sylvia and Tim agree in their opinion of modern art.

7. (A) They always work hard in the afternoon.
   (B) They don't do much after lunch.
   (C) After noon they never work.
   (D) It's never hard for them to work in the afternoon.

8. (A) It's hard for him to work when it gets warm.
   (B) Whenever it gets warm, he turns on the air-conditioner.
   (C) The air-conditioner only works when it isn't needed.
   (D) He likes to use the air-conditioner when it is warm.

9. (A) He did really poorly.
    (B) He's felt worse before.
    (C) The results could not have been better.
    (D) He's not too unhappy with the results.

10. (A) With so many members present, the committee couldn't reach a decision.
    (B) The committee should've waited until more members were present.
    (C) The issue shouldn't have been decided by all the committed members.
    (D) The issue wasn't decided because so many members were absent.

TOEFL REVIEW EXERCISE (Skills 1–10): In this exercise, listen carefully to each short dialogue and question on the recording, and then choose the best answer to the question.

  NOW BEGIN THE RECORDING AT TOEFL REVIEW EXERCISE (SKILLS 1–10).

1. (A) In a doctor's office
    (B) At a bar
    (C) In a travel agency
    (D) In a business office

2. (A) She bought some sheets.
    (B) She got a new piece of clothing.
    (C) She couldn't find anything because she's too short.
    (D) She was sure to greet her boss.

3. (A) The hotel was all right, except for the poor view.
    (B) The view from the hotel room was spectacular.
    (C) She would have preferred a better hotel.
    (D) Only a few hotels would have been better.

4. (A) Take a nap
    (B) Try the rest of the work
    (C) See a doctor
    (D) Have a bite to eat

5. (A) She's an exacting person.
    (B) She can't be expected to give you four of them.
    (C) She generally forgives others.
    (D) She isn't exact about what she gives to others.

6. (A) She's unable to take her vacation this year.
    (B) Her vacation next week has been postponed.
    (C) She'll go on vacation next week.
    (D) She'll return from vacation in a week.

7. (A) The waitress was sitting in the back of the restaurant.
    (B) They were waiting for a seat in the restaurant.
    (C) The customers had a table in the back.
    (D) The waitress sat down behind the table.

8. (A) It's hard for the market to sell its fruit.
    (B) All of the fresh fruit at the market is hard.
    (C) She hardly ever goes to the market to buy fresh fruit.
    (D) There was a scarcity of fresh fruit at the market.

9. (A) The man should never be late for school.
    (B) The man can always return to school.
    (C) The man should never go back to school.
    (D) If the man's late to school, he should go through the back door.

10. (A) She can't bear to try.
    (B) She is a daring person.
    (C) She doesn't want the man even to try.
    (D) She is challenging the man to make the effort.

FUNCTIONS

SKILL 11: LISTEN FOR EXPRESSIONS OF AGREEMENT

Expressions of agreement are common in the short dialogues, so you should become familiar with them. The following example shows agreement with a *positive* statement.

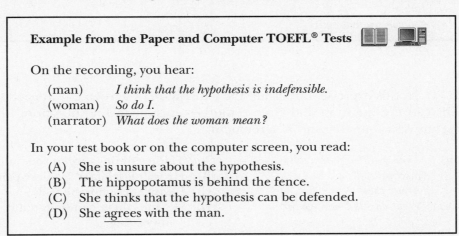

Example from the Paper and Computer TOEFL® Tests

On the recording, you hear:

(man)	*I think that the hypothesis is indefensible.*
(woman)	*So do I.*
(narrator)	*What does the woman mean?*

In your test book or on the computer screen, you read:

(A) She is unsure about the hypothesis.
(B) The hippopotamus is behind the fence.
(C) She thinks that the hypothesis can be defended.
(D) She agrees with the man.

The expression *So do I* is an expression that shows agreement with a *positive* statement, so the woman means that she *agrees* with the man. The best answer is therefore answer (D).

Other expressions are used to show agreement with negative statements.

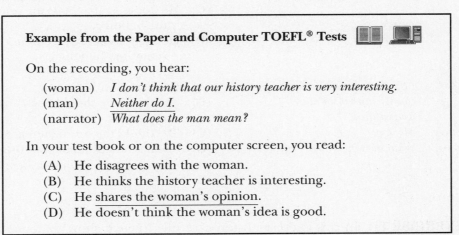

Example from the Paper and Computer TOEFL® Tests

On the recording, you hear:

(woman)	*I don't think that our history teacher is very interesting.*
(man)	*Neither do I.*
(narrator)	*What does the man mean?*

In your test book or on the computer screen, you read:

(A) He disagrees with the woman.
(B) He thinks the history teacher is interesting.
(C) He shares the woman's opinion.
(D) He doesn't think the woman's idea is good.

The expression *Neither do I* is an expression that shows agreement with a negative statement, so the man *shares the woman's opinion*. The best answer is therefore answer (C).

The following chart lists common expressions that show agreement. You should become familiar with these expressions:

EXPRESSIONS OF AGREEMENT	
Agreement with Positive Statements	Agreement with Negative Statements
So do I. *Me, too.* *I'll say!* *Isn't it!* *You can say that again!*	*Neither do I.* *I don't either.*

EXERCISE 11: In this exercise, underline the expression of agreement in each short dialogue. Then read the question and choose the best answer to that question. Remember that the best answer is one that shows agreement.

1. (woman) *These paintings are really fascinating!*
   (man) *Aren't they!*
   (narrator) *What does the man mean?*

   (A) These paintings aren't very interesting.
   (B) He isn't fascinated by these paintings.
   (C) He isn't sure how he feels.
   (D) He finds these paintings quite interesting.

2. (woman) *I don't really care for the way the building was renovated.*
   (man) *I don't either.*
   (narrator) *What does the man mean?*

   (A) He thinks the building was not renovated.
   (B) He has the same opinion of the building as the woman.
   (C) He doesn't care about the renovation of the building.
   (D) He suggests being careful in the renovated building.

3. (man) *I think that both candidates for county supervisor are unqualified.*
   (woman) *Me, too.*
   (narrator) *What does the woman mean?*

   (A) She agrees with the man.
   (B) She thinks he should become county supervisor.
   (C) She thinks the candidates are qualified.
   (D) She has no opinion about the candidates for county supervisor.

TOEFL EXERCISE 11: In this exercise, listen carefully to each short dialogue and question on the recording, and then choose the best answer to the question. You should pay attention to expressions of agreement.

  NOW BEGIN THE RECORDING AT TOEFL EXERCISE 11.

1. (A) The trip would cost too much.
   (B) She doesn't think that a trip would be a good idea.
   (C) She would like to take two trips rather than one.
   (D) She would also like to take a trip.

2. (A) He would like to see the elections for town council.
   (B) He agrees that Matt should be elected.
   (C) He thinks the elections should take place next month.
   (D) He disagrees with the woman.

3. (A) She is not sure which course she should take.
   (B) She's not sure if she should take a trip to France.
   (C) She knows that she is not ready for intermediate French.
   (D) She wants to take neither beginning nor intermediate French.

4. (A) The man should repeat what he said.
   (B) The man said something foolish.
   (C) She thinks that the food is the best she has ever tasted.
   (D) She agrees that the food is pretty bad.

5. (A) This party hasn't been any fun at all.
   (B) He wonders if the woman enjoyed herself.
   (C) He wants to know what she said.
   (D) He's enjoyed himself tremendously.

6. (A) She condones what happened.
   (B) She does not like what the man said.
   (C) She agrees with the man about what happened.
   (D) She says that she did not do it.

7. (A) He thinks the parties aren't loud.
   (B) He says that the neighbors don't have many parties.
   (C) He agrees that the upstairs neighbors are noisy.
   (D) The loud parties don't bother him.

8. (A) She doesn't like this meal too much.
   (B) This food tastes wonderful to her.
   (C) She's not sure if she likes it.
   (D) She can't stand this meal.

9. (A) She agrees that getting the car was not a good idea.
   (B) She imagines that she would like to have a similar car.
   (C) She thinks that the man is mistaken about the car.
   (D) She thinks the man has no imagination.

10. (A) He would like the woman to repeat what she said.
    (B) He thinks that one semester is enough time for the course.
    (C) He also thinks that the course should be extended.
    (D) He would like to take the course two semesters from now.

SKILL 12: LISTEN FOR EXPRESSIONS OF UNCERTAINTY AND SUGGESTION

Expressions of uncertainty and suggestion are common in the short dialogues, so you should become familiar with them. The following example shows an expression of uncertainty.

Example from the Paper and Computer TOEFL® Tests

On the recording, you hear:

(man)   *Do you know anything about the final exam in physics?*
(woman)   *It's going to be rather difficult, isn't it?*
(narrator) *What does the woman mean?*

In your test book or on the computer screen, you read:

(A) The exam is not going to be too difficult.
(B) She's positive that it's going to be hard.
(C) She thinks that it might be hard.
(D) She has no idea about the exam.

The tag question *isn't it* changes a definite statement into a statement that shows uncertainty, so the best answer is one that expresses uncertainty. The best answer to this question is answer (C) because the words *thinks* and *might* express uncertainty.

Other expressions that are common in the short dialogues are expressions of suggestion.

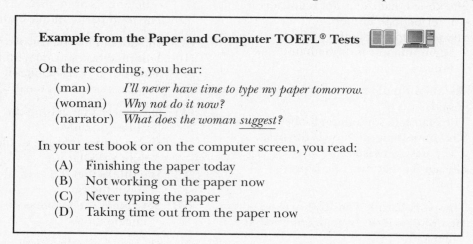

In this example, the expression *Why not* is an expression of suggestion, so the woman suggests *doing it now*. In this suggestion, the woman is referring to the paper that the man needs to type, so the best answer is answer (A).

The following chart lists common expressions that show uncertainty and suggestion:

EXPRESSIONS OF UNCERTAINTY AND SUGGESTION	
Uncertainty	Suggestion
...isn't it (tag)? *As far as I know.* *As far as I can tell.*	*Why not...?* *Let's...*

EXERCISE 12: In this exercise, underline the expression of uncertainty or suggestion in each short dialogue. Then read the question and choose the best answer to that question. Remember that the best answer is one that shows uncertainty or suggestion.

1. (man)   *Do you know what time they're leaving for the city?*
   (woman) *They have to leave at four o'clock, don't they?*
   (narrator) *What does the woman mean?*

   (A) She's not completely sure when they are leaving.
   (B) They are returning from the city at about 4:00.
   (C) She knows when they are leaving.
   (D) She doesn't have any idea when they are leaving.

2. (woman) *I'm so thirsty from all this walking.*
   (man)   *Let's stop and get a drink.*
   (narrator) *What does the man suggest?*

   (A) They should stop drinking.
   (B) They should go for a walk.
   (C) They should walk thirty miles.
   (D) They should take a break and have a drink.

3. (man)   *Is the exam still scheduled for*
                3:00 on Thursday?
    (woman)   *As far as I know.*
    (narrator) *What does the woman mean?*

(A) The exam is far away.
(B) She knows that the exam schedule has
     been changed.
(C) She is sure that the exam is set for
     Thursday.
(D) She thinks she knows when the
     test is.

TOEFL EXERCISE 12: In this exercise, listen carefully to each short dialogue and question on the recording, and then choose the best answer to the question. You should be particularly careful of expressions of uncertainty and suggestion.

 NOW BEGIN THE RECORDING AT TOEFL EXERCISE 12.

1. (A) He's sure about which chapters
         they are to read.
    (B) He thinks he knows what the
         assignment is.
    (C) He has to tell her how far she
         should go.
    (D) The professor told them to read
         the chapters after the exam.

2. (A) The man should take the pie out.
    (B) The man should try something
         else.
    (C) The man shouldn't try cherry pie.
    (D) The man should feel sorry.

3. (A) He knows the movie starts at 8:00.
    (B) He is not quite sure when the
         movie begins.
    (C) He thinks the start of the movie has
         been changed.
    (D) He will start the movie himself at
         8:00.

4. (A) Not doing the dishes now
    (B) Leaving the house with the dishes
    (C) Leaving later so that they can do
         the dishes now
    (D) Washing the dishes before they
         leave

5. (A) She's told Matt he'll go far.
    (B) Matt has far from enough talent.
    (C) She told Matt to roll farther.
    (D) She believes Matt has the ability for
         the part.

6. (A) They should go to the hospital.
    (B) Mary should visit the man.
    (C) The woman should try not to break
         her leg.
    (D) They should go on a trip with Mary.

7. (A) She knows where the children are.
    (B) The children have finished playing
         ball.
    (C) She's going to the park to find the
         children.
    (D) She believes that the children are
         in the park.

8. (A) The man should try to borrow
         some from a neighbor.
    (B) The man should take a check to
         Tom.
    (C) The man should work on his math
         assignment with Tom.
    (D) The man should check behind the
         door.

9. (A) He thinks the bill is due in the
         middle of the month.
    (B) The bill is approximately fifteen
         dollars.
    (C) He knows when they should pay the
         bill.
    (D) The bill is going to be fifteen days
         late.

10. (A) They should postpone their
         decision until morning.
    (B) They should go to sleep in the new
         house.
    (C) They should not buy such a big
         house.
    (D) They should decide where to go to
         sleep.

SKILL 13:   LISTEN FOR EMPHATIC EXPRESSIONS OF SURPRISE

Emphatic expressions of surprise are common in the short dialogues, so you should become familiar with them. When surprise is expressed, it implies that the speaker did not expect something to be true.

Example from the Paper and Computer TOEFL® Tests

On the recording, you hear:

    (woman)   *Did you see Paul driving around in his Mustang?*
    (man)   *Then he DID get a new car.*
    (narrator) *What had the man thought?*

In your test book or on the computer screen, you read:

    (A)   Paul would definitely get a Mustang.
    (B)   Paul did not know how to drive.
    (C)   Paul did not like Mustangs.
    (D)   Paul would not get a new car.

In this dialogue the emphatic form *he did get* is used to show the man's surprise that Paul got a new car. It means that the man expected that Paul *would not get* a new car, so the best answer is answer (D).

    The following chart outlines various ways to express emphatic surprise:

EXPRESSIONS OF EMPHATIC SURPRISE			
Verb	Emphatic Form	Example	Meaning
be	*be*, with emphasis	Then he *is* here!	I thought he was not here.
modal	modal, with emphasis	Then you *can* go!	I thought you could not go.
present tense	*do(es)*, with emphasis	Then you *do* play tennis!	I thought you did not play tennis.
past tense	*did*, with emphasis	Then she *did* read it.	I thought she had not read it.
perfect tense	*have*, with emphasis	Then he *has* gone there.	I thought he had not gone there.

EXERCISE 13:   In this exercise, underline the expression of emphatic surprise in each short dialogue. Then read the question and choose the best answer to that question. Remember that the best answer is one that shows surprise.

1. (man)   *I just got 600 on the TOEFL*   (A)   The man had not passed.
                 test!   (B)   The man would pass easily.
      (woman)   *Then you did pass.*   (C)   The man had already passed.
      (narrator) *What had the woman assumed?*   (D)   The man got the score he was expected
                                                         to get.

2. (woman)   *Would you like to go skiing this*   (A) The woman was a good skier.
                weekend?   (B) The woman was going skiing this
    (man)   *So you can ski!*   weekend.
    (narrator) *What had the man assumed?*   (C) The woman did not know how to ski.
                                                          (D) The woman did not intend to go skiing.

3. (man)   *I just got this letter from my*   (A) The man's sister never wrote to him.
                sister.   (B) The mail had not yet arrived.
    (woman)   *So the mail has come already.*   (C) The mail always came early.
    (narrator) *What had the woman assumed?*   (D) The mail had already arrived.

TOEFL EXERCISE 13: In this exercise, listen carefully to each short dialogue and question on the recording, and then choose the best answer to the question. You should be particularly careful of expressions of emphatic surprise.

 Now begin the recording at Toefl Exercise 13.

1. (A) Greg always comes to parties.   5. (A) He had been somewhere else.
    (B) Greg would come to the party later.   (B) He had been in the library.
    (C) Greg was unable to attend the   (C) He had been working on his
         party.   research project.
    (D) Greg would stay at the party for   (D) He would start working on his
         only a moment.   project in five hours.

2. (A) The woman always rode her   6. (A) He had changed apartments.
         motorcycle to school.   (B) He did not like his new apartment.
    (B) The woman was not coming to   (C) He was still in his old apartment.
         school today.   (D) He had moved from a house to an
    (C) The woman was an expert   apartment.
         motorcycle rider.
    (D) The woman did not know how to   7. (A) The woman did not like desserts.
         ride a motorcycle.   (B) The woman ate sweets regularly.
                                                   (C) The woman would not share her
3. (A) The man was not a very good cook.   chocolate cake.
    (B) The man never invited friends over   (D) The woman had eaten his piece of
         for dinner.   cake.
    (C) The man would never invite him
         over for dinner.   8. (A) The man was going to study hard.
    (D) The man was an excellent cook.   (B) The man already had a driver's
                                                        license.
4. (A) The woman had run more than   (C) The man would not take the test.
         three miles.   (D) The man had already taken the
    (B) The woman always got lots of   test.
         exercise.
    (C) The woman ran for three hours in
         the morning.
    (D) The woman had not gotten much
         exercise.

9. (A) She had registered in physics.
    (B) She would go to physics class later.
    (C) She had already taken a physics class.
    (D) She had not enrolled in physics.

10. (A) The pipes were not clear.
    (B) The plumber would be late.
    (C) The plumber had already cleared the pipes.
    (D) The pipes did not need to be cleared.

TOEFL EXERCISE (Skills 11–13): In this exercise, listen carefully to each short dialogue and question on the recording, and then choose the best answer to the question.

  NOW BEGIN THE RECORDING AT TOEFL EXERCISE (SKILLS 11–13).

1. (A) She plans to talk a lot this month.
    (B) She has a lot to say about the phone bill.
    (C) The bill is high because she has a lot to say.
    (D) She agrees with the man.

2. (A) Bill had never really been sick.
    (B) Bill was too sick to come to class.
    (C) Bill was sick of calculus class.
    (D) Bill had forgotten about the calculus class that morning.

3. (A) The man should go out tonight.
    (B) The man should stay home and relax.
    (C) The man should work on the paper tonight.
    (D) The man should go out Monday instead.

4. (A) The cafeteria was open in the morning.
    (B) The cafeteria did not serve breakfast.
    (C) The breakfast in the cafeteria was not very tasty.
    (D) The woman never ate breakfast in the cafeteria.

5. (A) He believes that it is acceptable to park there.
    (B) The parking lot is too far from their destination.
    (C) He knows that they won't get a ticket.
    (D) He knows where the parking lot is.

6. (A) He would be glad to say it over again.
    (B) He would like the woman to repeat what she said.
    (C) He says that he would like to take the class again.
    (D) He's happy the class is over, too.

7. (A) He finished all the problems.
    (B) He doesn't believe what the woman said.
    (C) He was able to finish some of the problems.
    (D) Both he and the woman were unsuccessful on the math problems.

8. (A) The man had mailed the package.
    (B) The man had forgotten to go to the post office.
    (C) The man had given the package to the woman to mail.
    (D) The man remembered the package after he went to the post office.

9. (A) They should take both cars.
    (B) The woman should try not to be afraid.
    (C) The woman should buy a bigger car.
    (D) They should go together in his car.

10. (A) He wants to know if the muffins taste good.
    (B) He thinks the muffins were recently prepared.
    (C) The muffins are not really fresh.
    (D) He's sure that the muffins were just made.

TOEFL REVIEW EXERCISE (Skills 1–13): In this exercise, listen carefully to each short dialogue and question on the recording, and then choose the best answer to the question.

 NOW BEGIN THE RECORDING AT TOEFL REVIEW EXERCISE (SKILLS 1–13).

1. (A) Write a message to the man
   (B) Make some phone calls
   (C) Respond to the man's questions
   (D) Get a new phone installed

2. (A) She's not sure if she's free.
   (B) She's marked it on her calendar.
   (C) She'll write a check for the calendar.
   (D) Her calendar says she has to have a meeting at 3:00.

3. (A) He barely rode the bicycle.
   (B) He didn't have enough money.
   (C) The bicycle didn't need to be paid for.
   (D) He paid for the bicycle.

4. (A) She fixed the television.
   (B) Bob made the television work.
   (C) The woman looked at Bob on television.
   (D) Bob works for the woman.

5. (A) He helped her say what she couldn't say.
   (B) She was unable to say anything about him.
   (C) He hasn't helped her very much.
   (D) What he said was very helpful.

6. (A) The man should spend more time on registration.
   (B) The man should walk more quickly through registration.
   (C) The man should send in his registration materials.
   (D) The man should try to avoid registering next semester.

7. (A) He couldn't find Paula's phone number, so he didn't call her.
   (B) He couldn't give Paula the list over the phone.
   (C) When he went to call Paula, he couldn't find the list.
   (D) He couldn't recollect the number that was on the list.

8. (A) She couldn't take her luggage to the store.
   (B) She stored her luggage at the train station.
   (C) She carried her luggage from the train station to the store.
   (D) There were no lockers for her bags.

9. (A) The woman had taken a different major.
   (B) The woman had chosen psychology as a major.
   (C) The woman was uninformed.
   (D) The woman needed to see a psychiatrist.

10. (A) She would like the man to repeat what he said.
    (B) She thinks the exam could have been a little more difficult.
    (C) She shares the same opinion of the exam as the man.
    (D) She believes that the exam was easy.

CONTRARY MEANINGS _____

SKILL 14: LISTEN FOR WISHES

Conversations about wishes can appear in the short dialogues. The important idea to remember about wishes is that a wish implies that *the opposite of the wish is true.*

Example from the Paper and Computer TOEFL® Tests

On the recording, you hear:

(woman)   *It's too bad that you have to stay here and work during the school break.*
(man)   *I really <u>wish</u> I <u>could go</u> with you and the others to Palm Springs.*
(narrator)   *What does the man mean?*

In your test book or on the computer screen, you read:

(A)   Maybe he will go with the others on the trip.
(B)   He is <u>unable to go</u> on the trip.
(C)   He's happy to be going on the trip.
(D)   He's going on the trip, but not with the others.

In this dialogue the man *wishes* that he *could go* with the others on the trip, so the implied meaning is that he is *unable to go*. The correct answer is therefore answer (B).

The following chart outlines the key points that you should know about wishes:

KEY INFORMATION ABOUT *WISHES*		
Point	Example	Meaning
• An *affirmative* wish implies a *negative* reality.	I wish I *had time* to help.	= no time to help
• A *negative* wish implies an *affirmative* reality.	I wish I *did not have time* to help.	= time to help
• A *past* tense verb implies a *present* reality.	I wish he *were* at home.*	= is not at home
• A *past perfect* tense verb implies a *past* reality.	I wish he *had been* at home.	= was not at home

*Remember that *were* is used instead of *was* in wishes. I wish I *were* going.

EXERCISE 14: In this exercise, underline the wish in each short dialogue. Then read the question and choose the best answer to that question. Remember that the best answer is one that implies the opposite of what is said.

1. (man)   *Do you think we'll be able to have the picnic today?*
    (woman)   *I wish the sky weren't so cloudy.*
    (narrator)   *What does the woman mean?*

    (A)   The sky is not very cloudy.
    (B)   The sky yesterday was cloudier than it is today.
    (C)   The sky is too cloudy.
    (D)   The sky is rather clear.

2. (woman)   *Did you enjoy the Thanksgiving dinner?*
    (man)   *I wish I hadn't eaten so much.*
    (narrator)   *What does the man mean?*

    (A)   He didn't eat very much.
    (B)   He plans on eating a lot.
    (C)   He thinks he is eating a lot.
    (D)   He ate too much.

3. (man)   *Are you coming to the party tonight?*

    (woman)   *I wish I could.*

    (narrator) *What does the woman mean?*

    (A) She is coming to the party.
    (B) She might come to the party.
    (C) She will try to come to the party.
    (D) She is not coming to the party.

TOEFL EXERCISE 14: In this exercise, listen carefully to each short dialogue and question on the recording, and then choose the best answer to the question. You should remember that a wish implies an opposite meaning.

 NOW BEGIN THE RECORDING AT TOEFL EXERCISE 14.

1. (A) The line is short.
    (B) There are not very many people in front of them.
    (C) The line in front of them is too long.
    (D) Not many people want to get tickets to the concert.

2. (A) The woman told him about the ticket.
    (B) He wanted the woman to get a ticket.
    (C) He was happy to find out about the ticket.
    (D) The woman did not tell him about the ticket.

3. (A) She is not working too many hours next week.
    (B) She doesn't have enough hours next week.
    (C) She is working too many hours next week.
    (D) She likes working so much.

4. (A) The department did not change the requirements.
    (B) She likes the new requirements.
    (C) She changed her apartment just before graduation.
    (D) She does not like the changes that the department made.

5. (A) He is going to the theater.
    (B) He doesn't have enough money.
    (C) He isn't afraid to go.
    (D) He doesn't want to spend the money.

6. (A) Harry did not prepare enough for the exam.
    (B) Harry studied hard for the exam.
    (C) He has not heard anything about Harry.
    (D) He had a bet with Harry.

7. (A) The algebra course that she is taking is not her favorite.
    (B) She doesn't need to take the algebra course.
    (C) She has a good schedule of courses this semester.
    (D) She's good at math, but she's taking the algebra course anyway.

8. (A) He was able to find a cheap apartment.
    (B) His apartment is too expensive.
    (C) He doesn't like the apartment's location.
    (D) The apartment is cheap because of its location.

9. (A) He arrived early at the auditorium.
    (B) He got one of the best seats in the auditorium.
    (C) He was not early enough to get a seat at the front.
    (D) He prefers sitting at the back.

10. (A) He'd like to work on his social skills at the game.
    (B) He wishes he could work on his term paper for sociology.
    (C) He can't attend the game because of his schoolwork.
    (D) Sociology is less important to him than football this weekend.

SKILL 15:   LISTEN FOR UNTRUE CONDITIONS

Conversations containing conditions can appear in the short dialogues. The important idea to remember about conditions is that a condition implies that the *opposite of the condition is true.*

Example from the Paper and Computer TOEFL® Tests

On the recording, you hear:

(man)	*Do you think that you'll be able to go to the party?*
(woman)	*If I had time, I would go.*
(narrator)	*What does the woman say about the party?*

In your test book or on the computer screen, you read:

(A)   Maybe she'll go.
(B)   She has time, so she'll go.
(C)   She is going even if she doesn't have time.
(D)   It's impossible to go.

In this question, the condition *If I had time* implies that the opposite is true: The woman does not have time for the party, so *it's impossible to go.* Therefore, the best answer to this question is answer (D).

The following box outlines the key points that you should know about untrue conditions:

KEY INFORMATION ABOUT *UNTRUE CONDITIONS*		
Point	Example	Meaning
• An *affirmative* condition implies a *negative* reality. • A *negative* condition implies an *affirmative* reality.	If she *were at home,* she could do it.* If she *weren't at home,* she could do it.	= not at home = at home
• A *past* tense implies a *present* reality. • A *past perfect* verb implies a *past* reality.	If I *had* money, I would buy it. If I *had had* money, I would have bought it.	= do not have money = did not have money
• *Had* can be used without *if.*	*Had I had* money, I would have bought it.**	= did not have money

*Remember that *were* is used instead of *was* in untrue conditions: "If I *were* there, I would help."
**This has the same meaning as "If I had had money...." Note that the subject and "had" are inverted.

EXERCISE 15: In this exercise, underline the condition in each short dialogue. Then read the question and choose the best answer to that question. Remember that the best answer is one that implies the opposite of what is said.

1. (man)   *Are you going to have something*
                 to eat?
   (woman)   *If the food looked fresh, I would*
                 eat some.
   (narrator) *What does the woman mean?*

   (A) She is not going to eat.
   (B) The food looks fresh.
   (C) She doesn't like fresh food.
   (D) She already ate something.

2. (woman)   *The flight must have taken*
                 longer than usual.
   (man)   *Had the flight left on time, we*
                 would not have arrived so late.
   (narrator) *What does the man say about*
                 the flight?

   (A) It arrived early.
   (B) It was unusually short.
   (C) It left on time.
   (D) It departed late.

3. (man)   *Are you sure you want to go*
                 out? You do not seem to be
                 feeling very well.
   (woman)   *If there were some aspirin in the*
                 medicine cabinet, I would not
                 need to go to the drugstore.
   (narrator) *What does the woman mean?*

   (A) She really is feeling fine.
   (B) There is plenty of aspirin in the
          medicine cabinet.
   (C) It is necessary to get some aspirin.
   (D) She does not need to go out.

TOEFL EXERCISE 15: In this exercise, listen carefully to each short dialogue and question on the recording, and then choose the best answer to the question. You should be particularly careful of untrue conditions.

 NOW BEGIN THE RECORDING AT TOEFL EXERCISE 15.

1. (A) The woman did not need to call him.
   (B) The woman called to let him know
          about the meeting.
   (C) He's not glad that the woman called.
   (D) He already knew about the meeting
          when the woman called.

2. (A) The man often drives too quickly.
   (B) The police do not stop the man too
          much.
   (C) The man drove rather slowly.
   (D) The police should not stop the
          man so often.

3. (A) She's so happy they don't have to
          work on Friday.
   (B) It would be nice if they could finish
          their work on Friday.
   (C) She wonders if the man would be
          nice enough to come in to work
          in her place on Friday.
   (D) It's too bad they must work on
          Friday.

4. (A) She did not put enough postage on
          the letter.
   (B) The letter arrived last week.
   (C) The letter did not need more
          postage.
   (D) She did not put any postage on the
          letter.

5. (A) He has a dog.
   (B) He doesn't pay attention to dogs.
   (C) He wishes he had a dog.
   (D) Dogs do not need much attention.

6. (A) They knew they had to prepare for
          the exam.
   (B) They didn't prepare for the exam.
   (C) As soon as they knew about the
          exam, they began to prepare for
          it.
   (D) They knew that the preparation for
          the exam would take a lot of
          time.

7. (A) It costs too much for him to go.
   (B) He agrees to go with them.
   (C) He is unworried about the cost of the restaurant.
   (D) The restaurant is rather inexpensive.

8. (A) When Joe saw the car coming, he tried to get out of the way.
   (B) Joe was able to get out of the way because he saw the car coming.
   (C) Joe jumped out of the way of the oncoming car.
   (D) Because Joe didn't see the car coming, he couldn't get out of the way.

9. (A) The woman didn't come.
   (B) The woman wanted to be there.
   (C) The woman was going to leave immediately.
   (D) The woman was not really there.

10. (A) Kathy didn't work as hard as possible because she didn't know what the reward was.
    (B) Kathy couldn't have put more effort into the project to win the prize.
    (C) Kathy won first prize because of her hard work on the art project.
    (D) Kathy worked so hard that she knew first prize was hers.

TOEFL EXERCISE (Skills 14–15): In this exercise, listen carefully to each short dialogue and question on the recording, and then choose the best answer to the question.

 NOW BEGIN THE RECORDING AT TOEFL EXERCISE (SKILLS 14–15).

1. (A) She enjoys violent movies.
   (B) She would have preferred a more violent movie.
   (C) She thinks the film was too violent.
   (D) She enjoyed the movie.

2. (A) He left the windows open.
   (B) The rain did not get in.
   (C) He forgot to close the windows.
   (D) The rain got into the house.

3. (A) Her family is unable to come to graduation.
   (B) It is possible that her family will come.
   (C) Her parents are coming to the ceremonies.
   (D) She is not graduating this year.

4. (A) He is going to miss the conference.
   (B) He will take his vacation next week.
   (C) He will attend the conference.
   (D) He won't miss his vacation.

5. (A) He enjoys chemistry lab.
   (B) He doesn't have chemistry lab this afternoon.
   (C) He isn't taking chemistry class.
   (D) He has to go to the lab.

6. (A) They filled up the gas tank at the last service station.
   (B) Although they filled up the tank, they still ran out of gas.
   (C) Even though they didn't stop at the service station, they didn't run out of gas.
   (D) They ran out of gas because they didn't stop at the gas station.

7. (A) His schedule is not really heavy.
   (B) He needs to add a few more courses.
   (C) He enrolled in more courses than he really wants.
   (D) He will register for a lot of courses next semester.

8. (A) She never took the bus to work.
   (B) She regularly takes the bus.
   (C) She doesn't know how to get to work.
   (D) She gets lost on the bus.

9. (A) She bought some eggs at the store.
    (B) She doesn't have any eggs to lend him.
    (C) He can borrow some eggs.
    (D) She didn't go to the store.

10. (A) Teresa is feeling a lot better.
    (B) The doctor didn't prescribe the medicine.
    (C) Teresa didn't follow the doctor's orders.
    (D) Teresa did exactly what the doctor said.

TOEFL REVIEW EXERCISE (Skills 1–15): In this exercise, listen carefully to each short dialogue and question on the recording, and then choose the best answer to the question.

 NOW BEGIN THE RECORDING AT TOEFL REVIEW EXERCISE (SKILLS 1–15).

1. (A) Drinking the hot tea
    (B) Making more tea in a few minutes
    (C) Letting the tea cool off a bit
    (D) Having the tea immediately

2. (A) In a bus station
    (B) In a store
    (C) In a restaurant
    (D) In a theater

3. (A) He's unhappy to end the semester.
    (B) He's glad to be finishing school.
    (C) He couldn't be happier to begin the semester.
    (D) The end of the semester is making him feel sad.

4. (A) The storm destroyed the house.
    (B) The house blocked the trees.
    (C) The stormy weather caused the trees to fall.
    (D) During the storm, someone knocked on the door of the house.

5. (A) The team hasn't won often.
    (B) He usually doesn't pay attention to the football team.
    (C) It's out of the ordinary for the team to lose.
    (D) He usually hears about the football games.

6. (A) He went to the office every morning.
    (B) He was not working.
    (C) He had to arrive at work earlier than 8 o'clock.
    (D) He had a job.

7. (A) He did not enjoy his vacation as much as possible.
    (B) He got lost on his vacation.
    (C) The vacation was really enjoyable.
    (D) He did not really lose his passport.

8. (A) It will take eight hours to get to Riverdale on the bus.
    (B) He believes he knows the correct bus.
    (C) He doesn't know where Riverdale is.
    (D) He assures the woman that he knows the way to Riverdale.

9. (A) The laboratory assistant completed one experiment.
    (B) The laboratory assistant couldn't finish one experiment.
    (C) The laboratory assistant didn't want to do more experiments.
    (D) None of the experiments could be completed.

10. (A) She would like the man to repeat what he said.
    (B) The semester is really over!
    (C) The semester will never end.
    (D) She has the same wish as the man.

IDIOMATIC LANGUAGE

SKILL 16: LISTEN FOR TWO- AND THREE-PART VERBS

Two- and three-part verbs appear in some questions in the short dialogues. These verbs are expressions that include a verb and one or more particles (such as *in*, *on*, or *at*); the particle changes the meaning of the verb. Questions involving two- and three-part verbs can be difficult for students because the addition of the particle changes the meaning of the verb in an idiomatic way.

Example from the Paper and Computer TOEFL® Tests

On the recording, you hear:

    (man)   *What time does the meeting start?*
    (woman)   *Didn't you hear that it was <u>called off</u> by the director?*
    (narrator) *What does the woman say about the meeting?*

In your test book or on the computer screen, you read:

    (A)   The director called a meeting.
    (B)   The director phoned her about the meeting.
    (C)   The director called the meeting to order.
    (D)   The director <u>canceled</u> the meeting.

In this question, the two-part verb *called off* has a different meaning from the verb *call*, which means *phone*. The two-part verb *call off* means *cancel*, so the best answer is answer (D).

NOTE: A list of common two- and three-part verbs and exercises using these verbs appear in Appendix B. You may want to study these two- and three-part verbs before you try the following exercises.

EXERCISE 16: In this exercise, underline the two- or three-part verb in each short dialogue. Then read the question and choose the best answer to that question. Remember that the best answer is one that is related to the meaning of the two- or three-part verb and might not seem to be related to the meaning of the verb without the particle.

1. (man)   *Did you have your history exam today?*
     (woman) *No, the professor put it off for another week.*
     (narrator) *What does the woman say about the exam?*

    (A)   She would like to put it out of her mind.
    (B)   The professor canceled it.
    (C)   It was moved to another location.
    (D)   It was delayed.

2. (woman) *Do we have any more soap?*
     (man)   *We've run out of it. Someone will have to go to the store.*
     (narrator) *What does the man mean?*

    (A)   He will run to the store.
    (B)   He needs soap to wash himself after running.
    (C)   There is no more soap.
    (D)   They have a store of soap at home.

3. (man)   *I need to take the written test to renew my driver's license.*

    (woman)   *Then, you'll have to brush up on the laws.*

    (narrator)   *What does the man need to do?*

(A) Reapply for his driver's license.
(B) Sweep around the lawn.
(C) Learn the laws for the first time.
(D) Review the information that will be on the test.

TOEFL EXERCISE 16: In this exercise, listen carefully to each short dialogue and question on the recording, and then choose the best answer to the question. You should be particularly careful of two- and three-part verbs.

 Now begin the recording at Toefl Exercise 16.

1. (A) Phone their neighbors
    (B) Call to their neighbors over the fence
    (C) Help the neighbors move in
    (D) Visit their neighbors

2. (A) The course is becoming more interesting.
    (B) The course used to be more interesting.
    (C) The course is about the same as it was.
    (D) He's not as bored in the class as the woman.

3. (A) Her headache is getting worse.
    (B) She felt better this morning than now.
    (C) She seems to be feeling better now.
    (D) She is just getting another headache now.

4. (A) The man should stop breaking his cigarettes in half.
    (B) The man should decrease the number of cigarettes he smokes.
    (C) The man should cut the ends off his cigarettes.
    (D) The man should stop smoking completely.

5. (A) The client presented his case to the lawyer.
    (B) The client was upset about the lawyer's rejection.
    (C) The client was annoyed because the lawyer returned the suitcase.
    (D) The client made the lawyer unhappy about the case.

6. (A) She gets along with lots of people.
    (B) She gets back at people who cross her.
    (C) She gets rid of people she doesn't want to spend time with.
    (D) She tries to get ahead of everyone else.

7. (A) He must try to find the children.
    (B) It is necessary for him to clean up after the children.
    (C) The children need to be watched.
    (D) He's going to see what the children have done.

8. (A) They are going on strike.
    (B) They are lying down on the job.
    (C) They are being released from their jobs.
    (D) They are relaxing too much at the factory.

9. (A) He is betting that the football team will win.
    (B) He really wants to succeed.
    (C) It is not so difficult to play on the football team.
    (D) He pulled a muscle while playing football.

10. (A) She's unsure why she tolerates the man.
    (B) She doesn't know where she put her keys.
    (C) She is actually the one who put the keys in the car.
    (D) She can't understand why the man did what he did.

Skill 17:   LISTEN FOR IDIOMS

Idioms appear in some questions in the short dialogues. Idioms are special expressions in a language that all speakers of the language know; these special expressions describe one situation in life but are applied to many different areas of life. Idiom questions can be difficult for students because they seem to be describing one situation when they are really describing a different situation.

Example from the Paper and Computer TOEFL® Tests

On the recording, you hear:

(man)	*Tom is a full-time student and is holding down a full-time job.*
(woman)	*He's really <u>burning the candle at both ends</u>.*
(narrator)	*What does the woman say about Tom?*

In your test book or on the computer screen, you read:

(A)   He's lighting a candle.
(B)   He's holding the candle at the top and the bottom.
(C)   He's <u>doing too much</u>.
(D)   He's working as a firefighter.

In this question, the idiom *burning the candle at both ends* has nothing to do with candles and nothing to do with burning or fires, so answers (A), (B), and (D) are not correct. Instead, this idiom is an expression that is used in a situation when someone is trying to do more than he or she really can do; after all, a candle usually only burns at one end, so a candle that burns at two ends is *doing too much*. Therefore, the best answer to the question above is answer (C).

NOTE: A list of common idioms and exercises using these idioms appear in Appendix C. You may want to study these idioms before you try the following exercises.

EXERCISE 17: In this exercise, underline the idiom in each short dialogue. Then, read the question and choose the best answer to that question. Remember that the best answer is one that might not seem to be related to the idiom in the last line.

1. (man)   *I have to take advanced biology from Professor Stanton next semester.*
   (woman)   *Don't worry about it. It's a piece of cake.*
   (narrator)   *What does the woman mean?*

   (A)   The man should try a piece of cake.
   (B)   The man should worry about the course.
   (C)   The man shouldn't take part in the course.
   (D)   The course is easy.

2. (woman)   *Thanks for changing the oil and putting air in the tires.*
   (man)   *It's all in a day's work.*
   (narrator)   *What does the man mean?*

   (A)   It will take him a whole day to do the job.
   (B)   This is a regular part of his job.
   (C)   He can do the work at the end of the day.
   (D)   He's too busy today to do the work.

3. (man)   *What was it like while the*   (A) The president dropped his pen.
               president was giving his speech?   (B) The audience was very quiet.
    (woman)   *You could hear a pin drop.*   (C) The speech contained several puns.
    (narrator) *What does the woman mean?*   (D) The president discussed dropping a
                                                           bomb.

TOEFL EXERCISE 17: In this exercise, listen carefully to each short dialogue and question on the recording, and then choose the best answer to the question. You should be particularly careful of idioms.

  NOW BEGIN THE RECORDING AT TOEFL EXERCISE 17.

1. (A) The man's never late.
    (B) It's good that the man was fifteen
         minutes late.
    (C) It's never good to be late for class.
    (D) It's good that the man went to class,
         on time or not.

2. (A) The woman's work is all in her
         head.
    (B) The woman has to do two
         experiments rather than one.
    (C) It's a good idea to work together.
    (D) The biology experiment concerns
         two-headed animals.

3. (A) She has no time to work now.
    (B) She doesn't want to work on the
         report either.
    (C) It's best to get it over with now.
    (D) There's no time to present the
         report now.

4. (A) She's very lucky to get the last
         book.
    (B) She's sorry she can't get the book
         today.
    (C) She always has good luck with
         books.
    (D) She just wanted to look at the book.

5. (A) The man doesn't like eating in
         restaurants.
    (B) She doesn't really like that
         restaurant.
    (C) Each of them has his own
         restaurant.
    (D) Everyone has different tastes.

6. (A) She'll do it immediately.
    (B) It is not possible to do it.
    (C) The man should have told her
         sooner.
    (D) She would have done it if the man
         had asked.

7. (A) Abbie used a feather in his art
         project.
    (B) He was knocked down.
    (C) He was really surprised.
    (D) Abbie's father knocked on the
         door.

8. (A) They are taking a boat trip
         together.
    (B) The six chapters are all about the
         boat.
    (C) Everyone has to do the same thing.
    (D) The man will read while he's on the
         boat.

9. (A) She is taller than the others.
    (B) She put her science project on top
         of the others.
    (C) She has a really good head on her
         shoulders.
    (D) She's the best of them all.

10. (A) The man needs to improve his
         penmanship.
    (B) The man doesn't really need to
         apply for the scholarship.
    (C) The man needs to fill out the
         application with dots and crosses.
    (D) The man needs to pay attention to
         every detail.

TOEFL EXERCISE (Skills 16–17): In this exercise, listen carefully to each short dialogue and question on the recording, and then choose the best answer to the question.

 NOW BEGIN THE RECORDING AT TOEFL EXERCISE (SKILLS 16–17).

1. (A) She gets lots of take-out dinners.
    (B) She and her roommate alternate cooking responsibilities.
    (C) Her roommate cooks more often than she does.
    (D) Her roommate does the cooking while she does other chores.

2. (A) He resembles his father.
    (B) He has a chipped tooth.
    (C) He lives one block from his father.
    (D) He and his father were playing a game with blocks.

3. (A) She's going somewhere else.
    (B) She does not like football.
    (C) She has a lot of work to do.
    (D) She is getting sick.

4. (A) He put his foot where he should not have.
    (B) He put the food that the teacher gave him into his mouth.
    (C) He said something embarrassing.
    (D) He told the teacher that his foot was hurt.

5. (A) She'd like the man to delay his trip.
    (B) She prefers that the man leave a few minutes earlier than he planned.
    (C) She wants to know if the man will stay in the market for only a few minutes.
    (D) She'd like to talk to the man for a few minutes.

6. (A) The man might start a fire in the park.
    (B) The man parked his car near the fire.
    (C) The man's thinking of doing something dangerous.
    (D) The man's playing a game in the park.

7. (A) The machines do not act very well.
    (B) The machines don't really bother her.
    (C) She would like them to stop the noise.
    (D) She wishes the machines would cut the wood.

8. (A) Fred has a dog that barks a lot.
    (B) Fred has hidden the money in a tree.
    (C) Fred has backed into a tree.
    (D) Fred has made a mistake.

9. (A) She will give him any help he needs.
    (B) He has to give away what he doesn't need.
    (C) He should not give up.
    (D) He should give back what he borrowed.

10. (A) She'd rather go swimming than do the homework.
    (B) The chemistry homework is really difficult.
    (C) She's doing the homework by the swimming pool.
    (D) The stream is drying up.

TOEFL REVIEW EXERCISE (Skills 1–17): In this exercise, listen carefully to each short dialogue and question on the recording, and then choose the best answer to the question.

 NOW BEGIN THE RECORDING AT TOEFL REVIEW EXERCISE (SKILLS 1–17).

1. (A) There's no more wood inside.
    (B) The wood in the fireplace should be put outside.
    (C) There's a fire outside.
    (D) He needs to bring some wood outside.

2. (A) She worked late at a conference.
    (B) Her meeting was canceled.
    (C) She called a conference at work.
    (D) She was late to a conference.

3. (A) In a hospital
   (B) At a police station
   (C) At the beach
   (D) In a locker room

4. (A) There was too much room on the dance floor.
   (B) He enjoyed the room where they went dancing.
   (C) The dance floor was too crowded.
   (D) The club needed more rooms for dancing.

5. (A) He could not understand the fax machine.
   (B) He wrote the letter that was sent.
   (C) The fax machine was easy for him to use.
   (D) He was not very good with figures.

6. (A) The woman hit her head on a nail.
   (B) The woman hit his new car.
   (C) The woman was exactly right.
   (D) The woman bought the new car.

7. (A) He would like the woman to help him find his paper.
   (B) He wants the woman to put the paper away.
   (C) He needs the woman to review the paper.
   (D) He would like the woman to write the paper for him.

8. (A) Information about the problem is unavailable.
   (B) No one has been informed.
   (C) Everybody knows what is going on.
   (D) Nobody is aware that the problem is serious.

9. (A) He did not sleep well.
   (B) He never woke up this morning.
   (C) The alarm failed to go off.
   (D) He needed a loud alarm to wake up.

10. (A) The pilot made an emergency landing.
    (B) The pilot was forced to leave the plane in a hurry.
    (C) The pilot fielded questions about the forced landing.
    (D) The plane was damaged when it landed forcefully.

LONG CONVERSATIONS
(PAPER TOEFL® TEST)

Two long conversations, each followed by a number of multiple-choice questions, appear in Part B of the Listening Comprehension section of the paper TOEFL test. You will hear the conversations and the questions on a recording; they are not written in your test book. You must choose the best answer to each multiple-choice question from the four choices that are written in your test book.

The conversations are often about some aspect of school life (how difficult a class is, how to write a research paper, how to register for a course). The conversations can also be about topics currently in the news in the United States (desalination of the water supply, recycling of used products, damage from a storm or some other type of natural phenomenon).

Example from the Paper TOEFL® Test

On the recording, you hear:

(narrator) *Questions 1 through 4. Listen to a conversation between a professor and a student.*

(man) *Hello, Professor Denton. Are you free for a moment? Could I have a word with you?*

(woman) *Come on in, Michael. Of course I have some time. These are my office hours, and this is the right time for you to come and ask questions. Now, how can I help you?*

(man) *Well, I have a quick question for you about the homework assignment for tomorrow. I thought the assignment was to answer the first three questions at the top of page 67 in the text, but when I looked, there weren't any questions there. I'm confused.*

(woman) *The assignment was to answer the first three questions at the top of page 76, not 67.*

(man) *Oh, now I understand. I'm glad I came in to check. Thanks for your help.*

(woman) *No problem. See you tomorrow.*

Questions:

1. On the recording, you hear:

     (narrator) *Who is the man?*

     In your test book, you read: (A)   A professor
                                     (B)   An office worker
                                     (C)   Professor Denton's assistant
                                     (D)   A student

2. On the recording, you hear:

     (narrator) *When does the man come to see Professor Denton?*

     In your test book, you read: (A)   During regular class hours
                                     (B)   Just before class time
                                     (C)   As soon as class is finished
                                     (D)   During office hours

---

3. On the recording, you hear:

   (narrator) *Why does the man come to see Professor Denton?*

   In your test book, you read: (A) To turn in an assignment
                                   (B) To ask a question
                                   (C) To pick up a completed test
                                   (D) To explain why he did not attend class

4. On the recording, you hear:

   (narrator) *What incorrect information did the man have?*

   In your test book, you read: (A) The date the assignment was due
                                   (B) The page number of the assignment
                                   (C) The length of the assignment
                                   (D) The numbers of the assignment questions

The first question asks you to determine who the man is. Since the man opens the conversation with *Professor Denton* and he asks about the page number of an assignment for tomorrow, he is probably a student. The best answer to this question is therefore answer (D). The second question asks about when the man comes to see the professor. The professor says that *These are my office hours,* so the best answer to this question is answer (D). The third question asks why the man comes to see the professor. Since the man says *I have a quick question for you,* the best answer to this question is answer (B). The last question asks what incorrect information the man had. The man thought that the assignment was on page 67 and not on page 76, so he was mistaken about the *page number* of the assignment. The best answer to this question is answer (B).

PROCEDURES FOR THE LONG CONVERSATIONS
(Paper TOEFL® Test)

1. **If you have time, preview the answers to the questions.** While you are looking at the answers, you should try to do the following:
    - Anticipate the **topics** of the conversations you will hear.
    - Anticipate the **questions** for each of the groups of answers.

2. **Listen carefully to the first line of the conversation.** The first line of the conversation often contains the main idea, subject, or topic of the conversation, and you will often be asked to answer such questions.

3. **As you listen to the conversation, draw conclusions about the situation of the conversation: who is talking, where the conversation takes place, or when it takes place.** You will often be asked to make such inferences about the conversation.

4. **As you listen to the conversation, follow along with the answers in your test book and try to determine the correct answers.** Detail questions are generally answered in order in the conversation, and the answers often sound the same as what is said on the recording.

5. **You should guess even if you are not sure.** Never leave any answers blank.

6. **Use any remaining time to look ahead at the answers to the questions that follow.**

The following skills will help you to implement these procedures in the long conversations on the paper TOEFL test.

BEFORE LISTENING _____

SKILL 18:   ANTICIPATE THE TOPICS

It is very helpful to your overall comprehension if you know what topics to expect in the long conversations. You should therefore try to anticipate the topics you will be hearing. For example, are the conversations about some aspect of school life, or some type of social issue, or a trip someone is planning? A helpful strategy is therefore to look briefly at the answers in the test book, before you actually hear the conversations on the recording, and try to determine the topics of the conversations that you will hear.

EXERCISE 18: Look at the answers to the five questions together, and try to anticipate the topic of the conversation for those five questions. (Of course, you cannot always determine exactly what the topic is, but you often can get a general idea.) Questions 1 through 5 have been answered for you.

1. (A) Find *work on campus*
    (B) *Work* in the *employment office*
    (C) Help *students* find *jobs*
    (D) Ask the woman questions

2. (A) In the library
    (B) In a classroom
    (C) In a campus office
    (D) In an apartment

3. (A) No more than ten
    (B) At least twenty
    (C) Not more than twenty
    (D) Up to ten

4. (A) Every morning
    (B) Afternoons and weekends
    (C) When he's in class
    (D) Weekdays

5. (A) Fill out a form
    (B) Give her some additional
         information
    (C) Tell her some news
    (D) Phone her

What is the topic of the conversation for questions 1 through 5?

_____looking for a job on campus_____

You can guess this because of the following clues:

- *work on campus*
- *employment office*
- *students*
- *jobs*

6. (A) Just before a vacation
    (B) Just after the end of a school
         semester
    (C) At the end of the summer
    (D) Just after a break from school

7. (A) A trip to visit the Eskimos
    (B) A trip the woman is planning to
         take
    (C) A trip the man has already taken
    (D) A camping trip the man and
         woman took

8. (A) Three hours
    (B) Three complete days
    (C) Three classes
    (D) Three weeks

9. (A) Sleeping outside on the ground
    (B) Spending time in a sauna or hot
         tub
    (C) Relaxing at the lodge
    (D) Enjoying excellent food

10. (A) She'd be scared, but she'd like to
         try.
    (B) She can't wait.
    (C) It would be quite exciting for her.
    (D) She'd prefer not to try.

What is the topic of the conversation for questions 6 through 10?

_____

11. (A) All kinds of pollution
    (B) How acid rain has harmed the
         earth
    (C) Pollution from cars and factories
    (D) The causes and possible effects of
         acid rain

12. (A) Nuclear power
    (B) Electricity
    (C) Burning coal and oil
    (D) Solar power

13. (A) From sulfur dioxide and water
         vapor
    (B) From sulfur dioxide and nitrogen
         oxide
    (C) From nitric acid and sulfur dioxide
    (D) From water vapor and nitric acid

14. (A) Only in North America
    (B) At the North and South Poles
    (C) In parts of several northern
         continents
    (D) In equatorial areas

15. (A) She should protect herself from the
         rain.
    (B) She should clean up the water
         supply.
    (C) She should read a novel.
    (D) She should get more information
         about acid rain.

What is the topic of the conversation for questions 11 through 15?

_____

SKILL 19:   ANTICIPATE THE QUESTIONS

It is very helpful to your ability to answer individual questions with the long conversations if you can anticipate what the questions will be and listen specifically for the answers to those questions.

Example from the Paper TOEFL® Test 📖

In your test book, you read:

    (A)   In the airport
    (B)   In the library
    (C)   In the dormitory
    (D)   In the travel agent's office

You try to anticipate the question:

Where does the conversation probably take place?

In this example, you can be quite certain that one of the questions will be about where the conversation takes place. Since you are sure that this is one of the questions, you can listen carefully for clues that will give you the answer. This example shows that a helpful strategy is therefore to look briefly at the answers in the test book, before you actually hear the conversations on the recording, and try to determine the questions that you will be asked to answer.

EXERCISE 19: Study the following answers and try to determine what the questions will be. (You should note that perhaps you will only be able to predict part of a question, rather than the complete question.) If you cannot predict the question in a short period of time, then move on to the next group of answers. Question 1 has been answered for you.

1. Question: ___What does (someone) want to do?___
    (A)   Find work on campus
    (B)   Work in the employment office
    (C)   Help students find jobs
    (D)   Ask the woman questions

2. Question: _____
    (A)   In the library
    (B)   In a classroom
    (C)   In a campus office
    (D)   In an apartment

3. Question: _____
    (A)   No more than ten
    (B)   At least twenty
    (C)   Not more than twenty
    (D)   Up to ten

4. Question: _____
    (A)   Every morning
    (B)   Afternoons and weekends
    (C)   When he's in class
    (D)   Weekdays

5. Question: _____
   (A) Fill out a form
   (B) Give her some additional information
   (C) Tell her some news
   (D) Phone her

6. Question: _____
   (A) Just before a vacation
   (B) Just after the end of a school semester
   (C) At the end of the summer
   (D) Just after a break from school

7. Question: _____
   (A) A trip to visit the Eskimos
   (B) A trip the woman is planning to take
   (C) A trip the man has already taken
   (D) A camping trip the man and woman took

8. Question: _____
   (A) Three hours
   (B) Three complete days
   (C) Three classes
   (D) Three weeks

9. Question: _____
   (A) Sleeping outside on the ground
   (B) Spending time in a sauna or hot tub
   (C) Relaxing at the lodge
   (D) Enjoying excellent food

10. Question: _____
    (A) She'd be scared, but she'd like to try.
    (B) She can't wait.
    (C) It would be quite exciting for her.
    (D) She'd prefer not to try.

11. Question: _____
    (A) All kinds of pollution
    (B) How acid rain has harmed the earth
    (C) Pollution from cars and factories
    (D) The causes and possible effects of acid rain

12. Question: _____
    (A) Nuclear power
    (B) Electricity
    (C) Burning coal and oil
    (D) Solar power

13. Question: _____
    (A) From sulfur dioxide and water vapor
    (B) From sulfur dioxide and nitrogen oxide
    (C) From nitric acid and sulfur dioxide
    (D) From water vapor and nitric acid

14. Question: _____
    (A) Only in North America
    (B) At the North and South Poles
    (C) In parts of several northern continents
    (D) In equatorial areas

15. Question: _____
    (A) She should protect herself from the rain.
    (B) She should clean up the water supply.
    (C) She should read a novel.
    (D) She should get more information about acid rain.

WHILE LISTENING

Skill 20:   DETERMINE THE TOPIC

As you listen to each long conversation, you should be thinking about the topic (subject) or main idea for each conversation. Since the first one or two sentences generally give the topic, you should be asking yourself what the topic is while you are listening carefully to the first part of the conversation.

Example from the Paper TOEFL® Test

On the recording, you hear:

(man)	*You can't believe what I just got!*
(woman)	*I bet you got that new car you've always wanted.*
(man)	*Now, how in the world did you figure that out?*

You think:

The topic of the conversation is the new car that the man just got.

EXERCISE 20: Listen to the first part of each of the conversations, and decide on the topic of each conversation.

  Now begin the recording at Exercise 20.

1. What is the topic of Conversation 1?

    _____

2. What is the topic of Conversation 2?

    _____

3. What is the topic of Conversation 3?

    _____

Skill 21:   DRAW CONCLUSIONS ABOUT *WHO, WHAT, WHEN, WHERE*

As you listen to each long conversation, you should be trying to set the situation in your mind. You should be thinking the following thoughts:

- *Who* is talking?
- *When* does the conversation probably take place?
- *Where* does the conversation probably take place?
- *What* is the source of information for the conversation?

Example from the Paper TOEFL® Test 📖

On the recording, you hear:

(man)	*Why do you have so many books?*
(woman)	*I need them for my paper on George Washington. Do you know how I can check them out?*
(man)	*Yes, you should go downstairs to the circulation desk and fill out a card for each book.*

You think:

Who is probably talking?	(two students)
Where are they?	(in the library)
What course are they discussing?	(American History)

EXERCISE 21: Listen to the first part of each of the conversations and try to imagine the situation. Then answer the questions in the text.

🎧   NOW BEGIN THE RECORDING AT EXERCISE 21.

Conversation 1
1. Who is probably talking?   _____

2. Where does the conversation take place?   _____

Conversation 2
1. Who is probably talking?   _____

2. When does the conversation take place?   _____

3. What is the source of the man's information? _____

Conversation 3
1. Who is probably talking?   _____

2. When does the conversation take place?   _____

3. What is the source of the information?   _____

SKILL 22:   LISTEN FOR ANSWERS IN ORDER

There are two possible methods to use while you listen to a long conversation:

- *You can just listen to the conversation (and ignore the answers).*
- *You can follow along with the answers while you listen.*

Some students prefer to just listen to the conversation while it is being spoken, and if that method works well for you, then that is what you should do. Other students find that they can answer more questions correctly if they read along with the answers while the conversation is being spoken. Because the detail questions are answered in order, it is possible to read along while you listen to the conversation on the recording.

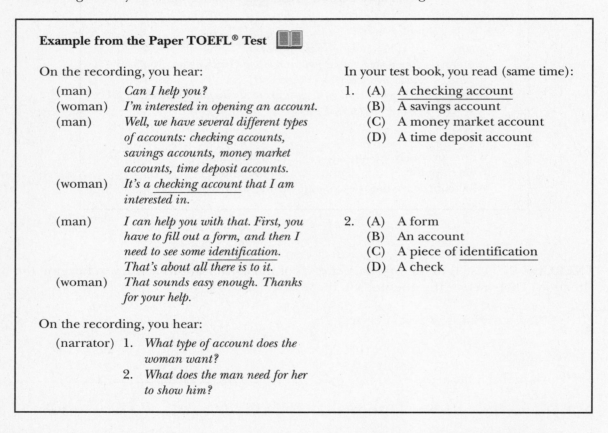

Example from the Paper TOEFL® Test

On the recording, you hear:

(man)	*Can I help you?*
(woman)	*I'm interested in opening an account.*
(man)	*Well, we have several different types of accounts: checking accounts, savings accounts, money market accounts, time deposit accounts.*
(woman)	*It's a checking account that I am interested in.*
(man)	*I can help you with that. First, you have to fill out a form, and then I need to see some identification. That's about all there is to it.*
(woman)	*That sounds easy enough. Thanks for your help.*

In your test book, you read (same time):

1. (A)   A checking account
    (B)   A savings account
    (C)   A money market account
    (D)   A time deposit account

2. (A)   A form
    (B)   An account
    (C)   A piece of identification
    (D)   A check

On the recording, you hear:

(narrator) 1. *What type of account does the woman want?*
2. *What does the man need for her to show him?*

When you read the answers to the first question, you can anticipate that the first question is: *What type of account?* As you listen, you determine that the woman wants *a checking account.* Therefore, you can anticipate that the best answer to the first question is (A).

When you read the answers to the second question, you can anticipate that the second question is going to ask *What thing...?* In the conversation, the man asks her to fill out a *form* and show some *identification,* so as you are listening you can anticipate that the correct answer to the second question is either (A) or (C). When you hear the question, you can determine that the best answer is answer (C).

TOEFL EXERCISE 22: Listen to each complete conversation and answer the questions that follow.

  Now begin the recording at Toefl Exercise 22.

1. (A) Find work on campus
    (B) Work in the employment office
    (C) Help students find jobs
    (D) Ask the woman questions

2. (A) In the library
    (B) In a classroom
    (C) In a campus office
    (D) In an apartment

3. (A) No more than ten
    (B) At least twenty
    (C) Not more than twenty
    (D) Up to ten

4. (A) Every morning
    (B) Afternoons and weekends
    (C) When he's in class
    (D) Weekdays

5. (A) Fill out a form
    (B) Give her some additional information
    (C) Tell her some news
    (D) Phone her

6. (A) Just before a vacation
    (B) Just after the end of a school semester
    (C) At the end of the summer
    (D) Just after a break from school

7. (A) A trip to visit the Eskimos
    (B) A trip the woman is planning to take
    (C) A trip the man has already taken
    (D) A camping trip the man and woman took

8. (A) Three hours
    (B) Three complete days
    (C) Three classes
    (D) Three weeks

9. (A) Sleeping outside on the ground
    (B) Spending time in a hot tub
    (C) Relaxing at the lodge
    (D) Enjoying excellent food

10. (A) She'd be scared, but she'd like to try.
    (B) She can't wait.
    (C) It would be quite exciting for her.
    (D) She'd prefer not to try.

11. (A) All kinds of pollution
    (B) How acid rain has harmed the earth
    (C) Pollution from cars and factories
    (D) The causes and possible effects of acid rain

12. (A) Nuclear power
    (B) Electricity
    (C) Burning coal and oil
    (D) Solar power

13. (A) From sulfur dioxide and water vapor
    (B) From sulfur dioxide and nitrogen oxide
    (C) From nitric acid and sulfur dioxide
    (D) From water vapor and nitric acid

14. (A) Only in North America
    (B) At the North and South Poles
    (C) In parts of several northern continents
    (D) In equatorial areas

15. (A) She should protect herself from the rain.
    (B) She should clean up the water supply.
    (C) She should read a novel.
    (D) She should get more information about acid rain.

TOEFL REVIEW EXERCISE (Skills 18–22): In this exercise, you will use all of the information that you learned in Skills 18 through 22.

Before the recording begins, you should read over the answers to questions 1 through 15 and do the following:

- *Anticipate the topics you will hear.*
- *Anticipate the questions.*

While you are listening to the conversations, you should do the following:

- *Listen for the topic in the first lines.*
- *Draw conclusions about the situation (who, what, when, where).*
- *Listen for the answers in order.*

 NOW BEGIN THE RECORDING AT TOEFL REVIEW EXERCISE (SKILLS 18–22).

1. (A) To a concert
   (B) To a rehearsal
   (C) To a lecture
   (D) To the library

2. (A) One
   (B) Two
   (C) Three
   (D) Four

3. (A) The bus does not go directly to the Music Building.
   (B) The bus goes very slowly to the Music Building.
   (C) The bus sometimes does not come.
   (D) The bus will not arrive for a while.

4. (A) Walk
   (B) Wait for the bus
   (C) Miss the lecture
   (D) Think of another plan

5. (A) Boring
   (B) Fantastic
   (C) Lengthy
   (D) Faithful

6. (A) By car
   (B) By plane
   (C) By train
   (D) By bicycle

7. (A) She went directly to Yellowstone.
   (B) She spent a few weeks in Laramie.
   (C) She stopped at the Devil's Tower National Monument.
   (D) She made a few stops before going on to Yellowstone.

8. (A) Laramie
   (B) Devil's Tower National Monument
   (C) Old Faithful
   (D) Wyoming

9. (A) Hear again about Yellowstone
   (B) Take a trip to Yellowstone
   (C) Get a job in a national park
   (D) Move to Yellowstone

10. (A) How and when we celebrate Thanksgiving
    (B) The traditional Thanksgiving dinner
    (C) When Thanksgiving began
    (D) Abraham Lincoln

11. (A) With colonists in Massachusetts
    (B) Alone and thinking about how Thanksgiving developed
    (C) With a big Thanksgiving dinner
    (D) In an untraditional manner

12. (A) The terrible winter
    (B) The corn harvest
    (C) The development of Thanksgiving Day
    (D) For getting the whole family together

13. (A) At many different times
    (B) In July
    (C) Any time in November
    (D) On a Thursday in November

LONG TALKS

(PAPER TOEFL® TEST)

Three talks, each followed by a number of multiple-choice questions, appear in Part C of the Listening Comprehension section of the paper TOEFL test. You will hear the talks and the questions on a recording; they are not written in your test book. You must choose the best answer to each question from the four choices that are written in your test book. Like the conversations in Part B, the talks are often about some aspect of school life or topics currently in the news. It is also very common for the talks to be shortened versions of lectures from courses taught in American colleges and universities.

Example from the Paper TOEFL® Test

On the recording, you hear:

(narrator)   ***Questions 1 through 4.*** *Listen to a talk about the settlement of America.*

(woman)   *The settling of the vast farmlands in central North America was delayed at least partly because of an error by one man. In the early nineteenth century, Lieutenant Zebulon Pike of the U.S. Army was sent out to explore and chart the huge expanses of land in the center of the continent. When he returned from his explorations, he wrote a report in which he erroneously stated that the vast plains in the central part of the continent were desertlike, comparable to the Sahara in Africa. In reality, however, these vast plains contained some of the most fertile farmland in the world. Because of Pike's mistake, the maps of the day depicted the central part of what is today the United States as a vast desert rather than the excellent and available farmland that it was. This mistaken belief about the nature of those lands caused settlers to avoid the central plains for years.*

Questions:

1. On the recording, you hear:

    (narrator)   *What is the topic of this talk?*

    In your test book, you read: (A)   Zebulon Pike's career
                                    (B)   A mistake that influenced the settlement of America
                                    (C)   A report for the army
                                    (D)   The farmlands

2. On the recording, you hear:

    (narrator)   *How did Pike describe the area that he explored?*

    In your test book, you read: (A)   As a desert
                                    (B)   As usable for army purposes
                                    (C)   As located in the Sahara
                                    (D)   As available for farmland

---

3. On the recording, you hear:

　　(narrator) *What was this area really like?*

In your test book, you read:　(A)　It was a vast desert.
　　　　　　　　　　　　　　　(B)　It was covered with farms.
　　　　　　　　　　　　　　　(C)　It was excellent farmland.
　　　　　　　　　　　　　　　(D)　It was similar to the Sahara.

4. On the recording, you hear:

　　(narrator) *This talk would probably be given in which of the following courses?*

In your test book, you read:　(A)　Agricultural Science
　　　　　　　　　　　　　　　(B)　American History
　　　　　　　　　　　　　　　(C)　Geology of the United States
　　　　　　　　　　　　　　　(D)　Military Science

The first question asks about the topic of the talk. The topic of the talk is found in the first sentence of the talk: *The settling of the vast farmlands in central North America was delayed at least partly because of an error by one man.* Therefore, the best answer to the question is (B). The second question is a detail question that asks how Pike described this area. It is stated in the talk that Pike *wrote a report in which he erroneously stated that the vast plains in the central part of the continent were desertlike....* Therefore, the best answer to this question is (A). The third question is an additional detail question that asks what the area was really like. Because the talk indicates that *in reality...these vast plains contained some of the most fertile farmland in the world,* the best answer to this question is (C). The fourth question is an inference question. It asks in which course this lecture would probably be given. The word *probably* indicates to you that the question is not answered directly in the talk. You must draw a conclusion from the information in the talk to answer this question. Because this talk refers to *the early nineteenth century* and discusses the *settling of the vast farmlands in central North America,* it would probably be given in an American History course. The best answer to this question is (B).

PROCEDURES FOR THE LONG TALKS
(Paper TOEFL® Test) 📖📖

1. **If you have time, preview the answers to the questions.** While you are looking at the answers, you should try to do the following:
   • Anticipate the **topics** of the talks you will hear.
   • Anticipate the **questions** for each of the groups of answers.

2. **Listen carefully to the first line of the talk.** The first line of the talk often contains the main idea, subject, or topic of the talk, and you will often be asked this type of question.

3. **As you listen to the talk, draw conclusions about the situation of the talk: who is talking, where or when the talk takes place, which course this lecture might be given in.** You will often be asked to make such inferences about the talk.

4. **As you listen to the talk, follow along with the answers in your test book and try to determine the correct answers.** Detail questions are generally answered in order in the talk, and the answers often sound the same as what is said on the recording.

5. **You should guess even if you are not sure.** Never leave any answers blank.

6. **Use any remaining time to look ahead at the answers to the questions that follow.**

The following skills will help you to implement these procedures in the long talks on the paper TOEFL test.

BEFORE LISTENING

SKILL 23:   ANTICIPATE THE TOPICS

It is very helpful to your overall comprehension if you know what topics to expect in the long talks. You should therefore try to anticipate the topics that you will be hearing (as you did with the long conversations). For example, are the talks about American history, or literature, or some aspect of school life? A helpful strategy is therefore to look briefly at the answers in the test book, before you actually hear the talks on the recording, and try to determine the topics of the talks that you will hear.

EXERCISE 23: Look at the answers to the five questions together, and try to anticipate the topic of the talk for those five questions. (Of course, you cannot always determine exactly what the topic is, but you often can get a general idea.) Questions 1 through 5 have been answered for you.

1. (A) During a *biology* laboratory
        session
   (B) In a biology study group
   (C) On the *first day of class*
   (D) Just before the final exam

2. (A) Once a week
   (B) Two times a week
   (C) Three times a week
   (D) For fifteen hours

3. (A) To do the first laboratory
        assignment
   (B) To take the first *exam*
   (C) To study the laboratory manual
   (D) To read one chapter of the text

4. (A) Room assignments
   (B) Exam topics
   (C) *Reading assignments*
   (D) The first lecture

5. (A) *Exams and lab work*
   (B) Reading and writing assignments
   (C) Class participation and grades on
        examinations
   (D) Lecture and laboratory attendance

What is the topic of the talk for questions 1 through 5?

the requirements of a biology class

You can guess this because of the following clues:

- *biology*
- *first day of class*
- *reading assignments*
- *exam(s)*
- *lab work*

6. (A) What caused the Ring of Fire
   (B) The volcanoes of the Ring of Fire
   (C) Hawaiian volcanoes
   (D) Different types of volcanoes

7. (A) The Ring of Fire
   (B) The characteristics of volcanoes in
       the Ring of Fire
   (C) The volcanoes of Hawaii
   (D) Mauna Loa

8. (A) In Hawaii
   (B) In the United States
   (C) Along the Ring of Fire
   (D) Within the Ring of Fire

9. (A) They are not so violent.
   (B) They are located along the Ring of
       Fire.
   (C) They contain a lot of gas.
   (D) They contain thick lava.

10. (A) A volcano on the Ring of Fire
    (B) An island in Hawaii
    (C) A long, low volcanic mountain
    (D) An explosive volcano

What is the topic of the talk for questions 6 through 10?

_____

11. (A) An artist
    (B) A tour guide
    (C) An Indian
    (D) Orville Wright

12. (A) Several
    (B) Sixty thousand
    (C) Sixteen million
    (D) Millions and millions

13. (A) The National Air and Space
        Museum
    (B) The Museum of Natural History
    (C) The American History Museum
    (D) The Smithsonian Arts and
        Industries Building

14. (A) The American History Museum
    (B) The Smithsonian Arts and
        Industries Building
    (C) The Washington Museum
    (D) The National Air and Space
        Museum

15. (A) To the White House
    (B) To the Smithsonian
    (C) To the mall
    (D) To various other museums

What is the topic of the talk for questions 11 through 15?

_____

SKILL 24:   ANTICIPATE THE QUESTIONS

It is very helpful to your ability to answer individual questions with the long talks if you can anticipate what the questions will be and listen specifically for the answers to those questions (as you did with the long conversations).

Example from the Paper TOEFL® Test

In your test book, you read:

    (A)   For three weeks
    (B)   For three days
    (C)   For three months
    (D)   For three hours

You try to anticipate the question:

How long does (something) last?

In this example, you can be quite certain that one of the questions will be about how long something lasts. Since you are sure that this is one of the questions, you can listen carefully for clues that will give you the answer. This example shows that a helpful strategy is therefore to look briefly at the answers in the test book, before you actually hear the talks on the recording, and try to determine the questions that you will be asked to answer.

EXERCISE 24: Study the following answers and try to determine what the questions will be. (You should note that perhaps you will only be able to predict part of a question, rather than the complete question.) If you cannot predict the question in a short period of time, then move on to the next group of answers. Question 1 has been answered for you.

1. Question: _When does the talk probably take place?_
    (A)   During a biology laboratory session
    (B)   In a biology study group
    (C)   On the first day of class
    (D)   Just before the final exam

2. Question: _____
    (A)   Once a week
    (B)   Two times a week
    (C)   Three times a week
    (D)   For fifteen hours

3. Question: _____
    (A)   To do the first laboratory assignment
    (B)   To take the first exam
    (C)   To study the laboratory manual
    (D)   To read one chapter of the text

4. Question: _____
    (A)   Room assignments
    (B)   Exam topics
    (C)   Reading assignments
    (D)   The first lecture

5. Question: _____
   (A) Exams and lab work
   (B) Reading and writing assignments
   (C) Class participation and grades on examinations
   (D) Lecture and laboratory attendance

6. Question: _____
   (A) What caused the Ring of Fire
   (B) The volcanoes of the Ring of Fire
   (C) Hawaiian volcanoes
   (D) Different types of volcanoes

7. Question: _____
   (A) The Ring of Fire
   (B) The characteristics of volcanoes in the Ring of Fire
   (C) The volcanoes of Hawaii
   (D) Mauna Loa

8. Question: _____
   (A) In Hawaii
   (B) In the United States
   (C) Along the Ring of Fire
   (D) Within the Ring of Fire

9. Question: _____
   (A) They are not so violent.
   (B) They are located along the Ring of Fire.
   (C) They contain a lot of gas.
   (D) They contain thick lava.

10. Question: _____
    (A) A volcano on the Ring of Fire
    (B) An island in Hawaii
    (C) A long, low volcanic mountain
    (D) An explosive volcano

11. Question: _____
    (A) An artist
    (B) A tour guide
    (C) An Indian
    (D) Orville Wright

12. Question: _____
    (A) Several
    (B) Sixty thousand
    (C) Sixteen million
    (D) Millions and millions

13. Question: _____
    (A) The National Air and Space Museum
    (B) The Museum of Natural History
    (C) The American History Museum
    (D) The Smithsonian Arts and Industries Building

14. Question: _____
     (A) The American History Museum
     (B) The Smithsonian Arts and Industries Building
     (C) The Washington Museum
     (D) The National Air and Space Museum

15. Question: _____
     (A) To the White House
     (B) To the Smithsonian
     (C) To the mall
     (D) To various other museums

WHILE LISTENING

SKILL 25:   DETERMINE THE TOPIC

As you listen to each long talk, you should be thinking about the topic (subject) or main idea for the talk (as you did with the long conversations). Since the first sentence is generally a topic sentence, you should be asking yourself what the topic is while you are listening carefully to the first part of the talk.

Example from the Paper TOEFL® Test

On the recording, you hear:

(man)   *The major earthquake that occurred east of Los Angeles in 1971 is still affecting the economy of the area today.*

You think:

The topic of the talk is the effect of the 1971 earthquake on Los Angeles today.

EXERCISE 25: Listen to the first part of each of the talks, and decide on the topic of each talk.

   NOW BEGIN THE RECORDING AT EXERCISE 25.

1. What is the topic of Talk 1?

    _____

2. What is the topic of Talk 2?

    _____

3. What is the topic of Talk 3?

    _____

SKILL 26: DRAW CONCLUSIONS ABOUT *WHO, WHAT, WHEN, WHERE*

As you listen to each talk, you should be trying to set the situation in your mind (as you did with the long conversations). You should be thinking the following thoughts:

- ***Who** is talking?*
- ***When** does the talk probably take place?*
- ***Where** does the talk probably take place?*
- ***What** course is the talk concerned with?*
- ***What** is the source of information for the talk?*

Example from the Paper TOEFL® Test 📖

On the recording, you hear:

(woman)   *The next stop on our tour of Atlanta will be the original home of Coca-Cola, at 107 Marietta Street. Coca-Cola was manufactured at this location until early in September of 1888.*

You think:

Who is probably talking?	(a tour guide)
Where are they?	(in Atlanta)
When does the talk take place?	(in the middle of a tour)

EXERCISE 26: Listen to the first part of each of the talks and try to imagine the situation. Then, answer the questions in the text.

  NOW BEGIN THE RECORDING AT EXERCISE 26.

Talk 1
1. Who is probably talking?   _____

2. Where does the talk probably take place?   _____

3. When does the talk probably take place?   _____

4. What course is being discussed?   _____

Talk 2
1. Who is probably talking?   _____

2. Where does the talk probably take place?   _____

3. When does the talk probably take place?   _____

4. What course is being discussed?   _____

Talk 3
1. Who is probably talking?   _____

2. Where does the talk take place?   _____

3. When does the talk take place?   _____

SKILL 27:   LISTEN FOR ANSWERS IN ORDER

There are two possible methods to use while you listen to the talks.

- *You can just listen to the talk (and ignore the answers).*
- *You can follow along with the answers while you listen.*

Some students prefer to just listen to the talk while it is being spoken, and if that method works well for you, then that is what you should do. Other students find that they can answer more questions correctly if they read along with the answers while the talk is being given. Because the detail questions are answered in order, it is possible to read along while you listen to the talk on the recording.

Example from the Paper TOEFL® Test

On the recording, you hear:

(woman)   *The Great Chicago Fire began on October 8, 1871, and according to legend began when a cow knocked over a lantern in Mrs. O'Leary's barn. No matter how it began, it was a disastrous fire. The preceding summer had been exceedingly dry in the Chicago area, and the extreme dryness accompanied by Chicago's infamous winds created an inferno that destroyed 18,000 buildings and killed more than 300 people before it was extinguished the following day.*

In your test book, you read (same time):

1. (A)   In a barn
    (B)   In Mrs. O'Leary's home
    (C)   In a cow pasture
    (D)   In a lantern factory

2. (A)   The dry weather prior to the fire made it worse.
    (B)   It happened during the summer.
    (C)   Chicago's winds made it worse.
    (D)   It killed many people.

On the recording, you hear:

(narrator) 1. *According to legend, where did the Great Chicago Fire begin?*
            2. *Which of the following is **not** true about the Great Chicago Fire?*

When you read the answers to the first question, you can anticipate that the first question is: *Where did something happen?* As you listen, you determine that the fire began *in Mrs. O'Leary's barn.* Therefore, you can anticipate that the best answer to the first question is (A).

If you read the answers to the second question while you listen to the talk, you can determine that answers (A), (C), and (D) are true. Answer (B) is not true: the fire did not begin in the summer, it began in *October,* which is in autumn. Therefore, answer (B) is the best answer to the question *Which of the following is **not** true about the Great Chicago Fire?*

TOEFL EXERCISE 27: Listen to each complete talk and answer the questions that follow.

  NOW BEGIN THE RECORDING AT TOEFL EXERCISE 27.

1. (A) During a biology laboratory session
    (B) In a biology study group
    (C) On the first day of class
    (D) Just before the final exam

2. (A) Once a week
    (B) Two times a week
    (C) Three times a week
    (D) For fifteen hours

3. (A) To do the first laboratory assignment
    (B) To take the first exam
    (C) To study the laboratory manual
    (D) To read one chapter of the text

4. (A) Room assignments
    (B) Exam topics
    (C) Reading assignments
    (D) The first lecture

5. (A) Exams and lab work
    (B) Reading and writing assignments
    (C) Class participation and grades on examinations
    (D) Lecture and laboratory attendance

6. (A) What caused the Ring of Fire
    (B) The volcanoes of the Ring of Fire
    (C) Hawaiian volcanoes
    (D) Different types of volcanoes

7. (A) The Ring of Fire
    (B) The characteristics of volcanoes in the Ring of Fire
    (C) The volcanoes of Hawaii
    (D) Mauna Loa

8. (A) In Hawaii
    (B) In the United States
    (C) Along the Ring of Fire
    (D) Within the Ring of Fire

9. (A) They are not so violent.
    (B) They are located along the Ring of Fire.
    (C) They contain a lot of gas.
    (D) They contain thick lava.

10. (A) A volcano on the Ring of Fire
     (B) An island in Hawaii
     (C) A long, low volcanic mountain
     (D) An explosive volcano

11. (A) An artist
     (B) A tour guide
     (C) An Indian
     (D) Orville Wright

12. (A) Several
     (B) Sixty thousand
     (C) Sixteen million
     (D) Millions and millions

13. (A) The National Air and Space Museum
     (B) The Museum of Natural History
     (C) The American History Museum
     (D) The Smithsonian Arts and Industries Building

14. (A) The American History Museum
     (B) The Smithsonian Arts and Industries Building
     (C) The Washington Museum
     (D) The National Air and Space Museum

15. (A) To the White House
     (B) To the Smithsonian
     (C) To the mall
     (D) To various other museums

TOEFL REVIEW EXERCISE (Skills 23–27): In this exercise, you will use all of the information that you learned in Skills 23 through 27.

Before the recording begins, you should read over the answers to questions 1 through 12 and do the following:

- *Anticipate the topics you will hear.*
- *Anticipate the questions.*

While you are listening to the talks, you should do the following:

- *Listen for the topic in the first sentence.*
- *Draw conclusions about the situation (who, what, when, where).*
- *Listen for the answers in order.*

 NOW BEGIN THE RECORDING AT TOEFL REVIEW EXERCISE (SKILLS 23–27).

1. (A) Other librarians
   (B) Undergraduate students
   (C) Students who are not in the business department
   (D) Graduate business students

2. (A) It opens at 7:00 a.m.
   (B) It closes at 7:00 p.m.
   (C) It closes at midnight.
   (D) It is always open.

3. (A) Computer area and business materials
   (B) Magazines and newspapers
   (C) Business department and library staff offices
   (D) First and second floors of the library

4. (A) Go home
   (B) Return to class
   (C) Work on the computers
   (D) Tour the library

5. (A) A student in health services
   (B) A drug abuse lecturer
   (C) A dermatologist
   (D) A representative of the tobacco industry

6. (A) How to reduce nicotine and other addictions
   (B) How stress affects the skin
   (C) The effects of alcohol on health
   (D) How to achieve optimal health

7. (A) Alcohol
   (B) Nicotine
   (C) Caffeine
   (D) A reduced supply of blood

8. (A) It increases the flow of blood to the skin.
   (B) It causes increased consumption of alcohol.
   (C) It prevents the skin from receiving enough nourishment.
   (D) It causes stress.

9. (A) Before the Civil War
   (B) At the end of the Civil War
   (C) At the beginning of the twentieth century
   (D) Within the last decade

10. (A) The Civil War ended.
    (B) The U.S. government issued a large amount of paper currency.
    (C) The price of gold plummeted.
    (D) The value of gold became inflated.

11. (A) The president
    (B) The president's brother
    (C) The president's brother-in-law
    (D) The president's wife

12. (A) Issue greenbacks
    (B) Sell gold
    (C) Corner the gold market
    (D) Hold its gold reserves

CASUAL CONVERSATIONS

(COMPUTER TOEFL® TEST)

Casual conversations appear in Part B of the Listening section of the computer TOEFL test. For each of the casual conversations in this part of the test, you will see a context-setting visual as you listen to a five- to seven-line conversation between two speakers. After you see the visual and listen to the conversation, you will see a series of two or three multiple-choice questions and the four answer choices for each question on the computer screen. You must click on the best answer choice to each question on the computer screen. Look at an example of a casual conversation from the computer TOEFL test.

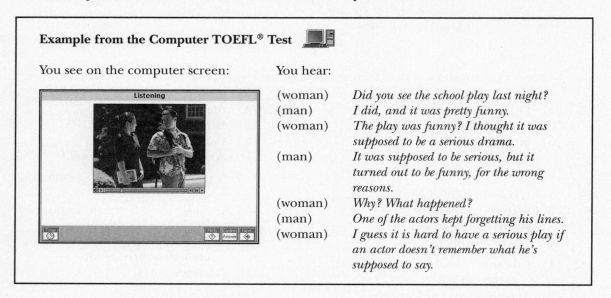

Example from the Computer TOEFL® Test

You see on the computer screen:

You hear:

(woman)   *Did you see the school play last night?*
(man)   *I did, and it was pretty funny.*
(woman)   *The play was funny? I thought it was supposed to be a serious drama.*
(man)   *It was supposed to be serious, but it turned out to be funny, for the wrong reasons.*
(woman)   *Why? What happened?*
(man)   *One of the actors kept forgetting his lines.*
(woman)   *I guess it is hard to have a serious play if an actor doesn't remember what he's supposed to say.*

After the conversation is complete, the first question and answer choices appear on the computer screen as the narrator states the question. This question is a regular multiple-choice question that asks about the type of play.

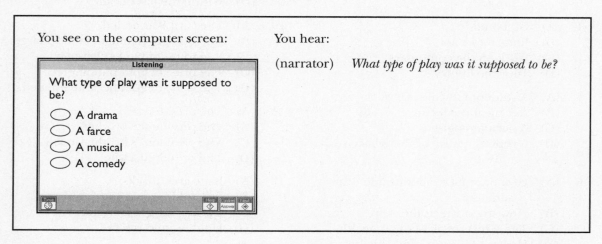

You see on the computer screen:

You hear:

(narrator)   *What type of play was it supposed to be?*

What type of play was it supposed to be?

◯ A drama
◯ A farce
◯ A musical
◯ A comedy

In the conversation, the woman says that she thought *it was supposed to be a serious drama*, and the man replies that *it was supposed to be serious*. From this, it can be determined that the play was supposed to be a *drama*. The first answer is the best answer, so you should click on the first answer.

After you have finished with the first question, another question appears on the computer screen. This question is a multiple-choice question that asks about the problem that occurred.

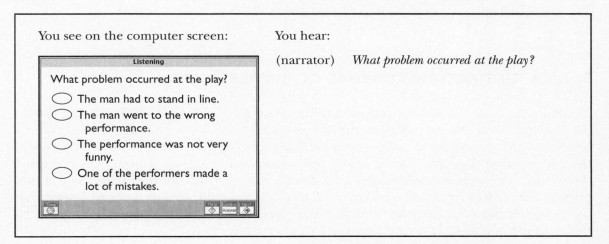

You see on the computer screen:

Listening

What problem occurred at the play?

◯ The man had to stand in line.
◯ The man went to the wrong performance.
◯ The performance was not very funny.
◯ One of the performers made a lot of mistakes.

You hear:

(narrator)   *What problem occurred at the play?*

In the conversation, the man states that *one of the actors kept forgetting his lines*. From this, it can be determined that *one of the performers made a lot of mistakes*. The last answer is the best answer, so you should click on the last answer.

PROCEDURES FOR THE CASUAL CONVERSATIONS
(Computer TOEFL® Test)

1. **Listen carefully to the casual conversation.** You may listen to the conversation one time only.

2. **Use the visual to help you focus on the context.** A context-setting visual appears on the screen at the beginning of each casual conversation. It shows you who is talking and where they are talking.

3. **Focus on the overall meaning of the casual conversation rather than on specific words or expressions.** The questions following a casual conversation generally test your overall comprehension of the conversation rather than the meaning of a specific word or expression.

4. **Listen to each question following the casual conversation as you read it on the screen.** Each listening question is both spoken and written on the computer screen.

5. **Do not panic if you do not understand every word of the casual conversation.** You can still answer the questions correctly without understanding each word of the conversation.

6. **Click on an answer on the computer screen when you have selected an answer.** You may still change your mind at this point and click on a different answer.

7. **Click on** Next . **Then click on** Confirm Answer **to record your answer.** After you click on this button, you cannot go back and change your answer.

8. **Be prepared for the next question.** After you click on Confirm Answer , the next question begins automatically.

The following language skill will help you to implement these procedures with the casual conversations on the computer TOEFL test.

SKILL 28: UNDERSTAND CASUAL CONVERSATIONS

As you listen to each casual conversation in Part B of the computer TOEFL test, you should be thinking about the overall ideas and the supporting details in the casual conversation. Questions that accompany casual conversations most commonly test the overall ideas of the conversation (i.e., *what are the man and woman discussing* and *what do they finally decide to do,* or *what is the woman's problem* and *what does the man suggest*), but they may also test supporting details from the passage (i.e., *what time will they leave,* or *how many assignments are there*). It is unusual for the questions that accompany a casual conversation to depend on the meaning of a specific vocabulary word, or idiom, or grammatical structure as the questions that accompany the short dialogues often do.

TOEFL EXERCISE 28: Look at the picture as you listen to each casual conversation. Do not look at the questions or answer choices until the conversation is complete. (On the computer TOEFL test, you will not be able to see the questions or answer choices during the conversation.)

Questions 1–3

1. Where is the man going?
   ◯ To listen to a concert
   ◯ To give a performance
   ◯ To attend a class
   ◯ To take part in a practice

2. How often does the orchestra meet for practice?
   ◯ Once each week
   ◯ Twice each week
   ◯ Three times each week
   ◯ Four times each week

3. How many musical instruments does the woman play?
   ◯ Zero
   ◯ One
   ◯ Two
   ◯ Three

Questions 4–5

4. What is the woman confused about?

- ◯ Where to get the syllabus
- ◯ How many papers to write
- ◯ When the papers are due
- ◯ Where to find the professor

5. What do they decide to do?

- ◯ Ask at the next class
- ◯ Write a paper before the next class
- ◯ Follow the course syllabus
- ◯ See the professor immediately

Questions 6–8

6. What is true about the man?

- ◯ He has a car.
- ◯ He has a parking sticker.
- ◯ He will never drive to school.
- ◯ He intends to get a car.

7. What does the woman say about parking on campus?

- ◯ There are enough spaces.
- ◯ It's hard to find space.
- ◯ All students have permanent parking stickers.
- ◯ The lots are difficult to find.

8. What does the man say that he needs?

- ◯ A daily parking sticker
- ◯ A different type of car
- ◯ A permanent parking sticker
- ◯ A private parking space

Questions 9–11

9. What was true about the exam?
    ⬭ It had fifteen true-false questions.
    ⬭ It was sixty minutes long.
    ⬭ It had only one type of question.
    ⬭ It took two hours.

10. How did the man feel about the true-false questions?
    ⬭ He minded doing them.
    ⬭ He liked them less than the essays.
    ⬭ He didn't think they were too bad.
    ⬭ He didn't know the answers to them.

11. How did the woman do on the essay questions?
    ⬭ She was rushed when she wrote them.
    ⬭ She didn't know the answers.
    ⬭ She had enough time to finish them.
    ⬭ She wrote her answers clearly.

ACADEMIC DISCUSSIONS

(COMPUTER TOEFL® TEST)

Academic discussions appear in Part B of the Listening section of the computer TOEFL test. For each of the academic discussions in this part of the test, you will see a series of context-setting and content visuals as you listen to a 120–150 second discussion by two to five speakers. After you see the visuals and listen to the discussion, you will hear a series of questions as you see each question and its answer choices on the computer screen. You must click on the best answer choice to each question on the computer screen.

A variety of types of questions are possible in this part of the test. Some of these types of questions may follow a discussion:

1. **Multiple-Choice Questions with One Correct Answer** ask you to select the best answer from four choices based upon the information given in the discussion. A multiple-choice question with one correct answer may ask about the main idea or a directly or indirectly answered detail from the passage.

2. **Multiple-Choice Questions with Two Correct Answers** ask you to select the two correct answers from four choices based upon the information given in the discussion. A multiple-choice question with two correct answers may ask about directly or indirectly answered details from the passage.

3. **Graphic Questions with Four Letters** ask you to click on one of four letters on a graphic that answers a question. A graphic question with four letters may ask about a directly or indirectly answered detail from the passage.

4. **Questions with Four Graphics** ask you to click on one of four graphics that answers a question. A question with four graphics may ask about a directly or indirectly answered detail from the passage.

5. **Matching Questions** ask you to match three categories of information from the passage with details from each of the categories. A matching question generally asks about the organization of ideas in the passage.

6. **Ordering Questions** ask you to put four pieces of information in the correct procedural or chronological order. An ordering question generally asks about the overall organization of ideas in the passage.

The following example of an academic discussion shows each of these types of questions. (On the actual computer TOEFL test, you will probably not see all of these types of questions accompanying one academic discussion.)

Example from the Computer TOEFL® Test

You see on the computer screen:

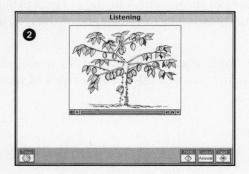

You hear:

(narrator)	*Listen to a discussion in a botany class. The discussion is on the cacao tree.*
(instructor)	❶ *Today, we're going to talk about the cacao tree and some of the products we get from this tree. Just what products do we get from the cacao tree? Joe?*
(Joe)	*The products we get from the cacao tree are some of my favorites: cocoa and chocolate.*
(instructor)	*And where are cacao trees found? Ellen?*
(Ellen)	*Cacao trees are native to the coastal areas of Mexico, Central America, and South America. Today, in addition to Mexico, Central, and South America, cacao trees are also found along the west coast of Africa and on a number of tropical islands.*
(instructor)	*Yes, it's true that cacao trees are found in coastal areas of Central and South America as well as in Africa.* ❷ *Let's look at this cacao tree. Can you describe the cacao tree for me? Taylor?*
(Taylor)	*You can see that the cacao tree has long, thick, shiny leaves; it's a type of evergreen tree.*
(instructor)	*What does it mean that it's an evergreen tree?*
(Taylor)	*An evergreen is any plant that keeps its leaves throughout the year. Many people think that only pines and firs are evergreens, but in reality, many plants with broad leaves are evergreens. Plants with thin, narrow leaves are generally not evergreen.*
(instructor)	*And what about the fruit of the cacao tree? Joe?*
(Joe)	*The fruit of the cacao tree is the size of a large cucumber and can be a variety of colors, depending on the type of tree.*

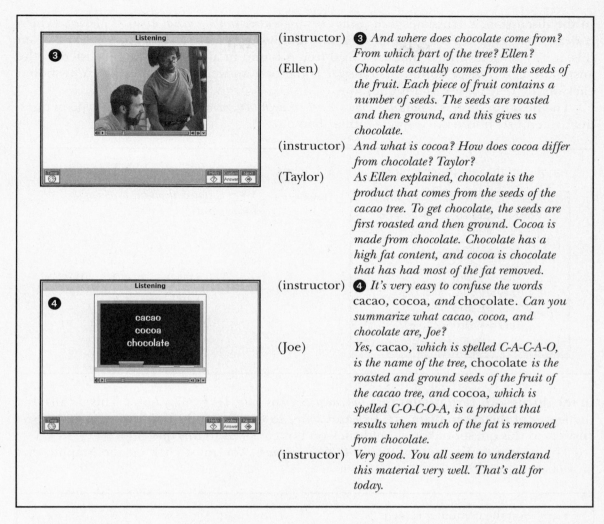

(instructor)	**3** *And where does chocolate come from? From which part of the tree? Ellen?*
(Ellen)	*Chocolate actually comes from the seeds of the fruit. Each piece of fruit contains a number of seeds. The seeds are roasted and then ground, and this gives us chocolate.*
(instructor)	*And what is cocoa? How does cocoa differ from chocolate? Taylor?*
(Taylor)	*As Ellen explained, chocolate is the product that comes from the seeds of the cacao tree. To get chocolate, the seeds are first roasted and then ground. Cocoa is made from chocolate. Chocolate has a high fat content, and cocoa is chocolate that has had most of the fat removed.*
(instructor)	**4** *It's very easy to confuse the words* cacao, cocoa, *and* chocolate. *Can you summarize what cacao, cocoa, and chocolate are, Joe?*
(Joe)	*Yes,* cacao, *which is spelled C-A-C-A-O, is the name of the tree,* chocolate *is the roasted and ground seeds of the fruit of the cacao tree, and* cocoa, *which is spelled C-O-C-O-A, is a product that results when much of the fat is removed from chocolate.*
(instructor)	*Very good. You all seem to understand this material very well. That's all for today.*

After the discussion is complete, the first question and answer choices appear on the computer screen as the narrator states the question. This question is a *multiple-choice question with one correct answer* that asks about a location.

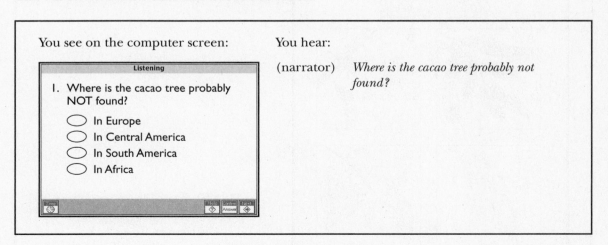

You see on the computer screen:

> **Listening**
>
> 1. Where is the cacao tree probably NOT found?
>   - ◯ In Europe
>   - ◯ In Central America
>   - ◯ In South America
>   - ◯ In Africa

You hear:

(narrator) *Where is the cacao tree probably not found?*

In the discussion, Ellen states that *cacao trees are native to the coastal areas of Mexico, Central America, and South America* and that *cacao trees are also found along the west coast of Africa*. From this, it can be determined that the cacao tree is found in all of the locations listed in the answers except *Europe*, so the first answer is the best answer to this question. You should click on the first answer to this question.

The next question is a *multiple-choice question with two correct answers*. In this type of question, you must choose two answers rather than one.

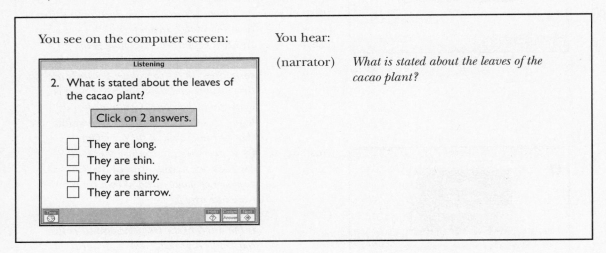

In the discussion, Taylor states that *the cacao tree has long, thick, shiny leaves*. This means that the leaves of the cacao plant are *long* and *shiny*, so the first and third answers are the best answers to this question. You should click on both answers to this question.

The next question is a *question with four graphics*. You must click on the graphic that answers the question.

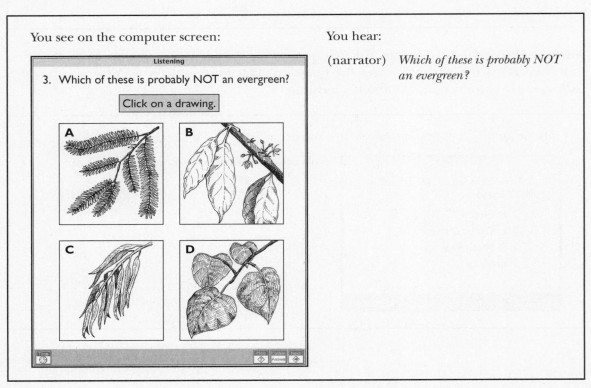

In the discussion, Taylor states that *plants with thin, narrow leaves are generally not evergreen.* From this, it can be determined that the plant with narrow leaves in drawing (C) is probably not an evergreen. You should click on drawing (C) to answer this question.

The next question is a *graphic question with four letters.* You must click on the letter on the graphic that answers the question.

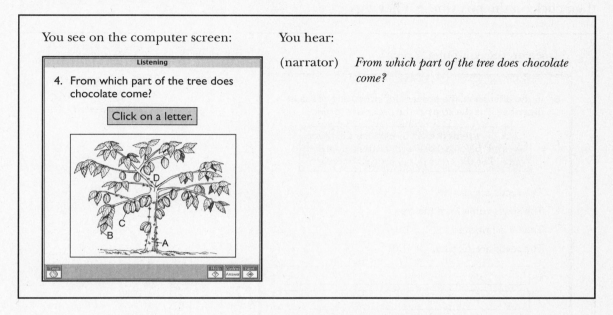

In the discussion, Ellen states that *chocolate actually comes from the seeds of the fruit.* Letter C, on the fruit, is therefore the best answer to this question. You should click on letter C to answer this question.

The next question is a *matching question.* You must click on each of the words and then click on the box where it belongs.

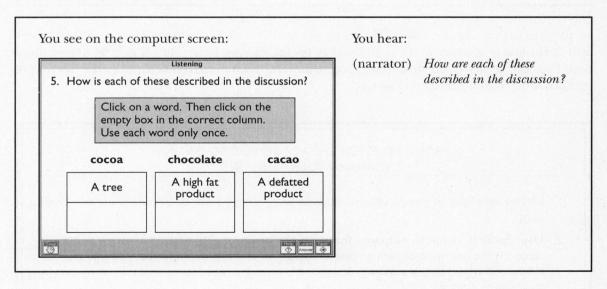

In the discussion, Taylor states that *chocolate is the product that comes from the seeds of the cacao tree* and that *chocolate has a high fat content, and cocoa is chocolate that has had most of the fat removed.* From this, it can be determined that cacao is a tree, chocolate is a high fat product, and cocoa is a defatted product.

The next question is an *ordering question.* You must click on each of the sentences and then click on the box where it belongs.

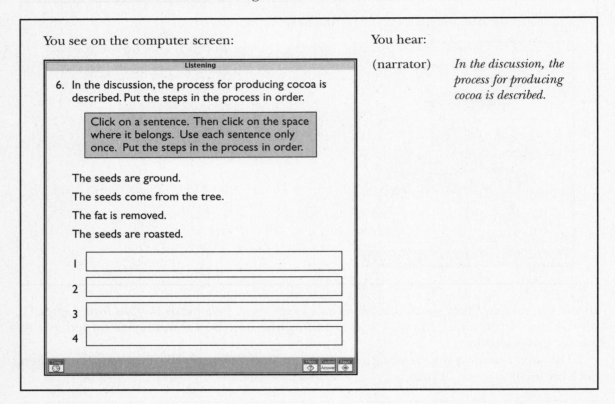

You see on the computer screen:

Listening

6. In the discussion, the process for producing cocoa is described. Put the steps in the process in order.

> Click on a sentence. Then click on the space where it belongs. Use each sentence only once. Put the steps in the process in order.

The seeds are ground.

The seeds come from the tree.

The fat is removed.

The seeds are roasted.

1 [ ]
2 [ ]
3 [ ]
4 [ ]

You hear:

(narrator)   *In the discussion, the process for producing cocoa is described.*

In the discussion, Taylor states that *to get chocolate, the seeds are first roasted and then ground* and that *cocoa is chocolate that has had most of the fat removed.* From this, it can be determined that first the seeds come from the tree, then the seeds are roasted, next the seeds are ground, and finally the fat is removed.

PROCEDURES FOR THE ACADEMIC DISCUSSIONS
(Computer TOEFL® Test)

1. **Listen carefully to the academic discussion.** You may listen to the discussion one time only.

2. **Use the first visual to help you focus on the context.** The first visual appears on the screen at the beginning of each academic discussion. It shows you how many people are talking and where they are talking. Anywhere from two to five people could be taking part in an academic discussion.

3. **Focus on the overall meaning of the academic discussion rather than on specific words or expressions.** The questions following an academic discussion generally test your overall comprehension rather than the meaning of a specific word or expression.

4. **Relate the remaining visuals to the academic discussion.** The remaining visuals are related to the portion of the discussion that you hear as you see the visual.

5. **Listen carefully to each question following the academic discussion as you read it on the screen.** Each listening question is both spoken and written on the computer screen.

6. **Understand the ordering of the questions that accompany an academic discussion.** The answers to the questions that accompany a discussion are generally found in order in the discussion. The answer to the first question will generally be found closer to the beginning of the discussion, and the answer to the last question will generally be found closer to the end of the discussion.

7. **Do not panic if you do not understand all of the details of the academic discussion.** You can still answer the questions correctly without understanding each detail of the discussion.

8. **Click on an answer on the computer screen when you have selected an answer.** You may still change your mind at this point and click on a different answer.

9. **Click on Next . Then click on Confirm Answer to record your answer.** After you click on this button, you cannot go back and change your answer.

10. **Be prepared for the next question.** After you click on Confirm Answer , the next question begins automatically.

Next you should move on to the language skills. The following language skills will help you to implement these procedures with the academic discussions on the computer TOEFL test.

SKILL 29: RECOGNIZE THE ORGANIZATION

As you listen to each academic discussion in Part B of the computer TOEFL test, you should be thinking about the organization of the passage because questions about the organization of the passage quite commonly accompany the academic discussions. The types of questions that test the organization of the passage are *matching* questions and *ordering* questions. Matching questions are used to test your understanding of the organization of a classification passage that discusses the various types or categories of a given topic. Ordering questions are used to test your understanding of the organization of a process or chronological passage that discusses either how something is accomplished or a series of historical events. Look at an example of part of a discussion with a classification organization, followed by a matching question.

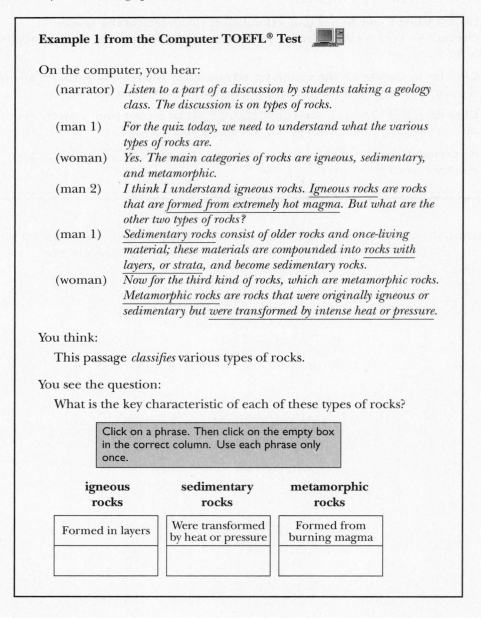

Example 1 from the Computer TOEFL® Test

On the computer, you hear:

(narrator) *Listen to a part of a discussion by students taking a geology class. The discussion is on types of rocks.*

(man 1) *For the quiz today, we need to understand what the various types of rocks are.*

(woman) *Yes. The main categories of rocks are igneous, sedimentary, and metamorphic.*

(man 2) *I think I understand igneous rocks. Igneous rocks are rocks that are formed from extremely hot magma. But what are the other two types of rocks?*

(man 1) *Sedimentary rocks consist of older rocks and once-living material; these materials are compounded into rocks with layers, or strata, and become sedimentary rocks.*

(woman) *Now for the third kind of rocks, which are metamorphic rocks. Metamorphic rocks are rocks that were originally igneous or sedimentary but were transformed by intense heat or pressure.*

You think:

This passage *classifies* various types of rocks.

You see the question:

What is the key characteristic of each of these types of rocks?

Click on a phrase. Then click on the empty box in the correct column. Use each phrase only once.

igneous rocks	sedimentary rocks	metamorphic rocks
Formed in layers	Were transformed by heat or pressure	Formed from burning magma

In the discussion, the students state that *igneous rocks…formed from extremely hot magma,* that *sedimentary rocks* are *rocks with layers, or strata,* and that *metamorphic rocks…were transformed by intense heat or pressure.* From this, it can be determined that igneous rocks formed from burning magma, that sedimentary rocks formed in layers, and that metamorphic rocks were transformed by heat or pressure.

Now look at an example of a part of a discussion with a process organization, followed by an ordering question.

Example 2 from the Computer TOEFL® Test

On the computer, you hear:

(narrator)	*Listen to a part of a discussion in a physics class. The class is discussing how the space shuttle is propelled into orbit.*
(instructor)	*Today, we'll be talking about the space shuttle and how it is propelled into orbit. First of all, can you tell me where the shuttle gets its power? Jack?*
(Jack)	*The shuttle has three sources of power. It has its main engines, of course, and it also has smaller engines in the shuttle and boosters attached to it.*
(instructor)	*And how does the shuttle actually get into orbit? Can you explain the process, Cathy?*
(Cathy)	*First, the main engines and the boosters work together to lift the shuttle off the ground.*
(instructor)	*Then, what happens to the boosters?*
(Cathy)	*The boosters separate from the shuttle and parachute back to Earth.*
(instructor)	*Now, Greg, after the shuttle has lifted off the ground, how does it get into orbit?*
(Greg)	*After the boosters have dropped off, the main engines power the shuttle until it is almost at orbital velocity.*
(instructor)	*Then how does the shuttle actually get into orbit?*
(Greg)	*That's when the smaller engines kick in and push the shuttle into orbit.*

You think:

This passage explains the *process* by which the shuttle is propelled into space.

You see the question:

The process by which the shuttle is propelled into space is explained in the discussion. Put the steps in the process in order.

> Click on a sentence. Then click on the space where it belongs. Use each sentence one time only.

The main engines put the shuttle almost into orbit.

The main engines and boosters lift the shuttle.

The smaller engines push the shuttle into orbit.

The boosters separate and parachute to Earth.

```
1 ┌─────────────────────────────────────────┐
  └─────────────────────────────────────────┘
2 ┌─────────────────────────────────────────┐
  └─────────────────────────────────────────┘
3 ┌─────────────────────────────────────────┐
  └─────────────────────────────────────────┘
4 ┌─────────────────────────────────────────┐
  └─────────────────────────────────────────┘
```

In the discussion, the students state that *first, the main engines and the boosters work together to lift the shuttle off the ground,* that *the boosters separate from the shuttle and parachute back to Earth,* that *the main engines power the shuttle until it is almost at orbital velocity,* and that *the smaller engines…push the shuttle into orbit.* From this, it can be determined that first the main engines and boosters lift the shuttle, next the boosters separate and parachute to Earth, then the main engines put the shuttle almost into orbit, and finally the smaller engines push the shuttle into orbit.

Now look at an example of a part of a lecture with both classification and chronological organization, followed by both a matching question and an ordering question.

Example 3 from the Computer TOEFL® Test

On the computer, you hear:

(narrator) *Listen to a part of a discussion by a group of students taking a music class. The discussion is on early periods of music.*

(woman 1) *There are four periods of music that we need to be familiar with. The first period was the Medieval period, from 1100 to 1300. The Medieval period was the period when organized instrumental music began.*

(man) *And after the Medieval period was the Renaissance period, which was the age of polyphonic church music. This period lasted for 300 years.*

(woman 2) *So the Renaissance period lasted from 1300 to 1600. Then which period was next?*

(woman 1) *After the Renaissance period there was the Baroque period from 1600 to 1750, followed by the Classical period from 1750 to 1850.*

(man) *And what type of music was featured in each of these periods?*

(woman 1) *The Baroque period featured the beginnings of opera and oratorio.*

(woman 2) *And the Classical period was the age of symphonies and concertos.*

You think:

This passage presents types or *classifications* of music in *chronological order.*

You see the question:

The students discuss a number of periods of music. Put the periods of music into the order in which they occurred.

Click on a phrase. Then click on the space where it belongs. Use each phrase one time only.

Baroque period
Renaissance period
Classical period
Medieval period

1 [   ]

2 [   ]

3 [   ]

4 [   ]

In the discussion, the students mention *the Medieval period, from 1100 to 1300, the Renaissance period, which...lasted from 1300 to 1600, the Baroque period from 1600 to 1750,* and *the Classical period from 1750 to 1850.* From this, it can be determined that first there was the Medieval period, then the Renaissance period, next the Baroque period, and finally the Classical period.

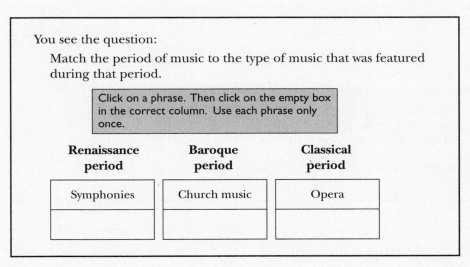

You see the question:

Match the period of music to the type of music that was featured during that period.

Click on a phrase. Then click on the empty box in the correct column. Use each phrase only once.

Renaissance period	**Baroque period**	**Classical period**
Symphonies	Church music	Opera

In the discussion, the students mention *the Renaissance period, which was the age of polyphonic church music,* and state that *the Baroque period featured the beginnings of opera* and that *the Classical period was the age of symphonies.* From this, it can be determined that the Renaissance period featured church music, the Baroque period featured opera, and the Classical period featured symphonies.

EXERCISE 29: Listen to each academic discussion, and try to determine how the information in the passage is organized.

1. a.   What type of organization is used in the first passage?

   ○ classification
   ○ ordering (process or chronology)
   ○ both classification and ordering

   b.   What are the main points in the organization?

   _____

   _____

   _____

2. a.   What type of organization is used in the second passage?

   ○ classification
   ○ ordering (process or chronology)
   ○ both classification and ordering

   b.   What are the main points in the organization?

   _____

   _____

   _____

3. a.   What type of organization is used in the third passage?

   ○ classification
   ○ ordering (process or chronology)
   ○ both classification and ordering

   b.   What are the main points in the organization?

   _____

   _____

   _____

TOEFL EXERCISE 29: Listen to each passage, and answer the questions that accompany it.

Questions 1–2

Listen to a discussion by a group of students taking a meteorology class. The discussion is on the formation of hail.

1. In the discussion, the students explain the initial stages in the formation of a hailstone from a drop of water. Summarize the process by putting the steps in order.

> Click on a sentence. Then click on the space where it belongs. Use each sentence one time only.

It picks up water.
It falls within the cloud.
It rises within a cloud.
It freezes for the first time.

1	
2	
3	
4	

2. In the discussion, the students explain how a hailstone hits the earth. Summarize the process by putting the steps in order.

> Click on a sentence. Then click on the space where it belongs. Use each sentence one time only.

It becomes too heavy.
It falls to the ground.
It rises and falls repeatedly in the cloud.
It adds new layers of ice.

1	
2	
3	
4	

Questions 3–5

Listen to a discussion in a physiology class. The discussion is on types of fractures.

3. How many breaks in the bone are there in each of these fractures?

Click on a phrase. Then click on the empty box in the correct column. Use each phrase only once.

double fracture	multiple fracture	single fracture
One break	Two breaks	Numerous breaks

4. How is each of these fractures described?

Click on a phrase. Then click on the empty box in the correct column. Use each phrase only once.

compound fracture	simple fracture	greenstick fracture
Complete fracture with no broken skin	Partial fracture	Complete fracture with broken skin

5. How serious is each of these fractures?

Click on a phrase. Then click on the empty box in the correct column. Use each phrase only once.

simple fracture	compound fracture	greenstick fracture
Less serious	Serious	More serious

Questions 6–7

Listen to a discussion by a group of students taking a law class. The students are discussing Clarence Darrow.

6.   With what event was each of the defendants associated?

> Click on a name. Then click on the empty box in the correct column. Use each expression only once.

John Scopes	Loeb and Leopold	Eugene Debs
Pullman strike	Evolution in the classroom	Murder trial

7.   A historical series of events in the life of Clarence Darrow is presented in the discussion. Put the events in the correct chronological order.

> Click on a sentence. Then click on the space where it belongs. Use each sentence one time only.

He arbitrated a coal strike.

He defended the murderers of a teenager.

He took part in the Monkey Trial.

He defended the railway union president.

1
2
3
4

Skill 30:   LISTEN FOR DIRECT AND INDIRECT DETAILS

As you listen to each academic discussion in Part B of the computer TOEFL test, you should focus on the details from the passage and indirect information that can be inferred from these details because questions about direct and indirect details quite commonly accompany the academic discussions. Multiple-choice questions are used to test direct and indirect details, and these multiple-choice questions may have one correct answer or two correct answers. Look at an example of a part of an academic discussion, followed by a multiple-choice question about a direct detail. This question has one correct answer.

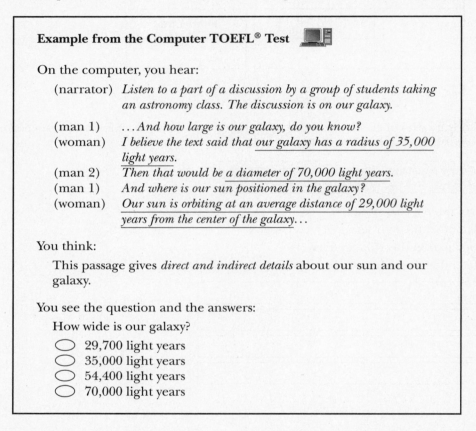

Example from the Computer TOEFL® Test

On the computer, you hear:

(narrator)   *Listen to a part of a discussion by a group of students taking an astronomy class. The discussion is on our galaxy.*

(man 1)   *...And how large is our galaxy, do you know?*
(woman)   *I believe the text said that our galaxy has a radius of 35,000 light years.*
(man 2)   *Then that would be a diameter of 70,000 light years.*
(man 1)   *And where is our sun positioned in the galaxy?*
(woman)   *Our sun is orbiting at an average distance of 29,000 light years from the center of the galaxy...*

You think:

This passage gives *direct and indirect details* about our sun and our galaxy.

You see the question and the answers:

How wide is our galaxy?

- ◯ 29,700 light years
- ◯ 35,000 light years
- ◯ 54,400 light years
- ◯ 70,000 light years

In the discussion, the speakers state that *our galaxy has a radius of 35,000 light years,* which is *a diameter of 70,000 light years.* This means that our galaxy is *70,000 light years* wide, so the last answer is the best answer to this question.

Now look at an example of a multiple-choice question about a direct detail. This question has two correct answers.

You see the question:

What is stated about our sun?

> [Click on 2 answers.]

- ☐ It orbits around the center of the galaxy.
- ☐ It has a diameter of 35,000 light years.
- ☐ It is just under 30,000 light years from the center of the galaxy.
- ☐ It has a radius of 29,000 light years.

In the discussion, the woman states that *our sun is orbiting at an average distance of 29,000 light years from the center of the galaxy*. This means that our sun *orbits around the center of the galaxy* and that it *is just under 30,000 light years from the center*. The first and third answers are therefore the best answers to this question.

Now look at an example of a multiple-choice question about an indirect detail. This question has one correct answer.

You see the question:

What can be inferred about our sun?

◯ It is close to the center of our galaxy.
◯ It moves erratically throughout the galaxy.
◯ It is almost as large as our galaxy.
◯ It is in the outer portion of our galaxy.

In the discussion, the speakers state that *our galaxy has a radius of 35,000 light years* and that *our sun is orbiting at an average distance of 29,000 light years from the center*. From this, it can be inferred that our sun *is in the outer portion of our galaxy*. The last answer is therefore the best answer to this question.

EXERCISE 30: Listen to each academic discussion, and try to focus on the direct and indirect details in the passage.

1. What are some of the **direct details** in the first passage?

   a. About when the performance is: _____

   b. About the characters they are playing: _____

   c. About the scene they are performing: _____

   What are some of the **indirect details** that can be inferred from the passage?

   d. About how familiar they are with their lines: _____

   e. About what they will do next: _____

2. What are some of the **direct details** in the second passage?

   a. About how iron pyrite is like gold: _____

   b. About the composition of iron pyrite: _____

   c. About the reaction of iron pyrite to heat: _____

   d. About the derivation of the word *pyrite*: _____

   What are some of the **indirect details** that can be inferred from the passage?

   e. About the people who mistook iron pyrite for gold: _____

   f. About the reaction of gold to heat: _____

   g. About the use of gold to create fires: _____

3. What are some of the **direct details** in the third passage?

    a.   About who named California: _____

    b.   About where the name California first appeared: _____

    c.   About what the fictional California was like: _____

    d.   About the inhabitants of the fictional California: _____

    What are some of the **indirect details** that can be inferred from the passage?

    e.   About when California was named: _____

    f.   About the real land of California: _____

TOEFL EXERCISE 30: Listen to each passage, and answer the questions that accompany it.

Questions 1–5

Listen to a discussion by some students who
are taking a drama class. They are discussing
their class project on the play *Our Town*.

1. When is the students' performance?
    ○ In three days
    ○ In ten days
    ○ In a few weeks
    ○ In three months

2. Which of these is not a character in the
    scene?
    ○ Emily
    ○ George
    ○ Thornton Wilder
    ○ The Stage Manager

3. It is most likely that the students are how
    familiar with their lines?
    ○ They haven't even looked at their
       lines.
    ○ They have read over their lines.
    ○ They have each memorized their
       own lines.
    ○ They have each memorized
       everyone's lines.

4. What is stated about the scene?

    | Click on 2 answers. |

    ☐ It takes place before a wedding.
    ☐ It takes place during a wedding.
    ☐ George and Emily are getting
       married.
    ☐ George and Emily are wedding guests.

5. What are the students probably going to
    discuss next?

    | Click on 2 answers. |

    ☐ Other plays
    ☐ Costumes
    ☐ Characters
    ☐ Props

Questions 6–12

Listen to a discussion about a geology class. The students are discussing iron pyrite.

6. In what way is iron pyrite similar to gold?
   ○ In color
   ○ In shape
   ○ In composition
   ○ In reaction to heat

7. It is implied in the discussion that what type of people thought iron pyrite was gold?
   ○ Adventurous people
   ○ Foolish people
   ○ Wealthy people
   ○ Practical people

8. What is iron pyrite composed of?

   | Click on 2 answers. |

   ☐ Gold
   ☐ Sulfur
   ☐ Pyrite
   ☐ Iron

9. How does iron pyrite react to heat?

   | Click on 2 answers. |

   ☐ It creates smoke.
   ☐ It emits a bad smell.
   ☐ It becomes golden.
   ☐ It develops a shine.

10. How does gold most likely react to heat?
    ○ It develops a cubical shape.
    ○ It smokes and smells.
    ○ It does not have a strong reaction.
    ○ It turns into iron pyrite.

11. Where did the word *pyrite* come from?
    ○ From a Latin word meaning "gold."
    ○ From a Latin word meaning "far."
    ○ From a Greek word meaning "iron."
    ○ From a Greek word meaning "fire."

12. What can be inferred from the discussion about gold in ancient cultures?
    ○ It was not mined.
    ○ It was not used to start fires.
    ○ It was valued less than iron pyrite.
    ○ It was called fool's gold.

Questions 13–18

Listen to a discussion in a history class. The discussion is on the history behind the name *California*.

13. Who gave the area of North America known as California its name?
    ○ An explorer
    ○ An Amazon
    ○ A knight
    ○ The son of a knight

14. In which of these years was the area of North America known as California most likely given its name?
    ○ In 1435
    ○ In 1535
    ○ In 1635
    ○ In 1735

15. How was the name *California* first used?
    ○ As the name of a fictional place
    ○ As the name of an Amazon tribe
    ○ As the name of an explorer's ship
    ○ As the name of a knight's son

16. What was the fictional California like?

    | Click on 2 answers. |

    ☐ It was in the Americas.
    ☐ It was an island.
    ☐ It was full of explorers.
    ☐ It had lots of gold.

17. What is not stated in the discussion about the inhabitants of the fictional California?

⊙ They were women.
⊙ They were Amazons.
⊙ They were warriors.
⊙ They were explorers.

18. What can be inferred about the California that Cortes visited?

| Click on 2 answers. |

☐ It did not have Amazons.
☐ It did not have any gold.
☐ It was not an island.
☐ It did not have any inhabitants.

SKILL 31:   VISUALIZE THE PASSAGE

As you listen to each academic discussion in Part B of the computer TOEFL test, you should try to visualize what you hear in the passage because visual questions about what is being described in the passage quite commonly accompany the academic discussions. There are two types of visual questions that may accompany an academic discussion. One type of visual question shows you four drawings and asks you to click on the one drawing of the four that answers a question. The other type of visual question shows you one drawing with four letters on it and asks you to click on the one letter of the four that answers a question. Look at an example of a part of a discussion and a visual question with four drawings.

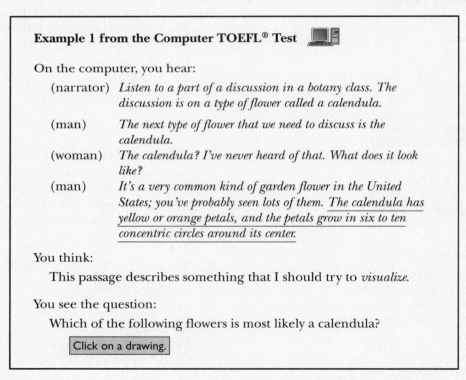

Example 1 from the Computer TOEFL® Test

On the computer, you hear:

(narrator) *Listen to a part of a discussion in a botany class. The discussion is on a type of flower called a calendula.*

(man) *The next type of flower that we need to discuss is the calendula.*

(woman) *The calendula? I've never heard of that. What does it look like?*

(man) *It's a very common kind of garden flower in the United States; you've probably seen lots of them. The calendula has yellow or orange petals, and the petals grow in six to ten concentric circles around its center.*

You think:

This passage describes something that I should try to *visualize.*

You see the question:

Which of the following flowers is most likely a calendula?

| Click on a drawing. |

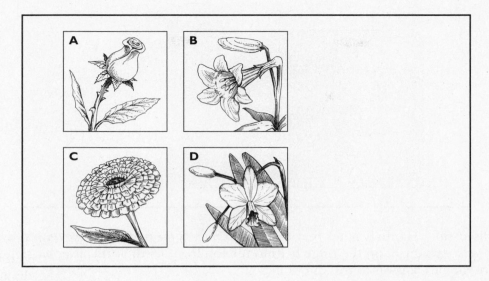

In the discussion, the man states that *the calendula has yellow or orange petals, and the petals grow in six to ten concentric circles around its center.* Answer C, with petals in concentric circles around the center, is therefore the best answer to this question.

Now look at an example of a part of a discussion and a visual question with one drawing and four letters.

Example 2 from the Computer TOEFL® Test

On the computer, you hear:

(narrator)	*Listen to a part of a discussion in a phonology class. The discussion is about how the English /t/ sound is produced.*
(instructor)	*The next sound we'll talk about is the /t/ sound. What type of sound is the /t/ sound? Hannah?*
(Hannah)	*The /t/ sound is an alveolar sound. This means that the /t/ sound is formed when the tip of the tongue is placed against the alveolar ridge and then is suddenly removed.*
(instructor)	*And where is the alveolar ridge?*
(Hannah)	*The alveolar ridge is the ridge in the mouth just behind the top front teeth.*
(instructor)	*That's exactly right. If you practice forming a /t/ sound, you can feel the tip of your tongue against the alveolar ridge....*

You think:

This passage has something that I should try to *visualize.*

You see the question:

Where is the alveolar ridge?

Click on a letter.

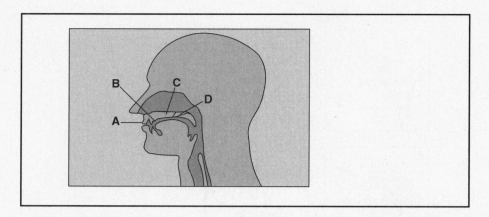

In the discussion, Hannah states that *the alveolar ridge is the ridge in the mouth just behind the top front teeth.* Answer B, on the ridge behind the top front teeth, is the alveolar ridge and is therefore the best answer to this question.

EXERCISE 31: Listen to each academic discussion, and try to visualize the information in the passage.

1. How do you visualize the two theories about the behavior of storms?

    a. Redfield's theory   b. Espy's theory

2. How do you visualize an opossum?

    a. A mother with a very young baby   b. A mother with an older child   c. An adult in a defensive position

3.   How do you visualize Chimney Rock?

   a. Its actual shape

   b. Its location in relation
       to the Platte River

   c. Its location in relation
       to the Rocky Mountains

TOEFL EXERCISE 31: Listen to each passage, and answer the questions that accompany it.

Questions 1–3

Listen to a discussion by a group of students in a meteorology class. The discussion is on theories about the behavior of storms.

1.   How did Redfield believe that the winds in storms behave?

   Click on a drawing.

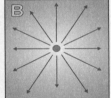
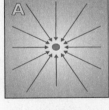
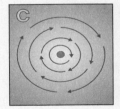
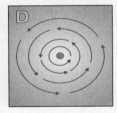

2.   How did Espy believe that the winds in storms behave?

   Click on a drawing.

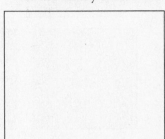

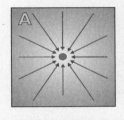
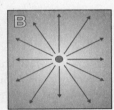
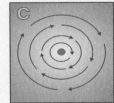
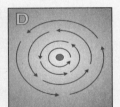

3. Which of these diagrams most closely represents what winds actually do during a storm?

Click on a drawing.

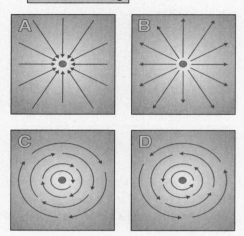

Questions 4–6

Listen to a group of students discussing information from a zoology class. The discussion is on the opossum.

4. Where would a one-month-old baby opossum most likely be found?

Click on a letter.

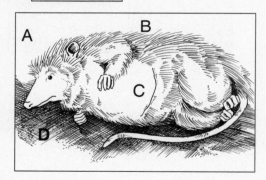

5. Where would a three-month-old opossum most likely be while its mother is walking around?

Click on a letter.

6. What does an opossum do when it is threatened?

Click on a drawing.

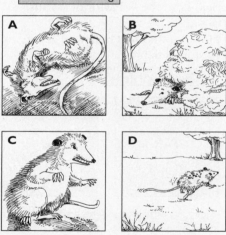

Questions 7–9

Listen to a discussion from an American history class. The discussion is on Chimney Rock.

7. Which of these most closely resembles Chimney Rock?

Click on a drawing.

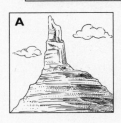

8. Where is Chimney Rock located in relation to the Platte River?

Click on a letter.

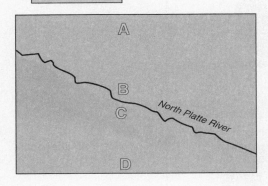

9. Where is Chimney Rock in relation to the Great Plains and the Rocky Mountains?

Click on a letter.

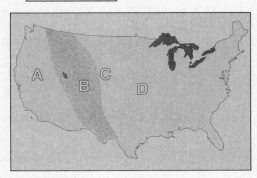

TOEFL REVIEW EXERCISE (Skills 29–31)

Questions 1–5

Listen to a discussion in an American history class. The discussion is about an early American coin.

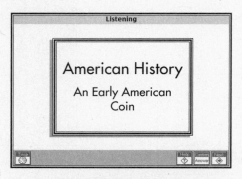

1. By what two names is this coin known?

    Click on 2 answers.

    ☐ The "I Fly" coin
    ☐ The Fugio coin
    ☐ The "Mind Your Business" coin
    ☐ The Franklin coin

2. When was this coin first issued?

    ◯ In the 16th century
    ◯ In the 17th century
    ◯ In the 18th century
    ◯ In the 19th century

3. For which part of the coin was Franklin given credit?

    Click on a letter.

4. What do the circles on the back of the coin look like?

    Click on a drawing.

    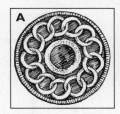
    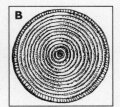
    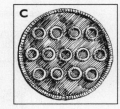
    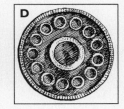

5. What words are on the back of the coin?

    ◯ Fugio
    ◯ Mind your business
    ◯ The 13 colonies
    ◯ We are one

Questions 6–10

Listen to a group of students discussing a presentation for a business class. The discussion is on the marketing of Kleenex.

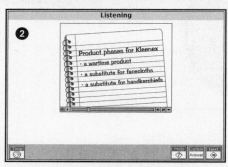

6. What are the students doing?

    ☐ Reviewing class lecture notes
    ☐ Preparing for a presentation
    ☐ Writing a paper
    ☐ Preparing for an exam

7. Match the use of the product to the period of time when that use predominated.

    > Click on a word or phrase. Then click on the empty box in the correct column. Use each word or phrase one time only.

facecloth	handkerchief	gas mask
Before 1920	In the 1920s	In the 1930s

8. What was the situation at Kimberly-Clark at the end of World War I?

    > Click on 2 answers.

    ☐ It had a large surplus of its product.
    ☐ It needed to develop a new product.
    ☐ It no longer needed to market its product.
    ☐ It needed to begin marketing its product.

9. How did Kimberly-Clark learn that its product had a use as a handkerchief?

    ☐ From customer letters
    ☐ From research scientists
    ☐ From marketing experts
    ☐ From famous actresses

10. Match the use of the product to the marketing strategy associated with that use.

    > Click on a word. Then click on the empty box in the correct column. Use each word one time only.

bandages	facecloths	handkerchiefs
Famous actresses	No marketing	Consumer testing

Questions 11–15

Listen to a discussion by a group of students in an oceanography class. The discussion is on atolls.

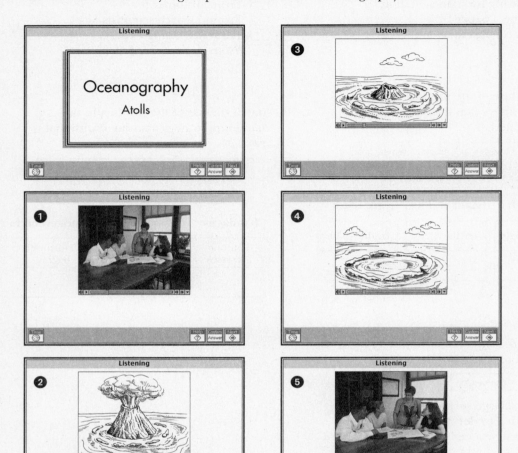

11. What is an atoll made of?

◯ A combination of coral and algae
◯ A combination of algae and volcanic ash
◯ Only of algae
◯ Only of coral

12. Which of these is an atoll?

| Click on a drawing. |

13. Where do atolls tend to grow?

| Click on 2 answers. |

☐ In tropical areas
☐ In arctic areas
☐ In warm water
☐ In cool water

14. In the discussion, the process of the formation of atolls is discussed. Summarize the process by putting the steps in order.

| Click on a sentence. Then click on the space where it belongs. Use each sentence one time only. |

Coral begins to grow.
A volcanic island forms.
The volcano disappears underwater.
The volcano erodes.

1
2
3
4

15. Where is the lagoon?

| Click on a letter. |

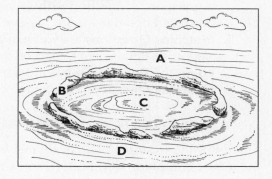

ACADEMIC LECTURES
(COMPUTER TOEFL® TEST)

Academic lectures appear in Part B of the Listening section of the computer TOEFL test. For each of the academic lectures in this part of the test, you will see a series of context-setting and content visuals as you listen to a 120–150 second lecture by a university professor. After you see the visuals and listen to the lecture, you will hear a series of questions as you see each question and its answer choices on the computer screen. You must click on the best answer choice to each question on the computer screen.

A variety of types of questions are possible in this part of the test. Some of these types of questions may follow a lecture:

1. **Multiple-Choice Questions with One Correct Answer** ask you to select the best answer from four choices, based upon the information given in the passage. A multiple-choice question with one correct answer may ask about the main idea or a directly or an indirectly answered detail from the passage.

2. **Multiple-Choice Questions with Two Correct Answers** ask you to select the two correct answers from four choices, based upon the information given in the passage. A multiple-choice question with two correct answers may ask about directly or indirectly answered details from the passage.

3. **Graphic Questions with Four Letters** ask you to click on one of four letters on a graphic that answers a question. A graphic question with four letters may ask about a directly or an indirectly answered detail from the passage.

4. **Questions with Four Graphics** ask you to click on one of four graphics that answers a question. A question with four graphics may ask about a directly or an indirectly answered detail from the passage.

5. **Matching Questions** ask you to match three categories of information from the passage with details from each of the categories. A matching question generally asks about the organization of ideas in the passage.

6. **Ordering Questions** ask you to put four pieces of information in the correct procedural or chronological order. An ordering question generally asks about the overall organization of ideas in the passage.

The following example of an academic lecture shows each of these types of questions. (On the actual computer TOEFL test, you will probably not see all of these types of questions accompanying one academic lecture.)

Example from the Computer TOEFL® Test

You see on the computer screen:

You hear:

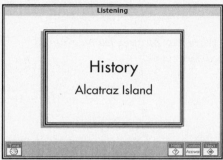

Listen to a lecture in a history class. The professor is talking about the history of Alcatraz Island.

❶ *Alcatraz is a large, rocky island in San Francisco Bay. It was named in 1775 by a Spanish explorer who first saw the rocky island when it was covered with pelicans. He named the island after the pelicans — the word Alcatraz is actually a derivation of the Spanish word for pelican.*

❷ *You can see Alcatraz Island in this photo. The island was acquired by the United States in 1848, when it was turned over to the military. It was first made into a fort to protect San Francisco because of its location due north of San Francisco just inside the entrance to San Francisco Bay. It was later turned into a military prison, and it remained part of the military system until 1934, when it was changed into a federal prison.*

Alcatraz served as a federal prison for twenty-nine years from 1934 until the prison was closed in 1963. During the time that it served as a federal prison, a number of famous prisoners served time there, including Al Capone, Machine Gun Kelly, and Robert Stroud, who was better known as the Birdman of Alcatraz because of the studies he conducted there on birds.

❸ *In 1963, the prison at Alcatraz was shut down, and, for the next nine years, the entire island was closed off and no one was allowed to go there. Then, in 1972, Alcatraz became part of the National Park system, and today the island is open to anyone who wishes to venture out there.*

After the lecture is complete, the first question and answer choices appear on the computer screen as the narrator states the question. This question is a *multiple-choice question with one correct answer* that asks about a period of time.

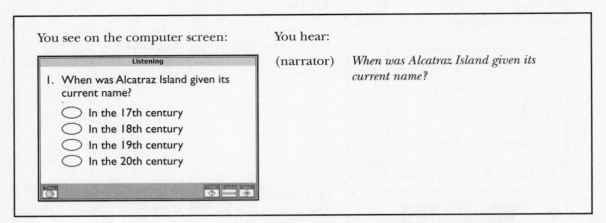

In the lecture, the professor states that Alcatraz *was named in 1775 by a Spanish explorer.* This means that the Spanish explorer named the island Alcatraz in the eighteenth century. The second answer is the correct answer, so you should click on this answer.

The next question is a *question with four graphics.* You must click on the graphic that answers the question.

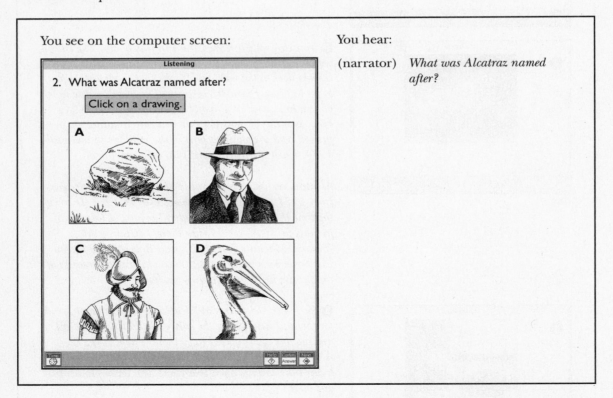

In the lecture, the professor states that *he named the island after the pelicans.* Drawing D, a pelican, is therefore the best answer to this question, so you should click on Drawing D to answer the question.

The next question is a *graphic question with four letters*. You must click on the letter on the graphic that answers the question.

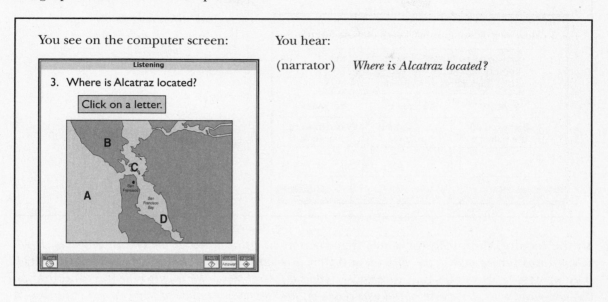

In the lecture, the professor mentions *its location due north of San Francisco just inside the entrance to San Francisco Bay*. Answer C, which is due north of San Francisco and just inside the entrance to the bay, is therefore the best answer to this question.

The next question is a *multiple-choice question with two correct answers*. You must choose the two answers that are correct.

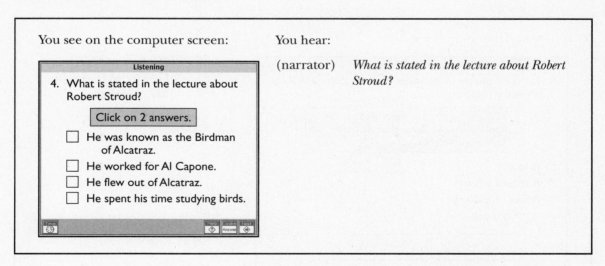

In the lecture, the professor mentions *Robert Stroud, who was better known as the Birdman of Alcatraz because of the studies he conducted there on birds*. This means that Robert Stroud *was known as the Birdman of Alcatraz* and that he *spent his time studying birds*. The first and last answers are therefore the best answers to this question, so you should click on the first and last answers to this question.

The next question is a *matching question*. You must click on each of the phrases and then click on the box where it belongs.

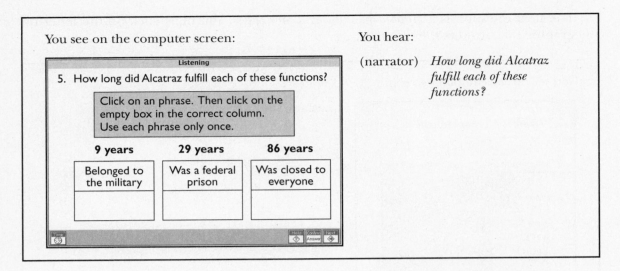

You see on the computer screen:

You hear:

(narrator)   *How long did Alcatraz fulfill each of these functions?*

In the lecture, the professor states that *the island was acquired by the United States in 1848, when it was turned over to the military* and that *it remained part of the military system until 1934.* The professor also states that *Alcatraz served as a federal prison for twenty-nine years* and that *for the next nine years, the entire island was closed off and no one was allowed to go there.* From this, it can be determined that Alcatraz belonged to the military for 86 years, that it was a federal prison for 29 years, and that it was closed to everyone for 9 years. You should click on each period of time and then click on the box where it belongs to answer this question.

The next question is an *ordering question.* You must click on each of the phrases and then click on the box where it belongs.

You see on the computer screen:

You hear:

(narrator)   *Put these people in the order in which they most likely arrived at Alcatraz.*

Listening

6. Put these people in the order in which they most likely arrived at Alcatraz.

> Click on a phrase. Then click on the space where it belongs. Use each phrase only once.

A tourist
A federal prisoner
A Spanish explorer
A military prisoner

1 [   ]
2 [   ]
3 [   ]
4 [   ]

In the lecture, the professor mentions the following: *1775* and *a Spanish explorer; 1848, when it was turned over to the military; a federal prison…from 1934 until…1963;* and *1972* and *the National Park system.* From this, it can be determined that the most likely order that these people arrived at Alcatraz was first a Spanish explorer, then a military prisoner, next a federal prisoner, and finally a tourist.

PROCEDURES FOR THE ACADEMIC LECTURES
(Computer TOEFL® Test)

1. **Listen carefully to the academic lecture.** You may listen to the lecture one time only.

2. **Use the first visual to help you focus on the context.** The first visual appears on the screen at the beginning of each academic lecture. It shows you that a professor is giving a lecture in an academic lecture hall.

3. **Focus on the overall meaning of the academic lecture rather than on specific words or expressions.** The questions following an academic lecture generally test your overall comprehension rather than the meaning of a specific word or expression.

4. **Relate the remaining visuals to the academic lecture.** The remaining visuals are related to the portion of the lecture that you hear as you see the visual.

5. **Listen carefully to each question following the academic lecture as you read it on the screen.** Each listening question is both spoken and written on the computer screen.

6. **Understand the ordering of the questions that accompany an academic lecture.** The answers to the questions that accompany a lecture are generally found in order in the lecture. The answer to the first question will generally be found closer to the beginning of the lecture, and the answer to the last question will generally be found closer to the end of the lecture.

7. **Do not panic if you do not understand all of the details of the academic lecture.** You can still answer the questions correctly without understanding each detail of the lecture.

8. **Click on an answer on the computer screen when you have selected an answer.** You may still change your mind at this point and click on a different answer.

9. **Click on** Next **. Then click on** Confirm Answer **to record your answer.** After you click on this button, you cannot go back and change your answer.

10. **Be prepared for the next question.** After you click on Confirm Answer , the next question begins automatically.

Next you should move on to the language skills. The following language skills will help you to implement these procedures with the academic lectures on the computer TOEFL test.

SKILL 32: RECOGNIZE THE ORGANIZATION

As you listen to each academic lecture in Part B of the computer TOEFL test, you should be thinking about the organization of the passage because questions about the organization of the passage quite commonly accompany the academic lectures. The types of questions that test the organization of the passage are *matching* questions and *ordering* questions. Matching questions are used to test your understanding of the organization of a classification passage that discusses the various types or categories of a given topic. Ordering questions are used to test your understanding of the organization of a process or chronological passage that discusses either how something is accomplished or a series of historical events. Look at an example of a part of a lecture with a classification organization, followed by a matching question.

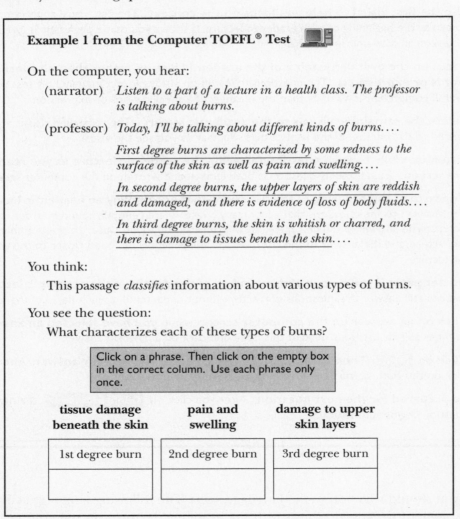

Example 1 from the Computer TOEFL® Test

On the computer, you hear:

(narrator) *Listen to a part of a lecture in a health class. The professor is talking about burns.*

(professor) *Today, I'll be talking about different kinds of burns....*

First degree burns are characterized by some redness to the surface of the skin as well as pain and swelling....

In second degree burns, the upper layers of skin are reddish and damaged, and there is evidence of loss of body fluids....

In third degree burns, the skin is whitish or charred, and there is damage to tissues beneath the skin....

You think:

This passage *classifies* information about various types of burns.

You see the question:

What characterizes each of these types of burns?

Click on a phrase. Then click on the empty box in the correct column. Use each phrase only once.

tissue damage beneath the skin	pain and swelling	damage to upper skin layers
1st degree burn	2nd degree burn	3rd degree burn

In the lecture, the professor states that *first degree burns are characterized by...pain and swelling*, that *in second degree burns, the upper layers of skin are reddish and damaged*, and that *in third degree burns,...there is damage to tissues beneath the skin*. From this, it can be determined that tissue damage beneath the skin occurs in third degree burns, pain and swelling occur in first degree burns, and damage to upper skin layers occurs in second degree burns.

Now look at an example of a part of a lecture with a chronological organization, followed by an ordering question.

Example 2 from the Computer TOEFL® Test

On the computer, you hear:

(narrator)   *Listen to a part of a lecture in a class on the history of aviation. The lecture is on early ballooning.*

(professor)   *Today, I'll be discussing some major events in the early history of ballooning. The first important event took place in June of 1783, when the Montgolfier brothers of France sent up a large, smoke-filled cloth balloon without any passengers....*

Only a few months later in the same year, French scientist Jean François Pilâtre de Rozier became the first person to go up in a balloon....

Two years later, French balloonist Jean-Pierre Blanchard and American doctor John Jeffries made the first balloon flight across the English Channel....

It was not until 1793 that the first balloon ascent in the United States took place when Jean Pierre Blanchard gave a demonstration in front of a large crowd that included President George Washington....

You think:

This passage presents a series of historical events in *chronological order.*

You see the question:

The professor describes a series of events. Put the events in order.

> Click on a phrase. Then click on the space where it belongs. Use each phrase one time only.

The first balloon trip across the English Channel
An unmanned, smoke-filled balloon
The first balloon ascent in the United States
The first manned balloon ascent

1 [   ]

2 [   ]

3 [   ]

4 [   ]

In the lecture, the professor mentions the following: *June of 1783* and *a large, smoke-filled cloth balloon without any passengers; only a few months later in the same year* and *the first person to go up in a balloon; two years later* and *the first balloon flight across the English Channel;* and *1793* and *the first balloon ascent in the United States.* From this, it can be determined that first there was an unmanned, smoke-filled balloon, then there was the first manned balloon ascent, next there was the first balloon trip across the English Channel, and finally there was the first balloon ascent in the United States.

Now look at an example of a part of a lecture with both classification and chronological organization, followed by both a matching question and an ordering question.

Example 3 from the Computer TOEFL® Test

On the computer, you hear:

(narrator)   *Listen to part of a lecture in a geography class. The lecture is on major rivers of the world.*

(professor)   *Today, I'll be talking about the major rivers and river systems of the world. The four longest are <u>the Nile River in Africa, which is 4,145 miles long, the Amazon River in South America, which is 4,007 miles long, the Mississippi River system in North America, which is 3,710 miles long, and the Yangtze River in China, which is 3,436 miles long</u>....*

You think:

This passage *classifies* information about different rivers. It also *orders* the rivers by length.

You see the question:

The professor discusses major rivers of the world. Put these rivers in order, from longest to shortest.

> Click on a name. Then click on the space where it belongs. Use each name one time only.

The Mississippi River
The Yangtze River
The Amazon River
The Nile River

1 [   ]

2 [   ]

3 [   ]

4 [   ]

In the lecture, the professor mentions *the Nile River...*, *which is 4,145 miles long, the Amazon River...*, *which is 4,007 miles long, the Mississippi River system...*, *which is 3,710 miles long, and the Yangtze River...*, *which is 3,436 miles long*. From this, it can be determined that the order of the rivers from longest to shortest is the Nile River, the Amazon River, the Mississippi River, and the Yangtze River.

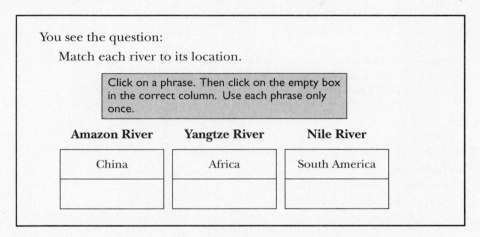

In the lecture, the professor mentions *the Nile River in Africa, the Amazon River in South America*, and *the Yangtze River in China*. From this, it can be determined that the Amazon River is in South America, the Yangtze River is in China, and the Nile River is in Africa.

EXERCISE 32: Listen to each academic lecture, and try to determine how the information in the passage is organized.

1. a. What type of organization is used in the first passage?
   - ⬭ classification
   - ⬭ ordering (process or chronology)
   - ⬭ both classification and ordering

   b. What are the main points in the organization?

   _____

   _____

   _____

2. a. What type of organization is used in the second passage?
    - ◯ classification
    - ◯ ordering (process or chronology)
    - ◯ both classification and ordering

    b. What are the main points in the organization?

    _____

    _____

    _____

3. a. What type of organization is used in the third passage?
    - ◯ classification
    - ◯ ordering (process or chronology)
    - ◯ both classification and ordering

    b. What are the main points in the organization?

    _____

    _____

    _____

TOEFL EXERCISE 32: Listen to each passage, and answer the questions that accompany it.

Questions 1–2

Listen to a lecture in a geography class. The professor is talking about lakes.

1. How are each of these lakes described in the lecture?

> Click on a name. Then click on the empty box in the correct column. Use each name only once.

Lake Superior	**Caspian Sea**	**Lake Baikal**
Largest lake	Deepest lake	Largest freshwater lake

2.   How was each of these lakes formed?

> Click on a name. Then click on the empty box in
> the correct column. Use each name only once.

Lake Superior	Caspian Sea	Lake Baikal
Cut off from the oceans	Carved out by glaciers	Created over a fault in the crust

Questions 3–5

Listen to a lecture in an archeology class. The professor is talking about the formation of fossils.

3.   In the lecture, the professor describes how the process of fossilization gets started. Summarize the process by putting the steps in order.

> Click on a sentence. Then click on the space where
> it belongs. Use each sentence one time only.

Soft tissues decompose.

Hard tissues become buried.

An animal dies.

Hard tissues remain.

1 _____

2 _____

3 _____

4 _____

4. In the lecture, the professor explains what happens to the buried bones. Summarize the
    process by putting the steps in order.

    > Click on a sentence. Then click on the space where
    > it belongs. Use each sentence one time only.

    Minerals eventually replace the bones.

    Layers of sediment cover the bones.

    Minerals from the ground water enter the bones.

    The bones sink to the level of the ground water.

    1 [   ]

    2 [   ]

    3 [   ]

    4 [   ]

5. In the lecture, the professor explains what happens after the hard tissue has fossilized
    underground. Summarize the process by putting the steps in order.

    > Click on a sentence. Then click on the space where
    > it belongs. Use each sentence one time only.

    The remains may be pushed close to the surface.

    The fossilized remains are buried.

    Humans may discover the remains.

    The earth moves the buried remains.

    1 [   ]

    2 [   ]

    3 [   ]

    4 [   ]

Questions 6–8

Listen to a lecture in a nutrition class. The professor is talking about olive oil.

6.   In the lecture, the professor describes the cold-press process. Summarize the process by putting the steps in order.

> Click on a sentence. Then click on the space where it belongs. Use each sentence one time only.

Virgin olive oil results.

The crushed olives are repressed.

The olives are pressed for the first time.

Cold-pressed olive oil results.

1	
2	
3	
4	

7.   What are the different grades of olive oil?

> Click on a phrase. Then click on the empty box in the correct column. Use each phrase only once.

light olive oil	virgin olive oil	pure olive oil
Olive oil of the highest quality	Olive oil affected by heating	Olive oil mixed with other oils

8.   What are the different types of oil produced by the cold-press process?

> Click on a phrase. Then click on the empty box in the correct column. Use each phrase only once.

cold-pressed olive oil	virgin olive oil	extra virgin olive oil
From the first pressing, with lower acid	From the first pressing, with higher acid	From a later pressing

Skill 33:   LISTEN FOR DIRECT AND INDIRECT DETAILS

As you listen to each academic discussion in Part B of the computer TOEFL test, you should focus on the details from the passage and indirect information that can be inferred from these details because questions about direct and indirect details quite commonly accompany the academic lectures. Multiple-choice questions are used to test direct and indirect details, and these multiple-choice questions may have one correct answer or two correct answers. Look at an example of a part of an academic lecture, followed by a multiple-choice question about a direct detail. This question has one correct answer.

Example from the Computer TOEFL® Test

On the computer, you hear:

(narrator)   *Listen to a part of a lecture in an astronomy class. The lecture is on Halley's comet.*

(professor)   *Halley's comet, which <u>passes by our planet every 76 years</u>, last came by our planet in 1986....*

This comet was named after <u>astronomer Edmund Halley</u>, who correctly <u>predicted its return in 1758, sixteen years after his death</u>....

You think:

This passage gives *direct and indirect details* about Edmund Halley and Halley's comet.

You see the question and the answers:

What is stated in the lecture about Halley's comet?

- ◯ It last came by in 1976.
- ◯ It comes by once every 76 years.
- ◯ It did not appear between 1758 and 1986.
- ◯ It gave its name to an astronomer.

In the lecture, the professor states that *Halley's comet...passes by our planet every 76 years.* This means that *it comes by once every 76 years.* The second answer is therefore the best answer to this question.

Now look at another example of a multiple-choice question about a direct detail. This question has two correct answers.

You see the question:

What does the lecturer say about Edmund Halley?

Click on 2 answers.

- ☐ He lived to the age of 76.
- ☐ He was an astronomer.
- ☐ He made an accurate prediction.
- ☐ He viewed the comet in 1758.

In the lecture, the professor mentions *astronomer Edmund Halley, who correctly predicted its return.* This means that Edmund Halley *was an astronomer* and *made an accurate prediction.* The second and third answers are therefore the best answers to this question.

Now look at an example of a multiple-choice question about an indirect detail. This question has one correct answer.

You see the question:

In what year did Edmund Halley most likely die?

- ◯ In 1742
- ◯ In 1758
- ◯ In 1774
- ◯ In 1986

In the lecture, the professor mentions *1758, sixteen years after his death.* From this, it can be determined that Edmund Halley most likely died sixteen years prior to 1758, in 1742. The first answer is therefore the best answer to this question.

EXERCISE 33: Listen to each academic lecture, and try to focus on the direct and indirect details in the passage.

1. What are some of the **direct details** in the first passage?

   a.   About conifers: _____

   b.   About the percent of trees that are conifers: _____

   c.   About the oldest tree: _____

   d.   About the biggest trees: _____

   e.   About the evolution of conifers: _____

   f.   About how evergreens differ from deciduous trees: _____

   What are some of the **indirect details** that can be inferred from the passage?

   g.   About where conifers are found: _____

   h.   About the giant redwoods: _____

2. What are some of the **direct details** in the second passage?

   a. About who is listening to the lecture: _____

   b. About the period of time discussed in the lecture:_____

   c. About the rules related to clothing: _____

   d. About the rules related to places to go: _____

   What are some of the **indirect details** that can be inferred from the passage?

   e. About the lifestyle of the teachers in the lecture: _____

   f. About where the teachers would spend evenings: _____

3. What are some of the **direct details** in the third passage?

   a. About how Venus compares to the Moon: _____

   b. About the highest temperatures on Venus: _____

   c. About the causes of the heat on Venus: _____

   d. About the components of Venus's atmosphere: _____

   e. About the components of Venus's clouds: _____

   f. About the causes of the brightness of Venus: _____

   What are some of the **indirect details** that can be inferred from the passage?

   g. About the size of Venus in relation to other planets: _____

   h. About the brightness of Venus in its full phase: _____

   i. About the clouds that surround Venus: _____

TOEFL EXERCISE 33: Listen to each passage, and answer the questions that accompany it.

Questions 1–8

Listen to a lecture in a botany class. The professor is talking about conifers.

1. What is true about all conifers?
    ◯ They have colorful flowers.
    ◯ Their leaves are wide.
    ◯ Their wood is red.
    ◯ They bear cones.

2. What percent of the world's trees are conifers?
    ◯ 20
    ◯ 33
    ◯ 50
    ◯ 67

3. It is implied in the lecture that most conifers are found in which hemisphere?
    ◯ The northern hemisphere
    ◯ The southern hemisphere
    ◯ The eastern hemisphere
    ◯ The western hemisphere

4. What is true about the biggest and oldest trees?

> Click on 2 answers.

☐ They are both found in the same state.
☐ They are both hundreds of feet high.
☐ They are both types of conifers.
☐ They are both over 4,000 years old.

5. Which of the following is most likely a giant redwood?

◯ A tree that weighs 2,000 pounds
◯ A tree that is 250 feet tall
◯ A tree with wide, flat leaves
◯ A tree with huge cones

6. What can be inferred from the lecture?

> Click on 2 answers.

☐ All conifers are evergreens.
☐ Some conifers are not evergreens.
☐ All conifers have needles.
☐ Some conifers do not have needles.

7. Why did needle-shaped leaves evolve?

◯ Because of a shortage of water
◯ Because of an overabundance of water
◯ Because of a shortage of sunlight
◯ Because of an overabundance of sunlight

8. What can be determined from the lecture about different types of trees?

> Click on 2 answers.

☐ Evergreen trees lose and replace their leaves at specific times in the year.
☐ Evergreen trees lose and replace their leaves throughout the year.
☐ Deciduous trees lose and replace their leaves at specific times in the year.
☐ Deciduous trees lose and replace their leaves throughout the year.

Questions 9–14

Listen to a lecture in an education class. The professor is talking about early teachers.

9. Who is listening to this lecture?

◯ Experienced teachers
◯ Students of American history
◯ School administrators
◯ Future teachers

10. The rules discussed in this lecture relate to what period of time?

◯ Late in the 18th century
◯ Early in the 19th century
◯ Early in the 20th century
◯ Late in the 20th century

11. It is implied in the lecture that the teachers discussed in the lecture had what kind of lifestyle?

◯ Very liberated
◯ Extremely controlled
◯ Rather varied
◯ Quite adventurous

12. What rules about clothing are discussed in the lecture?

> Click on 2 answers.

☐ The style of the trousers
☐ The color of the cloth
☐ The length of the skirts
☐ The type of material

13. Where would a teacher from the era discussed in the lecture most likely be at 9:00 in the evening?

◯ At home
◯ In the library
◯ At school
◯ On a date

14. Where were the teachers in the lecture forbidden to go?

   Click on 2 answers.

   ☐ To stores
   ☐ To bars
   ☐ To friends' houses
   ☐ To ice cream shops

Questions 15–22

Listen to a lecture in an astronomy class. The professor is talking about Venus.

15. It can be inferred from the lecture that Venus is how large in relation to the other planets in our solar system?

   ◯ It is the second largest planet.
   ◯ It is the fourth largest planet.
   ◯ It is the fifth largest planet.
   ◯ It is the sixth largest planet.

16. How does Venus compare with the Moon?

   ◯ From Earth, they appear similar in size.
   ◯ They have similar temperatures.
   ◯ From Earth, they both appear to have phases.
   ◯ They both have similar cloud cover.

17. What can be inferred about Venus when it is in a full phase?

   ◯ It is not visible from Earth.
   ◯ It is not at its brightest.
   ◯ It reaches its hottest temperatures.
   ◯ It is hidden behind the Moon.

18. What are the highest temperatures on Venus?

   Click on 2 answers.

   ☐ 500 degrees Centigrade
   ☐ 500 degrees Fahrenheit
   ☐ 900 degrees Centigrade
   ☐ 900 degrees Fahrenheit

19. Why is it hot on Venus?

   Click on 2 answers.

   ☐ Because of its brightness
   ☐ Because of its nearness to the Sun
   ☐ Because of its shape
   ☐ Because of its atmosphere

20. What is implied in the lecture about the clouds that surround Venus?

   ◯ They are very thick.
   ◯ They are invisible from Earth.
   ◯ They are similar to the clouds surrounding Earth.
   ◯ They have been discovered only recently.

21. Which of the following are true, according to the lecture?

   Click on 2 answers.

   ☐ Venus's atmosphere is made of carbon dioxide.
   ☐ Venus's atmosphere is made of sulfuric acid.
   ☐ Venus's clouds are made of carbon dioxide.
   ☐ Venus's clouds are made of sulfuric acid.

22. Why is Venus so bright?

   ◯ Because its inner core is so hot.
   ◯ Because its atmosphere is so thin.
   ◯ Because its clouds magnify the planet's inner light.
   ◯ Because its clouds reflect a lot of sunlight.

SKILL 34:   VISUALIZE THE PASSAGE

As you listen to each academic lecture in Part B of the computer TOEFL test, you should try to visualize what you hear in the passage because visual questions about what is being described in the passage quite commonly accompany the academic lectures. There are two types of visual questions that may accompany an academic lecture. One type of visual question shows you four drawings and asks you to click on the one drawing of the four that answers a question. The other type of visual question shows you one drawing with four letters on it and asks you to click on the one letter of the four that answers a question. Look at an example of a part of a lecture and a visual question with four drawings.

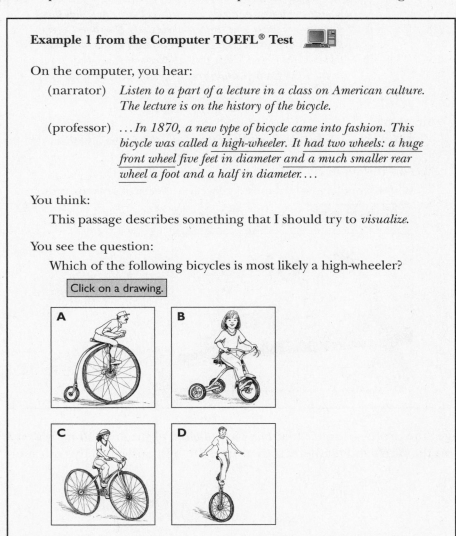

In the lecture, the professor states that a *high-wheeler... had two wheels: a huge front wheel... and a much smaller rear wheel.* Answer A, a bicycle with a large front wheel and a smaller rear wheel, is therefore the best answer to this question.

Now look at an example of a part of a lecture and a visual question with one drawing and four letters.

Example 2 from the Computer TOEFL® Test

On the computer, you hear:

(narrator)   *Listen to a part of a lecture in a zoology class. The lecture is on a kind of bird known as a lovebird.*

(professor) *...The next bird I'll be talking about is a type of parrot that is commonly called a lovebird. As you can probably guess, this bird is called a lovebird because it lives in pairs and demonstrates great affection for its partner....*

Something unusual about lovebirds is the method that they use to carry grass and straw to their nest. They don't carry the grass and straw in their beaks, in their claws, or under their wings. Instead, they pick up pieces of grass and straw in their tail feathers and carry the material to their nest in this way....

You think:

This passage describes something that I should try to *visualize*.

You see the question:

Where would a lovebird most likely carry pieces of grass or straw?

    Click on a letter.

In the lecture, the professor states that *they pick up pieces of grass and straw in their tail feathers*. Answer D, on the bird's tail feathers, is therefore the best answer to this question.

EXERCISE 34: Listen to each academic lecture, and try to visual the information in the passage.

1.   How do you visualize the Iroquois village?

  a. An Iroquois house   b. Where the clan is identified   c. The stockade that surrounds the village

2.   How do you visualize a plant affected by tropism?

  a. A plant affected by phototropism   b. A plant affected by geotropism   c. A plant affected by hydrotropism

3.   How do you visualize the sinkhole and its contents?

  a. The sinkhole today   b. The weapon found in the sinkhole   c. Where the weapon was found in the sinkhole

d. Where the water level
    was 12,000 years ago

e. Where the trap was found

TOEFL EXERCISE 34: Listen to each passage, and answer the questions that accompany it.

Questions 1–3

Listen to a lecture in a course on Native American studies. The lecture is on Iroquois houses.

1. How does the professor describe an Iroquois house?

    Click on a drawing.

2. What part of the house indicates what clan the inhabitants belong to?

    Click on a letter.

    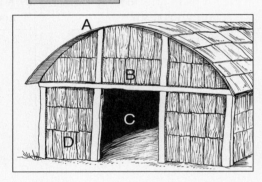

3. How does the professor describe the stockade surrounding an Iroquois village?

    Click on a drawing.

    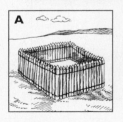
    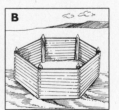
    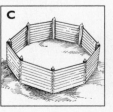
    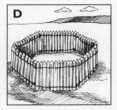

Questions 4–6

Listen to a lecture in a biology class. The lecture is on tropism in plants.

4. Which of these plants is exhibiting phototropism?

Click on a drawing.

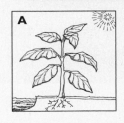

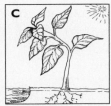
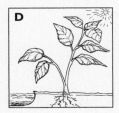

5. Which of these root systems is exhibiting geotropism?

Click on a drawing.

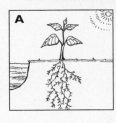
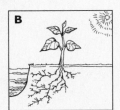
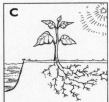
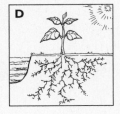

6. What is the stimulus for hydrotropism?

Click on a letter.

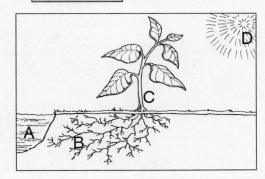

Questions 7–10

Listen to a lecture in an archeology class. The lecture is on some archeological finds at Little Salt Spring.

7. What type of weapon was found at the sinkhole?

Click on a drawing.

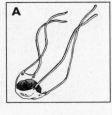
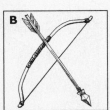

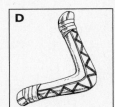

8. Where was the weapon found?

Click on a letter.

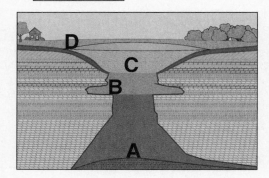

10. Where was the trap found?

Click on a letter.

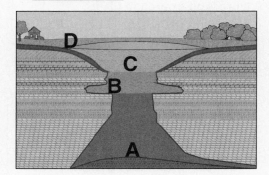

9. Where was the water level 12,000 years ago?

Click on a drawing.

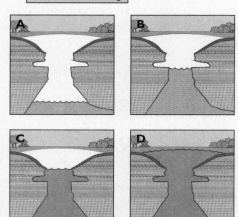

TOEFL REVIEW EXERCISE (Skills 32–34)

Questions 1–5

Listen to a lecture in an American history class. The lecture is on the St. Louis Arch.

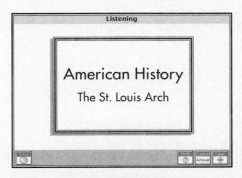

1. What does the professor say about the arch?

   Click on 2 answers.

   ☐ It is over 600 feet high.
   ☐ It is made of stainless steel.
   ☐ Its legs alone do not support it.
   ☐ It has solid legs.

2. Where is each of these features of the arch located?

   Click on a word. Then click on the empty box in the correct column. Use each word only once.

trams	museum	observatory
At the top	In the legs	Under the ground

3. Why is the arch named after Jefferson?

   ◯ He was responsible for building the arch.
   ◯ He lived in St. Louis.
   ◯ He was responsible for expanding the country.
   ◯ He traveled with Lewis and Clark.

4. It is implied in the lecture that it is approximately what distance between St. Louis and the Pacific Northwest?

   ◯ 1,000 miles
   ◯ 2,000 miles
   ◯ 4,000 miles
   ◯ 8,000 miles

5. The professor explains a historical series of events. Put the events in order.

   Click on a sentence. Then click on the space where it belongs. Use each sentence one time only.

   Thousands of settlers set out from St. Louis.
   The arch was built.
   Jefferson became president.
   Lewis and Clark set out to explore the west.

1	
2	
3	
4	

Questions 6–10

Listen to a lecture in a geology class. The lecture is on the structure of the earth.

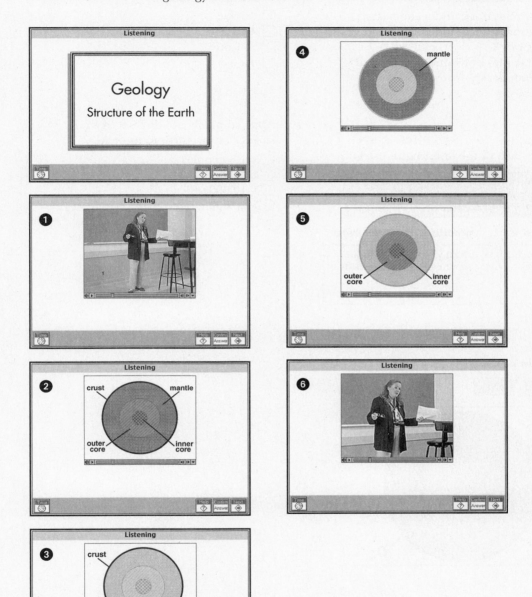

6. How thick is the crust?

    Click on 2 answers.

    ☐ It is 4 miles thick under the oceans.
    ☐ It is 4 miles thick under the land
       masses.
    ☐ It is 20 miles thick under the oceans.
    ☐ It is 20 miles thick under the land
       masses.

9. What minerals are in the core?

    Click on 2 answers.

    ☐ Nickel
    ☐ Quartz
    ☐ Silicates
    ☐ Iron

7. What are each of the layers composed of?

    Click on a word or phrase. Then click on
    the empty box in the correct column.
    Use each word or phrase only once.

outer core	mantle	inner core
Compressed minerals	Stony silicates	Liquid minerals

10. Approximately how far is it from the
    surface of the earth to its center?

    ◯ 1,800 miles
    ◯ 4,000 miles
    ◯ 10,000 miles
    ◯ 20,000 miles

8. Which layer is 1,800 miles wide?

    Click on a letter.

    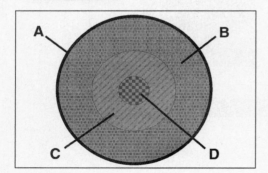

Questions 11–16

Listen to a lecture in a linguistics class. The professor is talking about the history of the letter *c*.

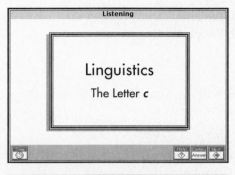

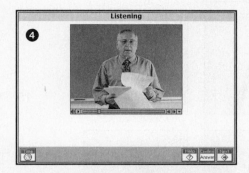

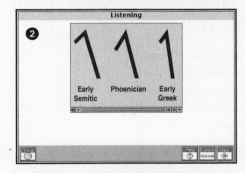

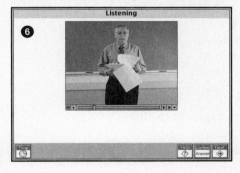

11. Which of the following letters was NOT a predecessor of the letter *c*?

   Click on a picture.

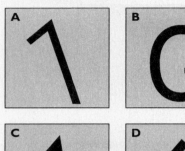

12. How was the third letter of the alphabet pronounced in Phoenician and early Greek?

   ◯ Like a *k*
   ◯ Like a *g*
   ◯ Like an *s*
   ◯ Like a *c*

13. In which language was the letter *g* created?

   ◯ Phoenician
   ◯ Early Greek
   ◯ Early Latin
   ◯ Classical Latin

14. The letter *c* took on an *s* sound because of an influence from which language?

   ◯ Saxon
   ◯ Greek
   ◯ French
   ◯ Phoenician

15. Which of the following English words begin with an *s* sound?

   Click on 2 answers.

   ☐ Coxswain
   ☐ Cytoplasm
   ☐ Curmudgeon
   ☐ Cephalization

16. The professor discusses stages in the history of the third letter of the alphabet. Put the following historical stages in order.

   Click on a sentence. Then click on the space where it belongs. Use each sentence one time only.

   It had only a *k* sound.
   It had only a *g* sound.
   It had both a *k* and an *s* sound.
   It had both a *k* and a *g* sound.

1	
2	
3	
4	

LISTENING POST-TEST (Paper) 📖

SECTION 1
LISTENING COMPREHENSION
Time—approximately 35 minutes
(including the reading of the directions for each part)

In this section of the test, you will have an opportunity to demonstrate your ability to understand conversations and talks in English. There are three parts to this section. Answer all the questions on the basis of what is <u>stated</u> or <u>implied</u> by the speakers you hear. Do <u>not</u> take notes or write in your test book at any time. Do not turn the pages until you are told to do so.

Part A

<u>Directions:</u> In Part A you will hear short conversations between two people. After each conversation, you will hear a question about the conversation. The conversations and questions will not be repeated. After you hear a question, read the four possible answers in your test book and choose the best answer. Then, on your answer sheet, find the number of the question and fill in the space that corresponds to the letter of the answer you have chosen.

Listen to an example.

On the recording, you hear:

(man)	*That exam was just awful.*
(woman)	*Oh, it could have been worse.*
(narrator)	*What does the woman mean?*

Sample Answer
Ⓐ
Ⓑ
Ⓒ
●

In your test book, you read: (A) The exam was really awful.
                                 (B) It was the worst exam she had ever seen.
                                 (C) It couldn't have been more difficult.
                                 (D) It wasn't that hard.

You learn from the conversation that the man thought the exam was very difficult and that the woman disagreed with the man. The best answer to the question, "What does the woman mean?" is (D), "It wasn't that hard." Therefore, the correct choice is (D).

Wait

1. (A) He'll correct the exams this afternoon.
   (B) The exam will be at noon.
   (C) He will collect the exams at 12:00.
   (D) The tests will be graded by noon.

2. (A) Martha applied for a visa last month.
   (B) Martha's visa will last for only a month.
   (C) Martha arrived last month without her visa.
   (D) One month ago Martha got her visa.

3. (A) The professor described what the students should do.
   (B) There was a long line to register for the required class.
   (C) It is a requirement for each professor to teach at least one course.
   (D) The professor required the class to prepare an outline.

4. (A) Chuck had improved.
   (B) This visit was better than the last.
   (C) Chuck looked at him in the hospital.
   (D) Chuck didn't seem to be doing very well.

5. (A) She thinks the tuition should be raised.
   (B) The semester's tuition is quite affordable.
   (C) She doesn't have enough money for her school fees.
   (D) She has more than enough for tuition.

6. (A) He thinks he got a good grade.
   (B) The history grades were all C or above.
   (C) No one got history grades.
   (D) There were no high scores.

7. (A) The parking lots were full before 10:00.
   (B) It was impossible to start class by 10:00.
   (C) He parked the car before class at 10:00.
   (D) The possibility of finding a place to park increased.

8. (A) She's found a new ring.
   (B) She needs to help him find something.
   (C) She's shopping for a carpet.
   (D) She's thankful she has a rag.

9. (A) In a department store
   (B) In a bank
   (C) In an accounting firm
   (D) In a checkout line

10. (A) Jane usually visits San Francisco for her vacations.
    (B) Jane's cousin often visits San Francisco.
    (C) Whenever there's a holiday, Jane's cousin goes to San Francisco.
    (D) Whenever there's a holiday, Jane leaves San Francisco.

11. (A) He'd really like to have something to eat.
    (B) Because he's weak, he can't eat.
    (C) It's been weeks since he's had anything to eat.
    (D) He hasn't felt like eating for weeks.

12. (A) Traffic should not be allowed.
    (B) She thinks that the traffic should stay outside.
    (C) She agrees that the traffic is noisy.
    (D) She'll stay outside with the man.

13. (A) The headings for today's reading assignment.
    (B) The chance to make the headlines.
    (C) Her reading ability.
    (D) The daily newspaper.

14. (A) The bus trip is only five minutes long.
    (B) The man missed the bus by five minutes.
    (C) The man should hurry to catch the bus.
    (D) The bus was five minutes late.

15. (A) It's not possible to pass the class.
    (B) She'll definitely fail.
    (C) It's always possible.
    (D) She shouldn't say anything about the class.

GO ON TO THE NEXT PAGE

16. (A) She gave Tom money to pay the rent.
    (B) She was given money for the rent.
    (C) Tom borrowed money for the rent.
    (D) She had some money to lend.

17. (A) The cake is extremely good.
    (B) He never tasted the cake.
    (C) He wished he hadn't tasted the cake.
    (D) The cake has never been very good.

18. (A) At the corner she ran into another car.
    (B) She ran to Carl because she cared.
    (C) She unexpectedly met one of her relatives.
    (D) Carl was running from place to place.

19. (A) She shouldn't leave her purse here.
    (B) She's probably in the apartment.
    (C) Her purse must not be in the apartment.
    (D) She left without taking her purse.

20. (A) The landlord failed to collect rent on the first of last month.
    (B) The tenants absolutely must pay rent at the beginning of the month.
    (C) The landlord will not fail to collect your rent on the first of next month.
    (D) It is important to call the landlord about rent on the first of the month.

21. (A) Taking the car out for a test drive
    (B) Listening to the noises
    (C) Fixing the car herself
    (D) Getting the car repaired

22. (A) Martha's jobs are easy.
    (B) It's easy to hold two jobs.
    (C) It's better for Martha to have two jobs.
    (D) Martha should slow down.

23. (A) The plane took off just after he arrived.
    (B) He arrived just after the plane took off.
    (C) He wasn't in time to catch the plane.
    (D) He arrived too late to catch the plane.

24. (A) He agrees with the woman's suggestion.
    (B) Parking is not free on the weekend.
    (C) It is not necessary for them to park.
    (D) He thinks they don't have to pay.

25. (A) He is eager to leave his job.
    (B) He is unhappy at the thought of retiring.
    (C) He couldn't be unhappier about retiring.
    (D) He is retiring too soon.

26. (A) He got the car he really wanted.
    (B) He didn't get a new car.
    (C) The car that he got was not his first choice.
    (D) He didn't really want a new car.

27. (A) Mr. Drew pointedly asked the president about the committee.
    (B) The president pointed to Mr. Drew's head.
    (C) Mr. Drew became head of the new commission.
    (D) Mr. Drew was committed to the president's appointments.

28. (A) She felt inferior.
    (B) She wasn't furious.
    (C) She felt there should have been more fairness.
    (D) She was extremely angry.

29. (A) The man would do the dishes.
    (B) The plates did not need to be washed.
    (C) The man would not be ready to go.
    (D) The dishes would not be done.

30. (A) He knew that grapes were cheaper than cherries.
    (B) He didn't know that grapes were cheaper than cherries.
    (C) He bought grapes because they were cheaper than cherries.
    (D) He didn't buy either grapes or cherries because of the price.

GO ON TO THE NEXT PAGE ➤

Part B

Directions: In this part of the test, you will hear longer conversations. After each conversation, you will hear several questions. The conversations and questions will not be repeated.

After you hear a question, read the four possible answers in your test book and choose the best answer. Then, on your answer sheet, find the number of the question and fill in the space that corresponds to the letter of the answer you have chosen.

Remember, you are <u>not</u> allowed to take notes or write in your test book.

31. (A) Attend a football game alone
    (B) Go to a sporting event
    (C) Eat in the cafeteria and study
    (D) See a play

32. (A) It's the final game of the season.
    (B) It's better than the drama department's play.
    (C) It's a very important game.
    (D) It's close to the cafeteria.

33. (A) A play
    (B) A game
    (C) A study group meeting
    (D) Dinner in the cafeteria

34. (A) Saturday night
    (B) After dinner in the cafeteria
    (C) Sunday afternoon
    (D) Maybe next weekend

35. (A) Trash orbiting Earth
    (B) A trip by an astronaut to the Moon
    (C) The overabundance of garbage on Earth
    (D) Becoming space scientists

36. (A) From a lecture
    (B) In a magazine article
    (C) In a book
    (D) On a television program

37. (A) 17,000 pounds
    (B) 3,000 tons
    (C) 3,000 pounds
    (D) 300 tons

38. (A) She will be able to travel in space.
    (B) The problem will take care of itself.
    (C) Scientists will find solutions to the problem.
    (D) The junk will fall to Earth.

GO ON TO THE NEXT PAGE

Part C

Directions: In this part of the test, you will hear several talks. After each talk, you will hear some questions. The talks and questions will not be repeated.

After you hear a question, read the four possible answers in your test book and choose the best answer. Then, on your answer sheet, find the number of the question and fill in the space that corresponds to the letter of the answer you have chosen.

Here is an example.

On the recording, you hear:

(narrator) *Listen to an instructor talk to his class about painting.*
(man)   *Artist Grant Wood was a guiding force in the school of painting known as American regionalist, a style reflecting the distinctive characteristics of art from rural areas of the United States. Wood began drawing animals on the family farm at the age of three, and when he was thirty-eight one of his paintings received a remarkable amount of public notice and acclaim. This painting, called "American Gothic," is a starkly simple depiction of a serious couple staring directly out at the viewer.*

Now listen to a sample question.

Sample Answer

(narrator) *What style of painting is known as American regionalist?*

Ⓐ
Ⓑ
Ⓒ
●

In your test book, you read: (A) Art from America's inner cities
(B) Art from the central region of the United States
(C) Art from various urban areas in the United States
(D) Art from rural sections of America

The best answer to the question "What style of painting is known as American regionalist?" is (D), "Art from rural sections of America." Therefore, the correct choice is (D).

Now listen to another sample question.

Sample Answer

(narrator) *What is the name of Wood's most successful painting?*

Ⓐ
Ⓑ
●
Ⓓ

In your test book, you read: (A) "American Regionalist"
(B) "The Family Farm in Iowa"
(C) "American Gothic"
(D) "A Serious Couple"

The best answer to the question, "What is the name of Wood's most successful painting?" is (C), "American Gothic." Therefore, the correct choice is (C).

Remember, you are <u>not</u> allowed to take notes or write in your test book.

Wait

39. (A) On the first day of class
    (B) In the middle of the semester
    (C) At the end of class
    (D) In the final week of the semester

40. (A) Later today
    (B) By Friday of this week
    (C) In two weeks
    (D) In three weeks

41. (A) Journal and magazine articles
    (B) Books from outside the library
    (C) Books listed in student journals
    (D) Both books and journals

42. (A) Two
    (B) Three
    (C) Five
    (D) Seven

43. (A) In winter
    (B) In spring
    (C) In summer
    (D) In fall

44. (A) Seasonable, with warm summers and
        cold winters
    (B) Fairly constant and moderate
    (C) Very humid
    (D) Extremely hot year-round

45. (A) They come from the Southwest.
    (B) They come most days of the year.
    (C) They are the hardest during the night.
    (D) They increase the humidity.

46. (A) Preparing for a trip
    (B) Writing a report about the weather
    (C) Beginning a study of the weather
    (D) Buying warm clothes for a trip

47. (A) Modern American Authors
    (B) United States History
    (C) American Democracy
    (D) Nineteenth-Century American
        Literature

48. (A) The death of Abraham Lincoln
    (B) The beauty of American democracy
    (C) The raising of plants
    (D) The maturity of poetry

49. (A) It's a poem about the author.
    (B) It's a poem about Abraham Lincoln.
    (C) It's a collection of twelve poems that
        remained unchanged.
    (D) It's a volume of poetry that grew with
        its author.

50. (A) "Leaves of Grass"
    (B) "Song of Myself"
    (C) "When Lilacs Last in the Dooryard
        Bloomed"
    (D) "American Democracy"

This is the end of Section 1.
Stop work on Section 1.

Turn off the recording.

LISTENING POST-TEST (Computer)

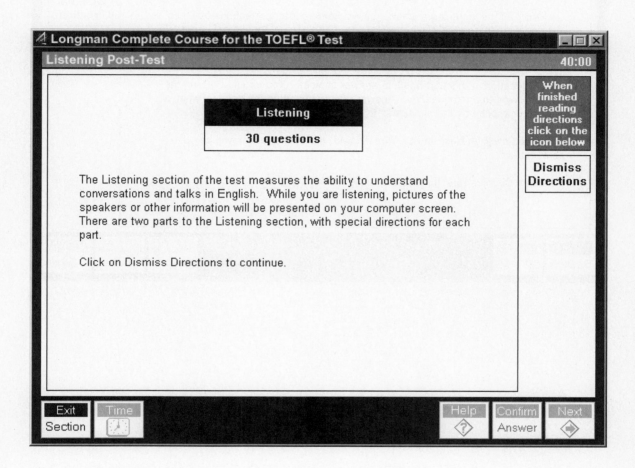

Longman Complete Course for the TOEFL® Test

Listening Post-Test   40:00

Listening
30 questions

The Listening section of the test measures the ability to understand conversations and talks in English. While you are listening, pictures of the speakers or other information will be presented on your computer screen. There are two parts to the Listening section, with special directions for each part.

Click on Dismiss Directions to continue.

When finished reading directions click on the icon below

Dismiss Directions

Exit Section

Time

Help

Confirm Answer

Next

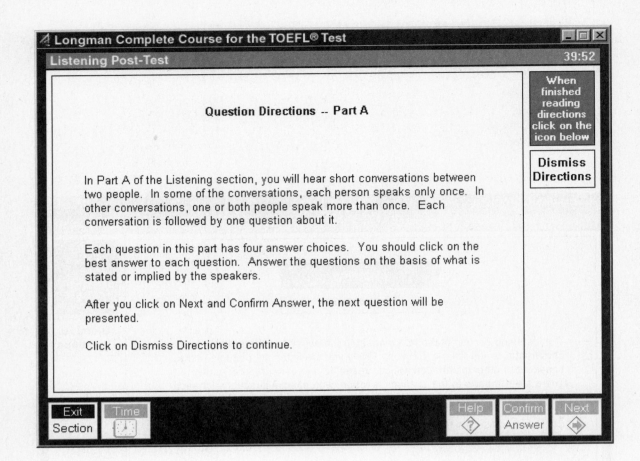

Longman Complete Course for the TOEFL® Test

When finished reading directions click on the icon below

Dismiss Directions

Question Directions -- Part A

In Part A of the Listening section, you will hear short conversations between two people. In some of the conversations, each person speaks only once. In other conversations, one or both people speak more than once. Each conversation is followed by one question about it.

Each question in this part has four answer choices. You should click on the best answer to each question. Answer the questions on the basis of what is stated or implied by the speakers.

After you click on Next and Confirm Answer, the next question will be presented.

Click on Dismiss Directions to continue.

Exit Section

Time

Help

Confirm Answer

Next

1. What does the man mean?

   ○ He needs to complete the math assignment first.
   ○ He'll be ready in a couple of hours.
   ○ He is going to history class now.
   ○ He was ready a few minutes ago.

2. What does the woman mean?

   ○ It's hard to lock the room.
   ○ Her cloak was delivered on time.
   ○ Someone struck the crockery and broke it.
   ○ It is now midday.

3. What does the man mean?

   ○ They were in the regular room.
   ○ The key was misplaced.
   ○ He's taking a different class.
   ○ He has the key to the classroom.

4. What does the woman mean?

   ○ She has no time to go to class.
   ○ They are already late for class.
   ○ She has to be on time for class.
   ○ It's too early to go to class.

5. What does the man mean?

   ○ The professor gives quizzes regularly.
   ○ The woman is really quite prepared.
   ○ It is unusual for this professor to give quizzes.
   ○ He doesn't think there's a class today.

6. What does the woman mean?
   ○ She knows where to take the next check.
   ○ She's not certain how much rent is.
   ○ She's not quite sure when to pay the rent.
   ○ She knows how far away the apartment is.

7. What does the man say about his nieces and nephews?
   ○ They were disappointed.
   ○ They didn't get any gifts.
   ○ They were unexcited.
   ○ They were really pleased.

8. What does the woman mean?
   ○ She's wearing a new dress.
   ○ She's exhausted.
   ○ She's ready to study for hours.
   ○ She has studied about the war for hours.

9. What does the man say about the party?
   ○ He went to it.
   ○ He knew about it.
   ○ He gave it.
   ○ He didn't know about it.

10. What did the man believe about the woman?
   ○ That she wouldn't take the trip
   ○ That she would go to the beach
   ○ That she really liked the beach
   ○ That she would take a break from her studies

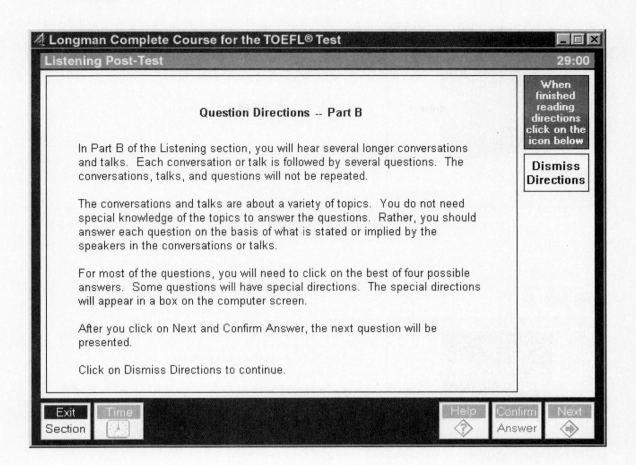

When finished reading directions click on the icon below

Dismiss Directions

Question Directions -- Part B

In Part B of the Listening section, you will hear several longer conversations and talks. Each conversation or talk is followed by several questions. The conversations, talks, and questions will not be repeated.

The conversations and talks are about a variety of topics. You do not need special knowledge of the topics to answer the questions. Rather, you should answer each question on the basis of what is stated or implied by the speakers in the conversations or talks.

For most of the questions, you will need to click on the best of four possible answers. Some questions will have special directions. The special directions will appear in a box on the computer screen.

After you click on Next and Confirm Answer, the next question will be presented.

Click on Dismiss Directions to continue.

Exit Section

Time

Help

Confirm Answer

Next

Questions 11–12

11. What problem does the man have?
    ○ He was absent from class.
    ○ He missed his doctor's appointment.
    ○ He has messy handwriting.
    ○ He will miss class later in the week.

12. What problem does the woman have?
    ○ Her notes are not very neat.
    ○ She doesn't have any notes.
    ○ She is sick.
    ○ She will be absent from class.

Questions 13–15

13. How often does the chess club meet?
    ○ Every week
    ○ Every three weeks
    ○ Every few months
    ○ Two times a year

14. How often are tournaments held?
    ○ Every week
    ○ Every three weeks
    ○ Every few months
    ○ Two times a year

15. Who competes in the tournaments?
    ○ All the members of the school's chess club
    ○ Players from various schools
    ○ Anyone who wants to participate
    ○ The best member of the school's chess club

Questions 16–20

Listen to a lecture in a botany class. The professor is talking about leaf arrangements.

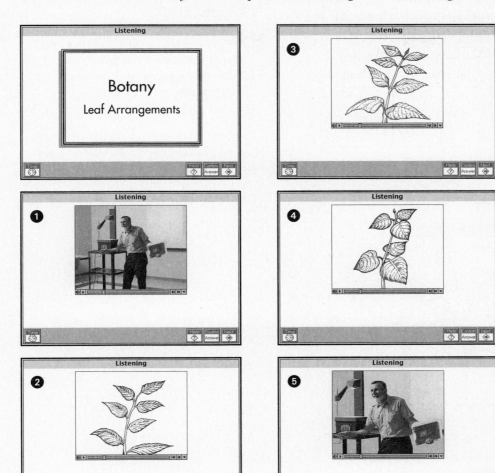

16. The professor discusses four types of leaf arrangements. Match the type of leaf arrangement to its description.

Click on a word. Then click on the empty box in the correct column. Use each word only once.

opposite	alternate	whorled
One leaf per node	Two leaves per node	Three leaves per node

17. Identify the node.

Click on the correct letter.

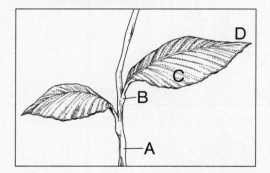

18. The professor describes how common these leaf arrangements are. Match the leaf arrangement to its description.

Click on a word. Then click on the empty box in the correct column. Use each word only once.

opposite	alternate	whorled
Least common	Neither most nor least common	Most common

19. What does the professor say about the botanical garden?

Click on 2 answers.

☐ It belongs to the university.
☐ It has quite a limited number of plants.
☐ The plants are not labeled.
☐ It has examples of all three leaf structures.

20. How many examples do the students have to find for their assignment?

◯ 3
◯ 6
◯ 9
◯ 12

Questions 21–25

Listen to a discussion from a geography class. The discussion is about the Great Salt Lake.

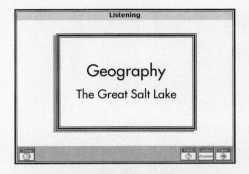

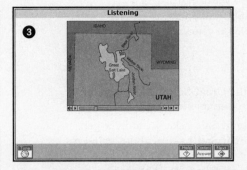

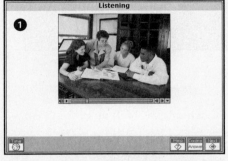

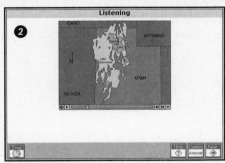

21. When did Lake Bonneville come into existence?

   ⬭ 10,000 years ago
   ⬭ 100,000 years ago
   ⬭ 1,000,000 years ago
   ⬭ 10,000,000 years ago

22. How does the Great Salt Lake compare in size to Lake Bonneville?

   ⬭ The Great Salt Lake is much larger.
   ⬭ The Great Salt Lake is about equal in size.
   ⬭ The Great Salt Lake is slightly smaller.
   ⬭ The Great Salt Lake is much smaller.

23. What is stated in the lecture about the water in the two lakes?

   Click on 2 answers.

   ☐ The Great Salt Lake is a saltwater lake.
   ☐ The Great Salt Lake is a freshwater lake.
   ☐ Lake Bonneville was a saltwater lake.
   ☐ Lake Bonneville was a freshwater lake.

24. In which direction does the water in the rivers flow?

   Click on the correct answer.

25. How much salt has built up in the Great Salt Lake?

   ⬭ 6 tons
   ⬭ 600 tons
   ⬭ 6 million tons
   ⬭ 6 billion tons

Questions 26–30

Listen to a lecture in an American history class. The professor is talking about Hawaii.

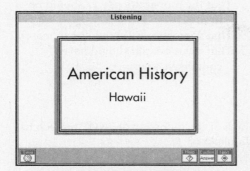

26. When did each person live?

> Click on a name. Then click on the empty box in the correct column. Use each name only once.

Kamehameha   **James Cook**   **Liliuokalani**

End of the 18th century	Beginning of the 19th century	End of the 19th century

27. What does the professor say about James Cook?

- ◯ He was the Earl of Sandwich.
- ◯ He fought to unite the islands under one king.
- ◯ He served as one of the kings of Hawaii.
- ◯ He named the islands after a British earl.

28. The professor explains a series of events. Put the events in order.

> Click on a sentence. Then click on the space where it belongs. Use each sentence one time only.

The monarchy disappeared.

Kamehameha became king.

The islands had different monarchs.

Liliuokalani became queen.

1 [   ]
2 [   ]
3 [   ]
4 [   ]

29. What did Liliuokalani believe, according to the professor?

- ◯ That the monarchy should end
- ◯ That the monarch's power should be limited
- ◯ That someone else should be monarch
- ◯ That the monarch should have complete power

30. Which of the following did NOT happen to Liliuokalani?

- ◯ She became queen in 1891.
- ◯ She ruled Hawaii until the end of her life.
- ◯ She received a pension from the government.
- ◯ She was removed from power.

SECTION TWO

STRUCTURE

STRUCTURE DIAGNOSTIC PRE-TEST
(Paper) 📖

SECTION 2
STRUCTURE AND WRITTEN EXPRESSION
Time—25 minutes
(including the reading of the directions)
Now set your clock for 25 minutes.

This section is designed to measure your ability to recognize language that is appropriate for standard written English. There are two types of questions in this section, with special directions for each type.

Structure

Directions: Questions 1–15 are incomplete sentences. Beneath each sentence you will see four words or phrases, marked (A), (B), (C), and (D). Choose the <u>one</u> word or phrase that best completes the sentence. Then, on your answer sheet, find the number of the question and fill in the space that corresponds to the letter of the answer you have chosen. Fill in the space so that the letter inside the oval cannot be seen.

Look at the following examples.

Example I

The president _____ the election by a landslide.

(A) won
(B) he won
(C) yesterday
(D) fortunately

Sample Answer

● Ⓑ Ⓒ Ⓓ

The sentence should read, "The president won the election by a landslide." Therefore, you should choose (A).

Example II

When _____ the conference?

(A) the doctor attended
(B) did the doctor attend
(C) the doctor will attend
(D) the doctor's attendance

Sample Answer

Ⓐ ● Ⓒ Ⓓ

The sentence should read, "When did the doctor attend the conference?" Therefore, you should choose (B).

Now begin work on the questions.

GO ON TO THE NEXT PAGE ➡

1. The North Pole _____ a latitude of 90 degrees north.

   (A) it has
   (B) is having
   (C) which is having
   (D) has

2. The city of Beverly Hills is surrounded on _____ the city of Los Angeles.

   (A) its sides
   (B) the sides are
   (C) it is the side of
   (D) all sides by

3. _____ greyhound, can achieve speeds up to thirty-six miles per hour.

   (A) The
   (B) The fastest
   (C) The fastest dog
   (D) The fastest dog, the

4. Marmots spend their time foraging among meadow plants and flowers or _____ on rocky cliffs.

   (A) gets sun
   (B) sunning
   (C) the sun
   (D) sunny

5. The greenhouse effect occurs _____ heat radiated from the Sun.

   (A) when does the Earth's atmosphere trap
   (B) does the Earth's atmosphere trap
   (C) when the Earth's atmosphere traps
   (D) the Earth's atmosphere traps

6. The Rose Bowl, _____ place on New Year's Day, is the oldest postseason collegiate football game in the United States.

   (A) takes
   (B) it takes
   (C) which takes
   (D) took

7. Experiments _____ represent a giant step into the medicine of the future.

   (A) using gene therapy
   (B) use gene therapy
   (C) they use
   (D) gene therapy uses

8. _____ off the Hawaiian coastline are living, others are dead.

   (A) While some types of coral reefs
   (B) Some types of coral reefs
   (C) There are many types of coral reefs
   (D) Coral reefs

9. Nimbostratus clouds are thick, dark gray clouds _____ forebode rain.

   (A) what
   (B) which
   (C) what they
   (D) which they

10. Some economists now suggest that home equity loans are merely a new trap to push consumers beyond _____.

    (A) they can afford
    (B) they can afford it
    (C) what is affordable
    (D) able to afford

11. People who reverse the letters of words _____ to read suffer from dyslexia.

    (A) when trying
    (B) if they tried
    (C) when tried
    (D) if he tries

12. Featured at the Henry Ford Museum _____ of antique cars dating from 1865.

    (A) is an exhibit
    (B) an exhibit
    (C) an exhibit is
    (D) which is an exhibit

GO ON TO THE NEXT PAGE

13. Rubber _____ from vulcanized silicones with a high molecular weight is difficult to distinguish from natural rubber.

    (A) is produced
    (B) producing
    (C) that produces
    (D) produced

14. _____ appears considerably larger at the horizon than it does overhead is merely an optical illusion.

    (A) The Moon
    (B) That the Moon
    (C) When the Moon
    (D) The Moon which

15. According to the World Health Organization, _____ any of the six most dangerous diseases to break out, it could be cause for quarantine.

    (A) were
    (B) they were
    (C) there were
    (D) were they

GO ON TO THE NEXT PAGE

Written Expression

Directions: In questions 16–40, each sentence has four underlined words or phrases. The four underlined parts of the sentence are marked (A), (B), (C), and (D). Identify the <u>one</u> underlined word or phrase that must be changed in order for the sentence to be correct. Then, on your answer sheet, find the number of the question and fill in the space that corresponds to the letter of the answer you have chosen.

Look at the following examples.

Example I   **Sample Answer**

The four <u>string</u> on a violin <u>are</u> <u>tuned</u>
  A   B   C   D

Ⓐ ● Ⓒ Ⓓ

in fifths.

The sentence should read, "The four strings on a violin are tuned in fifths." Therefore, you should choose (B).

Example II   **Sample Answer**

The <u>research</u> <u>for the</u> book *Roots* <u>taking</u>
    A   B   C

Ⓐ Ⓑ ● Ⓓ

Alex Haley <u>twelve years.</u>
                D

The sentence should read, "The research for the book *Roots* took Alex Haley twelve years." Therefore, you should choose (C).

Now begin work on the questions.

GO ON TO THE NEXT PAGE →

16. On the floor of the Pacific Ocean is hundreds of flat-topped mountains more than a
     $\overline{\quad A \quad}$ $\overline{B}$ $\overline{\quad C \quad}$ $\overline{D}$

    mile beneath sea level.

17. Because of the flourish with which John Hancock signed the Declaration of
     $\overline{A}$

    Independence, his name become synonymous with *signature*.
     $\overline{B}$ $\overline{C}$ $\overline{D}$

18. Segregation in public schools was declare unconstitutional by the Supreme Court
     $\overline{A}$ $\overline{B}$ $\overline{C}$

    in 1954.
     $\overline{D}$

19. Sirius, the Dog Star, is the most brightest star in the sky with an absolute magnitude
     $\overline{\quad A \quad}$ $\overline{B}$

    about twenty-three times that of the Sun.
     $\overline{\quad C \quad}$ $\overline{D}$

20. Killer whales tend to wander in family clusters that hunt, play, and resting together.
     $\overline{A}$ $\overline{B}$ $\overline{C}$ $\overline{D}$

21. Some of the most useful resistor material are carbon, metals, and metallic alloys.
     $\overline{A}$ $\overline{B}$ $\overline{C}$ $\overline{D}$

22. The community of Bethesda, Maryland, was previous known as Darcy's Store.
     $\overline{\quad A \quad}$ $\overline{B}$ $\overline{C}$ $\overline{D}$

23. Alloys of gold and copper have been widely using in various types of coins.
     $\overline{A}$ $\overline{B}$ $\overline{C}$ $\overline{D}$

24. J. H. Pratt used group therapy early in this century when he brought tuberculosis
     $\overline{A}$ $\overline{B}$ $\overline{C}$

    patients together to discuss its disease.
     $\overline{D}$

25. The United States has import all carpet wools in recent years because domestic
     $\overline{A}$ $\overline{B}$ $\overline{C}$

    wools are too fine and soft for carpets.
     $\overline{D}$

26. Irving Berlin wrote "Oh How I Hate to Get Up in the Morning" while serving in a
     $\overline{A}$ $\overline{B}$ $\overline{C}$

    U.S. Army during World War I.
     $\overline{D}$

GO ON TO THE NEXT PAGE ➤

27. Banks <u>are rushing</u> to merge because consolidations <u>enable them</u> to slash <u>theirs</u> costs
     A   B   C

and <u>expand</u>.
  D

28. <u>That</u> water has a very high specific heat <u>means</u> that without a large temperature
 A   B

change water can <u>add or lose</u> a large <u>number</u> of heat.
       C   D

29. Benny Goodman was <u>equally</u> talented as both a jazz <u>performer</u> <u>as well as</u> a
         A   B   C

<u>classical musician</u>.
   D

30. The state seal <u>still used</u> in Massachusetts <u>designed</u> by Paul Revere, <u>who also</u>
      A   B   C

designed <u>the first</u> Continental currency.
    D

31. Quarter horses were developed in eighteenth-century Virginia <u>to race</u> on
                   A

courses <u>short</u> of about a quarter <u>of a mile</u> <u>in length</u>.
   B   C   D

32. <u>No longer</u> <u>satisfied</u> with <u>the emphasis</u> of the Denishawn School, Martha Graham
  A   B   C

<u>has moved</u> to the staff of the Eastman School in 1925.
  D

33. William Hart was an <u>act</u> <u>best known</u> for <u>his</u> roles as western heroes in silent films.
       A   B   C

34. <u>Prior to</u> an extermination program <u>earlier</u> this century, <u>alive</u> wolves roamed
 A   B   C

<u>across nearly</u> all of North America.
  D

35. During the 1960s the Berkeley campus of the University of California <u>came to</u>
 A   B

national attention as a <u>result</u> its radical <u>political</u> activity.
       C   D

36. <u>Artist</u> Gutzon Borglum designed the Mount Rushmore Memorial and worked on
 A

<u>project</u> from 1925 <u>until</u> <u>his</u> death in 1941.
 B   C D

GO ON TO THE NEXT PAGE ➡

37. It is proving less <u>costly</u> and more <u>profitably</u> for drugmakers <u>to market</u> <u>directly</u> to
               A   B   C   D

patients.

38. Sapphires <u>weighing</u> <u>as</u> much as <u>two pounds</u> have on occasion <u>mined</u>.
              A   B   C   D

39. Like snakes, <u>lizards</u> can <u>be found</u> on all <u>others</u> continents <u>except</u> Antarctica.
        A   B   C   D

40. Banks, savings and loans, and finance companies <u>have recently</u> been <u>doing</u> home
                                              A   B

equity loans with <u>greater frequency</u> than <u>ever before</u>.
                   C   D

This is the end of the Structure and Written Expression Pre-Test.

Circle the number of each of the questions that you answered incorrectly or were not sure of. Then you will see which skills you should be sure to review.

1. SKILL 1	16. SKILL 22	31. SKILL 48
2. SKILL 2	17. SKILL 33	32. SKILL 35
3. SKILL 3	18. SKILL 31	33. SKILL 42
4. SKILL 6	19. SKILL 27	34. SKILL 50
5. SKILLS 7 and 15	20. SKILL 24	35. SKILL 57
6. SKILL 12	21. SKILL 21	36. SKILL 52
7. SKILLS 4 and 13	22. SKILL 47	37. SKILLS 47 and 49
8. SKILL 8	23. SKILL 51	38. SKILL 38
9. SKILL 12	24. SKILL 45	39. SKILL 60
10. SKILL 10	25. SKILL 30	40. SKILL 58
11. SKILL 14	26. SKILL 51	
12. SKILL 16	27. SKILL 44	
13. SKILLS 5 and 13	28. SKILL 40	
14. SKILL 9	29. SKILL 25	
15. SKILL 18	30. SKILL 37	

STRUCTURE DIAGNOSTIC PRE-TEST
(Computer) 🖥️

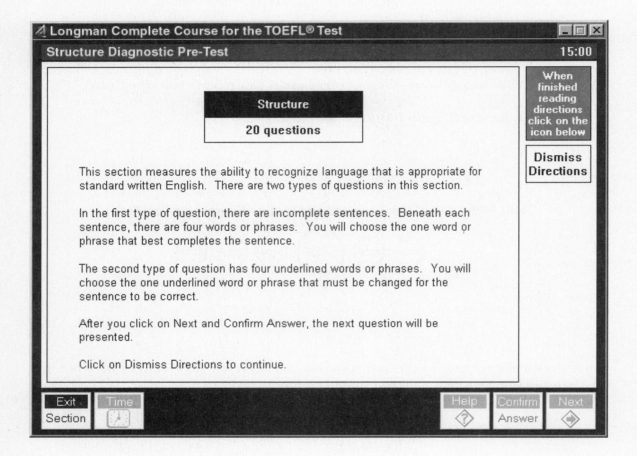

1. The music on a compact disk (CD) is record by lasers.

2. Aristotle believed that everything in the universe were composed of four basic elements: earth, water, air, and fire.

3. The 1980 explosion of _____ the first volcanic eruption in the continental United States in over 60 years.
   - ○ Mount St. Helens
   - ○ was Mount St. Helens
   - ○ it was Mount St. Helens
   - ○ Mount St. Helens was

4. One type of Australian frog lays up to 25 eggs at a time and then swallows they for protection.

5. Static electricity _____ one cloud to another or between clouds and the ground creates lightning.
   - ○ flows from
   - ○ the flow from
   - ⊗ flowing from
   - ○ is flowing from

6. The Spanish introduced not only horses and also cattle to the North American continent.

7. White blood cells are the largest of red blood cells and are more varied in size and in shape.

8. The Model T car, introduced in 1908, _____ $850.
   - ○ the price was
   - ○ a price of
   - ○ to be priced at
   - ○ was priced at

9. During the 1982–83 El Niño, 90 percent of Peru's fur seal pups have died.

10. St. Augustine, Florida, was founded in 1565 by Pedro Menendez and was raze 21 years later by Francis Drake.

11. _____ reacts with a chlorine atom, an electron is transferred from the outer shell of the sodium atom to the outer shell of the chlorine atom.
    - ○ A sodium atom
    - ○ For a sodium atom
    - ○ When a sodium atom
    - ○ It is a sodium atom

12. Antelopes are gregarious animals that travel in herds ranging in amount from a few to several thousand.

13. In 1821, Emma Willard opened officially the doors of the first school in the United States to offer college-level courses for women.

14. In 1858, the site _____ was to become the city of Denver was settled as a way station for outfitting gold prospectors.
    - ○ it
    - ○ of it
    - ○ what
    - ○ of what

15. <u>Typical</u> long bone, <u>such as</u> the femur, <u>consists of</u> a long shaft with <u>swellings</u> at each end.

16. <u>The</u> vacuum tube <u>did</u> an <u>important</u> contribution to the early <u>growth</u> of radio and television.

17. In the Antarctic Ocean _____ of plankton and crustacean forms of life.

   ⬯ an abundance
   ⊗ is an abundance
   ⬯ it is abundant
   ⬯ an abundance is

18. A <u>bimetallic</u> thermometer <u>relies</u> the different <u>rates</u> of expansion of two types of metal, <u>usually</u> brass and copper.

19. Tremendous <u>flooding</u> during the summer of 1993 <u>left</u> 8 million acres of nine midwestern states inundated and proved both <u>expensively</u> and <u>deadly</u>.

20. _____ to occur in the earth's crust, push-pull and shake waves would be generated simultaneously.

   ⊗ Were a break
   ⬯ If a break
   ⬯ A break was
   ⬯ If broken

Circle the number of each of the questions on the test that you *answered incorrectly* or *were unsure of.* Then you will see which skills you should be sure to focus on.

1.	SKILL 31	8.	SKILL 13	15.	SKILL 52
2.	SKILL 23	9.	SKILL 34	16.	SKILL 58
3.	SKILL 2	10.	SKILL 37	17.	SKILL 16
4.	SKILL 43	11.	SKILL 7	18.	SKILL 57
5.	SKILL 4	12.	SKILL 40	19.	SKILL 49
6.	SKILL 25	13.	SKILL 48	20.	SKILL 18
7.	SKILL 28	14.	SKILL 10		

STRUCTURE

Structure is tested in the second section on both the paper TOEFL test and the computer TOEFL test. This section consists of a number of multiple-choice questions that test your knowledge of the structure of English sentences and error recognition questions that test your knowledge of correct written expression. The paper and the computer structure sections are **similar** in the following ways:

- *the types of questions*
- *the language skills tested*

The paper and the computer structure sections are **different** in the following ways:

- *the number of questions*
- *the amount of time*
- *the ordering of the questions*
- *the strategies*
- *the scoring*

STRUCTURE ON THE PAPER TOEFL® TEST

On the paper TOEFL test, the second section is called Structure and Written Expression. This section consists of forty questions (though some tests may be longer). You have twenty-five minutes to complete the forty questions in this section.

There are two types of questions in the Structure and Written Expression section of the paper TOEFL test:

1. **Structure** (questions 1–15) consists of fifteen sentences in which part of each sentence has been replaced with a blank. Each sentence is followed by four answer choices. You must choose the answer that completes the sentence in a grammatically correct way.
2. **Written Expression** (questions 16–40) consists of twenty-five sentences in which four words or groups of words have been underlined. You must choose the underlined word or group of words that is *not* correct.

The questions on the paper test are presented in *linear* order. The fifteen structure questions (1–15) progress from easy to difficult. The twenty-five written expression questions (16–40) also progress from easy to difficult. Your score in this section is based on your answers to these forty questions.

GENERAL STRATEGIES
(Paper TOEFL® Test)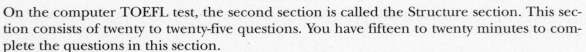

1. **Be familiar with the directions.** The directions on every paper TOEFL test are the same, so it is not necessary to spend time reading the directions carefully when you take the test. You should be completely familiar with the directions before the day of the test.

2. **Begin with questions 1 through 15.** Anticipate that questions 1 through 5 will be the easiest. Anticipate that questions 11 through 15 will be the most difficult. Do not spend too much time on questions 11 through 15. There will be easier questions that come later.

3. **Continue with questions 16 through 40.** Anticipate that questions 16 through 20 will be the easiest. Anticipate that questions 36 through 40 will be the most difficult. Do not spend too much time on questions 36 through 40.

4. **If you have time, return to questions 11 through 15.** You should spend extra time on questions 11 through 15 only after you spend all the time that you want on the easier questions that follow.

5. **Guess to complete the section before time is up.** There is no penalty for guessing, so it can only increase your score to guess the answers to questions that you do not have time to complete.

STRUCTURE ON THE COMPUTER TOEFL® TEST

On the computer TOEFL test, the second section is called the Structure section. This section consists of twenty to twenty-five questions. You have fifteen to twenty minutes to complete the questions in this section.

There are two types of questions in the Structure section of the computer TOEFL test:

1. **Structure** questions consist of sentences in which part of each sentence has been replaced with a blank. Each sentence is followed by four answer choices. You must choose the answer that completes the sentence in a grammatically correct way.

2. **Written Expression** questions consist of sentences in which four words or groups of words have been underlined. You must choose the underlined word or group of words that is *not* correct.

These two types of questions are intermixed in this section of the test.

The Structure section of the computer TOEFL test is *computer adaptive*. This means that the difficulty of the questions that you see is determined by how well you answer the questions. The section begins with a medium-level question, and the questions that follow will get easier or harder depending on whether or not you answer the questions correctly. Your answers to these questions count as only half of your structure score; the other half of your structure score comes from your answer to the writing question.

GENERAL STRATEGIES
(Computer TOEFL® Test)

1. **Be familiar with the directions.** The directions on every computer TOEFL test are the same, so it is not necessary to spend time reading the directions carefully when you take the test. You should be completely familiar with the directions before the day of the test.

2. **Be familiar with computer adaptivity.** This section of the computer TOEFL test is adaptive. This means that you will start with a medium-level question, and the difficulty of the questions will increase or decrease depending on whether or not your answers are correct.

3. **Dismiss the directions as soon as they come up.** The time starts when the directions come up. You should already be familiar with the directions, so you can click on `Dismiss Directions` as soon as it appears and save all your time for the questions.

4. **Think carefully about a question before you answer it.** You may not return to a question later in the test. You only have one opportunity to answer a given question.

5. **Click on an answer on the computer screen when you have selected an answer.** You may still change your mind at this point and click on a different answer.

6. **Click on** `Next` **and then click on** `Confirm Answer` **to record your answer.** After you click on the Confirm Answer button, you cannot go back and change your answer. A new question, either a structure question or a written expression question, will appear.

7. **Do not spend too much time on a question you are unsure of.** If you truly do not know the answer to a question, simply guess and go on. The computer will automatically move you into a level of questions that you can answer.

8. **Be very careful not to make careless mistakes.** If you carelessly choose an incorrect answer, the computer will move you to an easier level of questions. You will have to waste time working your way back to the appropriate level of questions.

9. **Monitor the time carefully on the title bar of the computer screen.** The title bar indicates the time remaining in the Structure section, the total number of questions in the section, and the current number.

10. **Do not randomly guess at the end of the section to complete all the questions in the section before time is up.** In a computer adaptive section such as Structure, random guessing to complete the section will only lower your score.

THE STRUCTURE QUESTIONS

(PAPER TOEFL® TEST AND COMPUTER TOEFL® TEST) 📖 🖥️

Multiple-choice questions that test your knowledge of the correct structure of English sentences appear on both the paper TOEFL test and the computer TOEFL test. Look at an example of a structure question from the paper TOEFL test.

Example from the Paper TOEFL® Test 📖

A camel _____ 30 gallons of water in ten minutes.

(A)   can drink
(B)   it can drink
(C)   a large drink of
(D)   with a drink of

In this example, you should notice that the sentence has a subject *camel* but needs a verb. Answer (A) is the correct answer because it contains the verb *can drink*. Answer (B) is incorrect because it has the extra subject *it*, and answers (C) and (D) are incorrect because they do not have verbs. You should therefore choose answer (A).

Now, look at an example of a structure question from the computer TOEFL test.

Example from the Computer TOEFL® Test 🖥️

_____, a firefighting specialist from Texas, has dealt with numerous major fires worldwide.

◯ Red Adair is
◯ For Read Adair
◯ Red Adair
◯ In Red Adair's life

In this example, you should notice that the sentence has a verb *has dealt* but needs a subject. The comma in front of the verb *has* indicates that *specialist* is an appositive and is not the subject. The third answer is the best answer because it contains the subject *Red Adair*. The first answer has an extra verb, and the second and fourth answers contain prepositional phrases, so these answers are incorrect. You should click on the third answer to this question.

PROCEDURES FOR THE STRUCTURE QUESTIONS
(Paper TOEFL® Test and Computer TOEFL® Test)

1. **First, study the sentence.** Your purpose is to determine what is needed to complete the sentence correctly.

2. **Then study each answer based on how well it completes the sentence.** Eliminate answers that do not complete the sentence correctly.

3. **Do not try to eliminate incorrect answers by looking only at the answers.** The incorrect answers are generally correct by themselves. The incorrect answers are generally incorrect only when used to complete the sentence.

Now, you should move on to the language skills. The following language skills will help you to implement these strategies and procedures in the structure questions of both the paper TOEFL test and the computer TOEFL test.

SENTENCES WITH ONE CLAUSE

Some sentences in English have just one subject and verb, and it is very important for you to find the subject and verb in these sentences. In some sentences it is easy to find the subject and verb. However, certain structures, such as objects of prepositions, appositives, and participles, can cause confusion in locating the subject and verb because each of these structures can look like a subject or verb. An object of the preposition or an appositive can be mistaken for a subject, while a participle can be mistaken for a verb.

Therefore, you should be able to do the following in sentences with one subject and verb: (1) be sure the sentence has a subject and a verb, (2) be careful of objects of prepositions and appositives when you are looking for the subject, and (3) be careful of present participles and past participles when you are looking for the verb.

SKILL 1:   BE SURE THE SENTENCE HAS A SUBJECT AND A VERB

You know that a sentence in English should have a subject and a verb. The most common types of problems that you will encounter in structure questions on the TOEFL test have to do with subjects and verbs: perhaps the sentence is missing either the subject or the verb or both, or perhaps the sentence has an extra subject or verb.

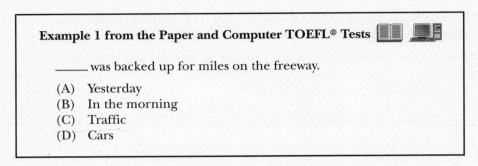

Example 1 from the Paper and Computer TOEFL® Tests

_____ was backed up for miles on the freeway.

(A)   Yesterday
(B)   In the morning
(C)   Traffic
(D)   Cars

In this example you should notice immediately that there is a verb *was*, but there is no subject. Answer (C) is the best answer because it contains the singular subject *traffic* that agrees with the singular verb *was*. Answer (A), *yesterday*, and answer (B), *in the morning*, are not subjects, so they are not correct. Although answer (D), *cars*, could be a subject, it is not correct because *cars* is plural and it does not agree with the singular verb *was*.

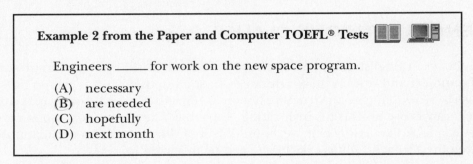

Example 2 from the Paper and Computer TOEFL® Tests

Engineers _____ for work on the new space program.

(A)   necessary
(B)   are needed
(C)   hopefully
(D)   next month

In this example you should notice immediately that the sentence has a subject *engineers* and that there is no verb. Because answer (B), *are needed,* is a verb, it is the best answer. Answers (A), (C), and (D) are not verbs, so they are not correct.

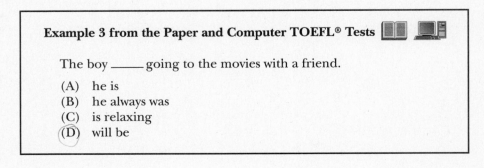

Example 3 from the Paper and Computer TOEFL® Tests

The boy _____ going to the movies with a friend.

(A)   he is
(B)   he always was
(C)   is relaxing
(D)   will be

This sentence has a subject *boy* and has part of a verb *going;* to be correct, some form of the verb *be* is needed to make the sentence complete. Answers (A) and (B) are incorrect because the sentence already has a subject *boy* and does not need the extra subject *he.* Answer (C) is incorrect because *relaxing* is an extra verb part that is unnecessary because of *going.* Answer (D) is the best answer; *will be* together with *going* is a complete verb.

The following chart outlines what you should remember about subjects and verbs:

SUBJECTS AND VERBS
A *sentence* in English must have at least one *subject* and one *verb.*

EXERCISE 1: Underline the subjects once and the verbs twice in each of the following sentences. Then indicate if the sentences are correct (C) or incorrect (I).

___I___ 1. Last week <u>went</u> fishing for trout at the nearby mountain lake.

___C___ 2. A schedule of the day's events <u>can be obtained</u> at the front desk.

___I___ 3. A <u>job</u> on the day shift or the night shift at the plant available. *N V*

___I___ 4. The new computer <u>program</u> has <u>provides</u> a variety of helpful applications.

___C___ 5. The box can <u>be</u> opened only with a special screwdriver.

_____ 6. The assigned text for history class it contains more than twenty chapters.

_____ 7. The papers in the wastebasket should be emptied into the trash can outside.

_____ 8. Departure before dawn on a boat in the middle of the harbor.

_____ 9. Yesterday found an interesting article on pollution.

_____ 10. The new machine is processes 50 percent more than the previous machine.

SKILL 2:   BE CAREFUL OF OBJECTS OF PREPOSITIONS

An object of a preposition is a noun, pronoun, gerund or noun clause that comes after a preposition, such as *in, at, of, to, by, behind, on,* and so on, to form a prepositional phrase.

(After his *exams*) Tom will take a trip (by *boat*).

This sentence contains two objects of prepositions. *Exams* is the object of the preposition *after,* and *boat* is the object of the preposition *by.*

An object of a preposition can cause confusion in structure questions on the TOEFL test because it can be mistaken for the subject of a sentence.

Example from the Paper and Computer TOEFL® Tests

With his friend _____ found the movie theater.

(A) has
(B) he
(C) later
(D) when

In this example you should look first for the subject and the verb. You should notice the verb *found* and should also notice that there is no subject. Do not think that *friend* is the subject; *friend* is the object of the preposition *with*, and one noun cannot be both a subject and an object at the same time. Because a subject is needed in this sentence, answer (B), *he*, is the best answer. Answers (A), (C), and (D) are not correct because they cannot be subjects.

The following chart outlines the key information that you should remember about objects of prepositions:

OBJECTS OF PREPOSITIONS
A *preposition* is followed by a noun, pronoun, gerund or noun clause that is called an *object of the preposition*. If a word is an *object of a preposition,* it is not the *subject.*

NOTE: A lengthy list of prepositions and practice in recognizing prepositions can be found in Appendix D at the back of the text. You may want to complete these exercises before continuing with Exercise 2.

EXERCISE 2: Each of the following sentences contains one or more prepositional phrases. Underline the subjects once and the verbs twice. Circle the prepositional phrases that come before the verb. Then indicate if the sentences are correct (C) or incorrect (I).

__C__ 1. The interviews (by radio broadcasters) were carried live by the station.

__I__ 2. (In the last possible moment) (before takeoff) took his seat in the airplane.   NS

_____ 3. At the neighborhood flower shop, flowers in quantities of a dozen or a half dozen can be delivered for free.

_____ 4. The progressive reading methods at this school are given credit for the improved test scores.

_____ 5. For the last three years at various hospitals in the county has been practicing medicine.   NS

_____ 6. In the past a career in politics was not considered acceptable in some circles.

_____ 7. Shopping in the downtown area of the city it has improved a lot in recent years.

_____ 8. At the building site the carpenters with the most experience were given the most intricate work.

_____ 9. For the fever and headache took two aspirin tablets. *NS*

_____ 10. The report with complete documentation was delivered at the conference.

Skill 3: BE CAREFUL OF APPOSITIVES

Appositives can cause confusion in structure questions on the TOEFL test because an appositive can be mistaken for the subject of a sentence. An appositive is a noun that comes before or after another noun and has the same meaning.

Sally, the best *student* in the class, got an A on the exam.

In this example *Sally* is the subject of the sentence and *the best student in the class* can easily be recognized as an appositive phrase because of the noun *student* and because of the commas. The sentence says that *Sally* and *the best student in the class* are the same person. Note that if you leave out the appositive phrase, the sentence still makes sense (*Sally got an A on the exam*).

The following example shows how an appositive can be confused with the subject of a sentence in structure questions on the TOEFL test.

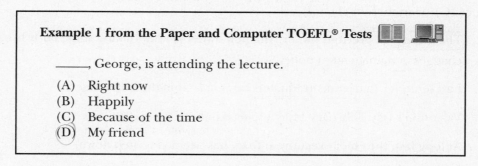

Example 1 from the Paper and Computer TOEFL® Tests

_____, George, is attending the lecture.

(A) Right now
(B) Happily
(C) Because of the time
(D) My friend

In this example you should recognize from the commas that *George* is not the subject of the sentence. *George* is an appositive. Because this sentence still needs a subject, the best answer is (D), *my friend*. Answers (A), (B), and (C) are incorrect because they are not subjects.

The next example shows that an appositive does not always come after the subject; an appositive can also come at the beginning of the sentence.

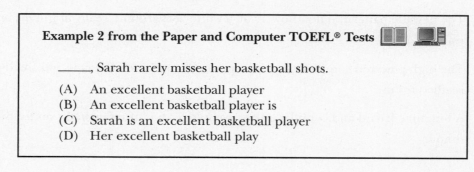

Example 2 from the Paper and Computer TOEFL® Tests

_____, Sarah rarely misses her basketball shots.

(A) An excellent basketball player
(B) An excellent basketball player is
(C) Sarah is an excellent basketball player
(D) Her excellent basketball play

In this example you can tell that *Sarah* is the subject and *misses* is the verb because there is no comma separating them. In the space you should put an appositive for Sarah, and Sarah is *an excellent basketball player*, so answer (A) is the best answer. Answers (B) and (C) are not correct because they each contain the verb *is*, and an appositive does not need a verb. Answer (D) contains a noun, *play*, that could possibly be an appositive, but *play* is not the same as *Sarah*, so this answer is not correct.

The following chart outlines the key information that you should remember about appositives:

APPOSITIVES
An *appositive* is a noun that comes before or after another noun and is generally set off from the noun with commas. If a word is an *appositive*, it is not the *subject*. The following appositive structures are both possible in English:
S,   APP,   V **Tom,   a really good mechanic,   is fixing   the car.**
APP,   S   V **A really good mechanic,   Tom   is fixing   the car.**

EXERCISE 3: Each of the following sentences contains an appositive. Underline the subjects once and the verbs twice. Circle the appositive phrases. Then indicate if the sentences are correct (C) or incorrect (I).

___C___ 1. (The son of the previous owner,) the new owner is undertaking some fairly broad changes in management policy.

___I___ 2. Last semester, (a friend,) graduated *cum laude* from the university.

___C___ 3. Valentine's Day, February 14, is a special holiday for sweethearts.

___I___ 4. At long last, the chief executive officer, has decided to step down.

___C___ 5. Tonight's supper, leftovers from last night, did not taste any better tonight than last night.

___C___ 6. The only entrance to the closet, the door was kept locked at all times.

___I___ 7. In the cold of winter, a wall heating unit, would not turn on.

___C___ 8. The new tile pattern, yellow flowers on a white background, really brightens up the room.

___I___ 9. The high-powered computer, the most powerful machine of its type, was finally readied for use.

___C___ 10. A longtime friend and confidant, the psychologist was often invited over for Sunday dinner.

Skill 4:   BE CAREFUL OF PRESENT PARTICIPLES

A present participle is the *-ing* form of the verb (*talking, playing*). In structure questions on the TOEFL test, a present participle can cause confusion because it can be either a part of the verb or an adjective. It is part of the verb when it is preceded by some form of the verb *be*.

The man *is talking* to his friend.
VERB

In this sentence *talking* is part of the verb because it is accompanied by *is*.

A present participle is an adjective when it is not accompanied by some form of the verb *be*.

The man *talking* to his friend has a beard.
ADJECTIVE

In this sentence *talking* is an adjective and not part of the verb because it is not accompanied by some form of *be*. The verb in this sentence is *has*.

The following example shows how a present participle can be confused with the verb in structure questions on the TOEFL test.

Example from the Paper and Computer TOEFL® Tests

The child _____ playing in the yard is my son.

(A)   now
(B)   is
(C)   he
(D)   was

In this example, if you look at only the first words of the sentence, it appears that *child* is the subject and *playing* is part of the verb. If you think that *playing* is part of the verb, you might choose answer (B), *is,* or answer (D), *was,* to complete the verb. However, these two answers are incorrect because *playing* is not part of the verb. You should recognize that *playing* is a participial adjective rather than a verb because there is another verb in the sentence *is*. In this sentence there is a complete subject *child* and a complete verb *is,* so this sentence does not need another subject or verb. The best answer here is (A).

The following chart outlines what you should remember about present participles:

PRESENT PARTICIPLES

A *present participle* is the *-ing* form of the verb. The **present participle** can be (1) **part of the verb** or (2) an **adjective.** It is part of the *verb* when it is accompanied by some form of the verb *be.* It is an *adjective* when it is not accompanied by some form of the verb *be.*
 	
    1. *The boy is **standing** in the corner.*
    2. *The boy **standing** in the corner was naughty.*

EXERCISE 4: Each of the following sentences contains one or more present participles. Underline the subjects once and the verbs twice. Circle the present participles and label them as adjectives or verbs. Then indicate if the sentences are correct (C) or incorrect (I).

__C__ 1. The companies (offering) the lowest prices will have the most customers.
ADJ.

__I__ 2. Those travelers are (completing) their trip on Delta should report to Gate Three.
VERB

__C__ 3. The artisans were demonstrating various handicrafts at booths throughout the fair.

__I__ 4. The fraternities are giving the wildest parties attract the most new pledges.

__C__ 5. The first team winning four games is awarded the championship.

__I__ 6. The speaker was trying to make his point was often interrupted vociferously.

__C__ 7. The fruits were rotting because of the moisture in the crates carrying them to market.

__C__ 8. Any students desiring official transcripts should complete the appropriate form.

__I__ 9. The advertisements were announcing the half-day sale received a lot of attention.

__C__ 10. The spices flavoring the meal were quite distinctive.

SKILL 5:   BE CAREFUL OF PAST PARTICIPLES

Past participles can cause confusion in structure questions on the TOEFL test because a past participle can be either an adjective or a part of a verb. The past participle is the form of the verb that appears with *have* or *be*. It often ends in *-ed*, but there are also many irregular past participles in English. (See Appendix F for a list of irregular past participles.)

The family *has purchased* a television.
VERB

The poem *was written* by Paul.
VERB

In the first sentence the past participle *purchased* is part of the verb because it is accompanied by *has*. In the second sentence the past participle *written* is part of the verb because it is accompanied by *was*.

A past participle is an adjective when it is not accompanied by some form of *be* or *have*.

The television *purchased* yesterday was expensive.
ADJECTIVE

The poem *written* by Paul appeared in the magazine.
ADJECTIVE

In the first sentence *purchased* is an adjective rather than a verb because it is not accompanied by a form of *be* or *have* (and there is a verb, *was*, later in the sentence). In the second sentence *written* is an adjective rather than a verb because it is not accompanied by a form of *be* or *have* (and there is a verb, *appeared*, later in the sentence).

The following example shows how a past participle can be confused with the verb in structure questions on the TOEFL test.

Example from the Paper and Computer TOEFL® Tests 📖 💻

The packages _____ mailed at the post office will arrive Monday.

(A) have
(B) were
(C) them
(D) just

In this example, if you look only at the first few words of the sentence, it appears that *packages* is the subject and *mailed* is either a complete verb or a past participle that needs a helping verb. But if you look further in the sentence, you will see that the verb is *will arrive*. You will then recognize that *mailed* is a participial adjective and is therefore not part of the verb. Answers (A) and (B) are incorrect because *mailed* is an adjective and does not need a helping verb such as *have* or *were*. Answer (C) is incorrect because there is no need for the object *them*. Answer (D) is the best answer to this question.

The following chart outlines what you should remember about past participles:

PAST PARTICIPLES

A *past participle* often ends in *-ed,* but there are also many irregular past participles. For many verbs, including *-ed* verbs, the *simple past* and the *past participle* are the same and can be easily confused. The *-ed* form of the verb can be (1) the *simple past,* (2) the *past participle* of a verb, or (3) an *adjective.*

    1. *She **painted** this picture.*
    2. *She has **painted** this picture.*
    3. *The picture **painted** by Karen is now in a museum.*

EXERCISE 5: Each of the following sentences contains one or more past participles. Underline the subjects once and the verbs twice. Circle the past participles and label them as adjectives or verbs. Then indicate if the sentences are correct (C) or incorrect (I).

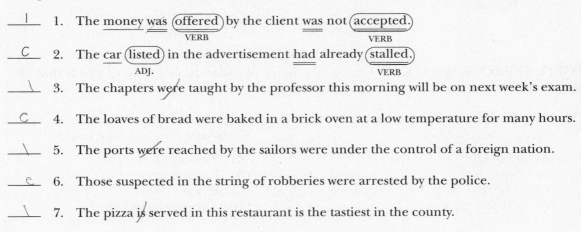

___I___ 1. The money was (offered) by the client was not (accepted.)
                    VERB   VERB

___C___ 2. The car (listed) in the advertisement had already (stalled.)
                    ADJ.   VERB

___I___ 3. The chapters were taught by the professor this morning will be on next week's exam.

___C___ 4. The loaves of bread were baked in a brick oven at a low temperature for many hours.

___I___ 5. The ports were reached by the sailors were under the control of a foreign nation.

___C___ 6. Those suspected in the string of robberies were arrested by the police.

___I___ 7. The pizza is served in this restaurant is the tastiest in the county.

___I___ 8. The courses are listed on the second page of the brochure have several prerequisites.

___C___ 9. All the tenants were invited to the Independence Day barbecue at the apartment complex.

___C___ 10. Any bills paid by the first of the month will be credited to your account by the next day.

EXERCISE (Skills 1–5): Underline the subjects once and the verbs twice in each of the following sentences. Then indicate if the sentences are correct (C) or incorrect (I).

___C___ 1. For three weeks at the beginning of the semester students with fewer than the maximum number of units can add additional courses.

___I___ 2. On her lunch hour *she* went to a nearby department store to purchase a wedding gift.

___I___ 3. The fir trees were grown for the holiday season were harvested in November.

___I__ˣ__ᶜ___ 4. In the grove the overripe oranges were falling on the ground.

___I___ 5. The papers being delivered at 4:00 will contain the announcement of the president's resignation.

___I___ 6. A specialty shop with various blends from around the world *is* in the shopping mall.

___C___ 7. The portraits exhibited in the Houston Museum last month are now on display in Dallas.

___I___ 8. With a sudden jerk of his hand *he* threw the ball across the field to one of the other players.

___I___ 9. Construction of the housing development it will be underway by the first of the month.

___C___ 10. Those applicants returning their completed forms at the earliest date have the highest priority.

TOEFL EXERCISE (Skills 1–5): Choose the letter of the word or group of words that best completes the sentence.

1. The North Platte River _____ from Wyoming into Nebraska.

   (A) it flowed
   (B) flows
   (C) flowing
   (D) with flowing water

2. _____ Biloxi received its name from a Sioux word meaning "first people."

   (A) The city of
   (B) Located in
   (C) It is in
   (D) The tour included

3. A pride of lions _____ up to forty lions, including one to three males, several females, and cubs.

   (A) can contain
   (B) it contains
   (C) contain
   (D) containing

4. _____ tea plant are small and white.

   (A) The
   (B) On the
   (C) Having flowers the
   (D) The flowers of the

5. The tetracyclines, _____ antibiotics, are used to treat infections.

   (A) are a family of
   (B) being a family
   (C) a family of
   (D) their family is

6. Any possible academic assistance from taking stimulants _____ marginal at best.

   (A) it is
   (B) there is
   (C) is
   (D) as

7. Henry Adams, born in Boston, _____ famous as a historian and novelist.

   (A) became
   (B) and became
   (C) he was
   (D) and he became

8. The major cause _____ the pull of the Moon on the Earth.

   (A) the ocean tides are
   (B) of ocean tides is
   (C) of the tides in the ocean
   (D) the oceans' tides

9. Still a novelty in the late nineteenth century, _____ limited to the rich.

   (A) was
   (B) was photography
   (C) it was photography
   (D) photography was

10. A computerized map of the freeways using information gathered by sensors embedded in the pavement _____ on a local cable channel during rush hours.

    (A) airs
    (B) airing
    (C) air
    (D) to air

SENTENCES WITH MULTIPLE CLAUSES _____

Many sentences in English have more than one clause. (A clause is a group of words containing a subject and a verb.) Whenever you find a sentence on the TOEFL test with more than one clause, you need to make sure that every subject has a verb and every verb has a subject. Next you need to check that the various clauses in the sentence are correctly joined. There are various ways to join clauses in English. Certain patterns appear frequently in English and on the TOEFL test. You should be very familiar with these patterns.

SKILL 6:   USE COORDINATE CONNECTORS CORRECTLY

When you have two clauses in an English sentence, you must connect the two clauses correctly. One way to connect two clauses is to use *and, but, or, so,* or *yet* between the clauses.

> Tom is singing, *and* Paul is dancing.

> Tom is tall, *but* Paul is short.

Tom <u>must write</u> the letter, *or* Paul <u>will do</u> it.

Tom <u>told</u> a joke, *so* Paul <u>laughed</u>.

Tom <u>is</u> tired, *yet* he <u>is not going</u> to sleep.

In each of these examples, there are two clauses that are correctly joined with a coordinate conjunction *and, but, or, so,* or *yet,* and a comma (,).

The following example shows how this sentence pattern could be tested in structure questions on the TOEFL test.

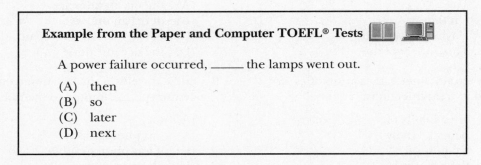

Example from the Paper and Computer TOEFL® Tests

A power failure occurred, _____ the lamps went out.

(A)   then
(B)   so
(C)   later
(D)   next

In this example you should notice quickly that there are two clauses, *a power failure occurred* and *the lamps went out.* This sentence needs a connector to join the two clauses. *Then, later,* and *next* are not connectors, so answers (A), (C), and (D) are not correct. The best answer is answer (B) because *so* can connect two clauses.

The following chart lists the coordinate connectors and the sentence pattern used with them:

COORDINATE CONNECTORS				
and	*but*	*or*	*so*	*yet*
S V,		(coordinate connector)	S V	
She laughed,		**but**	**she wanted to cry.**	

EXERCISE 6: Each of the following sentences contains more than one clause. Underline the subjects once and the verbs twice. Circle the connectors. Then indicate if the sentences are correct (C) or incorrect (I).

__C__   1.   The <u>software</u> <u>should be used</u> on a laptop computer, (and) this <u>computer</u> <u>is</u> a laptop.

__I__   2.   The rain <u>clouds</u> <u>can be seen</u> in the distance, (but) no <u>has fallen</u>.

_____   3.   They are trying to sell their house, it has been on the market for two months.

_____   4.   So the quality of the print was not good, I changed the typewriter ribbon.

__C__   5.   The lifeguard will warn you about the riptides, or she may require you to get out of the water.

_____   6.   You should have finished the work yesterday, yet is not close to being finished today.

_____ *c*   7. The phone rang again and again, so the receptionist was not able to get much work done.

_____ *c*   8. The missing wallet was found, but the cash and credit cards had been removed.

_____   9. Or you can drive your car for another 2,000 miles, you can get it fixed.

_____ 10. The chemist was awarded the Nobel Prize, he flew to Europe to accept it.

SKILL 7:   USE ADVERB *TIME* AND *CAUSE* CONNECTORS CORRECTLY

Sentences with adverb clauses have two basic patterns in English. Study the clauses and connectors in the following sentences:

<u>I</u> will <u>sign</u> the check *before* <u>you</u> <u>leave</u>.

Before <u>you</u> <u>leave</u>, <u>I</u> will <u>sign</u> the check.

In each of these examples, there are two clauses: *you leave* and *I will sign the check,* and the clause *you leave* is an adverb time clause because it is introduced with the connector *before.* In the first example the connector *before* comes in the middle of the sentence, and no comma (,) is used. In the second example the connector *before* comes at the beginning of the sentence. In this pattern, when the connector comes at the beginning of the sentence, a comma (,) is required in the middle of the sentence.

The following example shows how this sentence pattern could be tested in structure questions on the TOEFL test.

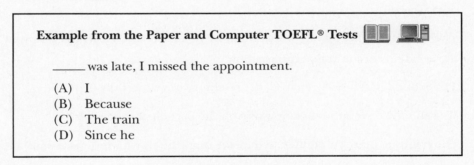

Example from the Paper and Computer TOEFL® Tests

_____ was late, I missed the appointment.

(A) I
(B) Because
(C) The train
(D) Since he

In this example you should recognize easily that there is a verb, *was,* that needs a subject. There is also another clause, *I missed the appointment.* If you choose answer (A) or answer (C), you will have a subject for the verb *was,* but you will not have a connector to join the two clauses. Because you need a connector to join two clauses, answers (A) and (C) are incorrect. Answer (B) is incorrect because there is no subject for the verb *was.* Answer (D) is the best answer because there is a subject, *he,* for the verb *was,* and there is a connector, *since,* to join the two clauses.

The following chart lists adverb *time* and *cause* connectors and the sentence patterns used with them:

ADVERB TIME AND CAUSE CONNECTORS					
TIME				CAUSE	
after	as soon as	once	when	as	now that
as	before	since	whenever	because	since
as long as	by the time	until	while	inasmuch as	
S V *Teresa went inside*		adverb connector *because*		S V *it was raining.*	
adverb connector *Because*		S V, *it was raining,*		S V *Teresa went inside.*	

EXERCISE 7: Each of the following sentences contains more than one clause. Underline the subjects once and the verbs twice. Circle the connectors. Then indicate if the sentences are correct (C) or incorrect (I).

__C__ 1. (Since) the bank closes in less than an hour, the deposits need to be tallied immediately.

__I__ 2. Their backgrounds are thoroughly investigated (before) are admitted to the organization.

_____ 3. The citizens are becoming more and more incensed about traffic accidents whenever the accidents occur at that intersection.

_____ 4. The ground had been prepared, the seedlings were carefully planted.

__C__ 5. We can start the conference now that all the participants have arrived.

__I__ 6. The building quite vulnerable to damage until the storm windows are installed.

__I__ 7. Once the address label for the package is typed, can be sent to the mail room.

__C__ 8. Because the recent change in work shifts was not posted, several workers missed their shifts.

__C__ 9. The mother is going to be quite upset with her son as long as he misbehaves so much.

__I__ 10. Inasmuch as all the votes have not yet been counted, the outcome of the election cannot be announced.

SKILL 8:   USE OTHER ADVERB CONNECTORS CORRECTLY

Adverb clauses can express the ideas of time and cause, as you saw in Skill 7; adverb clauses can also express a number of other ideas, such as contrast, condition, manner, and place. Because these clauses are adverb clauses, they have the same structure as the time and cause clauses in Skill 7. Study the following examples:

I will leave at 7:00 *if* I am ready.

Although I was late, I managed to catch the train.

In each of these examples, there are two clauses that are correctly joined with adverb connectors. In the first sentence, the adverb condition connector *if* comes in the middle of the sentence. In the second sentence, the adverb contrast connector *although* comes at the beginning of the sentence, and a comma (,) is used in the middle of the sentence.

The following example shows a way that this sentence pattern can be tested in the Structure section of the TOEFL test.

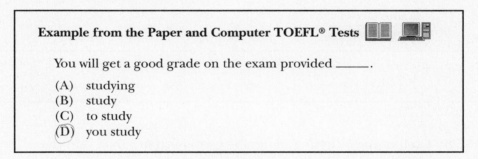

Example from the Paper and Computer TOEFL® Tests

You will get a good grade on the exam provided _____ .

(A)   studying
(B)   study
(C)   to study
(D)   you study

In this example you should quickly notice the adverb condition connector *provided*. This connector comes in the middle of the sentence; because it is a connector, it must be followed by a subject and a verb. The best answer to this question is answer (D), which contains the subject and verb *you study*.

The following chart lists adverb contrast, condition, manner, and place connectors and the sentence patterns used with them:

OTHER ADVERB CONNECTORS			
CONDITION	CONTRAST	MANNER	PLACE
if *in case* *provided* *providing* *unless* *whether*	*although* *even though* *though* *while* *whereas*	*as* *in that*	*where* *wherever*

S   V   (adverb connector)   S   V
Bob went to school   even though   he felt sick.
(adverb connector)   S   V,   S   V
Even though   Bob felt sick,   he went to school.

NOTE: A comma is often used in the middle of the sentence with a contrast connector.

*The Smith family arrived at 2:00, **while** the Jones family arrived an hour later.*

EXERCISE 8: Each of the following sentences contains more than one clause. Underline the subjects once and the verbs twice. Circle the connectors. Then indicate if the sentences are correct (C) or incorrect (I).

_C_   1. It is impossible to enter that program (if) you lack experience as a teacher.

_I_   2. The commandant left strict orders about the passes, several soldiers left the post anyway.

_I_   3. No one is admitted to the academy unless he or she the education requirements.

_C_   4. While most students turned the assignment in on time, a few asked for an extension.

_I_   5. I will take you wherever need to go to complete the registration procedures.

_____   6. I will wait here in the airport with you whether the plane leaves on time or not.

_____   7. Providing the envelope is postmarked by this Friday, your application still acceptable.

_____   8. As the nurse already explained, all visitors must leave the hospital room now.

_____   9. This exam will be more difficult than usual in that it covers two chapters instead of one.

_C_ 10. Though snow had been falling all day long, everyone got to the church on time for the wedding.

EXERCISE (Skills 6–8): Underline the subjects once and the verbs twice in each of the following sentences. Circle the connectors. Then indicate if the sentences are correct (C) or incorrect (I).

_____ 1. Until the registrar makes a decision about your status, you must stay in an unclassified category.

_____ 2. Or the bills can be paid by mail by the first of the month.

_____ 3. The parents left a phone number with the baby-sitter in case a problem with the children.

_____ 4. The furniture will be delivered as soon it is paid for.

_____ 5. Whenever you want to hold the meeting, we will schedule it.

_____ 6. The government was overthrown in a revolution, the king has not returned to his homeland.

_____ 7. Whereas most of the documents are complete, this form still needs to be notarized.

_____ 8. Trash will be collected in the morning, so you should put the trash cans out tonight.

_____ 9. It is impossible for the airplane to take off while is snowing so hard.

_____ 10. We did not go out to dinner tonight even though I would have preferred not to cook.

TOEFL EXERCISE (Skills 6–8): Choose the letter of the word or group of words that best completes the sentence.

1. The president of the United States appoints the cabinet members, _____ appointments are subject to Senate approval.

    (A) their
    (B) with their
    (C) because their
    (D) but their

2. The prisoners were prevented from speaking to reporters because _____.

    (A) not wanting the story in the papers
    (B) the story in the papers the superintendent did not want
    (C) the public to hear the story
    (D) the superintendent did not want the story in the papers

3. Like Thomas Berger's fictional character *Little Big Man,* Lauderdale managed to find himself where _____ of important events took place.

    (A) it was an extraordinary number
    (B) there was an extraordinary number
    (C) an extraordinary number
    (D) an extraordinary number existed

4. _____ sucked groundwater from below, some parts of the city have begun to sink as much as ten inches annually.

    (A) Pumps have
    (B) As pumps have
    (C) So pumps have
    (D) With pumps

5. Case studies are the target of much skepticism in the scientific community, _____ used extensively by numerous researchers.

   (A) they are
   (B) are
   (C) yet they
   (D) yet they are

6. According to the hypothesis in the study, the monarchs pick up the magnetic field of the _____ migrate by following magnetic fields.

   (A) target monarchs
   (B) target since monarchs
   (C) target since monarchs are
   (D) target

7. _____ show the relations among neurons, they do not preclude the possibility that other aspects are important.

   (A) Neural theories
   (B) A neural theory
   (C) Although neural theories
   (D) However neural theories

8. _____ or refinanced, the lender will generally require setting up an escrow account to ensure the payment of property taxes and homeowner's insurance.

   (A) A home is
   (B) A home is bought
   (C) When a home
   (D) When a home is bought

9. If ultraviolet radiation enters the Earth's atmosphere, _____ generally blocked by the ozone concentrated in the atmosphere.

   (A) it
   (B) it is
   (C) so it is
   (D) then it

10. Among human chromosomes, the Y chromosome is unusual _____ most of the chromosome does not participate in meiotic recombination.

   (A) in
   (B) so
   (C) and
   (D) in that

TOEFL REVIEW EXERCISE (Skills 1–8): Choose the letter of the word or group of words that best completes the sentence.

1. The three basic chords in _____ the tonic, the dominant, and the subdominant.

   (A) functional harmony
   (B) functional harmony is
   (C) functional harmony are
   (D) functional harmony they are

2. _____ Hale Telescope, at the Palomar Observatory in southern California, scientists can photograph objects several billion light years away.

   (A) The
   (B) With the
   (C) They use the
   (D) It is the

3. Without the proper card installed inside the computer, _____ impossible to run a graphics program.

   (A) is definitely
   (B) because of
   (C) it is
   (D) is

4. The charter for the Louisiana lottery was coming up for renewal, _____ spared no expense in the fight to win renewal.

   (A) the lottery committee
   (B) so the lottery committee and
   (C) so the lottery committee
   (D) the lottery committee made

5. While in reality Alpha Centauri is a triple star, _____ to the naked eye to be a single star.

    (A) it appears
    (B) but it appears
    (C) appears
    (D) despite it

6. The Sun's gravity severely distorted the path of the comet _____ entered its wildly erratic orbit around Jupiter.

    (A) it
    (B) when
    (C) after the comet came into it
    (D) once the comet

7. Each object _____ Jupiter's magnetic field is deluged with electrical charges.

    (A) enters
    (B) it enters
    (C) entering
    (D) enter

8. As its name suggests, the Prairie Wetlands Resource Center _____ the protection of wetlands on the prairies of the Dakotas, Montana, Minnesota, and Nebraska.

    (A) it focuses
    (B) focuses on
    (C) focusing
    (D) to focus on

9. One of the largest and most powerful birds of prey in the world, _____ a six-foot wingspan and legs and talons roughly the size of a man's arms and legs.

    (A) so the harpy has
    (B) the harpy having
    (C) with the harpy having
    (D) the harpy has

10. _____ creation of such a community was a desirable step, the requisite political upheaval had to be accepted.

    (A) Since the
    (B) The
    (C) Later, the
    (D) It was the

MORE SENTENCES WITH MULTIPLE CLAUSES _____

As we saw in Skills 6 through 8, many sentences in English have more than one clause. In Skills 9 through 12, we will see more patterns for connecting the clauses in sentences with multiple clauses. Because these patterns appear frequently in English and on the TOEFL test, you should be very familiar with them.

SKILL 9: USE NOUN CLAUSE CONNECTORS CORRECTLY

A noun clause is a clause that functions as a noun; because the noun clause is a noun, it is used in a sentence as either an object of a verb, an object of a preposition, or the subject of the sentence.

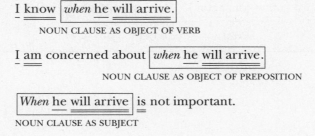

I know | *when* he will arrive.
NOUN CLAUSE AS OBJECT OF VERB

I am concerned about | *when* he will arrive.
NOUN CLAUSE AS OBJECT OF PREPOSITION

| *When* he will arrive | is not important.
NOUN CLAUSE AS SUBJECT

In the first example there are two clauses, *I know* and *he will arrive*. These two clauses are joined with the connector *when*. *When* changes the clause *he will arrive* into a noun clause that functions as the object of the verb *know*.

In the second example the two clauses *I am concerned* and *he will arrive* are also joined by the connector *when*. *When* changes the clause *he will arrive* into a noun clause that functions as the object of the preposition *about*.

The third example is more difficult. In this example there are two clauses, but they are a little harder to recognize. *He will arrive* is one of the clauses, and the connector *when* changes it into a noun clause that functions as the subject of the sentence. The other clause has the noun clause *when he will arrive* as its subject and *is* as its verb.

The following example shows how these sentence patterns could be tested in structure questions on the TOEFL test.

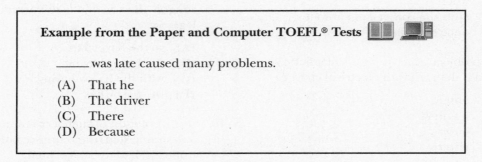

Example from the Paper and Computer TOEFL® Tests

_____ was late caused many problems.

(A) That he
(B) The driver
(C) There
(D) Because

In this example there are two verbs, *was* and *caused,* and each of these verbs needs a subject. Answer (B) is wrong because *the driver* is one subject, and two subjects are needed. Answers (C) and (D) are incorrect because *there* and *because* are not subjects. The best answer is answer (A). If you choose answer (A), the completed sentence would be: *That he was late caused many problems.* In this sentence *he* is the subject of the verb *was*, and the noun clause *that he was late* is the subject of the verb *caused*.

The following chart lists the noun clause connectors and the sentence patterns used with them:

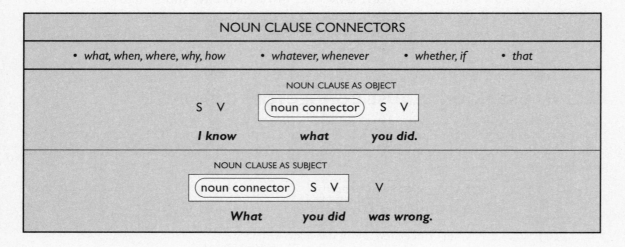

NOUN CLAUSE CONNECTORS
• *what, when, where, why, how*   • *whatever, whenever*   • *whether, if*   • *that*
NOUN CLAUSE AS OBJECT
S V   (noun connector) S V
I know   what   you did.
NOUN CLAUSE AS SUBJECT
(noun connector) S V   V
What   you did   was wrong.

EXERCISE 9: Each of the following sentences contains more than one clause. Underline the subjects once and the verbs twice. Circle the connectors. Put boxes around the noun clauses. Then indicate if the sentences are correct (C) or incorrect (I).

__C__ 1. When the season starts is determined by the weather.

__I__ 2. The manual how the device should be built.

__C__ 3. The schedule indicated if the teams would be playing in the final game.

__I__ 4. He refused to enter a plea could not be determined by the lawyer.

_____ 5. Talked about where we should go for lunch.

_____ 6. Why the condition of the patient deteriorated so rapidly it was not explained.

_____ 7. Whether or not the new office would be built was to be determined at the meeting.

_____ 8. That the professor has not yet decided when the paper is due.

_____ 9. The contract will be awarded is the question to be answered at the meeting.

__C__ 10. He always talked with whomever he pleased and did whatever he wanted.

SKILL 10:   USE NOUN CLAUSE CONNECTOR/SUBJECTS CORRECTLY

In Skill 9 we saw that noun clause connectors were used to introduce noun subject clauses or noun object clauses. In Skill 10 we will see that in some cases a noun clause connector is not just a connector; a noun clause connector can also be the subject of the clause at the same time.

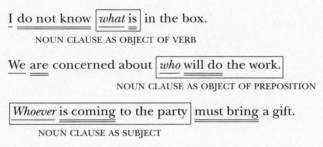

I do not know what is in the box.
    NOUN CLAUSE AS OBJECT OF VERB

We are concerned about who will do the work.
    NOUN CLAUSE AS OBJECT OF PREPOSITION

Whoever is coming to the party must bring a gift.
    NOUN CLAUSE AS SUBJECT

In the first example there are two clauses: *I do not know* and *what is in the box.* These two clauses are joined by the connector *what*. It is important to understand that in this sentence the word *what* serves two functions. It is both the subject of the verb *is* and the connector that joins the two clauses.

In the second example there are two clauses. In the first clause *we* is the subject of *are*. In the second clause *who* is the subject of *will do*. *Who* also serves as the connector that joins the two clauses. The noun clause *who will do the work* functions as the object of the preposition *about*.

In the last example there are also two clauses: *whoever* is the subject of the verb *is coming*, and the noun clause *whoever is coming to the party* is the subject of *must bring*. The word *whoever* serves two functions in the sentence: It is the subject of the verb *is coming*, and it is the connector that joins the two clauses.

The following example shows how this sentence pattern could be tested in structure questions on the TOEFL test.

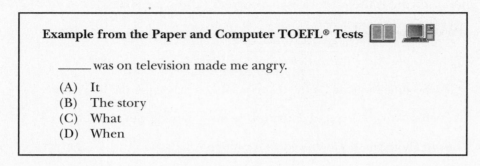

Example from the Paper and Computer TOEFL® Tests

_____ was on television made me angry.

(A) It
(B) The story
(C) What
(D) When

In this example you should notice immediately that there are two verbs, *was* and *made*, and each of those verbs needs a subject. Answers (A) and (B) are incorrect because *it* and *the story* cannot be the subject for both *was* and *made* at the same time. Answer (D) is incorrect because *when* is not a subject. In answer (C) *what* serves as both the subject of the verb *was* and the connector that joins the two clauses together; the noun clause *what was on television* is the subject of the verb *made*. Answer (C) is therefore the best answer.

The following chart lists the noun clause connector/subjects and the sentence patterns used with them:

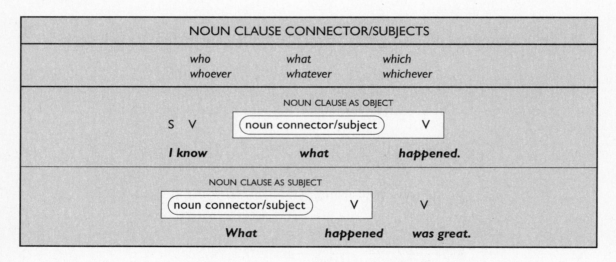

NOUN CLAUSE CONNECTOR/SUBJECTS

| who | what | which |
| whoever | whatever | whichever |

NOUN CLAUSE AS OBJECT

S   V   (noun connector/subject)   V

I know   *what*   *happened.*

NOUN CLAUSE AS SUBJECT

(noun connector/subject)   V   V

What   *happened*   *was great.*

EXERCISE 10: Each of the following sentences contains more than one clause. Underline the subjects once and the verbs twice. Circle the connectors. Put boxes around the noun clauses. Then indicate if the sentences are correct (C) or incorrect (I).

___C___ 1. The game show contestant was able to respond to (whatever) was asked.

___I___ 2. You should find out (which) the best physics department.

_____ 3. The employee was unhappy about what was added to his job description.

_____ 4. Whoever wants to take the desert tour during spring break signing up at the office.

_____ 5. The motorist was unable to discover who he had struck his car.

_____   6.   The voters should elect whichever of the candidates seems best to them.

_____   7.   It was difficult to distinguish between what was on sale and what was merely on display.

_____   8.   You should buy whatever the cheapest and most durable.

_____   9.   What was written in the letter angered him beyond belief.

_____ 10.   You can spend your time with whoever important to you.

SKILL 11:   USE ADJECTIVE CLAUSE CONNECTORS CORRECTLY

An adjective clause is a clause that describes a noun. Because the clause is an adjective, it is positioned directly after the noun that it describes.

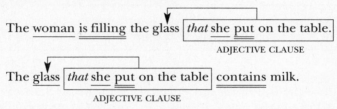

In the first example there are two clauses: *woman* is the subject of the verb *is filling,* and *she* is the subject of the verb *put. That* is the adjective clause connector that joins these two clauses, and the adjective clause *that she put on the table* describes the noun *glass.*

In the second example there are also two clauses: *glass* is the subject of the verb *contains,* and *she* is the subject of the verb *put.* In this sentence also, *that* is the adjective clause connector that joins these two clauses, and the adjective clause *that she put on the table* describes the noun *glass.*

The following example shows how these sentence patterns could be tested in structure questions on the TOEFL test.

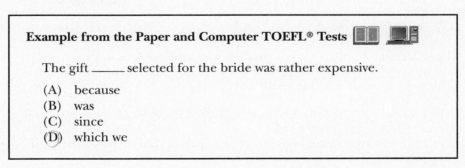

Example from the Paper and Computer TOEFL® Tests

     The gift _____ selected for the bride was rather expensive.

     (A)   because
     (B)   was
     (C)   since
     (D)   which we

In this example you should notice quickly that there are two clauses: *gift* is the subject of the verb *was,* and the verb *selected* needs a subject. Because there are two clauses, a connector is also needed. Answers (A) and (C) have connectors, but there are no subjects, so these answers are not correct. Answer (B) changes *selected* into a passive verb; in this case the sentence would have one subject and two verbs, so answer (B) is not correct. The best answer to this question is answer (D). The correct sentence should say: *The gift which we selected for the bride was rather expensive.* In this sentence *gift* is the subject of the verb *was,* *we* is the subject of the verb *selected,* and the connector *which* joins these two clauses.

The following chart lists the adjective clause connectors and the sentence patterns used with them:

ADJECTIVE CLAUSE CONNECTORS		
whom (for people)	*which* (for things)	*that* (for people or things)

S   V   （adjective connector）   S   V

I liked the book   which   you recommended.

S   （adjective connector）   S   V   V

The book   which   you recommended   was interesting.

NOTE: The adjective connectors can be omitted. This omission is very common in spoken English or in casual written English. It is not as common in formal English or in structure questions on the TOEFL test.

EXERCISE 11: Each of the following sentences contains more than one clause. Underline the subjects once and the verbs twice. Circle the connectors. Put boxes around the adjective clauses. Then indicate if the sentences are correct (C) or incorrect (I).

__C__ 1. It is important to fill out the form in the way (that) you have been instructed.

__I__ 2. The car (which) I have been driving for five years is for sale at a really good price.

__I__ 3. I just finished reading the novel whom the professor suggested for my book report.

__C__ 4. The plane that he was scheduled to take to Hawaii was delayed.

__I__ 5. The movie which we watched on cable last night it was really frightening.

__C__ 6. I made an appointment with the doctor whom you recommended.

__C__ 7. The enthusiasm with which he greeted me made me feel welcome.

__I__ 8. The story that you told me about Bob.

__I__ 9. The men with whom were having the discussion did not seem very friendly.

__C__ 10. I'm not really sure about taking part in the plans that we made last night.

SKILL 12:   USE ADJECTIVE CLAUSE CONNECTOR/SUBJECTS CORRECTLY

In Skill 11 we saw that adjective clause connectors were used to introduce clauses that describe nouns. In Skill 12 we will see that in some cases an adjective clause connector is not just a connector; an adjective clause connector can also be the subject of the clause at the same time.

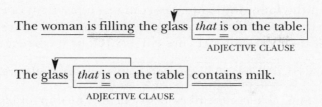

In the first example there are two clauses: *woman* is the subject of the verb *is filling*, and *that* is the subject of the verb *is*. These two clauses are joined with the connector *that*. Notice that in this example the word *that* serves two functions at the same time: it is the subject of the verb *is*, and it is the connector that joins the two clauses. The adjective clause *that is on the table* describes the noun *glass*.

In the second example, there are also two clauses: *glass* is the subject of the verb *contains*, and *that* is the subject of the verb *is*. In this example *that* also serves two functions: it is the subject of the verb *is*, and it is the connector that joins the two clauses. Because *that is on the table* is an adjective clause describing the noun *glass*, it directly follows *glass*.

The following example shows how these sentence patterns could be tested in structure questions on the TOEFL test.

Example from the Paper and Computer TOEFL® Tests

_____ is on the table has four sections.

(A) The notebook
(B) The notebook which
(C) Because the notebook
(D) In the notebook

In this example you should notice immediately that the sentence has two verbs, *is* and *has*, and each of them needs a subject. You know that *table* is not a subject because it follows the preposition *on; table* is the object of the preposition. The only answer that has two subjects is answer (B), so answer (B) is the correct answer. The correct sentence should say: *The notebook which is on the table has four sections.* In this sentence *notebook* is the subject of the verb *has*, and *which* is the subject of the verb *is*. *Which* is also the connector that joins the two clauses.

The following chart lists the adjective clause connector/subjects and the sentence patterns used with them:

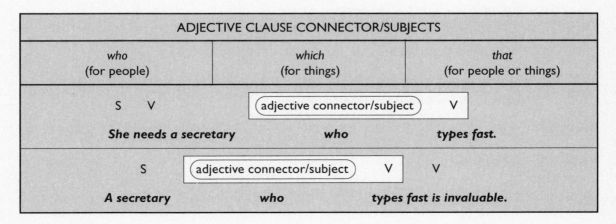

EXERCISE 12: Each of the following sentences contains more than one clause. Underline the subjects once and the verbs twice. Circle the connectors. Put boxes around the adjective clauses. Then indicate if the sentences are correct (C) or incorrect (I).

__C__ 1. The ice cream [that is served in the restaurant] has a smooth, creamy texture.

__I__ 2. The cars are trying to enter the freeway system are lined up for blocks.

__I__ 3. I have great respect for everyone who on the Dean's List.

__I__ 4. It is going to be very difficult to work with the man which just began working here.

__I__ 5. The door that leads to the vault it was tightly locked.

__C__ 6. The neighbors reported the man who was trying to break into the car to the police.

__I__ 7. These plants can only survive in an environment is extremely humid.

__I__ 8. The boss meets with any production workers who they have surpassed their quotas.

__C__ 9. The salesclerk ran after the woman who had left her credit card in the store.

__I__ 10. The shoes which matched the dress that was on sale.

EXERCISE (Skills 9–12): Each of the following sentences contains more than one clause. Underline the subjects once and the verbs twice. Circle the connectors. Put boxes around the clauses. Then indicate if the sentences are correct (C) or incorrect (I).

__I__ 1. No one explained to me whether was coming or not.

__C__ 2. The part of the structure that has already been built needs to be torn down.

__I__ 3. The girl who she just joined the softball team is a great shortstop.

__C__ 4. I have no idea about when the meeting is supposed to start.

__I__ 5. We have been told that we can leave whenever want.

__I__ 6. The racquet with whom I was playing was too big and too heavy for me.

__I__ 7. I will never understand that he did.

__I__ 8. He was still sick was obvious to the entire medical staff.

__I__ 9. What is most important in this situation it is to finish on time.

__C__ 10. The newspapers that were piled up on the front porch were an indication that the residents had not been home in some time.

TOEFL EXERCISE (Skills 9–12): Choose the letter of the word or group of words that best completes the sentence.

1. Dolphins form extremely complicated allegiances and _____ continually change.

   (A) enmities that
   (B) that are enmities
   (C) enmities that are
   (D) that enmities

2. Scientists are now beginning to conduct experiments on _____ trigger different sorts of health risks.

   (A) noise pollution can
   (B) that noise pollution
   (C) how noise pollution
   (D) how noise pollution can

3. The Apollo 11 astronauts _____ of the Earth's inhabitants witnessed on the famous first moonwalk on July 20, 1969, were Neil Armstrong and Buzz Aldrin.

   (A) whom
   (B) whom millions
   (C) were some
   (D) whom some were

4. At the end of the nineteenth century, Alfred Binet developed a test for measuring intelligence _____ served as the basis of modern IQ tests.

   (A) has
   (B) it has
   (C) and
   (D) which has

5. _____ have at least four hours of hazardous materials response training is mandated by federal law.

   (A) All police officers
   (B) All police officers must
   (C) That all police officers
   (D) For all police officers

6. A cloud's reservoir of negative charge extends upward from the altitude at _____ the freezing point.

   (A) temperatures hit
   (B) hit temperatures
   (C) which temperatures hit
   (D) which hit temperatures

7. In a 1988 advanced officers' training program, Sampson developed a plan to incorporate police in enforcing environmental protection laws whenever _____ feasible.

   (A) it is
   (B) is
   (C) has
   (D) it has

8. _____ will be carried in the next space shuttle payload has not yet been announced to the public.

   (A) It
   (B) What
   (C) When
   (D) That

9. During free fall, _____ up to a full minute, a skydiver will fall at a constant speed of 120 m.p.h.

   (A) it is
   (B) which is
   (C) being
   (D) is

10. The fact _____ the most important ratings period is about to begin has caused all the networks to shore up their schedules.

    (A) is that
    (B) of
    (C) that
    (D) what

TOEFL REVIEW EXERCISE (Skills 1–12): Choose the letter of the word or group of words that best completes the sentence.

1. _____ loom high above the northern and northeastern boundaries of the expanding city of Tucson.

   (A) The Santa Catalina mountains
   (B) Because the Santa Catalina mountains
   (C) The Santa Catalina mountains are
   (D) That the Santa Catalina mountains

2. Radioactive _____ provides a powerful way to measure geologic time.

   (A) it
   (B) dates
   (C) dating
   (D) can

3. _____ contained in the chromosomes, and they are thought of as the units of heredity.

   (A) Genes which are
   (B) Genes are
   (C) When genes
   (D) Because of genes

4. The benefit _____ the study is that it provides necessary information to anyone who needs it.

   (A) of
   (B) which
   (C) that
   (D) because

5. The same symptoms that occur _____ occur with cocaine.

   (A) amphetamines can
   (B) with amphetamines can
   (C) so amphetamines
   (D) with amphetamines they

6. Many companies across the country have molded the concepts _____ describes into an integrated strategy for preventing stress.

   (A) and Wolf
   (B) that Wolf
   (C) what Wolf
   (D) so Wolf

7. _____ in the first draft of the budget will not necessarily be in the final draft.

   (A) Although it appears
   (B) It appears
   (C) What appears
   (D) Despite its appearance

8. If a food label indicates that a food is mostly carbohydrate, it does not mean _____ is a good food to eat.

   (A) and it
   (B) and
   (C) that it
   (D) when

9. A need for space law to include commercial concerns has been recognized inasmuch _____ been expanding drastically in recent years.

   (A) the commercial launch industry
   (B) the commercial launch industry has
   (C) as has the commercial launch industry
   (D) as the commercial launch industry has

10. The report on the nuclear power plant indicated that when the plant had gone on line _____ unsafe.

   (A) and it had been
   (B) it had been
   (C) had been
   (D) that it had been

SENTENCES WITH REDUCED CLAUSES _____

It is possible in English for a clause to appear in a complete form or in a reduced form.

> My friend should be on the train *which is arriving at the station now.*
>
> *Although it was not really difficult,* the exam took a lot of time.

The first sentence shows an adjective clause in its complete form, *which is arriving at the station now,* and in its reduced form, *arriving at the station now.* The second sentence shows an adverb clause in its complete form, *although it was not really difficult,* and its reduced form, *although not really difficult.*

The two types of clauses that can reduce in English are: (1) adjective clauses and (2) adverb clauses. It is important to become familiar with these reduced clauses because they appear frequently on the TOEFL test.

SKILL 13:   USE REDUCED ADJECTIVE CLAUSES CORRECTLY

Adjective clauses can appear in a reduced form. In the reduced form, the adjective clause connector and the *be*-verb that directly follow it are omitted.

> The woman *who is waving to us* is the tour guide.
>
> The letter *which was written last week* arrived today.
>
> The pitcher *that is on the table* is full of iced tea.

Each of these sentences may be used in the complete form or in the reduced form. In the reduced form the connector *who, which,* or *that* is omitted along with the *be*-verb *is* or *was.*

If there is no *be*-verb in the adjective clause, it is still possible to have a reduced form. When there is no *be*-verb in the adjective clause, the connector is omitted and the verb is changed into the *-ing* form.

> *appearing*
> I don't understand the article *which appears in today's paper.*

In this example there is no *be*-verb in the adjective clause *which appears in today's paper,* so the connector *which* is omitted and the main verb *appears* is changed to the *-ing* form *appearing.*

It should be noted that not all adjective clauses can appear in a reduced form. An adjective clause can appear in a reduced form only if the adjective clause connector is followed directly by a verb. In other words, an adjective clause can only be reduced if the connector is also a subject.

> The woman *that I just met* is the tour guide.   (*does not reduce*)
> The letter *which you sent me* arrived yesterday.   (*does not reduce*)

In these two examples the adjective clauses cannot be reduced because the adjective clause connectors *that* and *which* are not directly followed by verbs; *that* is directly followed by the subject *I,* and *which* is directly followed by the subject *you.*

A final point to note is that some adjective clauses are set off from the rest of the sentence with commas, and these adjective clauses can also be reduced. In addition, when an adjective clause is set off with commas, the reduced adjective clause can appear at the front of the sentence.

> 1   The White House, *which is located in Washington,* is the home of the president.
> 2   The White House, *located in Washington,* is the home of the president.
> 3   *Located in Washington,* the White House is the home of the president.

> The president, *who is now preparing to give a speech,* is meeting with his advisors.
> The president, *now preparing to give a speech,* is meeting with his advisors.
> *Now preparing to give a speech,* the president is meeting with his advisors.

In these two examples, the adjective clauses are set off from the rest of the sentence with commas, so each sentence can be structured in three different ways: (1) with the complete clause, (2) with the reduced clause following the noun that it describes, and (3) with the reduced clause at the beginning of the sentence.

The following example shows how reduced adjective clauses could be tested in structure questions on the TOEFL test.

Example from the Paper and Computer TOEFL® Tests

_____ on several different television programs, the witness gave conflicting accounts of what had happened.

(A)   He appeared
(B)   Who appeared
(C)   Appearing ~~who appeared~~
(D)   Appears

In this example, answer (A) is incorrect because there are two clauses, *He appeared...* and *the witness gave...,* and there is no connector to join them. Answer (B) is incorrect because an adjective clause such as *who appeared...* cannot appear at the beginning of a sentence (unless it is in a reduced form). Answer (C) is the correct answer because it is the reduced form of the clause *who appeared,* and this reduced form can appear at the front of the sentence. Answer (D) is not the reduced form of a verb; it is merely a verb in the present tense; a verb such as *appears* needs a subject and a connector to be correct.

The following chart lists the structure for reduced adjective clauses and rules for how and when reduced forms can be used:

REDUCED ADJECTIVE CLAUSES		
with a *be*-verb in the adjective clause	~~(ADJECTIVE CONNECTOR/SUBJECT)~~ ~~(who which that)~~	~~(BE)~~
with no *be*-verb in the adjective clause	~~(ADJECTIVE CONNECTOR/SUBJECT)~~ ~~(who which that)~~	(VERB + *ING*)

- To reduce an adjective clause, omit the adjective clause connector/subject and the *be*-verb.
- If there is no *be*-verb, omit the connector/subject and change the main verb to the *-ing* form.
- Only reduce an adjective clause if the connector/subject is directly followed by the verb.
- If an adjective clause is set off with commas, the reduced clause can be moved to the front of the sentence.

EXERCISE 13: Each of the following sentences contains an adjective clause, in a complete or reduced form. Underline the adjective clauses. Then indicate if the sentences are correct (C) or incorrect (I).

_C_ 1. We will have to return the merchandise <u>purchased yesterday</u> at the Broadway.

_I_ 2. The children <u>sat in the fancy restaurant</u> found it difficult to behave.

_C_ 3. Serving a term of four years, the mayor of the town will face reelection next year.

_I_ 4. The brand new Cadillac, purchasing less than two weeks ago, was destroyed in the accident.

_I_ 5. The fans who supporting their team always come out to the games in large numbers.

_I_ 6. The suspect can be seen in the photographs were just released by the police.

_I_ 7. The food placing on the picnic table attracted a large number of flies.

_C_ 8. Impressed with everything she had heard about the course, Marie signed her children up for it.

_I_ 9. The passengers in the airport waiting room, heard the announcement of the canceled flight, groaned audibly.

_I_ 10. Dissatisfied with the service at the restaurant, the meal really was not enjoyable.

SKILL 14:   USE REDUCED ADVERB CLAUSES CORRECTLY

Adverb clauses can also appear in a reduced form. In the reduced form, the adverb connector remains, but the subject and *be*-verb are omitted.

> *Although ~~he is~~ rather unwell,* the speaker will take part in the seminar.

> *When ~~you are~~ ready,* you can begin your speech.

These two examples may be used in either the complete or reduced form. In the reduced form, the adverb connectors *although* and *when* remain; the subjects *he* and *you* as well as the *be*-verbs *is* and *are* are omitted.

If there is no *be*-verb in the adverb clause, it is still possible to have a reduced form. When there is no *be*-verb in the adverb clause, the subject is omitted and the main verb is changed into the *-ing* form.

> *feeling*
> *Although ~~he feels~~ rather sick,* the speaker will take part in the seminar.

> *giving*
> *When ~~you give~~ your speech,* you should speak loudly and distinctly.

In the first example the adverb clause *although he feels rather sick* does not include a *be*-verb; to reduce this clause, the subject *he* is omitted and the main verb *feels* is changed to *feeling*. In the second example the adverb clause *when you give your speech* also does not include a *be*-verb; to reduce this clause, the subject *you* is omitted and the main verb *give* is changed to *giving*.

The following example shows how this sentence pattern could be tested in structure questions on the TOEFL test.

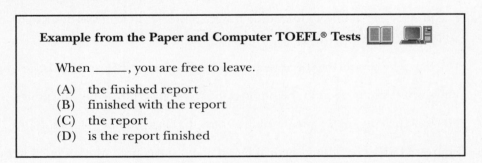

> **Example from the Paper and Computer TOEFL® Tests**
>
> When _____, you are free to leave.
>
> (A)   the finished report
> (B)   finished with the report
> (C)   the report
> (D)   is the report finished

In this example you should notice the adverb connector *when,* and you should know that this time word could be followed by either a complete clause or a reduced clause. Answers (A) and (C) contain the subjects *the finished report* and *the report* and no verb, so these answers are incorrect. In answer (D) the subject and verb are inverted, and this is not a question, so answer (D) is incorrect. The correct answer is answer (B); this answer is the reduced form of the clause *when you are finished with the report.*

It should be noted that not all adverb clauses can appear in a reduced form, and a number of adverb clauses can only be reduced if the verb is in the passive form.

Once you submit your thesis, you will graduate.   *Once ~~it is~~ submitted,* your thesis will be reviewed.
(active — does not reduce)   (passive — does reduce)

In the first example, the adverb clause *once you submit your thesis* does not reduce because clauses introduced by *once* only reduce if the verb is passive, and the verb *submit* is active. In the second example, the adverb clause *once it is submitted* does reduce to *once submitted* because the clause is introduced by *once* and the verb *is submitted* is passive.

The following chart lists the structures for reduced adverb clauses and which adverb clause connectors can be used in a reduced form:

REDUCED ADVERB CLAUSES					
with a *be*-verb in the adverb clause	(ADVERB CONNECTOR)		~~(SUBJECT)~~	~~(BE)~~	
with no *be*-verb in the adverb clause	(ADVERB CONNECTOR)		~~(SUBJECT)~~	(VERB + *ING*)	
	Time	Condition	Contrast	Place	Manner
reduces in ACTIVE	*after* *before* *since* *while*	*if* *unless* *whether*	*although* *though*		
reduces in PASSIVE	*once* *until* *when* *whenever*	*if* *unless* *whether*	*although* *though*	*where* *wherever*	*as*

- To reduce an adverb clause, omit the subject and the *be*-verb from the adverb clause.
- If there is no *be*-verb, then omit the subject and change the verb to the *-ing* form.

EXERCISE 14: Each of the following sentences contains a reduced adverb clause. Circle the adverb connectors. Underline the reduced clauses. Then indicate if the sentences are correct (C) or incorrect (I).

__C__ 1. (If) not completely satisfied, you can return the product to the manufacturer.

__I__ 2. Steve has had to learn how to cook and clean (since) left home.

__C__ 3. The ointment can be applied where needed.

__C__ 4. Tom began to look for a job after completing his master's degree in engineering.

__I__ 5. Although not selecting for the team, he attends all of the games as a fan.

__I__ 6. When purchased at this store, the buyer gets a guarantee on all items.

__C__ 7. The medicine is not effective unless taken as directed.

__I__ 8. You should negotiate a lot before buy a new car.

__C__ 9. Once purchased, the swimsuits cannot be returned.

__C__ 10. Though located near the coast, the town does not get much of an ocean breeze.

EXERCISE (Skills 13–14): Each of the following sentences contains a reduced clause. Underline the reduced clauses. Then indicate if the sentences are correct (C) or incorrect (I).

_____ 1. Though was surprised at the results, she was pleased with what she had done.

_____ 2. Wearing only a light sweater, she stepped out into the pouring rain.

_____ 3. The family stopped to visit many relatives while driving across the country.

_____ 4. The company president, needed a vacation, boarded a plane for the Bahamas.

_____ 5. When applying for the job, you should bring your letters of reference.

_____ 6. She looked up into the dreary sky was filled with dark thunderclouds.

_____ 7. Feeling weak after a long illness, Sally wanted to try to get back to work.

_____ 8. Before decided to have surgery, you should get a second opinion.

_____ 9. The construction material, a rather grainy type of wood, gave the room a rustic feeling.

_____ 10. The application will at least be reviewed if submitted by the fifteenth of the month.

TOEFL EXERCISE (Skills 13–14): Choose the letter of the word or group of words that best completes the sentence.

1. When _____ nests during spring nesting season, Canadian geese are fiercely territorial.

    (A) building
    (B) are building
    (C) built
    (D) are built

2. In 1870, Calvin, along with Adirondack hunter Alvah Dunning, made the first known ascent of Seward Mountain, _____ far from roads or trails.

    (A) a remote peak
    (B) it is a remote peak
    (C) a remote peak is
    (D) which a remote peak

3. Kokanee salmon begin to deteriorate and die soon _____ at the age of four.

    (A) they spawn
    (B) after spawning
    (C) spawn
    (D) spawned the salmon

4. _____ behind government secrecy for nearly half a century, the Hanford plant in central Washington produced plutonium for the nuclear weapons of the Cold War.

    (A) It is hidden
    (B) Hidden
    (C) Which is hidden
    (D) The plant is hiding

5. Until _____ incorrect, astronomers had assumed that the insides of white dwarfs were uniform.

    (A) they
    (B) their proof
    (C) the astronomers recently proven
    (D) recently proven

6. _____ artifacts from the early Chinese dynasties, numerous archeologists have explored the southern Silk Road.

    (A) They were searching for
    (B) It was a search for
    (C) Searched for
    (D) Searching for

7. In Hailey, the best-known lecturer was women's rights activist Abigail Scott Duniway of Portland, Oregon, who could usually be persuaded to speak _____ town visiting her son.

(A) she was in
(B) while in
(C) while she was
(D) was in

8. The National Restaurant _____ Washington, says that federal efforts to regulate workplace smoking would limit restaurants' ability to respond to the desires of their patrons.

(A) Association in
(B) Association is in
(C) Association which is in
(D) Association, based in

9. _____ in North American waterways a little over a decade ago, zebra mussels have already earned a nasty reputation for their expensive habit of clogging water pipes in the Great Lakes area.

(A) The first sighting
(B) Although first sighted
(C) Zebra mussels were first sighted
(D) First sighting

10. Small companies may take their goods abroad for trade shows without paying foreign value-added taxes by acquiring _____ an ATA carnet.

(A) a document calls
(B) a document called
(C) calls a document
(D) called a document

TOEFL REVIEW EXERCISE (Skills 1–14): Choose the letter of the word or group of words that best completes the sentence.

1. In the United States _____ approximately four million miles of roads, streets, and highways.

(A) there
(B) is
(C) they
(D) there are

2. _____ twelve million immigrants entered the United States via Ellis Island.

(A) More than
(B) There were more than
(C) Of more than
(D) The report of

3. The television, _____ so long been a part of our culture, has an enormous influence.

(A) has
(B) it has
(C) which
(D) which has

4. Psychologists have traditionally maintained that infants cannot formulate long-term memories until _____ the age of eight or nine months.

(A) they
(B) they reach
(C) to reach
(D) reach

5. _____ a cheese shop has since grown into a small conglomerate consisting of a catering business and two retail stores.

(A) In the beginning of
(B) It began as
(C) Its beginning which was
(D) What began as

6. Primarily a government contractor, _____ preferential treatment from government agencies as both a minority-group member and a woman.

(A) receives Weber
(B) Weber receives
(C) the reception of Weber
(D) according to Weber's reception

7. Because the project depends on _____ at the federal level, the city and county may have to wait until the budget cutting ends.

   (A) it happens
   (B) which happening
   (C) what happens
   (D) that it happens

8. _____ definitive study of a western hard-rock mining community cemetery appears to have been done is in Silver City, Nevada.

   (A) Most
   (B) The most
   (C) Where most
   (D) Where the most

9. One of the areas of multimedia that is growing quickly _____ is sound.

   (A) yet is easily overlooked
   (B) is easily overlooked
   (C) it is easily overlooked
   (D) that is easily overlooked

10. _____, early approaches for coping with workplace stress dealt with the problem only after its symptoms had appeared.

   (A) Although well-intending
   (B) Although it is a good intention
   (C) Although a good intention
   (D) Although well-intended

SENTENCES WITH INVERTED SUBJECTS AND VERBS

Subjects and verbs are inverted in a variety of situations in English. Inverted subjects and verbs occur most often in the formation of a question. To form a question with a helping verb (*be, have, can, could, will, would,* etc.), the subject and helping verb are inverted.

> He can go to the movies.
>
> Can he go to the movies?

> You would tell me the truth.
>
> Would you tell me the truth?

> She was sick yesterday.
>
> Was she sick yesterday?

To form a question when there is no helping verb in the sentence, the helping verb *do* is used.

> He goes to the movies.
>
> Does he go to the movies?

> You told me the truth.
>
> Did you tell me the truth?

There are many other situations in English when subjects and verbs are inverted, but if you just remember this method of inverting subjects and verbs, you will be able to handle the other situations. The most common problems with inverted subjects and verbs on the TOEFL test occur in the following situations: (1) with question words such as *what, when, where, why,* and *how;* (2) after some place expressions; (3) after negative expressions; (4) in some conditionals; and (5) after some comparisons.

SKILL 15:   INVERT THE SUBJECT AND VERB WITH QUESTION WORDS

There is some confusion about when to invert the subject and verb after question words such as *what, when, where, why,* and *how.* These words can have two very different functions in a sentence. First, they can introduce a question, and in this case the subject and verb that follow are inverted.

What is the homework?

When can I leave?

Where are you going?

Also, these words can join together two clauses, and in this case the subject and verb that follow are not inverted.

I do not know *what* the homework is.

When I can leave, I will take the first train.

Do you know *where* you are going?

In each of these examples there are two clauses joined by a question word. Notice that the subjects and verbs that follow the question words *what, when,* and *where* are not inverted in this case.

The following example shows how this sentence pattern could be tested in structure questions on the TOEFL test.

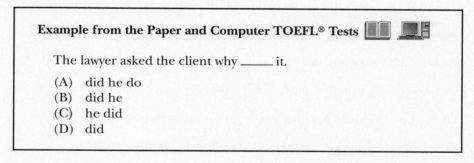

Example from the Paper and Computer TOEFL® Tests

The lawyer asked the client why _____ it.

(A)   did he do

(B)   did he

(C)   he did

(D)   did

In this example the question word *why* is used to connect the two clauses, so a subject and verb are needed after this connector; this is not a question, so the subject and verb should not be inverted. The best answer is therefore answer (C).

The following chart lists the question words and their sentence patterns:

INVERTED SUBJECTS AND VERBS WITH QUESTION WORDS
who   what   when   where   why   how
When the question word introduces a question, the subject and verb *are* inverted.
(question word)   V   S ? **What**   **are they?**
When the question word connects two clauses, the subject and verb that follow *are not* inverted.
S V   (question word)   S V. **I know**   **what**   **they are.**

EXERCISE 15: Each of the following sentences contains a question word. Circle the question words. Underline the subjects once and the verbs twice. Then indicate if the sentences are correct (C) or incorrect (I).

____I____ 1. The phone company is not certain (when) will the new directories be ready.

____C____ 2. The professor does not understand (why) so many students did poorly on the exam.

____I____ 3. How new students can get information about parking?

____C____ 4. Where is it cheapest to get typeset copies printed?

____I____ 5. Only the pilot can tell you how far can the plane go on one tank of fuel. *not question*

____C____ 6. What type of security does he prefer for his investments?

____C____ 7. Not even the bank president knows when the vault will be opened.

____I____ 8. How long it has been since you arrived in the United States?

____C____ 9. The jury doubts what the witness said under cross-examination.

____C____ 10. Do you know why he wants to take an extended leave of absence?

SKILL 16:   INVERT THE SUBJECT AND VERB WITH PLACE EXPRESSIONS

After ideas expressing place, the subject and the verb sometimes invert in English. This can happen with single words expressing place, such as *here, there,* or *nowhere.*

> *Here* is the book that you lent me.
> *There* are the keys that I thought I lost.
> *Nowhere* have I seen such beautiful weather.

In the first example the place word *here* causes the subject *book* to come after the verb *is*. In the second example the place word *there* causes the subject *keys* to come after the verb *are*. In the last example the place word *nowhere* causes the subject *I* to come after the verb *have*.

The subject and verb can also be inverted after <u>prepositional phrases expressing place</u>.

> *In the closet* <u>are</u> the <u>clothes</u> that you want.
>
> *Around the corner* <u>is</u> Sam's <u>house</u>.
>
> *Beyond the mountains* <u>lies</u> the <u>town</u> where you will live.

In the first example the prepositional phrase of place *in the closet* causes the subject *clothes* to come after the verb *are*. In the second example the prepositional phrase of place *around the corner* causes the subject *house* to come after the verb *is*. In the last example the prepositional phrase of place *beyond the mountains* causes the subject *town* to come after the verb *lies*.

It is important (and a bit difficult) to understand that the subject and verb will invert after place expressions at the beginning of a sentence only when the place expression is *necessary* to complete the sentence. Study the following examples:

> *In the forest* <u>are</u> many exotic <u>birds</u>.
>
> *In the forest* <u>I</u> <u>walked</u> for many hours.

In the first example the subject *birds* and verb *are* are inverted because the place expression *in the forest* is needed to complete the idea *many exotic birds are....* In the second example the subject *I* and the verb *walked* are not inverted because the idea *I walked for many hours* is complete without the place expression *in the forest*; the place expression is therefore not needed to complete the sentence.

The following example shows how this sentence pattern could be tested in structure questions on the TOEFL test.

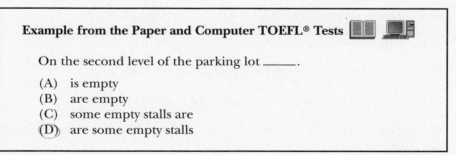

Example from the Paper and Computer TOEFL® Tests

On the second level of the parking lot _____.

(A) is empty
(B) are empty
(C) some empty stalls are
(D) are some empty stalls

This example begins with the place expression *on the second level of the parking lot,* which consists of two prepositional phrases, *on the second level* and *of the parking lot*. This sentence needs a subject and a verb to be complete, and the two answers that contain both a subject, *stalls,* and verb, *are,* are answers (C) and (D). The subject and verb should be inverted because the place expression is necessary to complete the idea *some empty stalls are....* The best answer is therefore answer (D).

The following chart lists the sentence patterns used with place expressions:

INVERTED SUBJECTS AND VERBS WITH PLACE EXPRESSIONS
When a place expression at the front of the sentence is *necessary* to complete the sentence, the subject and verb that follow *are* inverted.
(PLACE (necessary))   V   S
In the classroom   were some old desks.
When a place expression at the front of the sentence contains *extra* information that is *not* needed to complete the sentence, the subject and verb that follow *are not* inverted.
(PLACE (extra))   S   V
In the classroom,   I studied very hard.

EXERCISE 16: Each of the following sentences contains an expression of place at the beginning of the sentence. Circle the expressions of place. Look at the clauses that immediately follow the place expressions and underline the subjects once and the verbs twice. Then indicate if the sentences are correct (C) or incorrect (I).

__C__ 1. (In front of the house) were some giant trees.

__I__ 2. (There) a big house is on the corner.

__C__ 3. In the cave was a vast treasure of gems and jewels.

__I__ 4. To the north the stream is that the settlers will have to cross.

__C__ 5. Around the corner are the offices that you are trying to find.

____ 6. At the Italian restaurant was the food too spicy for my taste.

__I__ 7. Nowhere in the world farmers can grow such delicious food.

__I__ 8. In the backyard the two trees are that need to be pruned.

__C__ 9. Around the recreation hall and down the path are the tents where we will be staying this week.

__I__ 10. In the apartment next to mine, a man and a woman were having a heated discussion.

Skill 17:   INVERT THE SUBJECT AND VERB WITH NEGATIVES

The subject and verb can also be inverted after certain negatives and related expressions. When negative expressions, such as *no, not,* or *never,* come at the beginning of a sentence, the subject and verb are inverted.

Not once did I miss a question.

Never has Mr. Jones taken a vacation.

At *no time* can the woman talk on the telephone.

In the first example the negative expression *not once* causes the subject *I* to come after the helping verb *did*. In the second example the negative word *never* causes the subject *Mr. Jones* to come after the helping verb *has*. In the last example the negative expression *at no time* causes the subject *woman* to come after the helping verb *can*.

Certain words in English, such as *hardly, barely, scarcely,* and *only,* act like negatives. If one of these words comes at the beginning of a sentence, the subject and verb are also inverted.

Hardly ever does he take time off.

(This means that he *almost never* takes time off.)

Only once did the manager issue overtime paychecks.

(This means that the manager *almost never* issued overtime paychecks.)

In the first example the "almost negative" expression *hardly ever* causes the subject *he* to come after the helping verb *does*. In the second example the "almost negative" expression *only once* causes the subject *manager* to come after the helping verb *did*.

When a negative expression appears in front of a subject and verb in the middle of a sentence, the subject and verb are also inverted. This happens often with the negative words *neither* and *nor*.

I do not want to go, and *neither* does Tom.

The secretary is not attending the meeting, *nor* is her boss.

In the first example the negative *neither* causes the subject *Tom* to come after the helping verb *does*. In the second example the negative *nor* causes the subject *boss* to come after the verb *is*.

The following example shows how this sentence pattern could be tested in structure questions on the TOEFL test.

Example from the Paper and Computer TOEFL® Tests

Only in extremely dangerous situations _____ stopped.

(A)   will be the printing presses
(B)   the printing presses will be
(C)   that the printing presses will be
(D)   will the printing presses be

In this example you should notice that the sentence begins with the negative *only,* so an inverted subject and verb are needed. Answer (D) contains a correctly inverted subject and verb, with the helping verb *will,* the subject *printing presses,* and the main verb *be,* so answer (D) is the best answer.

The following chart lists the negative expressions and the sentence pattern used with them:

INVERTED SUBJECTS AND VERBS WITH NEGATIVES					
no	*not*	*never*	*neither*	*nor*	
barely	*hardly*	*only*	*rarely*	*scarcely*	*seldom*

When a negative expression appears *in front of* a subject and verb (at the beginning of a sentence or in the middle of a sentence) the subject and verb *are* inverted.

(negative expression)   V   S

Rarely   ***were they so happy.***

EXERCISE 17: Each of the following sentences contains a negative or "almost negative" expression. Circle the negative expressions. Look at the clauses that follow and underline the subjects once and the verbs twice. Then indicate if the sentences are correct (C) or incorrect (I).

_I_ 1. (Never) the boy wrote to his sisters.

_C_ 2. (On no occasion) did they say that to me.

_C_ 3. Steve did not win the prize, nor did he expect to do so.

_I_ 4. Only once in my life gone I have to New York City.

_I_ 5. Did he go out of the house at no time.

_I_ 6. Seldom their secretary has made such mistakes.

_C_ 7. No sooner had she hung up the phone than it rang again.

_I_ 8. Sheila did not arrive late for work, nor she left early.

_C_ 9. Barely had he finished the exam when the graduate assistant collected the papers.

_C_ 10. The police did not arrive in time to save the girl, and neither did the paramedics.

SKILL 18:   INVERT THE SUBJECT AND VERB WITH CONDITIONALS

In certain conditional structures, the subject and verb may also be inverted. This can occur when the helping verb in the conditional clause is *had, should,* or *were,* and the conditional connector *if* is omitted.

If he had taken more time, the results would have been better.

Had he taken more time, the results would have been better.

> I would help you *if* I were in a position to help.
>
> I would help you were I in a position to help.
>
> *If* you should arrive before 6:00, just give me a call.
>
> Should you arrive before 6:00, just give me a call.

In each of these examples you can see that when *if* is included, the subject and verb are in the regular order (*if he had taken, if I were, if you should arrive*). It is also possible to omit *if;* in this case, the subject and verb are inverted (*had he taken, were I, should you arrive*).

The following example shows how this sentence pattern could be tested in structure questions on the TOEFL test.

Example from the Paper and Computer TOEFL® Tests

The report would have been accepted _____ in checking its accuracy.

(A)   if more care

(B)   more care had been taken

(C)   had taken more care

(D)   had more care been taken

In this example a connector *if* and a subject and verb are needed, but *if* could be omitted and the subject and verb inverted. Answer (A) is incorrect because it contains the connector *if* and the subject *care* but no verb. Answer (B) is incorrect because it contains the subject *care* and the verb *had been taken* but does not have a connector. In answers (C) and (D), *if* has been omitted. Because it is correct to invert the subject *more care* and the helping verb *had,* answer (D) is correct.

The following chart lists the conditional verbs that may invert and the sentence patterns used with them:

INVERTED SUBJECTS AND VERBS WITH CONDITIONALS
had   *should*   *were*
When the verb in the conditional clause is *had, should,* or *were,* it is possible to omit *if* and invert the subject and verb.
(omitted *if*)   V   S **Were he   here, he would help.**
It is also possible to keep *if.* Then the subject and verb *are not* inverted.
if   S   V **If   he were   here, he would help.**

EXERCISE 18: Each of the following sentences contains a conditional with a stated or an implied *if*. Circle the conditionals, or put an asterisk (*) where *if* has been omitted. Look at the clauses that follow and underline the subjects once and the verbs twice. Then indicate if the sentences are correct (C) or incorrect (I).

___C___ 1. *Were our neighbors a bit more friendly, it would be somewhat easier to get to know them.

___I___ 2. There are plenty of blankets in the closet if should you get cold during the night.   *should you get cold*

___I___ 3. Has he enough vacation days left this year, he will take two full weeks off in December.   *not*

___C___ 4. Had we been informed of the decision, we might have had something to say about it.

___I___ 5. I would like to know could you help me pack these boxes.   *if you*

___I___ 6. He would have been in big trouble had not he remembered the assignment at the last minute.

___C___ 7. If your friends come to visit, will they stay in a hotel or at your house?

___C___ 8. He might be a little more successful today were he a little more willing to do some hard work.

___C___ 9. Should you ever visit this town again, I would be delighted to show you around.

___C___ 10. Do you think that she would give the speech were she asked to do so?

Skill 19:   INVERT THE SUBJECT AND VERB WITH COMPARISONS

An inverted subject and verb may also occur after a comparison. The inversion of a subject and verb after a comparison is optional, rather than required, and it is a rather formal structure. There have been a number of inverted comparisons on recent TOEFL tests, so you should be familiar with this structure.

My sister spends *more* hours in the office *than* John.

My sister spends *more* hours in the office *than* John does.

My sister spends *more* hours in the office *than* does John.

All three of these examples contain the comparison *more…than,* and all three are correct in English. It is possible to have the noun *John* alone, as in the first example; it is possible that the comparison is followed by the subject and verb *John does,* as in the second example; it is also possible that the comparison is followed by the inverted subject and verb *does John,* as in the third example.

The following example shows how this sentence pattern could be tested in structure questions on the TOEFL test.

> **Example from the Paper and Computer TOEFL® Tests** 📖 🖥️
>
> The results of the current experiment appear to be more consistent than _____ the results of any previous tests.
>
> (A) them
> (B) were
> (C) they were
> (D) were they

In this example you should notice the comparison *more consistent than,* and you should also understand that *the results of the current experiment* is being compared with *the results of any previous tests.* Because *the results of any previous tests* is the subject, only a verb is needed; the best answer to this question is therefore answer (B). We know that it is possible for a subject and a verb to be inverted after a comparison, and in this case the subject *the results of any previous tests* comes after the verb *were.*

The following chart lists the sentence patterns used with comparisons:

INVERTED SUBJECTS AND VERBS WITH COMPARISONS		
The subject and verb *may* invert after a comparison. The following structures are both possible.		
S V (comparison) S V We were more prepared than the other performers were.		
S V (comparison) V S We were more prepared than were the other performers.		
NOTE: A subject-verb inversion after a comparison sounds rather formal.		

EXERCISE 19: Each of the following sentences contains a comparison. Circle the comparisons. Look at the clauses that follow and underline the subjects once and the verbs twice. Then indicate if the sentences are correct (C) or incorrect (I).

__C__ 1. This candidate has received (more votes than) has any other candidate in previous years.

__I__ 2. Obviously we were much (more impressed with the performance than) did the other members of the audience.

__C__ 3. The film that we saw last night at the festival was far better than any of the other films.

__C__ 4. The vegetables at the market this morning were far fresher than were those at the market yesterday.

__I__ 5. I am afraid that is the condition of these tires as bad as the condition of the others.

_____ 6. We firmly believed that our team could achieve a much faster time than any of the others.

_____ 7. This apple pie is not as good as the last one that you made.

_____ 8. On the fishing trip, Bobby caught twice as many fish as anyone else did.

_____ 9. The final speaker gave us more details than had any of the previous speakers.

_____ 10. Do you know why does he need to sleep so many more hours than do the others?

EXERCISE (Skills 15–19): Each of these sentences contains a structure that could require an inverted subject and verb. Circle the structures that may require inverted subjects and verbs. Underline the subjects once and the verbs twice. Then indicate if the sentences are correct (C) or incorrect (I).

_____ 1. The town council is not sure why have the land developers changed their plans.

_____ 2. Never in the world I believed that this would happen.

_____ 3. The day might have been a little more enjoyable had the sun been out a little more.

_____ 4. Only once did the judge take the defense lawyer's suggestion.

_____ 5. Down the hall to the left the offices are that need to be painted.

_____ 6. Did the scientist explain what he put in the beaker?

_____ 7. Hardly ever it snows in this section of the country.

_____ 8. Elijah scored more points in yesterday's basketball final than had any other player in history.

_____ 9. In the state of California, earthquakes occur regularly.

_____ 10. He should ever call again, please tell him that I am not at home.

TOEFL EXERCISE (Skills 15–19): Choose the letter of the word or group of words that best completes the sentence.

1. Rarely _____ located near city lights or at lower elevations.

   (A) observatories are
   (B) are
   (C) in the observatories
   (D) are observatories

2. There are geographic, economic, and cultural reasons why _____ around the world.

   (A) diets differ
   (B) do diets differ
   (C) are diets different
   (D) to differ a diet

3. Were _____ millions of dollars each year replenishing eroding beaches, the coastline would be changing even more rapidly.

(A) the U.S. Army Corps of Engineers not spending
(B) the U.S. Army Corps of Engineers not spend
(C) the U.S. Army Corps of Engineers does not spend
(D) not spending the U.S. Army Corps of Engineers

4. Nowhere _____ more skewed than in the auto industry.

(A) that retail trade figures
(B) retail trade figures are
(C) are retail trade figures
(D) retail trade figures

5. New York City's Central Park is nearly twice as large _____ second smallest country, Monaco.

(A) as
(B) is the
(C) as is
(D) as is the

6. Potassium has a valence of positive one because it usually loses one electron when _____ with other elements.

(A) does it combine
(B) it combines
(C) in combining
(D) combination

7. The economic background of labor legislation will not be mentioned in this course, _____ be treated.

(A) trade unionism will not
(B) nor trade unionism will
(C) nor will trade unionism
(D) neither trade unionism will

8. _____ test positive for antibiotics when tanker trucks arrive at a milk processing plant, according to federal law, the entire truckload must be discarded.

(A) Should milk
(B) If milk
(C) If milk is
(D) Milk should

9. Located behind _____ the two lacrimal glands.

(A) each eyelid
(B) is each eyelid
(C) each eyelid are
(D) each eyelid which is

10. Only for a short period of time _____ run at top speed.

(A) cheetahs
(B) do cheetahs
(C) that a cheetah can
(D) can

TOEFL REVIEW EXERCISE (Skills 1–19): Choose the letter of the word or group of words that best completes the sentence.

1. _____ variety of flowers in the show, from simple carnations to the most exquisite roses.

(A) A wide
(B) There was a wide
(C) Was there
(D) Many

2. The wedges _____ dart board are worth from one to twenty points each.

(A) they are on a
(B) are on a
(C) are they on a
(D) on a

3. _____ producing many new movies for release after the new season begins.

   (A) His company is
   (B) His companies
   (C) The company
   (D) Why the company is

4. _____ that Emily Dickinson wrote, 24 were given titles and 7 were published during her lifetime.

   (A) Of the 1,800 poems
   (B) There were 1,800 poems
   (C) Because the 1,800 poems
   (D) The 1,800 poems

5. Since an immediate change was needed on an emergency basis, _____ by the governor to curtail railway expenditure.

   (A) so it was proposed
   (B) was proposed
   (C) because of the proposal
   (D) it was proposed

6. In the Morgan Library in New York City _____ of medieval and Renaissance manuscripts.

   (A) a collection is
   (B) in a collection
   (C) is a collection
   (D) which is a collection

7. Some fishing fleets might not have been so inefficient in limiting their catch to target species _____ more strict in enforcing penalties.

   (A) the government had been
   (B) if the government had
   (C) had the government been
   (D) if the government

8. The Dewey Decimal System, currently used in libraries throughout the world, _____ all written works into ten classes according to subject.

   (A) dividing
   (B) divides
   (C) it would divide
   (D) was divided

9. Individual differences in brain-wave activity may shed light on why some people are more prone to emotional stress disorders _____.

   (A) that others are
   (B) and others are
   (C) others are
   (D) than are others

10. _____ squeezed, the orange juice in a one-cup serving provides twice the minimum daily requirement for vitamin C.

   (A) It is freshly
   (B) If freshly
   (C) You freshly
   (D) If it freshly

THE WRITTEN EXPRESSION QUESTIONS

(PAPER TOEFL® TEST AND COMPUTER TOEFL® TEST)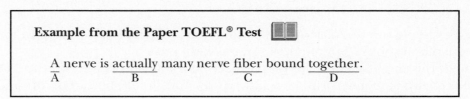

Written expression questions that test your knowledge of the correct way to express your-self in English writing appear on both the paper TOEFL test and the computer TOEFL test. Each question consists of one sentence in which four words or groups of words have been underlined. You must choose the underlined word or group of words that is not cor-rect. Look at an example of a written expression question from the paper TOEFL test.

Example from the Paper TOEFL® Test

A nerve is actually many nerve fiber bound together.
A　　　　　B　　　　　　　　C　　　　D

In this example, you should notice that the plural quantifier *many* is accompanied by the singular noun *fiber. Many* should be accompanied by the plural noun *fibers.* You should choose answer (C) because answer (C) is not correct.

Now, look at an example of a written expression question from the computer TOEFL test.

Example from the Computer TOEFL® Test

Venus emits very intense radio waves of thermally origin.

In this example, you should notice that the adverb *thermally* is used to describe the noun *origin.* The adjective *thermal* should be used to describe the noun. You should click on the word *thermally* to answer this question because *thermally* is not correct.

PROCEDURES FOR THE WRITTEN EXPRESSION QUESTIONS
(Paper TOEFL® Test and Computer TOEFL® Test)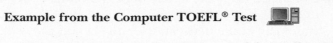

1. **First, look at the underlined words or groups of words.** You want to see if you can spot which of the four answer choices is *not* correct.

2. **If you have been unable to find the error by looking only at the four underlined expressions, then read the complete sentence.** Often an underlined expression is incorrect because of something in another part of the sentence.

Next, you should move on to the language skills. The following language skills will help you to implement the appropriate strategies and procedures in written expression ques-tions on both the paper TOEFL test and the computer TOEFL test.

PROBLEMS WITH SUBJECT/VERB AGREEMENT _____

Subject/verb agreement is simple: if the subject of a sentence is singular, then the verb must be singular; if the subject of the sentence is plural, then the verb must be plural. An *s* on a verb usually indicates that a verb is singular, while an *s* on a noun usually indicates that the noun is plural. (Do not forget irregular plurals of nouns, such as *women, children,* and *people.*)

The <u>boy</u> <u><u>walks</u></u> to school.

The <u>boys</u> <u><u>walk</u></u> to school.

In the first example the singular subject *boy* requires a singular verb, *walks.* In the second example the plural subject *boys* requires a plural verb, *walk.*

Although this might seem quite simple, there are a few situations on the TOEFL test when subject/verb agreement can be a little tricky. You should be careful of subject/verb agreement in the following situations: (1) after prepositional phrases, (2) after expressions of quantity, (3) after inverted verbs, and (4) after certain words, such as *anybody, everything, no one, something, each,* and *every.*

Skill 20:   MAKE VERBS AGREE AFTER PREPOSITIONAL PHRASES

Sometimes prepositional phrases can come between the subject and the verb. If the object of the preposition is singular and the subject is plural, or if the object of the preposition is plural and the subject is singular, there can be confusion in making the subject and verb agree.

The <u>key</u> (to the doors) <u><u>are</u></u>* in the drawer.

SINGULAR   PLURAL

The <u>keys</u> (to the door) <u><u>is</u></u>* in the drawer.

PLURAL   SINGULAR

(* indicates an error)

In the first example you might think that *doors* is the subject because it comes directly in front of the verb *are.* However, *doors* is not the subject because it is the object of the preposition *to.* The subject of the sentence is *key,* so the verb should be *is.* In the second example you might think that *door* is the subject because it comes directly in front of the verb *is.* You should recognize in this example that *door* is not the subject because it is the object of the preposition *to.* Because the subject of the sentence is *keys,* the verb should be *are.*

The following chart outlines the key information that you should understand about subject/verb agreement with prepositional phrases:

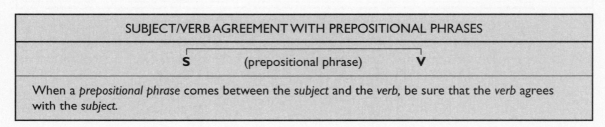

SUBJECT/VERB AGREEMENT WITH PREPOSITIONAL PHRASES
S   (prepositional phrase)   **V**
When a *prepositional phrase* comes between the *subject* and the *verb,* be sure that the *verb* agrees with the *subject.*

EXERCISE 20: Each of the following sentences has one or more prepositional phrases between the subject and verb. Circle the prepositional phrases. Underline the subjects once and the verbs twice. Then indicate if the sentences are correct (C) or incorrect (I).

_C_ 1. The climbers (on the sheer face) (of the mountain) need to be rescued.

_I_ 2. The interrogation, conducted (by three police officers,) have lasted for several hours.

_I_ 3. The tenants in the apartment next to mine is giving a party this evening.

_C_ 4. The president, surrounded by secret service agents, is trying to make his way to the podium.

_C_ 5. The buildings destroyed during the fire are being rebuilt at the taxpayers' expense.

_C_ 6. Because of the seriousness of the company's financial problems, the board of directors have called an emergency meeting.

_C_ 7. Manufacture of the items that you requested have been discontinued because of lack of profit on those items.

_I_ 8. Further development of any new ideas for future products has to be approved in advance.

_I_ 9. The scheduled departure time of the trains, posted on panels throughout the terminal buildings, are going to be updated.

_I_ 10. Any houses built in that development before 1970 have to be upgraded to meet current standards.

Skill 21:   MAKE VERBS AGREE AFTER EXPRESSIONS OF QUANTITY

A particular agreement problem occurs when the subject is an expression of quantity, such as *all*, *most*, or *some*, followed by the preposition *of*. In this situation, the subject (*all*, *most*, or *some*) can be singular or plural, depending on what follows the preposition *of*.

All (of the *book*) was interesting.

SINGULAR

All (of the *books*) were interesting.

PLURAL

All (of the *information*) was interesting.

UNCOUNTABLE

In the first example the subject *all* refers to the singular noun *book*, so the correct verb is therefore the singular verb *was*. In the second example the subject *all* refers to the plural noun *books*, so the correct verb is the plural verb *were*. In the third example the subject *all* refers to the uncountable noun *information*, so the correct verb is therefore the singular verb *was*.

The following chart outlines the key information that you should understand about subject/verb agreement after expressions of quantity:

SUBJECT/VERB AGREEMENT AFTER EXPRESSIONS OF QUANTITY
all *most* *some* *half*   OF THE (OBJECT)   **V**
When an expression of quantity is the subject, the verb agrees with the object.

EXERCISE 21: Each of the following sentences has a quantity expression as the subject. Underline the subjects once and the verbs twice. Circle the objects that the verbs agree with. Then indicate if the sentences are correct (C) or incorrect (I).

____C____ 1. The witnesses saw that most of the (fire) in the hills was extinguished.

____I____ 2. Some of the (animals) from the zoo was released into the animal preserve.

____I____ 3. All of the (students) in the class taught by Professor Roberts is required to turn in their term papers next Monday.

____I____ 4. Half of the (food) that we are serving to the guests are still in the refrigerator.

____C____ 5. We believe that some of the (time) of the employees is going to be devoted to quality control.

____C____ 6. All of the (witnesses) in the jury trial, which lasted more than two weeks, have indicated that they believed that the defendant was guilty.

____I____ 7. She did not know where most of the (people) in the room was from.

____I____ 8. In spite of what was decided at the meeting, half of the (procedures) was not changed.

____C____ 9. I was sure that all of the (questions) on the test were correct.

____C____ 10. Most of the (trouble) that the employees discussed at the series of meetings was resolved within a few weeks.

SKILL 22: MAKE INVERTED VERBS AGREE

We have seen that sometimes in English the subject comes after the verb. This can occur after question words (Skill 15), after place expressions (Skill 16), after negative expressions (Skill 17), after omitted conditionals (Skill 18), and after some comparisons (Skill 19). When the subject and verb are inverted, it can be difficult to locate them, and it can therefore be a problem to make them agree.

(Behind the house) was* the bicycles I wanted.

(Behind the houses) were* the bicycle I wanted.

In the first example it is easy to think that *house* is the subject, because it comes directly in front of the verb *was*. *House* is not the subject, however, because it is the object of the preposition *behind*. The subject of the sentence is *bicycles,* and the subject *bicycles* comes after the verb because of the place expression *behind the house*. Because the subject *bicycles* is plural, the verb should be changed to the plural *were*. In the second example the subject *bicycle* comes after the verb *were* because of the place expression *behind the houses*. Because the subject *bicycle* is singular, the verb should be changed to the singular *was*.

The following chart outlines the key information that you should understand about subject/verb agreement after inverted verbs:

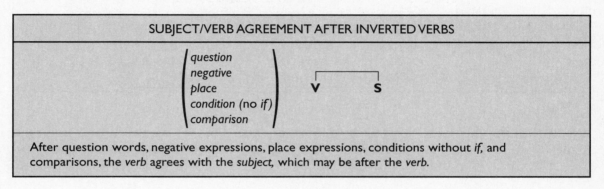

SUBJECT/VERB AGREEMENT AFTER INVERTED VERBS
question *negative* *place* *condition (no if)* *comparison*   **V   S**
After question words, negative expressions, place expressions, conditions without *if*, and comparisons, the *verb* agrees with the *subject,* which may be after the *verb*.

EXERCISE 22: Each of the following sentences contains an inverted subject and verb. Circle the word or group of words that causes the subject and verb to invert. Find the subject and verb that follow these words. Underline the subject once and the verb twice. Then indicate if the sentences are correct (C) or incorrect (I).

__C__ 1. (Only once) this morning were the letters delivered by the campus mail service.

__I__ 2. (Around the corner and to the right) is the rooms that have been assigned to that program.

__I__ 3. (What in the world is the children trying to do?

__I__ 4. (John would be studying the chapters were he able to get hold of the book.

__I__ 5. (This chapter has many more exercises than do the next one.

__I__ 6. (The computer programmer was unaware that there was so many mistakes in the program he had written.

__I__ 7. (Seldom in the history of television has two new comedies been so successful in one season.

__I__ 8. (How many huge mistakes have the teacher actually found in the research paper?

__C__ 9. (The new phone system is able to hold far more messages than was the phone system that had previously been used.

__I__ 10. (In the parking lot south of the stadium was the cars that were about to be towed.

Skill 23:   Make Verbs Agree After Certain Words

Certain words in English are always grammatically singular, even though they might have plural meanings.

Everybody are going* to the theater.

Even though we understand from this example that a lot of people are going to the theater, *everybody* is singular and requires a singular verb. The plural verb *are going* should be changed to the singular verb *is going*.

The following chart lists the grammatically singular words that have plural meanings:

SUBJECT/VERB AGREEMENT AFTER CERTAIN WORDS
These words or expressions are grammatically singular, so they take singular verbs:

anybody	*everybody*	*nobody*	*somebody*	*each* (+ noun)
anyone	*everyone*	*no one*	*someone*	*every* (+ noun)
anything	*everything*	*nothing*	*something*	

EXERCISE 23: Each of the following sentences contains one of the words that are grammatically singular but have plural meanings. Underline these words once and underline the verbs twice. Then indicate if the sentences are correct (C) or incorrect (I).

___I___   1.   It is impossible to believe that somebody actually admire that man.

___C___   2.   Each of the doctors in the building needs to have a separate reception area.

___I___   3.   The president felt that no one were better suited for the position of chief staff advisor.

___I___   4.   Everybody participating in the fund-raiser are to turn in the tickets by 8:00.

___C___   5.   Because of the low number of orders, nothing has to be done now.

___I___   6.   Every time someone take unnecessary breaks, precious moments of production time are lost.

___C___   7.   Anybody who goes to the top of the Empire State Building is impressed with the view.

___I___   8.   Every man, woman, and child in this line are required to sign the forms in order to complete the registration process.

___C___   9.   It is nice to believe that anything is possible if a person tries hard enough.

___I___   10.   The company reiterated to reporters that nobody have been dismissed because of the incident.

WRITTEN EXPRESSION QUESTIONS (Paper and Computer)   253

EXERCISE (Skills 20–23): Underline the subjects once and the verbs twice in each of the following sentences. Then indicate if the sentences are correct (C) or incorrect (I).

_____ 1. The contracts signed by the company has been voided because some stipulations were not met.

_____ 2. Ten miles beyond the river was the farmlands that they had purchased with their life savings.

_____ 3. Each package that is not properly wrapped have to be returned to the sender.

_____ 4. She would not have to enter the house through the bedroom window were the keys where they were supposed to be.

_____ 5. The proposal brought so much new work to the partnership that there was not enough hours to complete all of it.

_____ 6. The box of disks for the computer have been misplaced.

_____ 7. It is disconcerting to believe that every possible candidate has been rejected for one reason or another.

_____ 8. Only once have there been more excitement in this city about a sporting event.

_____ 9. Bobby has a bigger bicycle than does the other children in the neighborhood.

_____ 10. If nobody have bought that car from the dealer, then you should return and make another offer.

TOEFL EXERCISE (Skills 20–23): Choose the letter of the word or group of words that best completes the sentence.

1. Among bees _____ a highly elaborate form of communication.

   (A) occur
   (B) occurs
   (C) it occurs
   (D) they occur

2. _____ heated by solar energy have special collectors on the roofs to trap sunlight.

   (A) A home is
   (B) Homes are
   (C) A home
   (D) Homes

Choose the letter of the underlined word or group of words that is not correct.

_____ 3. Each number in a binary system are formed from only two symbols.
                        A   B   C   D

_____ 4. Scientists at the medical center is trying to determine if there is a relationship
                                        A   B   C
between saccharine and cancer.
         D

_____ 5. On the rim of the Kilauea volcano in the Hawaiian Islands are a hotel called the
A   B   C   D
Volcano Hotel.

_____ 6. The great digital advances of the electronic age, such as integrated circuitry and a
A   B
microcomputer, has been planted in tiny chips.
C   D

_____ 7. There are many frequently mentioned reasons why one out of four arrests involve a
A   B   C   D
juvenile.

_____ 8. Kepler's Laws, principles outlining planetary movement, was formulated based on
A   B   C
observations made without a telescope.
D

_____ 9. Only with a two-thirds vote by both houses are the U.S. Congress able to override a
A   B   C
presidential veto.
D

_____ 10. Of all the evidence that has piled up since Webster's paper was published, there is no
A   B
new ideas to contradict his original theory.
C   D

TOEFL REVIEW EXERCISE (Skills 1–23): Choose the letter of the word or group of words that best completes the sentence.

1. _____ several unsuccessful attempts, Robert Peary reached the North Pole on April 6, 1909.

   (A) After
   (B) He made
   (C) When
   (D) His

2. The musical instrument _____ is six feet long.

   (A) is called the bass
   (B) it is called the bass
   (C) called the bass
   (D) calls the bass

3. One problem with all languages _____ they are full of irregularities.

   (A) when
   (B) so
   (C) is that
   (D) in case

4. _____ of economic cycles been helpful in predicting turning points in cycles, they would have been used more consistently.

   (A) Psychological theories
   (B) Psychological theories have
   (C) Had psychological theories
   (D) Psychologists have theories

5. Hospital committees _____ spent weeks agonizing over which artificial kidney candidate would receive the treatments now find that the decision is out of their hands.

   (A) once
   (B) that once
   (C) have
   (D) once had

Choose the letter of the underlined word or group of words that is not correct.

_____ 6. More than half of the children in the 1,356-member district qualifies for
               A   B   C
      reduced-price or free lunches.
           D

_____ 7. Five miles beyond the hills were a fire with its flames reaching up to the sky.
                          A   B   C   D

_____ 8. Kettledrums, what were first played on horseback, were incorporated into the
                  A   B   C   D
      orchestra in the eighteenth century.

_____ 9. When is a flag hung upside down, it is an internationally recognized symbol of
                A   B   C   D
      distress.

_____ 10. The Museum of the Confederation in Richmond hosts an exhibition which
                                           A

      documenting the origins and history of the banner that most Americans think of as
       B   C   D
      the Confederate flag.

PROBLEMS WITH PARALLEL STRUCTURE _____

In good English an attempt should be made to make the language as even and balanced as possible. This balance is called "parallel structure." You can achieve parallel structure by making the forms of words as similar as possible. The following is an example of a sentence that is not parallel:

I like to sing and dancing.*

The problem in this sentence is not the expression *to sing,* and the problem is not the word *dancing.* The expression *to sing* is correct by itself, and the word *dancing* is correct by itself. Both of the following sentences are correct:

I like to sing.
I like dancing.

The problem in the incorrect example is that *to sing* and *dancing* are joined together in one sentence with *and.* They are different forms where it is possible to have similar forms; therefore the example is not parallel. It can be corrected in two different ways: we can make the first expression like the second, or we can make the second expression like the first.

I like to sing and to dance.
I like singing and dancing.

There are several situations in which you should be particularly careful of parallel structure. Parallel structures are required in the following situations: (1) with coordinate conjunctions, such as *and, but, or;* (2) with paired conjunctions, such as *both...and, either...or, neither...nor, not only...but also;* and (3) with comparisons.

SKILL 24: USE PARALLEL STRUCTURE WITH COORDINATE CONJUNCTIONS

The job of the coordinate conjunctions (*and, but, or*) is to join together equal expressions. In other words, what is on one side of these words must be parallel to what is on the other side. These conjunctions can join nouns, or verbs, or adjectives, or phrases, or subordinate clauses, or main clauses; they just must join together two of the same thing. Here are examples of two nouns joined by a coordinate conjunction:

> I need to talk to the manager *or* the assistant manager.
> She is not a teacher *but* a lawyer.
> You can choose from activities such as hiking *and* kayaking.

Here are examples of two verbs joined by a coordinate conjunction:

> He only eats *and* sleeps when he takes a vacation.
> She invites us to her home *but* never talks with us.
> You can stay home *or* go to the movies with us.

Here are examples of two adjectives joined by a coordinate conjunction:

> My boss is sincere *and* nice.
> The exam that he gave was short *but* difficult.
> Class can be interesting *or* boring.

Here are examples of two phrases joined by a coordinate conjunction:

> There are students in the classroom *and* in front of the building.
> The papers are on my desk *or* in the drawer.
> The checks will be ready not at noon *but* at 1:00.

Here are examples of two clauses joined by a coordinate conjunction:

> They are not interested in what you say *or* what you do.
> I am here because I have to be *and* because I want to be.
> Mr. Brown likes to go home early, *but* his wife prefers to stay late.

The following chart outlines the use of parallel structures with coordinate conjunctions:

PARALLEL STRUCTURE WITH COORDINATE CONJUNCTIONS		
(same structure)	*and* *but* *or*	(same structure)
(same structure), (same structure),	*and* *but* *or*	(same structure)

EXERCISE 24: Each of the following sentences contains words or groups of words that should be parallel. Circle the word that indicates that the sentence should have parallel parts. Underline the parts that should be parallel. Then indicate if the sentences are correct (C) or incorrect (I).

____I____ 1. She held jobs as <u>a typist</u>, <u>a housekeeper</u>, (and) <u>in a restaurant</u>.

____C____ 2. The report you are looking for could be <u>in the file</u> (or) <u>on the desk</u>.

_____ 3. She works very hard but usually gets below-average grades.

_____ 4. The speaker introduced himself, told several interesting anecdotes, and finishing with an emotional plea.

_____ 5. You should know when the program starts and how many units you must complete.

_____ 6. The term paper he wrote was rather short but very impressive.

_____ 7. She suggested taking the plane this evening or that we go by train tomorrow.

_____ 8. The dean or the assistant dean will inform you of when and where you should apply for your diploma.

_____ 9. There are papers to file, reports to type, and those letters should be answered.

_____ 10. The manager needed a quick but thorough response.

SKILL 25: USE PARALLEL STRUCTURE WITH PAIRED CONJUNCTIONS

The paired conjunctions *both...and, either...or, neither...nor,* and *not only...but also* require parallel structures.

> I know *both* <u>where you went</u> *and* <u>what you did</u>.
> *Either* <u>Mark</u> *or* <u>Sue</u> has the book.
> The tickets are *neither* <u>in my pocket</u> *nor* <u>in my purse</u>.
> He is *not only* <u>an excellent student</u> *but also* <u>an outstanding athlete</u>.

The following is not parallel and must be corrected:

> He wants *either* <u>to go by train</u> *or* <u>by plane</u>*.

It is not correct because *to go by train* is not parallel to *by plane*. It can be corrected in several ways.

> He wants *either* <u>to go by train</u> *or* <u>to go by plane</u>.
> He wants to go *either* <u>by train</u> *or* <u>by plane</u>.
> He wants to go by *either* <u>train</u> *or* <u>plane</u>.

When you are using these paired conjunctions, be sure that the correct parts are used together. The following are incorrect:

> I want *both* <u>this book</u> *or** <u>that one</u>.
> *Either* <u>Sam</u> *nor** <u>Sue</u> is taking the course.

These sentences are incorrect because the wrong parts of the paired conjunctions are used together. In the first example, *and* should be used with *both*. In the second example, *or* should be used with *either*.

The following chart outlines the use of parallel structure with paired conjunctions:

PARALLEL STRUCTURE WITH PAIRED CONJUNCTIONS			
both *either* *neither* *not only*	(same structure)	*and* *or* *nor* *but also*	(same structure)

EXERCISE 25: Each of the following sentences contains words or groups of words that should be parallel. Circle the word or words that indicate that the sentence should have parallel parts. Underline the parts that should be parallel. Then indicate if the sentences are correct (C) or incorrect (I).

___I___   1.   According to the syllabus, you can (either) <u>write a paper</u> (or) <u>you can take an exam</u>.

___C___   2.   It would be (both) <u>noticed</u> (and) <u>appreciated</u> if you could finish the work before you leave.

_____   3.   She would like neither to see a movie or to go bowling.

_____   4.   Either the manager or her assistant can help you with your refund.

_____   5.   She wants not only to take a trip to Europe but she also would like to travel to Asia.

_____   6.   He could correct neither what you said nor you wrote.

_____   7.   Both the tailor or the laundress could fix the damage to the dress.

_____   8.   He not only called the police department but also called the fire department.

_____ 9. You can graduate either at the end of the fall semester or you can graduate at the end of the spring semester.

_____ 10. The movie was neither amusing nor was it interesting.

SKILL 26:   USE PARALLEL STRUCTURE WITH COMPARISONS

When you make a comparison, you point out the similarities or differences between two things, and those similarities or differences must be in parallel form. You can recognize a comparison showing how two things are different from the *-er...than* or the *more...than*.

> My <u>school</u> is farth*er than* <u>your school</u>.
> <u>To be rich</u> is bett*er than* <u>to be poor</u>.
> <u>What is written</u> is *more* easily understood *than* <u>what is spoken</u>.

A comparison showing how two things are the same might contain *as...as* or expressions such as *the same as* or *similar to*.

> Their <u>car</u> is *as* big *as* <u>a small house</u>.
> <u>Renting those apartments</u> costs about *the same as* <u>leasing them</u>.
> The <u>work that I did</u> is *similar to* <u>the work that you did</u>.

The following chart outlines the use of parallel structures with comparisons:

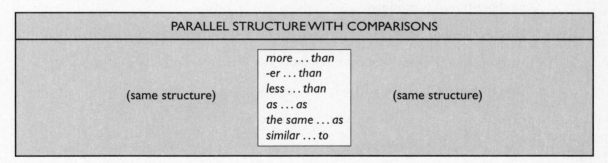

PARALLEL STRUCTURE WITH COMPARISONS		
(same structure)	more ... than -er ... than less ... than as ... as the same ... as similar ... to	(same structure)

EXERCISE 26:   Each of the following sentences contains words or groups of words that should be parallel. Circle the word or words that indicate that the sentence should have parallel parts. Underline the parts that should be parallel. Then indicate if each sentence is correct (C) or incorrect (I).

__C__ 1. His <u>research</u> for the thesis was (more useful than) <u>hers</u>.

__I__ 2. <u>Dining</u> in a restaurant is (more fun than) <u>to eat</u> at home.

_____ 3. I want a new secretary who is as efficient as the previous one.

_____ 4. What you do today should be the same as did yesterday.

_____ 5. This lesson is more difficult than we had before.

_____ 6. You have less homework than they do.

_____ 7. What you do has more effect than what you say.

_____ 8. Music in your country is quite similar to my country.

_____ 9. The collection of foreign journals in the university library is more extensive than the high school library.

_____ 10. How to buy a used car can be as difficult as buying a new car.

EXERCISE (Skills 24–26): Circle the word or words that indicate that the sentence should have parallel parts. Underline the parts that should be parallel. Then indicate if the sentences are correct (C) or incorrect (I).

_____ 1. After retirement he plans on traveling to exotic locations, dine in the finest restaurants, and playing a lot of golf.

_____ 2. She was both surprised by and pleased with the seminar.

_____ 3. What came after the break was even more boring than had come before.

_____ 4. He would find the missing keys neither under the bed or behind the sofa.

_____ 5. Depending on the perspective of the viewer, the film was considered laudable, mediocrity, or horrendous.

_____ 6. He exercised not only in the morning, but he also exercised every afternoon.

_____ 7. Working four days per week is much more relaxing than working five days per week.

_____ 8. Sam is always good-natured, generous, and helps you.

_____ 9. Either you have to finish the project, or the contract will be canceled.

_____ 10. The courses that you are required to take are more important than the courses that you choose.

TOEFL EXERCISE (Skills 24–26): Choose the letter of the word or group of words that best completes the sentence.

1. Truman Capote's *In Cold Blood* is neither journalistically accurate _____.

   (A) a piece of fiction
   (B) nor a fictitious work
   (C) or written in a fictitious way
   (D) nor completely fictitious

2. Vitamin C is necessary for the prevention and _____ of scurvy.

   (A) it cures
   (B) cures
   (C) cure
   (D) for curing

3. A baby's development is influenced by both heredity and _____.

    (A) by environmental factors
    (B) environmentally
    (C) the influence of the environment
    (D) environment

4. Because bone loss occurs earlier in women than _____, the effects of osteoporosis are more apparent in women.

    (A) men do
    (B) in men
    (C) as men
    (D) similar to men

Choose the letter of the underlined word or group of words that is not correct.

_____ 5. Fire extinguishers can contain liquefied gas, dry chemicals, or watery.
            A   B   C   D

_____ 6. The U.S. Congress consists of both the Senate as well as the House of Representatives.
                                A   B   C   D

_____ 7. The prison population in this state, now at an all time high, is higher than any state.
                      A   B   C   D

_____ 8. A well-composed baroque opera achieves a delicate balance by focusing alternately
            A   B   C
        on the aural, visual, emotional, and philosophy elements.
                                              D

_____ 9. Manufacturers may use food additives for preserving, to color, to flavor, or to fortify
                          A   B   C
        foods.
        D

_____ 10. A bankruptcy may be either voluntary nor involuntary.
            A   B   C   D

TOEFL REVIEW EXERCISE (Skills 1–26): Choose the letter of the word or group of words that best completes the sentence.

1. The growth of hair _____ cyclical process, with phases of activity and inactivity.

    (A) it is
    (B) is a
    (C) which is
    (D) a regular

2. The fire _____ to have started in the furnace under the house.

    (A) is believed
    (B) that is believed
    (C) they believe
    (D) that they believe

3. In Roman numerals, _____ symbols for numeric values.

    (A) are letters of the alphabet
    (B) letters of the alphabet are
    (C) which uses letters of the alphabet
    (D) in which letters of the alphabet are

4. The legal systems of most countries can be classified _____ common law or civil law.

    (A) as either
    (B) either as
    (C) either to
    (D) to either

5. One difference between mathematics and language is that mathematics is precise _____.

(A) language is not
(B) while language is not
(C) but language not
(D) while is language

6. Your criticism of the three short stories should not be less than 2,000 words, nor _____ more than 3,000.

(A) should it be
(B) it should be
(C) it is
(D) should be it

Choose the letter of the underlined word or group of words that is not correct.

_____ 7. In 1870, the attorney general was made head of the Department of Justice, given an
                                         A
enlarged staff, and endow with clear-cut law-enforcement functions.
     B   C   D

_____ 8. The General Sherman Tree, the largest of all the giant sequoias, are reputed to be
                                    A   B   C
the world's largest living thing.
                     D

_____ 9. The skeleton of a shark is made of cartilage rather than having bone.
                    A   B   C   D

_____ 10. At least one sample of each of the brands contains measurable amounts of aflatoxin,
                              A   B
and there is three which exceed the maximum.
        C   D

PROBLEMS WITH COMPARATIVES AND SUPERLATIVES _____

Sentences with incorrect comparatives and superlatives can appear on the TOEFL test. It is therefore important for you to know how to do the following: (1) form the comparative and superlative correctly; (2) use the comparative and superlative correctly; and (3) use the irregular *-er, -er* structure that has been appearing frequently on the TOEFL test.

SKILL 27:   FORM COMPARATIVES AND SUPERLATIVES CORRECTLY

The problem with some of the comparative and superlative sentences on the TOEFL test is that the comparative or superlative is formed incorrectly. You should therefore understand how to form the comparative and superlative to answer such questions correctly.

The comparative is formed with either *-er* or *more* and *than*. In the comparative, *-er* is used with short adjectives such as *tall,* and *more* is used with longer adjectives such as *beautiful.*

Bob is tall*er than* Ron.
Sally is *more* beautiful *than* Sharon.

The superlative is formed with *the,* either *-est* or *most,* and sometimes *in, of,* or a *that*-clause. In the superlative, *-est* is used with short adjectives such as *tall,* and *most* is used with longer adjectives such as *beautiful.*

> Bob is *the* tall*est* man *in* the room.
> Sally is *the most* beautiful *of* all the women at the party.
> The spider over there is *the* larg*est* one *that* I have ever seen.
> *The* fast*est* runner wins the race.   (no *in, of,* or *that*)

The following chart outlines the possible forms of comparatives and superlatives:

THE FORM OF COMPARATIVES AND SUPERLATIVES			
COMPARATIVE	$\begin{bmatrix} more \quad \text{(long adjective)} \\ \text{(short adjective)} + er \end{bmatrix}$	*than*	
SUPERLATIVE	*the*	$\begin{bmatrix} most \quad \text{(long adjective)} \\ \text{(short adjective)} + est \end{bmatrix}$	maybe *in, of, that*

EXERCISE 27: Each of the following sentences contains a comparative or superlative. Circle the comparative or superlative. Then indicate if the sentences are correct (C) or incorrect (I).

___I___ 1. Oxygen is (abundanter than) nitrogen.

___C___ 2. The directions to the exercise say to choose (the most appropriate) response.

_____ 3. The lesson you are studying now is the most importantest lesson that you will have.

_____ 4. Fashions this year are shorter and more colorful than they were last year.

_____ 5. The professor indicated that Anthony's research paper was more long than the other students' papers.

_____ 6. Alaska is the coldest than all the states in the United States.

_____ 7. The workers on the day shift are more rested than the workers on the night shift.

_____ 8. She was more happier this morning than she had been yesterday.

_____ 9. The quarterback on this year's football team is more versatile than the quarterback on last year's team.

_____ 10. She always tries to do the best and most efficient job that she can do.

SKILL 28:   USE COMPARATIVES AND SUPERLATIVES CORRECTLY

Another problem with the comparative and superlative on the TOEFL test is that they can be used incorrectly. The comparative and superlative have different uses, and you should understand these different uses to answer such questions correctly. The comparative is used to compare two equal things.

> The history class is *larger than* the math class.
> Mary is *more intelligent than* Sue.

In the first example *the history class* is being compared with *the math class*. In the second example *Mary* is being compared with *Sue*.

   The superlative is used when there are more than two items to compare and you want to show the one that is the best, the biggest, or in some way the most outstanding.

> The history class is *the largest* in the school.
> Mary is *the most intelligent* of all the students in the class.

In the first example *the history class* is compared with all the other classes in the school, and the history class is larger than each of the other classes. In the second example, *Mary* is compared with all the other students in the class, and Mary is more intelligent than each of the other students.

   The following chart outlines the uses of comparatives and superlatives:

THE USES OF COMPARATIVES AND SUPERLATIVES
The COMPARATIVE is used to compare *two equal things*.
The SUPERLATIVE is used to show which *one of many* is in some way the most outstanding.

EXERCISE 28: Each of the following sentences contains a comparative or superlative. Circle the comparative or superlative. Then indicate if the sentences are correct (C) or incorrect (I).

__C__   1. Harvard is probably (the most prestigious) university in the United States.

__I__   2. Rhonda is (more hard working) of the class.

_____   3. The engineers hired this year have more experience than those hired last year.

_____   4. The graduate assistant informed us that the first exam is the most difficult of the two.

_____   5. He bought the more powerful stereo speakers that he could find.

_____   6. The afternoon seminar was much more interesting than the morning lecture.

_____   7. The food in this restaurant is the best of the restaurant we visited last week.

_____   8. The plants that have been sitting in the sunny window are far healthier than the other plants.

_____   9. The photocopies are the darkest that they have ever been.

_____ 10. The first journal article is the longest of the second article.

SKILL 29:   USE THE IRREGULAR *-ER, -ER* STRUCTURE CORRECTLY

An irregular comparative structure that has been appearing frequently on the TOEFL test consists of two parallel comparatives introduced by *the.*

> *The harder* he tried, *the further* he fell behind.
> *The older* the children are, *the more* their parents expect from them.

The first example contains the two parallel comparatives, *the harder* and *the further.* The second example contains the two parallel comparatives, *the older* and *the more.*

   In this type of sentence, *the* and the comparison can be followed by a number of different structures.

> *The more* children you have, *the bigger* the house you need.
> *The harder* you work, *the more* you accomplish.
> *The greater* the experience, *the higher* the salary.

In the first example, *the more* is followed by the noun *children* and the subject and verb *you have,* while *the bigger* is followed by the noun *the house* and the subject and verb *you need.* In the second example, *the harder* is followed by the subject and verb *you work,* while *the more* is followed by the subject and verb *you accomplish.* In the third example, *the greater* is followed only by the noun *the experience,* while *the higher* is followed only by the noun *the salary.* You should note that this last example does not even contain a verb, yet it is a correct structure in English.

   The following chart outlines this irregular *-er, -er* structure:

THE *-ER, -ER* STRUCTURE					
THE	-er / more	(same structure),	THE	-er / more	(same structure)
This type of sentence *may* or *may not* include a verb.					

EXERCISE 29: Each of the following sentences contains the irregular *-er, -er* structure. Circle the two comparisons with *the.* Underline the parts that should be parallel. Then indicate if the sentences are correct (C) or incorrect (I).

___I___ 1. (The hotter) the food is, (harder) it is to eat.

___C___ 2. (The warmer) the weather, (the greater) the attendance at the outdoor concert.

_____ 3. The more you say, the worst the situation will be.

_____ 4. The more time they have to play, the happier the children are.

_____ 5. The thicker the walls, the noise that comes through is less.

_____ 6. If you run faster, the earlier you'll arrive.

_____ 7. The more you use the phone, the higher the bill will be.

_____ 8. The harder you serve, the easier it is to win the point.

_____ 9. The earliest you send in your tax forms, the sooner you will receive your refund.

_____ 10. The more people there are at the party, you'll have a good time.

EXERCISE (Skills 27–29): Circle the comparatives and superlatives in the following sentences. Then indicate if the sentences are correct (C) or incorrect (I).

_____ 1. The coffee is more stronger today than it was yesterday.

_____ 2. The tree that was struck by lightning had been the tallest of the two trees we had in the yard.

_____ 3. He will buy the most fuel-efficient car that he can afford.

_____ 4. The closest it gets to summer, the longer the days are.

_____ 5. The business department is bigger of the departments in the university.

_____ 6. I really do not want to live in the Southeast because it is one of the most hot areas in the United States.

_____ 7. It is preferable to use the most efficient and most effective method that you can.

_____ 8. Tonight's dinner was more filling than last night's.

_____ 9. The sooner the exam is scheduled, the less time you have to prepare.

_____ 10. The house is now the cleanest that it has ever been.

TOEFL EXERCISE (Skills 27–29): Choose the letter of the word or group of words that best completes the sentence.

1. The speed of light is _____ the speed of sound.

    (A) faster
    (B) much faster than
    (C) the fastest
    (D) as fast

2. The use of detail is _____ method of developing a controlling idea, and almost all students employ this method.

    (A) more common
    (B) common
    (C) most common
    (D) the most common

3. _____ in Stevenson's landscapes, the more vitality and character the paintings seem to possess.

    (A) The brushwork is loose
    (B) The looser brushwork
    (C) The loose brushwork is
    (D) The looser the brushwork is

Choose the letter of the underlined word or group of words that is not correct.

_____ 4. Certain types of snakes have been known to survive fasts more as a year long.
             A   B   C   D

_____ 5. The grizzly bear, which can grow up to eight feet tall, has been called a more
                    A   B   C   D
       dangerous animal of North America.

_____ 6. Climate, soil type, and availability of water are the most critical factors than selecting
                            A   B   C
       the best type of grass for a lawn.
        D

_____ 7. Peter Abelard, a logician and theologian, was the controversialest teacher of his age.
                     A   B   C   D

_____ 8. Protein molecules are the most complex than the molecules of carbohydrates.
                        A   B   C   D

_____ 9. The leek, a member of the lily family, has a mildest taste than the onion.
              A   B   C   D

_____ 10. The widely used natural fiber of all is cotton.
             A   B   C   D

TOEFL REVIEW EXERCISE (Skills 1–29): Choose the letter of the word or group of words that best completes the sentence.

1. _____, a liberal arts college specifically for deaf people, is located in Washington, D.C.

   (A) Gallaudet College
   (B) Gallaudet College is
   (C) About Gallaudet College
   (D) Because of Gallaudet College

2. _____ varieties of dogs at the show, including spaniels, poodles, and collies.

   (A) The several
   (B) Those
   (C) Several
   (D) There were several

3. While the discovery that many migratory songbirds can thrive in deforested wintering spots _____, the fact remains that these birds are dying at unusual rates.

   (A) it is heartening
   (B) hearten
   (C) heartening
   (D) is heartening

Choose the letter of the underlined word or group of words that is not correct.

_____ 4. The coyote is somewhat smaller in size than a timber wolf.
                           A   B   C D

_____ 5. The weather reports all showed that there were a tremendous storm front moving in.
                     A   B   C   D

_____ 6. Seldom cactus plants are found outside of North America.
            A   B   C   D

_____ 7. In a basketball game a player what is fouled receives one or two free throws.
                                    A   B   C   D

_____ 8. Until recently, California was largest producer of oranges in the United States.
                  A   B   C   D

_____ 9. An understanding of engineering theories and problems are impossible until basic
                                          A   B

arithmetic is fully mastered.
                C   D

_____ 10. The earliest the CVS (*chorionic villus sampling*) procedure in the pregnancy, the
                   A   B   C

greater the risk to the baby.
                D

PROBLEMS WITH THE FORM OF THE VERB _____

It is common in written expression questions on the TOEFL test for the verbs to be formed incorrectly. Therefore, you should check the form of the verb carefully. You should be familiar with the following verb forms: the base form, the present tense, the present participle, the past, and the past participle. The following are examples of each of these verb forms as they are used in this text:

BASE FORM	PRESENT	PRESENT PARTICIPLE	PAST	PAST PARTICIPLE
walk	*walk(s)*	*walking*	*walked*	*walked*
hear	*hear(s)*	*hearing*	*heard*	*heard*
cook	*cook(s)*	*cooking*	*cooked*	*cooked*
sing	*sing(s)*	*singing*	*sang*	*sung*
come	*come(s)*	*coming*	*came*	*come*
begin	*begin(s)*	*beginning*	*began*	*begun*

You should be particularly aware of the following three problematic situations with verbs because they are the most common and the easiest to correct: (1) check what comes after *have*; (2) check what comes after *be*; and (3) check what comes after *will, would,* and other modals.

> NOTE: A more complete list of verb forms and an exercise to practice their use are included at the back of the text in Appendix F. You may want to complete this exercise before you continue with skills 30 through 32.

SKILL 30:   AFTER *HAVE*, USE THE PAST PARTICIPLE

Whenever you see the helping verb *have* in any of its forms (*have, has, having, had*), be sure that the verb that follows it is in the past participle form.

They *had walk** to school.	(should be *had walked*)
We *have see** the show.	(should be *have seen*)
He *has took** the test.	(should be *has taken*)
*Having ate**, he went to school.	(should be *Having eaten*)
She *should have did** the work.	(should be *should have done*)

In addition, you should be sure that if you have a subject and a past participle, you also have the verb *have*. This problem is particularly common with those verbs (such as *sing, sang, sung*) that change from present to past to past participle by changing only the vowel.

My friend *sung** in the choir.	(should be *sang* or *has sung*)
He *become** angry at his friend.	(should be *became* or *has become*)
The boat *sunk** in the ocean.	(should be *sank* or *has sunk*)

The following chart outlines the use of verb forms after *have:*

VERB FORMS AFTER *HAVE*		
HAVE	+	past participle

EXERCISE 30: Each of the following sentences contains a verb in the past or a past participle. Underline the verbs or past participles twice. Then indicate if the sentences are correct (C) or incorrect (I).

___I___ 1.   The young girl drunk a glass of milk.

___C___ 2.   Before she left, she had asked her mother for permission.

_____ 3.   Having finished the term paper, he began studying for the exam.

_____ 4.   The secretary has broke her typewriter.

_____ 5.   The installer should have completes the task more quickly.

_____ 6.   He has often become angry during meetings.

_____ 7.   She has rarely rode her horse in the park.

_____ 8.   Having saw the film, he was quite disappointed.

_____ 9.   Tom has thought about taking that job.

_____ 10. You might have respond more effectively.

SKILL 31:   AFTER *BE*, USE THE PRESENT PARTICIPLE OR THE PAST PARTICIPLE

The verb *be* in any of its forms (*am, is, are, was, were, be, been, being*) can be followed by another verb. This verb should be in the present participle or the past participle form.

We *are do** our homework.	(should be *are doing*)
The homework *was do** early.	(should be *was done*)
Tom *is take** the book.	(should be *is taking*)
The book *was take** by Tom.	(should be *was taken*)

The following chart outlines the use of verb forms after *be*:

VERB FORMS AFTER *BE*
BE   +   (1) present participle (2) past participle

EXERCISE 31: Each of the following sentences contains a verb formed with *be*. Underline the verbs twice. Then indicate if the sentences are correct (C) or incorrect (I).

__I__   1.   At 12:00 Sam <u>is eat</u> his lunch.

__C__   2.   We <u>are meeting</u> them later today.

_____   3.   The message was took by the receptionist.

_____   4.   Being heard was extremely important to him.

_____   5.   The Smiths are build their house on some property that they own in the desert.

_____   6.   It had been noticed that some staff members were late.

_____   7.   The report should have been submit by noon.

_____   8.   Are the two companies merge into one?

_____   9.   He could be taking four courses this semester.

_____   10.   The score information has been duplicates on the back-up disk.

SKILL 32:   AFTER *WILL, WOULD,* OR OTHER MODALS, USE THE BASE FORM OF THE VERB

Whenever you see a modal, such as *will, would, shall, should, can, could, may, might,* or *must,* you should be sure that the verb that follows it is in its base form.

The boat *will leaving** at 3:00.	(should be *will leave*)
The doctor *may arrives** soon.	(should be *may arrive*)
The students *must taken** the exam.	(should be *must take*)

The following chart outlines the use of verb forms after modals:

VERBS FORMS AFTER MODALS
MODAL   +   base form of the verb

EXERCISE 32:   Each of the following sentences contains a verb formed with a modal. Underline the verbs twice. Then indicate if the sentences are correct (C) or incorrect (I).

__C__ 1.   The salesclerk <u>might lower</u> the price.

__I__ 2.   The television movie <u>will finishes</u> in a few minutes.

_____ 3.   Should everyone arrive by 8:00?

_____ 4.   The method for organizing files can be improved.

_____ 5.   The machine may clicks off if it is overused.

_____ 6.   Every morning the plants must be watered.

_____ 7.   The houses with ocean views could sell for considerably more.

_____ 8.   Would anyone liked to see that movie?

_____ 9.   I do not know when it will depart.

_____ 10.   She will work on the project only if she can has a full-time secretary.

EXERCISE (Skills 30–32):   Underline the verbs twice in the following sentences. Then indicate if the sentences are correct (C) or incorrect (I).

_____ 1.   I have gave you all the money that I have.

_____ 2.   The articles were put in the newspaper before he was able to stop production.

_____ 3.   All the tickets for the concert might already be sold.

_____ 4.   He was so thirsty that he drunk several large glasses of water.

_____ 5.   The deposit will has to be paid before the apartment can be rented.

_____ 6.   He objects to being held without bail.

_____ 7.   Having completed the first chapter of the manuscript, she decided to take a break.

_____ 8.   If Steve had really wanted to pass his exam, he would has studied much more.

_____ 9.   He thought that he should have be invited to attend the conference.

_____ 10.   Before the speaker finished, many guests had rose from their seats and started for the door.

TOEFL EXERCISE (Skills 30–32): Choose the letter of the underlined word or group of words that is not correct.

_____ 1. *Alice in Wonderland,* first published in 1865, has since being translated into thirty
          <u>A</u>   <u>B</u>   <u>C</u>   <u>D</u>
languages.

_____ 2. The Peace Corps was establish on March 1, 1961, by then President John F. Kennedy.
         <u>A</u>   <u>B</u> <u>C</u>   <u>D</u>

_____ 3. The advisor told himself, while listening to the speech, that a dozen other reporters
                  <u>A</u>   <u>B</u>
would has already asked that question.
<u>C</u>   <u>D</u>

_____ 4. At the start of the American Revolution, lanterns were hung in the Old North Church
                <u>A</u>   <u>B</u>   <u>C</u>
as a signal that the British were came.
                              <u>D</u>

_____ 5. Linus Pauling has wins two Nobel Prizes: the 1954 Nobel Prize in Chemistry and the
                    <u>A</u> <u>B</u>   <u>C</u>   <u>D</u>
1962 Nobel Peace Prize.

_____ 6. On the huge Ferris wheel constructed for a world exhibition in Chicago in 1893,
                <u>A</u>   <u>B</u>
each of the thirty-six cabs could held sixty people.
<u>C</u>   <u>D</u>

_____ 7. To overcome rejection of a skin graft, a system for matching donor and recipient
            <u>A</u>   <u>B</u>   <u>C</u>
tissues has be developed.
          <u>D</u>

_____ 8. Nails are commonly make of steel but also can contain substances such as aluminum
              <u>A</u>   <u>B</u>   <u>C</u> <u>D</u>
or brass.

_____ 9. A patient suffering from amnesia may had partial or total loss of memory.
                  <u>A</u>   <u>B</u> <u>C</u>   <u>D</u>

_____ 10. The idea of using pure nicotine to help smokers stop was first tries in the mid-1980's
                  <u>A</u>   <u>B</u>   <u>C</u>   <u>D</u>
with nicotine-laced chewing gum.

TOEFL REVIEW EXERCISE (Skills 1–32): Choose the letter of the word or group of words that best completes the sentence.

1. _____ separates Manhattan's Upper East Side from the Upper West Side.

   (A) Central Park
   (B) Where Central Park
   (C) Where is Central Park
   (D) Central Park which

2. Bioluminescent animals _____ the water or on land.

   (A) live
   (B) are living either
   (C) they are found in
   (D) can be found in

3. The purpose of a labor union is to improve the working conditions, _____, and pay of its members.

    (A) jobs are secure
    (B) to be secure
    (C) job security
    (D) the job's security

4. When _____ on July 4, 1789, the federal tariff, intended by the Founding Fathers to be the government's primary source of revenue, was remarkably evenhanded.

    (A) was first enacted
    (B) first enacted
    (C) was enacted first
    (D) it first

5. _____ inclined to push for such a reduction, it would probably not be successful.

    (A) The Office of Management
    (B) The Office of Management was
    (C) In the Office of Management
    (D) Were the Office of Management

Choose the letter of the underlined word or group of words that is not correct.

_____ 6. Helium has the most low boiling point of all substances.
            A   B   C   D

_____ 7. There is twenty-six bones in the human foot, fourteen of them in the toes.
          A   B   C   D

_____ 8. Extension of the countdown hold to fourteen hours was order to give crews
                                  A   B
       more time to repair wiring and clear away equipment.
           C   D

_____ 9. The study demonstrates that neither experience or awareness will improve chances of
              A   B   C   D
   success.

_____ 10. Some of the eye movements used in reading is actually unnecessary.
                             A   B   C D

PROBLEMS WITH THE USE OF THE VERB _____

Many different problems in using the correct verb tense are possible in English. However, four specific problems occur frequently on the TOEFL test, so you need to pay careful attention to these four: (1) knowing when to use the past with the present, (2) using *had* and *have* correctly, (3) using the correct tense with time expressions, and (4) using the correct tense with *will* and *would*.

SKILL 33:   KNOW WHEN TO USE THE PAST WITH THE PRESENT

One verb tense problem that is common both in student writing and on the TOEFL test is the switch from the past tense to the present tense for no particular reason. Often when a sentence has both a past tense and a present tense, the sentence is incorrect.

He *took* the money when he *wants** it.

This sentence says that *he took the money* (in the past) *when he wants it* (in the present). This meaning does not make any sense; it is impossible to do something in the past as a result of something you want in the present. This sentence can be corrected in several ways, depending on the desired meaning.

He *took* the money when he *wanted* it.
He *takes* the money when he *wants* it.

The first example means that *he took the money* (in the past) *when he wanted it* (in the past). This meaning is logical, and the sentence is correct. The second example means that *he takes the money* (habitually) *when he wants it* (habitually). This meaning is also logical, and the second example is also correct.

It is necessary to point out, however, that it is possible for a logical sentence in English to have both the past and the present tense.

I *know* that he *took* the money yesterday.

The meaning of this sentence is logical: *I know* (right now, in the present) that *he took the money* (yesterday, in the past). You can see from this example that it is possible for an English sentence to have both the past and the present tense. The error you need to avoid is the switch from the past to the present for no particular reason. Therefore, when you see a sentence on the TOEFL test with both the past tense and the present tense, you must check the meaning of the sentence carefully to see if it is logical in English.

The following chart outlines the use of the past tense with the present tense in English:

USING THE PAST WITH THE PRESENT
1. If you see a sentence with one verb in the *past* and one verb in the *present,* the sentence is probably incorrect.
2. However, it is possible for a correct sentence to have both *past* and *present* together.
3. If you see the *past* and *present* together, you must *check the meaning* to determine whether or not the sentence is correct.

EXERCISE 33: Each of the following sentences has at least one verb in the past and one verb in the present. Underline the verbs twice and decide if the meanings are logical. Then indicate if the sentences are correct (C) or incorrect (I).

___I___ 1. I tell him the truth when he asked me the question.

___C___ 2. I understand that you were angry.

_____ 3. When he was a child, he always goes to the circus.

_____ 4. Last semester he reads seven books and wrote five papers.

_____ 5. Steve wakes up early every morning because he went to work early.

_____ 6. Mark studied at the American University when he is in Washington, D.C.

_____ 7. He is telling the teacher why he did not have time to finish his homework.

_____ 8. He put some money in his account when he goes to the bank.

_____ 9. Tom keeps studying hard because he intended to go to dental school.

_____ 10. She is where she is today because she worked hard when she was a student.

SKILL 34:   USE *HAVE* AND *HAD* CORRECTLY

Two tenses that are often confused are the present perfect (*have* + past participle) and the past perfect (*had* + past participle). These two tenses have completely different uses, and you should understand how to differentiate them.

The present perfect (*have* + past participle) refers to the period of time *from the past until the present.*

> Sue *has lived* in Los Angeles for ten years.

This sentence means that Sue has lived in Los Angeles for the ten years up to now. According to this sentence, Sue is still living in Los Angeles.

Because the present perfect refers to a period of time from the past until the present, it is not correct in a sentence that indicates past only.

> *At the start of the nineteenth century,* Thomas Jefferson *has become** president of the United States.
> Every time Jim *worked* on his car, he *has improved** it.

In the first example, the phrase *at the start of the nineteenth century* indicates that the action of the verb was in the past only, but the verb indicates the period of time from the past until the present. Since this is not logical, the sentence is not correct. The verb in the first example should be the simple past *became.* The second example indicates that Jim *worked* on his car in the past, but he improved it in the period from the past until the present. This idea also is not logical. The verb in the second example should be the simple past *improved.*

The past perfect (*had* + past participle) refers to a period of time *that started in the past and ended in the past, before something else happened in the past.*

> Sue *had lived* in Los Angeles for ten years when she *moved* to San Diego.

This sentence means that Sue lived in Los Angeles for ten years in the past before she moved to San Diego in the past. She no longer lives in Los Angeles.

Because the past perfect begins in the past and ends in the past, it is generally not correct in the same sentence with the present tense.

> Tom *had finished* the exam when the teacher *collects** the papers.

This sentence indicates that *Tom finished the exam* (in the past) and that action ended *when the teacher collects the papers* (in the present). This is not logical, so the sentence is not correct. Tom finished the exam (in the past), and the action of finishing the exam ended when the teacher collected the papers. Therefore, the second verb in this example should be in the past tense, *collected*.

The following chart outlines the uses of the present perfect and the past perfect:

USING (*HAVE* + PAST PARTICIPLE) AND (*HAD* + PAST PARTICIPLE)			
TENSE	FORM	MEANING	USE
present perfect	*have* + past participle	past up to now	not with a past tense**
past perfect	*had* + past participle	before past up to past	not with a present tense
**Except when the time expression *since* is part of the sentence (see Skill 35).			

EXERCISE 34: Each of the following sentences contains *had* or *have*. Underline the verbs twice and decide if the meanings are logical. Then indicate if the sentences are correct (C) or incorrect (I).

__C__ 1. I have always liked the designs that are on the cover.

__I__ 2. Because her proposal had been rejected, she is depressed.

_____ 3. The students have registered for classes before the semester started.

_____ 4. When she had purchased the car, she contacted the insurance agent.

_____ 5. He said that he had finished the typing when you finish the reports.

_____ 6. She has enjoyed herself every time that she has gone to the zoo.

_____ 7. He drove to the post office after he had finished preparing the package.

_____ 8. After the votes were counted, it had been determined that Steve was the winner.

_____ 9. Last night all the waiters and waitresses have worked overtime.

_____ 10. He had fastened his seat belt before the airplane took off.

SKILL 35:   USE THE CORRECT TENSE WITH TIME EXPRESSIONS

Often in written expression questions on the TOEFL test there is a time expression that clearly indicates what verb tense is needed in the sentence.

> We moved to New York *in 1980.*
> We had left there *by 1990.*
> We have lived in San Francisco *since 1999.*

In the first example, the time expression *in 1980* indicates that the verb should be in the simple past (*moved*). In the second example, the time expression *by 1990* indicates that the verb should be in the past perfect (*had left*). In the third example, the time expression *since 1999* indicates that the verb should be in the present perfect (*have lived*).

Some additional time expressions that clearly indicate the correct tense are *ago, last,* and *lately.*

> She got a job *two years ago.*
> She started working *last week.*
> She has worked very hard *lately.*

In the first example, the time expression *two years ago* indicates that the verb should be in the simple past (*got*). In the second example, the time expression *last week* indicates that the verb should be in the simple past (*started*). In the third example, the time expression *lately* indicates that the verb should be in the present perfect (*has worked*).

The following chart lists time expressions that indicate the correct verb tense:

USING CORRECT TENSES WITH TIME EXPRESSIONS		
PAST PERFECT	SIMPLE PAST	PRESENT PERFECT
by (1920)	*(two years) ago* *last (year)* *in (1920)*	*since (1920)* *lately*

EXERCISE 35: Each of the following sentences contains a time expression. Circle the time expressions and underline the verbs twice. Then indicate if the sentences are correct (C) or incorrect (I).

___C___ 1. The phone <u>rang</u> incessantly (last night.)

___I___ 2. They <u>have finished</u> contacting everyone (by 4:00 yesterday.)

_____ 3. The Pilgrims have arrived in the New World in 1620.

_____ 4. Since the new law was passed, it has been difficult to estimate taxes.

_____ 5. The cashier put the money into the account two hours ago.

_____ 6. All the votes have been counted last week.

_____ 7. The students are writing many compositions lately.

_____ 8. The Senate votes on the law to ban cigarette smoking in public in 1990.

_____ 9. By the time the main course was served, all the guests had arrived and been seated.

_____ 10. I had not done much more work since I talked to you on Wednesday.

SKILL 36:   USE THE CORRECT TENSE WITH *WILL* AND *WOULD*

Certain combinations of verbs are very common in English. One is the combination of the simple present and *will*.

> I *know* that they *will arrive* soon.
> It *is* certain that he *will graduate*.

Another combination that is quite common is the combination of the simple past and *would*.

> I *knew* that he *would arrive*.
> It *was* certain that he *would graduate*.

It is important to stress that in the combination discussed here, the present should be used with *will* and the past should be used with *would*; they generally should not be mixed.

The common errors that must generally be avoided are the combination of the past with *will* and the combination of the present with *would*.

> I *know* that he *would* arrive* soon.
> It *was* certain that he *will* graduate*.

In the first example, the present, *know*, is illogical with *would*. It can be corrected in two different ways.

> I *knew* that he *would arrive* soon.
> I *know* that he *will arrive* soon.

In the second example, the past, *was*, is illogical with *will*. It can also be corrected in two different ways.

> It *was* certain that he *would graduate*.
> It *is* certain that he *will graduate*.

The following chart outlines the use of tenses with *will* and *would*:

USING CORRECT TENSES WITH *WILL* AND *WOULD*		
VERB	MEANING	USE
will	after the present	do not use with past
would	after the past	do not use with present
NOTE: There is a different modal *would* that is used to make polite requests. This type of *would* is often used with the present tense.		
I would like to know if you **have** a pencil that I could borrow.		

EXERCISE 36: Each of the following sentences contains *will* or *would*. Underline the verbs twice and decide if the meanings are logical. Then indicate if the sentences are correct (C) or incorrect (I).

___I___ 1. He knew that he will be able to pass the exam.

___C___ 2. I think that I will leave tomorrow.

_____ 3. Paul did not say when he will finish the project.

_____ 4. Jake doubts that he would have time to finish the project.

_____ 5. I know that I will go if I can afford it.

_____ 6. The police officer indicated that he would write a ticket if he has the time.

_____ 7. Students will often study in the library before they go to classes or before they go home.

_____ 8. He told me that he thought he will get the job in spite of his lack of education.

_____ 9. The executive vice president emphasizes at the conferences that the board would not change its position.

_____ 10. Students will register for classes according to who has the highest number of units.

EXERCISE (Skills 33–36): Underline the verbs twice in each of the following sentences. Then indicate if the sentences are correct (C) or incorrect (I).

_____ 1. When he receives the money from the insurance company two days ago, he had already rebuilt the house.

_____ 2. The position on the city council will be filled next week when the electorate votes.

_____ 3. The dentist fills the cavities every time the x-rays show that it was necessary.

_____ 4. When the bell rang, the students have left the class.

_____ 5. The space shuttle would be launched next month if the weather is good.

_____ 6. The special delivery package has arrived by noon yesterday.

_____ 7. It is probable that the students who were tested yesterday were quite successful.

_____ 8. After forty-five students had signed up for the class, the class was closed.

_____ 9. The parking at the arena was inadequate for the tremendous number of drivers who will want to park there.

_____ 10. They have not returned to Rhode Island since they left in 1970.

TOEFL EXERCISE (Skills 33–36): Choose the letter of the underlined word or group of words that is not correct.

_____ 1. In several of his paintings, Edward Hicks depicted the Quaker farm in Pennsylvania
            A
where he spends his youth.
 B   C   D

_____ 2. Florida has become the twenty-seventh state in the United States on March 3, 1845.
            A   B   C D

_____   3. After last week's meeting, the advertising department quickly realized that the
$\qquad$ A $\qquad$ B

product will need a new slogan.
C   D

_____   4. John F. Kennedy's grandfather, John F. Fitzgerald, serves two terms as the mayor of
$\qquad$ A $\qquad$ B $\qquad$ C

Boston in the beginning of the twentieth century.
D

_____   5. Fort Ticonderoga, a strategically important fortification during the Revolution, had
A

since been reconstructed and turned into a museum.
B $\qquad$ C $\qquad$ D

_____   6. In making their calculations, Institute researchers assume that the least costly form of
A $\qquad$ B

energy would be used.
C $\qquad$ D

_____   7. A twenty-one-year-old man became the second casualty yesterday when he loses
A $\qquad$ B   C

control of his truck.
D

_____   8. Most people had written with quill pens until pens with metal points become popular
A   B $\qquad$ C $\qquad$ D

in the middle of the nineteenth century.

_____   9. In a determined drive to pare its debt, Time Warner is launching a stock offering
A $\qquad$ B $\qquad$ C

plan that would potentially raise $2.8 billion.
D

_____ 10. The formula used in the study calls for either peroxide or metaldehyde, but
A $\qquad$ B $\qquad$ C

metaldehyde was not always available.
D

TOEFL REVIEW EXERCISE (Skills 1–36): Choose the letter of the word or group of words that best completes the sentence.

1. _____ in the United States declined from twenty million in 1910 to nine million in the 1970s.

   (A) For a number of horses
   (B) The number of horses
   (C) When the number of horses
   (D) That the number of horses

2. Because of his reservations about the issue, _____ refused to vote for it.

   (A) who
   (B) and
   (C) which the senator
   (D) the senator

3. Bats avoid running into objects by _____ high-frequency sounds and listening for echoes.

(A) the emission
(B) emitted
(C) emitting
(D) they emit

4. It has been estimated that if we intend to stay above the starvation level, _____ the food supply.

(A) so we will have to double
(B) and it must double
(C) which it must be doubled
(D) we must double

Choose the letter of the underlined word or group of words that is not correct.

_____ 5. To determine an object's force, the mass and speed of the object must be measure.
           $\underset{A}{\underline{\hspace{1.3cm}}}$ $\underset{B}{\underline{\hspace{1.3cm}}}$ $\underset{C}{\underline{\hspace{1cm}}}$ $\underset{D}{\underline{\hspace{1.3cm}}}$

_____ 6. The most common time for tornados to occur are in the afternoon or evening on a
           $\underset{A}{\underline{\hspace{1cm}}}$ $\underset{B}{\underline{\hspace{1cm}}}$ $\underset{C}{\underline{\hspace{0.5cm}}}$
hot, humid spring day.
$\underset{D}{\underline{\hspace{1cm}}}$

_____ 7. Automakers Nissan and Ford and several aerospace research facilities in Great Britain
                                                $\underset{A}{\underline{\hspace{1cm}}}$
are working lately to apply active noise cancellation to entire cars and planes.
$\underset{B}{\underline{\hspace{1cm}}}$ $\underset{C}{\underline{\hspace{1cm}}}$ $\underset{D}{\underline{\hspace{1cm}}}$

_____ 8. When a country in an early stage of development, investments in fixed capital
                    $\underset{A}{\underline{\hspace{1cm}}}$ $\underset{B}{\underline{\hspace{1cm}}}$ $\underset{C}{\underline{\hspace{0.5cm}}}$
are vital.
$\underset{D}{\underline{\hspace{1cm}}}$

_____ 9. John Chapman became famous in American folklore as "Johnny Appleseed" after he
                              $\underset{A}{\underline{\hspace{1cm}}}$
plants apple trees throughout the northeastern part of the United States.
$\underset{B}{\underline{\hspace{1cm}}}$ $\underset{C}{\underline{\hspace{1cm}}}$ $\underset{D}{\underline{\hspace{1cm}}}$

_____ 10. Inasmuch he kept mostly to himself, the author of *The Treasure of the Sierra Madre* was
                    $\underset{A}{\underline{\hspace{1cm}}}$ $\underset{B}{\underline{\hspace{0.5cm}}}$ $\underset{C}{\underline{\hspace{1cm}}}$ $\underset{D}{\underline{\hspace{0.5cm}}}$
known as "the mysterious B. Treuen."

PROBLEMS WITH PASSIVE VERBS_____

Sentences in which the error is an incorrect passive are common in written expression questions on the TOEFL test. You therefore need to be able to recognize the correct form of the passive and to be able to determine when a passive verb rather than an active verb is needed in a sentence.

The difference between an active and a passive verb is that the subject in an active sentence *does* the action of the verb, and the subject in a passive sentence *receives* the action of the verb. To convert a sentence from active to passive, two changes must be made. (1) The subject of the active sentence becomes the object of the passive sentence, while the object of the active sentence becomes the subject of the passive sentence. (2) The verb in the passive sentence is formed by putting the helping verb *be* in the same form as the verb in the active sentence and then adding the past participle of this verb.

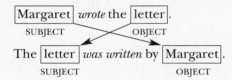

The first example is an active sentence. To convert this active sentence to a passive sentence, you must first make the subject of the active sentence, *Margaret,* the object of the passive sentence with *by.* The object of the active sentence, *letter,* becomes the subject of the passive sentence. Next, the passive verb can be formed. Because *wrote* is in the past tense in the active sentence, the past tense of *be (was)* is used in the passive sentence. Then the verb *wrote* in the active sentence is changed to the past participle *written* in the passive sentence.

It should be noted that in a passive sentence, *by + object* does not need to be included to have a complete sentence. The following are both examples of correct sentences.

> The letter was written yesterday *by Margaret.*
> The letter was written yesterday.

Notice that these passive sentences are correct if *by Margaret* is included (as in the first example) or if *by Margaret* is omitted (as in the second example).

NOTE: Exercises to practice active and passive forms can be found in Appendix G at the back of the text. You may want to complete these exercises before you begin Skill 37.

Skill 37:   USE THE CORRECT FORM OF THE PASSIVE

One way that the passive can be tested on the TOEFL test is simply with an incorrect form of the passive. The following are examples of passive errors that might appear on the TOEFL test:

> The portrait *was painting** by a famous artist.
> The project *will finished** by Tim.

In the first example, the passive is formed incorrectly because the past participle *painted* should be used rather than the present participle *painting*. In the second example, the verb *be* has not been included, and some form of *be* is necessary for a passive verb. The verb in the second sentence should be *will be finished*.

The following chart outlines the way to form the passive correctly:

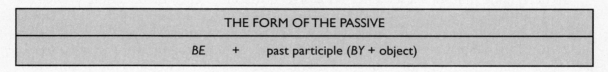

THE FORM OF THE PASSIVE
BE   +   past participle (*BY* + object)

EXERCISE 37: Each of the following sentences has a passive meaning. Underline twice the verbs that should be passive. Then indicate if the sentences are correct (C) or incorrect (I).

__I__   1.   The boy <u>had never be stung</u> by a bee.

__C__   2.   The suits <u>were hung</u> in the closet when they <u>were returned</u> from the cleaners.

_____   3.   Money is lending by the credit union to those who want to buy homes.

_____   4.   The record had been chose by dancers near the jukebox.

_____   5.   The topic for your research paper should have been approved by your advisor.

_____   6.   That song has been playing over and over again by Steve.

_____   7.   Their utility bills have been increased again and again.

_____   8.   The patients who are too sick to sit up are being assisted by the orderlies.

_____   9.   The offices were thoroughly clean last evening by the night crew.

_____   10.   The car that was struck in the intersection yesterday is being repaired today.

Skill 38:   RECOGNIZE ACTIVE AND PASSIVE MEANINGS

When there is no object (with or without *by*) after a verb, you must look at the meaning of the sentence to determine if the verb should be active or passive. Sentences with an incorrect passive verb and no *by* + *object* to tell you that the verb should be passive are the most difficult passive errors to recognize on the TOEFL test. Study the examples:

> We <u>mailed</u> *the package* at the post office.
> The letter <u>was mailed</u> *by us* today before noon.
> The letter <u>was mailed</u> today before noon.
> The letter <u>mailed</u>* today before noon.

The first three examples above are correct. The first example has the active verb *mailed* used with the object *package;* the second example has the passive verb *was mailed* used with *by us;* the third sentence has the passive verb *was mailed* used without an object.

The fourth example is the type of passive error that appears most often on the TOEFL test. This type of sentence has the following characteristics: (1) an incorrect passive verb that looks like a correct active verb, and (2) no *by + object* to tell you that a passive is needed. To correct the fourth example, the active verb needs to be changed to the passive *was mailed*.

To determine that such a sentence is incorrect, you must study the meaning of the subject and the verb. You must ask yourself if the subject *does* the action of the verb (so an active verb is needed) or if the subject *receives* the action of the verb (so a passive verb is needed). In the incorrect example, you should study the meaning of the subject and verb, *the letter mailed*. You should ask yourself if *a letter mails itself* (the letter *does* the action) or if someone *mails a letter* (the letter *receives* the action of being mailed). Since a letter does not mail itself, the passive is required in this sentence.

The following chart outlines the difference in meaning between active and passive verbs:

ACTIVE AND PASSIVE MEANINGS	
ACTIVE	The subject *does* the action of the verb.
PASSIVE	The subject *receives* the action of the verb.

EXERCISE 38: Each of the following sentences contains at least one active verb; however, some of the verbs should be passive. Underline the verbs twice. Then indicate if the sentences are correct (C) or incorrect (I).

___I___ 1. The car <u>parked</u> in a no-parking zone.

___C___ 2. The physics exam <u>began</u> just a few minutes ago.

___I___ 3. Everything to organize the picnic has already done. *been*

___C___ 4. The police investigated him because of his unusual actions.

___I___ 5. The package containing the necessary samples has just sent. *been*

___I___ 6. The vacation to Europe will plan carefully before the scheduled departure date. *be*

___I___ 7. The coffee turned bitter when it left on the stove for so long.

___I___ 8. The soccer game won in the closing minutes. *was*

___I___ 9. The clothes made to rival the latest fashions of the season.

___I___ 10. When the roads are icy, the buses do not drive.

EXERCISE (Skills 37–38): Underline the verbs twice in the following sentences. Then indicate if the sentences are correct (C) or incorrect (I).

_____ I   1.   After the old radiator had be replaced, the travelers continued their cross-country trip.

_____ I   2.   During the lightning storm, he struck in the head by a falling tree.

_____ I   3.   While I am on vacation, the pets should be feeds every morning and evening.

_____ C   4.   A book being written now by a team of writers will be published in the fall.

_____ I   5.   I found out that the real estate agent had already been leased the condominium.

_____ I   6.   The house that Mrs. Martin has always wanted to buy has just placed on the market.

_____ I   7.   The foundation should have been finishing by the construction workers before they left the construction site.

_____ I   8.   We must leave that money in the checking account because the bills pay on the first of the month.

_____ I   9.   The horses can't be taken out now because they have been rode for the past few hours.

_____ C 10.   It is being announced by a presidential aide that a lawyer from Virginia has been named attorney general.

TOEFL EXERCISE (Skills 37–38): Choose the letter of the word or group of words that best completes the sentence.

1.   _____ discussed by the board of directors when it was proposed again by the supervisors.

   (A)   The problem had already
   (B)   The problem is already
   (C)   The problem had already been
   (D)   The problem has already

2.   Much of the carnage of elephants, giraffes, and big cats _____ uncaring hunters.

   (A)   must commit by
   (B)   must be committed
   (C)   must have committed
   (D)   must have been committed by

3.   The x-ray treatments _____ up to the time that he was dismissed from the hospital.

   (A)   gave daily
   (B)   were given daily
   (C)   basically have given
   (D)   daily had been given

Choose the letter of the underlined word or group of words that is not correct.

_____ 4. Particular <u>issues</u> that <u>concern</u> teenagers <u>were</u> <u>covering</u> in the half-hour program.
               A   B   C   D

_____ 5. Electrical <u>impulses</u> <u>may</u> also <u>picked</u> up <u>by the</u> optic nerve.
                    A   B   C   D

_____ 6. Workers <u>training</u> for a specific job <u>have</u> a strong possibility of <u>being</u> <u>replace</u> by a
                   A   B   C   D
machine.

_____ 7. <u>On</u> June 30, 1992, international timekeepers in Paris <u>were added</u> an extra <u>second</u> to
       A   B   C
the day.
  D

_____ 8. The report <u>could not be</u> <u>turned</u> in on time because all the <u>needed</u> work <u>lost</u>.
                   A   B   C   D

_____ 9. In English these questions <u>have be</u> <u>formed</u> by <u>changing</u> the word order of a
                                 A   B   C
statement, whereas in some languages the word order <u>remains</u> the same.
                                                             D

_____ 10. He <u>was not able</u> <u>to define</u> the process <u>by which</u> the body <u>had protected</u> by the
             A   B   C   D
immunologic system.

TOEFL REVIEW EXERCISE (Skills 1–38): Choose the letter of the word or group of words that best completes the sentence.

1. _____ Big Dipper, a seven-star constellation in the shape of a cup, is part of Ursa Major.

   (A) The
   (B) It is the
   (C) With the
   (D) That the

2. The Military Academy at West Point _____ on the west bank of the Hudson River, north of New York City.

   (A) located
   (B) is located
   (C) which is located
   (D) whose location is

3. _____ impressive chapter in the book was the chapter on Stuart's scientific theories.

   (A) It was the most
   (B) The most
   (C) Most
   (D) Most of the

Choose the letter of the underlined word or group of words that is not correct.

_____ 4. The first fish <u>have appeared</u> on the earth approximately 500 <u>million</u> years ago.
                A   B   C   D

_____ 5. Only <u>rarely</u> sound waves are of <u>a single</u> frequency <u>encountered</u> in practice.
               A   B   C   D

_____ 6. <u>Cameos</u> can <u>be carved</u> not only <u>from</u> onyx and sardonyx <u>or</u> from agate.
           A   B   C   D

_____ 7. Although <u>most of</u> the wild horses on the western range <u>have already been</u> rounded
                  A   B

up, the <u>most remote</u> the area, the greater <u>the possibility</u> that wild horses can still be
          C   D

found.

_____ 8. During this period, $206 <u>was spend</u> annually <u>on food</u> by families in the <u>lower third</u>
                            A   B   C   D

income bracket.

_____ 9. The dangers of noise <u>are</u>, unfortunately, not as clear-cut <u>than</u> <u>are those</u> from
                            A   B   C

<u>most other</u> health hazards.
   D

_____ 10. In a <u>recent survey</u> of Americans, more than 75 percent <u>expressed</u> the view that the
                A   B

government <u>it should</u> take <u>a more</u> active role in health care.
            C   D

PROBLEMS WITH NOUNS _____

The same types of problems with nouns appear often in written expression questions on the TOEFL test. You should be familiar with these problems so that you will recognize them easily. You should be able to do the following: (1) use the correct singular or plural noun, (2) distinguish countable and uncountable nouns, (3) recognize irregular singular and plural nouns, and (4) distinguish the person from the thing.

SKILL 39:   USE THE CORRECT SINGULAR OR PLURAL NOUN

A problem that is common in written expression questions on the TOEFL test is a singular noun used where a plural noun is needed, or a plural noun used where a singular noun is needed.

                  On the table there were many *dish**.
                  The lab assistant finished every *tests**.

In the first example, *many* indicates that the plural *dishes* is needed. In the second example, *every* indicates that the singular *test* is needed.

In written expression questions on the TOEFL test, you should watch very carefully for key words, such as *each, every, a, one,* and *single,* that indicate that a noun should be singular. You should also watch carefully for such key words as *many, several, both, various,* and *two* (or any other number except *one*) that indicate that a noun should be plural.

The following chart lists the key words that indicate to you whether a noun should be singular or plural:

KEY WORDS FOR SINGULAR AND PLURAL NOUNS					
For Singular Nouns	*each*	*every*	*single*	*one*	*a*
For Plural Nouns	*both*	*two*	*many*	*several*	*various*

EXERCISE 39: Each of the following sentences contains at least one key word to tell you if a noun should be singular or plural. Circle the key words. Draw arrows to the nouns they describe. Then indicate if the sentences are correct (C) or incorrect (I).

___I___ 1. The automotive shop stocked (many) part for the (various) types of Hondas.

___C___ 2. (Every) receipt must be removed from the cashier's drawer and tallied.

___I___ 3. The salesclerk demonstrated various additional way that the machine could be used.

___I___ 4. The woman found it difficult to believe that both of the piece of jewelry had disappeared.

___I___ 5. The unhappy man became more and more discouraged with each passing days.

___I___ 6. An extended cruise would be a nice way to spend a vacation one days.

___C___ 7. The manager was surprised that not a single worker was available on Tuesday.

___I___ 8. The housekeeper cleaned the room and took two of the occupant's dress to the laundry.

___I___ 9. When the first bill was defeated, the Senate immediately began work on a different bills.

___C___ 10. There were several boxes in the cupboard, and each box contained a dozen glasses.

Skill 40:   DISTINGUISH COUNTABLE AND UNCOUNTABLE NOUNS

In English, nouns are classified as countable or uncountable. For certain questions on the TOEFL test, it is necessary to distinguish countable and uncountable nouns in order to use the correct modifiers with them.

As the name implies, countable nouns are nouns that can be counted. Countable nouns can come in quantities of one, or two, or a hundred, etc. The noun *book* is countable because you can have one book or several books.

Uncountable nouns, on the other hand, are nouns that cannot be counted because they come in some indeterminate quantity or mass. A noun such as *milk* or *happiness* cannot be counted; you cannot have one milk or two milks, and you cannot find one happiness or two happinesses. Uncountable nouns are often liquid items, such as *water, oil,* or *shampoo.* Uncountable nouns can also refer to abstract ideas, such as *security, excitement,* or *hope.*

It is important for you to recognize the difference between countable and uncountable nouns when you come across such key words as *much* and *many.*

He has seen *much** foreign *films.*
He didn't have *many** *fun* at the movies.

In the first example, *much* is incorrect because *films* is countable. This sentence should say *many foreign films.* In the second example, *many* is incorrect because *fun* is uncountable. This sentence should say *much fun.*

The following chart lists the key words that indicate to you whether a noun should be countable or uncountable:

KEY WORDS FOR COUNTABLE AND UNCOUNTABLE NOUNS				
For Countable Nouns	*many*	*number*	*few*	*fewer*
For Uncountable Nouns	*much*	*amount*	*little*	*less*

EXERCISE 40: Each of the following sentences contains at least one key word to tell you if a noun should be countable or uncountable. Circle the key words. Draw arrows to the nouns they describe. Then indicate if the sentences are correct (C) or incorrect (I).

_C_ 1. He received (little) notice that the bill would have to be paid in full.

_I_ 2. The police had (few) opportunities to catch the thief who had committed a large (amount) of crimes.

_C_ 3. You will have fewer problems with your income taxes if you get professional help.

_C_ 4. After the strike, the company dismissed many employees.

_I_ 5. Because the bottom corner of the pocket was torn, much coins fell out.

_C_ 6. Since he bought the new adapter, he has had less trouble with the machine.

_I_ 7. There are much new items to purchase before leaving, and there is such a short amount of time.

_I_ 8. The less time you take on the assignment, the less pages you will complete.

_C_ 9. A few soldiers who had been in heavy combat were brought back for a little rest.

_I_ 10. It is better to go shopping in the late evening because there are less people in the market, and you can accomplish a number of tasks in a short period of time.

Skill 41:   RECOGNIZE IRREGULAR PLURALS OF NOUNS

Many nouns in English have irregular plurals, and these irregular forms can cause confusion in written expression questions on the TOEFL test. The irregular forms that are the most problematic are plural forms that do not end in *s*.

> Different *criteria* was* used to evaluate the performers.

In this example the plural noun *criteria* looks singular because it does not end in *s;* you might incorrectly assume that it is singular because there is no final *s*. However, *criteria* is a plural noun, so the singular verb *was used* is incorrect. The verb should be the plural form *were used*.

The following chart lists the irregular plurals that you should become familiar with:

IRREGULAR PLURALS			
Vowel change	*man / men* *woman / women*	*foot / feet* *tooth / teeth*	*goose / geese* *mouse / mice*
Add -*EN*	*child / children*	*ox / oxen*	
Same as singular	*deer / deer* *fish / fish*	*salmon / salmon* *sheep / sheep*	*trout / trout*
-*IS* ➝ -*ES*	*analysis / analyses* *axis / axes* *crisis / crises*	*diagnosis / diagnoses* *hypothesis / hypotheses* *parenthesis / parentheses*	*synthesis / syntheses* *thesis / theses*
Ends in -*A*	*bacterium / bacteria* *curriculum / curricula*	*datum / data* *phenomenon / phenomena*	*criterion / criteria*
-*US* ➝ -*I*	*alumnus / alumni* *bacillus / bacilli* *cactus / cacti*	*fungus / fungi* *nucleus / nuclei* *radius / radii*	*stimulus / stimuli* *syllabus / syllabi*

> NOTE: Additional exercises to practice these irregular plurals of nouns appear in Appendix H at the back of the text. You may want to complete these exercises before you begin Exercise 41.

EXERCISE 41: Each of the following sentences contains at least one noun with an irregular plural. Circle the nouns with irregular plurals. Then indicate if the sentences are correct (C) or incorrect (I).

___I___ 1. (Parentheses) is needed around that expression.

___C___ 2. He wants to go on a fishing trip this weekend because he has heard that the (fish) are running.

___I___ 3. The syllabi for the courses is included in the packet of materials.

___I___ 4. The diagnosis that he heard today were not very positive.

_____C____ 5. The crisis is not going to be resolved until some of the pressure is relieved.

_____c____ 6. All of the alumni are attending the reception at the president's house.

_____l____ 7. A flock of geese were seen heading south for the winter.

_____l____ 8. The teeth in the back of his mouth needs to be capped.

_____l____ 9. The fungi has spread throughout the garden.

_____c___ 10. The sheepdog is chasing after the sheep which are heading over the hill.

SKILL 42:   DISTINGUISH THE PERSON FROM THE THING

Nouns in English can refer to persons or things. Sometimes in written expression questions on the TOEFL test the person is used in place of the thing, or the thing is used in place of the person.

> Ralph Nader is an *authorization** in the field of consumer affairs.
> There are many job opportunities in *accountant**.

In the first example, *authorization* is incorrect because *authorization* is a thing and Ralph Nader is a person. The person *authority* should be used in this sentence. In the second example, *accountant* is incorrect because *accountant* is a person and the field in which an accountant works is *accounting*. The thing *accounting* should be used in this sentence.

The following chart outlines what you should remember about the person or thing:

PERSON OR THING
It is common to confuse a person with a thing in written expression questions on the TOEFL test.

EXERCISE 42:   Some of the following sentences contain incorrectly used *persons* or *things*. Circle the incorrectly used words. Then indicate if the sentences are correct (C) or incorrect (I).

_____I____ 1. In the evening he relaxes in front of the fire and writes long (poets.)

_____C____ 2. Service in the restaurant was slow because one cook had called in sick.

_____l____ 3. The sculpture worked from sunrise until sunset on his new project.

_____l____ 4. She has received several awards for her research in engineer.

_____c____ 5. The economist's radical views were printed in a column in the Sunday newspaper.

_____c____ 6. You must have remarkable looks to work as a model for *Vogue*.

_____l____ 7. He had several critics to offer about the new play.

_C_   8.   The gardener worked feverishly after the frost to save as many plants as possible.

_I_   9.   The company hired a statistic to prepare marketing studies for the new product.

_I_   10.   The famous acting has appeared in more than fifty Broadway plays.

EXERCISE (Skills 39–42): Study the nouns in the following sentences. Then indicate if the sentences are correct (C) or incorrect (I).

_I_   1.   The professor does not give many exam in chemistry class, but the ones she gives are difficult.

_I_   2.   His thesis includes an analyses of the hypotheses.

_I_   3.   It was his dream to be a musical in the New York Philharmonic.

_C_   4.   For the reception, the caterers prepared a large amount of food to serve a large number of people.

_I_   5.   Many job opportunities exist in the field of nurse if you will accept a low-paying position.

_C_   6.   For each business trip you make, you can choose from many different airlines.

_____   7.   The stimulus for his career change is his acknowledgment that he is in a dead-end job.

_C_   8.   She wants to undergo a series of treatments, but she thinks it costs a little too much money.

_I_   9.   The television producer that was shown last night on the CBS network from 9:00 to 11:00 was one of the best shows of the season.

_C_   10.   Various sight-seeing excursion were available from the tourist agency.

TOEFL EXERCISE (Skills 39–42): Choose the letter of the underlined word or group of words that is not correct.

_D_   1.   As a compilation of <u>useful details</u>, a <u>weekly</u> magazine commends <u>itself</u> in several
                                  A   B   C
          <u>respect</u>.
           D

_D_   2.   Through aquaculture, or fish farming, <u>more than</u> 500 <u>million tons of fish</u>
                                                    A   B
          <u>are produced</u> each <u>years</u>.
                C   D

_A_   3.   The legal system has <u>much</u> safeguards to protect <u>the right</u> of a <u>defendant</u> to an
                                  A   B   C
          impartial <u>jury</u>.
                      D

_C_ 4. The mystery bookstore was largely a phenomena of the last decade.
         A B   C   D

_B_ 5. The *Song of Hiawatha,* by Longfellow, tells the story of the Indian heroism who
               A   B C

   married Minehaha.
    D

_C_ 6. Uranus is the seventh planets from the Sun.
    A B   C   D

_C_ 7. The sycamore has broad leaves with a large amount of pointed teeth.
         A B   C   D

_A_ 8. The first of two such investigation requires the students to read continuously over a
             A   B

   period of four hours.
    C   D

_C_ 9. A quantitative analysis, using both the computer and quantitative techniques,
           A   B

   are used to optimize financial decisions.
    C   D

_C_ 10. To enter the FBI National Academy, an application must be between the ages of
    A   B   C   D

   twenty-three and thirty-four.

TOEFL REVIEW EXERCISE (Skills 1–42): Choose the letter of the word or group of words that best completes the sentence.

1. Presidential _____ held every four years on the first Tuesday after the first Monday in November.

 (A) electing
 (B) elections are
 (C) is elected
 (D) elected and

2. Studies of carcinogenesis in animals can provide data on _____ in human susceptibility.

 (A) differences are
 (B) that differences are
 (C) differences have
 (D) differences

3. Those who favor the new law say that the present law does not set spending limits on lobbyists' gifts to politicians, nor _____ statewide funds.

 (A) it limits
 (B) limits it
 (C) does it limit
 (D) does it

4. The population of the earth is increasing at a tremendous rate and _____ out of control.

 (A) they have become
 (B) are soon going to be
 (C) soon will be
 (D) why it will be

5. Starting in 1811, traders and manufacturers were more easily able to send goods upriver in _____ provided the necessary power to counteract the flow of the waters.

 (A) steamboats
 (B) which
 (C) that
 (D) that steamboats

Choose the letter of the underlined word or group of words that is not correct.

_____ 6. Temperature <u>indicates</u> on a bimetallic <u>thermometer</u> by the <u>amount</u> <u>that</u> the
                    A   B   C   D
          bimetallic strip bends.

_____ 7. <u>Many</u> of the food <u>consumed</u> by penguins <u>consists</u> of fish <u>obtained from</u> the ocean.
          A   B   C   D

_____ 8. Before the newspaper became <u>widespread</u>, a town <u>crier</u> <u>has walked</u> throughout a
                                        A   B   C
          village or town <u>singing out</u> the news.
                            D

_____ 9. All of NASA's <u>manned</u> spacecraft <u>project</u> are <u>headquartered</u> at the Lyndon B.
                    A   B   C   D
          Johnson Space Center in Houston.

_____ 10. Fungi <u>cause</u> <u>more serious</u> plant <u>diseased</u> than <u>do other</u> parasites.
                 A   B   C   D

PROBLEMS WITH PRONOUNS _____

Pronouns are words, such as *he, she,* or *it,* that take the place of nouns. When you see a pronoun in written expression questions on the TOEFL test, you need to check that it serves the correct function in the sentence (as a subject or object, for example) and that it agrees with the noun it is replacing. The following pronoun problems are the most common on the TOEFL test: (1) distinguishing subject and object pronouns, (2) distinguishing possessive pronouns and possessive adjectives, and (3) checking pronoun reference for agreement.

SKILL 43:   DISTINGUISH SUBJECT AND OBJECT PRONOUNS

Subject and object pronouns can be confused on the TOEFL test, so you should be able to recognize these two types of pronouns:

SUBJECT	OBJECT
I	me
you	you
he	him
she	her
it	it
we	us
they	them

A subject pronoun is used as the subject of a verb. An object pronoun can be used as the object of a verb or the object of a preposition. Compare the following two sentences.

Sally gave *the book* to *John.*

She gave *it* to *him.*

In the second sentence the subject pronoun *she* is replacing the noun *Sally.* The object of the verb *it* is replacing the noun *book,* and the object of the preposition *him* is replacing the noun *John.*

The following are examples of the types of subject or object pronoun errors that you might see on the TOEFL test.

Him* and the girl are going shopping.
The gift was intended for you and *I*.*

In the first example, the object pronoun *him* is incorrect because this pronoun serves as the subject of the sentence. The object pronoun *him* should be changed to the subject pronoun *he.* It can be difficult to recognize that *him* is the subject because the verb *are* has a double subject, *him* and *girl.* In the second example, the subject pronoun *I* is incorrect because this pronoun serves as the object of the preposition *for.* The subject pronoun *I* should be changed to the object pronoun *me.* It can be difficult to recognize that *I* is the object of the preposition *for* because the preposition *for* has two objects: the correct object *you* and the incorrect object *I.*

EXERCISE 43: Each of the following sentences contains at least one subject or object pronoun. Circle the pronouns. Then indicate if the sentences are correct (C) or incorrect (I).

_C_ 1. The worst problem with (it) is that (he) cannot afford (it.)

_I_ 2. (They) saw Steve and (I) at the movies last night after class.

_____ 3. Perhaps you would like to go to the seminar with they and their friends.

_____ 4. The mother took her son to the doctor's office because he was feeling sick.

_____ 5. I did not know that you and her were working together on the project.

_____ 6. She did not buy the sweater because it had a small hole in it.

_____ 7. The man leading the seminar gave me all the information I needed to make a decision.

_____ 8. The cords connecting the computer to its printer need to be replaced before them wear down.

_____ 9. He is going to the party with you and me if you do not mind.

_____ 10. You and her ought to return the books to the library because they are already overdue.

SKILL 44:   DISTINGUISH POSSESSIVE ADJECTIVES AND PRONOUNS

Possessive adjectives and pronouns both show who or what "owns" a noun. However, possessive adjectives and possessive pronouns do not have the same function, and these two kinds of possessives can be confused on the TOEFL test. A possessive adjective describes a noun: it must be accompanied by a noun. A possessive pronoun takes the place of a noun: it cannot be accompanied by a noun.

They lent me *their* book.
ADJECTIVE

They lent me *theirs*.
PRONOUN

Notice that in the first example the possessive adjective *their* is accompanied by the noun *book*. In the second example the possessive pronoun *theirs* is not accompanied by a noun.

These examples show the types of errors that are possible with possessive adjectives and possessive pronouns on the TOEFL test.

Each morning they read *theirs** newspapers.
Could you give me *your**?

In the first example, the possessive pronoun *theirs* is incorrect because it is accompanied by the noun *newspapers,* and a possessive pronoun cannot be accompanied by a noun. The possessive adjective *their* is needed in the first example. In the second example, the possessive adjective *your* is incorrect because it is not accompanied by a noun, and a possessive adjective must be accompanied by a noun. The possessive pronoun *yours* is needed in the second example.

The following chart outlines the possessives and their uses:

POSSESSIVE ADJECTIVES	POSSESSIVE PRONOUNS
my *your* *his* *her* *its* *our* *their*	*mine* *yours* *his* *hers* — *ours* *theirs*
must be accompanied by a noun	*cannot* be accompanied by a noun

EXERCISE 44: Each of the following sentences contains at least one possessive pronoun or adjective. Circle the possessives in these sentences. Then indicate if the sentences are correct (C) or incorrect (I).

___I___   1.   If she borrows (your) coat, then you should be able to borrow (her).

___C___   2.   Each pot and pan in (her) kitchen has (its) own place on the shelf.

_____   3.   Mary and Mark invited theirs parents to see their new apartment.

_____ 4. When my roommate paid her half of the rent, I paid mine.

_____ 5. All students need to bring theirs own pencils and answer sheets to the exam.

_____ 6. All her secretaries are working late tonight to finish her report.

_____ 7. The horse trotting around the track won its race a few minutes ago.

_____ 8. Before the report is finalized, the information in their notes and our must be proofed.

_____ 9. She worked all day cooking food and making decorations for her son's birthday party.

_____ 10. The weather in the mountains this weekend will be extremely cold, so please take yours heavy jackets.

SKILL 45:   CHECK PRONOUN REFERENCE FOR AGREEMENT

After you have checked that the subject and object pronouns and the possessives are used correctly, you should also check each of these pronouns and possessives for agreement. The following are examples of errors of this type that you might find on the TOEFL test:

> The boys will cause trouble if you let _him*_.
> Everyone must give _their*_ name.

In the first example, the singular pronoun _him_ is incorrect because it refers to the plural noun _boys_. This pronoun should be replaced with the plural pronoun _them_. In the second example, the plural possessive adjective _their_ is incorrect because it refers to the singular _everyone_. This adjective should be replaced with the singular _his_ or _his or her_.

The following chart outlines what you should remember about checking pronoun reference:

PRONOUN AGREEMENT
1. Be sure that every pronoun and possessive agrees with the noun it refers to.
2. You generally check _back_ in the sentence for agreement.

EXERCISE 45: Each of the following sentences contains at least one pronoun or possessive. Circle the pronouns and possessives. Draw arrows to the nouns they refer to. Then indicate if the sentences are correct (C) or incorrect (I).

__I__ 1. If a person really wants to succeed, (they) must always work hard.

__C__ 2. If you see the students from the math class, could you return (their) exam papers to (them?)

_____ 3. Some friends and I went to see a movie, and afterwards we wrote a critique about them.

_____ 4. If you have a problem, you are welcome to discuss it with me before you try to resolve them.

_____ 5. I know you had a terrible time last week, but you must try to forget about it.

_____ 6. At the start of the program, each student needs to see his advisor about his schedule.

_____ 7. In spite of its small size, these video recorders produce excellent tapes.

_____ 8. Whatever the situation, you should reflect profoundly about them before coming to a decision.

_____ 9. The people I admire most are those who manage to solve their own problems.

_____ 10. If anyone stops by while I am at the meeting, please take a message from them.

EXERCISE (Skills 43–45): Circle the pronouns and possessives in the following sentences. Then indicate if the sentences are correct (C) or incorrect (I).

_____ 1. Helicopters are being used more and more in emergency situations because of its ability to reach out-of-the-way places.

_____ 2. The worker was fired by the chemical company because his refused to work with certain dangerous chemicals.

_____ 3. If you have car trouble while driving on the freeway, you should pull your car over to the side of the freeway and wait for help.

_____ 4. The administration will not install the new security system because they cost so much.

_____ 5. Some parents prefer to send their children to private schools because they believe the children will be better educated.

_____ 6. The air traffic controller was not blamed for the accident because he had strictly followed the correct procedures.

_____ 7. The new student has been assigned to work on the project with you and I.

_____ 8. Many different kinds of aspirin are on the market, but theirs effectiveness seems to be equal.

_____ 9. You must bring a tent and a sleeping bag for your trip to the Sierras.

_____ 10. Each of the team members had their new uniform.

TOEFL EXERCISE (Skills 43–45): Choose the letter of the underlined word or group of words that is not correct.

_____ 1. Superman <u>made</u> <u>their</u> comic <u>debut</u> in 1938 <u>in</u> *Action Comics*.
            A   B   C   D

_____ 2. Commercial letters of credit are <u>often used</u> to finance <u>export</u> trade, but <u>them</u> can
                                              A   B   C
have <u>other uses</u>.
       D

_____ 3. When children <u>experience</u> <u>too much</u> frustration, <u>its</u> behavior <u>ceases</u> to be integrated.
                          A   B   C   D

_____ 4. On March 30, 1981, President Reagan <u>was shot</u> <u>as</u> <u>his</u> was <u>leaving</u> a Washington hotel.
                                                A   B   C   D

_____ 5. Although the destruction that <u>it causes</u> is often terrible, cyclones <u>benefit</u> a
                                          A   B
<u>much wider</u> belt than <u>they</u> devastate.
       C   D

_____ 6. President Andrew Jackson had <u>an official</u> cabinet, but <u>him</u> <u>preferred</u> the advice of <u>his</u>
                                         A   B   C   D
informal advisors, the Kitchen Cabinet.

_____ 7. After <u>Clarence Day's</u> book *Life with Father* was <u>rewritten</u> as a play, <u>they</u> ran for <u>six years</u>
                  A   B   C   D
on Broadway.

_____ 8. <u>Almost</u> <u>half</u> of the Pilgrims did not survive <u>theirs</u> <u>first</u> winter in the New World.
            A   B   C   D

_____ 9. There was <u>no</u> <u>indication</u> from the Senate that <u>he</u> would agree with the decision <u>made</u>
                      A   B   C   D
in the House.

_____ 10. A baby learns the meanings of words as <u>they</u> are spoken by <u>others</u> and <u>later</u> uses <u>him</u>
                                                    A   B   C   D
in sentences.

TOEFL REVIEW EXERCISE (Skills 1–45): Choose the letter of the word or group of words that best completes the sentence.

1. _____ worst phase of the Depression, more than thirteen million Americans had no jobs.

   (A) It was in the
   (B) During the
   (C) While the
   (D) The

2. When reading a book, you must keep your point of view separate from the point of view in _____ you are studying.

   (A) that
   (B) the material and
   (C) the materials that
   (D) the materials that are

3. Speech consists not merely of sounds but _____ that follow various structural patterns.

    (A) of organized sound patterns
    (B) organized sound patterns
    (C) that sound patterns are organized
    (D) in organizing sound patterns

Choose the letter of the underlined word or group of words that is not correct.

_____ 4. The <u>latest</u> medical report indicated that the patient's temperature was <u>near normal</u>
           A   B
and <u>their</u> lungs <u>were</u> partially cleared.
      C   D

_____ 5. Most oxygen atoms <u>have</u> eight neutrons, but a small <u>amount</u> have <u>nine or ten</u>.
        A   B   C   D

_____ 6. When Paine expressed <u>his</u> <u>belief</u> in independence, he <u>praised</u> by <u>the public</u>.
                        A B   C   D

_____ 7. A <u>vast quantity</u> of <u>radioactive material</u> <u>is</u> made when <u>does a hydrogen bomb explode</u>.
            A   B   C   D

_____ 8. Genes have <u>several alternative</u> <u>form</u>, or alleles, <u>which</u> are <u>produced by</u> mutations.
                   A   B   C   D

_____ 9. A star that has used up <u>its</u> energy and has <u>lost</u> its <u>heat</u> <u>became</u> a black dwarf.
                      A   B   C D

_____ 10. Each <u>lines</u> of poetry <u>written</u> in blank verse <u>has</u> ten syllables, which are <u>alternately</u>
              A   B   C   D
stressed and unstressed.

PROBLEMS WITH ADJECTIVES AND ADVERBS _____

Many different problems with adjectives and adverbs are possible in written expression questions on the TOEFL test. To identify these problems, you must first be able to recognize adjectives and adverbs.

Often adverbs are formed by adding *-ly* to adjectives, and these *-ly* adverbs are very easy to recognize. The following examples show adverbs that are formed by adding *-ly* to adjectives:

ADJECTIVE	ADVERB
recent	*recently*
public	*publicly*
evident	*evidently*

However, there are many adverbs in English that do not end in *-ly*. These adverbs can be recognized from their meanings. They can describe *when* something happens (*often, soon, later*), *how* something happens (*fast, hard, well*), or *where* something happens (*here, there, nowhere*).

There are three skills involving adjectives and adverbs that will help you on written expression questions on the TOEFL test: (1) knowing when to use adjectives and adverbs, (2) using adjectives rather than adverbs after linking verbs, and (3) positioning adjectives and adverbs correctly.

SKILL 46:   USE BASIC ADJECTIVES AND ADVERBS CORRECTLY

Sometimes in written expression questions on the TOEFL test, adjectives are used in place of adverbs, or adverbs are used in place of adjectives. Adjectives and adverbs have very different uses. Adjectives have only one job: they describe nouns or pronouns.

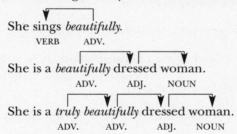

She is a *beautiful* woman.
ADJ.   NOUN

She is *beautiful*.
PRO.   ADJ.

In the first example, the adjective *beautiful* describes the noun *woman*. In the second example, the adjective *beautiful* describes the pronoun *she*.

Adverbs do three different things. They describe verbs, adjectives, or other adverbs.

She sings *beautifully*.
VERB   ADV.

She is a *beautifully* dressed woman.
ADV.   ADJ.   NOUN

She is a *truly beautifully* dressed woman.
ADV.   ADV.   ADJ.   NOUN

In the first example, the adverb *beautifully* describes the verb *sings*. In the second example, the adverb *beautifully* describes the adjective *dressed* (which describes the noun *woman*). In the third example, the adverb *truly* describes the adverb *beautifully*, which describes the adjective *dressed* (which describes the noun *woman*).

The following are examples of incorrect sentences as they might appear on the TOEFL test.

They were seated at a *largely** table.
ADV.   NOUN

The child talked *quick** to her mother.
VERB   ADJ.

We read an *extreme** long story.
ADJ.   ADJ.

In the first example, the adverb *largely* is incorrect because the adjective *large* is needed to describe the noun *table*. In the second example, the adjective *quick* is incorrect because the adverb *quickly* is needed to describe the verb *talked*. In the last example, the adjective *extreme* is incorrect because the adverb *extremely* is needed to describe the adjective *long*.

The following chart outlines the important information that you should remember about the basic use of adjectives and adverbs:

BASIC USE OF ADJECTIVES AND ADVERBS	
ADJECTIVES	Adjectives describe *nouns* or *pronouns*.
ADVERBS	Adverbs describe *verbs*, *adjectives*, or other *adverbs*.

EXERCISE 46: Each of the following sentences has at least one adjective or adverb. Circle the adjectives and adverbs, and label them. Draw arrows to the words they describe. Then indicate if the sentences are correct (C) or incorrect (I).

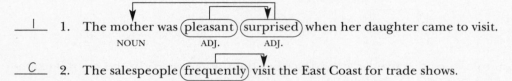

__I__   1. The mother was (pleasant) (surprised) when her daughter came to visit.
                   NOUN   ADJ.   ADJ.

__C__   2. The salespeople (frequently) visit the East Coast for trade shows.
                         ADV.   VERB

_____   3. He was driving an expensively sports car.

_____   4. There is a special program on television this evening.

_____   5. She was chosen for the leading part because she sings so well.

_____   6. The car was not complete ready at 3:00.

_____   7. It was difficult to believe that what we read in the newspaper was a truly story.

_____   8. Points will be subtracted for each incorrect answered question.

_____   9. The production manager quietly requested a completely report of the terribly incident.

_____ 10. The children finished their homework quickly so that they could watch television.

SKILL 47:   USE ADJECTIVES AFTER LINKING VERBS

Generally an adverb rather than an adjective will come directly after a verb because the adverb is describing the verb.

                  She spoke *nicely.*
                  VERB   ADV.

In this example, the verb *spoke* is followed by the adverb *nicely*. This adverb describes the verb *spoke*.

However, you must be very careful if the verb is a *linking* verb. A *linking* verb is followed by an adjective rather than an adverb.

She looks *nice.*
SUB.   ADJ.

In this example, the linking verb *looks* is followed by the adjective *nice.* This adjective describes the subject *she.*

You should be sure to use an adjective rather than an adverb after a linking verb. Be careful, however, because the adjective that goes with the linking verb does not always directly follow the linking verb.

He seems *unusually nice.*
SUB.   ADV.   ADJ.

In this example, the adjective *nice,* which describes the subject *he,* is itself described by the adverb *unusually.* From this example, you should notice that it is possible to have an adverb directly after a linking verb, but only if the adverb describes an adjective that follows.

The following chart lists commonly used linking verbs and outlines the different uses of adjectives and adverbs after regular verbs and linking verbs:

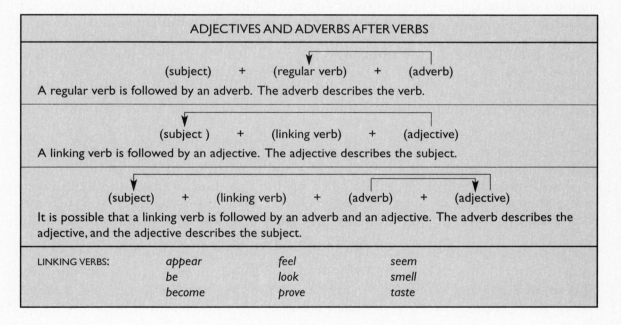

ADJECTIVES AND ADVERBS AFTER VERBS
(subject)   +   (regular verb)   +   (adverb) A regular verb is followed by an adverb. The adverb describes the verb.
(subject)   +   (linking verb)   +   (adjective) A linking verb is followed by an adjective. The adjective describes the subject.
(subject)   +   (linking verb)   +   (adverb)   +   (adjective) It is possible that a linking verb is followed by an adverb and an adjective. The adverb describes the adjective, and the adjective describes the subject.
LINKING VERBS: appear   feel   seem be   look   smell become   prove   taste

EXERCISE 47: Each of the following sentences contains at least one adjective or adverb. Circle the adjectives and adverbs, and label them. Draw arrows to the words they describe. Then indicate if the sentences are correct (C) or incorrect (I).

___I___ 1. The parents seem (angrily) about the child's report card.
                                          ADV.

___C___ 2. The speaker talked (knowingly) about (prehistoric) fossils.
                                          ADV.   ADJ.

_____ 3. After she drank the lemonade, the cake tasted too sweetly to her.

_____ 4. Throughout dinner we were bored because he spoke incessantly.

_____ 5. Sam felt terribly depressed after the accident.

_____ 6. The neighbor appeared calm in spite of the fact that his house was on fire.

_____ 7. He looked quite unhappily at the thought of leaving his job.

_____ 8. Marla jumped up quick when she heard the gunshot.

_____ 9. Even though we were not really hungry, the food smelled delicious.

_____ 10. The history course that I took last semester proved more difficultly than I had expected.

Skill 48:   POSITION ADJECTIVES AND ADVERBS CORRECTLY

Adjectives and adverbs can appear in incorrect positions in written expression questions on the TOEFL test. There are two common errors of this type that you should beware of: (1) the position of adjectives with the nouns they describe, and (2) the position of adverbs with objects.

In English it is correct to place a one-word adjective in front of the noun it describes. On the TOEFL test, however, an incorrect sentence might have an adjective after the noun it describes.

The information *important** is on the first page.

NOUN   ADJ.

In this example, the adjective *important* should come before the noun *information* because *important* describes *information*.

A second problem you should be aware of is the position of adverbs with objects of verbs. When a verb has an object, an adverb describing the verb should not come between the verb and its object.

He <u>has taken</u> *recently** an English course.

ADV.   OBJECT

This example is incorrect because the adverb *recently* comes between the verb *has taken* and its object *an English course*. There are many possible corrections for this sentence.

Recently he has taken an English course.
He has *recently* taken an English course.
He has taken an English course *recently*.

You can see from these examples that there are many possible correct positions for the adverb. What is important for you to remember is that an adverb that describes a verb cannot come between the verb and its object.

The following chart outlines the key points that you should remember about the position of adjectives and adverbs:

THE POSITION OF ADJECTIVES AND ADVERBS	
ADJECTIVES	A one-word *adjective* comes before the noun it describes. It does not come directly after.
ADVERBS	An *adverb* can appear in many positions. It cannot be used between a verb and its object.

EXERCISE 48: Each of the following sentences contains at least one adjective or adverb. Circle the adjectives and adverbs, and label them. Draw arrows to the words they describe. Then indicate if the sentences are correct (C) or incorrect (I).

__I__   1.   The store opened with a sale (fantastic.)
                                        ADJ.

__C__   2.   The pharmacist has (always) filled our order (quickly.)
                       ADV.   ADV.

_____   3.   The political candidates expressed their opposing views.

_____   4.   The lawyer has selected carefully a new case.

_____   5.   Frequently the coffee has tasted bitter.

_____   6.   The wedding reception was held at a restaurant expensive.

_____   7.   The salesclerk has often traveled to New York.

_____   8.   Following the failure of the first set of plans, the manager has altered subsequently them.

_____   9.   The students had to study many hours daily during the program intensive.

_____ 10.   The naval officer was asked to transfer to a foreign country.

EXERCISE (Skills 46–48): Circle the adjectives and adverbs in the following sentences. Draw arrows to the words they describe. Then indicate if the sentences are correct (C) or incorrect (I).

_____   1.   They were unable to see where their friends were sitting in the theater because of the lights dim.

_____   2.   After the comprehensive exam, she looked exhaustedly by the experience.

_____   3.   The project was remarkable close to being finished.

_____   4.   Mark always does his homework careful.

_____ 5.   The program proved far more interesting than I had imagined it would be.

_____ 6.   The student had attended regularly all the lectures in the series.

_____ 7.   The patient became healthy after the operation.

_____ 8.   The grandparents speak proudly about all their offspring.

_____ 9.   The manager seemed certainly that the project would be finished under budget.

_____ 10.   The firefighters worked feverishly, and they put out immediately the fire.

TOEFL EXERCISE (Skills 46–48):   Choose the letter of the underlined word or group of words that is not correct.

_____ 1.   Modern art is on display at the Guggenheim Museum, a building with an unusually
                        A   B   C   D

           design.

_____ 2.   By the beginning of the 1980s fifteen states had adopted already no-fault insurance
                           A   B   C   D

           laws.

_____ 3.   Heart attacks are fatally in 75 percent of occurrences.
                  A   B   C   D

_____ 4.   In spite of a tremendous amount of electronic gadgetry, air traffic control still
                      A   B   C

           depends heavy on people.
                  D

_____ 5.   Only recently have Gooden's industrially designers and engineers been able to
                  A   B

           optimize Watertred's unusual tread patterns for mass production.
                       C   D

_____ 6.   A baboon's arms appear as lengthily as its legs.
              A   B   C   D

_____ 7.   A serious problem is how to communicate reliable with a submerged submarine.
                A   B   C   D

_____ 8.   Americans are destroying rapidly wetlands, faster than an acre every two minutes.
              A   B   C   D

_____ 9.   The central banking system of the United States consists of twelve banks district.
              A   B   C   D

_____ 10.   Telegraph service across the Atlantic was successful established in 1866.
                  A   B   C   D

TOEFL REVIEW EXERCISE (Skills 1–48): Choose the letter of the word or group of words that best completes the sentence.

1. Patty Berg, the top tournament winner in women's golf, _____ eighty-three golf tournaments from 1935 through 1964.

    (A) she won
    (B) winning
    (C) won
    (D) who won

2. _____ with about fifteen times its weight in air does gasoline allow the carburetor to run smoothly.

    (A) It is mixed
    (B) To mix it
    (C) When mixed
    (D) Only when mixed

Choose the letter of the underlined word or group of words that is not correct.

_____ 3. The Colorado River reaches their maximum height during April and May.
                          A   B   C   D

_____ 4. Plant proteins tend to have few amino acids than proteins from animal sources.
                A   B   C   D

_____ 5. The Viking spacecraft has landed on Mars in July of 1976.
              A   B   C   D

_____ 6. Admiral Byrd commanded airplane expeditions over both the Arctic or the Antarctic.
                      A   B   C   D

_____ 7. The advertising campaign will be based on the recent completed study.
             A   B   C   D

_____ 8. Coronary occlusion results from a disease in which fatty substances with a large
                                    A   B

        amount of cholesterol is deposited in the arteries.
             C   D

_____ 9. Her money gave back as soon as she threatened to take the matter to court.
                   A   B   C   D

_____ 10. Other sites of fossil discoveries throughout Wyoming, ranging from the fiery
             A   B

        Tyrannosaurus rex to the milder *Triceratops*, have proven equally excite.
                                C   D

MORE PROBLEMS WITH ADJECTIVES _____

The previous section dealt with various problems related to both adjectives and adverbs. This section deals with a few problems that are related only to adjectives: (1) *-ly* adjectives, (2) predicate adjectives, and (3) *-ed* and *-ing* adjectives.

SKILL 49: RECOGNIZE *-LY* ADJECTIVES

Generally when a word ends in *-ly* in English, it is an adverb. However, there are a few words ending in *-ly* that are adjectives, and these *-ly* adjectives can cause confusion in written expression questions on the TOEFL test.

The manager turned in his *weekly* report.
ADJ.   NOUN

This example is correct, but it appears to be incorrect; it appears that there is an *-ly* adverb in front of the noun *report*. However, *weekly* is an adjective that describes the noun *report*.

The following chart lists common *-ly* adjectives that can appear in English:

-LY ADJECTIVES				
costly	likely	daily	quarterly	northerly
early	lively	hourly	weekly	easterly
friendly	lonely	monthly	yearly	southerly
kindly	manly	nightly	lovely	westerly

EXERCISE 49: Each of the following sentences contains at least one adjective or adverb ending in *-ly*. Circle the *-ly* words, and label them as either adjectives or adverbs. Draw arrows to the words they describe. Then indicate if the sentences are correct (C) or incorrect (I).

_C_ 1. Federal taxes are (yearly) taxes which must be paid every April.
ADJ.

_I_ 2. At the fashion show, the new (seasonally) fashions will be shown.
ADV.

_____ 3. Do you want to go to the early movie or the lately movie?

_____ 4. She offered me some friendly advice about how to deal with the terribly problem.

_____ 5. The quarterly reports need to be turned in at the next weekly meeting.

_____ 6. He did not have a manly reaction to the negatively comments.

_____ 7. The likely outcome of the purchase of the costly car is that he will not be able to pay his monthly bills.

_____ 8. The days she spent at the beach house were lonely and solitarily.

_____ 9. She takes her daily medication on a regularly schedule.

_____ 10. The kindly neighbor paid hourly visits to her unhealthily friend.

SKILL 50:   USE PREDICATE ADJECTIVES CORRECTLY

Certain adjectives appear only in the predicate of the sentence; that is, they appear after a linking verb such as *be,* and they cannot appear directly in front of the nouns that they describe.

> The snake on the rock was *alive.*
> The *alive** snake was lying on the rock.

In the first example, the predicate adjective *alive* is used correctly after the linking verb *was* to describe the subject *snake.* In the second example, the predicate adjective *alive* is used incorrectly in front of the noun *snake.* In this position, the adjective *live* should be used.

The following chart lists some common predicate adjectives and the corresponding forms that can be used in front of the noun:

PREDICATE ADJECTIVES	
PREDICATE ADJECTIVES	FORMS USED IN FRONT OF A NOUN
alike *alive* *alone* *afraid* *asleep*	*like, similar* *live, living* *lone* *frightened* *sleeping*
A predicate adjective appears after a linking verb such as *be.* It cannot appear directly in front of the noun that it describes.	

EXERCISE 50: Each of the following sentences contains a predicate adjective or its related form. Circle the predicate adjectives or related forms. Then indicate if the sentences are correct (C) or incorrect (I).

__C__ 1. The two brothers do not look at all (alike.)

__I__ 2. My friend brought the (alive) lobster to my house and expected me to cook it.

_____ 3. Are you going to be lone in the house tonight?

_____ 4. The afraid child cried for his mother.

_____ 5. Everyone else was asleep by the time I arrived home.

_____ 6. We completed our two projects in a like manner.

_____ 7. All of the crash victims were alive when they were found.

_____ 8. She tried to walk quietly by the asleep dogs without waking them.

_____ 9.   Were you feeling afraid when you heard the noise?

_____ 10. According to the report, the president was shot by an alone gunman.

Skill 51:   Use -ED and -ING Adjectives Correctly

Verb forms ending in *-ed* and *-ing* can be used as adjectives. For example, the verbal adjectives *cleaned* and *cleaning* come from the verb *to clean*.

The woman *cleans* the car.
VERB

The *cleaning* woman worked on the car.
ADJECTIVE

The woman put the *cleaned* car back in the garage.
ADJECTIVE

In the first example, *cleans* is the verb of the sentence. In the second example, *cleaning* is a verbal adjective describing *woman*. In the third example, *cleaned* is a verbal adjective describing *car*.

Verbal adjectives ending in *-ed* and *-ing* can be confused in written expression questions on the TOEFL test.

The *cleaning** car…
The *cleaned** woman…

The difference between an *-ed* and an *-ing* adjective is similar to the difference between the active and the passive (see Skills 37 and 38). An *-ing* adjective (like the active) means that the noun it describes is *doing* the action. The above example about *the cleaning car* is not correct because a car cannot do the action of cleaning: you cannot say that *a car cleans itself*. An *-ed* adjective (like the passive) means that the noun it describes is *receiving* the action from the verb. The above example about *the cleaned woman* is not correct because in this example a woman does not receive the action of the verb *clean*: this sentence does not mean that *someone cleaned the woman*.

The following chart outlines the key information that you should remember about *-ed* and *-ing* adjectives:

-ED AND -ING ADJECTIVES			
TYPE	MEANING	USE	EXAMPLE
-ING	active	It *does* the action of the verb.	…the happily *playing* children … (The children *play*.)
-ED	passive	It *receives* the action of the verb.	…the frequently *played* record … (Someone *plays* the record.)

EXERCISE 51: Each of the following sentences contains either an *-ed* or an *-ing* verbal adjective. Circle the verbal adjectives. Draw arrows to the words they describe. Then indicate if the sentences are correct (C) or incorrect (I).

__I__   1. The teacher gave a quiz on the just (completing) lesson.

__C__   2. There is a (fascinating) movie at the theater tonight.

_____   3. They thought that it had been a very satisfied dinner.

_____   4. The empty bottles are to the left, and the filling bottles are to the right.

_____   5. For lunch at the restaurant she ordered a mixed salad.

_____   6. The students thought that it was an interesting assignment.

_____   7. The shoppers were impressed by the reducing prices.

_____   8. He can't afford to take long vacations to exotic places because he is a worked man.

_____   9. I recently received several annoying phone calls from the insurance agent.

_____ 10. Today the bookkeeper will work on the unpaying bills.

EXERCISE (Skills 49–51): Circle the adjectives in each of the following sentences. Draw arrows to the nouns or pronouns they describe. Then indicate if the sentences are correct (C) or incorrect (I).

_____   1. Her kindly words of thanks made me feel appreciating.

_____   2. After the earthquake, assistance was sent to the damaging areas.

_____   3. Your view has some validity; however, we do not have alike opinions on the matter.

_____   4. It is likely that the early seminar will not be the most interested.

_____   5. I prefer a live theater show to a movie.

_____   6. The thesis of your essay was not very well developed.

_____   7. The asleep children were wakened by the loud sound of the crashing thunder.

_____   8. During the nightly news show there was a lively and fascinating debate.

_____   9. His car was struck by an uninsured motorist.

_____ 10. The girl was all alone and feeling lonely in the darkened, frightened house.

TOEFL EXERCISE (Skills 49–51): Choose the letter of the underlined word or group of words that is not correct.

_____ 1. As the only major American river that flowed in a west direction, the Ohio was the
         A   B   C
preferred route for settlers.
   D

_____ 2. During the annually salmon migration from the sea to fresh water, Alaska's McNeil
                     A   B
River becomes a gathering place for brown bears waiting eagerly to catch their fill.
                 C   D

_____ 3. Edelman stresses the mounting evidence showing that greatly variation on a
                            A   B   C
microscopic scale is likely.
                     D

_____ 4. Perhaps the most welcoming and friendly of the park's wild places is the live oak
                         A   B   C
forest that surrounds the district's alone visitors' center in Gulf Breeze.
                                     D

_____ 5. Halley's comet, viewing through a telescope, was quite impressive.
                        A   B   C   D

_____ 6. The state of deep asleep is characterized by rapid eye movement, or REM, sleep.
                     A   B   C   D

_____ 7. Among the disputing sections of the Monteverdi opera are the sinfonia, the
         A   B   C   D
prologue, and the role of Ottone.

_____ 8. Most probably because of the likable rapport between anchors, the night newscast on
              A   B   C
the local ABC affiliate has recently moved well beyond its competitors in the ratings
                            D
battle.

_____ 9. Signing at the outset of a business deal, a contract offers the participants a certain
         A   B   C
degree of legal protection from costly mistakes.
                                D

_____ 10. The story presented by Fischer is a headlong tale told so effectively that
                                             A   B
its momentum carries the reader right through the live endnotes.
   C   D

TOEFL REVIEW EXERCISE (Skills 1–51): Choose the letter of the word or group of words that best completes the sentence.

1. During the early nineteenth century, the Spanish missions in Alta, California _____ to be an integral part of the economy and productive capacity of the region.

   (A) proved
   (B) they proved
   (C) they proved it
   (D) proved it

2. Still other hurdles remain before _____ suitable for private cars.

   (A) fuel cells
   (B) become
   (C) fuel cells become
   (D) that fuel cells become

3. The daughters of Joseph LaFlesche were born into the generation of Omaha forced to abandon tribal traditions, _____ on the reservation, and to adapt to the white man's ways.

   (A) they matured
   (B) to mature
   (C) maturing
   (D) to maturity

4. Among the most revealing aspects of mining towns _____ their paucity of public open space.

   (A) was
   (B) were
   (C) it was
   (D) so

Choose the letter of the underlined word or group of words that is not correct.

_____ 5. Factor analysis <u>is used</u> to discover <u>how many</u> abilities are <u>involve</u> in intelligence test
               A   B   C   D
        performance.

_____ 6. One of the <u>early</u> orders of marine mammals, manatees <u>have evolved</u> more than fifty
                 A   B
        <u>million</u> years ago <u>from</u> land animals.
           C   D

_____ 7. Dolphins and chimps are <u>like</u> <u>in</u> <u>that</u> they <u>have been shown</u> to have language skills.
                       A B C   D

_____ 8. In the appendix at the <u>end</u> of the chapter <u>are</u> the instructions <u>to be used</u> for the
                           A   B   C
        <u>completion correct</u> of the form.
             D

_____ 9. <u>Used</u> sound <u>that varies</u> not only in time <u>but in space</u>, whales at close range may
         A   B   C
        <u>communicate with</u> sonarlike "pictures."
            D

_____ 10. The 1898 Trans-Mississippi International Exposition <u>has</u> the distinction <u>of being</u> the
                                             A   B
        last major fair <u>which held</u> <u>during</u> the Victorian period.
                 C   D

PROBLEMS WITH ARTICLES

Articles are very difficult to learn because there are many rules, many exceptions, and many special cases. It is possible, however, to learn a few rules that will help you to use articles correctly much of the time.

Nouns in English can be either countable or uncountable. If a noun is countable, it must be either singular or plural. In addition to these general types of nouns, there are two types of articles: definite (specific) and indefinite (general).

ARTICLES	COUNTABLE SINGULAR NOUNS	COUNTABLE PLURAL NOUNS	UNCOUNTABLE NOUNS
INDEFINITE (General)	*a* dollar *an* apple	_____ dollars _____ apples	_____ money _____ juice
DEFINITE (Specific)	*the* dollar *the* apple	*the* dollars *the* apples	*the* money *the* juice

SKILL 52:   USE ARTICLES WITH SINGULAR NOUNS

You can see from the chart that if a noun is either countable plural or uncountable, it is possible to have either the definite article *the* or no article (indefinite). With **all** countable singular nouns, however, you must have an article (unless you have another determiner such as *my* or *each*).

> I have *money.*   (uncountable — no article needed)
> I have *books.*   (countable plural — no article needed)
> I have a *book.*   (countable singular — article needed)

The following chart outlines the key information that you should remember about articles with singular nouns:

ARTICLES WITH SINGULAR NOUNS
A singular noun **must** have an article (*a, an, the*) or some other determiner such as *my* or *each*. (A plural noun or an uncountable noun **may** or **may not** have an article.)

EXERCISE 52: The following sentences contain different types of nouns. Circle only the countable singular nouns. Mark where articles (or determiners) have been omitted. Then indicate if the sentences are correct (C) or incorrect (I).

__I__ 1.   She is taking ⱽ(trip) with friends.

__C__ 2.   In my (yard) there are flowers, trees, and grass.

_____ 3.   The manager sent memo to his employees.

_____ 4.   There is car in front of the building.

_____ 5.   The child and his friends are having milk and cookies.

_____ 6. She is studying to be an actress in films.

_____ 7. My neighbor was arrested for throwing rocks through windows.

_____ 8. We have machinery that prints ten pages each minute.

_____ 9. Teacher has many students during a semester.

_____ 10. Can you heat water for tea?

SKILL 53: DISTINGUISH *A* AND *AN*

The basic difference between *a* and *an* is that *a* is used in front of consonants and *an* is used in front of vowels (*a, e, i, o, u*):

a book	*an* orange
a man	*an* illness
a page	*an* automobile

There are two exceptions to this rule: *u* and *h*. When *u* is pronounced like the consonant *y* (as in *usual*), it is preceded by the article *a* rather than *an*. When *h* is not pronounced (as in *honor*), it is preceded by the article *an* rather than *a*. Pronounce the following examples:

a university	*an* unhappy man	*a* hospital	*an* honor
a unit	*an* understanding	*a* heart	*an* herb

The following chart outlines the key information about the use of *a* and *an*:

A AND AN	
A	A is used in front of a singular noun with a *consonant* sound.
AN	An is used in front of a singular noun with a *vowel* sound.
Be careful of nouns beginning with H or U. They may have a vowel or a consonant sound.	

EXERCISE 53: Each of the following sentences contains *a* or *an*. Circle each *a* or *an*. Underline the beginning of the word that directly follows. Pronounce the word. Then indicate if the sentences are correct (C) or incorrect (I).

__I__ 1. The dishwasher quit his job because he was making only four dollars (a) hour.

__C__ 2. It was (an) unexpected disappointment to receive (a) rejection letter from the university.

_____ 3. It is raining, so you should bring a umbrella.

_____ 4. He bought a half gallon of milk and a box of a hundred envelopes.

_____ 5. An objection was raised because it was such a unacceptable idea.

_____ 6.   The workers at the plant do not belong to a union.

_____ 7.   The police officer was not wearing an uniform when she arrested the suspect.

_____ 8.   If you do not give me a hand, finishing the project on time will be an impossibility.

_____ 9.   She was upset when a honest mistake was made.

_____ 10.   She opened a account at a local department store.

SKILL 54:   MAKE ARTICLES AGREE WITH NOUNS

The definite article (*the*) is used for both singular and plural nouns, so agreement is not a problem with the definite article. However, because the use of the indefinite article is different for singular and plural nouns, you must be careful of agreement between the indefinite article and the noun. One very common agreement error is to use the singular indefinite article (*a* or *an*) with a plural noun.

> He saw *a** new *movies.*
> They traveled to *a** nearby *mountains.*
> Do you have *another** books?*

In these examples, you should not have *a* or *an* because the nouns are plural. The following sentences are possible corrections of the sentences above.

> He saw a new movie.   (singular)
> He saw new movies.   (plural)
>
> They traveled to a nearby mountain.   (singular)
> They traveled to nearby mountains.   (plural)
>
> Do you have another book?   (singular)
> Do you have other books?   (plural)

The following chart states the key point for you to remember about the agreement of articles with nouns:

AGREEMENT OF ARTICLES WITH NOUNS
You should never use *a* or *an* with a plural noun.

EXERCISE 54: Each of the following sentences contains *a* or *an*. Circle each *a* or *an*. Draw an arrow to the noun it describes. Then indicate if the sentences are correct (C) or incorrect (I).

__C__ 1.   She went to school in (a) local community.

__I__   2.   The doctor used (an) other pills.

_____ 3.   It is necessary to have a farm or land of your own.

_____ 4.   He must contact a members of the club.

_____ 5. You will need a pen or a pencil.

_____ 6. He is responsible for bringing a number of items.

_____ 7. You must write a report on a subjects of your choice.

_____ 8. They crossed through several forests and a stream.

_____ 9. There will be another important lessons tomorrow.

_____ 10. He could not give me a good reasons for what he did.

SKILL 55: DISTINGUISH SPECIFIC AND GENERAL IDEAS

With countable singular nouns it is possible to use either the definite or the indefinite article, but they have different meanings. The definite article is used to refer to one specific noun.

> Tom will bring _the_ book tomorrow.
> (There is one specific book that Tom will bring tomorrow.)

> He will arrive on _the_ first Tuesday in July.
> (There is only one first Tuesday in July.)

> He sailed on _the_ Pacific Ocean.
> (There is only one Pacific Ocean.)

The indefinite article is used when the noun could be one of several different nouns.

> Tom will bring _a_ book tomorrow.
> (Tom will bring any one book.)

> He will arrive on _a_ Tuesday in July.
> (He will arrive on one of four Tuesdays in July.)

> He sailed on _an_ ocean.
> (He sailed on any one of the world's oceans.)

   The following chart outlines the key information that you should understand about specific and general ideas:

SPECIFIC AND GENERAL IDEAS		
ARTICLE	MEANING	USES
A or AN	general idea	Use when there are _many_, and you do not _know_ which one it is. Use when there are _many_, and you do not _care_ which one it is.
THE	specific idea	Use when it is _the only one_. Use when there are _many_, and you _know_ which one it is.

EXERCISE 55: Each of the following sentences contains one or more articles. Circle the articles. Draw arrows to the nouns they describe. Then indicate if the sentences are correct (C) or incorrect (I).

__I__   1. He took (a) trip on (a) Snake River.

__C__   2. I'll meet you at (the) library later.

_____   3. The ball hit a child on a head.

_____   4. He had a best grade in the class on the exam.

_____   5. The people who came here yesterday were here again today.

_____   6. She was a most beautiful girl in the room.

_____   7. The trip that I took last year to the Bahamas was the only vacation I had all year.

_____   8. I need a piece of paper so that I can finish the report that I am working on.

_____   9. A basketball player threw the ball to a center of the court.

_____   10. The sixth-grade class went on a field trip to visit a Lincoln Memorial.

EXERCISE (Skills 52–55): Circle the articles in the following sentences. Then indicate if the sentences are correct (C) or incorrect (I).

_____   1. He took a money from his wallet to pay for sweater.

_____   2. The notebook that he left had an important assignment in it.

_____   3. Because of previous disagreements, they are trying to arrive at an understanding.

_____   4. The appearance of room could be improved by adding a green plants.

_____   5. The Senate passed law banning smoking in public workplaces.

_____   6. Each chemistry student should bring laboratory manual to a next class.

_____   7. She admitted that she made mistake but said that she had made a honest effort.

_____   8. His absence from the board meeting was a strong indications of his desire to leave the company.

_____   9. The car needed gas, so the driver stopped at a service station.

_____   10. Anyone taking group tour to the Hawaiian Islands must pay fee before a first of the month.

TOEFL EXERCISE (Skills 52–55): Choose the letter of the underlined word or group of words that is not correct.

_____ 1. On a trip down to the bottom of the Grand Canyon, the equipment will in all
        A   B   C
probability be carried by a burros.
                  D

_____ 2. Ford designed the first large-scale assembly line at plant in Highland Park, Michigan.
               A   B   C   D

_____ 3. In the human body, blood flows from a heart through the arteries, and it returns
    A   B   C
through the veins.
        D

_____ 4. The scholarship that Wilson received to study history at Cambridge presented an
        A   B   C   D
unique opportunity.

_____ 5. Observations from Earth indicate that at the solar surface, the outward magnetic field
                                 A   B
is a strongest at the polar regions.
   C   D

_____ 6. A radar images of Venus add details about a planet dominated by volcanoes and lava.
    A   B   C   D

_____ 7. In 1863 and 1864, the U.S. Congress passed the National Bank Acts, which set up a
                                A   B
system of privately owned banks chartered by a federal government.
          C   D

_____ 8. An human ear responds to a wide range of frequencies.
    A   B   C   D

_____ 9. Bacteria that live in soil and water play a vital role in recycling carbon, nitrogen,
                     A   B
sulfur, and another chemical elements used by living things.
         C   D

_____ 10. During the U.S. Civil War, an American balloonist organized a balloon corps in Army.
       A   B   C   D

TOEFL REVIEW EXERCISE (Skills 1–55): Choose the letter of the word or group of words that best completes the sentence.

1. In economics, "diminishing returns" describes _____ resource inputs and production.

   (A) among
   (B) when it is
   (C) among them
   (D) the relationship between

2. When lava reaches the surface, its temperature can be ten times _____ boiling water.

   (A) the temperature
   (B) that of
   (C) it is
   (D) more

3. Rarely _____ remove the entire root of a dandelion because of its length and sturdiness.

    (A) can the casual gardener
    (B) the casual gardener
    (C) the casual gardener will
    (D) does the casual gardener's

Choose the letter of the underlined word or group of words that is not correct.

_____ 4. Operas can be broadly classified as either comedies or they are tragedies.
                        A   B   C   D

_____ 5. Tungsten has the highest melting point of all metals, and for this reason it is often
                          A

use in equipment that must withstand high temperatures.
B   C   D

_____ 6. Whereas there are forty-three ant species in Great Britain, the same amount of ant
         A   B   C

species can be found in a single tree in Peru.
                    D

_____ 7. People voice theirs opinions first in small groups or among friends and
              A   B   C

acquaintances.
D

_____ 8. Inside the Lincoln Memorial is a large statue of Lincoln make from white marble.
                       A   B   C   D

_____ 9. Detailed photometric data of the area just north of Triton's equatorial region
             A

indicate the existence of a thin, transparent layers of frost.
B   C   D

_____ 10. U.S. census figures indicate that people with only an elementary education can earn
                   A   B

just half as much as college graduations.
C   D

PROBLEMS WITH PREPOSITIONS _____

Prepositions can be used in two ways: in a literal way and in an idiomatic way. In the literal use, the preposition means exactly what you expect.

> The boy ran *up* the hill.
> She went *in* the house.

In the first example, the preposition *up* means that the boy went in the direction *up* rather than *down*. In the second example, the preposition *in* means that she went *into* rather than *out of* the house.

    In the idiomatic use, which is what appears most often on the TOEFL test, the preposition appears in an idiomatic expression; that is, its meaning in this expression has nothing to do with the literal meaning.

> I call *up* my friend.
> He succeeded *in* passing the course.

In the first example, the word *up* has nothing to do with the direction *up*. *To call up someone* means *to telephone* someone. In the second example, the word *in* has nothing to do with the meaning of *into* or *inside;* it is simply idiomatic that the word *in* is used after the verb *succeed*.

    It is impossible to list all potential idiomatic expressions with their prepositions because there are so many expressions that could appear on the TOEFL test. However, in this chapter you can practice recognizing problems with prepositions in TOEFL-type questions. Then, when you are working in written expression questions on the TOEFL test, you should be aware that idiomatic errors with prepositions are common in that section. There are two common types of problems with prepositions that you should expect: (1) incorrect prepositions and (2) omitted prepositions.

SKILL 56:   RECOGNIZE INCORRECT PREPOSITIONS

Sometimes an incorrect preposition is given in a sentence in written expression questions on the TOEFL test.

> The game was called *on** because of rain.
> I knew I could count *in** you to do a good job.

The first example should say that the game was *called off* because of rain. The expression *called off* means *canceled,* and that is the meaning that makes sense in this sentence. *To call on someone* is *to visit someone,* and this meaning does not make sense in this example. In the second example, it is not correct in English to *count in someone*. The correct expression is to *count on someone*.

EXERCISE 56: Each of the following sentences contains at least one preposition. Circle the prepositions. Then indicate if the sentences are correct (C) or incorrect (I).

__C__ 1. (After) school many students participate (in) sports.

__I__ 2. I know I can rely (in) you to be here (on) time.

_____ 3. If you need more light to read, turn on the lamp next to you.

_____ 4. Parents always try to bring at their children to be thoughtful.

_____ 5. I'll have to consult to my attorney before making a decision.

_____ 6. Walt has lost his keys, so he must look for them.

_____ 7. I just don't approve at your cheating on the exam.

_____ 8. Smoking is forbidden, so you should put out your cigarette.

_____ 9. Failure to pass the test will result to the loss of your license.

_____ 10. It is unlawful for parolees to associate with known felons.

SKILL 57:   RECOGNIZE WHEN PREPOSITIONS HAVE BEEN OMITTED

Sometimes a necessary preposition has been omitted from a sentence in written expression questions on the TOEFL test.

Can you *wait** me after the game?
I *plan** attending the meeting.

The first example is incorrect because it is necessary to say *wait for me*. The second example is incorrect because it is necessary to say *plan on attending*.

EXERCISE 57: Prepositions have been omitted in some of the following sentences. Mark where prepositions have been omitted. Then indicate if the sentences are correct (C) or incorrect (I).

__I__ 1. If you take this job, it will be necessary to deal^Vother departments.

__C__ 2. Each child took one cookie from the plate.

_____ 3. In the discussion, Rob sided the rest.

_____ 4. The board turned his suggestion for the project because it was too costly.

_____ 5. He can always depend his friends.

_____ 6. While Mrs. Sampson went shopping, a baby-sitter looked the children.

_____ 7. I know Steve believes what you told him.

_____ 8. Children should beware strangers.

_____ 9. It was difficult to make a decision about buying a house.

_____ 10. Tom blamed his brother the dent in the car.

EXERCISE (Skills 56–57): Circle the prepositions in the following sentences. Mark where they have been omitted. Then indicate if the sentences are correct (C) or incorrect (I).

_____ 1. The students must hand in their homework.

_____ 2. It will be difficult to forgive you of breaking your promise.

_____ 3. Elizabeth excels math and science.

_____ 4. She insisted on going to work in spite of her cold.

_____ 5. Bob reminds me to his father because he looks just like him.

_____ 6. If you are cold, you should put on your sweater.

_____ 7. Mr. Sanders is not here now, but he will call you when he returns.

_____ 8. I do not want to interfere your plans.

_____ 9. Alan waited Marie after school.

_____ 10. Bill laughs me whenever he looks me.

TOEFL EXERCISE (Skills 56–57): Choose the letter of the underlined word or group of words that is not correct.

_____ 1. Amelia Earhart, the first woman to fly solo across the Atlantic, disappeared on June
A   B   C
1937 while attempting to fly around the world.
D

_____ 2. The occurrence edema indicates the presence of a serious illness.
A   B   C   D

_____ 3. Atomic nuclei are believed to be composed by protons and neutrons in equal
A   B   C   D
numbers for the lighter elements.

_____ 4. According legend, Betsy Ross designed and sewed the first American flag.
A   B   C   D

_____ 5. The middle ear is attached for the back of the throat by the eustachian tube.
A   B   C   D

_____ 6. Plants that sprout, grow, bloom, produce seeds, and die within one year are classified
A   B   C
for annuals.
D

_____ 7. A marionette is controlled by means strings connected to wooden bars.
A   B   C   D

_____ 8. In July of 1861, Pat Garrett killed Billy the Kid in a house close Fort Sumner.
      A   B   C   D

_____ 9. Many comfort heating systems using steam as a working fluid operate at the
                                        A   B   C   D
         convection principle.

_____ 10. Mars's two small moons are irregularly shaped and covered for craters.
                  A   B   C   D

TOEFL REVIEW EXERCISE (1–57): Choose the letter of the word or group of words that best completes the sentence.

1. In any matter, heat tends to flow _____ to the cooler parts.

   (A) hotter parts
   (B) there are hotter parts
   (C) from the hotter parts
   (D) toward the hotter parts

2. Certain authorities claim that the costumes that people wear to parties _____ into their personalities.

   (A) give subtle insights
   (B) they give subtle insights
   (C) which give subtle insights
   (D) subtle insights

3. _____ Army camps near Washington, D.C., in 1861, Julia Ward Howe wrote "The Battle Hymn of the Republic."

   (A) She visited
   (B) After visiting
   (C) When visited
   (D) When was she visiting

Choose the letter of the underlined word or group of words that is not correct.

_____ 4. The body depends in food as its primary source of energy.
                  A   B   C D

_____ 5. Regular programming was interrupted to broadcast a special news bulletins.
                  A   B   C   D

_____ 6. Sulfa drugs had been used to treat bacterial infection until penicillin becomes widely
                              A   B   C   D
         available.

_____ 7. Plans for both the International Monetary Fund or the World Bank were drawn up at
             A   B   C   D
         the Bretton Woods Conference.

_____ 8. Seldom Antarctic icebergs will move far enough north to disturb South Pacific
                A   B   C
         shipping lanes.
         D

——— 9. In 1958, a largest recorded wave, with a height of 500 meters, occurred in Lituya Bay,
                  A   B   C   D

Alaska.

———10. Exercise in swimming pools is particularly helpful because of the buoyant
                                        A   B   C

effect water.
      D

PROBLEMS WITH USAGE

In English certain groups of words have similar uses, and these words are sometimes confused in written expression questions on the TOEFL test. Although various usage problems are possible on the TOEFL test, the following problems are the most common: (1) when to use *make* and *do;* (2) when to use *like, unlike,* and *alike;* and (3) when to use *other, another,* and *others.*

SKILL 58:   DISTINGUISH *MAKE* AND *DO*

Make and *do* can be confused in English because their meanings are so similar. Since the difference between *make* and *do* is tested on the TOEFL test, you should learn to distinguish them.

    Make often has the idea of *creating* or *constructing.* The following expressions show some of the possible uses of *make:*

> She likes to *make* her own clothes.
> Would you like to *make* a cake for dessert?
> If you *make* a mistake, you should correct it.
> He was unable to *make* a response to the threat.

Do often has the idea of *completing* or *performing.* The following expressions show some of the possible uses of *do:*

> This morning she *did* all the dishes.
> The students *are doing* the assignments.
> The janitors *did* the work they were assigned.
> You can *do* your laundry at the laundromat.

These are only some of the uses of *make* and *do.* Many uses of *make* and *do* are idiomatic and therefore difficult to classify.

EXERCISE 58: Each of the following sentences contains *make* or *do*. Circle *make* or *do*. Draw arrows to the nouns that complete the expressions. Then indicate if the sentences are correct (C) or incorrect (I).

__I__   1. The biology student (did) several mistakes in the lab report.

__C__   2. I hope that you will be able to (do) me a favor this afternoon.

_____   3. No matter what job she has, she always makes her best.

_____   4. The runner did a strong effort to increase her speed in the mile race.

_____   5. It is comforting to think that your work can make a difference.

_____   6. His grade was not very good because he had not done his homework.

_____   7. In this job you will make more money than in your previous job.

_____   8. He was unable to do dinner because no one had done the lunch dishes.

_____   9. It is a pleasure to work with someone who always makes the right thing.

_____   10. If you make a good impression at your job interview, you will get the job.

SKILL 59:   DISTINGUISH *LIKE, ALIKE,* AND *UNLIKE*

Like, alike, and *unlike* are easily confused because they look so similar and they have many different uses. There are several structures with *like, alike,* and *unlike* that you should be familiar with.

The first structures you should already be familiar with are the adjectives *alike* and *like* (see Skill 50). Study the use of *alike* and *like* in the following examples.

> John and Tom are *alike.*
> John and Tom worked in a *like* manner.

In both these examples, *alike* and *like* are adjectives that mean *similar.* In the first example, *alike* is a predicate adjective describing *John* and *Tom.* Because *alike* is a predicate adjective, it can only be used after a linking verb such as *are.* In the second example, *like* is the adjective form that is used immediately before the noun *manner.*

The next structures you should be familiar with are the prepositions *like* and *unlike,* which have opposite meanings. Because they are prepositions, they must be followed by objects.

> John is (*like* Tom).
> John is (*unlike* Tom).

In the first example, the preposition *like* is followed by the object *Tom.* It means that Tom and John are similar. In the second example, the preposition *unlike* is followed by the object *Tom.* It means that Tom and John are not similar.

The prepositions *like* and *unlike* can also be used at the beginning of a sentence.

> (*Like* Tom), John is tall.
> (*Unlike* Tom), John is tall.

In the first example, the preposition *like* is followed by the object *Tom*. It means that Tom is tall. In the second example, the preposition *unlike* is followed by the object *Tom*. It means that Tom is not tall.

The following chart outlines the structures and meanings of sentences with *like, alike,* and *unlike:*

LIKE, ALIKE, AND UNLIKE			
	GRAMMAR	MEANING	USE
like *alike*	adjective adjective	similar similar	As an adjective, *like* is used before a noun. As an adjective, *alike* is used after a linking verb.
like *unlike*	preposition preposition	similar different	Both prepositions are followed by objects. They can both be used in many positions, including at the beginning of the sentence.

EXERCISE 59: Each of the following sentences contains *like, alike,* or *unlike.* Circle the *like* words. Then indicate if the sentences are correct (C) or incorrect (I).

_____I_____ 1. The two routes you have chosen for the trip are (like.)

_____C_____ 2. The science books this semester are (like) the books used last semester.

_____ 3. Alike the restaurant where we usually eat, this new restaurant has early-bird specials.

_____ 4. Unlike the traditional red fire engines, the new fire engines are yellow.

_____ 5. The two girls were embarrassed because they were wearing alike dresses.

_____ 6. The new piece that the pianist is preparing is unlike any she has ever played before.

_____ 7. Like the Washington Zoo, the San Diego Zoo had several panda bears.

_____ 8. The insurance package offered by that company is exactly alike the package our company offers.

_____ 9. Any further work done in a like fashion will be rejected.

_____ 10. It is unfortunate that the covers for this year's and last year's albums are so alike.

Skill 60:   DISTINGUISH *OTHER, ANOTHER,* AND *OTHERS*

Other, another, and *others* are very easy to confuse. To decide how to use each of them correctly, you must consider three things: (1) if it is singular or plural, (2) if it is definite (*the*) or indefinite (*a, an*), and (3) if it is an adjective (it appears with a noun) or if it is a pronoun (it appears by itself).

	SINGULAR	PLURAL
INDEFINITE	I have *another* book. (ADJ) I have *another*. (PRO)	I have *other* books. (ADJ) I have *others*. (PRO)
DEFINITE	I have *the other* book. (ADJ) I have *the other*. (PRO)	I have *the other* books. (ADJ) I have *the others*. (PRO)

Notice that you use *another* only to refer to an indefinite, singular idea. *Others* is used only as a plural pronoun (not accompanied by a noun). In all other cases, *other* is correct.

EXERCISE 60: Each of the following sentences contains *other, another,* or *others.* Circle *other, another,* or *others.* Then indicate if the sentences are correct (C) or incorrect (I).

____C____ 1. It is essential to complete the first program before working on the (others.)

____I____ 2. The waitress will bring you (the another) bowl of soup if you want.

_____ 3. You should pack another pair of shoes in case that pair gets soaked.

_____ 4. It is difficult to find others workers who are willing to work such long hours.

_____ 5. Since the lamp you wanted is out of stock, you must choose another.

_____ 6. The other desk clerk must have put that message in your mailbox.

_____ 7. If your identification card is lost or stolen, you cannot get another.

_____ 8. Because they were not pleased with the hotel accommodations last year, they have decided to try a other hotel this year.

_____ 9. As some students moved into the registration area, others took their places in line.

_____ 10. The printer will not function unless it has another cartridges.

EXERCISE (Skills 58–60): Circle the words in the following sentences that are commonly confused on the TOEFL test. Then indicate if the sentences are correct (C) or incorrect (I).

_____ 1. When the car's odometer reached 100,000, she decided that it was time to buy another car.

_____ 2. Every time someone does an error in the program, several extra hours of work are created.

_____ 3. Like the fashions shown in this magazine, the fashions in the other magazine are quite expensive.

_____ 4. Because the main highway is crowded at this hour, the driver should try to find another routes to the stadium.

_____ 5.   Although the two signatures are supposed to be exactly the same, they are not at all like.

_____ 6.   The decorators did the shopping for the material and made curtains for the windows.

_____ 7.   Before the administrator reads the stack of papers on his desk, he should sign the others that are on the file cabinet.

_____ 8.   The committee is doing the arrangements for the Saturday evening banquet.

_____ 9.   When he made several other big mistakes, he did his apologies to the others in the office.

_____ 10.   Perhaps the designer could select others styles if these are inappropriate.

TOEFL EXERCISE (Skills 58–60): Choose the letter of the underlined word or group of words that is not correct.

_____ 1.   The buffalo and the bison $\underset{A}{are}$ $\underset{B}{like}$ $\underset{C}{except\ for}$ the $\underset{D}{size}$ and shape of the head and shoulders.

_____ 2. $\underset{A}{Other}$ $\underset{B}{interesting}$ aspect of tachistopic training in recent years $\underset{C}{has\ been}$ the newfound $\underset{D}{use}$ by professional teams.

_____ 3. $\underset{A}{Only\ about}$ 3 percent of oil wells $\underset{B}{actually}$ $\underset{C}{do}$ $\underset{D}{a}$ profit.

_____ 4. $\underset{A}{Dislike}$ sumac $\underset{B}{with}$ red berries, sumac with white berries $\underset{C}{is}$ $\underset{D}{poisonous}$.

_____ 5.   Pittsburgh has reduced $\underset{A}{its}$ smog by requiring $\underset{B}{more}$ complete oxidation of fuel in cars, and $\underset{C}{others}$ cities can $\underset{D}{do}$ the same thing.

_____ 6. $\underset{A}{Alike}$ $\underset{B}{all}$ $\underset{C}{other}$ mammals, dolphins $\underset{D}{have}$ lungs.

_____ 7.   Up to World War II $\underset{A}{almost\ all}$ important research in physics had been $\underset{B}{made}$ in universities, $\underset{C}{with\ only}$ university funds $\underset{D}{for\ support}$.

_____ 8.   Because the plan $\underset{A}{that\ was\ made}$ yesterday is $\underset{B}{no\ longer}$ feasible, the manager $\underset{C}{had\ to}$ choose another $\underset{D}{alternatives}$.

_____ 9.   Particles with $\underset{A}{unlike}$ charges attract each other, $\underset{B}{while}$ particles with $\underset{C}{alike}$ charges repel each $\underset{D}{other}$.

_____ 10. $\underset{A}{One\ another}$ surprising method of forest $\underset{C}{conservation\ is}$ $\underset{D}{controlled\ cutting}$ of trees.

TOEFL REVIEW EXERCISE (Skills 1–60): Choose the letter of the word or group of words that best completes the sentence.

1. Wild Bill Hickok _____ for the Union Army during the Civil War by posing as a Confederate officer.

    (A) spied
    (B) spying
    (C) a spy
    (D) was spied

2. _____ was unusable as farmland and difficult to traverse, the Badlands is an area in South Dakota.

    (A) So named because it
    (B) Because of
    (C) It
    (D) Naming it

Choose the letter of the underlined word or group of words that is not correct.

_____ 3. Titania, photographed by *Voyager 2* in 1986, has significantly fewer craters than
     A   B   C
   another moons of Uranus.
   D

_____ 4. The author Francis Scott Key Fitzgerald is better know as F. Scott Fitzgerald.
   A   B C D

_____ 5. The result of the failure to plan for the future is that a child from an urban area must
                A   B
   be took to the country to see nature.
   C   D

_____ 6. This machine can print on a single pieces of paper, but only if the lever is facing the
   A   B   C   D
   front of the machine.

_____ 7. The development of permanent teeth, alike that of deciduous teeth, begins before
            A B   C
   birth.
   D

_____ 8. A crowd of several hundred fan watched the ceremony from behind a fence.
      A   B C   D

_____ 9. Unlike other architects of the early modern movement, Alvar Aalto stressed
   A   B
   informality, personal expression, romantic, and regionality in his work.
               C   D

_____ 10. Color blindness may exist at birth or may occur later in life as a result for disease or
    A   B   C   D
   injury.

STRUCTURE POST-TEST (Paper) 📖

SECTION 2
STRUCTURE AND WRITTEN EXPRESSION
Time—25 minutes
(including the reading of the directions)
Now set your clock for 25 minutes.

This section is designed to measure your ability to recognize language that is appropriate for standard written English. There are two types of questions in this section, with special directions for each type.

Structure

Directions: Questions 1–15 are incomplete sentences. Beneath each sentence you will see four words or phrases, marked (A), (B), (C), and (D). Choose the <u>one</u> word or phrase that best completes the sentence. Then, on your answer sheet, find the number of the question and fill in the space that corresponds to the letter of the answer you have chosen. Fill in the space so that the letter inside the oval cannot be seen.

Look at the following examples.

Example I   **Sample Answer**
                                                                 ●
The president _____ the election by a landslide.   Ⓑ
                                                                 Ⓒ
(A) won   Ⓓ
(B) he won
(C) yesterday
(D) fortunately

The sentence should read, "The president won the election by a landslide." Therefore, you should choose (A).

Example II   **Sample Answer**
                                                                 Ⓐ
When _____ the conference?   ●
                                                                 Ⓒ
(A) the doctor attended   Ⓓ
(B) did the doctor attend
(C) the doctor will attend
(D) the doctor's attendance

The sentence should read, "When did the doctor attend the conference?" Therefore, you should choose (B).

Now, begin work on the questions.

GO ON TO THE NEXT PAGE ➜

1. _____ range in color from pale yellow to bright orange.

   (A) Canaries
   (B) Canaries which
   (C) That canaries
   (D) Canaries that are

2. Carnivorous plants _____ insects to obtain nitrogen.

   (A) are generally trapped
   (B) trap generally
   (C) are trapped generally
   (D) generally trap

3. A federal type of government results in _____.

   (A) a vertical distribution of power
   (B) power is distributed vertically
   (C) vertically distributed
   (D) the distribution of power is vertical

4. February normally has twenty-eight days, but every fourth year, _____ has twenty-nine.

   (A) there
   (B) its
   (C) is a leap year
   (D) a leap year, it

5. Evidence suggests that one-quarter of operations _____ bypass surgery may be unnecessary.

   (A) they involve
   (B) involve
   (C) involving
   (D) which they involve

6. _____ a tornado spins in a counterclockwise direction in the northern hemisphere, it spins in the opposite direction in the southern hemisphere.

   (A) However
   (B) Because of
   (C) Although
   (D) That

7. The Caldecott Medal, _____ for the best children's picture book, is awarded each January.

   (A) is a prize which
   (B) which prize
   (C) which is a prize
   (D) is a prize

8. Sports medicine is a medical specialty that deals with the identification and treatment of injuries to persons _____.

   (A) sports are involved
   (B) involved in sports
   (C) they are involved in sports
   (D) sports involve them

9. The Wilmington Oil Field, in Long Beach, California, is one of _____ oil fields in the continental United States.

   (A) productive
   (B) the most productive
   (C) most are productive
   (D) productivity

10. Thunder occurs as _____ through air, causing the heated air to expand and collide with layers of cooler air.

    (A) an electrical charge
    (B) passes an electrical charge
    (C) the passing of an electrical charge
    (D) an electrical charge passes

11. The population of Houston was ravaged by yellow fever in 1839 _____ in 1867.

    (A) it happened again
    (B) and again
    (C) was ravaged again
    (D) again once more

GO ON TO THE NEXT PAGE →

12. Researchers have long debated _____ Saturn's moon Titan contains hydrocarbon oceans and lakes.

    (A) over it
    (B) whether the
    (C) whether over
    (D) whether

13. According to Bernoulli's principle, the higher the speed of a fluid gas, _____ the pressure.

    (A) it will be lower
    (B) lower than the
    (C) the lower
    (D) lower it is

14. The flight instructor, _____ at the air base, said that orders not to fight had been issued.

    (A) when interviewed
    (B) when he interviewed
    (C) when to interview
    (D) when interviewing

15. In the northern and central parts of the state of Idaho _____ and churning rivers.

    (A) majestic mountains are found
    (B) are majestic mountains found
    (C) are found majestic mountains
    (D) finding majestic mountains

GO ON TO THE NEXT PAGE

Written Expression

Directions: In questions 16–40, each sentence has four underlined words or phrases. The four underlined parts of the sentence are marked (A), (B), (C), and (D). Identify the <u>one</u> underlined word or phrase that must be changed in order for the sentence to be correct. Then, on your answer sheet, find the number of the question and fill in the space that corresponds to the letter of the answer you have chosen.

Look at the following examples.

Example I

The four <u>string</u> on a violin <u>are</u> <u>tuned</u>
 A   B   C   D

in fifths.

Sample Answer

Ⓐ
●
Ⓒ
Ⓓ

The sentence should read, "The four strings on a violin are tuned in fifths." Therefore, you should choose (B).

Example II

The <u>research</u> <u>for the book</u> *Roots* <u>taking</u>
     A   B   C

Alex Haley <u>twelve years.</u>
          D

Sample Answer

Ⓐ
Ⓑ
●
Ⓓ

The sentence should read, "The research for the book *Roots* took Alex Haley twelve years." Therefore, you should choose (C).

Now, begin work on the questions.

GO ON TO THE NEXT PAGE ➡

16. Light can travels from the Sun to the Earth in eight minutes and twenty seconds.
$\underset{A}{}$ $\underset{B}{}$ $\underset{C}{}$ $\underset{D}{}$

16. Light can <u>travels</u> from <u>the Sun</u> to the Earth <u>in eight minutes</u> and twenty seconds.
    A   B   C

17. Every human <u>typically</u> <u>have</u> twenty-three <u>pairs</u> of chromosomes in <u>most cells</u>.
                 A   B   C   D

18. In the <u>sport</u> of fencing, three <u>type</u> of swords <u>are used</u>: the foil, the epee, and
    A   B   C   D
    the sabre.

19. The Internal Revenue Service <u>uses</u> computers to check tax return <u>computations</u>, to
                                  A   B
    determine the reasonableness of deductions, and <u>for verifying</u> the accuracy of
                                                     C
    <u>reported income</u>.
    D

20. There <u>was</u> four groups of <u>twenty rats</u> <u>each involved</u> in the <u>test</u>.
          A   B   C   D

21. The type of jazz <u>known as</u> "swing" was <u>introduced</u> by Duke Ellington when <u>he wrote</u>
                     A   B   C
    and <u>records</u> "It Don't Mean a Thing If It Ain't Got That Swing."
        D

22. The bones of mammals, <u>not alike</u> <u>those</u> of <u>other</u> vertebrates, <u>show</u> a high degree
                          A   B   C   D
    of differentiation.

23. The United States <u>receives</u> a <u>large amount</u> of revenue from <u>taxation</u> of <u>a</u> tobacco
                      A   B   C   D
    products.

24. <u>Much</u> fats are composed of <u>one molecule</u> of glycerin <u>combined with</u> three molecules
    A   B   C
    of <u>fatty acids</u>.
       D

25. The <u>capital</u> of the Confederacy was <u>originally</u> in Mobile, but <u>they were</u> <u>moved</u>
        A   B   C   D
    to Richmond.

26. A pearl develops <u>when</u> a tiny grain of sand or some <u>another</u> <u>irritant</u> accidentally
                     A   B   C
    <u>enters into</u> the shell of a pearl oyster.
    D

27. The English horn is <u>an alto</u> oboe with <u>a pitch</u> one fifth lower <u>as</u> <u>that</u> of the
                           A   B   C D

    soprano oboe.

28. In the Milky Way galaxy, <u>the most</u> <u>recent</u> observed supernova <u>appeared</u> <u>in</u> 1604.
                                 A   B   C D

29. <u>Although</u> the name suggests <u>otherwise</u>, the ship <u>known as</u> *Old Ironsides* was built of
    A   B   C

    oak and cedar rather than <u>it was built</u> of iron.
                                   D

30. Never <u>in the history</u> of humanity <u>there have</u> been <u>more people</u> <u>living</u> on this
              A   B   C   D

    relatively small planet.

31. Because of <u>the mobile</u> of Americans today, <u>it</u> is difficult for <u>them</u> to put down
                A   B   C

    <u>real roots.</u>
    D

32. For five <u>years after</u> the Civil War, Robert E. Lee <u>served to</u> president of Washington
                A   B

    College, <u>which</u> later <u>was called</u> Washington and Lee.
           C   D

33. Doctors <u>successfully</u> used hypnosis <u>during</u> World War II <u>to treat</u> <u>fatigue battle.</u>
               A   B   C   D

34. The lobster, <u>like</u> <u>many</u> crustaceans, can cast off <u>a damaging</u> appendage and
              A   B   C

    regenerate a new appendage to <u>nearly normal size.</u>
                                  D

35. The main cause of the <u>oceans' tides</u> <u>is</u> the <u>gravitation</u> pull of <u>the Moon.</u>
                          A   B   C   D

36. <u>The curricula</u> of American public schools <u>are</u> <u>set in</u> individual states; they
   A   B C

    <u>do not determine</u> by the federal government.
          D

37. The fact that the sophisticated technology <u>has become</u> part of <u>revolution</u> in travel
                                      A   B

    <u>delivery systems</u> has not made travel schedules <u>less hectic.</u>
       C   D

GO ON TO THE NEXT PAGE

38. Balanchine's <u>plotless</u> ballets, <u>such</u> *Jewels* and *The Four Temperaments,* <u>present</u> dance
           A   B   C

    <u>purely</u> as a celebration of the movement of the human body.
     D

39. In a solar battery, a photosensitive <u>semiconducting</u> substance <u>such as</u> silicon crystal
                                          A   B

    is <u>the source of</u> <u>electrician.</u>
         C   D

40. <u>In early days</u> hydrochloric acid was <u>done</u> by <u>heating</u> a mixture of sodium chloride
         A   B   C

    with iron sulfate.
     D

**This is the end of Section 2.
If you finish before 25 minutes has ended,
check your work on Section 2 only.**

STRUCTURE POST-TEST (Computer)

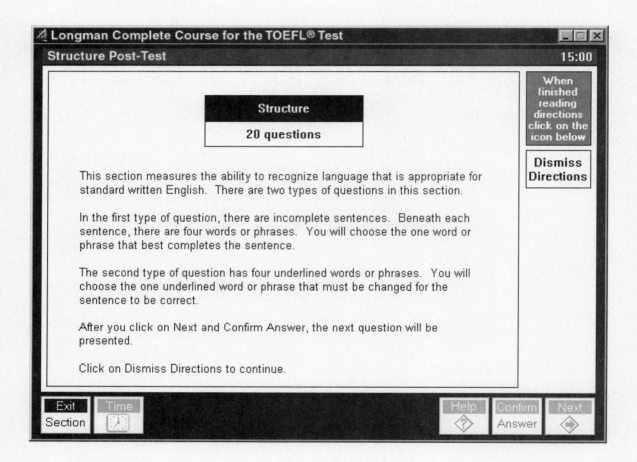

1. Alaska has more active glaciers <u>as the rest</u> of the <u>inhabited</u> world <u>combined</u>.

2. Benjamin Franklin <u>believed</u> that the turkey <u>rather</u> than the eagle should <u>became</u> <u>the</u> symbol of the United States.

3. Indiana's Lost River _____ underground for a distance of 22 miles.
   ◯ travels
   ◯ traveling
   ◯ to travel
   ◯ it travels

4. <u>Passengers</u> <u>have ridden</u> the first Ferris <u>wheel</u> at the Columbian Exposition in Chicago <u>in</u> 1893.

5. The Cro-Magnons entered the area <u>that is</u> today Europe and <u>quickly</u> eliminated or absorbed <u>theirs</u> Neanderthal <u>predecessors</u>.

6. Fossil fuels like coal, oil, and gas produce carbon dioxide when _____ burned.
   ◯ are
   ◯ they
   ◯ they are
   ◯ are they

7. The <u>best-known</u> members of the cabbage vegetable <u>group</u> <u>includes</u> <u>head</u> cabbage, cauliflower, broccoli, kale, collard, and brussel sprouts.

8. <u>An</u> hiccup is a <u>spasmodic</u> contraction of the diaphragm, <u>which</u> leads to a massive <u>intake</u> of air.

9. <u>Alike</u> a bar <u>magnet</u>, the earth has two <u>magnetic poles</u>.

10. Flintlock muskets _____ sharp bayonets were standard weapons during the American Revolution.
    ◯ tip with
    ◯ tipped with
    ◯ the tips of
    ◯ were tipped with

11. Not <u>until</u> Harvard College was <u>founded</u> in 1636 <u>was</u> there <u>any</u> colleges in America.

12. In general, the cells of large animals and plants are <u>only</u> <u>slightly</u> larger, if <u>at all</u>, than <u>smaller</u> plants and animals.

13. The light from an electrical lamp includes many different wave lengths, _____ in a laser is concentrated on only one wave length.
    ◯ all the energy
    ◯ it is all the energy
    ◯ while all the energy
    ◯ while all the energy is

14. A <u>supersonic</u> airplane can <u>fly</u> <u>faster than</u> <u>a</u> speed of sound.

15. The first <u>gummed</u> postage <u>stamps</u> <u>issued</u> in New York City <u>in</u> 1842.

16. The temperatures _____ take place vary widely for different materials.
    ◯ which melting and freezing
    ◯ at which melting and freezing
    ◯ which they melt and freeze
    ◯ at which they melt and freeze

17. The common octopus lives <u>lone</u>, in a den <u>just</u> <u>big enough</u> for <u>its</u> body.

18. Not until Nellie Tayloe Ross was elected governor of Wyoming in 1924 _____ as governor of a U. S. state.
    ◯ a woman served
    ◯ a woman serving
    ◯ to serve a woman
    ◯ did a woman serve

19. <u>Only</u> <u>about</u> 25 percent of diamonds prove <u>suitably</u> for <u>gemstones</u>.

20. An ice <u>crystal</u> is the <u>nuclei</u> <u>on which</u> a hailstone is <u>built</u>.

SECTION THREE

READING

3 △ 3 △ 3 △ 3 △ 3 △ 3 △ 3 △ 3

READING DIAGNOSTIC PRE-TEST (Paper) 📖

SECTION 3
READING COMPREHENSION
Time—55 minutes
(including the reading of the directions)
Now set your clock for 55 minutes.

This section is designed to measure your ability to read and understand short passages similar in topic and style to those that students are likely to encounter in North American universities and colleges.

Directions: In this section you will read several passages. Each one is followed by a number of questions about it. You are to choose the <u>one</u> best answer, (A), (B), (C), or (D), to each question. Then, on your answer sheet, find the number of the question and fill in the space that corresponds to the letter of the answer you have chosen.

Answer all questions about the information in a passage on the basis of what is <u>stated</u> or <u>implied</u> in that passage.

Read the following passage:

John Quincy Adams, who served as the sixth president of the United States from 1825 to 1829, is today recognized for his masterful statesmanship and diplomacy. He dedicated his life to public service, both in the presidency and in the various other political offices that he
Line held. Throughout his political career he demonstrated his unswerving belief in freedom of
(5) speech, the antislavery cause, and the right of Americans to be free from European and Asian domination.

Example I

To what did John Quincy Adams devote his life?

(A) Improving his personal life
(B) Serving the public
(C) Increasing his fortune
(D) Working on his private business

Sample Answer

Ⓐ ● Ⓒ Ⓓ

According to the passage, John Quincy Adams "dedicated his life to public service." Therefore, you should choose (B).

Example II

In line 4, the word "unswerving" is closest in meaning to

(A) moveable
(B) insignificant
(C) unchanging
(D) diplomatic

Sample Answer

Ⓐ Ⓑ ● Ⓓ

The passage states that John Quincy Adams demonstrated his unswerving belief "throughout his career." This implies that the belief did not change. Therefore, you should choose (C).

Now begin work on the questions.

GO ON TO THE NEXT PAGE ➡

Questions 1–9

Carbon tetrachloride is a colorless and inflammable liquid that can be produced by combining carbon disulfide and chlorine. This compound is widely used in industry today because of its effectiveness as a solvent as well as its use in the production of propellants.

Line
(5)
Despite its widespread use in industry, carbon tetrachloride has been banned for home use. In the past, carbon tetrachloride was a common ingredient in cleaning compounds that were used throughout the home, but it was found to be dangerous: when heated, it changes into a poisonous gas that can cause severe illness and even death if it is inhaled. Because of this dangerous characteristic, the United States revoked permission for the home use of carbon tetrachloride in 1970. The United States has taken similar action with various other chemical compounds.

1. The main point of this passage is that

   (A) carbon tetrachloride can be very dangerous when it is heated
   (B) the government banned carbon tetrachloride in 1970
   (C) although carbon tetrachloride can legally be used in industry, it is not allowed in home products
   (D) carbon tetrachloride used to be a regular part of cleaning compounds

2. The word "widely" in line 2 could most easily be replaced by

   (A) grandly
   (B) extensively
   (C) largely
   (D) hugely

3. The word "banned" in line 4 is closest in meaning to

   (A) forbidden
   (B) allowed
   (C) suggested
   (D) instituted

4. According to the passage, before 1970 carbon tetrachloride was

   (A) used by itself as a cleanser
   (B) banned in industrial use
   (C) often used as a component of cleaning products
   (D) not allowed in home cleaning products

5. It is stated in the passage that when carbon tetrachloride is heated, it becomes

   (A) harmful
   (B) colorless
   (C) a cleaning compound
   (D) inflammable

6. The word "inhaled" in line 7 is closest in meaning to

   (A) warmed
   (B) breathed in
   (C) carelessly used
   (D) blown

7. The word "revoked" in line 8 could most easily be replaced by

   (A) gave
   (B) granted
   (C) instituted
   (D) took away

8. It can be inferred from the passage that one role of the U.S. government is to

   (A) regulate product safety
   (B) prohibit any use of carbon tetrachloride
   (C) instruct industry on cleaning methodologies
   (D) ban the use of any chemicals

9. The paragraph following the passage most likely discusses

   (A) additional uses for carbon tetrachloride
   (B) the banning of various chemical compounds by the U.S. government
   (C) further dangerous effects of carbon tetrachloride
   (D) the major characteristics of carbon tetrachloride

GO ON TO THE NEXT PAGE

Questions 10–19

The next artist in this survey of American artists is James Whistler; he is included in this survey of American artists because he was born in the United States, although the majority of his artwork was completed in Europe. Whistler was born in Massachusetts in 1834, but nine years later his father moved the family to St. Petersburg, Russia, to work on the construction of a railroad. The family returned to the United States in 1849. Two years later Whistler entered the U.S. military academy at West Point, but he was unable to graduate. At the age of twenty-one, Whistler went to Europe to study art despite familial objections, and he remained in Europe until his death.

Whistler worked in various art forms, including etchings and lithographs. However, he is most famous for his paintings, particularly *Arrangement in Gray and Black No. 1: Portrait of the Artist's Mother* or *Whistler's Mother,* as it is more commonly known. This painting shows a side view of Whistler's mother, dressed in black and posing against a gray wall. The asymmetrical nature of the portrait, with his mother seated off-center, is highly characteristic of Whistler's work.

10. The paragraph preceding this passage most likely discusses
    (A) a survey of eighteenth-century art
    (B) a different American artist
    (C) Whistler's other famous paintings
    (D) European artists

11. Which of the following best describes the information in the passage?
    (A) Several artists are presented.
    (B) One artist's life and works are described.
    (C) Various paintings are contrasted.
    (D) Whistler's family life is outlined.

12. Whistler is considered an American artist because
    (A) he was born in America
    (B) he spent most of his life in America
    (C) he served in the U.S. military
    (D) he created most of his famous art in America

13. The word "majority" in line 2 is closest in meaning to
    (A) seniority
    (B) maturity
    (C) large pieces
    (D) high percentage

14. It is implied in the passage that Whistler's family was
    (A) unable to find any work at all in Russia
    (B) highly supportive of his desire to pursue art
    (C) working class
    (D) military

15. The word "objections" in line 7 is closest in meaning to
    (A) protests
    (B) goals
    (C) agreements
    (D) battles

16. In line 8, the "etchings" are
    (A) a type of painting
    (B) the same as a lithograph
    (C) an art form introduced by Whistler
    (D) an art form involving engraving

17. The word "asymmetrical" in line 11 is closest in meaning to
    (A) proportionate
    (B) uneven
    (C) balanced
    (D) lyrical

18. Which of the following is NOT true according to the passage?
    (A) Whistler worked with a variety of art forms.
    (B) *Whistler's Mother* is not the official name of his painting.
    (C) Whistler is best known for his etchings.
    (D) *Whistler's Mother* is painted in somber tones.

19. Where in the passage does the author mention the types of artwork that Whistler was involved in?
    (A) Lines 1–3
    (B) Lines 4–5
    (C) Lines 6–7
    (D) Lines 8–10

GO ON TO THE NEXT PAGE

Questions 20–30

The locations of stars in the sky relative to one another do not appear to the naked eye to change, and as a result stars are often considered to be fixed in position. Many unaware stargazers falsely assume that each star has its own permanent home in the nighttime sky.

Line
(5)
In reality, though, stars are always moving, but because of the tremendous distances between stars themselves and from stars to Earth, the changes are barely perceptible here. An example of a rather fast-moving star demonstrates why this misconception prevails; it takes approximately 200 years for a relatively rapid star like Bernard's star to move a distance in the skies equal to the diameter of the earth's moon. When the apparently negligible movement of the stars is contrasted with the movement of the planets, the stars are seemingly unmoving.

20. Which of the following is the best title for this passage?

    (A) What the Eye Can See in the Sky
    (B) Bernard's Star
    (C) Planetary Movement
    (D) The Evermoving Stars

21. The expression "naked eye" in line 1 most probably refers to

    (A) a telescope
    (B) a scientific method for observing stars
    (C) unassisted vision
    (D) a camera with a powerful lens

22. According to the passage, the distances between the stars and Earth are

    (A) barely perceptible
    (B) huge
    (C) fixed
    (D) moderate

23. The word "perceptible" in line 5 is closest in meaning to which of the following?

    (A) Noticeable
    (B) Persuasive
    (C) Conceivable
    (D) Astonishing

24. In line 6, a "misconception" is closest in meaning to a(n)

    (A) idea
    (B) proven fact
    (C) erroneous belief
    (D) theory

25. The passage states that in 200 years Bernard's star can move

    (A) around Earth's moon
    (B) next to Earth's moon
    (C) a distance equal to the distance from Earth to the Moon
    (D) a distance seemingly equal to the diameter of the Moon

26. The passage implies that from Earth it appears that the planets

    (A) are fixed in the sky
    (B) move more slowly than the stars
    (C) show approximately the same amount of movement as the stars
    (D) travel through the sky considerably more rapidly than the stars

27. The word "negligible" in line 8 could most easily be replaced by

    (A) negative
    (B) insignificant
    (C) rapid
    (D) distant

28. Which of the following is NOT true according to the passage?

    (A) Stars do not appear to the eye to move.
    (B) The large distances between stars and the earth tend to magnify movement to the eye.
    (C) Bernard's star moves quickly in comparison with other stars.
    (D) Although stars move, they seem to be fixed.

29. The paragraph following the passage most probably discusses

    (A) the movement of the planets
    (B) Bernard's star
    (C) the distance from Earth to the Moon
    (D) why stars are always moving

30. This passage would most probably be assigned reading in which course?

    (A) Astrology
    (B) Geophysics
    (C) Astronomy
    (D) Geography

GO ON TO THE NEXT PAGE

Questions 31–40

It has been noted that, traditionally, courts have granted divorces on fault grounds: one spouse is deemed to be at fault in causing the divorce. More and more today, however, divorces are being granted on a no-fault basis.

Line
(5)
Proponents of no-fault divorce argue that when a marriage fails, it is rarely the case that one marriage partner is completely to blame and the other blameless. A failed marriage is much more often the result of mistakes by both partners.

Another argument in favor of no-fault divorce is that proving fault in court, in a public arena, is a destructive process that only serves to lengthen the divorce process and that dramatically increases the negative feelings present in a divorce. If a couple can reach a decision to divorce without first

(10)
deciding which partner is to blame, the divorce settlement can be negotiated more easily and equitably and the postdivorce healing process can begin more rapidly.

31. What does the passage mainly discuss?

   (A) Traditional grounds for divorce
   (B) Who is at fault in a divorce
   (C) Why no-fault divorces are becoming more common
   (D) The various reasons for divorces

32. The word "spouse" in line 1 is closest in meaning to a

   (A) judge
   (B) problem
   (C) divorce decree
   (D) marriage partner

33. According to the passage, no-fault divorces

   (A) are on the increase
   (B) are the traditional form of divorce
   (C) are less popular than they used to be
   (D) were granted more in the past

34. It is implied in the passage that

   (A) there recently has been a decrease in no-fault divorces
   (B) not all divorces today are no-fault divorces
   (C) a no-fault divorce is not as equitable as a fault divorce
   (D) people recover more slowly from a no-fault divorce

35. The word "Proponents" in line 4 is closest in meaning to which of the following?

   (A) Advocates
   (B) Recipients
   (C) Authorities
   (D) Enemies

36. The passage states that a public trial to prove the fault of one spouse can

   (A) be satisfying to the wronged spouse
   (B) lead to a shorter divorce process
   (C) reduce negative feelings
   (D) be a harmful process

37. Which of the following is NOT listed in this passage as an argument in favor of no-fault divorce?

   (A) Rarely is only one marriage partner to blame for a divorce.
   (B) A no-fault divorce generally costs less in legal fees.
   (C) Finding fault in a divorce increases negative feelings.
   (D) A no-fault divorce settlement is generally easier to negotiate.

38. The word "present" in line 9 could most easily be replaced by

   (A) existing
   (B) giving
   (C) introducing
   (D) resulting

39. The word "settlement" in line 10 is closest in meaning to

   (A) development
   (B) serenity
   (C) discussion
   (D) agreement

40. The tone of this passage is

   (A) emotional
   (B) enthusiastic
   (C) expository
   (D) reactionary

GO ON TO THE NEXT PAGE

Questions 41–50

Whereas literature in the first half of the eighteenth century in America had been largely religious and moral in tone, by the latter half of the century the revolutionary fervor that was coming to life in the colonies began to be reflected in the literature of the time, which in turn served to further
Line   influence the population. Although not all writers of this period supported the Revolution, the two
(5)   best-known and most influential writers, Ben Franklin and Thomas Paine, were both strongly supportive of that cause.

Ben Franklin first attained popular success through his writings in his brother's newspaper, the *New England Current.* In these articles he used a simple style of language and common sense argumentation to defend the point of view of the farmer and the Leather Apron man. He continued
(10)   with the same common sense practicality and appeal to the common man with his work on *Poor Richard's Almanac* from 1733 until 1758. Firmly established in his popular acceptance by the people, Franklin wrote a variety of extremely effective articles and pamphlets about the colonists' revolutionary cause against England.

Thomas Paine was an Englishman working as a magazine editor in Philadelphia at the time of
(15)   the Revolution. His pamphlet *Common Sense,* which appeared in 1776, was a force in encouraging the colonists to declare their independence from England. Then throughout the long and desperate war years he published a series of *Crisis* papers (from 1776 until 1783) to encourage the colonists to continue on with the struggle. The effectiveness of his writing was probably due to his emotional yet oversimplified depiction of the cause of the colonists against England as a classic struggle of good
(20)   and evil.

41. The paragraph preceding this passage most likely discusses

    (A) how literature influences the population
    (B) religious and moral literature
    (C) literature supporting the cause of the American Revolution
    (D) what made Thomas Paine's literature successful

42. The word "fervor" in line 2 is closest in meaning to

    (A) war
    (B) anxiety
    (C) spirit
    (D) action

43. The word "time" in line 3 could best be replaced by

    (A) hour
    (B) period
    (C) appointment
    (D) duration

44. It is implied in the passage that

    (A) some writers in the American colonies supported England during the Revolution
    (B) Franklin and Paine were the only writers to influence the Revolution
    (C) because Thomas Paine was an Englishman, he supported England against the colonies
    (D) authors who supported England did not remain in the colonies during the Revolution

45. The pronoun "he" in line 8 refers to

    (A) Thomas Paine
    (B) Ben Franklin
    (C) Ben Franklin's brother
    (D) Poor Richard

46. The expression "point of view" in line 9 could best be replaced by

    (A) perspective
    (B) sight
    (C) circumstance
    (D) trait

GO ON TO THE NEXT PAGE →

47. According to the passage, the tone of *Poor Richard's Almanac* is

   (A) pragmatic
   (B) erudite
   (C) theoretical
   (D) scholarly

48. The word "desperate" in line 16 could best be replaced by

   (A) unending
   (B) hopeless
   (C) strategic
   (D) combative

49. Where in the passage does the author describe Thomas Paine's style of writing?

   (A) Lines 4–6
   (B) Lines 8–9
   (C) Lines 14–15
   (D) Lines 18–20

50. The purpose of the passage is to

   (A) discuss American literature in the first half of the eighteenth century
   (B) give biographical data on two American writers
   (C) explain which authors supported the Revolution
   (D) describe the literary influence during revolutionary America

This is the end of the Reading Diagnostic Pre-Test.

Circle the number of each of the questions that you answered incorrectly or were not sure of. Then you will see which skills you should be sure to review.

1. SKILL 1	18. SKILL 4	35. SKILL 9
2. SKILL 11	19. SKILL 12	36. SKILL 3
3. SKILL 10	20. SKILL 1	37. SKILL 4
4. SKILL 3	21. SKILL 11	38. SKILL 11
5. SKILL 3	22. SKILL 3	39. SKILL 10
6. SKILL 9	23. SKILL 9	40. SKILL 13
7. SKILL 10	24. SKILL 9	41. SKILL 7
8. SKILL 6	25. SKILL 3	42. SKILL 10
9. SKILL 7	26. SKILL 6	43. SKILL 11
10. SKILL 7	27. SKILL 11	44. SKILL 6
11. SKILL 2	28. SKILL 4	45. SKILL 5
12. SKILL 3	29. SKILL 7	46. SKILL 11
13. SKILL 9	30. SKILL 13	47. SKILL 3
14. SKILL 6	31. SKILL 1	48. SKILL 10
15. SKILL 10	32. SKILL 10	49. SKILL 12
16. SKILL 8	33. SKILL 3	50. SKILL 13
17. SKILL 9	34. SKILL 6	

READING DIAGNOSTIC PRE-TEST
(Computer)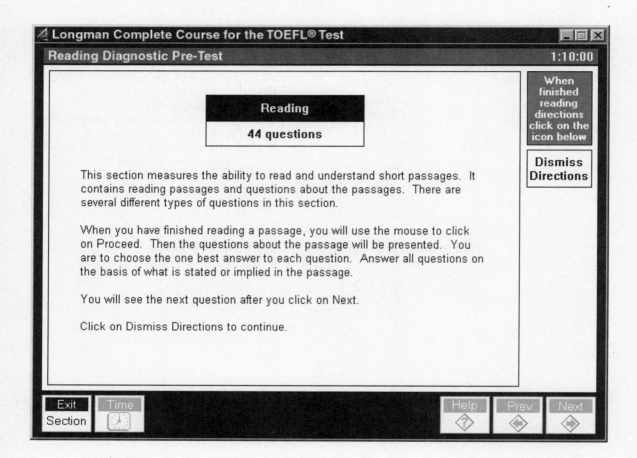

PASSAGE ONE (Questions 1–11)

The final battle of the War of 1812 was the Battle of New Orleans. This battle gave a clear demonstration of the need for effective communication during wartime; it also showed the disastrous results that can come to pass when communication is inadequate.

The War of 1812 was fought between Great Britain and the very young country of the United States only a relatively few years after the United States had won its independence from Britain. The United States had declared war against Britain in June of 1812, mostly because of interference with U.S. shipping by the British and because of the shanghaiing of U.S. sailors for enforced service on British vessels. The war lasted for a little more than two years, when a peace treaty was signed at Ghent, in Belgium, on the 24th of December, 1814.

Unfortunately, the news that the Treaty of Ghent had been signed and that the war was officially over was not communicated in a timely manner over the wide distance to where the war was being contested. Negotiations for the treaty and the actual signing of the treaty took place in Europe, and news of the treaty had to be carried across the Atlantic to the war front by ship. A totally unnecessary loss of life was incurred as a result of the amount of time that it took to inform the combatants of the treaty.

10A Early in January of 1815, some two weeks after the peace treaty had been signed, British troops in the southern part of the United States were unaware that the war had officially ended. **10B** Over 5,000 British troops attacked U.S. troops. **10C** During the ensuing battle, known as the Battle of New Orleans, the British suffered a huge number of casualties, around 2,000, and the Americans lost 71, all in a battle fought only because news of the peace treaty that had already been signed in Ghent had not yet reached the battlefield. **10D**

1. The main idea of this passage is that
   ○ the War of Independence was unnecessary
   ○ the War of 1812 was unnecessary
   ○ the Treaty of Ghent was unnecessary
   ○ the Battle of New Orleans was unnecessary

2. Look at the word it in paragraph 1. Click on the word or phrase that it refers to.

3. Look at the expression come to pass in paragraph 1. This expression could best be replaced by
   ○ happen
   ○ overthrow
   ○ self-destruct
   ○ circumvent

4. According to the passage, when did the United States win its independence from Britain?
   ○ Shortly before the War of 1812
   ○ During the War of 1812
   ○ Just after the War of 1812
   ○ Long after the War of 1812

5. According to the passage, some U.S. sailors were
   ○ taken forcibly to Shanghai
   ○ made to go to Ghent
   ○ forced to work on British ships
   ○ responsible for causing the War of 1812

6. Click on the sentence in paragraph 2 that indicates when the War of 1812 officially ended.

7. It is NOT stated in the passage that Ghent was
   ○ where negotiations took place
   ○ the site of the final battle
   ○ where the treaty was signed
   ○ far from the battlefield

8. Look at the word contested in paragraph 3. Click on the word or phrase in paragraph 4 that is closest in meaning to contested.

9. It can be determined from the passage that, of the following dates, the Battle of New Orleans was most probably fought

○ on December 10, 1814
○ on December 24, 1814
○ on January 1, 1815
○ on January 8, 1815

10. The following sentence could be added to paragraph 4.

These U.S. troops were in fortified entrenchments outside the city.

Where would it best fit into the paragraph? Click on the square (■) to add the sentence to the paragraph.

11. Click on the paragraph that describes the battle that took place after the signing of the treaty.

PASSAGE TWO (Questions 12–21)

Although only a small percentage of the electromagnetic radiation that is emitted by the Sun is ultraviolet (UV) radiation, the amount that is emitted would be enough to cause severe damage to most forms of life on Earth were it all to reach the surface of the earth. Fortunately, all of the Sun's ultraviolet radiation does not reach the earth because of a layer of oxygen, called the ozone layer, encircling the earth in the stratosphere at an altitude of about 15 miles above the earth. The ozone layer absorbs much of the Sun's ultraviolet radiation and prevents it from reaching the earth.

Ozone is a form of oxygen in which each molecule consists of three atoms (O_3) instead of the two atoms (O_2) usually found in an oxygen molecule. Ozone forms in the stratosphere in a process that is initiated by ultraviolet radiation from the Sun. UV radiation from the Sun splits oxygen molecules with two atoms into free oxygen atoms, and each of these unattached oxygen atoms then joins up with an oxygen molecule to form ozone. UV radiation is also capable of splitting up ozone molecules; thus, ozone is constantly forming, splitting, and reforming in the stratosphere. When UV radiation is absorbed during the process of ozone formation and reformation, it is unable to reach Earth and cause damage there.

Recently, however, the ozone layer over parts of the earth has been diminishing. Chief among the culprits in the case of the disappearing ozone, those that are really responsible, are the chloroflurocarbons (CFCs). CFCs meander up from Earth into the stratosphere, where they break down and release chlorine. The released chlorine reacts with ozone in the stratosphere to form chlorine monoxide (ClO) and oxygen (O_2). The chlorine then becomes free to go through the cycle over and over again. One chlorine atom can, in fact, destroy hundreds of thousands of ozone molecules in this repetitious cycle.

12. According to the passage, ultraviolet radiation from the Sun

- ○ is causing severe damage to the earth's ozone layer
- ○ is only a fraction of the Sun's electromagnetic radiation
- ○ creates electromagnetic radiation
- ○ always reaches the earth

13. Look at the word encircling in paragraph 1. This word is closest in meaning to

- ○ rotating
- ○ attacking
- ○ raising
- ○ surrounding

14. It is stated in the passage that the ozone layer

- ○ enables ultraviolet radiation to reach the earth
- ○ reflects ultraviolet radiation
- ○ shields the earth from a lot of ultraviolet radiation
- ○ reaches down to the earth

15. Click on the drawing of the ozone molecule.

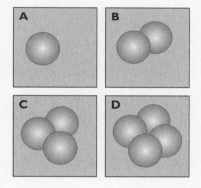

16. Look at the word free in paragraph 2. Click on another word or phrase in paragraph 2 that could best be replaced by free.

17. Ultraviolet radiation causes oxygen molecules to

- ○ rise to the stratosphere
- ○ burn up ozone molecules
- ○ split up and reform as ozone
- ○ reduce the number of chloroflurocarbons

18. Look at the word it in paragraph 2. Click on the word or phrase in paragraph 2 that it refers to.

19. Look at the word culprits in paragraph 3. This word is closest in meaning to which of the following?

   ○ Guilty parties
   ○ Detectives
   ○ Group members
   ○ Leaders

20. Click on the drawing that shows what happens after a chlorine molecule reacts with an ozone molecule.

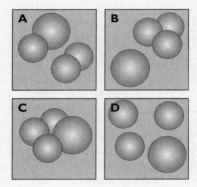

21. Click on the sentence in paragraph 3 that explains how much damage chlorine can do.

PASSAGE THREE (Questions 22–34)

Esperanto is what is called a planned, or artificial, language. It was created more than a century ago by Polish eye doctor Ludwik Lazar Zamenhof. Zamenhof believed that a common language would help to alleviate some of the misunderstandings among cultures.

In Zamenhof's first attempt at a universal language, he tried to create a language that was as uncomplicated as possible. This first language included words such as *ab, ac, ba, eb, be,* and *ce*. This did not result in a workable language in that these monosyllabic words, though short, were not easy to understand or to retain.

Next, Zamenhof tried a different way of constructing a simplified language. He made the words in his language sound like words that people already knew, but he simplified the grammar tremendously. One example of how he simplified the language can be seen in the suffixes: all nouns in this language end in *o*, as in the noun *amiko*, which means "friend," and all adjectives end in *-a*, as in the adjective *bela*, which means "pretty." Another example of the simplified language can be seen in the prefix *mal-*, which makes a word opposite in meaning; the word *malamiko* therefore means "enemy," and the word *malbela* therefore means "ugly" in Zamenhof's language.

In 1887, Zamenhof wrote a description of this language and published it. He used a penname, Dr. Esperanto, when signing the book. He selected the name Esperanto because this word means "a person who hopes" in his language. Esperanto clubs began popping up throughout Europe, and by 1905 Esperanto had spread from Europe to America and Asia.

In 1905, the First World Congress of Esperanto took place in France, with approximately 700 attendees from 20 different countries. Congresses were held annually for nine years, and 4,000 attendees were registered for the Tenth World Esperanto Congress scheduled for 1914, when World War I erupted and forced its cancellation.

31A Esperanto has had its ups and downs in the period since World War I. **31B** Today, years after it was introduced, it is estimated that perhaps a quarter of a million people are fluent in it. **31C** Current advocates would like to see its use grow considerably and are taking steps to try to make this happen. **31D**

22. The topic of this passage is
    - ◯ a language developed in the last few years
    - ◯ one man's efforts to create a universal language
    - ◯ how language can be improved
    - ◯ using language to communicate internationally

23. According to the passage, Zamenhof wanted to create a universal language
    - ◯ to resolve cultural differences
    - ◯ to provide a more complex language
    - ◯ to build a name for himself
    - ◯ to create one world culture

24. Look at the word simplified in paragraph 3. Click on the word or phrase in paragraph 2 that is closest in meaning to simplified.

25. It can be inferred from the passage that the Esperanto word *malespera* means
    - ◯ hopelessness
    - ◯ hope
    - ◯ hopeless
    - ◯ hopeful

26. Look at the expression popping up in paragraph 4. This expression could best be replaced by
    - ◯ leaping
    - ◯ shouting
    - ◯ hiding
    - ◯ opening

27. Click on the sentence in paragraph 4 that explains why Zamenhof chose the name that he did for his language.

28. It can be inferred from the passage that the Third World Congress of Esperanto took place
    - ○ in 1905
    - ○ in 1907
    - ○ in 1909
    - ○ in 1913

29. According to the passage, what happened to the Tenth World Esperanto Congress?
    - ○ It had 4,000 attendees.
    - ○ It was scheduled for 1915.
    - ○ It had attendees from 20 countries.
    - ○ It never took place.

30. Look at the expression ups and downs in paragraph 6. This expression is closest in meaning to
    - ○ tops and bottoms
    - ○ floors and ceilings
    - ○ take offs and landings
    - ○ highs and lows

31. The following sentence could be added to paragraph 6.

    This may seem like a large number, but it is really quite small when compared with the billion English speakers and billion Mandarin Chinese speakers in today's world.

    Where would it best fit into the paragraph? Click on the square (■) to add the sentence to the paragraph.

32. Click on the paragraph that describes the predecessor to Esperanto.

33. This passage would most likely be assigned reading in a course on
    - ○ European history
    - ○ English grammar
    - ○ world government
    - ○ applied linguistics

34. The paragraph following the passage most likely discusses
    - ○ how current supporters of Esperanto are encouraging its growth
    - ○ another of Zamenhof's accomplishments
    - ○ the disadvantages of using an artificial language
    - ○ attempts to reconvene the World Congress of Esperanto in the 1920s

Paul Bunyan is perhaps America's best-known folk hero. A fictional logger of incredible strength, he was most likely based on an actual nineteenth century logger from the northern United States or Canada. As a folk hero, he struck a chord with Americans on some level, perhaps because he was incredibly strong but also because he was hard-working and capable, ingenious in solving problems, and fun-loving.

Though there is evidence that Paul Bunyan tales were part of oral tradition in the nineteenth century, Paul Bunyan stories did not appear in written form until the early twentieth century. Journalist James McGillivray included descriptions of Bunyan in a series of essays entitled "The Round River Drive," which appeared in a number of Midwestern newspapers between 1906 and 1910. However, it was through an extensive advertising campaign that Paul Bunyan moved solidly into print.

Recognizing the appeal of Paul Bunyan as a figure for his company's advertising, William Laughead, an advertising executive for the Red River Lumber Company, initiated a campaign that consisted of a series of publications featuring Paul Bunyan. For several decades, the company distributed these publications free of charge and made no attempt to obtain a copyright on them. In fact, the company vigorously encouraged other writers to make use of Paul Bunyan because it felt that the use of this character enhanced the name recognition of the Red River Lumber Company inasmuch as the name of the folk hero and the name of the company had become interwoven.

41A The Bunyan stories published by Red River and further circulated by others were tall tales of gigantic proportions. **41B** In these tales, Bunyan is depicted as a man of superhuman proportions, who is strong, hard-working, entrepreneurial, and innovative. **41C** In one story, for example, Paul is credited with digging the Great Lakes in order to create a watering hole for his giant ox, Babe. **41D** In another of these tales, Paul caused an entire winter of blue snow to fall by swearing a blue streak after he injured himself by smashing his thumb with a large hammer. **41E**

Fascination with Paul Bunyan has continued to grow, and today he is a standard of American folklore. The prevalence of Bunyan as a figure of folklore today is evidenced by references to him in countless stories, cartoons, poems, and songs as well as the numerous community festivals and logging competitions featuring Paul Bunyan that can be found throughout the sections of the country where logging has a strong tradition.

35. This purpose of this passage is to
○ present the actual feats of a real-life logger
○ discuss a "larger than life" folk hero
○ describe logging in North America
○ provide an overview of American folktales

36. It is NOT stated in the passage that Paul Bunyan is known for his
○ unusual strength
○ dedication to work
○ ingenuity in difficult situations
○ serious nature

37. The passage states that Paul Bunyan tales first appeared
○ in oral stories
○ in a series of essays
○ in newspapers
○ in advertising

38. Which of the following CANNOT be inferred about the Red River Lumber Company's advertising campaign featuring Paul Bunyan?
○ It endured for quite a time.
○ The company did not protect its ownership of the stories.
○ The campaign did little to enhance the company's profitability.
○ The company wanted the name Paul Bunyan to be known as widely as possible.

39. Look at the word them in paragraph 3. Click on the word that them refers to.

40. Look at the word interwoven in paragraph 3. This word could best be replaced by
   - ○ unfashionable
   - ○ mixed together
   - ○ not compatible
   - ○ too separate

41. The following sentence could be added to paragraph 4.

   A third story in the series describes Paul's role in establishing the Mississippi River.

   Where would it best fit into the paragraph? Click on the square (■) to add the sentence to the paragraph.

42. Click on the sentence in paragraph 4 that discusses a weather phenomenon that Paul Bunyan supposedly caused.

43. Look at the word countless in paragraph 5. Click on another word in paragraph 5 that is close in meaning to countless.

44. Click on the paragraph that describes the plots of some of the tales of Paul Bunyan.

Circle the number of each of the questions on the test that you *answered incorrectly* or *were unsure of.* Then you will see which skills you should be sure to focus on.

1. SKILL 1	16. SKILL 11	31. SKILL 14
2. SKILL 5	17. SKILL 3	32. SKILL 2
3. SKILL 10	18. SKILL 5	33. SKILL 13
4. SKILL 3	19. SKILL 8	34. SKILL 7
5. SKILL 3	20. SKILL 3	35. SKILL 13
6. SKILL 12	21. SKILL 12	36. SKILL 4
7. SKILL 4	22. SKILL 1	37. SKILL 3
8. SKILL 10	23. SKILL 3	38. SKILL 4
9. SKILL 6	24. SKILL 10	39. SKILL 5
10. SKILL 14	25. SKILL 6	40. SKILL 9
11. SKILL 2	26. SKILL 11	41. SKILL 14
12. SKILL 3	27. SKILL 12	42. SKILL 12
13. SKILL 9	28. SKILL 6	43. SKILL 9
14. SKILL 3	29. SKILL 3	44. SKILL 2
15. SKILL 3	30. SKILL 11	

READING

Reading is tested in the third section on both the paper TOEFL test and the computer TOEFL test. This section consists of reading passages followed by a number of questions. The paper and the computer reading sections are **similar** in the following ways:

- *the types of passages*
- *the language skills tested*
- *the ordering of the questions*

The paper and the computer reading sections are **different** in the following ways:

- *the types of questions*
- *the number of questions*
- *the amount of time*
- *the strategies and procedures*

READING ON THE PAPER TOEFL® TEST

On the paper TOEFL test, the third section is called Reading Comprehension. This section consists of five passages and fifty questions (although some tests may be longer). You have fifty-five minutes to complete the fifty questions in this section.

There is only one type of question in the Reading Comprehension section of the paper TOEFL test:

Multiple-Choice questions ask you to select the best answer to questions about the information given in the reading passages. A multiple-choice question on the paper test may ask about the main ideas, directly answered details, indirectly answered details, vocabulary, or overall review ideas.

The questions on the paper test are presented in *linear* order. The passages progress from easy to difficult, and the questions are presented in the order in which they appear in the passage.

GENERAL STRATEGIES FOR READING
(Paper TOEFL® Test)

1. **Be familiar with the directions.** The directions on every paper TOEFL test are the same, so it is not necessary to spend time reading the directions carefully when you take the test. You should be completely familiar with the directions before the day of the test.

2. **Do not spend too much time reading the passages.** You do not have time to read each passage in depth, and it is quite possible to answer the questions correctly without first reading the passages in depth.

---

3. **Do not worry if a reading passage is on a topic you are unfamiliar with.** All of the information that you need to answer the questions is included in the passages. You do not need any background knowledge to answer the questions.

4. **Do not spend too much time on a question you are unsure of.** If you do not know the answer to a question, simply guess and go on. You can return to this question later in the section if you have time.

5. **Guess to complete the section before time is up.** There is no penalty for guessing, so it can only increase your score to guess the answers to questions that you do not have time to complete.

Now look at a reading passage from the paper TOEFL test, followed by a number of multiple-choice questions.

Example from the Paper TOEFL Test

Obsidian is a distinctive type of igneous rock that forms as a result of the melting of deep crustal granite rocks into magma. Because of the speed at which the magma cools, crystallization does not occur, and a solid, shiny, volcanic, glass-like rock results. Most commonly a solid, shiny black in color, obsidian can also take on a golden or silvery sheen or be striped in a rainbow of hues.

Line
(5)

Obsidian is generally found in small outcrops, though large masses of it can be found in a few notable locations. Two such sites are the giant Valles Caldera in New Mexico, where the obsidian flows are hundreds of feet thick, and the Glass Buttes in Oregon, which are composed entirely of obsidian.

(10)

Because of its properties, obsidian was prized in many ancient cultures. Obsidian is easily worked into shapes with razor-sharp edges even sharper than the edges formed from flint and was thus used in the production of simple hunting weapons. It can also be polished to an extremely high luster and was thus held in a high regard in a number of cultures as a semiprecious stone in jewelry and other embellishments.

(15)

Now look at the first question, which is a multiple-choice question that asks about a direct detail from the passage.

1. What is stated in the passage about obsidian?

   (A) It results from rapidly cooling magma.
   (B) It is crystalline.
   (C) It is a sedimentary rock.
   (D) It has a dull finish.

To answer this question, you should find the part of the passage that states that *because of the speed at which the magma cools, crystallization does not occur, and a solid, shiny, volcanic, glass-like rock results.* From this, it can be determined that obsidian *results from rapidly cooling magma,* and that it is not crystalline, that it is a volcanic rather than sedimentary rock, and that it has a shiny finish rather than a dull finish. Answer (A) is therefore the best answer to this question.

Now look at the second question, which is a multiple-choice question that asks about a vocabulary word from the passage.

---

2. The word "sites" in line 10 is closest in meaning to

   (A) pieces
   (B) layers
   (C) places
   (D) distances

To answer this question, you should find the word *sites* in line 10 in the passage and read the context around it. The passage mentions *a few notable locations* and *two such sites.* From this context, you can determine that *sites* is close in meaning to *locations,* or *places.* Answer (C) is therefore the best answer to this question.

Now look at the third question, which is a multiple-choice question that asks you to infer an indirect detail from the passage.

---

3. It can be inferred from the passage that obsidian would least likely have been used to make

   (A) a spear
   (B) an arrowhead
   (C) a ring
   (D) a belt

The passage states that *obsidian was...used in the production of simple hunting weapons* and that it was *held in high regard in a number of cultures as a semiprecious stone in jewelry.* From this, it can be inferred that obsidian would likely have been used to make a *spear* or an *arrowhead,* which are types of weapons, or a *ring,* which is a type of jewelry, and that obsidian, which is a rock, would have been least likely to have been used to make a *belt,* which is an article of clothing. Answer (D) is therefore the best answer to this question.

Now look at the fourth question, which is a multiple-choice question that asks where in the passage a piece of information can be found.

---

4. Where in the passage does the author discuss the variety of colors in which obsidian is found?

   (A) Lines 1–3
   (B) Lines 5–7
   (C) Lines 8–9
   (D) Lines 18–20

To answer this question, you should skim each of the line numbers in the answer choices for information about the *colors* of obsidian. Lines 5–7 mention that obsidian is *black in color,* that it can *take on a golden or silvery sheen,* and that is can be *striped in a rainbow of hues.* This sentence clearly discusses the *colors* of obsidian, so answer (B) is the best answer to this question.

PROCEDURES FOR A READING PASSAGE
(Paper TOEFL® Test) 📖

1. **Skim the reading passage to determine the main idea and the overall organization of ideas in the passage.** You do not need to understand every detail in each passage to answer the questions correctly. It is therefore a waste of time to read the passage with the intent of understanding every single detail before you try to answer the questions.

2. **Look ahead at the questions to determine what language skills are being tested in the questions.** Questions related to different language skills are answered in different ways.

3. **Find the section of the passage that deals with each question.** The language skill tells you exactly where to look in the passage to find correct answers.
   • For *main idea* questions, look at the first line of each paragraph.
   • For *directly* and *indirectly answered detail* questions, choose a key word in the question, and skim for that key word (or a related idea) in order in the passage.
   • For *pronoun* questions, the question will tell you where the pronoun is located in the passage.
   • For *transition* questions, look at the beginning or the end of the passage.
   • For *vocabulary* questions, the question will tell you where the word is located in the passage.
   • For *where-in-the-passage* questions, the answer choices give you the four possible locations of the correct answer.
   • For *tone, purpose,* and *course* questions, look at the first line of each paragraph.

4. **Read the part of the passage that contains the answer carefully.** The answer will probably be in a very predictable place in the passage.

5. **Choose the best answer to each question from the four choices listed in your test book.** You can choose the best answer according to what is given in the appropriate section of the passage, eliminate definitely wrong answers, and mark your best guess on the answer sheet.

READING ON THE COMPUTER TOEFL® TEST 🖥️

On the computer TOEFL test, the third section is called the Reading section. This section consists of four to five passages and forty-four to sixty questions. You have seventy to ninety minutes to complete the questions in this section.

There are three types of questions in the Reading section of the computer TOEFL test:

1. **Multiple-Choice** questions ask you to select the best answer to questions about the information given in the reading passages. A multiple-choice question on the computer test may ask about the main ideas, directly answered details, indirectly answered details, vocabulary, or overall review ideas.

2. **Click-on** questions ask you to find a word, phrase, sentence, or paragraph in a passage that answers a question and to click on that word, phrase, sentence, or paragraph. They may also ask you to click on one of four pictures following a passage. In a click-on question, you may be asked to click on a vocabulary word with a specific meaning, a reference for a particular pronoun, a sentence or picture that answers a detail question, or a paragraph that develops a main idea.

3. **Insertion** questions ask you to find the most logical place in a passage to insert a specific piece of information. In an insertion question, you may be asked to insert a sentence that expresses a main idea, a supporting detail or an example, a transition, or a concluding idea into the appropriate place in a passage.

The questions in the Reading section of the computer test are presented in *linear* order. The passages progress from easy to difficult, and the questions are presented in the order in which they appear in the passage.

GENERAL STRATEGIES FOR READING
(Computer TOEFL® Test) 🖥️

1. **Be familiar with the directions.** The directions on every computer TOEFL test are the same, so it is not necessary to spend time reading the directions carefully when you take the test. You should be completely familiar with the directions before the day of the test.

2. **Dismiss the directions as soon as they come up.** The time starts when the directions come up. You should already be familiar with the directions, so you can click on `Dismiss Directions` as soon as it appears and save all your time for the questions.

3. **Understand that this section of the test is linear rather than computer adaptive.** This means that the ordering of the passages and questions is specified (and is not based on how you have answered previous questions, as it is in the Structure section and the Listening section of the computer test). The reading passages progress from easy to difficult, and the questions are presented in the order in which they appear in the passage.

4. **Do not spend too much time reading the passages.** You do not have time to read each passage in depth, and it is possible to answer the questions correctly without first reading the passages in depth. You must scroll through each passage completely and then click on `Proceed` before you will be allowed to continue with the questions.

5. **Do not worry if a reading passage is on a topic you are unfamiliar with.** All of the information that you need to answer the questions is included in the passage. You do not need any background knowledge to answer the questions.

6. **Do not spend too much time on a question you are unsure of.** If you do not know the answer to a question, simply guess, click on `Next`, and go on. You can click on `Previous` to return to this question later while you are still working on the same passage.

7. **Monitor the time carefully on the title bar of the computer screen.** The title bar indicates the time remaining in the section, the total number of questions in the section, and the current number.

8. **Guess to complete the section before time is up.** Because this section is linear rather than adaptive, it can only increase your score to guess the answers to questions that you do not have time to complete.

Now look at an example of a passage from the computer TOEFL test, followed by the various types of questions that appear in the reading section of the computer test. The first question is a *multiple-choice* question about a stated detail from the passage.

Reading

Amelia Bloomer (1818–1894) was an important writer and crusader for women's rights in the nineteenth century. Married to a newspaper editor, she started her own journal, *Lily,* in 1849 to espouse her ideas on rights for women. While she was effective in her work in a number of areas of women's rights, she is best known today for her attempts to improve the style of women's clothing.

Women's fashions in the middle of the nineteenth century were impractical, uncomfortable, and occasionally unhealthy. The preferred silhouette was a tiny waist flaring out into a wide, wide skirt. This minuscule waist was achieved through corsets; a woman was wrapped in a heavily-boned corset, and the laces of the corset were tightly laced, pulled, and secured to the point where her breathing was inhibited and damage to her ribs was possible. The flared-out skirts were created with hoop skirts and petticoats.

Amelia introduced a style of clothing for women that was considerably more practical but also proved quite scandalous. Her outfit consisted of a knee-length tunic with a flared skirt over a very wide-legged pant that was cinched at the ankle. Even though the tunic came down to the knee and the legs were completely hidden beneath the voluminous folds of the pants, society was shocked by an outfit that acknowledged women's legs.

1. It is stated in the passage that Amelia Bloomer
   - ○ lived in the eighteenth century
   - ○ kept a private journal
   - ○ did not believe in women's suffrage
   - ○ tried to effect a change in women's fashions

To answer this question, you should look at the part of the passage at the end of paragraph 1 that mentions Amelia's *attempts to improve the style of women's clothing*. From this, it can be determined that Amelia *tried to effect a change in women's fashions,* so the last answer is the best answer. You should click on the last answer to this question.

The second question is a *click-on-a-sentence* question that asks you to find where a specific piece of information can be found in paragraph 1. For this question, you should look at paragraph 1.

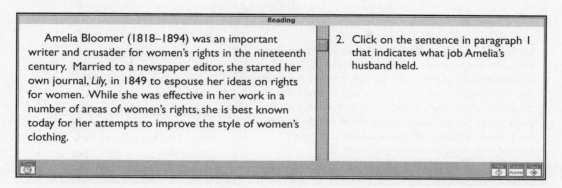

To answer this question, you should look at the second sentence of paragraph 1, which states that Amelia was *married to a newspaper editor*. From this, it can be determined that Amelia's husband held the position of newspaper editor. You should click on the second sentence of paragraph 1 to answer this question.

The third question is a *click-on-a-word* question that asks you to find a vocabulary word in paragraph 2 with a similar meaning.

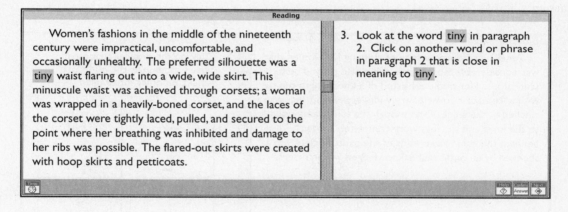

To answer this question, you should see the phrase *a tiny waist* in paragraph 2, and you should notice the context around it. You should notice the phrase in the following sentence that mentions *this minuscule waist*. From this context, you can determine that *minuscule* is close in meaning to *tiny*, so you should click on the word *minuscule* to answer this question.

The fourth question is an *insertion* question in which you must add a piece of information to paragraph 2.

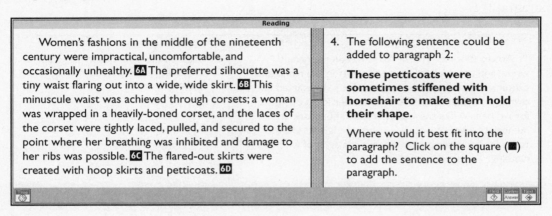

To answer this question, you should study the sentence to be inserted and should look at the context around each of the insertion boxes in paragraph 2. Because the last sentence of the paragraph ends with *petticoats* and the sentence to be inserted begins with *These petticoats,* the sentence should be inserted after the last sentence of the paragraph. You should click on **6D** to answer this question.

The fifth question is a *click-on-a-drawing* question that asks about a direct detail from the passage.

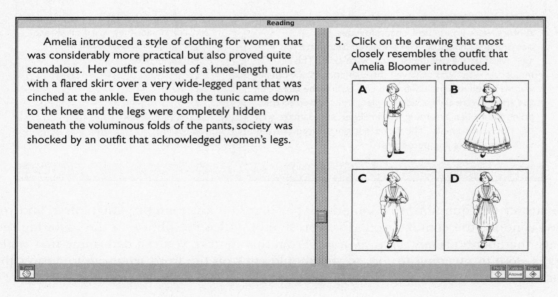

To answer this question, you should skim through the passage to find the part of the passage that discusses Amelia's outfit. In paragraph 3, the passage states that *her outfit consisted of a knee-length tunic with a flared skirt over a very wide-legged pant that was cinched at the ankle.* Drawing D most closely resembles this description, so you should click on drawing (D) to answer this question.

The sixth question is a *click-on-a-paragraph* question that asks you to indicate which paragraph discusses a certain topic.

Reading

Amelia Bloomer (1818–1894) was an important writer and crusader for women's rights in the nineteenth century. . . . .

Women's fashions in the middle of the nineteenth century were impractical, uncomfortable, and occasionally unhealthy. . . . .

Amelia introduced a style of clothing for women that was considerably more practical but also proved quite scandalous. . . . .

6. Click on the paragraph that describes the style of clothing that women commonly wore during Amelia's lifetime.

To answer this question, you should look at the question, which asks about the paragraph that describes *the style of clothing that women commonly wore,* and you should look at the first line of each paragraph to see which paragraph discusses this idea. The first sentence of paragraph 2 indicates that paragraph 2 discusses *women's fashions in the middle of the nineteenth century.* From this, you can determine that paragraph 2 is the best answer, so you should click on paragraph 2 to answer this question.

PROCEDURES FOR A READING PASSAGE
(Computer TOEFL® Test)

1. **Scroll through the reading passage to determine the main idea and the overall organization of ideas in the passage.** You do not need to understand every detail in each passage to answer the questions correctly. It is therefore a waste of time to read the passage with the intent of understanding every single detail before you try to answer the questions. When you have finished scrolling quickly through the passage, click on **Proceed** to begin the first question.

2. **As a question comes up on the screen, look at the language skill that is being tested.** The language skill tells you exactly where to look in the passage to find correct answers.
   - For *main idea* questions, look at the first line of each paragraph.
   - For *click-on-a-paragraph* questions, look at the first line of each paragraph.
   - For *directly* and *indirectly answered detail* questions, choose a key word in the question, and skim for that key word (or a related idea) in order in the passage.
   - For *pronoun* questions, the pronoun will be highlighted in the passage.
   - For *transition* questions, look at the beginning or the end of the passage.
   - For *vocabulary* questions, the vocabulary will be highlighted in the passage.
   - For *click-on-a-sentence* questions, the paragraph where the answer can be found is given in the question.
   - For *tone, purpose,* and *course* questions, look at the first line of each paragraph.
   - For *insertion* questions, look at the context before and after each insertion box.

3. **Read the part of the passage that contains the answer carefully.** The answer will probably be in a very predictable place in the passage.

4. **Choose the best answer to each question.** You can choose the best answer according to what is given in the appropriate section of the passage, or you can eliminate definitely wrong answers and select your best guess.

5. **Click on the answer on the computer screen when you have selected an answer.** You may still change your mind at this point and click on a different answer. You may also return later to a question within the same reading passage (although it can be time-consuming to click back through too many questions).

Next, you should move on to the language skills. The following language skills will help you to implement these strategies and procedures in the reading section of both the paper TOEFL test and the computer TOEFL test.

QUESTIONS ABOUT THE IDEAS OF THE PASSAGE

It is very common for reading passages in the reading section of both the paper TOEFL test and the computer TOEFL test to have questions about the overall ideas in the passage. The most common type of question asks about the main idea, topic, title, or subject. There may also be questions about how the information in the passage is organized or about which type of information is included in a particular paragraph.

Skill 1: ANSWER MAIN IDEA QUESTIONS CORRECTLY

Almost every reading passage on the paper TOEFL test or computer TOEFL test will have a multiple-choice question about the main idea of a passage. Such a question may be worded in a variety of ways; you may, for example, be asked to identify the *topic, subject, title, primary idea,* or *main idea.* These questions are all really asking what primary point the author is trying to get across in the passage. Since TOEFL passages are generally written in a traditionally organized manner, it is relatively easy to find the main ideas by studying the topic sentences, which are most probably found at the beginning of each paragraph.

If a passage consists of only one paragraph, you should study the beginning of that paragraph to determine the main idea. Look at a multiple-choice example from the paper TOEFL test that asks about the topic of a passage with one paragraph.

Example from the Paper TOEFL Test

The passage:

> In the philosophy of John Dewey, a sharp distinction is made between <u>intelligence</u> and <u>reasoning</u>. According to Dewey, intelligence is the only absolute way to achieve a
>
> *Line* balance between realism and idealism, between practicality
> *(5)* and wisdom of life. Intelligence involves "interacting with other things and knowing them," while reasoning is merely the act of an observer, "…a mind that beholds or grasps objects outside the world of things…." With reasoning, a level of mental certainty can be achieved, but it is through intelligence
> *(10)* that control is taken of events that shape one's life.

The question:

What is the ***topic*** of this passage?

(A) The intelligence of John Dewey
(B) Distinctions made by John Dewey
(C) Dewey's ideas on the ability to reason
(D) How <u>intelligence</u> differs from <u>reasoning</u> in Dewey's works

This question asks about the *topic* of the passage. Because this passage has only one paragraph, you should look at the first sentence of the passage to answer this question. The first sentence of this passage discusses a distinction between the ideas of *intelligence* and *reasoning* in the philosophy of John Dewey, so this is probably the topic. A quick check of the rest of the sentences in the passage confirms that the topic is in fact the difference between *intelligence* and *reasoning*. Now you should check each of the answers to determine which one comes closest to the topic that you have determined. Answer (A) mentions only intelligence, so it is not the topic. Answer (B) mentions distinctions that John Dewey made, but it does not say specifically what type of distinctions. Answer (C) mentions only reasoning, so answer (C) is incomplete. The best answer is therefore (D); the idea of *how intelligence differs from reasoning* comes from the first sentence of the passage, which mentions *a sharp distinction…between intelligence and reasoning*.

If a passage consists of more than one paragraph, you should study the beginning of each paragraph to determine the main idea. Look at a multiple-choice example from the computer TOEFL test that asks about the title of a passage with more than one paragraph.

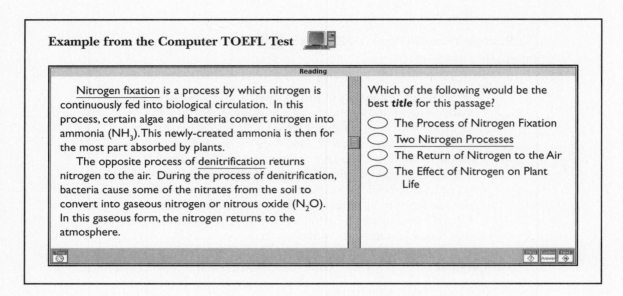

This question asks you about the best *title* for the passage. In a passage with more than one paragraph, you should be sure to read the first sentence of each paragraph to determine the subject, topic, title, or main idea. In this example, the first sentence of the first paragraph indicates that the first paragraph is about the process of *nitrogen fixation*. If you look only at the first paragraph, you might choose the incorrect first answer, which would be a good title for the first paragraph only. The first sentence of the second paragraph indicates that the process of *denitrification* is discussed in the second paragraph. The third answer is incorrect because the return of nitrogen to the air is the process of denitrification, and this is discussed in the second paragraph only. The last answer is incorrect because the effect of nitrogen on plant life is not discussed in this passage. The best answer to this question is the second answer; the *two nitrogen processes* are *nitrogen fixation,* which is discussed in the first paragraph, and *denitrification,* which is discussed in the second paragraph.

The following chart outlines the key information that you should remember about main idea questions:

MAIN IDEA QUESTIONS		
HOW TO IDENTIFY THE QUESTION	on both paper and computer tests	*What is the **topic** of the passage?* *What is the **subject** of the passage?* *What is the **main idea** of the passage?* *What is the author's **main point** in the passage?* *With what is the author **primarily concerned**?* *Which of the following would be the **best title**?*
WHERE TO FIND THE ANSWER	The answer to this type of question can generally be determined by looking at the first sentence of each paragraph.	
HOW TO ANSWER THE QUESTION	1. Read the first line of each paragraph. 2. Look for a common theme or idea in the first lines. 3. Pass your eyes quickly over the rest of the passage to check that you have really found the topic sentence(s). 4. Eliminate any definitely wrong answers and choose the best answer from the remaining choices.	

TOEFL EXERCISE 1: Study each of the passages and choose the best answers to the questions that follow. In this exercise, each passage is followed by several main idea, topic, or title questions so that the students can practice this type of question. On the TOEFL test, one passage would probably not have two such questions because they are so similar.

PASSAGE ONE (Questions 1–2)

Fort Knox, Kentucky, is the site of a U.S. army post, but it is even more renowned for the Fort Knox Bullion Depository, the massive vault that contains the bulk of the U.S. government's gold deposits. Completed in 1936, the vault is housed in a two-story building constructed of granite, steel, and concrete; the vault itself is made of steel and concrete and has a door that weighs more than twenty tons. Naturally, the most up-to-date security devices available are in place at Fort Knox, and the army post nearby provides further protection.

Line (5)

1. Which of the following best describes the topic of the passage?

   (A) The city of Fort Knox, Kentucky
   (B) The federal gold depository
   (C) The U.S. army post at Fort Knox
   (D) Gold bullion

2. Which of the following would be the best title for this passage?

   (A) The Massive Concrete Vault
   (B) Fort Knox Security
   (C) Where the United States Keeps Its Gold
   (D) A Visit to Kentucky

PASSAGE TWO (Questions 3–4)

One identifying characteristic of minerals is their relative hardness, which can be determined by scratching one mineral with another. In this type of test, a harder mineral can scratch a softer one, but a softer mineral is unable to scratch the harder one. The Mohs' hardness scale is used to rank minerals according to hardness. Ten minerals are listed in this scale, ranging from talc with a hardness of 1 to diamond with a hardness of 10. On this scale, quartz (number 7) is harder than feldspar (number 6) and is therefore able to scratch it; however, feldspar is unable to make a mark on quartz.

Line (5)

3. Which of the following best states the subject of this passage?

   (A) The hardness of diamonds
   (B) Identifying minerals by means of a scratch test
   (C) Feldspar on the Mohs' scale
   (D) Recognizing minerals in their natural state

4. The main idea of this passage is that

   (A) the hardness of a mineral can be determined by its ability to make a mark on other minerals
   (B) diamonds, with a hardness of 10 on the Mohs' scale, can scratch all other minerals
   (C) a softer mineral cannot be scratched by a harder mineral
   (D) talc is the first mineral listed on the Mohs' scale

PASSAGE THREE (Questions 5–6)

Hurricanes generally occur in the North Atlantic from May through November, with the peak of the hurricane season in September; only rarely will they occur from December through April in that part of the ocean. The main reason for the occurrence of hurricanes during this
Line period is that the temperature on the water's surface is at its warmest and the humidity of the air
(5) is at its highest.

Of the tropical storms that occur each year in the North Atlantic, only about five, on the average, are powerful enough to be called hurricanes. To be classified as a hurricane, a tropical storm must have winds reaching speeds of at least 117 kilometers per hour, but the winds are often much stronger than that; the winds of intense hurricanes can easily surpass 240 kilometers
(10) per hour.

5. The passage mainly discusses

    (A) how many hurricanes occur each year
    (B) the strength of hurricanes
    (C) the weather in the North Atlantic
    (D) hurricanes in one part of the world

6. The best title for this passage would be

    (A) The North Atlantic Ocean
    (B) Storms of the Northern Atlantic
    (C) Hurricanes: The Damage and Destruction
    (D) What Happens from May through November

PASSAGE FOUR (Questions 7–9)

Henry Wadsworth Longfellow (1807–1882) was perhaps the best-known American poet of the nineteenth century. His clear writing style and emphasis on the prevalent values of the period made him popular with the general public if not always with the critics. He was particularly recognized for
Line his longer narrative poems *Evangeline, The Song of Hiawatha,* and *The Courtship of Miles Standish,* in
(5) which he told stories from American history in terms of the values of the time.

Evangeline was set during the French and Indian War (1754–1763), when the British forced French settlers from Nova Scotia; two lovers, Gabriel and Evangeline, were separated by the British, and Evangeline devoted her lifetime to the search for Gabriel. With its emphasis on sentimental, undying love, *Evangeline* was immensely popular with the public.
(10) In *The Song of Hiawatha,* Longfellow depicted the noble life of the American Indian through the story of the brave Hiawatha and his beloved wife Minehaha. The tear-inspiring poem follows Hiawatha through the tragedies and triumphs of life, ending with the death of Minehaha and Hiawatha's departure into the sunset in his canoe.

The Courtship of Miles Standish takes place during the early period of the settlement of New
(15) England, a period which was viewed as a time of honor and romance. In this poem centered around a love triangle, Miles Standish asks his friend John Alden to propose to Priscilla Mullins for him; John Alden ends up marrying Priscilla Mullins himself, and it takes time for his friendship with Miles Standish to recover. As with Longfellow's other narrative poems, the emphasis on high ideals and romance made the poem extremely popular.

7. Which of the following best describes the main idea of the passage?

    (A) American history is often depicted in poetry.

    (B) Longfellow described American history even though people really did not enjoy it.

    (C) The popularity of Longfellow's poems results from his stress on the values of the people.

    (D) Longfellow wrote long narrative poems that were not always popular with the critics.

8. The best title of the passage is

    (A) Longfellow's Popular Appeal

    (B) Historical Narrative Poems

    (C) The Lyric, Dramatic, and Narrative Poems of Longfellow

    (D) Longfellow and the Critics

9. The subject of the fourth paragraph is

    (A) nobility and honor in the poems of Longfellow

    (B) the love triangle involving Miles Standish

    (C) the popular appeal of *The Courtship of Miles Standish*

    (D) the period of the early settlement of New England

SKILL 2: RECOGNIZE THE ORGANIZATION OF IDEAS

In the Reading section of both the paper TOEFL test and the computer TOEFL test, there may be questions about the organization of ideas in a passage. On the paper and the computer tests, you may be asked to determine how the ideas in one paragraph (or paragraphs) relate to the ideas in another paragraph (or paragraphs). On the computer TOEFL test, you may also see a question that asks you to click on the paragraph in a passage that contains certain ideas. Look at an example from the paper TOEFL test that asks you to determine how the information in the passage is organized.

Example from the Paper TOEFL Test

The passage:

        If asked who invented the game of baseball, most Americans would probably reply that it was their belief that Abner Doubleday did. They believe this because the story
Line about Doubleday is part of the tradition of baseball.
(5)   Doubleday was given credit for this invention early in the twentieth century when sporting-goods manufacturer Spaulding inaugurated a commission to research the question of who invented baseball. In 1908, a report was published by the commission in which Abner Doubleday, a U.S. Army
(10) officer from Cooperstown, New York, was given credit for the invention of the game. The National Baseball Hall of Fame was established in Cooperstown in honor of Doubleday.

        Today, most sports historians are in agreement that Doubleday really did not have much to do with the
(15) development of baseball. Instead, baseball seems to be a close relative of the English game of rounders and probably has English rather than American roots.

The question:

In this passage

(A)   an idea is <u>presented</u> and then <u>refuted</u>
(B)   a concept is followed by examples
(C)   a cause is followed by an effect
(D)   a belief is supported with reasons

This question is about how the information is organized in the passage. To answer this question, it is necessary to look at the main ideas of each of the three paragraphs. The main idea of the first paragraph is found in the first sentence of the first paragraph: that *if asked who invented the game of baseball, most Americans would probably reply that it was their belief that Abner Doubleday did.* The main idea of the second paragraph is found in the first line of the second paragraph: that *Doubleday was given credit for this invention.* The main idea of the third paragraph is found in the first line of the third paragraph: that *most sports historians are in agreement that Doubleday really did not have much to do with the development of baseball.* If you study the information in the first lines of the paragraphs, you can determine that the third paragraph contradicts or *refutes* the information that is *presented* in the first two paragraphs. Answer (A) is therefore the best answer to this question.

Now look at an example of a click-on question from the computer TOEFL test that asks you to select the paragraph that discusses a certain idea.

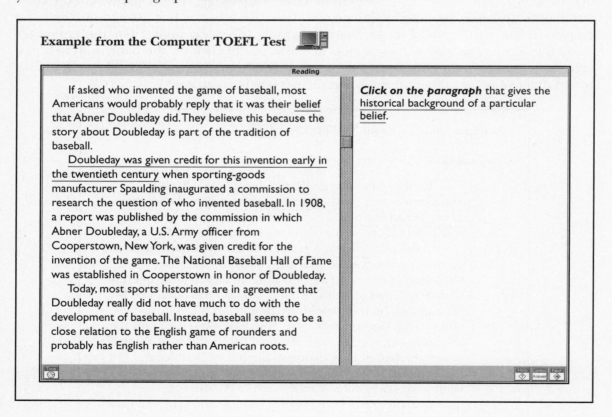

Example from the Computer TOEFL Test

Reading

If asked who invented the game of baseball, most Americans would probably reply that it was their <u>belief</u> that Abner Doubleday did. They believe this because the story about Doubleday is part of the tradition of baseball.

<u>Doubleday was given credit for this invention early in the twentieth century</u> when sporting-goods manufacturer Spaulding inaugurated a commission to research the question of who invented baseball. In 1908, a report was published by the commission in which Abner Doubleday, a U.S. Army officer from Cooperstown, New York, was given credit for the invention of the game. The National Baseball Hall of Fame was established in Cooperstown in honor of Doubleday.

Today, most sports historians are in agreement that Doubleday really did not have much to do with the development of baseball. Instead, baseball seems to be a close relation to the English game of rounders and probably has English rather than American roots.

Click on the paragraph that gives the <u>historical background</u> of a particular <u>belief.</u>

This question asks you to *click on the paragraph* that discusses the *historical background* of a particular *belief.* To answer this question you must also look at the main ideas of the paragraphs. The first sentence of the first paragraph mentions a *belief,* and the first sentence of the second paragraph states that *Doubleday was given credit for this invention early in the twentieth century.* From this, it can be determined that the second paragraph gives the *historical background* of the *belief* that is discussed in the first paragraph, so you should click on the second paragraph to answer this question.

The following chart outlines the key information that you should remember about questions on the organization of ideas:

ORGANIZATION OF IDEAS 📖 💻		
HOW TO IDENTIFY THE QUESTION	on both paper and computer tests 📖 💻	*How is the information in the passage* **organized**? *How is the information in the second paragraph* **related** *to the information in the first paragraph?*
	on computer test only 💻	**Click on the paragraph** *that…*
WHERE TO FIND THE ANSWER	The answer to this type of question can generally be determined by looking at the first sentence of the appropriate paragraphs.	
HOW TO ANSWER THE QUESTION	1. Read the first line of each paragraph. 2. Look for words that show relationships among the paragraphs. 3. Choose the answer that best expresses the relationship.	

TOEFL EXERCISE 2: Study each of the passages and choose the best answers to the questions that follow.

PASSAGE ONE (Questions 1–2)

Conflict within an organization is not always viewed as undesirable. In fact, various managers have widely divergent ideas on the value that conflict can have.

According to the traditional view of conflict, conflict is harmful to an organization.
Line
(5)
Managers with this traditional view of conflict see it as their role in an organization to rid the organization of any possible sources of conflict.

The interactionist view of conflict, on the other hand, holds that conflict can serve an important function in an organization by reducing complacency among workers and causing positive changes to occur. Managers who hold an interactionist view of conflict may actually take steps to stimulate conflict within the organization.

1. How is the information in the passage organized?

    (A) The origin of ideas about conflict is presented.
    (B) Contrasting views of conflict are presented.
    (C) Two theorists discuss the strengths and weaknesses of their views on conflict.
    (D) Examples of conflict within organizations are presented.

2. Click on the paragraph that supports the view that organizational conflict can be beneficial.

PASSAGE TWO (Questions 3–4)

IQ, or intelligence quotient, is defined as the ratio of a person's mental age to chronological age, with the ratio multiplied by 100 to remove the decimal. Chronological age is easily determined; mental age is generally measured by some kind of standard test and is not so simple
Line to define.
(5)   In theory, a standardized IQ test is set up to measure an individual's ability to perform intellectual operations such as reasoning and problem solving. These intellectual operations are considered to represent intelligence.

In practice, it has been impossible to arrive at consensus as to which types of intellectual operations demonstrate intelligence. Furthermore, it has been impossible to devise a test without
(10) cultural bias, which is to say that any IQ tests so far proposed have been shown to reflect the culture of the test makers. Test takers from that culture would, it follows, score higher on such a test than test takers from a different culture with equal intelligence.

3. What type of information is included in the first paragraph?

    (A) An argument
    (B) A definition
    (C) An opinion
    (D) A theory

4. Click on the paragraph that describes the application of IQ in the real world.

PASSAGE THREE (Questions 5–6)

The largest lake in the western United States is the Great Salt Lake, an inland saltwater lake in northwestern Utah, just outside the state capital of Salt Lake City. Rivers and streams feed into the Great Salt Lake, but none drain out of it; this has a major influence on both the salt content
Line and the size of the lake.
(5)   Although the Great Salt Lake is fed by freshwater streams, it is actually saltier than the oceans of the world. The salt comes from the more than two million tons of minerals that flow into the lake each year from the rivers and creeks that feed it. Sodium and chloride—the components of salt—comprise the large majority of the lake's mineral content.

The Great Salt Lake can vary tremendously from its normal size of 1,700 square miles,
(10) depending on long-term weather conditions. During periods of heavy rains, the size of the lake can swell tremendously from the huge amounts of water flowing into the lake from its feeder rivers and streams; in 1980 the lake even reached a size of 2,400 square miles. During periods of dry weather, the size of the lake decreases, sometimes drastically, due to evaporation.

5. How is the information in the passage organized?

    (A) Two unusual characteristics of the Great Salt Lake are discussed.
    (B) Contrasting theories about the Great Salt Lake's salt levels are presented.
    (C) The process by which the Great Salt Lake gets its salt is outlined.
    (D) The reasons for the variations in the Great Salt Lake's size are given.

6. Click on the paragraph that explains where the Great Salt Lake gets its salt.

TOEFL EXERCISE (Skills 1–2): Study each of the passages and choose the best answers to the questions that follow.

PASSAGE ONE (Questions 1–2)

Common types of calendars can be based on the Sun or on the Moon. The solar calendar is based on the solar year. Since the solar year is 365.2422 days long, solar calendars consist of regular years of 365 days and have an extra day every fourth year, or leap year, to make up for the additional fractional amount. In a solar calendar, the waxing and waning of the Moon can take place at various stages of each month.

Line
(5)

The lunar calendar is synchronized to the lunar month rather than the solar year. Since the lunar month is twenty-nine and a half days long, most lunar calendars have alternating months of twenty-nine and thirty days. A twelve-month lunar year thus has 354 days, 11 days shorter than a solar year.

1. What is the main idea of the passage?

    (A) All calendars are the same.
    (B) The solar calendar is based on the Sun.
    (C) Different calendars have dissimilar bases.
    (D) The lunar month is twenty-nine and a half days long.

2. How is the information in the passage organized?

    (A) Characteristics of the solar calendar are outlined.
    (B) Two types of calendars are described.
    (C) The strengths and weakness of the lunar calendar are described.
    (D) The length of each existing calendar is contrasted.

PASSAGE TWO (Questions 3–6)

Vaccines are prepared from harmful viruses or bacteria and administered to patients to provide immunity to specific diseases. The various types of vaccines are classified according to the method by which they are derived.

Line
(5)   The most basic class of vaccines actually contains disease-causing microorganisms that have been killed with a solution containing formaldehyde. In this type of vaccine, the microorganisms are dead and therefore cannot cause disease; however, the antigens found in and on the microorganisms can still stimulate the formation of antibodies. Examples of this type of vaccine are the ones that fight influenza, typhoid fever, and cholera.

A second type of vaccine contains the toxins produced by the microorganisms rather than
(10)   the microorganisms themselves. This type of vaccine is prepared when the microorganism itself does little damage but the toxin within the microorganism is extremely harmful. For example, the bacteria that cause diphtheria can thrive in the throat without much harm, but when toxins are released from the bacteria, muscles can become paralyzed and death can ensue.

A final type of vaccine contains living microorganisms that have been rendered harmless.
(15)   With this type of vaccine, a large number of antigen molecules are produced and the immunity that results is generally longer lasting than the immunity from other types of vaccines. The Sabin oral antipolio vaccine and the BCG vaccine against tuberculosis are examples of this type of vaccine.

3. Which of the following expresses the main idea of the passage?

   (A) Vaccines provide immunity to specific diseases.
   (B) Vaccines contain disease-causing microorganisms.
   (C) Vaccines are derived in different ways.
   (D) New approaches in administering vaccines are being developed.

4. How many types of vaccines are presented in the passage?

   (A) Two
   (B) Three
   (C) Four
   (D) Five

5. Click on the paragraph that discusses vaccines made from dead organisms.

6. Click on the paragraph that discusses vaccines that do not contain the disease-causing microorganism.

PASSAGE THREE (Questions 7–10)

A hoax, unlike an honest error, is a deliberately-concocted plan to present an untruth as the truth. It can take the form of a fraud, a fake, a swindle, or a forgery, and can be accomplished in almost any field: successful hoaxes have been foisted on the public in fields as varied as politics,
Line   religion, science, art, and literature.
(5)   A famous scientific hoax occurred in 1912 when Charles Dawson claimed to have uncovered a human skull and jawbone on the Piltdown Common in southern England. These human remains were said to be more than 500,000 years old and were unlike any other remains from that period; as such, they represented an important discovery in the study of human evolution. These remains, popularly known as the Piltdown Man and scientifically named *Eoanthropus dawsoni* after
(10)   their discoverer, confounded scientists for several decades.

It took more than forty years for the hoax to be uncovered. In 1953, a chemical analysis was used to date the bones, and it was found that the bones were modern bones that had been skillfully aged. A further twist to the hoax was that the skull belonged to a human and the jaws to an orangutan.

7. The topic of this passage could best be described as

   (A) the Piltdown Man
   (B) Charles Dawson's discovery
   (C) *Eoanthropus dawsoni*
   (D) a definition and example of a hoax

8. The author's main point is that

   (A) various types of hoaxes have been perpetrated
   (B) Charles Dawson discovered a human skull and jawbone
   (C) Charles Dawson was not an honest man
   (D) the human skull and jawbone were extremely old

9. Click on the paragraph that defines a hoax.

10. Click on the paragraph that explains how one particular hoax was resolved.

DIRECTLY ANSWERED QUESTIONS

Many questions in the Reading section of both the paper TOEFL test and the computer TOEFL test will require answers that are directly stated in the passage. This means that you should be able to find the answer to this type of question without having to draw a conclusion. The directly answered questions that are commonly asked are (1) stated detail questions, (2) "unstated" detail questions, and (3) pronoun reference questions.

Skill 3: ANSWER STATED DETAIL QUESTIONS CORRECTLY

A stated detail question asks about one piece of information in the passage rather than the passage as a whole. The answers to these questions are generally given in order in the passage, and the correct answer is often a restatement of what is given in the passage. This means that the correct answer often expresses the same idea as what is written in the passage, but the words are not exactly the same. The questions that test stated details are generally multiple-choice questions. On the computer test, there may also be a type of stated detail question that asks you to click on an appropriate drawing. Look at a multiple-choice example from the paper TOEFL test that asks about a stated detail from the passage.

Example from the Paper TOEFL Test

The passage:

> Williamsburg is a historic city in Virginia that was settled by English colonists in 1633, twenty-six years after the first permanent English colony in America was settled at
> *Line* Jamestown. In the beginning, the colony at Williamsburg was
> *(5)* named Middle Plantation because of its location in the middle of a peninsula between two rivers, the York and the James. The site for Williamsburg had been selected by the colonists because the soil drainage was better there than at the Jamestown location, and there were fewer mosquitoes.

The question:

The passage *indicates* that Jamestown

(A) was settled in 1633
(B) was settled twenty-six years after Williamsburg
(C) was the first permanent English colony in America
(D) was originally named Middle Plantation

This question asks what the passage *indicates* about *Jamestown,* so you know that the answer to this question will be directly stated in the passage. You should skim through the passage to find the part of the passage that discusses *Jamestown.* The answer to this question is found in the statement that *Williamsburg was settled by English colonists in 1633, twenty-six years after the first permanent English colony in America was settled at Jamestown.* Answer (A) is incorrect because it was Williamsburg that was settled in 1633. Answer (B) is incorrect because Jamestown was settled *before* rather than *after* Williamsburg. Answer (D) is incorrect because the name *Middle Plantation* referred to Williamsburg. The best answer to this question is answer (C) because the passage directly states that Jamestown *was the first permanent English colony in America.*

Now look at a multiple-choice example of a stated detail question from the computer TOEFL test.

Example from the Computer TOEFL Test

Reading

Williamsburg is a historic city in Virginia that was settled by English colonists in 1633, twenty-six years after the first permanent English colony in America was settled at Jamestown. In the beginning, the colony at Williamsburg was named Middle Plantation because of its location in the middle of a peninsula between two rivers, the York and the James. The site for Williamsburg had been selected by the colonists because the soil drainage was better there than at the Jamestown location, and there were fewer mosquitoes.

According to the passage, the colonists <u>chose</u> Williamsburg because

- it was in England
- there were no nearby rivers
- there were lots of mosquitoes
- the soil drained well

This question asks what is true *according to the passage* about why the colonists *chose* Williamsburg, so you know that the answer will be directly stated in the passage. You should skim through the passage to find the part of the passage that discusses this topic. The answer to this question is found in the statement that *the site for Williamsburg had been selected by the colonists because the soil drainage was better there.* The first answer is not correct because Williamsburg was in America rather than England, the second answer is not correct because Williamsburg was located close to two rivers, and the third answer is not correct because there were fewer mosquitoes. It is stated in the passage that *the soil drained well,* so the last answer is the best answer. You should click on the last answer to this question.

Next, look at a click-on question from the computer TOEFL test that asks you to select one of four drawings that answers a stated detail question.

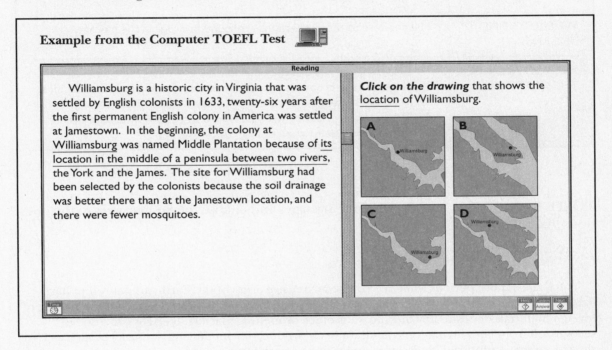

Example from the Computer TOEFL Test

Reading

Williamsburg is a historic city in Virginia that was settled by English colonists in 1633, twenty-six years after the first permanent English colony in America was settled at Jamestown. In the beginning, the colony at Williamsburg was named Middle Plantation because of its location in the middle of a peninsula between two rivers, the York and the James. The site for Williamsburg had been selected by the colonists because the soil drainage was better there than at the Jamestown location, and there were fewer mosquitoes.

Click on the drawing that shows the location of Williamsburg.

A   Williamsburg

B   Williamsburg

C   Williamsburg

D   Williamsburg

This question asks you to *click on the drawing* that shows the *location* of Williamsburg, so you know that the answer is directly stated in the passage. The passage mentions *Williamsburg* and *its location in the middle of a peninsula between two rivers.* Drawing (A) is incorrect because it shows only one river. Drawing (B) is incorrect because Williamsburg is not in the middle of the peninsula. Drawing (C) is incorrect because there is only one river. Drawing (D) is the one that has Williamsburg on a peninsula between two rivers and is therefore the best answer to the question. You should click on drawing (D) to answer this question.

The following chart outlines the key information that you should remember about stated detail questions:

STATED DETAIL QUESTIONS 📖 💻		
HOW TO IDENTIFY THE QUESTION	on both paper and computer tests 📖 💻	*According* to the passage,... It is *stated* in the passage... The passage *indicates* that... Which of the following is *true*...?
	on computer test only 💻	*Click on the drawing* that...
WHERE TO FIND THE ANSWER	The answers to these questions are found in order in the passage.	
HOW TO ANSWER THE QUESTION	1. Choose a key word in the question. 2. Skim in the appropriate part of the passage for the key word or idea. 3. Read the sentence that contains the key word or idea carefully. 4. Eliminate the definitely wrong answers and choose the best answer from the remaining choices.	

TOEFL EXERCISE 3: Study each of the passages and choose the best answers to the questions that follow.

PASSAGE ONE (Questions 1–4)

Ice ages, those periods when ice covered extensive areas of the Earth, are known to have occurred at least six times. Past ice ages can be recognized from rock strata that show evidence of foreign materials deposited by moving walls of ice or melting glaciers. Ice ages can also be
Line
(5)   recognized from land formations that have been produced from moving walls of ice, such as U-shaped valleys, sculptured landscapes, and polished rock faces.

1. According to the passage, what happens during an ice age?

   (A) Rock strata are recognized by geologists.
   (B) Evidence of foreign materials is found.
   (C) Ice covers a large portion of the Earth's surface.
   (D) Ice melts six times.

2. The passage covers how many different methods of recognizing past ice ages?

   (A) One
   (B) Two
   (C) Three
   (D) Four

3. According to the passage, what in the rock strata is a clue to geologists of a past ice age?

(A) Ice
(B) Melting glaciers
(C) U-shaped valleys
(D) Substances from other areas

4. Click on the drawing that shows the type of valley mentioned in the passage that results from melting glaciers.

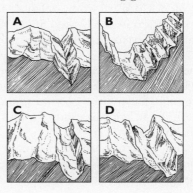

PASSAGE TWO (Questions 5–7)

The human heart is divided into four chambers, each of which serves its own function in the cycle of pumping blood. The atria are the thin-walled upper chambers that gather blood as it flows from the veins between heartbeats. The ventricles are the thick-walled lower chambers that *Line* receive blood from the atria and push it into the arteries with each contraction of the heart. The *(5)* left atrium and ventricle work separately from those on the right. The role of the chambers on the right side of the heart is to receive oxygen-depleted blood from the body tissues and send it on to the lungs; the chambers on the left side of the heart then receive the oxygen-enriched blood from the lungs and send it back out to the body tissues.

5. The passage indicates that the ventricles

(A) have relatively thin walls
(B) send blood to the atria
(C) are above the atria
(D) force blood into the arteries

6. According to the passage, when is blood pushed into the arteries from the ventricles?

(A) As the heart beats
(B) Between heartbeats
(C) Before each contraction of the heart
(D) Before it is received by the atria

7. Click on the drawing that highlights the part of the heart that gets blood from the body tissues and passes it on to the lungs.

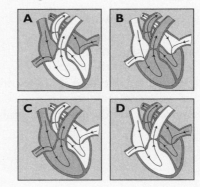

PASSAGE THREE (Questions 8–11)

The Golden Age of Railroads refers to the period from the end of the Civil War to the beginning of World War I when railroads flourished and, in fact, maintained a near monopoly in mass transportation in the United States. One of the significant developments during the period *Line* was the notable increase in uniformity, particularly through the standardization of track gauge (5)   and time.

At the end of the Civil War, only about half of the nation's railroad track was laid at what is now the standard gauge of 1.4 meters; much of the rest, particularly in the southern states, had a 1.5-meter gauge. During the postwar years, tracks were converted to the 1.4-meter gauge, and by June 1, 1886, the standardization of tracks was completed, resulting in increased efficiency and (10)   economy in the rail system.

A further boon to railroad efficiency was the implementation of standard time in 1883. With the adoption of standard time, four time zones were established across the country, thus simplifying railroad scheduling and improving the efficiency of railroad service.

8. Click on the drawing that shows the period of the Golden Age of Railroads.

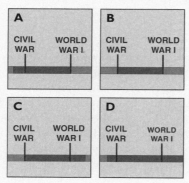

10. The passage mentions that which of the following occurred as a result of uniformity of track gauge?

   (A) The Civil War
   (B) Improved economy in the transportation system
   (C) Standardization of time zones
   (D) Railroad schedules

11. The passage indicates that standard time was implemented

   (A) before the Civil War
   (B) on June 1, 1886
   (C) after World War I
   (D) before standardized track gauge was established throughout the United States

9. According to the passage, the Golden Age of Railroads

   (A) was a result of World War I
   (B) was a period when most of U.S. mass transportation was controlled by the railroads
   (C) resulted in a decrease in uniformity of track gauge
   (D) resulted in standardization of train stations

Skill 4: FIND "UNSTATED" DETAILS

You will sometimes be asked in the reading section of both the paper TOEFL test and the computer TOEFL test to find an answer that is *not stated* or *not mentioned* or *not true* in the passage. This type of question really means that three of the answers are *stated, mentioned,* or *true* in the passage, while one answer is not.

You should note that there are two kinds of answers to this type of question: (1) there are three true answers and one that is not *true* according to the passage, or (2) there are three true answers and one that is not *mentioned* in the passage. Look at a multiple-choice example from the paper TOEFL test that asks you to find the one answer that is not *true*.

Example from the Paper TOEFL Test

The passage:

      In English, there are many different kinds of expressions that people use to give a name to anything whose name is unknown or momentarily forgotten. The word *gadget* is one
Line   such word. It was first used by British sailors in the 1850s and
(5)   probably came from the French word *gachette*, which was a small hook. In everyday use, the word has a more general meaning. Other words are also used to give a name to something unnamed or unknown, and these words tend to be somewhat imaginative. Some of the more commonly used
(10)   expressions are a *what-d'ye-call-it*, a *whatsis*, a *thingamabob*, a *thingamajig*, a *doodad*, or a *doohickey*.

The question:

Which of the following is ***NOT true*** about the word *gadget*?

  (A) It is used to name something when the name is not known.
  (B) It was used at the beginning of the nineteenth century.
  (C) It most likely came from a word in the French language.
  (D) Its first known use was by British sailors.

This question asks for the one answer that is *not true* about the *word "gadget,"* so three of the answers are true and one answer is *not.* You should look for the word *gadget* in the passage and find information that is untrue. Answers (A), (C), and (D) are all true according to the passage, so these answers are not correct. Answer (B) is the one answer that is *not true:* the passage states that *the word "gadget"...was first used by British sailors in the 1850s,* which is in the middle of the nineteenth century, so answer (B) is the best answer to this question.

Now, look at a multiple-choice example from the computer TOEFL test that asks you to find the one answer that is not mentioned.

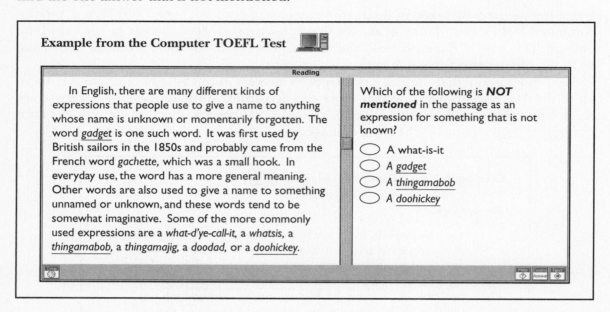

Example from the Computer TOEFL Test

Reading

In English, there are many different kinds of expressions that people use to give a name to anything whose name is unknown or momentarily forgotten. The word *gadget* is one such word. It was first used by British sailors in the 1850s and probably came from the French word *gachette,* which was a small hook. In everyday use, the word has a more general meaning. Other words are also used to give a name to something unnamed or unknown, and these words tend to be somewhat imaginative. Some of the more commonly used expressions are a *what-d'ye-call-it,* a *whatsis,* a *thingamabob,* a *thingamajig,* a *doodad,* or a *doohickey.*

Which of the following is **NOT mentioned** in the passage as an expression for something that is not known?

○ A what-is-it
○ A *gadget*
○ A *thingamabob*
○ A *doohickey*

This question asks for the one answer that is not mentioned, so three of the answers are listed in the passage and one is not. You should look for the three answers that are mentioned. Since *gadget, thingamabob,* and *doohickey* are listed in the passage, the second, third and fourth answers are incorrect. A *what-is-it* is not listed in the passage, so the first answer is the best answer to this question. You should click on the first answer to answer this question.

The following chart outlines the key information that you should remember about "unstated" detail questions:

"UNSTATED" DETAIL QUESTIONS		
HOW TO IDENTIFY THE QUESTION	on both paper and computer tests	*Which of the following is **not stated**...?* *Which of the following is **not mentioned**...?* *Which of the following is **not discussed**...?* *All of the following are true **except**....*
WHERE TO FIND THE ANSWER	The answers to these questions are found in order in the passage.	
HOW TO ANSWER THE QUESTION	1. Choose a key word in the question. 2. Scan the appropriate place in the passage for the key word (or related idea). 3. Read the sentence that contains the key word or idea carefully. 4. Look for answers that are definitely true according to the passage. Eliminate those answers. 5. Choose the answer that is not true or not discussed in the passage.	

TOEFL EXERCISE 4: Study each of the passages and choose the best answers to the questions that follow.

PASSAGE ONE (Questions 1–2)

Blood plasma is a clear, almost colorless liquid. It consists of blood from which the red and white blood cells have been removed. It is often used in transfusions because a patient generally needs the plasma portion of the blood more than the other components.

Line
(5)

Plasma differs in several important ways from whole blood. First of all, plasma can be mixed for all donors and does not have to be from the right blood group, as whole blood does. In addition, plasma can be dried and stored, while whole blood cannot.

1. All of the following are true about blood plasma EXCEPT that

   (A) it is a deeply colored liquid
   (B) blood cells have been taken out of it
   (C) patients are often transfused with it
   (D) it is generally more important to the patient than other parts of whole blood

2. Which of the following is NOT stated about whole blood?

   (A) It is different from plasma.
   (B) It cannot be dried.
   (C) It is impossible to keep it in storage for a long time.
   (D) It is a clear, colorless liquid.

PASSAGE TWO (Questions 3–4)

Elizabeth Cochrane Seaman was an American journalist at the turn of the century who wrote for the newspaper *New York World* under the pen name Nellie Bly, a name which was taken from the Stephen Foster song *Nelly Bly*. She achieved fame for her exposés and in particular for the bold and adventuresome way that she obtained her stories.

Line
(5)

She felt that the best way to get the real story was from the inside rather than as an outside observer who could be treated to a prettified version of reality. On one occasion she pretended to be a thief so that she would get arrested and see for herself how female prisoners were really treated. On another occasion she faked mental illness in order to be admitted to a mental hospital to get the real picture on the treatment of mental patients.

3. Which of the following is NOT true about Nellie Bly?

   (A) Nellie Bly's real name was Elizabeth Cochrane Seaman.
   (B) Nellie Bly was mentally ill.
   (C) The name Nellie Bly came from a song.
   (D) The name Nellie Bly was used on articles that Seaman wrote.

4. Which of the following is NOT mentioned as something that Nellie Bly did to get a good story?

   (A) She acted like a thief.
   (B) She got arrested by the police.
   (C) She pretended to be ill.
   (D) She worked as a doctor in a mental hospital.

PASSAGE THREE (Questions 5–6)

Dekanawida's role as a supreme lawgiver in the Iroquois tribe has given him the status of demigod within the Indian nation. Born into the Huron tribe, Dekanawida caused great fear in his parents, who tried to drown him in his youth after a prophecy was made indicating that he would bring great sorrow to the Huron nation. Dekanawida was to survive this attempted drowning but later left his parents' home and tribe to live among the Iroquois.

One of his achievements with the Iroquois was the institution of a law among the Iroquois that virtually ended blood feuds among the nation's families. Wampum, strings of beads made of polished shells, was a valued commodity in the Iroquois culture; according to policies established by Dekanawida, wampum had to be paid to the family of a murder victim by the family of the killer. Since the killer was also put to death, the family of the killer had to pay the victim's family in wampum for two deaths, the death of the murder victim and the death of the killer. These strict policies implemented by Dekanawida helped to establish him as a wise lawgiver and leader of the Iroquois nation.

Line
(5)

(10)

5. According to the passage, Dekanawida was NOT

(A) a lawmaker
(B) a Huron by birth
(C) a near deity
(D) drowned when he was young

6. Which of the following is NOT mentioned in the passage about wampum?

(A) It was used extensively by the Huron.
(B) It had a high value to the Iroquois.
(C) It was given to a murder victim's family.
(D) It was made of polished shells.

Skill 5: FIND PRONOUN REFERENTS

In the reading section of both the paper TOEFL test and the computer TOEFL test, you will sometimes be asked to determine to which noun a pronoun refers. Pronoun reference questions are worded a bit differently on the paper TOEFL test and the computer TOEFL test; on the paper test, pronoun reference questions are multiple-choice questions, while on the computer test, pronoun reference questions are click-on questions.

Either type of pronoun reference question tests the same language skill. In a pronoun reference question, it is important to understand that a noun is generally used first in a passage, and the pronoun that refers to it comes after. Whenever you are asked which noun a pronoun refers to, you should look *before* the pronoun to find the noun.

Look at a multiple-choice example of a pronoun reference question from the paper TOEFL test.

Example from the Paper TOEFL Test

The passage:

Carnivorous plants, such as the sundew and the Venus-flytrap, are generally found in humid areas where there is an inadequate supply of nitrogen in the soil. In order to survive,
Line these plants have developed mechanisms to trap insects within
(5) their foliage. **They** have digestive fluids to obtain the necessary nitrogen from the insects. These plants trap the insects in a variety of ways. The sundew has sticky hairs on its leaves; when an insect lands on these leaves, it gets caught up in the sticky hairs, and the leaf wraps itself around the insect.
(10) The leaves of the Venus-flytrap function more like a trap, snapping suddenly and forcefully shut around an insect.

The question:

The pronoun **They** in line 5 *refers* to

(A) humid areas
(B) these plants
(C) insects
(D) digestive fluids

This question asks about the *referent* for the pronoun *they*. To answer this question, you should look before the pronoun *they* for plural nouns that the pronoun could refer to. *Humid areas, insects,* and *these plants* come before the pronoun, so they are possible answers; *digestive fluids* comes after the pronoun, so it is probably not the correct answer. Then you should try the three possible answers in the sentence in place of the pronoun. You should understand from the context that *these plants* have *digestive fluids* to obtain the necessary nitrogen from the insects, so the best answer to this question is answer (B).

Now look at a click-on example of a pronoun reference question from the computer TOEFL test.

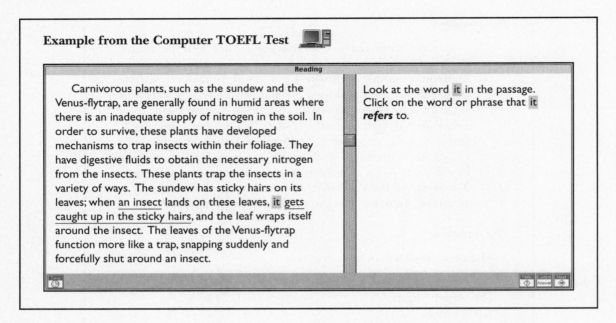

This question asks you to find the *referent* for the pronoun *it*. To answer this question, you should look before the pronoun *it* for singular nouns that the pronoun could refer to. *A variety, the sundew,* and *an insect* come before the pronoun, so they are possible answers. Next you should try the three possible answer in the sentence in place of the pronoun. *An insect gets caught up in the sticky hairs,* while a *variety* or *sundew* does not, so *insect* is the best answer to this question. You should click on *insect* to answer this question.

The following chart outlines the key information that you should remember about pronoun referents:

PRONOUN REFERENTS		
HOW TO IDENTIFY THE QUESTION	on paper test only	*The **pronoun** "..." in line X **refers** to which of the following?*
	on computer test only	*Look at the word X. Click on the word or phrase that X **refers** to.*
WHERE TO FIND THE ANSWER	on paper test only	The line where the pronoun is located is given in the question. The noun that the pronoun refers to is generally found *before* the pronoun.
	on computer test only	The pronoun is highlighted in the passage. The noun that the pronoun refers to is generally found *before* the pronoun.
HOW TO ANSWER THE QUESTION	1. Locate the pronoun in the passage. 2. Look *before* the pronoun for nouns that agree with the pronoun. 3. Try each of the nouns in the context in place of the pronoun. 4. Eliminate any definitely wrong answers and choose the best answer from the remaining choices.	

TOEFL EXERCISE 5: Study each of the passages and choose the best answers to the questions that follow.

PASSAGE ONE (Questions 1–2)

The full moon that occurs nearest the equinox of the Sun has become known as the harvest moon. It is a bright moon which allows farmers to work late into the night for several nights; they can work when the moon is at its brightest to bring in the fall harvest. The harvest moon, of
Line course, occurs at different times of the year in the northern and southern hemispheres. In the
(5) northern hemisphere, the harvest moon occurs in September at the time of the autumnal equinox. In the southern hemisphere, the harvest moon occurs in March at the time of the vernal equinox.

1. The pronoun "It" in line 2 refers to

(A) the equinox
(B) the Sun
(C) the harvest moon
(D) the night

2. Look at the word they in the passage. Click on the word or phrase that they refers to.

PASSAGE TWO (Questions 3–4)

Mardi Gras, which means "Fat Tuesday" in French, was introduced to America by French colonists in the early eighteenth century. From that time it has grown in popularity, particularly in New Orleans, and today it is actually a legal holiday in several southern states. The Mardi Gras
Line celebration in New Orleans begins well before the actual Mardi Gras Day. Parades, parties, balls,
(5) and numerous festivities take place throughout the week before Mardi Gras Day; tourists from various countries throughout the world flock to New Orleans for the celebration, where they take part in a week of nonstop activities before returning home for some much-needed rest.

3. The pronoun "it" in line 2 refers to

(A) Mardi Gras
(B) French
(C) that time
(D) New Orleans

4. Look at the word they in the passage. Click on the word or phrase that they refers to.

PASSAGE THREE (Questions 5–6)

The financial firm Dow Jones and Company computes business statistics every hour on the hour of each of the business days of the year, and these statistics are known as the Dow Jones averages. They are based on a select group of stocks and bonds that are traded on the New York
Line Stock Exchange. The Dow Jones averages are composed of four different types of averages: the
(5) average price of the common stock of thirty industrial firms, the average price of the common stock prices of twenty transportation companies, the average price of the common stock prices of fifteen utility companies, and an overall average of all the sixty-five stocks used to compute the first three averages. Probably the average that is the most commonly used is the industrial average; it is often used by an investor interested in checking the state of the stock market before
(10) making an investment in an industrial stock.

5. The pronoun "They" in line 3 refers to

    (A) the business days
    (B) these statistics
    (C) stocks and bonds
    (D) four different types

6. Look at the word it in the passage. Click on the word or phrase that it refers to.

TOEFL EXERCISE (Skills 3–5): Study each of the passages and choose the best answers to the questions that follow.

PASSAGE ONE (Questions 1–5)

> The United States does not have a national university, but the idea has been around for quite some time. George Washington first recommended the idea to Congress; he even selected an actual site in Washington, D.C., and then left an endowment for the proposed national
>
> *Line* university in his will. During the century following the Revolution, the idea of a national
> *(5)* university continued to receive the support of various U.S. presidents, and philanthropist Andrew Carnegie pursued the cause at the beginning of the present century. Although the original idea has not yet been acted upon, it continues to be proposed in bills before Congress.

1. According to the passage, the national university of the United States

    (A) has been around for a while
    (B) does not exist
    (C) is a very recent idea
    (D) is an idea that developed during the present century

2. Look at the word he in the passage. Click on the word or phrase that he refers to.

3. The passage indicates that George Washington did NOT do which of the following?

    (A) He suggested the concept for a national university to Congress.
    (B) He chose a location for the national university.
    (C) He left money in his will for a national university.
    (D) He succeeded in establishing a national university.

4. Which of the following is NOT mentioned in the passage about Andrew Carnegie?

    (A) He was interested in doing charity work and good deeds for the public.
    (B) He was a member of Congress.
    (C) He was interested in the idea of a national university.
    (D) He was active in the early twentieth century.

5. The pronoun "it" in line 7 refers to

    (A) the cause
    (B) the beginning of the present century
    (C) the original idea
    (D) Congress

PASSAGE TWO (Questions 6–11)

      The La Brea tarpits, located in Hancock Park in the Los Angeles area, have proven to be an extremely fertile source of Ice Age fossils. Apparently, during the period of the Ice Age, the tarpits were covered by shallow pools of water; when animals came there to drink, they got caught in the sticky tar and perished. The tar not only trapped the animals, leading to their death, but it also served as a remarkably effective preservant, allowing near-perfect skeletons to remain hidden until the present era.

      In 1906, the remains of a huge prehistoric bear discovered in the tarpits alerted archeologists to the potential treasure lying within the tar. Since then thousands and thousands of well-preserved skeletons have been uncovered, including the skeletons of camels, horses, wolves, tigers, sloths, and dinosaurs.

Line
(5)

(10)

6. Which of the following is NOT true about the La Brea tarpits?

  (A) They contain fossils that are quite old.
  (B) They are found in Hancock Park.
  (C) They have existed since the Ice Age.
  (D) They are located under a swimming pool.

7. The pronoun "they" in line 3 refers to

  (A) the La Brea tarpits
  (B) Ice Age fossils
  (C) shallow pools of water
  (D) animals

8. Click on the drawing that shows how the Ice Age animals mentioned in the passage died at the La Brea tarpits.

9. Look at the word it in paragraph 1. Click on the word or phrase that it refers to.

10. When did archeologists become aware of the possible value of the contents of the tarpits?

  (A) During the Ice Age
  (B) Thousands and thousands of years ago
  (C) Early in the twentieth century
  (D) Within the past decade

11. Which of the following is NOT mentioned as an example of a skeleton found in the tarpits?

  (A) A bear
  (B) A sloth
  (C) A horse
  (D) A snake

PASSAGE THREE (Questions 12–17)

When the president of the United States wants to get away from the hectic pace in Washington, D.C., Camp David is the place to go. Camp David, in a wooded mountain area about 70 miles from Washington, D.C., is where the president goes to find solitude. It consists of living
Line space for the president, the first family, and the presidential staff as well as sporting and
(5) recreational facilities.

Camp David was established by President Franklin Delano Roosevelt in 1942. He found the site particularly appealing in that its mountain air provided relief from the summer heat of Washington and its remote location offered a more relaxing environment than could be achieved in the capital city.
(10) When Roosevelt first established the retreat, he called it Shangri-La, which evoked the blissful mountain kingdom in James Hilton's novel *Lost Horizon*. Later, President Dwight David Eisenhower renamed the location Camp David after his grandson David Eisenhower.

Camp David has been used for a number of significant meetings. In 1943 during World War II, President Roosevelt met there with Great Britain's Prime Minister Winston Churchill. In 1959
(15) at the height of the Cold War, President Eisenhower met there with Soviet Premier Nikita Khrushchev; in 1978 President Jimmy Carter sponsored peace talks between Israel's Prime Minister Menachem Begin and Egypt's President Anwar el-Sadat at the retreat at Camp David.

12. Which of the following is NOT discussed about Camp David?

 (A) Its location
 (B) Its cost
 (C) Its facilities
 (D) Its uses

13. Look at the word It in paragraph 1. Click on the word or phrase that It refers to.

14. According to the passage, who founded Camp David?

 (A) George Washington
 (B) The first family
 (C) Franklin Delano Roosevelt
 (D) Dwight David Eisenhower

15. The pronoun "he" in line 10 refers to

 (A) Camp David
 (B) Roosevelt
 (C) James Hilton
 (D) President Dwight David Eisenhower

16. Which of the following is NOT true about President Eisenhower?

 (A) He had a grandson named David.
 (B) He attended a conference with Nikita Khrushchev.
 (C) He named the presidential retreat Shangri-La.
 (D) He visited Camp David.

17. Khrushchev was at Camp David in

 (A) 1942
 (B) 1943
 (C) 1959
 (D) 1978

TOEFL REVIEW EXERCISE (Skills 1–5): Study each of the passages and choose the best answers to the questions that follow.

PASSAGE ONE (Questions 1–5)

Lincoln's now famous Gettysburg Address was not, on the occasion of its delivery, recognized as the masterpiece that it is today. Lincoln was not even the primary speaker at the ceremonies, held at the height of the Civil War in 1863, to dedicate the battlefield at Gettysburg. *Line* The main speaker was orator Edward Everett, whose two-hour speech was followed by Lincoln's *(5)* shorter remarks. Lincoln began his small portion of the program with the words that today are immediately recognized by most Americans: "Four score and seven years ago our fathers brought forth on this continent a new nation, conceived in liberty and dedicated to the proposition that all men are created equal." At the time of the speech, little notice was given to what Lincoln had said, and Lincoln considered his appearance at the ceremonies rather unsuccessful. After his *(10)* speech appeared in print, appreciation for his words began to grow, and today it is recognized as one of the all-time greatest speeches.

1. The main idea of this passage is that

   (A) the Gettysburg Address has always been regarded as a masterpiece
   (B) at the time of its delivery the Gettysburg Address was truly appreciated as a masterpiece
   (C) it was not until after 1863 that Lincoln's speech at Gettysburg took its place in history
   (D) Lincoln is better recognized today than he was at the time of his presidency

2. Which of the following is NOT true about the ceremonies at Gettysburg during the Civil War?

   (A) Everett was the main speaker.
   (B) Everett gave a two-hour speech.
   (C) Lincoln was the closing speaker of the ceremonies.
   (D) Lincoln's speech was longer than Everett's.

3. According to the passage, when Lincoln spoke at the Gettysburg ceremonies,

   (A) his words were immediately recognized by most Americans
   (B) he spoke for only a short period of time
   (C) he was enthusiastically cheered
   (D) he was extremely proud of his performance

4. When did Lincoln's Gettysburg Address begin to receive public acclaim?

   (A) After it had been published
   (B) Immediately after the speech
   (C) Not until the present day
   (D) After Lincoln received growing recognition

5. Look at the word it in the passage. Click on the word or phrase that it refers to.

PASSAGE TWO (Questions 6–12)

Hay fever is a seasonal allergy to pollens. The term "hay fever," however, is a less than adequate description since such an attack can be brought on by sources other than hay-producing grasses and since an attack of this allergy does not incur fever.

Line
(5)
The causes of hay fever can be quite varied. Hay fever is generally caused by air-borne pollens, particularly ragweed pollen. The amount of pollen in the air is largely dependent on geographical location, weather, and season. In the eastern section of the United States, for example, there are generally three periods when pollen from various sources can cause intense hay fever suffering: in the springtime months of March and April, when pollen from trees is prevalent, in the summer months of June and July, when grass pollen fills the air, and at the end

(10)
of August, when ragweed pollen is at its most concentrated levels.

What results from an attack of hay fever is not a fever. Instead, a person with hay fever will suffer symptoms such as red and itching eyes, a swollen and runny nose, and repeated bouts of sneezing.

6. Which of the following would be the best title for the passage?

    (A) The Relationship between Season and Allergies
    (B) Misconceptions and Facts about Hay Fever
    (C) Hay Fever in the Eastern United States
    (D) How Ragweed Causes Hay Fever

7. According to the passage, which of the following helps to explain why the term "hay fever" is somewhat of a misnomer?

    (A) A strong fever occurs after an attack.
    (B) The amount of pollen in the air depends on geographical location.
    (C) Hay fever is often caused by ragweed pollen.
    (D) Grass pollen is prevalent in June and July.

8. Which of the following is NOT discussed in the passage as a determining factor of the amount of pollen in the air?

    (A) Place
    (B) Climate
    (C) Time of year
    (D) Altitude

9. Which of the following is NOT true about hay fever in the eastern United States?

    (A) Suffering from hay fever is equally severe year-round.
    (B) Pollen from trees causes hay fever suffering in the spring.
    (C) Grass pollen fills the air earlier in the year than ragweed pollen.
    (D) Ragweed pollen is most prevalent at the end of the summer.

10. Click on the drawing that represents a potential cause of hay fever.

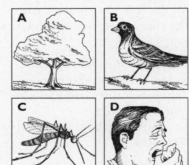

11. Which of the following is NOT a symptom of hay fever?

    (A) A high fever
    (B) A runny nose
    (C) Red eyes
    (D) Persistent sneezing

12. Click on the paragraph that outlines how, when, and where hay fever develops.

PASSAGE THREE (Questions 13–19)

Theories about the movement of the continents have evolved over time as the ability to conduct scientific study of the continents has improved. Thus, today's theory of plate tectonics, rather than contradicting its predecessor, had its roots in the older theory of continental drift.

Line
(5)   According to the theory of continental drift, the continents are not fixed in position but instead move slowly across the surface of the earth, constantly changing in position relative to one another. This theory was first proposed in the eighteenth century when mapmakers noticed how closely the continents of the earth fit together when they were matched up. It was suggested then that the present-day continents had once been one large continent that had broken up into pieces which drifted apart.

(10)   Today the modern theory of plate tectonics has developed from the theory of continental drift. The theory of plate tectonics suggests that the crust of the earth is divided into six large, and many small, tectonic plates that drift on the lava that composes the inner core of the earth. These plates consist of ocean floor and continents that quite probably began breaking up and moving relative to one another more than 200 million years ago.

13. The topic of this passage is

    (A) continental drift
    (B) the theory of plate tectonics
    (C) the development of ideas about the movement of the earth's surface
    (D) eighteenth-century mapmakers

14. The passage states that the theory of continental drift developed as a result of

    (A) the fixed positions of the continents
    (B) the work of mapmakers
    (C) the rapid movement of continents
    (D) the fit of the earth's plates

15. Look at the word they in paragraph 2. Click on a word or phrase that they refers to.

16. Which of the following is NOT true about the theory of plate tectonics?

    (A) It is not as old as the theory of continental drift.
    (B) It evolved from the theory of continental drift.
    (C) It postulates that the earth's surface is separated into plates.
    (D) It was proposed by mapmakers.

17. According to the passage, what constitutes a tectonic plate?

    (A) Lava
    (B) Only the continents
    (C) The inner core of the earth
    (D) The surface of the land and the floor of the oceans

18. Which of the following best describes the organization of the passage?

    (A) Two unrelated theories are presented.
    (B) Two contrasting opinions are stated.
    (C) A theory is followed by an example.
    (D) One hypothesis is developed from another.

19. Click on the paragraph that describes the earlier theory.

INDIRECTLY ANSWERED QUESTIONS

Some questions in the Reading section of both the paper TOEFL test and the computer TOEFL test will require answers that are not directly stated in the passage. To answer these multiple-choice questions correctly, you will have to draw conclusions from information that is given in the passage. Two common types of indirectly answered questions are (1) implied detail questions, and (2) transition questions.

SKILL 6: ANSWER IMPLIED DETAIL QUESTIONS CORRECTLY

You will sometimes be asked to answer a multiple-choice question about a reading passage by drawing a conclusion from a specific detail or details in the passage. Questions of this type contain the words *implied, inferred, likely,* or *probably* to let you know that the answer to the question is not directly stated. In this type of question, it is important to understand that you do not have to "pull the answer out of thin air." Instead, some information will be given in the passage, and you will draw a conclusion from that information. Look at a multiple-choice example of an implied detail question from the paper TOEFL test.

Example from the Paper TOEFL Test

The passage:

     The Hawaiian language is a melodious language in which all words are derived from an alphabet of only twelve letters, the five vowels *a, e, i, o, u* and the seven consonants *h,*
Line *k, l, m, n, p, w.* Each syllable in the language ends in a vowel,
(5) and two consonants never appear together, so vowels have a much higher frequency in the Hawaiian language than they do in English.
     This musical-sounding language can be heard regularly by visitors to the islands. Most Hawaiians speak English, but it
(10) is quite common to hear English that is liberally spiced with words and expressions from the traditional language of the culture. A visitor may be greeted with the expression *aloha* and may be referred to as a *malihini* because he is a newcomer to the island. The visitor may attend an outside *luau* where
(15) everyone eats too much and be invited afterwards to dance the *hula.*

The question:

Which of the following is ***probably NOT*** a Hawaiian word?

  (A)   *mahalo*
  (B)   *mahimahi*
  (C)   *meklea*
  (D)   *moana*

This question asks which word is *probably NOT* a Hawaiian word. To answer this question, you should refer to the part of the passage where it states that in the Hawaiian language *two consonants never appear together.* From this, you can draw the conclusion that answer (C), *meklea,* is probably not a Hawaiian word because the consonants *k* and *l* appear together, so answer (C) is the best answer to this question.

Now look at a multiple-choice example of an implied detail question from the computer TOEFL test.

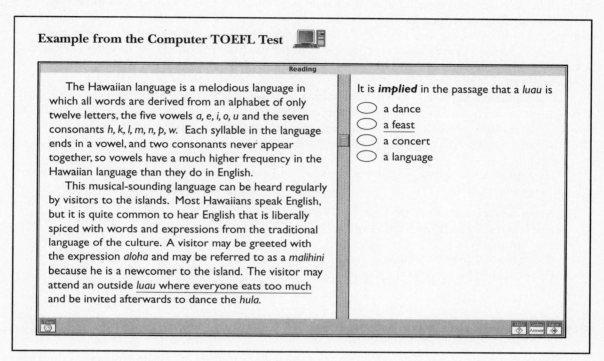

This question asks what is *implied* in the passage about a *luau*. To answer this question, you should refer to the part of the passage where it mentions a *luau where everyone eats too much.* From this, you can draw the conclusion that a *luau* is a *feast,* which is a very large meal. The second answer is therefore the best answer to this question.

The following chart outlines the key information that you should remember about implied detail questions:

IMPLIED DETAIL QUESTIONS		
HOW TO IDENTIFY THE QUESTION	on both paper and computer tests	It is **implied** in the passage that... It can be **inferred** from the passage that... It is most **likely** that... What **probably** happened...?
WHERE TO FIND THE ANSWER	The answers to these questions are generally found in order in the passage.	
HOW TO ANSWER THE QUESTION	1. Choose a key word in the question. 2. Scan the passage for the key word (or a related idea). 3. Carefully read the sentence that contains the key word. 4. Look for an answer that could be true, according to that sentence.	

TOEFL EXERCISE 6: Study each of the passages and choose the best answers to the questions that follow.

PASSAGE ONE (Questions 1–2)

Eskimos need efficient and adequate means to travel across water in that the areas where they live are surrounded by oceans, bays, and inlets and dotted with lakes and seas. Two different types of boats have been developed by the Eskimos, each constructed to meet specific needs.

Line
(5)   The kayak is something like a canoe that has been covered by a deck. A kayak is generally constructed with one opening in the deck for one rider; however, some kayaks are made for two. Because the deck of a kayak is covered over except for the hole (or holes) for its rider (or riders), a kayak can tip over in the water and roll back up without filling with water and sinking. One of the primary uses of the kayak is for hunting.

The umiak is not closed over, as is the kayak. Instead, it is an open boat that is built to hold
(10)   ten to twelve passengers. Eskimos have numerous uses for the umiak which reflect the size of the boat; e.g. the umiak is used to haul belongings from campsite to campsite, and it is used for hunting larger animals that are too big to be hunted in a kayak.

1. It is implied in the passage that if a kayak has two holes, then

    (A) it accommodates two riders
    (B) it is less stable than a kayak with one hole
    (C) it is as large as an umiak
    (D) it cannot be used on the ocean

2. It can be inferred from the passage that an example of the animals mentioned might be

    (A) a kangaroo
    (B) a snake
    (C) a whale
    (D) a salmon

PASSAGE TWO (Questions 3–5)

Two types of trees from the same family of trees share honors in certain respects as the most impressive of trees. Both evergreen conifers, the California redwood (*Sequoia sempervirens*) and the giant sequoia (*Sequoiandendron giganteum*) are found growing natively only in the state of
Line   California. The California redwood is found along the northern coast of the state, while the giant
(5)   sequoia is found inland and at higher elevations, along the western slopes of the Sierra Nevadas.

The California redwood is the tallest living tree and is in fact the tallest living thing on the face of the earth; the height of the tallest redwood on record is 385 feet (120 meters). Though not quite as tall as the California redwood, with a height of 320 feet (100 meters), the giant sequoia is nonetheless the largest and most massive of living things; giant sequoias have been measured at
(10)   more than 100 feet (30 meters) around the base, with weights of more than 6,000 tons.

3. It is implied in the passage that

    (A) the leaves of only the California redwood turn brown in the autumn
    (B) the leaves of only the giant sequoia turn brown in the winter
    (C) the leaves of both types of trees in the passage turn brown in the winter
    (D) the leaves of neither type of tree in the passage turn brown in the winter

4. It can be inferred from the passage that the Sierra Nevadas are

    (A) a type of giant redwood
    (B) a coastal community
    (C) a group of lakes
    (D) a mountain range

5. Which of the following is implied in the passage?

    (A) The giant sequoia is taller than the California redwood.
    (B) The California redwood is not as big around as the giant sequoia.
    (C) The California redwood weighs more than the giant sequoia.
    (D) Other living things are larger than the giant sequoia.

PASSAGE THREE (Questions 6–8)

Probably the most recognized board game around the world is the game of Monopoly. In this game, players vie for wealth by buying, selling, and renting properties; the key to success in the game, in addition to a bit of luck, is for a player to acquire monopolies on clusters of properties in order to force opponents to pay exorbitant rents and fees.

Line Although the game is now published in countless languages and versions, with foreign (5) locations and place names appropriate to the target language adorning its board, the beginnings of the game were considerably more humble. The game was invented in 1933 by Charles Darrow, during the height of the Great Depression. Darrow, who lived in Germantown, Pennsylvania, was himself unemployed during those difficult financial times. He set the original game not as might (10) be expected in his hometown of Germantown, but in Atlantic City, New Jersey, the site of numerous pre-Depression vacations, where he walked along the Boardwalk and visited Park Place. Darrow made the first games by hand and sold them locally until Parker Brothers purchased the rights to Monopoly in 1935 and took the first steps toward the mass production of today.

6. The French version of Monopoly might possibly include a piece of property entitled

    (A) Atlantic City, New Jersey
    (B) Germantown, Pennsylvania
    (C) Boardwalk
    (D) the Eiffel Tower

7. It is implied that Darrow selected Atlantic City as the setting for Monopoly because

    (A) it brought back good memories
    (B) his family came from Atlantic City
    (C) the people of Germantown might have been angered if he had used Germantown
    (D) Atlantic City was larger than Germantown

8. Parker Brothers is probably

    (A) a real estate company
    (B) a game manufacturing company
    (C) a group of Charles Darrow's friends
    (D) a toy design company

Skill 7: ANSWER TRANSITION QUESTIONS CORRECTLY

You will sometimes be asked on both the paper TOEFL test and the computer TOEFL test to answer a multiple-choice question about what probably came before the reading passage (in the *preceding* paragraph) or what probably comes after the reading passage (in the *following* paragraph). Of course, the topic of the *preceding* or *following* paragraph is not directly stated, and you must draw a conclusion to determine what is probably in these paragraphs.

This type of question is a *transition* question. It asks you to demonstrate that you understand that good writing contains *transitions* from one paragraph to the next. A paragraph may start out with the idea of the previous paragraph as a way of linking the ideas in the two paragraphs. A paragraph may also end with an idea that will be further developed in the following paragraph. Look at a multiple-choice example of a transition question from the paper TOEFL test that asks you to identify what was probably in the *preceding* paragraph.

Example from the Paper TOEFL Test

The passage:

      Another myth of the oceans concerns Davy Jones, who in folklore is a mean-spirited sovereign of the ocean's depths. The name "Jones" is thought by some etymologists to have
Line   been derived from the name "Jonah," the Hebrew prophet
(5)   who spent three days in a whale's belly.

      According to tradition, any object that goes overboard and sinks to the bottom of the ocean is said to have gone to Davy Jones's locker, the ocean-sized, mythical receptacle for anything that falls into the water. Needless to say, any sailor on
(10)   the seas is not so eager to take a tour of Davy Jones's locker, although it might be a rather interesting trip considering all the treasures located there.

The question:

The paragraph *preceding* this passage most probably discusses

(A)   the youth of Davy Jones
(B)   Davy Jones's career as a sailor
(C)   a different traditional story from the sea
(D)   preparing to travel on the ocean

This question asks about the topic of the *preceding* paragraph, so you must look at the beginning of the passage and draw a conclusion about what probably came before. Since the passage begins with the expression *another myth of the oceans,* you should understand that the new passage is going to present a *second* myth of the oceans and the previous passage probably presented the *first* myth of the oceans. A myth is a traditional story, so the best answer to this question is answer (C), which discusses *a different traditional story from the sea.*

Now look at a multiple-choice example from the computer TOEFL test that asks you to identify what is probably in the *following* paragraph.

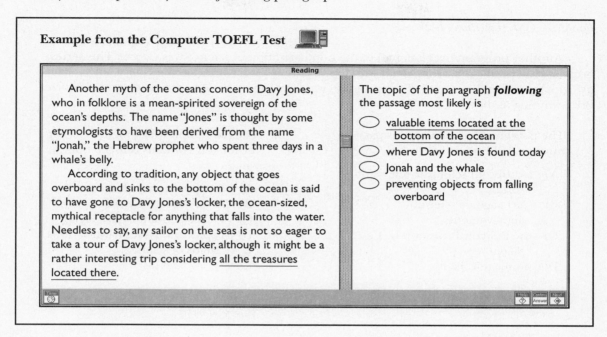

Example from the Computer TOEFL Test

Reading

Another myth of the oceans concerns Davy Jones, who in folklore is a mean-spirited sovereign of the ocean's depths. The name "Jones" is thought by some etymologists to have been derived from the name "Jonah," the Hebrew prophet who spent three days in a whale's belly.

According to tradition, any object that goes overboard and sinks to the bottom of the ocean is said to have gone to Davy Jones's locker, the ocean-sized, mythical receptacle for anything that falls into the water. Needless to say, any sailor on the seas is not so eager to take a tour of Davy Jones's locker, although it might be a rather interesting trip considering <u>all the treasures located there.</u>

The topic of the paragraph *following* the passage most likely is

○ <u>valuable items located at the bottom of the ocean</u>

○ where Davy Jones is found today

○ Jonah and the whale

○ preventing objects from falling overboard

This question asks about the topic of the *following* paragraph, so you must look at the end of the passage and draw a conclusion about what probably comes after. The passage ends with the mention of *all the treasures located there*, and *there* is in Davy Jones's locker, or at the bottom of the ocean; this is probably going to be the topic of the next paragraph. The first answer, which discusses *valuable items located at the bottom of the ocean* is therefore the best answer, so you should click on the first answer to this question.

The following chart outlines the key information that you should remember about transition questions:

TRANSITION QUESTIONS		
HOW TO IDENTIFY THE QUESTION	on both paper and computer tests	The paragraph **preceding** the passage probably... What is most likely in the paragraph **following** the passage?
WHERE TO FIND THE ANSWER	The answer can generally be found *in the first line* of the passage for a *preceding* question. The answer can generally be found *in the last line* for a *following* question.	
HOW TO ANSWER THE QUESTION	1. Read the *first* line for a *preceding* question. 2. Read the *last* line for a *following* question. 3. Draw a conclusion about what comes *before* or *after*. 4. Choose the answer that is reflected in the *first* or *last* line of the passage.	

TOEFL EXERCISE 7: Study each of the passages and choose the best answers to the questions that follow.

PASSAGE ONE (Questions 1–2)

Another program instrumental in the popularization of science was *Cosmos*. This series, broadcast on public television, dealt with topics and issues from varied fields of science. The principal writer and narrator of the program was Carl Sagan, a noted astronomer and Pulitzer Prize-winning author.

1. The paragraph preceding this passage most probably discusses

    (A) a different scientific television series
    (B) Carl Sagan's scientific achievements
    (C) the Pulitzer Prize won by Carl Sagan
    (D) public television

2. The paragraph following this passage most likely contains information on what?

    (A) The popularity of science
    (B) The program *Cosmos*
    (C) The astronomer Carl Sagan
    (D) Topics and issues from various fields of science

PASSAGE TWO (Questions 3–4)

When a strong earthquake occurs on the ocean floor rather than on land, a tremendous force is exerted on the seawater and one or more large, destructive waves called *tsunamis* can be formed. *Tsunamis* are commonly called tidal waves in the United States, but this is really an
Line inappropriate name in that the cause of the *tsunami* is an underground earthquake rather than
(5) the ocean's tides.

Far from land, a *tsunami* can move through the wide open vastness of the ocean at a speed of 600 miles (900 kilometers) per hour and often can travel tremendous distances without losing height and strength. When a *tsunami* reaches shallow coastal water, it can reach a height of 100 feet (30 meters) or more and can cause tremendous flooding and damage to coastal areas.

3. The paragraph preceding the passage most probably discusses

    (A) *tsunamis* in various parts of the world
    (B) the negative effects of *tsunamis*
    (C) land-based earthquakes
    (D) the effect of tides on *tsunamis*

4. Which of the following is most likely the topic of the paragraph following the passage?

    (A) The causes of *tsunamis*
    (B) The destructive effects of *tsunamis* on the coast
    (C) The differences between *tsunamis* and tidal waves
    (D) The distances covered by *tsunamis*

PASSAGE THREE (Questions 5–6)

While draft laws are federal laws, marriage laws are state laws rather than federal; marriage regulations are therefore not uniform throughout the country. The legal marriage age serves as an example of this lack of conformity. In most states, both the man and the woman must be at *Line* least eighteen years old to marry without parental consent; however, the states of Nebraska and *(5)* Wyoming require the couple to be at least nineteen, while the minimum age in Mississippi is twenty-one. If parental permission is given, then a couple can marry at sixteen in some states, and a few states even allow marriage before the age of sixteen, though a judge's permission, in addition to the permission of the parents, is sometimes required in this situation. Some states which allow couples to marry at such a young age are now considering doing away with such early *(10)* marriages because of the numerous negative effects of these young marriages.

5. The paragraph preceding the passage most probably discusses

    (A) state marriage laws
    (B) the lack of uniformity in marriage laws
    (C) federal draft laws
    (D) the minimum legal marriage age

6. The topic of the paragraph following the passage is most likely to be

    (A) disadvantages of youthful marriages
    (B) reasons why young people decide to marry
    (C) the age when parental consent for marriage is required
    (D) a discussion of why some states allow marriages before the age of sixteen

TOEFL EXERCISE (Skills 6–7): Study each of the passages and choose the best answers to the questions that follow.

PASSAGE ONE (Questions 1–4)

The most conservative sect of the Mennonite Church is the Old Order Amish, with 33,000 members living mainly today in the states of Pennsylvania, Ohio, and Indiana. Their lifestyle reflects their belief in the doctrines of separation from the world and simplicity of life. The Amish *Line* have steadfastly rejected the societal changes that have occurred in the previous three hundred *(5)* years, preferring instead to remain securely rooted in a seventeenth-century lifestyle. They live on farms without radios, televisions, telephones, electric lights, and cars; they dress in plainly styled and colored old-fashioned clothes; and they farm their lands with horses and tools rather than modern farm equipment. They have a highly communal form of living, with barn raisings and quilting bees as commonplace activities.

1. The paragraph preceding this passage most probably discusses

    (A) other, more liberal sects of Mennonites
    (B) where Mennonites live
    (C) the communal Amish lifestyle
    (D) the most conservative Mennonites

2. Which of the following would probably NOT be found on an Amish farm?

    (A) A hammer
    (B) A cart
    (C) A long dress
    (D) A refrigerator

3. It can be inferred from the passage that a quilting bee

(A) involves a group of people
(B) is necessary when raising bees
(C) always follows a barn raising
(D) provides needed solitude

4. Which of the following is most likely the topic of the paragraph following the passage?

(A) The effects of the communal lifestyle on the Old Order Amish
(B) How the Old Order Amish differ from the Mennonites
(C) The effect of modern technology on the Old Order Amish
(D) The doctrines of the Old Order Amish

PASSAGE TWO (Questions 5–8)

Various other Native American tribes also lived on the Great Plains. The Sioux, a group of seven Native American tribes, are best known for the fiercely combative posture against encroaching White civilization in the 1800s. Although they are popularly referred to as Sioux, these Native American tribes did not call themselves Sioux; the name was given to them by an enemy tribe. The seven Sioux tribes called themselves by some variation of the word *Dakota,* which means "allies" in their language. Four tribes of the eastern Sioux community living in Minnesota were known by the name *Dakota.* The Nakota included two tribes that left the eastern woodlands and moved out onto the plains. The Teton Sioux, or Lakota, moved even farther west to the plains of the present-day states of North Dakota, South Dakota, and Wyoming.

*Line
(5)*

5. The paragraph preceding this passage most probably discusses

(A) how the Sioux battled the white man
(B) one of the tribes of the plains
(C) where the Sioux lived
(D) Native American tribes on the East Coast

6. Which of the following represents a likely reaction of the Sioux in the 1800s to the encroaching white civilization?

(A) The Sioux would probably help the whites to settle in the West.
(B) The Sioux would probably attack the white settlers.
(C) The Sioux would probably invite the whites to smoke a peace pipe.
(D) The Sioux would probably join together in hunting parties with the white settlers.

7. It is implied in the passage that the seven Sioux tribes called each other by some form of the word *Dakota* because they were

(A) united in a cause
(B) all living in North Dakota
(C) fiercely combative
(D) enemies

8. It can be inferred from the passage that the present-day states of North and South Dakota

(A) are east of Minnesota
(B) are home to the four tribes known by the name *Dakota*
(C) received their names from the tribes living there
(D) are part of the eastern woodlands

PASSAGE THREE (Questions 9–12)

The extinction of many species of birds has undoubtedly been hastened by modern man; since 1600 it has been estimated that approximately 100 bird species have become extinct over the world. In North America, the first species known to be annihilated was the great auk, a
Line flightless bird that served as an easy source of food and bait for Atlantic fishermen through the
(5) beginning of the nineteenth century.

Shortly after the great auk's extinction, two other North American species, the Carolina parakeet and the passenger pigeon, began dwindling noticeably in numbers. The last Carolina parakeet and the last passenger pigeon in captivity both died in September 1914. In addition to these extinct species, several others such as the bald eagle, the peregrine falcon, and the
(10) California condor are today recognized as endangered; steps are being taken to prevent their extinction.

9. The number of bird species that have become extinct in the United States since 1600 most probably is

    (A) more than 100
    (B) exactly 100
    (C) less than 100
    (D) exactly three

10. The passage implies that the great auk disappeared

    (A) before 1600
    (B) in the 1600s
    (C) in the 1800s
    (D) in the last fifty years

11. It can be inferred from the passage that the great auk was killed because

    (A) it was eating the fishermen's catch
    (B) fishermen wanted to eat it
    (C) it flew over fishing areas
    (D) it baited fishermen

12. The paragraph following this passage most probably discusses

    (A) what is being done to save endangered birds
    (B) what the bald eagle symbolizes to Americans
    (C) how several bird species became endangered
    (D) other extinct species

TOEFL REVIEW EXERCISE (Skills 1–7): Study each of the passages and choose the best answers to the questions that follow.

PASSAGE ONE (Questions 1–8)

The Mason-Dixon Line is often considered by Americans to be the demarcation between the North and the South. It is in reality the boundary that separates the state of Pennsylvania from Maryland and parts of West Virginia. Prior to the Civil War, this southern boundary of
Line Pennsylvania separated the nonslave states to the north from the slave states to the south.
(5) The Mason-Dixon Line was established well before the Civil War, as a result of a boundary dispute between Pennsylvania and Maryland. Two English astronomers, Charles Mason and Jeremiah Dixon, were called in to survey the area and officially mark the boundary between the two states. The survey was completed in 1767, and the boundary was marked with stones, many of which remain to this day.

1. The best title for this passage would be

   (A) Dividing the North and the South
   (B) The Meaning of the Mason-Dixon
        Line
   (C) Two English Astronomers
   (D) The History of the Mason-Dixon
        Line

2. Look at the word It in paragraph 1.
   Click on the word or phrase that It
   refers to.

3. Click on the drawing that shows the
   location of the Mason-Dixon Line.

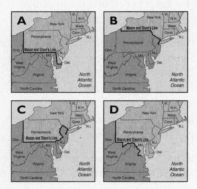

4. It can be inferred from the passage that
   before the Civil War

   (A) Pennsylvania was south of the
        Mason-Dixon Line
   (B) Pennsylvania was a nonslave state
   (C) the states south of the Mason-
        Dixon Line had the same opinion
        about slavery as Pennsylvania
   (D) the slave states were not divided
        from the nonslave states

5. The passage states all of the following
   about Mason and Dixon EXCEPT that

   (A) they came from England
   (B) they worked as astronomers
   (C) they caused the boundary dispute
        between Pennsylvania and
        Maryland
   (D) they surveyed the area of the
        boundary between Pennsylvania
        and Maryland

6. The passage indicates that the Mason-
   Dixon Line was identified with

   (A) pieces of rock
   (B) fences
   (C) a stone wall
   (D) a border crossing

7. Click on the paragraph that explains why
   the Mason-Dixon Line was established.

8. The paragraph following the passage
   most probably discusses

   (A) where the Mason-Dixon Line is
        located
   (B) the Mason-Dixon Line today
   (C) the effect of the Civil War on
        slavery
   (D) what happened to Charles Mason
        and Jeremiah Dixon

PASSAGE TWO (Questions 9–14)

    Manic depression is another psychiatric illness that mainly affects the mood. A patient
suffering from this disease will alternate between periods of manic excitement and extreme
depression, with or without relatively normal periods in between. The changes in mood suffered
Line by a manic-depressive patient go far beyond the day-to-day mood changes experienced by the
(5) general population. In the period of manic excitement, the mood elevation can become so
intense that it can result in extended insomnia, extreme irritability, and heightened
aggressiveness. In the period of depression, which may last for several weeks or months, a patient
experiences feelings of general fatigue, uselessness, and hopelessness, and, in serious cases, may
contemplate suicide.

9. The paragraph preceding this passage most probably discusses

(A) when manic depression develops
(B) a different type of mental disease
(C) how moods are determined
(D) how manic depression can result in suicide

10. The topic of this passage is

(A) various psychiatric illnesses
(B) how depression affects the mood
(C) the intense period of manic excitement
(D) the mood changes of manic depression

11. Click on the drawing of the person who is most likely a manic-depressive patient in a manic phase.

12. The passage indicates that most people

(A) never undergo mood changes
(B) experience occasional shifts in mood
(C) switch wildly from highs to lows
(D) become highly depressed

13. Look at the word it in the passage. Click on the word or phrase it refers to.

14. The passage implies that

(A) changes from excitement to depression occur frequently and often
(B) only manic-depressive patients experience aggression
(C) the depressive phase of this disease can be more harmful than the manic phase
(D) suicide is inevitable in cases of manic depression

PASSAGE THREE (Questions 15–23)

Unlike earlier campaigns, the 1960 presidential campaign featured a politically innovative and highly influential series of televised debates in the contest between the Republicans and the Democrats. Debates that could be viewed by such a wide audience had never before been part of *Line* the presidential campaigns, and through these debates, the far-reaching medium of television
(5) showed how effective it could be in influencing the outcome of an election.

The two parties to face off in the election selected very different candidates. John Kennedy, a young senator from Massachusetts without much experience and recognition in national politics, established an early lead among democratic hopefuls, and was nominated on the first ballot at the Los Angeles convention to be the representative of the Democratic party in the
(10) presidential elections. The older and more experienced Richard Nixon, then serving as vice president of the United States under Eisenhower, received the nomination of the Republican party. Both Nixon and Kennedy campaigned vigorously throughout the country and then took the unprecedented step of appearing in face-to-face debates on television.

Experts in the politics of presidential elections contend that the debates were a pivotal force
(15) in the elections. In front of a viewership of more than 100 million citizens, Kennedy masterfully overcame Nixon's advantage as the better-known and more experienced candidate and reversed the public perception of him as too inexperienced and immature for the presidency. In an election that was extremely close, it was perhaps these debates that brought victory to Kennedy.

15. The paragraph preceding the passage most likely discussed

   (A) presidential elections prior to 1960
   (B) planning for the 1960 election
   (C) the history of television prior to 1960
   (D) the outcome of the 1960 presidential election

16. Which of the following best expresses the main idea of the passage?

   (A) Kennedy defeated Nixon in the 1960 presidential election.
   (B) Television debates were instrumental in the outcome of the 1960 presidential election.
   (C) Television debates have long been a part of campaigning.
   (D) Kennedy was the leading Democratic candidate in the 1960 presidential election.

17. Look at the word it in paragraph 1. Click on the word or phrase that it refers to.

18. The passage implies that Kennedy

   (A) was a long shot to receive the Democratic presidential nomination
   (B) won the Democratic presidential nomination fairly easily
   (C) was not a front runner in the race for the Democratic presidential nomination
   (D) came from behind to win the Democratic presidential nomination

19. The passage states that the television debates between presidential candidates in 1960

   (A) did not influence the selection of the president
   (B) were the final televised debates
   (C) were fairly usual in the history of presidential campaigns
   (D) were the first presidential campaign debates to be televised

20. Which of the following is NOT mentioned about Richard Nixon?

   (A) He was serving as vice president.
   (B) He was the Republican party's candidate for president.
   (C) He campaigned strongly all over the country.
   (D) He was nominated on the first ballot.

21. The passage states that in the debates with Nixon, Kennedy demonstrated to the American people that he was

   (A) old enough to be president
   (B) more experienced than Nixon
   (C) better known than Nixon
   (D) too inexperienced to serve as president

22. The pronoun "him" in line 17 refers to

   (A) John Kennedy
   (B) Richard Nixon
   (C) Eisenhower
   (D) the better-known and more experienced candidate

23. Click on the paragraph that describes the two candidates in the election.

VOCABULARY QUESTIONS

In the reading section of both the paper TOEFL test and the computer TOEFL test, there will be a number of vocabulary questions. On the paper test, the vocabulary questions will always be multiple-choice questions. On the computer test, vocabulary questions may be multiple-choice questions, or they may be click-on questions: you may be asked to look at one word in a passage and click on another word with a similar or opposite meaning, or you may be asked to click on a word with a given meaning.

To answer a vocabulary question, it is, of course, helpful if you know the meaning of the word that is being tested. However, it is not always *necessary* for you to know the meaning of the word; often there are skills that you can use to help you find the correct answer to the question: (1) finding definitions from structural clues, (2) determining meanings from word parts, and (3) using context clues to determine meanings.

SKILL 8: FIND DEFINITIONS FROM STRUCTURAL CLUES

When you are asked to determine the meaning of a word in the reading section of either the paper TOEFL test or the computer TOEFL test, it is possible (1) that the passage provides information about the meaning of the word, and (2) that there are structural clues to tell you that the definition of a word is included in the passage. Look at a multiple-choice example from the paper TOEFL test where a structural clue to the meaning of the tested word is included in the passage.

Example from the Paper TOEFL Test

The passage:

> One of the leading schools of psychological thought in the twentieth century is **behaviorism**—the belief that the role of the psychologist is to study behavior, which is observable,
> *Line* rather than conscious or unconscious thought, which is not.
> *(5)* Probably the best-known proponent of behaviorism is B.F. Skinner, who is famous for his research on how positive and negative reinforcement influence behavior. He came to believe that positive reinforcement such as praise, food, or money were more effective in promoting good behavior than
> *(10)* negative reinforcement, or punishment.

The question:

In "**behaviorism**" in line 2, a psychologist is concerned with

    (A)   conscious thought patterns
    (B)   unconscious thought patterns
    (C)   observable actions
    (D)   unobservable actions

This question asks about the meaning of the word *behaviorism*. To answer this question, you should look at the part of the passage following the word *behaviorism*. The dash punctuation (—) indicates that a definition or further information about behaviorism is going to follow. In the information following the dash, you should see that the behaviorist is interested in *behavior, which is observable,* so the best answer to this question is answer (C).

Now look at a multiple-choice example from the computer TOEFL test where a structural clue to the meaning of the tested word is included in the passage.

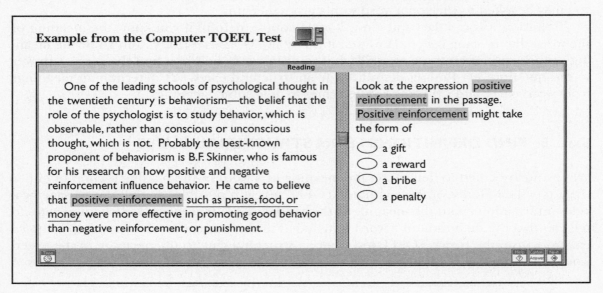

Example from the Computer TOEFL Test

Reading

One of the leading schools of psychological thought in the twentieth century is behaviorism—the belief that the role of the psychologist is to study behavior, which is observable, rather than conscious or unconscious thought, which is not. Probably the best-known proponent of behaviorism is B.F. Skinner, who is famous for his research on how positive and negative reinforcement influence behavior. He came to believe that positive reinforcement such as praise, food, or money were more effective in promoting good behavior than negative reinforcement, or punishment.

Look at the expression positive reinforcement in the passage. Positive reinforcement might take the form of

- a gift
- a reward
- a bribe
- a penalty

This question asks about the meaning of the expression *positive reinforcement*. To answer this question, you should look at the part of the passage following the expression *positive reinforcement*. The expression *such as* indicates that examples of *positive reinforcement* are going to follow. Your job is to look at the examples of positive reinforcement and draw a conclusion about what positive reinforcement might be. Since *praise, food,* or *money* might be given in return for a job well done, then *positive reinforcement* must be a *reward*. You should click on the second answer to this question.

Next look at a click-on example from the computer TOEFL test where a structural clue to the meaning of the tested word is included in the passage.

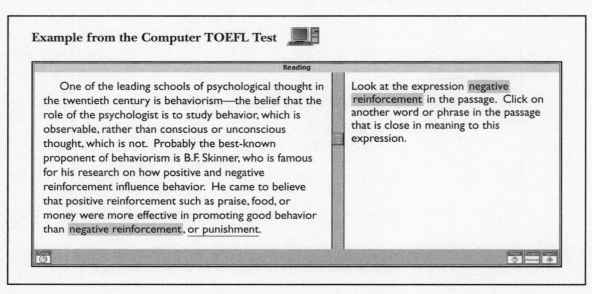

Example from the Computer TOEFL Test

Reading

One of the leading schools of psychological thought in the twentieth century is behaviorism—the belief that the role of the psychologist is to study behavior, which is observable, rather than conscious or unconscious thought, which is not. Probably the best-known proponent of behaviorism is B.F. Skinner, who is famous for his research on how positive and negative reinforcement influence behavior. He came to believe that positive reinforcement such as praise, food, or money were more effective in promoting good behavior than negative reinforcement, or punishment.

Look at the expression negative reinforcement in the passage. Click on another word or phrase in the passage that is close in meaning to this expression.

This question asks about a similar meaning to the expression *negative reinforcement*. To answer this question, you should look at the part of the passage around the expression *negative reinforcement*. The word *or* following *negative reinforcement* tells you that the idea is going to be restated in different words. You can see in the passage that another word for *negative reinforcement* is *punishment,* so you should click on *punishment* to answer this question.

The following chart outlines the key information that you should remember about structural clues to help you to understand unknown vocabulary words:

STRUCTURAL CLUES 📖 💻		
HOW TO IDENTIFY THE QUESTION	on both paper and computer tests 📖 💻	*What is the **meaning** of "X" in line Y?* *The word "X" in line Y is **closest in meaning** to…* *The word "X" in line Y **could best be replaced** by…*
	on computer test only 💻	*Look at the word X in paragraph Y. Click on another word that is **close in meaning** to X.* *Click on the word in paragraph Y that **could best be replaced** by…*
TYPES OF CLUES	punctuation	comma, parentheses, dashes
	restatement	*or, that is, in other words, i.e.*
	examples	*such as, for example, e.g.*
WHERE TO FIND THE ANSWER	Information to help you determine what something means will generally be found after the punctuation clue, the restatement clue, or the example clue.	
HOW TO ANSWER THE QUESTION	1. Find the word in the passage. 2. Locate any structural clues. 3. Read the part of the passage after the structural clue carefully. 4. Eliminate any definitely wrong answers and choose the best answer from the remaining choices.	

TOEFL EXERCISE 8:   Study each of the passages and choose the best answers to the questions that follow.

PASSAGE ONE (Questions 1–4)

The teddy bear is a child's toy, a nice soft stuffed animal suitable for cuddling. It is, however, a toy with an interesting history behind it.

Line   Theodore Roosevelt, or Teddy as he was commonly called, was president of the United
(5)   States from 1901 to 1909. He was an unusually active man with varied pastimes, one of which was hunting. One day the president was invited to take part in a bear hunt; and inasmuch as Teddy was president, his hosts wanted to ensure that he caught a bear. A bear was captured, clanked over the head to knock it out, and tied to a tree; however, Teddy, who really wanted to hunt a bear, refused to shoot the bear and, in fact, demanded that the bear be extricated from the ropes; that is, he demanded that the bear be set free.

(10)   The incident attracted a lot of attention among journalists. First a cartoon—drawn by Clifford K. Berryman to make fun of this situation—appeared in the *Washington Post,* and the cartoon was widely distributed and reprinted throughout the country. Then toy manufacturers began producing a toy bear which they called a "teddy bear." The teddy bear became the most widely recognized symbol of Roosevelt's presidency.

1. According to line 1 of the passage, what is a "teddy bear"?

   (A) A ferocious animal
   (B) The president of the United States
   (C) A famous hunter
   (D) A plaything

2. Look at the word pastimes in paragraph 2. This word could best be replaced by

   ⬭ past occurrences
   ⬭ previous jobs
   ⬭ hunting trips
   ⬭ leisure activities

3. Look at the word extricated in paragraph 2. Click on another word or phrase in paragraph 2 that is close in meaning to extricated.

4. In line 10, a "cartoon" could best be described as

   (A) a newspaper
   (B) a type of teddy bear
   (C) a drawing with a message
   (D) a newspaper article

PASSAGE TWO (Questions 5–8)

     A supernova occurs when all of the hydrogen in the core of a huge star is transformed to iron and explodes. All stars die after their nuclear fuel has been exhausted. Stars with little mass die gradually, but those with relatively large mass die in a sudden explosion, a supernova. The

Line   sudden flash of light can then be followed by several weeks of extremely bright light, perhaps as
(5)   much light as twenty million stars.
     Supernovae are not very common; they occur about once every hundred years in any galaxy, and in 1987 a supernova that could be seen by the naked eye occurred in the Magellan Cloud, a galaxy close to the Milky Way. Scientists periodically detect supernovae in other galaxies; however, no supernovae have occurred in the Milky Way (the galaxy that includes Earth) since 1604. One
(10)   very impressive supernova occurred in the Milky Way on July 4, 1054. There was a great explosion followed by three months of lighted skies, and historical chronicles of the time were full of accounts and unusual explanations for the misunderstood phenomenon—many people believed that it meant that the world was coming to an end.

5. A "supernova" in line 1 is which of the following?

   (A) The iron component of a star
   (B) The core of a star
   (C) The hydrogen in a star
   (D) The explosion of a star

6. According to the passage, which of the following best describes the "Magellan Cloud" in line 7?

   (A) A galaxy inside the Milky Way
   (B) A cloud composed of hydrogen
   (C) A galaxy near Earth's galaxy
   (D) A cloud in the sky above the Earth

7. Look at the expression Milky Way in paragraph 2. The Milky Way is

    ⬭ part of Earth
    ⬭ a galaxy close to Earth
    ⬭ the galaxy that is home to Earth
    ⬭ a creamy-colored cloud in the sky

8. Click on the word in paragraph 2 that is closest in meaning to "unusual occurrence."

Skill 9: DETERMINE MEANINGS FROM WORD PARTS

When you are asked to determine the meaning of a long word that you do not know in the reading section of either the paper TOEFL test or the computer TOEFL test, it is sometimes possible to determine the meaning of the word by studying the word parts. Look at a multiple-choice example from the paper TOEFL test where the answer can be determined from a word part.

Example from the Paper TOEFL Test

The passage:

> Ring Lardner was born into a wealthy, educated, and cultured family. For the bulk of his career, he worked as a reporter for newspapers in South Bend, Boston, St. Louis, and
> *Line* Chicago. However, it is for his short stories of lower middle-
> (5) class Americans that Ring Lardner is perhaps best known. In these stories, Lardner *vividly* creates the language and the ambiance of this lower class, often using the misspelled words, grammatical errors, and incorrect diction that typified the language of the lower middle class.

The question:

The word "**vividly**" in line 6 is closest in meaning to

(A) in a cultured way
(B) in a correct way
(C) in a lifelike way
(D) in a brief way

This question asks about the meaning of the word *vividly*. To answer this question, you should notice that the word *vividly* contains the word part *viv-*, which means *life*. Answer (C) is therefore the best answer to this question.

Now look at a multiple-choice example from the computer TOEFL test where the answer can be determined from a word part.

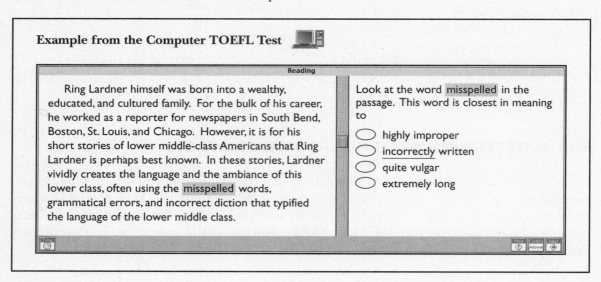

This question asks about the meaning of the word *misspelled*. To answer this question, you should notice that the word *misspelled* contains that word part *mis-*, which means *error* or *incorrect*. The second answer is therefore the best answer to this question. You should click on the second answer to this question.

Next, look at a click-on example from the computer TOEFL test where the answer can be determined from a word part.

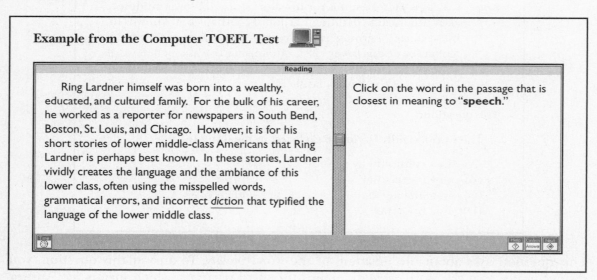

This question asks you to find a word that is close in meaning to *speech*. To answer this question, you should find the word *diction*, which contains the word part *dic-*, in the passage. The word part *dic-* means *speak,* so *diction* is the best answer to this question. You should click on *diction* to answer this question.

The following chart contains a few word parts that you will need to know to complete the exercises in this part of the text. A more complete list of word parts and exercises to practice them can be found in Appendix I at the back of the text.

A SHORT LIST OF WORD PARTS					
PART	MEANING	EXAMPLE	PART	MEANING	EXAMPLE
CONTRA	(against)	contrast	DIC	(say)	dictate
MAL	(bad)	malcontent	DOMIN	(master)	dominant
MIS	(error)	mistake	JUD	(judge)	judgment
SUB	(under)	subway	MOR	(death)	mortal
DEC	(ten)	decade	SPEC	(see)	spectator
MULTI	(many)	multiple	TERR	(earth)	territory
SOL	(one)	solo	VER	(turn)	divert
TRI	(three)	triple	VIV	(live)	revive

TOEFL EXERCISE 9: Study each of the passages and choose the best answers to the questions that follow.

PASSAGE ONE (Questions 1–5)

Juan Rodriguez Cabrillo was a Portuguese-born explorer who is credited with the exploration of the coast of what is today the state of California. Sketchy military records from the period show that early in his career he served with the Spanish army from 1520 to 1524 in Spain's
Line
(5) quest for subjugation of the people in what are today Cuba, Mexico, and Guatemala. Little is known of his activities over the next decades, but apparently he succeeded in rising up through the ranks of the military; in 1541, he was ordered by Antonio de Mendoza, the Spanish ruler of Mexico, to explore the western coast of North America. Cabrillo set out in June of 1542 in command of two ships, the *San Salvador* and the *Victoria*; he reached San Diego Bay on September 28, 1542, and claimed the terrain for Spain. The peninsula where he landed is today named
(10) Cabrillo Point in his honor; the area has been established as a national monument and park, and local residents each year hold a celebration and reenactment of Cabrillo's landing.

From San Diego, Cabrillo continued northward for further exploration of the spectacular California coastline. By November 1542, he had reached as far north as San Francisco Bay, although he missed the entrance of the bay due to a huge storm. Soon after, with the approach of
(15) winter, he veered south and turned back to Mexico. He made it as far south as the Channel Islands off the coast of what is today Santa Barbara. Cabrillo, who died on San Miguel Island in the Channel Islands, never made it back to Mexico.

1. The word "subjugation" in line 4 is closest in meaning to

    (A) religion
    (B) flag
    (C) control
    (D) agreement

2. Look at the word decades in paragaph 1. This word is closest in meaning to

    ◯ months
    ◯ centuries
    ◯ long epoch
    ◯ ten-year periods

3. In line 9, the word "terrain" is closest in meaning to

    (A) land
    (B) population
    (C) minerals
    (D) prosperity

4. Look at the word spectacular in paragraph 2. This word is closest in meaning to which of the following?

○ Ruggedly handsome
○ Visually exciting
○ Completely uneven
○ Unendingly boring

5. Look at the word veered in paragraph 2. Click on another word in paragraph 2 that is close in meaning to veered.

PASSAGE TWO (Questions 6–10)

      Checks and balances are an important concept in the formation of the U.S. system of government as presented in the Constitution of the United States. Under this conception of government, each branch of government has built-in checks and limitations placed on it by one *Line* or more different branches of government in order to ensure that any one branch is not able to *(5)* usurp total dominance over the government. Under the Constitution, the United States has a tripartite government, with power divided equally among the branches: the presidency, the legislature, and the judiciary. Each branch is given some authority over the other two branches to balance the power among the three branches. An example of these checks and balances is seen in the steps needed to pass a law. Congress can pass a law with a simple majority, but the president *(10)* can veto such a law. Congress can then counteract the veto with a two-thirds majority. However, even if Congress passes a law with a simple majority or overrides a presidential veto, the Supreme Court can still declare the law unconstitutional if it finds that the law is contradictory to the guidelines presented in the Constitution.

6. The expression "dominance over" in line 5 is closest in meaning to

(A) understanding of
(B) dispute over
(C) authority over
(D) rejection of

7. Look at the word tripartite in the passage. This word suggests that something is

○ divided into three
○ totally democratic
○ powerfully constructed
○ evenly matched

8. The "judiciary" in line 7 is

(A) the electorate
(B) the authority
(C) the legal system
(D) the government

9. Look at the word counteract in the passage. This word is closest in meaning to

○ vote for
○ debate
○ surpass
○ work against

10. "Contradictory to" in line 12 is closest in meaning to which of the following expressions?

(A) In agreement with
(B) Opposite to
(C) Supported by
(D) Similar to

Skill 10: USE CONTEXT TO DETERMINE MEANINGS OF DIFFICULT WORDS

On both the paper TOEFL test and the computer TOEFL test, you may be asked to determine the meaning of a difficult word in a reading passage, a word that you are not expected to know. In this case, the passage will probably give you a clear indication of what the word means. Look at a multiple-choice example from the paper TOEFL test where the context helps you to understand the meaning of an unknown word.

Example from the Paper TOEFL Test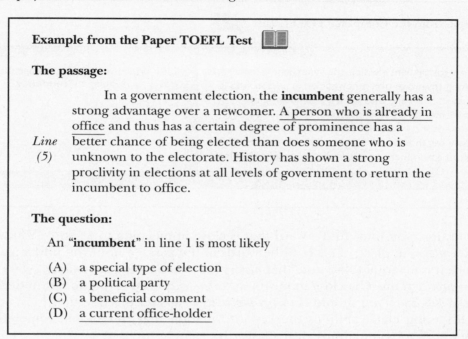

The passage:

In a government election, the **incumbent** generally has a strong advantage over a newcomer. A person who is already in office and thus has a certain degree of prominence has a
Line better chance of being elected than does someone who is
(5) unknown to the electorate. History has shown a strong proclivity in elections at all levels of government to return the incumbent to office.

The question:

An "**incumbent**" in line 1 is most likely

(A) a special type of election
(B) a political party
(C) a beneficial comment
(D) a current office-holder

This question asks about the meaning of the word *incumbent*. In this question, you are not expected to know the meaning of the word *incumbent*. Instead, you should understand from the context *a person who is already in office* that an *incumbent* is *a current office-holder.* Answer (D) is therefore the best answer to this question.

Now look at a multiple-choice example from the computer TOEFL test where the context helps you to understand the meaning of an unknown word.

Example from the Computer TOEFL Test

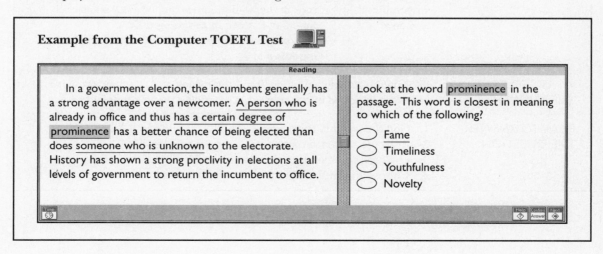

Reading

In a government election, the incumbent generally has a strong advantage over a newcomer. A person who is already in office and thus has a certain degree of prominence has a better chance of being elected than does someone who is unknown to the electorate. History has shown a strong proclivity in elections at all levels of government to return the incumbent to office.

Look at the word prominence in the passage. This word is closest in meaning to which of the following?

○ Fame
○ Timeliness
○ Youthfulness
○ Novelty

This question asks about the meaning of the word *prominence*. In this question, you are not expected to know the meaning of the word *prominence*. Instead, you should look at the context, which contrasts *a person who…has a certain degree of prominence* with *someone who is unknown*. From this context, you can determine that *prominence* is closest in meaning to *fame*. You should click on the first answer to this question.

Next, look at a click-on example from the computer TOEFL test where the context helps you to understand the meaning of an unknown word.

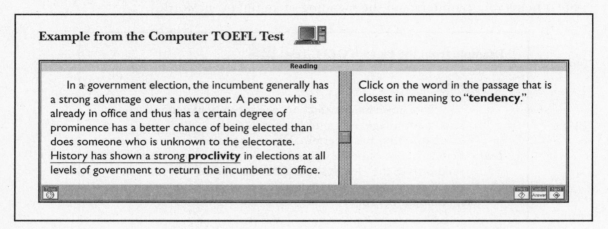

In this question, you must find a word that is close in meaning to *tendency*. You should try the word *tendency* in place of each of the words in the passage until you find a place where it fits. Since it is meaningful to state that *history has shown a strong tendency…*, you can determine that *proclivity* must be close in meaning to *tendency* even if you do not understand the meaning of *proclivity*. You should click on *proclivity* to answer this question.

The following chart outlines the key information that you should remember about vocabulary questions containing difficult words:

VOCABULARY QUESTIONS CONTAINING DIFFICULT WORDS		
HOW TO IDENTIFY THE QUESTION	on both paper and computer tests	*What is the **meaning** of "X" in line Y?* *The word "X" in line Y is **closest in meaning** to…*
	on computer test only	*Look at the word X in paragraph Y. Click on another word that is **close in meaning** to X.* *Click on the word in paragraph Y that **is closest in meaning** to X.*
WHERE TO FIND THE ANSWER	Information to help you understand the meaning of an unknown word can often be found in the context surrounding the unknown word.	
HOW TO ANSWER THE QUESTION	1. Find the word in the passage. 2. Read the sentence that contains the word carefully. 3. Look for context clues to help you understand the meaning. 4. Choose the answer that the context indicates.	

TOEFL EXERCISE 10: Study each of the passages and choose the best answers to the questions that follow.

PASSAGE ONE (Questions 1–4)

The black widow is the most dangerous spider living in the United States. It is most common in the southern parts of the country, but it can be found throughout the country. The black widow got its name because the female has been known to kill the male after mating and, as a result, becomes a widow.

Line (5) The black widow is rather distinctive in appearance; it has a shiny globular body, the size and shape of a pea, and is marked on its underbelly with a red or yellow spot. The female is considerably more ample than the male, roughly four times larger on the average.

If a human is bitten by a black widow, the spider's poison can cause severe illness and pain. Black widow bites have occasionally proved deadly, but it is certainly not the norm for black
(10) widow bites to be mortal.

1. In line 3, the word "widow" means

   (A) a type of poison
   (B) the dead male spider
   (C) the human victim of the spider
   (D) a female whose mate has died

2. Click on the word in paragraph 2 that is closest in meaning to "spherical."

3. The word "ample" in line 7 indicates that the spider is

   (A) feminine
   (B) large
   (C) dotted with colors
   (D) normal

4. Look at the word deadly in paragraph 3. Click on another word in paragraph 3 that is close in meaning to deadly.

PASSAGE TWO (Questions 5–8)

Tornadoes occur throughout the world, but for reasons that scientists are not fully able to discern, the great majority occur in the United States. Approximately 700 tornadoes a year occur within the United States, and this comprises three-quarters of the worldwide total. Most of the
Line U.S. tornadoes take place in the Midwest and in the southern states that border the Gulf of
(5) Mexico.

In general, a tornado cuts a path of a few hundred yards and lasts less than an hour; an average tornado might propel itself at a speed of 15 or 20 miles per hour and therefore cover a distance of 20 or so miles. Tornadoes, however, can be much worse than average. The most devastating tornado on record occurred on March 18, 1925, in the states of Missouri, Illinois, and
(10) Indiana. The path of this tornado was more than 200 miles long and a mile wide. Traveling at an average speed of 60 miles per hour, the winds at the center of the storm swirled around at considerably more than 200 miles per hour. A total of 689 people died, and countless more were injured, at the hands of this killer storm.

5. Click on the word in paragraph 1 that is closest in meaning to "understand."

6. The word "propel" in line 7 could best be replaced by

   (A) move
   (B) develop
   (C) destroy
   (D) inhibit

7. Which of the following is closest in meaning to the word "devastating" in line 9?

    (A) Described
    (B) Delicate
    (C) Destructive
    (D) Determined

8. Look at the word swirled in paragraph 2. This word is closest in meaning to

    ◯ decreased
    ◯ rose
    ◯ settled
    ◯ circled

SKILL 11: USE CONTEXT TO DETERMINE MEANINGS OF SIMPLE WORDS

On both the paper TOEFL test and the computer TOEFL test, you may be asked to determine the meaning of a simple word in a reading passage, a word that you see often in everyday English. In this type of question, you should *not* give the normal, everyday meaning of the word; instead, a secondary meaning of the word is being tested, so you must determine the meaning of the word in this situation. Look at a multiple-choice example from the paper TOEFL test where a secondary meaning is the best answer to the question.

Example from the Paper TOEFL Test

The passage:

> Faced with serious threats to its future, the company is taking **steps** to improve its outlook. The company has brought in a new crop of trainees to staff some of its empty positions.
> *Line*   In addition, the company has created a new committee to
> *(5)*   research various proposals and has appointed a key member of its management team to chair the committee.

The question:

The word "**steps**" in line 1 could best be replaced by

    (A) stairs
    (B) walks
    (C) actions
    (D) footprints

In this question, you are asked to choose a word that could replace *steps*. You should understand that *steps* is a normal, everyday word that is not being used in its normal, everyday way. Because the primary meaning of *steps* is *stairs,* this answer is not the correct answer. To answer this type of question, you must see which answer best fits into the context in the passage. You cannot say that *a company is taking stairs,* or *walks,* or *footprints,* but you can say that *a company is taking actions.* Answer (C) is therefore the best answer to this question.

Now look at a multiple-choice example from the computer TOEFL test where a secondary meaning is the best answer to the question.

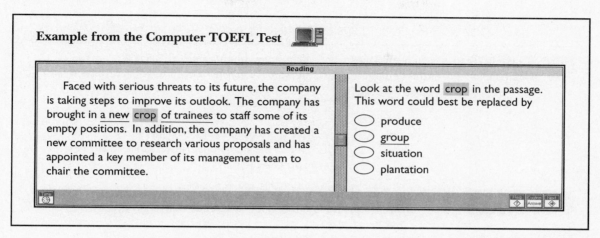

In this question, you are asked to choose which word could replace *crop*. You should again understand that the word *crop* is not being used in its primary meaning. The primary meaning of *crop* might be *produce,* so this answer is not correct. To answer this type of question, you must see which answer best fits into the context in the passage. A company would not have *a new produce of trainees, a new situation of trainees,* or *a new plantation of trainees,* but a company might have *a new group of trainees. Group* is the word that best fits into the context and is therefore the best answer to this question, so you should click on the second answer to answer this question.

Next, look at a click-on example from the computer TOEFL test where a secondary meaning is the best answer to the question.

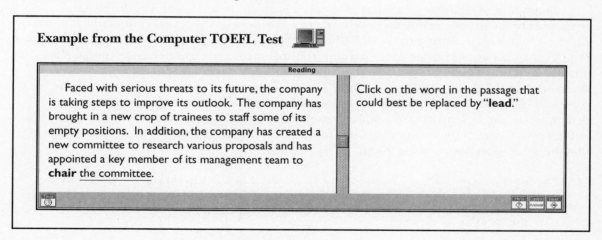

In this question, you are asked to find a word that could best be replaced by *lead.* You should try the word *lead* in place of each of the words in the passage until you find a place where it fits. Since it is possible to *lead a committee,* you can determine that *chair* could best be replaced by *lead* in this context. You should click on *chair* to answer this question.

The following chart outlines the key information that you should remember about vocabulary questions containing simple words:

VOCABULARY QUESTIONS CONTAINING SIMPLE WORDS		
HOW TO IDENTIFY THE QUESTION	on both paper and computer tests	*What is the **meaning** of "X" in line Y?* *The word "X" in line Y **could best be replaced** by…*
	on computer test only	*Look at the word* X *in paragraph Y. Click on another word that **could best be replaced** by…* *Click on the word in paragraph Y that **could best be replaced** by…*
WHERE TO FIND THE ANSWER	Information to help you understand the secondary meaning of a simple word can often be found in the context surrounding the word.	
HOW TO ANSWER THE QUESTION	1. Find the word in the passage. 2. Read the sentence that contains the word carefully. 3. Look for context clues to help you understand the meaning. 4. Choose the answer that the context indicates.	

TOEFL EXERCISE 11: Study each of the passages and choose the best answers to the questions that follow.

PASSAGE ONE (Questions 1–3)

The "piece of eight" was the nickname of the Spanish "peso," which was the rough equivalent of the American dollar in early America; the peso was accepted coin in much of the Americas, particularly during the period when the stores of Spanish ships were regularly stripped
Line by pirates on the waters off the Americas and "redistributed" throughout coastal towns. The
(5) nickname "piece of eight" derived from the fact that the peso was equal to eight "reals" and therefore had the numeral 8 stamped on it. The "piece of eight" was sometimes actually cut into pieces, or bits, and one popular size was one-quarter of a "piece of eight," or two bits. As a consequence, the U.S. quarter of a dollar is sometimes referred to today as two-bits, particularly in the western part of the country. A visitor to that area, if told "It'll be two-bits," should take it
(10) that the price of an item is being given.

1. The word "rough" in line 1 is closest in meaning to

   (A) unsmooth
   (B) mean
   (C) approximate
   (D) heavy

2. Look at the word stores in the passage. Stores are probably

   ○ departments
   ○ markets
   ○ shops
   ○ supplies

3. Look at the expression take it in the passage. This expression could best be replaced by

   ○ hold
   ○ understand
   ○ possess
   ○ grab

PASSAGE TWO (Questions 4–7)

Although *Wealth of Nations* by Adam Smith appeared in 1776, it includes many of the ideas that economists still consider the foundation of private enterprise. The ideas put forth by Smith compose the basis of the philosophies of the school of thought called classical economics.

Line
(5)   According to Smith's ideas, free competition and free trade are vital in fostering the growth of an economy. The role of government in the economy is to ensure the ability of companies to compete freely.

Smith, who was himself a Scot, lived during the period of the revolutions in America and in France. During this epoch, the predominant political thought was a strong belief in freedom and independence in government. Smith embraced economic ideas of free trade and competition

(10)   which are right in line with these political ideas.

4. A "school" in line 3 is

    (A) a common belief
    (B) a college
    (C) a university
    (D) an educational institution

5. Which of the following is closest in meaning to the word "free" in line 4?

    (A) Cheap
    (B) No cost
    (C) Uncontrolled
    (D) Democratic

6. Look at the word embraced in paragraph 3. This word could best be replaced by

    ◯ hugged
    ◯ believed in
    ◯ encircled
    ◯ handed over

7. Click on the word in paragraph 3 that could best be replaced by "agreement."

TOEFL EXERCISE (Skills 8–11): Study each of the passages and choose the best answers to the questions that follow.

PASSAGE ONE (Questions 1–5)

Cardamom is not as widely used as a spice in the United States as it is in other parts of the world. This fruit of the ginger plant provides an oil that basically has been used solely as a stimulant in American and English medicines. Other cultures have recognized the multipurpose

Line
(5)   benefits of this aromatic fruit. In Asia it is used to season sauces such as curry; in Middle Eastern countries it is steeped to prepare a flavorful, golden-colored tea; in parts of Northern Europe it is used as a spice in various types of pastry.

1. Click on the word in the passage that could best be replaced by "only."

2. The word "multipurpose" in line 3 is closest in meaning to

   (A) health
   (B) singular
   (C) recognized
   (D) varied

3. Which of the following is closest in meaning to the word "season" in line 4?

   (A) Divide
   (B) Forecast
   (C) Spice
   (D) Put a time limit

4. Look at the word curry in the passage. Curry is

   ⃝ the fruit of the ginger plant
   ⃝ a spicy type of sauce
   ⃝ a culture in the area of the Middle East
   ⃝ a type of golden-colored tea

5. Click on the word in the passage that could best be replaced by "steamed."

PASSAGE TWO (Questions 6–13)

The life span of an elephant that dies from natural causes is about sixty-five years. Of course, an elephant can perish from a number of "unnatural causes"; e.g., it can be killed by hunters, most probably for the valuable ivory in its tusks; it can die from diseases that spread throughout an elephant herd; or it can die from drought or from the lack of food that almost certainly accompanies the inadequate supply of water.

Line
(5)

If, however, an elephant survives these disasters, it falls prey to old age in its mid-sixties. Around this age, the cause of death is attributed to the loss of the final set of molars. When this last set of teeth is gone, the elephant dies from malnutrition because it is unable to obtain adequate nourishment. In old age, elephants tend to search out a final home where there is shade for comfort from the sun and soft vegetation for cushioning; the bones of many old elephants have been found in such places.

(10)

6. Look at the word perish in paragraph 1. Click on another word in paragraph 1 that is close in meaning to perish.

7. The word "unnatural" in line 2 is closest in meaning to

   (A) wild
   (B) violent
   (C) domesticated
   (D) abnormal

8. Look at the word drought in paragraph 1. A drought means

   ⃝ a drowning
   ⃝ a lack of food
   ⃝ an inadequate supply of water
   ⃝ an overabundance of animals

9. Which of the following could be used to replace the word "survives" in line 6?

   (A) Rises to
   (B) Succumbs to
   (C) Denies
   (D) Lives through

10. Look at the word molars in paragraph 2. Click on the word in paragraph 2 that is close in meaning to molars.

11. In line 8, "malnutrition" is used to describe a condition related to

   (A) good health
   (B) illness
   (C) poor eating
   (D) dental problems

12. Look at the expression a final home in paragraph 2. This expression is closest in meaning to

○ a place to die
○ a comfortable house
○ a place for sale
○ the only remaining place to live

13. The word "shade" in line 10 is closest in meaning to

(A) color
(B) heat
(C) diminished light
(D) a front porch

PASSAGE THREE (Questions 14–21)

The American flag is the end product of a long evolution. Each of its component parts has its own history.

The very first American flag was hoisted in the skies over Boston on January 1, 1776, by the American forces there. This first flag consisted of thirteen red and white stripes representing the number of American colonies. It also included the British Cross of St. George and Cross of St. Andrew. It could be considered rather ironic that these symbols of British rule were included on the American flag in that the American colonists were fighting for independence from the British.

The origin of the stars on the current flag is obscure; that is, the stars could possibly have been taken from the flag of Rhode Island, or they could have been taken from the coat of arms of the Washington family. According to legend, this first flag with stars was sewn by Betsy Ross, a Philadelphia seamstress who was famous for her clever needlework. This version of the flag contained thirteen stars and thirteen stripes, one for each of the thirteen colonies battling for independence.

The original idea was to add one star and one stripe for each state that joined the new, young country. However, by 1818, the number of states had grown to twenty, and it did not work well to keep adding stripes to the flag. As a result, Congress made the decision to revert to the original thirteen stripes representing the thirteen original colonies and adding a star each time a new state was admitted. This has been the policy ever since.

Line (5) and *(10)* and *(15)* are line markers in the passage.

14. The word "product" in line 1 is closest in meaning to

(A) goods
(B) merchandise
(C) banner
(D) result

15. Look at the word hoisted in paragraph 2. Something that is hoisted is

○ created
○ found
○ raised
○ made

16. The word "ironic" in line 6 could most easily be replaced by

(A) steellike
(B) normal
(C) unexpected
(D) nationalistic

17. Look at the word obscure in paragraph 3. Click on another word in paragraph 3 that is opposite in meaning to obscure.

18. In line 12, the word "seamstress" is used to describe someone who

(A) works at home
(B) sews
(C) is a part of high society
(D) practices medicine

19. Click on the word in paragraph 4 that could best be replaced by "function."

20. Click on the word in paragraph 4 that could best be replaced by "continue."

21. The expression "revert to" in line 17 means

(A) return to
(B) add to
(C) rejoice over
(D) forget about

TOEFL REVIEW EXERCISE (Skills 1–11): Study each of the passages and choose the best answers to the questions that follow.

PASSAGE ONE (Questions 1–9)

Bigfoot is a humanlike creature reportedly living in the Pacific Northwest. Bigfoot sightings have been noted most often in the mountainous areas of Northern California, Oregon, and Washington in the United States. The creature has also been spotted numerous times in British
Line Columbia in Canada, where it is known as Sasquatch.
(5)   The creature described by witnesses is tall by human standards, measuring 7 to 10 feet (2 to 3 meters) in height. It resembles an ape with its thick, powerful, fur-covered arms and short, strong neck; however, its manner of walking erect is more like that of *Homo sapiens*.
    Although there have been hundreds of reported sightings of Bigfoot, most experts have not seen enough evidence to be convinced of its existence. The fact that some purported evidence
(10) has been proven fake may have served to discredit other more credible information.

1. Which of the following best states the topic of the passage?

   (A) Differences between Bigfoot and Sasquatch
   (B) A description of Bigfoot
   (C) Where Bigfoot, or Sasquatch, can be found
   (D) The creature Bigfoot and its questionable existence

2. The word "noted" in line 2 is closest in meaning to which of the following?

   (A) Reported
   (B) Written in a letter
   (C) Refuted
   (D) Discussed

3. It is implied in the passage that Bigfoot would probably NOT like to live

   (A) in Oregon
   (B) in the Pacific Northwest
   (C) on coastal plains
   (D) in mountainous areas

4. Which of the following is NOT true about the appearance of Bigfoot?

   (A) Its arms and neck look like those of an ape.
   (B) Its arms are covered with fur.
   (C) It is short-necked.
   (D) It walks like an ape.

5. Click on the drawing that shows how Bigfoot compares in height to an average man.

6. Look at the word that in paragraph 2. Click on the word or phrase that that refers to.

7. The expression "Homo sapiens" in line 8 is closest in meaning to

(A) apes
(B) creatures
(C) humans
(D) furry animals

8. According to the passage, how do experts feel about the evidence concerning Bigfoot's existence?

(A) They feel certain as to its existence.
(B) They are not yet certain.
(C) They are sure that it does not exist.
(D) They feel that all the evidence is fake.

9. Click on the paragraph that explains how knowledgeable people feel about the existence of Bigfoot.

PASSAGE TWO (Questions 10–18)

The next hormone is epinephrine, or adrenaline. This hormone is a natural secretion of the adrenal glands, which are located just above the kidneys in the human body. Its primary function in the human body is to help the body to cope with sudden surges of stress. When a

Line
(5) person unexpectedly finds himself in a stressful situation filled with fear or anger, a large amount of epinephrine is released into the blood and the body responds with an increased heartbeat, higher blood pressure, and conversion of glycogen into glucose for energy to enable the body to deal with the stress.

It is possible to extract epinephrine from the adrenal glands of animals or to synthesize it chemically in order to put it to further use. It is used in the treatment of severe asthma, where it
(10) relaxes the large muscles of the bronchi, the large air passages leading into the lungs. It is also used in cases of severe allergic reaction or cardiac arrest.

10. The paragraph preceding the passage most probably discusses

(A) further uses of epinephrine
(B) the treatment of cardiac arrest
(C) a different hormone
(D) the secretions of the adrenal glands

11. What is another name for epinephrine?

(A) Adrenal glands
(B) Stressful situation
(C) Bronchi
(D) Adrenaline

12. Click on the drawing that shows where epinephrine is produced in the human body.

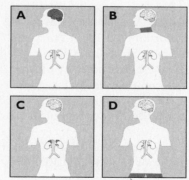

13. Look at the word cope in paragraph 1. Click on another word or phrase in paragraph 1 that is close in meaning to cope.

14. Which of the following is NOT mentioned as a result of the release of epinephrine in the blood?

   (A) Severe asthma
   (B) An increase in blood pressure
   (C) Higher heartbeat
   (D) Increased energy

15. It is implied in the passage that increased heartbeat

   (A) harms the body
   (B) causes the release of epinephrine into the body
   (C) is helpful in combating the stressful situation
   (D) is useful in treating asthma

16. The passage indicates that epinephrine is used in the treatment of all of the following EXCEPT

   (A) asthma
   (B) high blood pressure
   (C) serious allergic reactions
   (D) heart problems

17. Look at the word bronchi in paragraph 2. Bronchi are

   ○ large muscles
   ○ air passages
   ○ part of the lungs
   ○ part of the heart

18. Which of the following best expresses the organization of the information in the passage?

   (A) Epinephrine and adrenaline
   (B) Various effects of epinephrine on the body
   (C) Causes of sudden stress
   (D) Epinephrine's natural functions and further applications

PASSAGE THREE (Questions 19–25)

A massive banking crisis occurred in the United States in 1933. In the two preceding years, a large number of banks had failed, and fear of lost savings had prompted many depositors to remove their funds from banks. Problems became so serious in the state of Michigan that
Line Governor William A. Comstock was forced to declare a moratorium on all banking activities in
(5) the state on February 14, 1933. The panic in Michigan quickly spread to other states, and on March 6, President Franklin D. Roosevelt declared a banking moratorium throughout the United States that left the entire country without banking services.

Congress immediately met in a special session to solve the banking crisis, and on March 9 it passed the Emergency Banking Act of 1933 to assist financially healthy banks to reopen. By March
(10) 15, banks controlling 90 percent of the country's financial reserves were again open for business.

19. The passage states that all the following occurred prior to 1933 EXCEPT that

   (A) many banks went under
   (B) many bank patrons were afraid of losing their deposits
   (C) a lot of money was withdrawn from accounts
   (D) Governor Comstock canceled all banking activities in Michigan

20. Look at the word failed in paragraph 1. This word could best be replaced by which expression?

   ○ Not passed a test
   ○ Forgotten something important
   ○ Gone out of business
   ○ Paid little interest

21. The word "moratorium" in line 4 is closest in meaning to which of the following?

    (A) Death
    (B) Temporary cessation
    (C) Murder
    (D) Slow decline

22. The passage indicates that the moratorium declared by Roosevelt affected

    (A) the banks in Michigan
    (B) the banks in most of the U.S.
    (C) only the financially unhealthy banks
    (D) all the banks in the U.S.

23. Look at the word it in paragraph 2. Click on the word or phrase that it refers to.

24. Which of the following can be inferred from the passage?

    (A) Congress did not give any special priority to the banking situation.
    (B) The Emergency Banking Act helped all banks to reopen.
    (C) Ten percent of the country's money was in financially unhealthy banks.
    (D) Ninety percent of the banks reopened by the middle of March.

25. Which of the following best describes the organization of the passage?

    (A) A theme followed by an example
    (B) A problem and a solution
    (C) Opposing viewpoints of an issue
    (D) A problem and its causes

OVERALL REVIEW QUESTIONS

Often in the reading section of both the paper TOEFL test and the computer TOEFL test, the last question or two for a particular reading passage are overall questions that ask about the passage as a whole rather than one small detail. The most common type of overall review questions are questions that ask where in the passage something is found, questions about the tone of the passage, questions about the author's purpose in writing the passage, questions about which course the passage might be a part of, or questions about where a particular piece of information might be inserted into the passage.

SKILL 12: DETERMINE WHERE SPECIFIC INFORMATION IS FOUND

Sometimes the final question accompanying a reading passage (or one paragraph of a passage) will ask you to determine where in the passage a piece of information is found. This type of question is worded differently on the paper TOEFL test and on the computer TOEFL test. On the paper test, there will be a multiple-choice question that asks where certain information is found. The answer choices will list possible locations for that information. On the computer test, the question asks you to click on the sentence that contains certain information. Look at a multiple-choice example from the paper TOEFL that asks you to identify where certain information is found.

Example from the Paper TOEFL Test

The passage:

Meteor Crater, a great crater approximately forty miles east of Flagstaff, Arizona, is generally thought by scientists to have formed as a result of the impact of a 60,000-ton meteor
Line   about 50,000 years ago. The meteor, made of nickel and iron,
(5)   disintegrated on impact and spread half a billion tons of rock over the surface of the land. The massiveness of the meteor can only be imagined from the mammoth size of the crater, which measures a mile in diameter and three miles around the top. The rim of the crater rises more than 150 feet above
(10)   the plain where the meteor impacted and is visible for more than ten miles on a clear day.

The question:

Where in the passage does the author discuss the composition of the meteor?

(A)   Lines 1–3
(B)   Lines 4–5
(C)   Lines 6–8
(D)   Lines 9–11

This question asks you to find *where in the passage* there is information about the *composition* of the crater. You should skim through the lines of the passage listed in the answers to the question looking for the word *composition* or something that means *composition*. In line 4, you should find the expression *made of,* and you should recognize that *composition* is what something is *made of.* Answer (B) is therefore the best answer to this question.

Now look at a click-on example from the computer TOEFL test that asks you to indicate where certain information is found.

Example from the Computer TOEFL Test

Reading

Meteor Crater, a great crater approximately forty miles east of Flagstaff, Arizona, is generally thought by scientists to have formed as a result of the impact of a 60,000-ton meteor about 50,000 years ago. The meteor, made of nickel and iron, disintegrated on impact and spread half a billion tons of rock over the surface of the land. The massiveness of the meteor can only be imagined from the mammoth size of the crater, which measures a mile in diameter and three miles around the top. The rim of the crater rises more than 150 feet above the plain where the meteor impacted and is visible for more than ten miles on a clear day.

Click on the sentence in the passage that mentions the distance from which the crater can be seen.

This question asks you to *click on the sentence* in the passage that discusses the *distance* from which the crater can be *seen*. You should skim through the passage looking for the key words or ideas *distance* and *seen*. In the last sentence, you should recognize that *visible* means *seen* and that *ten miles* is a *distance*. The last sentence in the passage is the best answer, so you should click on the last sentence to answer the question.

The following chart outlines the key information that you should remember when you are trying to determine where in the passage something is found:

QUESTIONS ABOUT WHERE IN THE PASSAGE 📖 💻		
HOW TO IDENTIFY THE QUESTION	on paper test only 📖	***Where*** *in the passage…?*
	on computer test only 💻	***Click on the sentence*** *that indicates….*
WHERE TO FIND THE ANSWER	on paper test only 📖	The answer can be in any of the lines listed in the answers to the question.
	on computer test only 💻	The answer will be one of the sentences in the paragraph listed in the question.
HOW TO ANSWER THE QUESTION	1. Choose a key word or idea in the question. 2. Skim the appropriate part(s) of the passage looking for the key word or idea. 3. Choose the answer that contains the key word or idea.	

TOEFL EXERCISE 12: Study each of the passages and choose the best answers to the questions that follow.

PASSAGE ONE (Questions 1–4)

Beavers generally live in family clusters consisting of six to ten members. One cluster would probably consist of two adults, one male and one female, and four to eight young beavers, or kits. A female beaver gives birth each spring to two to four babies at a time. These baby beavers live
Line with their parents until they are two years old. In the springtime of their second year they are
(5) forced out of the family group to make room for the new babies. These two-year-old beavers then proceed to start new family clusters of their own.

1. Where in the passage does the author give the name of a baby beaver?

   (A) Line 1
   (B) Line 2
   (C) Line 3
   (D) Lines 4–5

2. Click on the sentence in the passage that mentions the time of year when new baby beavers are born.

3. Click on the sentence in the passage that states the age at which beavers must go out on their own.

4. Where in the passage does the author indicate why the young beavers must leave their parents' home?

   (A) Line 1
   (B) Line 2
   (C) Line 3
   (D) Lines 4–5

PASSAGE TWO (Questions 5–7)

Chamber music received its name because it was originally intended to be performed in small rooms in private homes rather than huge concert halls or theaters. Today it has evolved into small ensemble music in which each performer in the ensemble plays an individual part.

Line
(5)

The compositions written for this type of performance can easily be classified into three distinct periods, each with its style of music and instrumentation. In the earliest period (1450–1650), the viol and other instrumental families developed considerably, and instrumental music took its first steps toward equal footing with vocal music. In the second period (1650–1750), trio sonatas dominated. These ensemble compositions were often written for two violins and a cello; the harpsichord was also featured in various compositions of this period. In

(10)

the modern period (after 1750), the preponderance of chamber music was written for the string quartet, an ensemble composed of two violins, a viola, and a cello.

5. Where in the passage does the author discuss the modern definition of chamber music?

   (A) Lines 2–3
   (B) Lines 4–5
   (C) Lines 8–9
   (D) Lines 9–11

6. Click on the sentence in paragraph 2 that describes the first of the three periods of compositions for chamber music.

7. Click on the sentence in paragraph 2 that discusses which instruments were used in ensembles for three instruments.

PASSAGE THREE (Questions 8–10)

It is common practice to coat metals such as iron and steel with a protective layer of zinc or an alloy made from zinc mixed with aluminum, cadmium, or tin in a process known as "galvanization." The purpose of galvanization is to prevent the corrosion of the iron or steel.

Line
(5)

The most common method to galvanize metal is the hot-dip galvanizing process. In this process, the iron or steel is dipped into a hot bath of a zinc alloy to form a protective coating approximately .003 inches thick. Another method of galvanizing that is not as common is the process known as electrogalvanizing; in this process the metal is placed in a solution composed of zinc sulphate and water and is then charged electrically. This causes a thin layer of zinc to coat the metal.

(10)

Zinc is effective in galvanizing metals such as iron or steel in that zinc reacts more easily with oxygen than iron does. If iron is unprotected, it reacts with the oxygen in the air to form iron oxide, or rust, which leads to the corrosion of the iron. If, however, the iron is coated with zinc, as it is in the galvanization process, then it is the zinc rather than the iron which interacts with the oxygen to form zinc oxide, and the iron is not subject to corrosion.

8. Where in the passage does the author list the components of a zinc alloy?

   (A) Lines 1–2
   (B) Lines 4–6
   (C) Lines 9–10
   (D) Lines 11–12

9. Where in the passage does the author present the less routinely used process of galvanization?

   (A) Lines 1–2
   (B) Line 4
   (C) Lines 6–8
   (D) Lines 10–11

10. Click on the sentence in paragraph 2 that explains how the hot-dip galvanizing process is carried out.

Skill 13: DETERMINE THE TONE, PURPOSE, OR COURSE

Other types of review questions occur occasionally in the reading section of both the paper TOEFL test and the computer TOEFL test. Possible questions of this type are multiple-choice questions that ask about (1) the *tone* of the passage, (2) the author's *purpose* in writing the passage, and (3) the *course* in which the passage might be used.

A question about the *tone* is asking if the author is showing any emotion in his or her writing. The majority of the passages on the TOEFL test are factual passages presented without any emotion; the tone of this type of passage could be simply *informational, explanatory,* or *factual*. Sometimes the author shows some emotion, and you must be able to recognize that emotion to answer a question about tone correctly. If the author is being funny, then the tone might be *humorous;* if the author is making fun of something, the tone might be *sarcastic;* if the author feels strongly that something is right or wrong, the tone might be *impassioned*. Look at a multiple-choice example from the paper TOEFL test that asks about the *tone* of a passage.

Example from the Paper TOEFL Test

The passage:

Military awards have long been considered symbolic of royalty, and thus when the United States was a young nation just finished with revolution and eager to distance itself from

Line anything tasting of monarchy, there was strong sentiment
(5) against military decoration. For a century, from the end of the Revolutionary War until the Civil War, the United States awarded no military honors. The institution of the Medal of Honor in 1861 was a source of great discussion and concern. From the Civil War until World War I, the Medal of Honor was
(10) the only military award given by the United States government, and today it is awarded only in the most extreme cases of heroism. Although the United States is still somewhat wary of granting military awards, several awards have been instituted since World War I.

The question:

The *tone* of this passage is

(A) angered
(B) humorous
(C) outraged
(D) informational

This question asks about the *tone* of the passage. To determine the tone of a passage, you should look for any indications of emotion on the part of the author. In this passage, the author uses historical facts, using time expressions such as *for a century, in 1861,* and *since World War I,* to make a point about America's sentiment against military awards; the author does not make any kind of emotional plea. The best answer to this question is therefore answer (D), an *informational* tone. There is nothing in the passage to indicate anger (A), or humor (B), or outrage (C) on the part of the author.

A question about *purpose* is asking what the author is trying to do in the passage. You can draw a conclusion about the author's purpose by referring to the main idea and the organization of details in the passage. For example, if the main idea is that George Washington's early life greatly influenced his later career and if the details give a history of his early life, the author's purpose could be *to show how George Washington's early life influenced his later career.* However, the answer to a purpose question is often considerably more general than the main idea. A more general author's purpose for the main idea about George Washington would be *to demonstrate the influence of early experiences on later life* (without any mention of George Washington). Now look at a multiple-choice example from the computer TOEFL test that asks about the author's *purpose* in writing a passage.

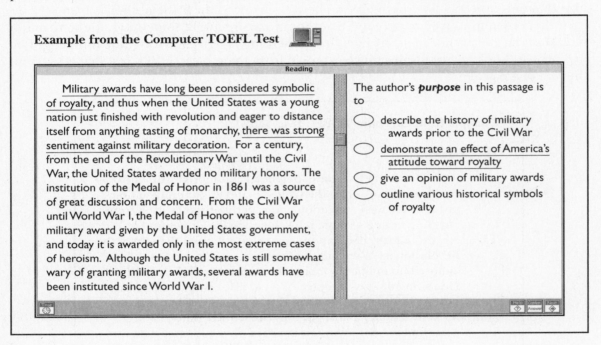

Example from the Computer TOEFL Test

Reading

Military awards have long been considered symbolic of royalty, and thus when the United States was a young nation just finished with revolution and eager to distance itself from anything tasting of monarchy, there was strong sentiment against military decoration. For a century, from the end of the Revolutionary War until the Civil War, the United States awarded no military honors. The institution of the Medal of Honor in 1861 was a source of great discussion and concern. From the Civil War until World War I, the Medal of Honor was the only military award given by the United States government, and today it is awarded only in the most extreme cases of heroism. Although the United States is still somewhat wary of granting military awards, several awards have been instituted since World War I.

The author's **purpose** in this passage is to

○ describe the history of military awards prior to the Civil War

○ demonstrate an effect of America's attitude toward royalty

○ give an opinion of military awards

○ outline various historical symbols of royalty

This question asks about the author's *purpose* in writing the passage. To answer this question correctly, you should refer to the main idea of this passage as outlined in the first sentence. The main idea is that *there was strong sentiment against military awards in the United States* because *military awards have been considered symbolic of royalty.* The author gives historical facts about military awards as details to support the main idea. Since the purpose is determined from the main idea and overall organization of details, the author's purpose is to describe, explain, or demonstrate that America's sentiment against military awards is because of its negative sentiment against royalty. The second answer is therefore the best answer to this question, so you should click on the second answer. You should notice that the correct answer is considerably more general than the main idea: according to the second answer, the purpose is to *demonstrate an effect* (America's dislike of military awards) *of America's attitude toward royalty.*

A question about the *course* is asking you to decide which university course might have this passage as assigned reading. You should draw a conclusion about the course by referring to the topic of the passage and organization of details. For example, if the passage is about George Washington and the details give historical background on his early life, then this would probably be assigned reading in an American history class. However, if the passage is about George Washington and the details show the various influences that he had on the formation of the American government, then the passage might be assigned reading in a government or political science class. Now look at a multiple-choice example from the computer TOEFL test that asks about the *course*.

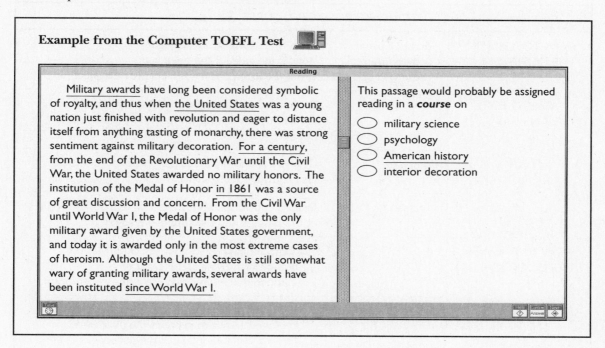

Example from the Computer TOEFL Test

Reading

Military awards have long been considered symbolic of royalty, and thus when the United States was a young nation just finished with revolution and eager to distance itself from anything tasting of monarchy, there was strong sentiment against military decoration. For a century, from the end of the Revolutionary War until the Civil War, the United States awarded no military honors. The institution of the Medal of Honor in 1861 was a source of great discussion and concern. From the Civil War until World War I, the Medal of Honor was the only military award given by the United States government, and today it is awarded only in the most extreme cases of heroism. Although the United States is still somewhat wary of granting military awards, several awards have been instituted since World War I.

This passage would probably be assigned reading in a **course** on

◯ military science
◯ psychology
◯ American history
◯ interior decoration

This question asks about the *course* in which you might be assigned this reading passage. To draw a conclusion about the course, you should refer to the topic of the passage and the overall organization of details. Since this passage is about American *military awards* in *the United States,* and the details discuss the history of American military awards using such time expressions as *for a century, in 1861,* and *since World War I,* you can determine that this passage might be assigned in a course on *American history.* You should click on the third answer to this question.

The following chart outlines the key information that you should remember about questions on the tone, purpose, or course:

TONE, PURPOSE, OR COURSE 📖 🖥		
HOW TO IDENTIFY THE QUESTION	on both paper and computer tests 📖 🖥	*What is the **tone** of the passage?* *What is the author's **purpose** in this passage?* *In which **course** would this reading be assigned?*
WHERE TO FIND THE ANSWER	*tone*	Look for clues throughout the passage that show if the author is showing some emotion rather than just presenting facts.
	purpose	Draw a conclusion about the purpose from the main idea and supporting ideas.
	course	Draw a conclusion about the course from the topic of the passage and the supporting ideas.
HOW TO ANSWER THE QUESTION	*tone*	1. Skim the passage looking for clues that the author is showing some emotion. 2. Choose the answer that identifies the emotion.
	purpose	1. Study the main idea in the topic sentence and the details used to support the main idea. 2. Draw a conclusion about the purpose.
	course	1. Study the main idea in the topic sentence and the details used to support the main idea. 2. Draw a conclusion about the course.

TOEFL EXERCISE 13: Study each of the passages and choose the best answers to the questions that follow.

PASSAGE ONE (Questions 1–3)

Truman Capote's *In Cold Blood* (1966) is a well-known example of the "nonfiction novel," a popular type of writing based upon factual events in which the author attempts to describe the underlying forces, thoughts, and emotions that lead to actual events. In Capote's book, the
Line author describes the sadistic murder of a family on a Kansas farm, often showing the point of view
(5) of the killers. To research the book, Capote interviewed the murderers, and he maintains that his book presents a faithful reconstruction of the incident.

1. The purpose of this passage is to

    (A) discuss an example of a particular
         literary genre
    (B) tell the story of *In Cold Blood*
    (C) explain Truman Capote's reasons
         for writing *In Cold Blood*
    (D) describe how Truman Capote
         researched his nonfiction novel

2. Which of the following best describes the
    tone of the passage?

    (A) Cold
    (B) Sadistic
    (C) Emotional
    (D) Descriptive

3. This passage would probably be assigned
    reading in which of the following
    courses?

    (A) Criminal Law
    (B) American History
    (C) Modern American Novels
    (D) Literary Research

PASSAGE TWO (Questions 4–6)

        Up to now, confessions that have been obtained from defendants in a hypnotic state have
not been admitted into evidence by courts in the United States. Experts in the field of hypnosis
have found that such confessions are not completely reliable. Subjects in a hypnotic state may
Line   confess to crimes they did not commit for one of two reasons. Either they fantasize that they
(5)   committed the crimes, or they believe that others want them to confess.
        A landmark case concerning a confession obtained under hypnosis went all the way to the
U.S. Supreme Court. In the case of *Layra* v. *Denno,* a suspect was hypnotized by a psychiatrist for
the district attorney; in a posthypnotic state the suspect signed three separate confessions to a
murder. The Supreme Court ruled that the confessions were invalid because the confessions had
(10)   been the only evidence against him.

4. Which of the following best describes the
    author's purpose in this passage?

    (A) To explain the details of a specific
         court case
    (B) To demonstrate why confessions
         made under hypnosis are not
         reliable
    (C) To clarify the role of the Supreme
         Court in invalidating confessions
         from hypnotized subjects
    (D) To explain the legal status of
         hypnotically induced confessions

5. The tone of this passage could best be
    described as

    (A) outraged
    (B) judicial
    (C) hypnotic
    (D) informative

6. This passage would probably be assigned
    reading in a course on

    (A) American law
    (B) psychiatric healing
    (C) parapsychology
    (D) philosophy

PASSAGE THREE (Questions 7–9)

The rate at which the deforestation of the world is proceeding is alarming. In 1950 approximately 25 percent of the earth's land surface had been covered with forests, and less than twenty-five years later the amount of forest land was reduced to 20 percent. This decrease from 25 percent to 20 percent from 1950 to 1973 represents an astounding 20 million square kilometers of forests. Predictions are that an additional 20 million square kilometers of forest land will be lost by 2020.

Line (5)

The majority of deforestation is occurring in tropical forests in developing countries, fueled by the developing countries' need for increased agricultural land and the desire on the part of developed countries to import wood and wood products. More than 90 percent of the plywood used in the United States, for example, is imported from developing countries with tropical rain forests. By the mid-1980s, solutions to this expanding problem were being sought, in the form of attempts to establish an international regulatory organization to oversee the use of tropical forests.

(10)

7. The author's main purpose in this passage is to

   (A) cite statistics about an improvement on the earth's land surface
   (B) explain where deforestation is occurring
   (C) make the reader aware of a worsening world problem
   (D) blame developing countries for deforestation

8. Which of the following best describes the tone of the passage?

   (A) Concerned
   (B) Disinterested
   (C) Placid
   (D) Exaggerated

9. This passage would probably be assigned reading in which of the following courses?

   (A) Geology
   (B) Geography
   (C) Geometry
   (D) Marine Biology

SKILL 14: DETERMINE WHERE TO INSERT A PIECE OF INFORMATION

On the computer TOEFL test, there may be a question following a particular paragraph or at the end of the reading passage that asks where a particular piece of information should be inserted. In this type of question, you must click on one of a number of squares in a passage to indicate that the piece of information should be inserted in that position. Look at an example from the computer TOEFL test that asks where to insert a piece of information.

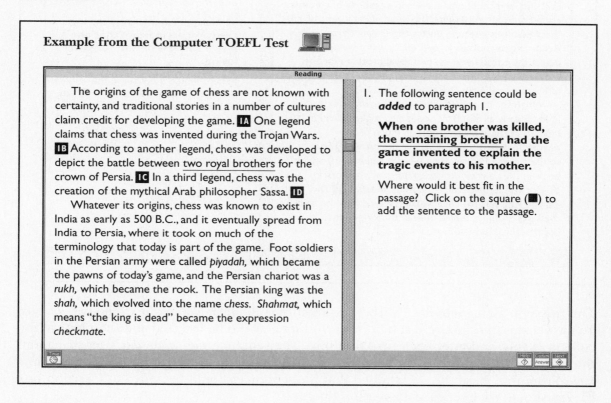

Example from the Computer TOEFL Test

Reading

The origins of the game of chess are not known with certainty, and traditional stories in a number of cultures claim credit for developing the game. **IA** One legend claims that chess was invented during the Trojan Wars. **IB** According to another legend, chess was developed to depict the battle between two royal brothers for the crown of Persia. **IC** In a third legend, chess was the creation of the mythical Arab philosopher Sassa. **ID**

Whatever its origins, chess was known to exist in India as early as 500 B.C., and it eventually spread from India to Persia, where it took on much of the terminology that today is part of the game. Foot soldiers in the Persian army were called *piyadah,* which became the pawns of today's game, and the Persian chariot was a *rukh,* which became the rook. The Persian king was the *shah,* which evolved into the name *chess. Shahmat,* which means "the king is dead" became the expression *checkmate.*

1. The following sentence could be *added* to paragraph 1.

   When one brother was killed, the remaining brother had the game invented to explain the tragic events to his mother.

   Where would it best fit in the passage? Click on the square (■) to add the sentence to the passage.

This question asks you to decide where a sentence could be *added* to one of the paragraphs. To answer this question, you should study the sentence to be inserted and then look at the context before and after each insertion box. The sentence mentions *one brother* and *the remaining brother,* and the context before insertion box **IC** mentions *two royal brothers.* From this, it can be determined that the sentence should be added at insertion box **IC**. You should click on **IC** to answer this question.

Now look at another example from the computer TOEFL test that asks where to insert a piece of information.

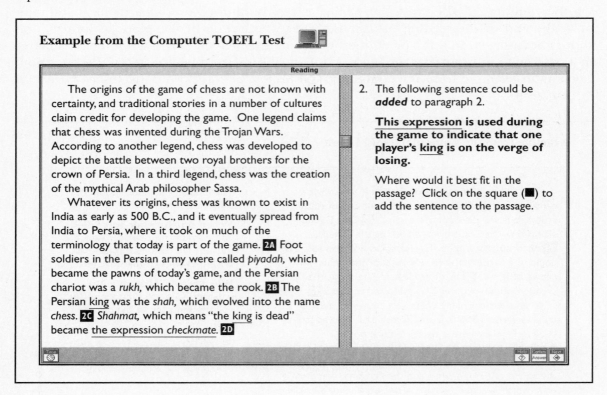

Example from the Computer TOEFL Test

Reading

The origins of the game of chess are not known with certainty, and traditional stories in a number of cultures claim credit for developing the game. One legend claims that chess was invented during the Trojan Wars. According to another legend, chess was developed to depict the battle between two royal brothers for the crown of Persia. In a third legend, chess was the creation of the mythical Arab philosopher Sassa.

Whatever its origins, chess was known to exist in India as early as 500 B.C., and it eventually spread from India to Persia, where it took on much of the terminology that today is part of the game. **2A** Foot soldiers in the Persian army were called *piyadah,* which became the pawns of today's game, and the Persian chariot was a *rukh,* which became the rook. **2B** The Persian king was the *shah,* which evolved into the name *chess.* **2C** *Shahmat,* which means "the king is dead" became the expression *checkmate.* **2D**

2. The following sentence could be *added* to paragraph 2.

This expression is used during the game to indicate that one player's king is on the verge of losing.

Where would it best fit in the passage? Click on the square (■) to add the sentence to the passage.

This question asks you to decide where a sentence could be *added* to one of the paragraphs. To answer this question, you should study the sentence to be inserted and then look at the context before and after each insertion box. The sentence mentions *this expression* about the *king,* and the context before insertion box **2D** mentions the *king* and *the expression checkmate.* From this, it can be determined that the sentence should be added at insertion box **2D**. You should click on **2D** to answer this question.

The following chart outlines the key information that you should remember when you are trying to determine where to insert a particular sentence:

QUESTIONS ABOUT INSERTING INFORMATION		
HOW TO IDENTIFY THE QUESTION	on computer test only	*The following sentence could be **added**…* *Click on the square to **add** the sentence to the passage.*
WHERE TO FIND THE ANSWER	The places where the sentence may be inserted are marked in the passage.	
HOW TO ANSWER THE QUESTION	1. Look at the sentence to be inserted for any key words or ideas at the beginning or the end of the sentence. 2. Read the context before and after the insertion squares for any ideas that relate to the sentence to be inserted. 3. Choose the insertion square that is most related to the sentence to be inserted.	

TOEFL EXERCISE 14: Study each of the passages and choose the best answers to the questions that follow.

PASSAGE ONE (Questions 1–3)

1A Something unusual about lions is that they hunt in groups. **1B** Group hunting is beneficial to lions because it means that much larger prey can be captured by the lions and that individual lions expend much less energy during a hunt. **1C**

Line   There is a standard pattern to the process of hunting in groups. **2A** The process is initiated
(5) by a single female, who stations herself at a raised elevation to serve as a lookout to spot potential prey. **2B** When prey is spotted, a group of young lionesses advances on the herd and pushes the herd in the direction of a different lioness who has hidden herself downwind. **2C** It is up to this concealed female to choose the weakest member of the herd for the kill. **2D**

     3A As can be seen from this description of the process, it is the females rather than the male
(10) or males in the pride that take part in the kill. **3B** While the young and strong females are on the attack, the males stay behind to protect the rest of the pride from attack from predators such as hyenas. **3C**

1. The following sentence could be added to paragraph 1.

   Other cats do not.

   Where would it best fit into the paragraph? Click on the square (■) to add the sentence to the paragraph.

2. The following sentence could be added to paragraph 2.

   This is usually accomplished by knocking the prey to the ground and breaking its neck.

   Where would it best fit into the paragraph? Click on the square (■) to add the sentence to the paragraph.

3. The following sentence could be added to paragraph 3.

   The males have a defensive rather than an offensive role.

   Where would it best fit into the paragraph? Click on the square (■) to add the sentence to the paragraph.

PASSAGE TWO (Questions 4–5)

     A number of products that we commonly use today were developed quite by accident. Two of many possible examples of this concept are the leotard and the popsicle, each of which came about when an insightful person recognized a potential benefit in a negative situation.

Line   The first of these accidental inventions is the leotard, a close-fitting, one-piece garment
(5) worn today by dancers, gymnasts, and acrobats, among others. **4A** In 1828, a circus performer named Nelson Hower was faced with the prospect of missing his performance because his costume was at the cleaners. **4B** Instead of canceling his part of the show, he decided to perform in his long underwear. **4C** Soon, other circus performers began performing the same way. **4D** When popular acrobat Jules Leotard adopted the style, it became known as the leotard.

(10)   **5A** Another product invented by chance was the popsicle. **5B** In 1905, eleven-year-old Frank Epperson stirred up a drink of fruit-flavored powder and soda water and then mistakenly left the drink, with the spoon in it, out on the back porch overnight. **5C** As the temperature dropped that night, the soda water froze around the spoon, creating a tasty treat. **5D** Years later, remembering how enjoyable the treat had been, Epperson went into business producing popsicles. **5E**

4. The following sentence could be added to paragraph 2.

   They enjoyed the comfort of performing in underwear rather than costumes.

   Where would it best fit into the paragraph? Click on the square (■) to add the sentence to the paragraph.

5. The following sentence could be added to paragraph 3.

   It was a taste sensation that stayed on his mind.

   Where would it best fit into the paragraph? Click on the square (■) to add the sentence to the paragraph.

PASSAGE THREE (Questions 6–7)

Uranium, a radioactive metal named after the planet Uranus, is a primary source of energy in nuclear power plants and certain nuclear weapons. It occurs naturally in three different isotopes, which differ in their facility in undergoing nuclear fission.

Line
(5)   **6A** The three naturally occurring isotopes of uranium are U-234, U-235, and U-238. **6B** Each of these isotopes has the same atomic number of 92, which is the number of protons in the nucleus. **6C** However, each has a different number of neutrons and thus has a different atomic mass, which is the sum of the number of protons and neutrons. **6D**

Of these three naturally occurring isotopes of uranium, U-238 is by far the most common, while U-235 is the most capable of undergoing nuclear fission. **7A** More than 99% of all naturally
(10)   occurring uranium is U-238, while U-234 and U-235 each make up less than 1%. **7B** Nuclear fission can occur when a U-235 nucleus is struck by a neutron, and the nucleus splits, releasing energy and releasing two or more neutrons. **7C** However, nuclear fission rarely involves a U-238 nucleus or a U-234 nucleus because it is unusual for either of these nuclei to break apart when struck by a neutron. **7D**

6. The following sentence could be added to paragraph 2.

   U-234 has 92 protons and 142 neutrons for an atomic mass of 234, U-235 has 92 protons and 143 neutrons for a total of 235, and U-238 has 92 protons and 146 neutrons for a total of 238.

   Where would it best fit into the paragraph? Click on the square (■) to add the sentence to the paragraph.

7. The following sentence could be added to paragraph 3.

   These neutrons can create a chain reaction by causing other U-235 nuclei to break up.

   Where would it best fit into the paragraph? Click on the square (■) to add the sentence to the paragraph.

TOEFL EXERCISE (Skills 12–14): Study each of the passages and choose the best answers to the questions that follow.

PASSAGE ONE (Questions 1–7)

3A The causes of schizophrenia are not clear, but schizophrenia has long been attributed to faulty parenting. **3B** In cases where schizophrenia developed, the parents were often considered responsible. **3C** However, recent studies are now pointing to heredity and prenatal environmental
Line factors as the chief culprits in this disease. **3D**
(5)   Recent studies of identical twins have been used to demonstrate that heredity plays a role in the development of schizophrenia. These studies have shown that in cases where one identical twin is afflicted with schizophrenia, the other twin has a 50 percent probability of also suffering from it.
       5A However, heredity is not believed to be the only culprit. **5B** Studies of the fingerprints of
(10) identical twins have lent credence to the theory that prenatal environmental factors are likely contributors to the development of schizophrenia. **5C** In studies of pairs of identical twins in which one is afflicted with schizophrenia and one is not, abnormalities were found in the fingerprints of one-third of the twins, always in the afflicted twin. **5D** Since fingers develop in the second trimester of pregnancy, the hypothesis has been proposed that the abnormalities in the
(15) fingerprints were due to a second-trimester trauma that affected only one of the twins and that this same trauma was a factor in the onset of schizophrenia. **5E**

1. The author's purpose in this passage is to

   (A) enumerate examples
   (B) cause the development of schizophrenia
   (C) prove that faulty parenting is the main cause of schizophrenia
   (D) refute a common misconception

2. Where in the passage does the author discuss the traditionally held view about the cause of schizophrenia?

   (A) Lines 1–2
   (B) Lines 3–4
   (C) Lines 6–8
   (D) Lines 9–11

3. The following sentence can be added to paragraph 1.

   They were faulted for having been uncaring, or manipulative, or emotionally abusive.

   Where would it best fit into the paragraph? Click on the square (■) to add the sentence to the paragraph.

4. Where in the passage does the author present the idea that people may inherit the tendency for schizophrenia?

   (A) Lines 3–4
   (B) Line 9
   (C) Lines 11–13
   (D) Lines 13–16

5. The following sentence can be added to paragraph 3.

   Further research into this hypothesis is ongoing.

   Where would it best fit into the paragraph? Click on the square (■) to add the sentence to the paragraph.

6. Click on the sentence in paragraph 3 that gives the fraction of twins under study with irregular fingerprints.

7. This passage would probably be assigned reading in which of the following courses?

   (A) Criminology
   (B) Public Administration
   (C) Statistics
   (D) Psychology

PASSAGE TWO (Questions 8–13)

[10A] To Americans, the Pony Express was a fixture of the Old West; most Americans are rather surprised to find out that in reality the Pony Express was in existence for only a short period of time, about a year and a half. [10B] A short-lived forefather of "express" mail service, the
Line   Pony Express operated between St. Joseph, Missouri, and Sacramento, California, a distance of
(5)   just under 2,000 miles. [10C] Letters and small packages could be delivered in under 10 days instead of the 3 to 4 weeks that it had taken prior to the institution of the Pony Express. [10D]

In 1860, St. Joseph was the westernmost terminal of the country's railroad system; mail destined for the West Coast could come to St. Joe by train, but the only way to get it farther west was on horseback. The Pony Express service was established on April 3, 1860, to fill this need: a
(10)   letter carried on horseback with only minimal downtime for changes in horses and riders could cover 200 miles in one twenty-four hour period.

The Pony Express system consisted of approximately 80 riders, 400 horses, and 190 stations every 10 to 15 miles along the route. One rider took a mail pouch and carried it for 75 miles, changing his tired horse for a fresh one at every station; he then passed the pouch to another
(15)   rider. Riders traveled day and night, and the mail never stopped.

[12A] On October 24, 1861, only a year and a half after the start of the Pony Express, the first transcontinental telegraph opened for business, ending the need for the Pony Express. [12B] The Pony Express officially closed for business on October 26, 1861. [12C] Obviously, its owners were quick to recognize that the need for their services no longer existed. [12D]

8. In which course would this passage most likely be assigned reading?

   (A) Veterinary Medicine
   (B) Speech Communication
   (C) Audiology
   (D) American History

9. Where in the passage does the author mention the amount of time it took to deliver a letter before the Pony Express?

   (A) Lines 1–3
   (B) Lines 5–6
   (C) Lines 9–11
   (D) Lines 12–13

10. The following sentence could be added to paragraph 1.

    This brief existence started in 1860 and was over before the end of 1861.

    Where would it best fit into the paragraph? Click on the square (■) to add the sentence to the paragraph.

11. Where in the passage does the author mention the technological device that put the Pony Express out of business?

    (A) Lines 5–6
    (B) Lines 9–11
    (C) Lines 12–13
    (D) Lines 16–17

12. The following sentence could be added to paragraph 4.

    Only two days later, the Pony Express went out of business.

    Where would it best fit into the paragraph? Click on the square (■) to add the sentence to the paragraph.

13. What is the author's purpose in writing this passage?

    (A) To warn of the dire effects of ending the Pony Express
    (B) To describe a little-known reality about a historical subject
    (C) To incite readers to action on behalf of the Pony Express
    (D) To describe the development of express mail service

PASSAGE THREE (Questions 14–18)

The grand jury is an important part of the American legal system. **16A** The grand jury is composed of private citizens who are appointed to serve for a designated period of time. **16B** Grand juries, which hold meetings in private, serve one of two functions: charging or
Line investigatory. **16C** A grand jury that is serving a charging function listens to evidence presented by
(5) the prosecutor and decides whether or not the prosecution has adequate evidence to charge a suspect with a crime; if the grand jury feels that there is adequate evidence, then it issues an indictment, and the suspect must then proceed with a trial. **16D** A grand jury that is serving an investigatory function investigates cases of suspected dishonesty, often by public officials. **16E**

The primary reason for the existence of the grand jury is that it is supposed to ensure that
(10) citizens are not subject to unfair prosecution; under the grand jury system, prosectors must first convince an unbiased group of citizens that there is justification for the charges that they want to bring. However, the grand jury system has come under attack from numerous directions. Grand juries are routinely criticized for being too slow and too costly; the grand jury system really means that there are two trials, the grand jury hearing to decide whether or not there should be a trial
(15) and then the actual trial itself. Another criticism of the grand jury results from the fact that the meetings are held in private; the grand jury is not open to public scrutiny and is therefore not publicly responsible for its actions, and this has cast doubt on some of its findings. A final common criticism of the grand jury is that the evidence it hears is one-sided, from the perspective of the prosecution, so that the grand jury serves as the right arm of the prosecution rather than
(20) as a defender of the rights of a suspect.

14. In which course might this passage be assigned reading?

   (A) Sociology of Criminal Behavior
   (B) Introduction to Law
   (C) American History
   (D) Research Methodologies

15. Click on the sentence in paragraph 1 that mentions who serves on a grand jury.

16. The following sentence could be added to paragraph 1.

   The investigatory function of the grand jury is different from the charging function.

   Where would it best fit into the paragraph? Click on the square (■) to add the sentence to the paragraph.

17. Where in the passage does the author discuss the problem associated with holding grand jury meetings in private?

   (A) Lines 4–6
   (B) Lines 7–8
   (C) Lines 10–12
   (D) Lines 15–17

18. How does the author seem to feel about the grand jury system?

   (A) Quite assured as to its usefulness
   (B) Somewhat doubtful about its effectiveness
   (C) Highly supportive of its use
   (D) Extremely negative about all aspects

TOEFL REVIEW EXERCISE (Skills 1–14): Study each of the passages and choose the best answers to the questions that follow.

PASSAGE ONE (Questions 1–11)

Another noteworthy trend in twentieth-century music in the United States was the use of folk and popular music as a base for more serious compositions. **10A** The motivation for these borrowings from traditional music might be a desire on the part of a composer to return to simpler forms, to enhance patriotic feelings, or to establish an immediate rapport with an audience. **10B** For whatever reason, composers such as Aaron Copland and Charles Ives offered compositions featuring novel musical forms flavored with refrains from traditional Americana. **10C** Copland drew upon folk music, particularly as sources for the music he wrote for the ballets *Billy the Kid, Rodeo,* and *Appalachian Spring.* **10D** Ives employed the whole gamut of patriotic songs, hymns, jazz, and popular songs in his compositions.

Line (5)

1. The paragraph preceding this passage most probably discusses

    (A) nineteenth-century music
    (B) one development in music in the last century
    (C) the works of Aaron Copland
    (D) the history of folk and popular music

2. Which of the following best describes the main idea of the passage?

    (A) Traditional music flavored some American musical compositions in the twentieth century.
    (B) Ives and Copland have used folk and popular music in their compositions.
    (C) A variety of explanations exist as to why a composer might use traditional sources of music.
    (D) Traditional music is composed of various types of folk and popular music.

3. It can be inferred from this passage that the author is not sure

    (A) when Ives wrote his compositions
    (B) that Ives and Copland actually borrowed from traditional music
    (C) why certain composers borrowed from folk and popular music
    (D) if Copland really featured new musical forms

4. Look at the word novel in the passage. This word could best be replaced by

    ☐ literary
    ☐ new
    ☐ cultural
    ☐ bookish

5. Look at the word he in the passage. Click on the word or phrase that he refers to.

6. Which of the following is NOT listed in the passage as a source for Ives's compositions?

    (A) National music
    (B) Religious music
    (C) Jazz
    (D) American novels

7. Click on the word in the passage that could best be replaced by "range."

8. Click on the sentence in the passage that gives reasons composers might use traditional melodies in their compositions.

9. Click on the sentence in the passage that lists examples of titles of Copland's works.

10. The following sentence could be added to the passage.

Ives drew inspiration from an even wider array of music than did Copland.

Where would it best fit into the paragraph? Click on the square (■) to add the sentence to the paragraph.

11. The passage would most probably be assigned reading in which of the following courses?

(A) American History
(B) The History of Jazz
(C) Modern American Music
(D) Composition

PASSAGE TWO (Questions 12–21)

The rattlesnake has a reputation as a dangerous and deadly snake with a fierce hatred for humanity. Although the rattlesnake is indeed a venomous snake capable of killing a human, its nature has perhaps been somewhat exaggerated in myth and folklore.

Line
(5) The rattlesnake is not inherently aggressive and generally strikes only when it has been put on the defensive. In its defensive posture the rattlesnake raises the front part of its body off the ground and assumes an S-shaped form in preparation for a lunge forward. At the end of a forward thrust, the rattlesnake pushes its fangs into the victim, thereby injecting its venom. **19A** There are more than 30 species of rattlesnakes, varying in length from 20 inches to 6 feet. **19B** In the United States there are only a few deaths annually from rattlesnakes, with a
(10) mortality rate of less than 2 percent of those attacked. **19C**

12. Which of the following would be the best title for this passage?

(A) The Exaggerated Reputation of the Rattlesnake
(B) The Dangerous and Deadly Rattlesnake
(C) The Venomous Killer of Humans
(D) Myth and Folklore about Killers

13. According to the passage, which of the following is true about rattlesnakes?

(A) They are always ready to attack.
(B) They are always dangerous and deadly.
(C) Their fierce nature has been underplayed in myth and folklore.
(D) Their poison can kill people.

14. Click on the word in paragraph 1 that is closest in meaning to "partially."

15. The word "posture" in line 5 is closest in meaning to which of the following?

(A) Mood
(B) Fight
(C) Position
(D) Strike

16. Click on the drawing that shows a rattlesnake that is ready to defend itself.

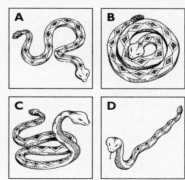

17. It can be inferred from the passage that

(A) all rattlesnake bites are fatal
(B) all rattlesnake bites are not equally harmful
(C) the few deaths from rattlesnake bites are from six-foot snakes
(D) deaths from rattlesnake bites have been steadily increasing

18. Look at the word mortality in paragraph 3. This word is closest in meaning to

   ◯ percentage
   ◯ illness
   ◯ death
   ◯ survival

19. The following sentence could be added to paragraph 3.

   They also vary in toxicity of venom.

   Where would it best fit into the paragraph? Click on the square (■) to add the sentence to the paragraph.

20. The author's purpose in this passage is to

   (A) warn readers about the extreme danger from rattlesnakes
   (B) explain a misconception about rattlesnakes
   (C) describe a rattlesnake attack
   (D) clarify how rattlesnakes kill humans

21. Click on the paragraph that explains what people believe about rattlesnakes.

PASSAGE THREE (Questions 22–30)

For a century before the Erie Canal was built, there was much discussion among the general population of the Northeast as to the need for connecting the waterways of the Great Lakes with the Atlantic Ocean. A project of such monumental proportions was not going to be undertaken
Line   and completed without a supreme amount of effort.
(5)   The man who was instrumental in accomplishing the feat that was the Erie Canal was DeWitt Clinton. As early as 1812, he was in the nation's capital petitioning the federal government for financial assistance on the project, emphasizing what a boon to the economy of the country the canal would be; his efforts with the federal government, however, were not successful.
         In 1816, Clinton asked the New York State Legislature for the funding for the canal, and this
(10)   time he did succeed. A canal commission was instituted, and Clinton himself was made head of it. One year later, Clinton was elected governor of the state, and soon after, construction of the canal was started.
         The canal took eight years to complete, and Clinton was on the first barge to travel the length of the canal, the *Seneca Chief,* which departed from Buffalo on October 26, 1825, and
(15)   arrived in New York City on November 4. Because of the success of the Erie Canal, numerous other canals were built in other parts of the country.

22. The information in the passage

   (A) gives a cause followed by an effect
   (B) is in chronological order
   (C) lists opposing viewpoints of a problem
   (D) is organized spatially

23. When did Clinton ask the U.S. government for funds for the canal?

   (A) One hundred years before the canal was built
   (B) In 1812
   (C) In 1816
   (D) In 1825

24. The word "boon" in line 7 is closest in meaning to which of the following?

   (A) Detriment
   (B) Disadvantage
   (C) Benefit
   (D) Cost

25. Look at the expression financial assistance in paragraph 2. Click on the word or phrase in paragraph 3 that is closest in meaning to financial assistance.

26. Look at the word it in paragraph 3. Click on the word or phrase that it refers to.

27. In what year did the actual building of the canal get underway?

   (A) In 1812
   (B) In 1816
   (C) In 1817
   (D) In 1825

28. Click on the drawing that most closely resembles the *Seneca Chief*.

29. Click on the paragraph that mentions a committee that worked to develop the canal.

30. The paragraph following the passage most probably discusses

   (A) the century before the building of the Erie Canal
   (B) canals in different U.S. locations
   (C) the effect of the Erie Canal on the Buffalo area
   (D) Clinton's career as governor of New York

READING POST-TEST (Paper) 📖

SECTION 3
READING COMPREHENSION
Time—55 minutes
(including the reading of the directions)
Now set your clock for 55 minutes.

This section is designed to measure your ability to read and understand short passages similar in topic and style to those that students are likely to encounter in North American universities and colleges.

Directions: In this section you will read several passages. Each one is followed by a number of questions about it. You are to choose the one best answer, (A), (B), (C), or (D), to each question. Then, on your answer sheet, find the number of the question and fill in the space that corresponds to the letter of the answer you have chosen.

Answer all questions about the information in a passage on the basis of what is <u>stated</u> or <u>implied</u> in that passage.

Read the following passage:

> John Quincy Adams, who served as the sixth president of the United States from 1825 to 1829, is today recognized for his masterful statesmanship and diplomacy. He dedicated his life to public service, both in the presidency and in the various other political offices that he *Line* held. Throughout his political career he demonstrated his unswerving belief in freedom of *(5)* speech, the antislavery cause, and the right of Americans to be free from European and Asian domination.

Example I   **Sample Answer**
                                                                              Ⓐ
To what did John Quincy Adams devote his life?   ●
                                                                              Ⓒ
(A) Improving his personal life   Ⓓ
(B) Serving the public
(C) Increasing his fortune
(D) Working on his private business

According to the passage, John Quincy Adams "dedicated his life to public service." Therefore, you should choose (B).

Example II   **Sample Answer**
                                                                              Ⓐ
In line 4, the word "unswerving" is closest in meaning to   Ⓑ
                                                                              ●
(A) moveable   Ⓓ
(B) insignificant
(C) unchanging
(D) diplomatic

The passage states that John Quincy Adams demonstrated his unswerving belief "throughout his career." This implies that the belief did not change. Therefore, you should choose (C).

Now begin work on the questions.

GO ON TO THE NEXT PAGE ➡

3 △ 3 △ 3 △ 3 △ 3 △ 3 △ 3 △ 3

Questions 1–10

A solar eclipse occurs when the Moon moves in front of the Sun and hides at least some part of the Sun from the earth. In a partial eclipse, the Moon covers part of the Sun; in an annular eclipse, the Moon covers the center of the Sun, leaving a bright ring of light around the Moon; in a total eclipse, the Sun is completely covered by the Moon.

Line
(5)

It seems rather improbable that a celestial body the size of the Moon could completely block out the tremendously immense Sun, as happens during a total eclipse, but this is exactly what happens. Although the Moon is considerably smaller in size than the Sun, the Moon is able to cover the Sun because of their relative distances from Earth. A total eclipse can last up to 7 minutes, during which time the Moon's shadow moves across Earth at a rate of about .6 kilometers per second.

1. This passage mainly

   (A) describes how long an eclipse will last
   (B) gives facts about the Moon
   (C) explains how the Sun is able to obscure the Moon
   (D) informs the reader about solar eclipses

2. In which type of eclipse is the Sun obscured in its entirety?

   (A) A partial eclipse
   (B) An annular eclipse
   (C) A total eclipse
   (D) A celestial eclipse

3. The word "ring" in line 3 could best be replaced by

   (A) piece of gold
   (B) circle
   (C) jewel
   (D) bell

4. A "celestial body" in line 5 is most probably one that is found

   (A) within the Moon's shadow
   (B) somewhere in the sky
   (C) on the surface of the Sun
   (D) inside Earth's atmosphere

5. What is the meaning of "block out" in line 5?

   (A) Square
   (B) Cover
   (C) Evaporate
   (D) Shrink

6. According to the passage, how can the Moon hide the Sun during a total eclipse?

   (A) The fact that the Moon is closer to Earth than the Sun makes up for the Moon's smaller size.
   (B) The Moon can only obscure the Sun because of the Moon's great distance from the earth.
   (C) Because the Sun is relatively close to Earth, the Sun can be eclipsed by the Moon.
   (D) The Moon hides the Sun because of the Moon's considerable size.

GO ON TO THE NEXT PAGE ➡

7. The word "relative" in line 8 could best be replaced by

   (A) familial
   (B) infinite
   (C) comparative
   (D) paternal

8. The passage states that which of the following happens during an eclipse?

   (A) The Moon hides from the Sun.
   (B) The Moon is obscured by the Sun.
   (C) The Moon begins moving at a speed of .6 kilometers per second.
   (D) The Moon's shadow crosses Earth.

9. The word "rate" in line 9 is closest in meaning to

   (A) form
   (B) speed
   (C) distance
   (D) rotation

10. Where in the passage does the author mention the rate of a total eclipse?

   (A) Lines 1–2
   (B) Lines 2–4
   (C) Lines 5–6
   (D) Lines 8–9

GO ON TO THE NEXT PAGE

Questions 11–20

While the bald eagle is one national symbol of the United States, it is not the only one. Uncle Sam, a bearded gentleman costumed in the red, white, and blue stars and stripes of the nation's flag, is another well-known national symbol. According to legend, this character is based on Samuel
Line Wilson, the owner of a meat-packing business in Troy, New York. During the War of 1812, Sam
(5) Wilson's company was granted a government contract to supply meat to the nation's soldiers; this meat was supplied to the army in barrels stamped with the initials U.S., which stood for United States. However, the country was at that time relatively young, and the initials U.S. were not commonly used. Many people questioned what the initials represented, and the standard reply became "Uncle Sam," for the owner of the barrels. It is now generally accepted that the figure of
(10) Uncle Sam is based on Samuel Wilson, and the U.S. Congress has made it official by adopting a resolution naming Samuel Wilson as the inspiration for Uncle Sam.

11. The paragraph preceding this passage most probably discusses

   (A) the War of 1812
   (B) the bald eagle, which symbolizes the United States
   (C) Sam Wilson's meat-packing company
   (D) the costume worn by Uncle Sam

12. Which of the following is the most appropriate title for this passage?

   (A) The Bald Eagle
   (B) The Symbols of the United States
   (C) Samuel Wilson
   (D) Uncle Sam—Symbol of the Nation

13. Which of the following is NOT mentioned about Uncle Sam's appearance?

   (A) He wears facial hair.
   (B) There is some blue in his clothing.
   (C) He is bald.
   (D) His clothes have stripes in them.

14. The word "costumed" in line 2 could most easily be replaced by

   (A) dressed
   (B) nationalized
   (C) hidden
   (D) seen

15. Sam Wilson was the proprietor of what type of business?

   (A) A costume company
   (B) A meat-packing company
   (C) A military clothier
   (D) A barrel-making company

16. The word "granted" in line 5 means

   (A) refused
   (B) underbid for
   (C) told about
   (D) given

17. According to the passage, what was in the barrels stamped U.S.?

   (A) Sam Wilson
   (B) Food for the army
   (C) Weapons to be used in the war
   (D) Company contracts

18. The word "initials" in line 6 means

   (A) nicknames
   (B) family names
   (C) first letters of words
   (D) company names

19. The word "official" in line 10 is closest in meaning to

   (A) authorized
   (B) professional
   (C) dutiful
   (D) accidental

20. In 1812, people most probably answered that the letters "U.S." written on the barrels stood for "Uncle Sam" because

   (A) Congress required it
   (B) Samuel Wilson was their favorite uncle
   (C) Sam Wilson preferred it
   (D) they were not exactly sure what the letters meant

GO ON TO THE NEXT PAGE ➤

Questions 21–31

Most people think of deserts as dry, flat areas with little vegetation and little or no rainfall, but this is hardly true. Many deserts have varied geographical formations ranging from soft, rolling hills to stark, jagged cliffs, and most deserts have a permanent source of water. Although deserts do not
Line receive a high amount of rainfall—to be classified as a desert, an area must get less than twenty-five
(5) centimeters of rainfall per year—there are many plants that thrive on only small amounts of water, and deserts are often full of such plant life.

Desert plants have a variety of mechanisms for obtaining the water needed for survival. Some plants, such as cactus, are able to store large amounts of water in their leaves or stems; after a rainfall these plants absorb a large supply of water to last until the next rainfall. Other plants, such as the
(10) mesquite, have extraordinarily deep root systems that allow them to obtain water from far below the desert's arid surface.

21. What is the main topic of the passage?
    (A) Deserts are dry, flat areas with few plants.
    (B) There is little rainfall in the desert.
    (C) Many kinds of vegetation can survive with little water.
    (D) Deserts are not really flat areas with little plant life.

22. The passage implies that
    (A) the typical conception of a desert is incorrect
    (B) all deserts are dry, flat areas
    (C) most people are well informed about deserts
    (D) the lack of rainfall in deserts causes the lack of vegetation

23. The passage describes the geography of deserts as
    (A) flat
    (B) sandy
    (C) varied
    (D) void of vegetation

24. The word "source" in line 3 means
    (A) supply
    (B) storage space
    (C) need
    (D) lack

25. According to the passage, what causes an area to be classified as a desert?
    (A) The type of plants
    (B) The geographical formations
    (C) The amount of precipitation
    (D) The source of water

26. The word "thrive" in line 5 means
    (A) suffer
    (B) grow well
    (C) minimally survive
    (D) decay

27. The word "mechanisms" in line 7 could most easily be replaced by
    (A) machines
    (B) pumps
    (C) sources
    (D) methods

28. Which of the following is mentioned in the passage about cacti?
    (A) They have deep root systems.
    (B) They retain water from one rainfall to the next.
    (C) They survive in the desert because they do not need water.
    (D) They get water from deep below the surface of the desert.

29. "Mesquite" in line 10 is probably
    (A) a type of tree
    (B) a desert animal
    (C) a type of cactus
    (D) a geographical formation in the desert

30. The word "arid" in line 11 means
    (A) deep
    (B) dry
    (C) sandy
    (D) superficial

31. Where in the passage does the author describe desert vegetation that keeps water in its leaves?
    (A) Lines 1–2
    (B) Lines 3–6
    (C) Lines 7–9
    (D) Lines 9–11

GO ON TO THE NEXT PAGE

Questions 32–41

American jazz is a conglomeration of sounds borrowed from such varied sources as American and African folk music, European classical music, and Christian gospel songs. One of the recognizable characteristics of jazz is its use of improvisation: certain parts of the music are written out and played the same way by various performers, and other improvised parts are created spontaneously during a performance and vary widely from performer to performer.

The earliest form of jazz was ragtime, lively songs or *rags* performed on the piano, and the best-known of the ragtime performers and composers was Scott Joplin. Born in 1868 to former slaves, Scott Joplin earned his living from a very early age playing the piano in bars along the Mississippi. One of his regular jobs was in the Maple Leaf Club in Sedalia, Missouri. It was there that he began writing the more than 500 compositions that he was to produce, the most famous of which was "The Maple Leaf Rag."

Line (5)

(10)

32. This passage is about

    (A) jazz in general and one specific type of jazz
    (B) the various sources of jazz
    (C) the life of Scott Joplin
    (D) the major characteristics of jazz

33. The word "conglomeration" in line 1 could best be replaced by

    (A) disharmony
    (B) mixture
    (C) purity
    (D) treasure

34. In line 3, the word "improvisation" involves which of the following?

    (A) Playing the written parts of the music
    (B) Performing similarly to other musicians
    (C) Making up music while playing
    (D) Playing a varied selection of musical compositions

35. According to the passage, ragtime was

    (A) generally performed on a variety of instruments
    (B) the first type of jazz
    (C) extremely soothing and sedate
    (D) performed only at the Maple Leaf Club in Sedalia

36. Which of the following statements is true according to the passage?

    (A) Scott Joplin was a slave when he was born.
    (B) Scott Joplin's parents had been slaves before Scott was born.
    (C) Scott Joplin had formerly been a slave, but he no longer was after 1868.
    (D) Scott Joplin's parents were slaves when Scott was born.

37. The word "living" in line 8 could most easily be replaced by

    (A) money
    (B) life-style
    (C) enjoyment
    (D) health

GO ON TO THE NEXT PAGE

38. The word "regular" in line 9 could best be replaced by

    (A) popular
    (B) steady
    (C) unusual
    (D) boring

39. The word "which" in line 10 refers to

    (A) regular jobs
    (B) the Maple Leaf Club
    (C) Sedalia, Missouri
    (D) 500 compositions

40. The name of Scott Joplin's most famous composition probably came from

    (A) the name of a saloon where he performed
    (B) the maple tree near his Sedalia home
    (C) the name of the town where he was born
    (D) the school where he learned to play the piano

41. The paragraph following the passage probably discusses

    (A) Sedalia, Missouri
    (B) the Maple Leaf Club
    (C) the numerous compositions of Scott Joplin
    (D) the life of Scott Joplin

GO ON TO THE NEXT PAGE

Questions 42–50

The idea of determinism, that no event occurs in nature without natural causes, has been postulated as a natural law yet is under attack on both scientific and philosophical grounds. Scientific laws assume that a specific set of conditions will unerringly lead to a predetermined outcome.

Line
(5) However, studies in the field of physics have demonstrated that the location and speed of minuscule particles such as electrons are the result of random behaviors rather than predictable results determined by pre-existing conditions. As a result of these studies, the principle of indeterminacy was formulated in 1925 by Werner Heisenberg. According to this principle, only the probable behavior of an electron can be predicted. The inability to absolutely predict the behavior of electrons casts doubt on the universal applicability of a natural law of determinism. Philosophically, the principal

(10) opposition to determinism emanates from those who see humans as creatures in possession of free will. Human decisions may be influenced by previous events, but the ultimate freedom of humanity may possibly lead to unforeseen choices, those not preordained by preceding events.

42. It is implied in the passage that a natural law

(A) is something that applies to science only
(B) can be incontrovertibly found in the idea of determinism
(C) is philosophically unacceptable
(D) is a principle to which there is no exception

43. The word "unerringly" in line 3 could be most easily replaced by

(A) fortunately
(B) effortlessly
(C) without mistake
(D) with guidance

44. The idea of determinism is refuted in this passage based on

(A) scientific proof
(B) data from the science and philosophy of determinism
(C) principles or assumptions from different fields of study
(D) philosophical doubt about free will

45. The word "minuscule" in line 4 is closest in meaning to

(A) charged
(B) fast-moving
(C) circular
(D) tiny

46. According to the passage, which of the following is NOT true about the principle of indeterminacy?

(A) It was formulated based on studies in physics.
(B) It is philosophically unacceptable.
(C) It has been in existence for more than a decade.
(D) It is concerned with the random behavior of electrons.

GO ON TO THE NEXT PAGE

47. The expression "emanates from" in line 10 could most easily be replaced by

(A) derives from
(B) differs from
(C) is in contrast to
(D) is subordinate to

48. It is implied in the passage that free will is

(A) accepted by all philosophers
(B) a direct outcome of Werner's principle of indeterminacy
(C) the antithesis of determinism
(D) a natural law

49. The word "unforeseen" in line 12 is closest in meaning to

(A) forewarned
(B) blind
(C) unappreciated
(D) unpredictable

50. Where in the passage does the author mention who developed the contrary principle to determinism?

(A) Lines 1–2
(B) Lines 6–7
(C) Lines 8–9
(D) Lines 9–13

This is the end of Section 3.

GO ON TO THE NEXT PAGE

READING POST-TEST (Computer)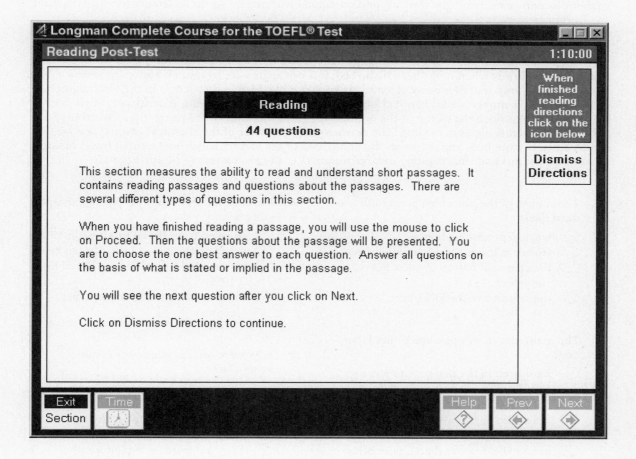

Longman Complete Course for the TOEFL® Test   　_ □ ✕

Reading Post-Test   1:10:00

Reading

44 questions

This section measures the ability to read and understand short passages. It contains reading passages and questions about the passages. There are several different types of questions in this section.

When you have finished reading a passage, you will use the mouse to click on Proceed. Then the questions about the passage will be presented. You are to choose the one best answer to each question. Answer all questions on the basis of what is stated or implied in the passage.

You will see the next question after you click on Next.

Click on Dismiss Directions to continue.

When finished reading directions click on the icon below

Dismiss Directions

Exit Section | Time | Help ? | Prev ◆ | Next ◆

PASSAGE ONE (Questions 1–10)

These stories of killer bees in the news in recent years have attracted a lot of attention as the bees have made their way from South America to North America. Killer bees are reputed to be extremely aggressive in nature, although experts say that their aggression may have been somewhat inflated.

The killer bee is a hybrid of the very mild European strain of honeybee and the considerably more aggressive African bee, which was created when the African strain was imported into Brazil in 1955. The African bees were brought into Brazil because their aggression was considered an advantage: they were far more productive than their European counterparts in that they spent a higher percentage of their time working and continued working longer in inclement weather than did the European bees.

These killer bees have been known to attack humans and animals, and some fatalities have occurred. Experts point out, however, that the mixed breed known as the killer bee is actually not at all as aggressive as the pure African bee. They also point out that the attacks have a chemical cause. A killer bee stings only when it has been disturbed; it is not aggressive by nature. However, after a disturbed bee stings and flies away, it leaves its stinger embedded in the victim. In the vicera attached to the embedded stinger is the chemical isoamyl acetate, which has an odor that attracts other bees. As other bees approach the victim of the original sting, the victim tends to panic, thus disturbing other bees and causing them to sting. The new stings create more of the chemical isoamyl acetate, which attracts more bees and increases the panic level of the victim. Killer bees tend to travel in large clusters or swarms and thus respond in large numbers to the production of isoamyl acetate.

1. The subject of the preceding paragraph was most likely
   - ways of producing honey
   - stories in the media about killer bees
   - the chemical nature of killer bee attacks
   - the creation of the killer bee

2. The main idea of this passage is that killer bees
   - have been in the news a lot recently
   - have been moving unexpectedly rapidly through the Americas
   - are not as aggressive as their reputation suggests
   - are a hybrid rather than a pure breed

3. Look at the word inflated in paragraph 1. This word could best be replaced by
   - exaggerated
   - blown
   - aired
   - burst

4. It can be inferred from the passage that the killer bee
   - traveled from Brazil to Africa in 1955
   - was a predecessor of the African bee
   - was carried from Africa to Brazil in 1955
   - did not exist early in the twentieth century

5. Why were African bees considered beneficial?
   - They produced an unusual type of honey.
   - They spent their time traveling.
   - They were very aggressive.
   - They hid from inclement weather.

6. Look at the word hybrid in paragraph 2. Click on the expression in paragraph 3 that is closest in meaning to hybrid.

7. It is stated in the passage that killer bees

⬭ are more deadly than African bees
⬭ are less aggressive than African bees
⬭ never attack animals
⬭ always attack African bees

8. Look at the word They in paragraph 3. Click on the word or phrase that They refers to.

9. What is NOT mentioned in the passage as a contributing factor in an attack by killer bees?

⬭ Panic by the victim
⬭ An odorous chemical
⬭ Disturbance of the bees
⬭ Inclement weather

10. Click on the sentence in paragraph 3 that describes the size of the groups in which killer bees move.

Clara Barton is well known for her endeavors as a nurse on the battlefield during the Civil War and for her role in founding the American Red Cross. She is perhaps not as well known, however, for her role in establishing a bureau for tracing missing soldiers following the Civil War.

At the close of the Civil War, the United States did not have in place any agency responsible for accounting for what had happened to the innumerable men who had served in the military during the war, and many families had no idea as to the fate of their loved ones. Families were forced to agonize endlessly over where their loved ones were, what kind of shape they were in, whether or not they would return, and what had happened to them.

15A Clara Barton developed a system for using print media to publish the names of soldiers known to have been wounded or killed during various battles of the Civil War. **15B** She made numerous unsuccessful attempts to interest various government officials in her plan. **15C** However, it was not until Henry Wilson, a senator from the state of Massachusetts, took up her cause and presented her plan to President Lincoln that her plan was implemented. **15D**

With Lincoln's assistance, Clara Barton was set up in a small government office with funding for a few clerks and the authority to examine military records. She and her clerks gathered and compiled information from military records and battlefield witnesses and published it in newspapers and magazines. Clara Barton operated this missing persons bureau for four years, from the end of the war in 1865 until 1869. During this period, she and her staff put out more than 100,000 printed lists, answered more than 60,000 letters, and accounted for more than 20,000 missing soldiers.

11. The purpose of this passage is
   ○ to praise Clara Barton's work as a battlefield nurse
   ○ to outline Clara Barton's role in establishing the American Red Cross
   ○ to malign the role of the U.S. government at the end of the Civil War
   ○ to present one of Clara Barton's lesser-known accomplishments

12. Which of the following is NOT mentioned as one of Clara Barton's accomplishments?
   ○ That she treated wounded Civil War soldiers
   ○ That she was integral to the establishment of the American Red Cross
   ○ That she served as an elected government official
   ○ That she continued to work for the good of soldiers and their families after the Civil War

13. Look at the word close in paragraph 2. This word could best be replaced by
   ○ near
   ○ battle
   ○ end
   ○ shut

14. What is stated in the passage about the issue of missing persons following the Civil War?
   ○ The U.S. government was not officially prepared to deal with the issue.
   ○ President Lincoln did not recognize that there was an issue.
   ○ One U.S. government agency was responsible for the issue.
   ○ U.S. citizens were unaware of the issue.

15. The following sentence could be added to paragraph 3.

   She was prepared to publish names that she herself had gathered on the battlefield as well as information gathered from others.

   Where would it best fit into the paragraph? Click on the square (■) to add the sentence to the paragraph.

16. Look at the expression print media in paragraph 3. Click on the expression in paragraph 4 that is closest in meaning to print media.

17. It can be inferred from the passage that the budget for Barton's missing persons agency was

   ○ quite lavish
   ○ open-ended
   ○ limited in scope
   ○ from private sources

18. Look at the word it in paragraph 4. Click on the word or phrase in paragraph 4 that it refers to.

19. Which of the following did Clara Barton and her staff accomplish, according to the passage?

   ○ They searched military records.
   ○ They responded to 100,000 letters.
   ○ They printed a list with 100,000 names.
   ○ They talked with 20,000 missing soldiers.

20. Click on the sentence in paragraph 4 that indicates the duration of the existence of Clara Barton's missing persons agency.

21. Click on the paragraph that describes Clara Barton's efforts to establish a missing persons bureau.

PASSAGE THREE (Questions 22–34)

Federal Express is a company that specializes in rapid overnight delivery of high-priority packages. The first company of its type, Federal Express was founded by the youthful Fred Smith in 1971, when he was only 28 years old. Smith had actually developed the idea for the rapid delivery service in a term paper for an economics class when he was a student at Yale University. The term paper reputedly received a less-than-stellar grade because of the infeasibility of the project that Smith had outlined. The model that Smith proposed had never been tried; it was a model that was efficient to operate but at the same time was very difficult to institute.

Smith achieved efficiency in his model by designing a system that was separate from the passenger system and could, therefore, focus on how to deliver packages most efficiently. His strategy was to own his own planes so that he could create his own schedules and to ship all packages through the centralized hub city of Memphis, a set-up which resembles the spokes on the wheel of a bicycle. With this combination of his own planes and hub set-up, he could get packages anywhere in the United States overnight.

What made Smith's idea difficult to institute was the fact that the entire system had to be created before the company could begin operations. He needed a fleet of aircraft to collect packages from airports every night and deliver them to Memphis, where they were immediately sorted and flown out to their new destinations; he needed a fleet of trucks to deliver packages to and from the various airports; he needed facilities and trained staff all in place to handle the operation. Smith had a $4 million inheritance from his father, and he managed to raise an additional $91 million dollars from venture capitalists to get the company operating.

32A When Federal Express began service in 1973 in 25 cities, the company was not an immediate success, but success did come within a relatively short period of time. **32B** The company lost $29 million in the first 26 months of operations. **32C** By late 1976, Federal Express was carrying an average of 19,000 packages per night and had made a profit of $3.6 million. **32D**

22. The most appropriate title for this passage is
   ◯ The Problems and Frustrations of a Business Student
   ◯ The Importance of Business Studies
   ◯ The Capitalization of Federal Express
   ◯ The Implementation of a Successful Business

23. Look at the word developed in paragraph 1. This word could best be replaced by
   ◯ come up with
   ◯ come about
   ◯ come across
   ◯ come into

24. What is stated in the passage about Smith's term paper?
   ◯ Smith submitted it through a delivery service.
   ◯ It was written by a student of Smith's.
   ◯ Its grade was mediocre.
   ◯ The professor thought it had great potential.

25. What was a key idea of Smith's?
   ◯ That he should focus on passenger service
   ◯ That package delivery should be separate from passenger service
   ◯ That packages could be delivered on other companies' planes
   ◯ That passenger service had to be efficient

26. Click on the drawing that most closely resembles a hub.

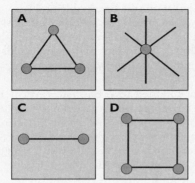

27. It can be inferred from the passage that Smith selected Memphis as his hub city because it
    ○ was near the middle of the country
    ○ had a large number of passenger aircraft
    ○ already had a large package delivery service
    ○ was a favorite passenger airport

28. Look at the word they in paragraph 3. Click on the word or phrase that they refers to.

29. It is NOT mentioned in the passage that, in order to set up his company, Smith needed
    ○ airplanes
    ○ trucks
    ○ personnel
    ○ faculty

30. Click on the sentence in paragraph 3 that explains how Smith raised the capital he needed.

31. How long did it take Federal Express to become profitable?
    ○ Two months
    ○ One year
    ○ Three years
    ○ Six years

32. The following sentence could be added to paragraph 4.

    However, the tide was to turn relatively quickly.

    Where would it best fit into the paragraph? Click on the square (■) to add the sentence to the paragraph.

33. Click on the paragraph that explains what made Smith's model effective.

34. The tone of the passage in describing Smith's accomplishments is
    ○ unflattering
    ○ sincere
    ○ unconvincing
    ○ snobbish

PASSAGE FOUR (Questions 35–44)

Perhaps better known than the Cullinan Diamond is the Hope Diamond, a valuable and rare blue gem with a background of more than 300 years as a world traveler. The 112-carat blue stone that later became the Hope Diamond was mined in India sometime before the middle of the seventeenth century and was first known to be owned by Shah Jahan, who built the Taj Mahal in memory of his beloved wife. From India, the celebrated blue stone has changed hands often, moving from location to location in distant corners of the world.

In the middle of the seventeenth century, a trader from France named Jean Baptiste Tavernier acquired the large blue diamond, which was rumored to have been illegally removed from a temple. Tavernier returned to France with the big blue gem, where the stone was purchased by the Sun King, Louis XIV. Louis XIV had it cut down from 112 to 67 carats to make its shape symmetrical and to maximize its sparkle. The newly cut diamond, still huge by any standards, was passed down through the royal family of France, until it arrived in the hands of Louis XVI and Marie Antoinette. During the French Revolution, Louis XVI and his wife met their fate on the guillotine in 1793, and the big blue diamond disappeared from public sight.

The diamond somehow managed to get from France to England, where banker Henry Hope purchased it from a gem dealer early in the nineteenth century. The huge blue stone was cut into a 45.5 carat oval, and at this point it took on the name by which it is known today. The diamond stayed in the Hope family for around a century, when deep indebtedness brought on by a serious gambling habit on the part of one of Henry Hope's heirs forced the sale of the diamond.

From England, the Hope Diamond may have made its way into the hands of the Sultan of Turkey; whatever route it took to get there, it eventually went on to the United States when American Evelyn Walsh McLean purchased it in 1911. Mrs. McLean certainly enjoyed showing the diamond off; guests in her home were sometimes astounded to notice the huge stone embellishing the neck of Mrs. McLean's Great Dane as the huge pet trotted around the grounds of her Washington, D.C. home. The Hope Diamond later became the property of jeweler Harry Winston, who presented the stunning 45.5-carat piece to the Smithsonian in 1958. The Hope Diamond is now taking a well-earned rest following its rigorous travel itinerary and is on display at the Smithsonian Institution in Washington, D.C., where it has been since 1958.

35. The paragraph preceding the passage most likely discussed
    ○ why gems are considered valuable
    ○ how the Hope Diamond was mined
    ○ a diamond other than the Hope Diamond
    ○ methods for mining diamonds

36. The main idea of this passage is that the Hope Diamond
    ○ came from India
    ○ has moved around a lot
    ○ has been cut several times
    ○ now resides in the Smithsonian

37. Look at the word it in paragraph 2. Click on the word or phrase that it refers to.

38. Click on the sentence in paragraph 2 that describes what happened to the royal French owners of the diamond.

39. It can be inferred from the passage that the author is not certain
    ○ who bought the Hope Diamond in England
    ○ who sold the Hope Diamond in England
    ○ how the Hope Diamond went from France to England
    ○ how big the Hope Diamond was in the nineteenth century

40. Look at the word dealer in paragraph 3. A dealer is most likely a
    ○ card player
    ○ miner
    ○ cutter
    ○ businessman

41. It can be determined from the passage that Henry Hope most likely had how many carats cut off the Hope Diamond?

⬭ 21.5
⬭ 45.5
⬭ 66.5
⬭ 67

42. According to the passage, Mrs. McLean

⬭ donated the Hope Diamond to the Smithsonian
⬭ let her dog wear the Hope Diamond
⬭ purchased the Hope Diamond from the French
⬭ had the Hope Diamond cut to its present size of 45.5 carats

43. Which country is NOT mentioned in the passage as a place where the Hope Diamond spent some time?

⬭ India
⬭ France
⬭ England
⬭ Denmark

44. Click on the paragraph that discusses the period when the Hope Diamond received its current name.

SECTION FOUR

WRITING

WRITING

Writing sometimes appears on the paper TOEFL test and always appears on the computer TOEFL test. On both forms of the test, writing consists of an essay question which must be answered by the test-taker in thirty minutes. The paper and the computer writing sections are **similar** in the following ways:

- *the type of question*
- *the amount of time*
- *the way the writing is scored*

The paper and the computer writing sections are **different** in the following ways:

- *the frequency with which writing is tested*
- *the place where writing appears on the test*
- *the method for writing an answer*
- *the computation of the writing score in the overall score*

WRITING ON THE PAPER TOEFL TEST

On the paper TOEFL test, the writing section is called the Test of Written English (TWE). The TWE is given at the beginning of the TOEFL test, before the Listening Comprehension, Structure and Written Expression, and Reading Comprehension. On the TWE, you are given a specific topic, and you are asked to write an answer to the question. You have thirty minutes to write your answer on a lined sheet of paper.

The TWE only appears on some of the paper TOEFL tests. The dates when the TWE will be given are published in the *Bulletin of Information for TOEFL, TWE, and TSE*. You should check the bulletin when you apply for the paper TOEFL test to determine whether or not the TWE will be given on the date when you will take the test.

WRITING ON THE COMPUTER TOEFL TEST

On the computer TOEFL test, the fourth section is called the Writing section. The Writing section appears every time that the computer TOEFL test is given. In this section, you are given a specific topic, and you are asked to write an answer to the question. You have thirty minutes either to type your answer on the computer or to write your answer on a lined sheet of paper. You should type your answer on the computer only if you are comfortable working on a computer; if you decide to write your answer by hand, then be sure to write neatly.

STRATEGIES FOR WRITING _____

Because you must write a complete essay in such a short period of time on either the paper test or the computer test, it is best for you to aim to write a basic, clear, concise, and well-organized essay. The following strategies will help you in the writing section of both the paper TOEFL test and the computer TOEFL test.

GENERAL STRATEGIES FOR WRITING
(Paper TOEFL Test and Computer TOEFL Test)

1. **Read the question carefully, and answer the question exactly as it is asked.** Take some time at the beginning of the test to be sure that you understand exactly what the question is asking.

2. **Organize your response very clearly.** You should think of having an introduction, body paragraphs that develop the introduction, and a conclusion to end your essay. Use transitions to help the reader understand the organization of ideas.

3. **Whenever you make any general statement, be sure to support that statement.** You can use examples, reasons, facts, or similar details to support any general statement.

4. **Stick to vocabulary and sentence structures that you know.** This is not the time to try out new words or structures.

5. **Finish writing your essay a few minutes early so that you have time to proof what you wrote.** You should spend the last three to five minutes checking your essay for errors.

THE WRITING SCORE _____

The writing score on both the paper TOEFL test and the computer TOEFL test is determined in the same way: the writing is given a score from 1 to 6, where 1 is the lowest score and 6 is the highest score. The following table outlines what each of these scores means:

WRITING SCORES

---

6. The writer has very strong organizational, structural, and grammatical skills.

---

5. The writer has good organizational, structural, and grammatical skills. However, the essay contains some errors.

---

4. The writer has adequate organizational, structural, and grammatical skills. The essay contains a number of errors.

---

3. The writer shows evidence of organizational, structural, and grammatical skills that still need to be improved.

---

2. The writer shows a minimal ability to convey ideas in written English.

---

1. The writer is not capable of conveying ideas in written English.

There is a major difference between the paper and the computer tests in how this writing score of 1 to 6 relates to the overall score. On the paper TOEFL test, the writing score is completely separate from the overall TOEFL score; you will receive a score of 1 to 6 on the TWE, and this will not count as part of the overall score. On the computer TOEFL test, however, the writing score counts as one-half of the score in the Structure section.

SAMPLE ESSAYS

This section contains six essays, one demonstrating each of the six possible scores. These essays can give you some idea of the type of essay you need to write to achieve a good score. They can also demonstrate some of the major errors you should avoid when you work on the writing section.

The strengths and weaknesses of each essay have been outlined at the end of each. It would be helpful to study each answer in order to understand what is good and what is not so good in each of these essays.

This is the topic that was used:

Sample Essay Topic
Time — 30 minutes

Do you agree or disagree with the following statement?

Some people place a high value on loyalty to the employer. To others, it is perfectly acceptable to change jobs every few years to build a career. Discuss these two positions. Then indicate which position you agree with and why.

Use specific reasons and details to support your answer.

The following essay received a score of 6:

Different cultures place varying values on loyalty to the employer. In some countries, most notably in Asia, there is a high degree of loyalty to one company. However, in most European countries and the United States, loyalty to one's employer is not highly valued; instead it is considered more rationel and reasonable for an employee to change jobs whenever it is waranted to achieve the optimal overall career. Both of these positions have advantages and disadvantages.

In cultures that value loyalty to the employer, a kind of family relationship seems to develop between employer and employee. It is a reciprocal arrangement which the employer is concerned with asisting the employee to develop to his/her full potential and the employee is concerned about optimizing the welfare of the company. The negative aspect to absolute loyalty to one company is that an employee may stay in one job that he/she has outgrow and may miss out on opportunities to develop in new directions. From the employer's point of view, the employee may be burdened with employees whose skills no longer match the needs of the company.

In cultures in which it is quite acceptable to change jobs every few years, employees can build the career they choose for themself. They can stay with one company as long as it is mutually beneficial to company and employee. As long as good relationship exists and the employee's career is advancing at an acceptable pace, the employee can rmain with a company. But at any time the employee is free to move to another company, perhaps to achieve a higher position, to move into a new area, or to find a work situation that is more suitable to his/her personality. The disadvantage of this situation is employees tend to move around a lot.

Although both these systems have advantages and disadvantages, it is much better for employees have the opportunity to move from job to job if it is necessary to have a better career.

THE "6" ESSAY

Strengths of This Essay

1. It discusses all aspects of the topic.

2. It is clearly organized.

3. The ideas are well developed.

4. It has good, correct sentence structure.

5. It has only a few spelling and grammar errors.

Weaknesses of This Essay

1. The concluding paragraph is rather weak.

The following essay received a score of 5:

Some people place high value on loyalty to employer. They believe the company is responsible for the employee's career. The company will make decisions for the employee about his job. The company will decide to raise employee to new position or keep him in the old position. In this way the company will have overall plan for the good of the company and everyone in the company.

Other people believe it is perfectly acceptable to change jobs every few years to build a career. They believe employee is responsible for his own career. The employee will make decisions about his career. Employee will decide when to move to other company. Employee will choose what is good for employee rather than the company.

The best system is one when employer takes responsibility for the careers of employees. Employer should take responsibility. It is his duty. Employee knows that employer is watching out for his career. Then employee will work hard and do good job. He will be loyal to the company. This system works out best for everyone. It is best for both the company and employees.

```
┌─────────────────────────────────────────────────────┐
│                    THE "5" ESSAY                     │
│ ─────────────────────────────────────────────────── │
│                                                      │
│  Strengths of This Essay                             │
│  1.  It discusses the topic fully.                   │
│  2.  It is clearly organized.                        │
│  3.  It has correct sentence structure.              │
│                                                      │
│  Weaknesses of This Essay                            │
│  1.  The sentence structure is very simple.          │
│  2.  There are some grammatical errors, particularly │
│      with articles.                                  │
│                                                      │
└─────────────────────────────────────────────────────┘
```

The following essay received a score of 4:

Every one is not in agreement about how loyal people should be to their employers. Some people place a high value on loyalty to the employer. These people believe that they should work hard for their employer and so their employer will take care of them. To others it is perfectly acceptable to change jobs every few years to build a career. They believe that having only one employer and one job in a career will not be the best for them.

In my culture people stay with one employer for their whole life. They have a job they will work their hardest at that job because it is the only job they will have. They do not look for another job they already have one because that would be unloyal. This way is better because when you old the company will take care you and your family.

```
┌─────────────────────────────────────────────────────┐
│                    THE "4" ESSAY                     │
│ ─────────────────────────────────────────────────── │
│                                                      │
│  Strengths of This Essay                             │
│  1.  It answers the question fairly well.            │
│  2.  It is clearly organized.                        │
│                                                      │
│  Weaknesses of This Essay                            │
│  1.  It copies too directly from the question.       │
│  2.  The ideas are not very well developed.          │
│  3.  There are several examples of incorrect         │
│      sentence structure.                             │
│                                                      │
└─────────────────────────────────────────────────────┘
```

The following essay received a score of 3:

Some people stay with one employeer for their entire career, but anothers build a career by changing jobs every few years. There are three reasens people should staying with on employer for their entire career.

First, the people should staying with one employer because it is best for the workers. If workers stay with one employer they will not having to move and they can learning all abou the company and advence in the company.

Second, people should staying with one employer because it is best for the compeny. The people will knowing how to do their jobs and they will having a big producton and the compeny will be very success.

Finally, people should staying with one employer because it is best for soceity. If people stay with one compeny then all the compenies will being very success. If all the compenie are very success then soceity will be success.

THE "3" ESSAY

Strengths of This Essay

1. It is clearly organized.
2. It has good, correct sentence structure.

Weaknesses of This Essay

1. It does not discuss the topic completely.
2. There are errors in spelling and grammar.

The following essay received a score of 2:

First, there is a disadvantage to place a high value on loyalty to the employer if your employer is no a good employer and your job is no a good job then you should no be loyal to a bad employer. Many employer are no good employers and if you are loyal to a bad employer it is a waste because a bad employer he will no be good to you.

Next, there is a advantage to change jobs every few years to build a carere if you get boring with your job and you want to move from one job to other so yo can get a better job instead of stay in your old boring job.

Finally, people should decide for themself where they want to work, if they decide one plce when they very young, how can they be sure whe they are older that they will still want to work there?

THE "2" ESSAY

Strengths of This Essay

1. The overall organization is clear.
2. The writer's main point is clear.

Weaknesses of This Essay

1. The sentence structure is poor.
2. There are numerous errors in spelling and grammar.
3. The ideas are not very well developed.

The following essay received a score of 1:

I think people should staying only one job for his hole careere. Because it is important loyal to your jop. If you not loyal. Th company didn't be able has good business. If the employees keep change. New employees alway needs be train, and so on.

THE "1" ESSAY

Weaknesses of This Essay

1. It does not discuss the topic completely.
2. The ideas are disorganized and difficult to follow.
3. There are many errors in spelling and grammar.
4. There are many errors in sentence structure.
5. It is too short.

BEFORE WRITING

SKILL 1: DECODE THE TOPIC

The first and most important step when writing an essay on the TOEFL test is to decode the topic to determine what the intended outline is. Writing topics generally give very clear clues about how your answer should be constructed. It is important to follow the clear clues that are given in the topic when you are planning your answer. You probably will not be given much credit for a response that does not cover the topic in the way that is intended. Study the following essay topic:

Essay Topic

Some people prefer large weddings with lots of people, while others prefer small weddings with only very close friends and family. Discuss the advantages of each type of wedding. Then indicate which you prefer and why.

As you read this topic, you should think about the organization of the intended response that will be expected by test graders. Your essay should start with an introduction, and that introduction should mention *large weddings, small weddings,* and their *advantages.* This introduction should be followed by supporting paragraphs describing the *advantages of large weddings* and the *advantages of small weddings.* In the final paragraph, you should discuss whether *you prefer large weddings* or *small weddings* and *why.* This final paragraph serves as your conclusion because it brings together the ideas in the previous paragraphs about large and small weddings. The following is an appropriate outline for an essay on the topic above:

Paragraph 1:   INTRODUCTORY PARAGRAPH
(mentioning the advantages of large and small weddings)

Paragraph 2:   FIRST SUPPORTING PARAGRAPH
(listing and discussing the advantages of large weddings)

Paragraph 3:   SECOND SUPPORTING PARAGRAPH
(listing and discussing the advantages of small weddings)

Paragraph 4:   CONCLUDING PARAGRAPH
(whether you prefer large or small weddings and why)

The following chart outlines the key information that you should remember about decoding writing topics:

THE WRITING TOPIC

Each writing topic shows you exactly *what* you should discuss and *how* you should organize your response. You must decode the topic carefully to determine the intended way of organizing your response.

EXERCISE 1: For each of the following writing topics, indicate the type of information that you will include in each paragraph of your response.

> 1.   What type of novel do you enjoy reading most? Use reasons and examples to support your response.

INTRODUCTION: *the type of novel I enjoy reading most*
SUPPORTING PARAGRAPH 1:   *the first reason I enjoy this type of novel (with an example)*
SUPPORTING PARAGRAPH 2:   *the second reason I enjoy this type of novel (with an example)*
SUPPORTING PARAGRAPH 3:   *the third reason I enjoy this type of novel (with an example)*
CONCLUSION: *summary of the reasons I enjoy this type of novel*

> 2.   Some students prefer to study alone, while other students prefer to study with others. Discuss the advantages of each type of studying. Then indicate which you prefer and why.

> 3.   Do you agree or disagree with the following statement?
>
>   *Patience is the most important characteristic in a boss.*
>
> Use specific reasons and examples to support your response.

> 4.   Some people work better during the day, while other people work better at night. Which kind of person are you, and why? Use reasons and examples to support your response.

5. Do you agree or disagree with the following statement?

    Time should never be wasted.

    Use specific reasons and examples to support your response.

6. What type of company would you most like to see built in your hometown or city. Give reasons to support your response.

7. Some people live for today, while other people live for the future. Which type of person are you? Use reasons and examples to support your response.

8. Do you agree or disagree with the following statement?

    A knowledge of history is absolutely essential.

    Use specific reasons and examples to support your response.

Skill 2: DEVELOP SUPPORTING IDEAS

After you have decoded a writing topic to determine the overall organization of your response, you need to plan how to develop your ideas. You need to provide as much support as possible for the ideas in your essay, using reasons and examples and making your answer as personal as possible. To have an effective essay, you need strong support.

Essay Topic

Why is it important to you to learn English? Support your response with reasons and examples.

As you read this topic, you should quickly determine that the overall organization of your response should be an introduction, supporting paragraphs about your reasons for learning English, and a conclusion. You should take a few minutes before you begin writing to develop your ideas.

INTRODUCTION   *my reasons for learning English*

SUPPORTING PARAGRAPH 1   *for educational opportunities*
    (examples)   • *going to university abroad, going to graduate school abroad*
    (reason)   • *necessary to learn English in order to study abroad*
    (personal story)   • *the opportunity that I have to get a graduate degree abroad with a scholarship from my company*

SUPPORTING PARAGRAPH 2   *for professional opportunities*
    (examples)   • *getting an entry-level job in a multinational company, advancing to a higher position in the company*
    (reason)   • *necessary to learn English in order to succeed in a multinational company*
    (personal story)   • *the low, entry-level job in a multinational company that I got after I was interviewed in English*

CONCLUSION   *the educational and professional opportunities that result from learning English*

In this example, there are two main reasons for learning English: *for educational opportunities* and *for professional opportunities*. Each of these ideas is supported by examples, a reason, and personal information.

The following chart outlines the key information that you should remember about the development of supporting ideas.

SUPPORTING IDEAS

Support your essay with *reasons* and *examples*, and *personalize* your essay as much as possible. The more support you have, the stronger your essay will be.

EXERCISE 2: For each of the following topics, develop ideas to support it, using reasons, examples, and personal information.

1. What have you done that has most surprised the people around you? Use reasons and examples to support your response.

2. Some people like to visit new and different places, while others prefer to remain in places they know. Which type of person are you? Support your response with reasons and examples.

3. Do you agree or disagree with the following statement?

   A teacher should always stick to the subject matter of the course.

   Use specific reasons and examples to support your response.

4. What advice would you give to someone who is just beginning the study of the English language? Give reasons and examples to support your response.

5. Some people prefer to marry when they are young, while others prefer to wait until they are older to marry. Discuss the advantages of each position. Then indicate which you think is better and why.

6. Do you agree or disagree with the following statement?

    It is better to save your money for the future than to enjoy it now.

    Use specific reasons and examples to support your response.

7. At the end of your life, how would you most like to be remembered? Support your response with reasons and examples.

8. Some people dream of reaching unlikely goals, while other people set more reasonable and reachable goals. Which kind of person do you tend to be? Use examples to support your response.

WHILE WRITING

SKILL 3: WRITE THE INTRODUCTORY PARAGRAPH

The purpose of the introduction is first to interest the reader in your topic and then to explain clearly to the reader what you are going to discuss. When finished with your introduction, the reader should be eager to continue on with your essay, and the reader should have an exact idea of your topic and how you are going to organize the discussion of your topic. You do not need to give the outcome of your discussion in the introduction; you can save that for the conclusion.

Essay Topic

Do you agree or disagree with the following statement?

> *To succeed, you should focus more on cooperation than on competition.*

Support your response with specific examples.

The following paragraph shows one possible introduction to an essay on this topic in which the author agrees with the statement.

INTRODUCTION 1

In my work in a marketing company, it is very clear that employees in the company compete with each other in order to be selected to work on the best projects and in order to advance in the company. However, in spite of this intense competition among employees, the most important key to the success of the company, and therefore to the success of the employees working within the company, is for employees to cooperate in order to produce the most effective marketing campaigns. Two examples in which I have taken part, a marketing campaign for an office supply company and a marketing campaign for a dance theater, demonstrate the value of cooperation among employees.

The first part of this introduction gives background information about the writer to interest the reader in the essay. The first two sentences tell the reader that the writer works in a marketing company and recognizes that, while both competition and cooperation exist among the employees of the marketing company, cooperation is the most important. From the last sentence of the introduction, it can be determined that the writer will discuss two examples from the marketing company that demonstrate the value of cooperation.

The next paragraph shows another way that the essay on the above topic could be introduced. In this essay, the author disagrees with the statement.

INTRODUCTION 2
    As a student in the university, I find that, while on many occasions it is beneficial to cooperate with other students, it is most important for me always to compete with other students for the top grades in the courses I take. The following two situations from my university studies indicate the importance of competition to a student in my position.

The first part of this introduction informs the reader that the writer is a university student who regularly competes for top grades; it also shows that the writer believes that competition is more important than cooperation. From the last sentence of the introduction, it can be determined that the writer will continue the essay by discussing two situations from the university that demonstrate the importance of competition.

The following chart outlines the key information that you should remember about writing introductory paragraphs.

THE INTRODUCTORY PARAGRAPH

1. Begin the introduction with *background* information about how the topic relates to you in order to get the reader *interested* in your essay.
2. End the introduction with a statement or statements that show the reader how the rest of the essay will be *organized*.

EXERCISE 3: Write introductory paragraphs for essays on the following topics. In each introductory paragraph, circle the *background* information that shows how the topic relates to you. Underline the information that shows how the rest of the essay will be *organized*.

> 1. Do you agree or disagree with the following statement?
>
>   *It is better to stick with what you know than to try out new things.*
>
>   Use specific reasons and examples to support your response.

> 2. What course that you have taken have you enjoyed the most, and why? Use reasons and examples to support your response.

3. In some courses, there are numerous exams throughout the course, while in other courses there is only one final exam. Discuss the advantages of each type of course. Then indicate which you prefer and why.

4. Do you agree or disagree with the following statement?

    Parents always know what is best for their children.

    Use specific reasons and examples to support your response.

5. What is the strongest advantage that technology can bring us? Support your response with reasons and examples.

6. Some people are very casual about handling their money, while other people budget their money carefully. Which type of person are you? Support your response with reasons and examples.

7. Do you agree or disagree with the following statement?

    It is the responsibility of government to support the arts.

    Use specific reasons and examples to support your response.

8. What person, other than a family member, has influenced you the most in your life? Support your response with reasons and examples.

SKILL 4: WRITE UNIFIED SUPPORTING PARAGRAPHS

A good way to write a clear and effective supporting paragraph is to begin with a sentence to introduce the main idea of the passage, support the main idea with strong details, and connect the ideas together in a unified paragraph. The following outline shows a paragraph topic and its supporting ideas.

---

to be a good employee, have a good understanding of your job
- *understand your responsibilities*
- *understand the rules you must follow*
- *understand the decisions you can make*

Various methods can be used to connect ideas together in a unified paragraph: repeating a key word, rephrasing the key word, referring to the key word with a pronoun or possessive, and adding transition expressions or sentences. The paragraph based on the outline above contains examples of each of these methods of unifying the ideas in a paragraph.

If you want to be a good employee, one characteristic that you must

have is a clear understanding of the job you have. First of all, you must
              (1) job   (4) transition expression

know what your responsibilities are in the position you hold. For example,
                  (1) rephrasing of job   (4) transition expression

you must know exactly what tasks you must do in your job. You must also
            (2) tasks   (1) job

know exactly how these tasks should be done and when they should be done.
        (2) tasks   (2) pronoun for tasks

After this, you must understand the organizational rules that you must
(4) transition expression   (3) rules

follow in your position. Every organization has rules to follow, such as when
      (1) rephrasing of job   (3) rules   (4) transition expression

to take breaks or what to do when you are sick, and it is important for you to

understand these clearly. In addition to understanding your duties and the
      (3) pronoun for rules

rules you must observe in your job, you must also have a clear
            (5) transition sentence

understanding of which decisions you can and cannot make. Some types of

decisions my be yours to make, while other kinds of decisions may be up to

your supervisor. In summary, for you to be a good employee, it is
        (4) transitions expression

important for you to understand all of these aspects of your job.
                                  (1) job

This paragraph contains numerous examples of devices that make the paragraph more unified. (1) The key word *job* is repeated numerous times and rephrased as *position*. (2) The key word *tasks* is repeated and is replaced with the pronoun *they*. (3) The key word *rules* is repeated and then is replaced with the pronoun *these*. (4) There are numerous transition expressions: *first of all, for example, after this, such as,* and *in summary.* (5) There is a transition sentence relating the first two supporting ideas about duties and rules to the third supporting idea about decisions.

The following chart outlines the key information that you should remember when you are writing supporting paragraphs.

UNIFIED SUPPORTING PARAGRAPHS

Introduce each supporting paragraph with a *topic sentence* and support that paragraph with lots of *details*. Make sure that the ideas in the paragraph are unified by using a mixture of the following methods:
- repeating a key word
- rephrasing a key word
- replacing a key word with a pronoun or possessive
- adding transition words, phrases, or sentences

NOTE: See 7B on page 501 for examples of transition expressions.

EXERCISE 4: Read the paragraph. Then answer these questions.

1. (A) Find the word *employee* in the passage. How many times does it appear?
    (B) How is the word *employee* restated in the second sentence?

2. (A) Find the word *priorities* in the passage. How many times does it appear?
    (B) Which pronoun refers to the noun *priorities*?

3. (A) Find the word *manner* in the passage. *Manner* is a rephrasing of which word in the previous sentence?
    (B) What pronoun refers to *manner*?

4. (A) Find the transition expression that indicates the first way you must understand your organization.
    (B) Find the transition sentence that relates the first way to the second way you must understand your organization.

5. (A) Find the transition expression that precedes examples of priorities.
    (B) Find the transition expression that precedes examples of manner.
    (C) Find the transition expression that precedes examples of inflexible style.

     Another characteristic that you must have if you are going to be a good employee is a clear understanding of your organization. First of all, for you to be a good worker, you must understand where the organization places

Line (5) its priorities. You must, for example, know if the organization most values product quality, on-time production, customer satisfaction, or cost savings. If you understand the organization's priorities, then you will be able to do your job in accordance with them. However, in addition to understanding an organization's priorities if you want to be a good employee, you must also understand the style for getting work done within

(10) the organization. The manner of getting work done could, for instance, be casual or formal, with perhaps very formal or informal ways of dressing or communicating. It could also be either flexible or inflexible. In a very rigid type of organization, you follow the rules to the letter (i.e., arriving at your desk precisely on time, taking breaks exactly as prescribed, and leaving as the

(15) clock strikes the hour); in a less rigid organization, the rules are not followed so precisely.

Now write a paragraph beginning with *The recent news event that has affected me most* . . . . Then follow these directions:

1. Circle each key word the first time that it appears in the paragraph. Draw a line from the key word to any repetitions, rephrases, or pronoun references to that key word.
2. Underline any transition phrases once.
3. Underline any transition sentences twice.

Skill 5: WRITE THE CONCLUDING PARAGRAPH

The purpose of the conclusion is to close your essay by summarizing the main points of your discussion. When finished with your conclusion, the reader should clearly understand your exact ideas on the topic and the reasons you feel the way that you do about the topic.

The ideas in your conclusion should be closely related to the ideas that you began in the introduction. While in the introduction you should indicate what you intend to discuss in the essay, in the conclusion you should indicate the outcome or results of the discussion. Refer to the essay topic and sample introductions in Skill 3 on page 487.

Essay Topic

Do you agree or disagree with the following statement?

> To succeed, you should focus more on cooperation than on competition.

Support your response with specific examples.

The following paragraph is a conclusion to the essay that began with INTRODUCTION 1 (in Skill 3) on page 487.

CONCLUSION 1

Even though there is intense competition among employees to advance in the company, the key ingredient for the success of the company is cooperation among employees to complete the company's various projects. The truth of this statement should be clear from the examples of the marketing campaigns for the office supply company and the dance theater, where strong teamwork caused one campaign to succeed and lack of teamwork caused the other campaign to be less successful.

In this conclusion, the writer clearly indicates the belief that cooperation is more important than competition. The writer also refers to the two examples from the essay that support this position.

The next paragraph is a conclusion to the essay that began with INTRODUCTION 2 (in Skill 3) on page 488.

CONCLUSION 2

If I had not competed so strongly in these two situations, my life would be very different from what it is today. I would never have been admitted to the top university in my country, and I would certainly never have earned a scholarship for my studies there. It is because I believe so strongly in competition that I was able to succeed in this way.

In this conclusion, the writer clearly indicates the strong belief that competition is very important. The writer also summarizes the two examples from the essay that support this position.

The following chart outlines the key information that you should remember about writing concluding paragraphs.

THE CONCLUDING PARAGRAPH
1. *Summarize* the key points in your discussion.   2. Be sure that your overall *idea* and the *reasons* for the idea are very clear.

EXERCISE 5: Write concluding paragraphs for the essays that you introduced in Skill 3. In each concluding paragraph, circle your overall idea. Underline the key points of your discussion.

> 1.   Do you agree or disagree with the following statement?
>
>   *It is better to stick with what you know than to try out new things.*
>
>   Use specific reasons and examples to support your response.

> 2.   What course that you have taken have you enjoyed the most, and why? Use reasons and examples to support your response.

> 3.   In some courses, there are numerous exams throughout the course, while in other courses there is only one final exam. Discuss the advantages of each type of course. Then indicate which you prefer and why.

4. Do you agree or disagree with the following statement?

    Parents always know what is best for their children.

    Use specific reasons and examples to support your response.

5. What is the strongest advantage that technology can bring us? Support your response with reasons and examples.

6. Some people are very casual about handling their money, while other people budget their money carefully. Which type of person are you? Support your response with reasons and examples.

7. Do you agree or disagree with the following statement?

    It is the responsibility of government to support the arts.

    Use specific reasons and examples to support your response.

8. What person, other than a family member, has influenced you the most in your life? Support your response with reasons and examples.

Skill 6: CONNECT THE SUPPORTING PARAGRAPHS IN THE ESSAY

To make your essay as clear as possible, you should show as clearly as you can how the ideas in the supporting paragraphs in your essay are related. This can be accomplished (1) with transition expressions such as *the first, the most important,* or *a final way,* or (2) with transition sentences that include the idea of the previous paragraph and the idea of the current paragraph. It is best to use a combination of these two types of transitions. The following example shows how transitions can be used to show the relationships among the supporting paragraphs in an essay.

ESSAY OUTLINE

(introduction)   *characteristics of a good class*
(supporting paragraph 1)   • *an organized teacher*
(supporting paragraph 2)   • *interesting lectures*
(supporting paragraph 3)   • *clear and reasonable assignments*

TRANSITIONS

(to introduce SP1)   *One important characteristic of a good class is an organized teacher.*

(to introduce SP2)   *In addition to having a teacher who is organized, a good class must also have a teacher who gives interesting lectures.*

(to introduce SP3)   *A final characteristic of a good class is that the assignments are clear and reasonable.*

The first supporting paragraph is introduced with the transition *One important characteristic* to show that this is the first of the characteristics of a good class that you are going to discuss in your essay. The second supporting paragraph is introduced with a transition sentence that shows how this paragraph is related to the previous paragraph; it includes a reference to the first supporting paragraph *a teacher who is organized* and a reference to the second supporting paragraph *a teacher who gives interesting lectures.* The third supporting paragraph is introduced with the transition expression *A final characteristic* to show that this is the last of the three characteristics of a good class.

The following chart outlines the important information to remember about connecting the supporting paragraphs of your essay:

WELL-CONNECTED SUPPORTING PARAGRAPHS

1. The supporting paragraphs of an essay can be connected with *transition expressions* or with *transition sentences.*
2. It is best to use a combination of these two types of transitions.

EXERCISE 6: For each outline of an essay, write sentences to introduce each of the supporting paragraphs. You should use a combination of transition expressions and transitions sentences.

1. INTRO: *courses I've enjoyed the most*
   SP1: sociology
   SP2: philosophy
   SP3: psychology

   SP1: *One course I have enjoyed is sociology.*

   SP2: *Even more than sociology, I have really enjoyed philosophy.*

   SP3: *Of all the courses, the one that I have enjoyed the most is psychology.*

2. INTRO: *places in the United States that I would like to see*
   SP1: • the Grand Canyon
   SP2: • Niagara Falls
   SP3: • the Petrified Forest

   SP1: _____

   SP2: _____

   SP3: _____

3. INTRO: *best type of part-time job while in school*
   SP1: one that pays a lot
   SP2: one that is related to my future career
   SP3: one that has flexible hours

   SP1: _____

   SP2: _____

   SP3: _____

4. INTRO: *the world's most important priorities*
   SP1: feeding the hungry
   SP2: taking care of the environment
   SP3: finding cures for diseases
   SP4: ending war and violence

   SP1: _____

   SP2: _____

   SP3: _____

   SP4: _____

5. INTRO: *assignments I most dislike*
    SP1: writing long research papers
    SP2: working on group assignments
    SP3: giving speeches

    SP1: _____

    SP2: _____

    SP3: _____

6. INTRO: *advantages of learning to cook*
    SP1: saving money
    SP2: preparing exactly what you want
    SP3: being able to cook for family and friends

    SP1: _____

    SP2: _____

    SP3: _____

7. INTRO: *what my parents taught me*
    SP1: to be honest with myself
    SP2: to make the most of what I have
    SP3: to strive for more than I think I can do

    SP1: _____

    SP2: _____

    SP3: _____

8. INTRO: *overused excuses for tardiness*
    SP1: "I overslept."
    SP2: "My alarm clock broke."
    SP3: "My car wouldn't start."
    SP4: "The bus was late."

    SP1: _____

    SP2: _____

    SP3: _____

    SP4: _____

AFTER WRITING

Skill 7: EDIT SENTENCE STRUCTURE

7A. Simple Sentence Structure

A *simple* sentence is a sentence that has only one **clause**[1]. Two types of sentence structure errors are possible in sentence with only one clause: (1) the clause can be missing a subject or a verb, and (2) the clause can be introduced by a subordinate clause connector.

The first type of incorrect simple sentence is a sentence that is missing a subject or a verb. (Note that an asterisk is used to indicate that the sentence contains an error.)

> Every day is necessary to sign in and sign out.*
>   VERB

> His recommendation about the project.*
>   SUBJECT

The first sentence is incorrect because it has the verb *is* but is missing a subject. The second sentence is incorrect because it has the subject *recommendation* but is missing a verb.

A sentence structure with both a subject and a verb is not always correct. If the one clause in the sentence includes both a subject and a verb but is introduced by a subordinate clause connector, then the sentence is also incomplete.

> When the storm with thunder and lightning will leave the area.*
>   SUBJECT   VERB

> How the driver of the car managed to avoid an accident.*
>   SUBJECT   VERB

The first sentence includes both the subject *storm* and the verb *will leave*, but this sentence is not correct because it is introduced by the subordinate clause connector *When*. The second sentence includes both the subject *driver* and the verb *managed*, but this sentence is not correct because it is introduced by the subordinate clause connector *How*.

The following chart outlines what you should remember about editing simple sentences:

SIMPLE SENTENCES
1. A simple sentence is a sentence with *one clause*.
2. A simple sentence must have both a *subject* and a *verb*.
3. A simple sentence may not be introduced by a *subordinate clause connector*.

---

[1]A **clause** is a group of words that has both a subject and a verb. Simple sentences with only one main clause are covered in great detail in Skills 1–5 of the Structure section on pages 200–209.

EXERCISE 7A: Underline the subjects once and the verbs twice. Put boxes around the subordinate clause connectors. Then indicate if the sentences are correct (C) or incorrect (I).

___I___   1.   The vague meaning of the underlined expression.

_____   2.   When you finally found out the whole truth.

_____   3.   His reaction to the film was priceless.

_____   4.   Usually leaves quite early in the morning.

_____   5.   An indication to everyone of the importance of the project.

_____   6.   Surprisingly, no one has collected the prize.

_____   7.   Why the committee met for so long.

_____   8.   Absolutely cannot submit the forms today.

_____   9.   The refusal of the judge to accept the petition.

_____   10.   The idea shocked me.

_____   11.   Since each of the participants was fully trained.

_____   12.   In a moment of anguish forgot about his promise.

_____   13.   A discussion by all interested parties has been scheduled.

_____   14.   A situation needing a considerable amount of attention.

_____   15.   Only that the books were overdue at the library.

_____   16.   The dean finally decided.

_____   17.   To put off the announcement for one more day.

_____   18.   If the outcome had been better.

_____   19.   Actually, the results have not yet been posted.

_____   20.   What the other students were able to do.

7B. Compound Sentence Structure

A *compound* sentence is a sentence that has more than one **main clause**[2]. The main clauses in a compound sentence can be connected correctly with either a coordinate conjunction (*and, but, so, or, yet*) and a comma or with a semi-colon (*;*).

> Tom drove too fast. He got a ticket for speeding.
> Tom drove too fast, so he got a ticket for speeding.
> Tom drove too fast; he got a ticket for speeding.

In the first example, the two main clauses *Tom drove too fast* and *He got a ticket for speeding* are not connected into a compound sentence. In the second example, the two main clauses are combined into a compound sentence with the coordinate conjunction *so* and a comma. In the third example, the same two clauses are combined into a compound sentence with a semi-colon.

It is possible to use adverb transitions in compound sentences. It is important to note that adverb transitions are not conjunctions, so either a semi-colon or a coordinate conjunction with a comma is needed.

> Tom drove too fast. As a result, he got a ticket for speeding.
> Tom drove too fast, and he got a ticket for speeding as a result.
> Tom drove too fast; as a result, he got a ticket for speeding.

In the first example, the two main clauses *Tom drove too fast* and *he got a ticket for speeding* are not combined into a compound sentence even though the adverb transition *As a result* is used. In the second example, the two main clauses are combined into a compound sentence with the coordinate conjunction *and* and a comma; the adverb transition *as a result* is included at the end of the compound sentence. In the third example, the same two main clauses are combined into a compound sentence with a semi-colon, and the adverb transition is set off from the second main clause with a comma.

The following chart lists some commonly used adverb transitions:

ADVERB TRANSITIONS			
TIME	CAUSE	CONTRAST	CONDITION
afterwards *next* *then* *finally*	*as a result* *consequently* *therefore*	*however* *in contrast*	*otherwise*

---

[2]A **main clause** is an independent clause that has both a subject and a verb. It is not introduced by a subordinate connector. Compound sentences are covered in Skill 6 of the Structure section on pages 209–211.

EXERCISE 7B: Underline the subjects once and the verbs twice in the main clauses. Put boxes around the punctuation, transitions, and connectors that join the main clauses. Then indicate if the sentences are correct (C) or incorrect (I).

__I__   1.   The <u>researcher</u> <u><u>completed</u></u> the study, the <u>results</u> <u><u>were</u></u> quite surprising.

_____   2.   The meeting did not take place today, so it will have to be rescheduled.

_____   3.   I expected the exam to be on Tuesday, however it was on Monday instead.

_____   4.   The department's sales were very high; as a result, the manager has been given a bonus.

_____   5.   We finished the last details and then we submitted the final report.

_____   6.   The employees often come late to work, but this does not seem to be a problem.

_____   7.   The team won its last three games. Next, it will compete in the championship tournament.

_____   8.   The light bulb in the lamp has burned out I need to replace the bulb.

_____   9.   The manager is hiring some more employees, then we will not have to work so much.

_____   10.   The textbook chapter was quite long, yet I finished it by 10:00.

_____   11.   You must turn in the paper by Friday, otherwise your grade will be lowered.

_____   12.   The decision has not yet been made. Therefore, we must wait to learn the final outcome.

_____   13.   Afterwards construction on the highway was completed, traffic moved more smoothly.

_____   14.   This course requires a lot of work; in contrast, the other course required very little.

_____   15.   Our flight is scheduled to board soon, we must head over to the gate now.

_____   16.   The building has a tower; the tower is on the north side of the building.

_____   17.   We have to see the professor now, or we will have to wait until next week.

_____   18.   I have worked hard for several months; finally, I will be able to rest.

_____   19.   The bookstore is open for another hour we should go there right now.

_____   20.   It has been raining steadily for days, consequently, the streets are flooded.

7C. Complex Sentence Structure

A *complex* sentence is a sentence that has at least one main clause and one **subordinate clause**[3]. Noun, adjective, and adverb clauses are all types of subordinate clauses. Each of these sentences is a complex sentence because it contains a subordinate clause:

They do not understand (what I said).
NOUN CLAUSE

The professor (who wrote the book) is giving the lectures.
ADJECTIVE CLAUSE

Final grades will be available (after the semester ends).
ADVERB CLAUSE

The first complex sentence contains the subordinate noun clause *what I said*. The second complex sentence contains the subordinate adjective clause *who wrote the book*. The final complex sentence contains the subordinate adverb clause *after the semester ends*.

A variety of errors with complex sentence structures can occur in student writing, but the following two errors occur with great frequency: (1) repeated subjects after adjective clauses, and (2) repeated subjects after noun clauses as subjects.

The movie (that we saw last night) it* was really funny.
S   ADJECTIVE CLAUSE   S   V

(What she told me yesterday) it* was quite confusing.
NOUN CLAUSE - S   S   V

The first sentence is incorrect because it contains an extra subject. The correct subject *movie* comes before the adjective clause *that we saw last night,* and an extra subject *it* comes after the adjective clause. To correct this sentence, you should omit the extra subject *it.* The second sentence is also incorrect because it contains an extra subject. The noun clause *What she told me yesterday* is a subject, and this noun clause subject is followed by an extra subject *it.* To correct this sentence, you should omit the extra subject *it.*

The following chart outlines what you should remember about editing complex sentences:

COMPLEX SENTENCES
1. When a subject comes before an adjective clause, do not add an extra subject after the adjective clause.
2. When a noun clause is used as a subject, do not add an extra subject after the noun clause.

---

[3]A **subordinate clause** is a dependent clause. It has both a subject and a verb and is introduced by a subordinate connector. Complex sentences with subordinate noun, adverb, and adjective clauses are covered in great detail in Skills 7–12 of the Structure section on pages 211–226.

EXERCISE 7C: Underline the subjects once and the verbs twice in the main clauses. Put parentheses around the subordinate noun and adjective clauses. Then indicate if the sentences are correct (C) or incorrect (I).

__I__   1.   The <u>tickets</u> (that I ordered) <u>they</u> <u><u>will be delivered</u></u> tomorrow.

_____   2.   How I will be able to get all this work done is unclear.

_____   3.   The excuse that you gave me was not very credible.

_____   4.   What the lecturer said it was really quite amusing.

_____   5.   The place where we agreed to meet it was quite secluded.

_____   6.   The person whose friendship I cherish most is a friend from my childhood.

_____   7.   Who is responsible for the accident it is unknown.

_____   8.   That the story is on the front page of the paper it is indisputable.

_____   9.   The contractor who painted the house he did a very careful job.

_____   10.   Why she was the one who got the job is a mystery to me.

_____   11.   What happened just before our arrival it is unknown.

_____   12.   The clothes that we purchased at the sale were quite a good bargain.

_____   13.   The room in which the seminar will be held is rather tiny.

_____   14.   What will happen to her next it is what concerns me the most.

_____   15.   The receptionist who regularly answers the phone is out of the office.

_____   16.   What the manager wrote in the report it was highly complimentary.

_____   17.   The classmate who presented the report he did a great job.

_____   18.   How such a thing could happen is not clear to me.

_____   19.   The situation in which I found myself was one in which all of the facts are not known.

_____   20.   Why he has done what I told him not to do with the money that I gave him it is not certain.

EXERCISE 7 (A-C): Find and correct the sentence structure errors in the following essay. (The number in parentheses at the end of each paragraph indicates the number of errors in that paragraph.) The essay discusses the following topic.

> Some people prefer to take vacations in quiet, natural places, while others prefer to spend their vacation time in big cities. Discuss the advantages of each type of vacation. Then indicate which you prefer and why.

1.   What you need to do before going on a vacation it is to decide where you will go on your vacation. You may decide to go to a quiet place with a quiet and natural setting, instead you may decide to go to a big city with a fast-paced life. Each of these types of vacation something to offer. (3 errors)

2.   The reasons that it can be a good idea to go to a quiet and natural location for a vacation they are numerous. First of all, a vacation in a natural setting allowing you to relax and slow down the pace of your life for a while. Instead of hurrying from place to place as you are used to doing. You can spend your time doing nothing more than enjoying the beauty of the location. Then, after are thoroughly relaxed, what you can do it is to take part in outdoor activities such as hiking or swimming. All of this will leave you completely relaxed and free of stress by the end of your vacation. (5 errors)

3.   It can be nice to go to a quiet and natural spot for a vacation, however it can also be quite an adventure to go to a big and fast-paced city for a vacation. The main reason that it can be a good idea to take a vacation in a big city it is to take part in so many activities that are unavailable in your hometown. On a big city vacation, numerous cultural events that might not be available in your hometown, such as theatrical performances, concerts, and art and museum exhibits, they are available. On a big city vacation, will also have access to some of the world's finest restaurants and shopping. After your big city vacation has ended. You will have a whole range of new experiences that are not part of your daily life. (5 errors)

4.   For me, the type of vacation that I decide to take it depends on my life prior to the vacation. I work as a legal assistant in a law office, this job is often repetitious and dull but is sometimes quite frantic just prior to a major case. After a slow and boring period of work. All I want is to head to a fast-paced vacation in a big city. However, if my job been frantic and busy prior to my vacation, then want to head to a quiet and beautiful place where I can relax. Thus, I enjoy different types of vacations, the type of vacation depends on the pace of my life before the vacation. (6 errors)

Skill 8: EDIT WRITTEN EXPRESSION

8A. Inversions and Agreement

Errors in inversions and agreement are covered in the Structure section of this book. You may want to review these skills.

> Skills 15–19: Sentences with Inverted Subjects and Verbs
> Skills 20–23: Problems with Subject/Verb Agreement

EXERCISE 8A: Find and correct the errors in the following essay. (The number in parentheses at the end of each paragraph indicates the number of errors in that paragraph.) The essay discusses the following topic.

> Some people prefer to work for a company, while others prefer to work for themselves. Discuss the advantages of each position. Then indicate which you prefer and why.

1.   Something very important for students to decide as they near the end of their studies are whether should they work for another company or go into business for themselves. As a university student, this decision about my future are one that I face soon myself. To me, each of these positions have clear advantages, in particular depending on the stage of your career. (4 errors)

2.   There is numerous advantages to working for another company, particularly early in your career. One of the advantages are that working in someone else's company provide a situation with the security of a regular paycheck and less responsibility than you would have you were to be the owner of the company. Also, not until you start your own business you need to come up with the finances to back the company. Thus, all of this indicate that it is better to work for other people early in your career while you are gaining the knowledge and experience you need to start your own company. (6 errors)

3.   Then, later in your career, it may be advantageous for you to go into business for yourself. The main reason for going into business for yourself are that in your own company you are able to decide on what direction do you want your company to go. However, only when you have gained enough knowledge and experience are it a good idea to go into business for yourself. This is when will you be ready to deal with the responsibility, pressure, and financial needs of owning a company. (4 errors)

4.   Nothing are more important to me than having my own company one day. However, what seems very clear to me now is that beginning my career working in someone else's company are best. In this situation, not only I can work with more security and less pressure, but I can also build up my financial resources and learn from others. Then, I should manage to gain enough experience, knowledge, and confidence and build up my financial resources, I hope eventually to open my own company, where can I determine exactly how would I like the company to operate. (6 errors)

8B. Parallel, Comparative, and Superlative Structures

Errors in parallel, comparative, and superlative structures are covered in the Structure section of this book. You may want to review these skills.

Skills 24–26: Problems with Parallel Structure
Skills 27–29: Problems with Comparatives and Superlatives

EXERCISE 8B: Find and correct the errors in the following essay. (The number in parentheses at the end of each paragraph indicates the number of errors in that paragraph.) The essay discusses the following topic.

> Do you agree or disagree with the following statement?
>
> *The primary reason to get an education is to succeed financially.*
>
> Support your response with reasons and examples.

1. I am a university student, and I am studying in the university for a number of reasons. Of course, one of my reasons for going to school, studying hard, and obtain a university degree is to succeed financially; the more money I make, it will be better for me. However, financial success is not my most importantest reason for going to the university. Instead, I am going to the university for a much broad reason than that: I believe that a university education will give me a much rich and better life, not just in a financial way. (5 errors)

2. One way that a university education makes your life enjoyabler is to give you the opportunity to have a career that you really desire and appreciative. Having a career that you like is much better than a job that just pays the bills. I, for example, am studying to be a marine biologist. I will have the better career for me; I will be rewarded not only in terms of money and also in terms of enjoyment of my career. (5 errors)

3. Another way that a university education can enrich your life is to provide a broadest knowledge, understand, and appreciation of the world around you than you already have. It provides you with an understanding of both the history of your own culture and to influence history on the present. It also provides you with an understanding of other cultures and shows you that other cultures are neither exactly the same as nor they are completely different from your own culture. Finally, it provides you with an understanding of the universe around you and showing you how the universe functions. (5 errors)

4. Thus, in getting a university education, I can say that financial success is certainly one goal that I have. However, the goal of financial success is not as important as I have another goal. My primary goal in getting a university education is the goal of achieving a more full life, certainly one with financial security but more importantly one that is rewarding both in terms of professional opportunities or in terms of awareness and understanding of life around me. The closer I get to achieving this goal, I will be happier. (4 errors)

8C. Verbs

Errors in verbs are covered in the Structure section of this book. You may want to review these skills.

Skills 30–32: Problems with the Form of the Verb
Skills 33–36: Problems with the Use of the Verb
Skills 37–38: Problems with Passive Verbs

EXERCISE 8C: Find and correct the errors in the following essay. (The number in parentheses at the end of each paragraph indicates the number of errors in that paragraph.) The essay discusses the following topic.

> When something unexpected happens, how do you react? Use examples to support your response.

1.   When something unexpected happens, different people reacted in a variety of ways. I wish I could reacted calmly to unexpected situations. However, unfortunately, I usually react with panic. The following example shows my usual reaction to situations when I have be completely unprepared for them. (3 errors)

2.   This example of the way that I react to unexpected situations has occurred in history class last week. The professor had told us that we will be covering the material in Chapters 10 through 12 in class on Thursday. By the time I arrived in class, I have read all of the assigned material, and I understood most of what I had study. While I was relax in my chair at the beginning of class, the professor announces that there would be a pop quiz on the material in the assigned chapters. I was preparing on the material because I have studied all of it thoroughly before class. (8 errors)

3.   However, I was face with an unexpected situation, and I do not react well to unexpected situations. Instead of feeling relaxed at the announcement of the unexpected quiz because I was so prepared, I was completely fill with anxiety by the situation. As the professor was write the questions on the board, I become more and more nervous. I was unable to think clearly, and I knew that I would done a bad job on the quiz because this was what always happens to me when I feel panic. As I stared at the questions on the board, I had been unable to think of the correct answers. It was as if I had not prepare at all for class. Then, the professor collected the papers from the class, including my basically blank piece of paper. Just after the papers had been collecting, the answers to all the questions came to me. (9 errors)

4.   You can seen from this example that my usual reaction to something unexpected is to panic. In the future, I hoped that I will learn to react more calmly, but up to now I had not learned to react this way. On the basis of my past behavior, however, it seems that I currently had a stronger tendency to react with panic than with calm. (4 errors)

8D. Nouns and Pronouns

Errors in nouns and pronouns are covered in the Structure section of this book. You may want to review these skills.

Skills 39–42: Problems with Nouns
Skills 43–45: Problems with Pronouns

EXERCISE 8D: Find and correct the errors in the following essay. (The number in parentheses at the end of each paragraph indicates the number of errors in that paragraph.) The essay discusses the following topic.

> What part of your high school experience was the most valuable? Use reasons and examples to support your response.

1.   *I was not a very good athleticism in high school, but I wanted with all of mine heart to be on the football team. My desire to be on the team had little to do with athletics and was perhaps not for the best of reasons; the strong stimuli for I to make the team was that team members were well-known in the school and he became very popular. This desire to be on the football team in high school, and the fact that through hard worker I managed to accomplish something that I wanted so much, even if its was something petty, turned out to be the single most valuable experiences of my years in high school. (8 errors)*

2.   *I had to work very hard to make the football team in high school, and for some time this seemed like an impossible goals. A large amount of students in my school, more than a hundred and fifty of them, spent many of theirs afternoons trying out for a team with less than forty positions. After a lot of hard work on my part, and after I had demonstrated to the coaches that he could count on me to keep going long after everyone was exhausted, I managed to make the team as a secondary play. Even with so many effort, I was never going to be a sports phenomena or even a member of the first team, but I did accomplish my goal of making the team.*
(8 errors)

3.   *The valuable lesson that I learned through this experience was not the joy of competitor or the much benefits of teamwork, several lesson very commonly associated with participation in team sports. Instead, the valuable lesson that I learned was that hard work and determination could be very important in helping I accomplish each goals that I want to reach. Even if others have more talent, I can work harder than it does and still perhaps find successor where them do not.*
(8 errors)

8E. Adjectives and Adverbs

Errors in adjectives and adverbs are covered in the Structure section of this book. You may
want to review these skills.

Skills 46–48: Problems with Adjectives and Adverbs
Skills 49–51: More Problems with Adjectives
Skills 52–55: Problems with Articles

EXERCISE 8E: Find and correct the errors in the following essay. (The number in parentheses at the end of each paragraph indicates the number of errors in that paragraph.)
The essay discusses the following topic.

> Some students prepare early, while other students procrastinate.
> Which type of student are you? Support your response with reasons
> and examples.

1.   I understand that it seems importantly for a students to prepare early their
assignments rather than procrastinate in getting assignments done. However,
although I understand this clear, I always seem to wait until the finally minute to
get assigning projects done. There are two reasons why I regular procrastinate on
my assignments academic in spite of the fact that this is not a best way to get
my work done. (9 errors)

2.   One reason that I tend to be a eternal procrastinator is that I work much more
efficient under pressure than I do when I am not under pressure. For example, I can
accomplish so much more in a two-hour period when I have a definitely deadline in
two hours than I can during an alike period without the pressure of a deadline
strict. Without a deadline, the two-hour period seems to fly by with minimally
accomplishment, but with an rapid approached deadline I seem quite capably of
making every minute of the two-hour period count. (10 errors)

3.   Another reason that I tend to procrastinate is that if I start preparing early, it
takes generally more of my time. If, for example, I have paper due in six weeks, I can
start working on the paper now and work on it on a day basis, and that paper will
take up a lot of my time and energy during the followed six weeks. However, if I wait
to begin work on the paper until week before it is due, I have to go off some place
where I can be lone and spend all of my time and energy that week on the paper, but
it will only take one week of my time valuable and not six weeks. (7 errors)

4.   In summary, it seems that I always wait until the last minute to complete an
assignments because I am afraid that I will waste too much time by starting early.
It would be good idea, however, for me to make a effort to get work done efficient
and early so that I do not always have to feel tensely about getting work done at a
last minute. (6 errors)

8F. Prepositions and Usage

Errors in prepositions and usage are covered in the Structure section of this book. You may want to review these skills.

Skills 56–57: Problems with Prepositions
Skills 58–60: Problems with Usage

EXERCISE 8F: Find and correct the errors in the following essay. (The number in parentheses at the end of each paragraph indicates the number of errors in that paragraph.) The essay discusses the following topic.

> Some people avoid confrontations at all costs, while other people seem to seek them out. Discuss each type of person. Then indicate which type of person you are and why.

1. Some people make their best to avoid confrontations, while another people often seem to get involved confrontations. There can be problems with either type of behavior; thus, I always try to be dislike people at either extreme and remain moderate in my approach at confrontation. (5 errors)

2. To some people, confrontation should be avoided for all costs. These people will make nothing even after something terribly wrong has happened to them. They, for example, stay silent when they are pushed around or when they are blamed something they did not do. Unfortunately, it is quite probable that others will take advantage from people alike this. Thus, people who avoid confrontations will find that they do not get as much out life as they deserve because other always take advantage of them. (7 errors)

3. Alike people who avoid confrontations, others individuals go to the opposite extreme; they take part for confrontations too easily. When something small happens accidentally, they become enraged and do a big deal of it as if they had been terribly wronged. Perhaps, for example, someone accidentally bumps in them or mistakenly says something offensive; in this type of situation, they create a serious confrontation. While it is true that other people will try hard not to provoke this type of person, it is also true that other will do an effort to avoid spending much time in the company of such a person. Thus, people who get involved in confrontations easily will find it hard to develop close friendships and relationships with anothers. (8 errors)

4. I try to make the right thing by avoiding either extreme type of behavior. I always try to behave in an alike manner, without overreacting or underreacting. If someone offends me with chance, I try to brush it and keep in going as if nothing had happened me. If someone intentionally succeeds on bothering me, however, I try to react without anger but with a reaction that shows that behavior alike this is unacceptable. In this way, I do not do the mistake of wasting time on unimportant situations, but I prevent others instances of bad behavior toward me for recurring. (11 errors)

COMPLETE TESTS

COLMPLETE TEST (Paper)

SECTION 1
LISTENING COMPREHENSION
Time—approximately 35 minutes
(including the reading of the directions for each part)

In this section of the test, you will have an opportunity to demonstrate your ability to understand conversations and talks in English. There are three parts to this section. Answer all the questions on the basis of what is <u>stated</u> or <u>implied</u> by the speakers you hear. Do <u>not</u> take notes or write in your test book at any time. Do not turn the pages until you are told to do so.

Part A

<u>Directions:</u> In Part A you will hear short conversations between two people. After each conversation, you will hear a question about the conversation. The conversations and questions will not be repeated. After you hear a question, read the four possible answers in your test book and choose the best answer. Then, on your answer sheet, find the number of the question and fill in the space that corresponds to the letter of the answer you have chosen.

Listen to an example.

Sample Answer
Ⓐ
Ⓑ
Ⓒ
●

On the recording, you hear:

(man)	*That exam was just awful.*
(woman)	*Oh, it could have been worse.*
(narrator)	*What does the woman mean?*

In your test book, you read:
(A) The exam was really awful.
(B) It was the worst exam she had ever seen.
(C) It couldn't have been more difficult.
(D) It wasn't that hard.

You learn from the conversation that the man thought the exam was very difficult and that the woman disagreed with the man. The best answer to the question, "What does the woman mean?" is (D), "It wasn't that hard." Therefore, the correct choice is (D).

Wait

1. (A) Carla does not live very far away.
   (B) What Carla said was unjust.
   (C) He does not fear what anyone says.
   (D) Carla is fairly rude to others.

2. (A) She thinks it's an improvement.
   (B) The fir trees in it are better.
   (C) It resembles the last one.
   (D) It is the best the man has ever done.

3. (A) He graduated last in his class.
   (B) He is the last person in his family to graduate.
   (C) He doesn't believe he can improve gradually.
   (D) He has finally finished his studies.

4. (A) He's surprised there were five dresses.
   (B) It was an unexpectedly inexpensive dress.
   (C) He would like to know what color dress it was.
   (D) The dress was not cheap.

5. (A) Leave the car somewhere else.
   (B) Ignore the parking tickets.
   (C) Add more money to the meter.
   (D) Pay the parking attendant.

6. (A) He does not like to hold too many books at one time.
   (B) There is no bookstore in his neighborhood.
   (C) It's not possible to obtain the book yet.
   (D) He needs to talk to someone at the bookstore.

7. (A) It was incomplete.
   (B) It finished on time.
   (C) It was about honor.
   (D) It was too long.

8. (A) She needs to use the man's notes.
   (B) Yesterday's physics class was quite boring.
   (C) She took some very good notes in physics class.
   (D) She would like to lend the man her notes.

9. (A) It's her birthday today.
   (B) She's looking for a birthday gift.
   (C) She wants to go shopping with her dad.
   (D) She wants a new wallet for herself.

10. (A) He prefers cold water.
    (B) His toes are too big.
    (C) The pool felt quite refreshing.
    (D) He didn't go for a swim.

11. (A) She just left her sister's house.
    (B) Her sister is not at home.
    (C) She's not exactly sure where her sweater is.
    (D) She doesn't know where her sister lives.

12. (A) She doesn't have time to complete additional reports.
    (B) She cannot finish the reports that she is already working on.
    (C) She is scared of having responsibility for the reports.
    (D) It is not time for the accounting reports to be compiled.

13. (A) He's had enough exercise.
    (B) He's going to give himself a reward for the hard work.
    (C) He's going to stay on for quite some time.
    (D) He would like to give the woman an exercise machine as a gift.

14. (A) He cannot see the huge waves.
    (B) The waves are not coming in.
    (C) He would like the woman to repeat what she said.
    (D) He agrees with the woman.

15. (A) The exam was postponed.
    (B) The man should have studied harder.
    (C) Night is the best time to study for exams.
    (D) She is completely prepared for the exam.

GO ON TO THE NEXT PAGE

16. (A) Students who want to change schedules should form a line.
    (B) It is only possible to make four changes in the schedule.
    (C) It is necessary to submit the form quickly.
    (D) Problems occur when people don't wait their turn.

17. (A) In a mine
    (B) In a jewelry store
    (C) In a clothing store
    (D) In a bank

18. (A) A visit to the woman's family
    (B) The telephone bill
    (C) The cost of a new telephone
    (D) How far away the woman's family lives

19. (A) She hasn't met her new boss yet.
    (B) She has a good opinion of her boss.
    (C) Her boss has asked her about her impressions of the company.
    (D) Her boss has been putting a lot of pressure on her.

20. (A) The recital starts in three hours.
    (B) He intends to recite three different poems.
    (C) He received a citation on the third of the month.
    (D) He thinks the performance begins at three.

21. (A) Choose a new dentist
    (B) Cure the pain himself
    (C) Make an appointment with his dentist
    (D) Ask his dentist about the right way to brush

22. (A) It is almost five o'clock.
    (B) The man doesn't really need the stamps.
    (C) It is a long way to the post office.
    (D) It would be better to go after five o'clock.

23. (A) The article was placed on reserve.
    (B) The woman must ask the professor for a copy.
    (C) The woman should look through a number of journals in the library.
    (D) He has reservations about the information in the article.

24. (A) He needs to take a nap.
    (B) He hopes the woman will help him to calm down.
    (C) The woman just woke him up.
    (D) He is extremely relaxed.

25. (A) She doesn't think the news report is false.
    (B) She has never before reported on the news.
    (C) She never watches the news on television.
    (D) She shares the man's opinion about the report.

26. (A) Management will offer pay raises on Friday.
    (B) The policy has not yet been decided.
    (C) The manager is full of hot air.
    (D) The plane has not yet landed.

27. (A) He doesn't believe that it is really snowing.
    (B) The snow had been predicted.
    (C) The exact amount of snow is unclear.
    (D) He expected the woman to go out in the snow.

28. (A) She's going to take the test over again.
    (B) She thinks she did a good job on the exam.
    (C) She has not yet taken the literature exam.
    (D) She's unhappy with how she did.

29. (A) The door was unlocked.
    (B) It was better to wait outside.
    (C) He could not open the door.
    (D) He needed to take a walk.

30. (A) He nailed the door shut.
    (B) He is heading home.
    (C) He hit himself in the head.
    (D) He is absolutely correct.

GO ON TO THE NEXT PAGE ➤

Part B

Directions: In this part of the test, you will hear longer conversations. After each conversation, you will hear several questions. The conversations and questions will not be repeated.

After you hear a question, read the four possible answers in your test book and choose the best answer. Then, on your answer sheet, find the number of the question and fill in the space that corresponds to the letter of the answer you have chosen.

Remember, you are <u>not</u> allowed to take notes or write in your test book.

31. (A) The haircut is unusually short.
    (B) This is Bob's first haircut.
    (C) Bob doesn't know who gave him the haircut.
    (D) After the haircut, Bob's hair still touches the floor.

32. (A) It is just what he wanted.
    (B) He enjoys having the latest style.
    (C) He dislikes it immensely.
    (D) He thinks it will be cool in the summer.

33. (A) A broken mirror
    (B) The hairstylist
    (C) The scissors used to cut his hair
    (D) Piles of his hair

34. (A) "You should become a hairstylist."
    (B) "Please put it back on."
    (C) "It'll grow back."
    (D) "It won't grow fast enough."

35. (A) Every evening
    (B) Every week
    (C) Every Sunday
    (D) Every month

36. (A) That she was eighty-five years old
    (B) That a storm was coming
    (C) That she was under a great deal of pressure
    (D) That she wanted to become a weather forecaster

37. (A) In her bones
    (B) In her ears
    (C) In her legs
    (D) In her head

38. (A) Call his great-grandmother less often
    (B) Watch the weather forecasts with his great-grandmother
    (C) Help his great-grandmother relieve some of her pressures
    (D) Believe his great-grandmother's predictions about the weather

GO ON TO THE NEXT PAGE

1 □ 1 □ 1 □ 1 □ 1 □ 1 □ 1 □ 1

Part C

Directions: In this part of the test, you will hear several talks. After each talk, you will hear some questions. The talks and questions will not be repeated.

After you hear a question, read the four possible answers in your test book and choose the best answer. Then, on your answer sheet, find the number of the question and fill in the space that corresponds to the letter of the answer you have chosen.

Here is an example.

On the recording, you hear:

(narrator) *Listen to an instructor talk to his class about painting.*
(man) *Artist Grant Wood was a guiding force in the school of painting known as American regionalist, a style reflecting the distinctive characteristics of art from rural areas of the United States. Wood began drawing animals on the family farm at the age of three, and when he was thirty-eight one of his paintings received a remarkable amount of public notice and acclaim. This painting, called "American Gothic," is a starkly simple depiction of a serious couple staring directly out at the viewer.*

Now listen to a sample question.

Sample Answer

(narrator) *What style of painting is known as American regionalist?*

Ⓐ
Ⓑ
Ⓒ
●

In your test book, you read: (A) Art from America's inner cities
(B) Art from the central region of the United States
(C) Art from various urban areas in the United States
(D) Art from rural sections of America

The best answer to the question, "What style of painting is known as American regionalist?" is (D), "Art from rural sections of America." Therefore, the correct choice is (D).

Now listen to another sample question.

Sample Answer

(narrator) *What is the name of Wood's most successful painting?*

Ⓐ
Ⓑ
●
Ⓓ

In your test book, you read: (A) "American Regionalist"
(B) "The Family Farm in Iowa"
(C) "American Gothic"
(D) "A Serious Couple"

The best answer to the question, "What is the name of Wood's most successful painting?" is (C), "American Gothic." Therefore, the correct choice is (C).

Remember, you are <u>not</u> allowed to take notes or write in your test book.

39. (A) In a car
    (B) On a hike
    (C) On a tram
    (D) In a lecture hall

40. (A) It means they have big tears.
    (B) It means they like to swim.
    (C) It means they look like crocodiles.
    (D) It means they are pretending to be sad.

41. (A) They are sad.
    (B) They are warming themselves.
    (C) They are getting rid of salt.
    (D) They regret their actions.

42. (A) Taking photographs
    (B) Getting closer to the crocodiles
    (C) Exploring the water's edge
    (D) Getting off the tram

43. (A) Water Sports
    (B) Physics
    (C) American History
    (D) Psychology

44. (A) To cut
    (B) To move fast
    (C) To steer a boat
    (D) To build a ship

45. (A) To bring tea from China
    (B) To transport gold to California
    (C) To trade with the British
    (D) To sail the American river system

46. (A) A reading assignment
    (B) A quiz on Friday
    (C) A research paper for the end of the semester
    (D) Some written homework

47. (A) Writers
    (B) Actors
    (C) Athletes
    (D) Musicians

48. (A) He or she would see butterflies.
    (B) He or she would break a leg.
    (C) He or she would have shaky knees.
    (D) He or she would stop breathing.

49. (A) By staring at the audience
    (B) By breathing shallowly
    (C) By thinking about possible negative outcomes
    (D) By focusing on what needs to be done

50. (A) At two o'clock
    (B) At four o'clock
    (C) At six o'clock
    (D) At eight o'clock

**This is the end of Section 1.
Stop work on Section 1.**

Turn off the recording.

**Read the directions for Section 2 and begin work.
Do NOT read or work on any other section
of the test during the next 25 minutes.**

2 • 2 • 2 • 2 • 2 • 2 • 2 • 2 • 2

SECTION 2
STRUCTURE AND WRITTEN EXPRESSION
Time—25 minutes
(including the reading of the directions)
Now set your clock for 25 minutes.

This section is designed to measure your ability to recognize language that is appropriate for standard written English. There are two types of questions in this section, with special directions for each type.

Structure

Directions: Questions 1–15 are incomplete sentences. Beneath each sentence you will see four words or phrases, marked (A), (B), (C), and (D). Choose the <u>one</u> word or phrase that best completes the sentence. Then, on your answer sheet, find the number of the question and fill in the space that corresponds to the letter of the answer you have chosen. Fill in the space so that the letter inside the oval cannot be seen.

Look at the following examples.

Example I

The president _____ the election by a landslide.

(A) won
(B) he won
(C) yesterday
(D) fortunately

Sample Answer

● Ⓑ Ⓒ Ⓓ

The sentence should read, "The president won the election by a landslide." Therefore, you should choose (A).

Example II

When _____ the conference?

(A) the doctor attended
(B) did the doctor attend
(C) the doctor will attend
(D) the doctor's attendance

Sample Answer

Ⓐ ● Ⓒ Ⓓ

The sentence should read, "When did the doctor attend the conference?" Therefore, you should choose (B).

Now begin work on the questions.

GO ON TO THE NEXT PAGE

1. _____, the outermost layer of skin, is about as thick as a sheet of paper over most of the skin.

    (A) It is the epidermis
    (B) In the epidermis
    (C) The epidermis
    (D) The epidermis is

2. Sam Spade in *The Maltese Falcon* and Rick Blaine in *Casablanca* _____ of Humphrey Bogart's more famous roles.

    (A) they are two
    (B) two of them are
    (C) two of them
    (D) are two

3. The compound microscope has not one _____ two lenses.

    (A) and also
    (B) but
    (C) and there are
    (D) but there are

4. During the Precambrian period, the Earth's crust formed, and life _____ in the seas.

    (A) first appeared
    (B) first to appear
    (C) is first appearing
    (D) appearing

5. The hard palate forms a partition _____ and nasal passages.

    (A) the mouth
    (B) between the mouth
    (C) is between the mouth
    (D) it is between the mouth

6. Conditions required for seed germination include abundant water, an adequate supply of oxygen, and _____.

    (A) the temperatures must be appropriate
    (B) having appropriate temperatures
    (C) appropriate temperatures
    (D) appropriately temperate

7. When fluid accumulates against the eardrum, a second more insidious type of _____.

    (A) *otitis media* may develop
    (B) developing *otitis media*
    (C) the development of *otitis media*
    (D) to develop *otitis media*

8. Some general theories of motivation _____ of central motives, from which other motives develop.

    (A) identify a limited number
    (B) identification of a limited amount
    (C) identify a limited amount
    (D) identifying a limited number

9. Before the Statue of Liberty arrived in the United States, newspapers invited the public to help determine where _____ placed after its arrival.

    (A) should the statue be
    (B) the statue being
    (C) it should be the statue
    (D) the statue should be

10. Hydroelectric power can be produced by _____ and using tidal flow to run turbines.

    (A) water basins are dammed
    (B) damming water basins
    (C) to dam water basins
    (D) dams in water basins

11. Abraham Lincoln and Jefferson Davis, _____ of the Union and the Confederacy during the Civil War, were both born in Kentucky.

    (A) they were opposing presidents
    (B) were opposing presidents
    (C) opposing presidents
    (D) presidents opposed

GO ON TO THE NEXT PAGE →

12. A stock _____ at an inflated price is called a watered stock.

    (A) issued
    (B) is issued
    (C) it is issued
    (D) which issued

13. The leaves of the white mulberry provide food for silkworms, _____ silk fabrics are woven.

    (A) whose cocoons
    (B) from cocoons
    (C) whose cocoons are from
    (D) from whose cocoons

14. Not only _____ generate energy, but it also produces fuel for other fission reactors.

    (A) a nuclear breeder reactor
    (B) it is a nuclear breeder reactor
    (C) does a nuclear breeder reactor
    (D) is a nuclear breeder reactor

15. D.W. Griffith pioneered many of the stylistic features and filmmaking techniques _____ as the Hollywood standard.

    (A) that established
    (B) that became established
    (C) what established
    (D) what became established

GO ON TO THE NEXT PAGE

Written Expression

Directions: In questions 16–40, each sentence has four underlined words or phrases. The four underlined parts of the sentence are marked (A), (B), (C), and (D). Identify the <u>one</u> underlined word or phrase that must be changed in order for the sentence to be correct. Then, on your answer sheet, find the number of the question and fill in the space that corresponds to the letter of the answer you have chosen.

Look at the following examples.

Example I   **Sample Answer**

<u>The</u> four <u>string</u> on a violin <u>are</u> <u>tuned</u>
 A   B   C   D

in fifths.

Ⓐ
●
Ⓒ
Ⓓ

The sentence should read, "The four strings on a violin are tuned in fifths." Therefore, you should choose (B).

Example II   **Sample Answer**

The <u>research</u> <u>for the</u> book *Roots* <u>taking</u>
      A   B   C

Alex Haley <u>twelve years</u>.
               D

Ⓐ
Ⓑ
●
Ⓓ

The sentence should read, "The research for the book *Roots* took Alex Haley twelve years." Therefore, you should choose (C).

Now begin work on the questions.

GO ON TO THE NEXT PAGE ➔

16. Mosquitoes will <u>accepts</u> the <u>malaria</u> parasite at <u>only one</u> stage of the parasite's
A   B   C

<u>complex</u> life cycle.
D

17. The <u>counterpart</u> of a negative <u>electrons</u> is the <u>positive</u> proton.
     A   B   C   D

18. The ankle joint <u>occur</u> where the <u>lower</u> ends of the tibia and fibula slot <u>neatly</u> <u>around</u>
                A   B   C   D

the talus.

19. In the United States and Canada, <u>motor vehicle</u> laws <u>affect</u> the <u>operate</u> of
                                A   B   C

motorcycles <u>as well as</u> automobiles.
D

20. The neocortex <u>is</u>, in evolutionary <u>terms</u>, <u>most</u> recent <u>layer</u> of the brain.
             A   B   C   D

21. There <u>are</u> more than eighty-four million <u>specimens</u> in the National Museum of
      A   B

Natural History's <u>collection</u> of biological, geological, archeological, and
                   C

<u>anthropology</u> treasures.
D

22. <u>After</u> George Washington married <u>widow</u> Martha Custis, the couple <u>came to</u> <u>resides</u>
A   B   C   D

at Mount Vernon.

23. At this stage in <u>their</u> development, <u>rubberized</u> asphalt can <u>hardly</u> be classified <u>as</u>
                  A   B   C   D

cutting edge.

24. Rhesus monkeys <u>exhibit</u> patterns of <u>shy</u> similar <u>to</u> <u>those</u> in humans.
               A   B   C D

25. In space, with <u>no</u> gravity for muscles to work <u>against</u>, <u>the body</u> becomes <u>weakly</u>.
            A   B   C   D

26. Fort Jefferson, in the Dry Tortugas <u>off</u> the southern tip of Florida, can be <u>reach</u>
                            A   B   C

<u>only by</u> boat or plane.
D

GO ON TO THE NEXT PAGE

27. A zoom lens produces an inverted real image, either on the film in a camera and on
       A   B   C   D

    the light-sensitive tube of a television camera.

28. Supersonic flight is flight that is faster the speed of sound.
             A   B C   D

29. The Betataken House Ruins at Navajo National Monument is among the largest and
                                                      A   B

    most elaborate cliff dwellings in the country.
            C   D

30. It is a common observation that liquids will soak through some materials but not
            A   B   C

    through other.
          D

31. The number of wild horses on Assateague are increasing lately, resulting in
               A   B   C

    overgrazed marsh and dune grasses.
        D

32. The newsreels of Hearst Metronome News, which formed part of every moviegoer's
                                                        A

    experience in the era before television, offer an unique record of the events of the
                             B   C   D

    1930s.

33. Unlikely gas sport balloons, hot air balloons do not have nets.
       A   B   C   D

34. Born in Massachusetts in 1852, Albert Farbanks has begun making banjos in Boston
      A   B   C

    in the late 1870s.
        D

35. Dwight David Eisenhower, military officer and thirty-fourth president of the United
                                   A

    States, lived in the White House and of least thirty-seven other residences.
          B   C   D

36. Methane in wetlands comes from soil bacteria that consumes organic plant matter.
                      A   B   C   D

37. Alois Alzheimer made the first observers of the telltale signs of the disease that today
                            A   B

    bears his name.
     C   D

GO ON TO THE NEXT PAGE

38. Edward MacDowell <u>remembers</u> as the <u>composer</u> of such <u>perennial</u> favorites as "To a
                  A   B   C   D

   Wild Rose" and "To a Water Lily."

39. Animism is the <u>belief</u> that objects and natural <u>phenomena</u> such as rivers, rocks, and
                 A   B

   wind are <u>live</u> and have <u>feelings</u>.
        C   D

40. Newtonian physics <u>accounts</u> <u>for</u> the <u>observing</u> <u>orbits</u> of the planets and the moons.
                    A   B   C   D

This is the end of Section 2.
If you finish before 25 minutes has ended,
check your work on Section 2 only.

At the end of 25 minutes, go on to Section 3.
Use exactly 55 minutes to work on Section 3.

SECTION 3
READING COMPREHENSION
Time—55 minutes
(including the reading of the directions)
Now set your clock for 55 minutes.

This section is designed to measure your ability to read and understand short passages similar in topic and style to those that students are likely to encounter in North American universities and colleges.

Directions: In this section you will read several passages. Each one is followed by a number of questions about it. You are to choose the <u>one</u> best answer, (A), (B), (C), or (D), to each question. Then, on your answer sheet, find the number of the question and fill in the space that corresponds to the letter of the answer you have chosen.

Answer all questions about the information in a passage on the basis of what is <u>stated</u> or <u>implied</u> in that passage.

Read the following passage:

> John Quincy Adams, who served as the sixth president of the United States from 1825 to 1829, is today recognized for his masterful statesmanship and diplomacy. He dedicated his life to public service, both in the presidency and in the various other political offices that he
> *Line* held. Throughout his political career he demonstrated his unswerving belief in freedom of
> *(5)* speech, the antislavery cause, and the right of Americans to be free from European and Asian domination.

Example I   **Sample Answer**

To what did John Quincy Adams devote his life?

(A) Improving his personal life
(B) Serving the public
(C) Increasing his fortune
(D) Working on his private business

According to the passage, John Quincy Adams "dedicated his life to public service." Therefore, you should choose (B).

Example II   **Sample Answer**

In line 4, the word "unswerving" is closest in meaning to

(A) moveable
(B) insignificant
(C) unchanging
(D) diplomatic

The passage states that John Quincy Adams demonstrated his unswerving belief "throughout his career." This implies that the belief did not change. Therefore, you should choose (C).

Now begin work on the questions.

GO ON TO THE NEXT PAGE

Questions 1–10

The hippopotamus is the third largest land animal, smaller only than the elephant and the rhinoceros. Its name comes from two Greek words which mean "river horse." The long name of this animal is often shortened to the easier to handle term "hippo."

Line
(5) The hippo has a natural affinity for the water. It does not float on top of the water; instead, it can easily walk along the bottom of a body of water. The hippo commonly remains underwater for three to five minutes and has been known to stay under for up to half an hour before coming up for air.

In spite of its name, the hippo has relatively little in common with the horse and instead has a number of interesting similarities in common with the whale. When a hippo comes up after a stay at the bottom of a lake or river, it releases air through a blowhole, just like a whale. In addition, the
(10) hippo resembles the whale in that they both have thick layers of blubber for protection and they are almost completely hairless.

1. The topic of this passage is

   (A) the largest land animals
   (B) the derivations of animal names
   (C) the characteristics of the hippo
   (D) the relation between the hippo and the whale

2. It can be inferred from the passage that the rhinoceros is

   (A) smaller than the hippo
   (B) equal in size to the elephant
   (C) a hybrid of the hippo and the elephant
   (D) one of the two largest types of land animals

3. The possessive "Its" in line 2 refers to

   (A) hippopotamus
   (B) elephant
   (C) rhinoceros
   (D) horse

4. It can be inferred from the passage that the hippopotamus is commonly called a hippo because the word "hippo" is

   (A) simpler to pronounce
   (B) scientifically more accurate
   (C) the original name
   (D) easier for the animal to recognize

5. The word "float" in line 4 is closest in meaning to

   (A) sink
   (B) drift
   (C) eat
   (D) flap

6. According to the passage, what is the maximum time that hippos have been known to stay underwater?

   (A) Three minutes
   (B) Five minutes
   (C) Thirty minutes
   (D) Ninety minutes

7. The expression "has relatively little in common" in line 7 could best be replaced by

   (A) has few interactions
   (B) is not normally found
   (C) has minimal experience
   (D) shares few similarities

8. The passage states that one way in which a hippo is similar to a whale is that

   (A) they both live on the bottoms of rivers
   (B) they both have blowholes
   (C) they are both named after horses
   (D) they both breathe underwater

9. The word "blubber" in line 10 is closest in meaning to

   (A) fat
   (B) metal
   (C) water
   (D) skin

10. The passage states that the hippo does not
    (A) like water
    (B) resemble the whale
    (C) have a protective coating
    (D) have much hair

GO ON TO THE NEXT PAGE

Questions 11–19

John James Audubon, nineteenth-century artist and naturalist, is known as one of the foremost authorities on North American birds. Born in Les Cayes, Haiti, in 1785, Audubon was raised in France and studied art under French artist Jacques-Louis David. After settling on his father's
Line Pennsylvania estate at the age of eighteen, he first began to study and paint birds.
(5) In his young adulthood, Audubon undertook numerous enterprises, generally without a tremendous amount of success; at various times during his life he was involved in a mercantile business, a lumber and grist mill, a taxidermy business, and a school. His general mode of operating a business was to leave it either unattended or in the hands of a partner and take off on excursions through the wilds to paint the natural life that he saw. His business career came to end in 1819 when
(10) he was jailed for debt and forced to file for bankruptcy.
It was at that time that Audubon began seriously to pursue the dream of publishing a collection of his paintings of birds. For the next six years he painted birds in their natural habitats while his wife worked as a teacher to support the family. His *Birds of America*, which included engravings of 435 of his colorful and lifelike water colors, was published in parts during the period from 1826 to 1838 in
(15) England. After the success of the English editions, American editions of his work were published in 1839, and his fame and fortune were ensured.

11. This passage is mainly about

    (A) North American birds
    (B) Audubon's route to success as a painter of birds
    (C) the works that Audubon published
    (D) Audubon's preference for travel in natural habitats

12. The word "foremost" in line 1 is closest in meaning to

    (A) prior
    (B) leading
    (C) first
    (D) largest

13. In the second paragraph, the author mainly discusses

    (A) how Audubon developed his painting style
    (B) Audubon's involvement in a mercantile business
    (C) where Audubon went on his excursions
    (D) Audubon's unsuccessful business practices

14. The word "mode" in line 7 could best be replaced by

    (A) method
    (B) vogue
    (C) average
    (D) trend

15. Audubon decided not to continue to pursue business when

    (A) he was injured in an accident at a grist mill
    (B) he decided to study art in France
    (C) he was put in prison because he owed money
    (D) he made enough money from his paintings

16. The word "pursue" in line 11 is closest in meaning to

    (A) imagine
    (B) share
    (C) follow
    (D) deny

GO ON TO THE NEXT PAGE →

17. According to the passage, Audubon's paintings

    (A) were realistic portrayals
    (B) used only black, white, and gray
    (C) were done in oils
    (D) depicted birds in cages

18. The word "support" in line 13 could best be replaced by

    (A) tolerate
    (B) provide for
    (C) side with
    (D) fight for

19. It can be inferred from the passage that after 1839 Audubon

    (A) unsuccessfully tried to develop new businesses
    (B) continued to be supported by his wife
    (C) traveled to Europe
    (D) became wealthy

GO ON TO THE NEXT PAGE

Questions 20–29

Schizophrenia is often confused with multiple personality disorder yet is quite distinct from it. Schizophrenia is one of the more common mental disorders, considerably more common than multiple personality disorder. The term "schizophrenia" is composed of roots which mean "a splitting

Line
(5)
of the mind," but it does not refer to a division into separate and distinct personalities, as occurs in multiple personality disorder. Instead, schizophrenic behavior is generally characterized by illogical thought patterns and withdrawal from reality. Schizophrenics often live in a fantasy world where they hear voices that others cannot hear, often voices of famous people. Schizophrenics tend to withdraw from families and friends and communicate mainly with the "voices" that they hear in their minds.

It is common for the symptoms of schizophrenia to develop during the late teen years or early
(10)
twenties, but the causes of schizophrenia are not well understood. It is believed that heredity may play a part in the onset of schizophrenia. In addition, abnormal brain chemistry also seems to have a role; certain brain chemicals, called neurotransmitters, have been found to be at abnormal levels in some schizophrenics.

20. The paragraph preceding the passage most probably discusses

   (A) the causes of schizophrenia
   (B) multiple personality disorder
   (C) the most common mental disorder
   (D) possible cures for schizophrenia

21. Which of the following is true about schizophrenia and multiple personality disorder?

   (A) They are relatively similar.
   (B) One is a psychological disorder, while the other is not.
   (C) Many people mistake one for the other.
   (D) Multiple personality disorder occurs more often than schizophrenia.

22. "Disorder" in line 3 is closest in meaning to which of the following?

   (A) Disruption
   (B) Untidiness
   (C) Misalignment
   (D) Disease

23. It can be inferred from the passage that a "schism" is

   (A) a division into factions
   (B) a mental disease
   (C) a personality trait
   (D) a part of the brain

24. What is NOT true about schizophrenia, according to the passage?

   (A) It is characterized by separate and distinct personalities.
   (B) It often causes withdrawal from reality.
   (C) Its symptoms include illogical thought patterns.
   (D) Its victims tend to hear voices in their minds.

25. According to the passage, how do schizophrenics generally relate to their families?

   (A) They are quite friendly with their families.
   (B) They become remote from their families.
   (C) They have an enhanced ability to understand their families.
   (D) They communicate openly with their families.

26. It can be inferred from the passage that it would be least common for schizophrenia to develop at the age of

   (A) fifteen
   (B) twenty
   (C) twenty-five
   (D) thirty

GO ON TO THE NEXT PAGE

27. The word "onset" in line 11 is closest in meaning to

    (A) start
    (B) medication
    (C) effect
    (D) age

28. The word "abnormal" in line 11 is closest in meaning to

    (A) unstable
    (B) unregulated
    (C) uncharted
    (D) unusual

29. Where in the passage does the author explain the derivation of the term "schizophrenia"?

    (A) Lines 3–5
    (B) Lines 5–6
    (C) Lines 9–10
    (D) Lines 11–13

GO ON TO THE NEXT PAGE

Questions 30–39

People are often surprised to learn just how long some varieties of trees can live. If asked to estimate the age of the oldest living trees on Earth, they often come up with guesses in the neighborhood of two or perhaps three hundred years. The real answer is considerably larger than

Line that, more than five thousand years.
(5) The tree that wins the prize for its considerable maturity is the bristlecone pine of California. This venerable pine predates wonders of the ancient world such as the pyramids of Egypt, the Hanging Gardens of Babylon, and the Colossus of Rhodes. It is not nearly as tall as the giant redwood that is also found in California, and, in fact, it is actually not very tall compared with many other trees, often little more than five meters in height. This relatively short height may be one of the

(10) factors that aid the bristlecone pine in living to a ripe old age—high winds and inclement weather cannot easily reach the shorter trees and cause damage. An additional factor that contributes to the long life of the bristlecone pine is that this type of tree has a high percentage of resin, which prevents rot from developing in the tree trunk and branches.

30. The best title for this passage would be

    (A) The Size of the Bristlecone Pine
    (B) Three-Hundred-Year-Old Forests
    (C) The Wonders of the Ancient World
    (D) An Amazingly Enduring Tree

31. The word "estimate" in line 2 is closest in meaning to

    (A) measure
    (B) approximate
    (C) evaluate
    (D) view

32. The expression "in the neighborhood of" in lines 2– 3 could best be replaced by

    (A) of approximately
    (B) on the same block as
    (C) with the friendliness of
    (D) located close to

33. It can be inferred from the passage that most people

    (A) are quite accurate in their estimates of the ages of trees
    (B) have two to three hundred trees in their neighborhoods
    (C) do not really have any idea how old the oldest trees on Earth are
    (D) can name some three-hundred-year-old trees

34. According to the passage, approximately how old are the oldest trees on Earth?

    (A) Two hundred years old
    (B) Three hundred years old
    (C) Five hundred years old
    (D) Five thousand years old

35. The word "venerable" in line 6 is closest in meaning to which of the following?

    (A) Ancient
    (B) Incredible
    (C) Towering
    (D) Unrecognizable

GO ON TO THE NEXT PAGE

36. The author mentions the Egyptian pyramids as an example of something that is

    (A) far away
    (B) believed to be strong
    (C) extremely tall
    (D) known to be old

37. Which of the following is true about the bristlecone pine?

    (A) It is as tall as the great pyramids.
    (B) It is never more than five meters in height.
    (C) It is short in comparison to many other trees.
    (D) It can be two to three hundred feet tall.

38. The word "inclement" in line 10 could best be replaced by

    (A) sunny
    (B) bad
    (C) unusual
    (D) strong

39. The passage states that resin

    (A) assists the tree trunks to develop
    (B) is found only in the bristlecone pine
    (C) flows from the branches to the tree trunk
    (D) helps stop rot from starting

GO ON TO THE NEXT PAGE

Questions 40–50

The organization that today is known as the Bank of America did start out in America, but under quite a different name. Italian American A.P. Giannini established this bank on October 17, 1904, in a renovated saloon in San Francisco's Italian community of North Beach under the name
Line Bank of Italy, with immigrants and first-time bank customers comprising the majority of his first
(5) customers. During its development, Giannini's bank survived major crises in the form of a natural disaster and a major economic upheaval that not all other banks were able to overcome.

One major test for Giannini's bank occurred on April 18, 1906, when a massive earthquake struck San Francisco, followed by a raging fire that destroyed much of the city. Giannini obtained two wagons and teams of horses, filled the wagons with the bank's reserves, mostly in the form of gold,
(10) covered the reserves with crates of oranges, and escaped from the chaos of the city with his clients' funds protected. In the aftermath of the disaster, Giannini's bank was the first to resume operations. Unable to install the bank in a proper office setting, Giannini opened up shop on the Washington Street Wharf on a makeshift desk created from boards and barrels.

In the period following the 1906 fire, the Bank of Italy continued to prosper and expand. By
(15) 1918 there were twenty-four branches of the Bank of Italy, and by 1928 Giannini had acquired numerous other banks, including a Bank of America located in New York City. In 1930 he consolidated all the branches of the Bank of Italy, the Bank of America in New York City, and another Bank of America that he had formed in California into the Bank of America National Trust and Savings Association.
(20) A second major crisis for the bank occurred during the Great Depression of the 1930s. Although Giannini had already retired prior to the darkest days of the Depression, he became incensed when his successor began selling off banks during the bad economic times. Giannini resumed leadership of the bank at the age of sixty-two. Under Giannini's leadership, the bank weathered the storm of the Depression and subsequently moved into a phase of overseas development.

40. According to the passage, Giannini
    (A) opened the Bank of America in 1904
    (B) worked in a bank in Italy
    (C) set up the Bank of America prior to setting up the Bank of Italy
    (D) later changed the name of the Bank of Italy

41. Where did Giannini open his first bank?
    (A) In New York City
    (B) In what used to be a bar
    (C) On Washington Street Wharf
    (D) On a makeshift desk

42. According to the passage, which of the following is NOT true about the San Francisco earthquake?
    (A) It happened in 1906.
    (B) It occurred in the aftermath of a fire.
    (C) It caused problems for Giannini's bank.
    (D) It was a tremendous earthquake.

43. The word "raging" in line 8 could best be replaced by
    (A) angered
    (B) localized
    (C) intense
    (D) feeble

44. It can be inferred from the passage that Giannini used crates of oranges after the earthquake
    (A) to hide the gold
    (B) to fill up the wagons
    (C) to provide nourishment for his customers
    (D) to protect the gold from the fire

45. The word "chaos" in line 10 is closest in meaning to
    (A) legal system
    (B) extreme heat
    (C) overdevelopment
    (D) total confusion

GO ON TO THE NEXT PAGE

46. The word "consolidated" in line 17 is closest in meaning to

    (A) hardened
    (B) merged
    (C) moved
    (D) sold

47. The passage states that after his retirement, Giannini

    (A) began selling off banks
    (B) caused economic misfortune to occur
    (C) supported the bank's new management
    (D) returned to work

48. The expression "weathered the storm of" in line 23 could best be replaced by

    (A) found a cure for
    (B) rained on the parade of
    (C) survived the ordeal of
    (D) blew its stack at

49. Where in the passage does the author describe Giannini's first banking clients?

    (A) Lines 2–5
    (B) Lines 7–8
    (C) Lines 12–13
    (D) Lines 14–16

50. The paragraph following the passage most likely discusses

    (A) bank failures during the Great Depression
    (B) a third major crisis of the Bank of America
    (C) the international development of the Bank of America
    (D) how Giannini spent his retirement

This is the end of Section 3.

If you finish in less than 55 minutes,
check your work on Section 3 only.
Do NOT read or work on any other section of the test.

TEST OF WRITTEN ENGLISH:
TWE ESSAY TOPIC
Time—30 minutes

Do you agree or disagree with the following statement?

People should never live at home with their parents after the age of twenty-five.

Use specific reasons and details to support your answer.

COMPLETE TEST (Computer)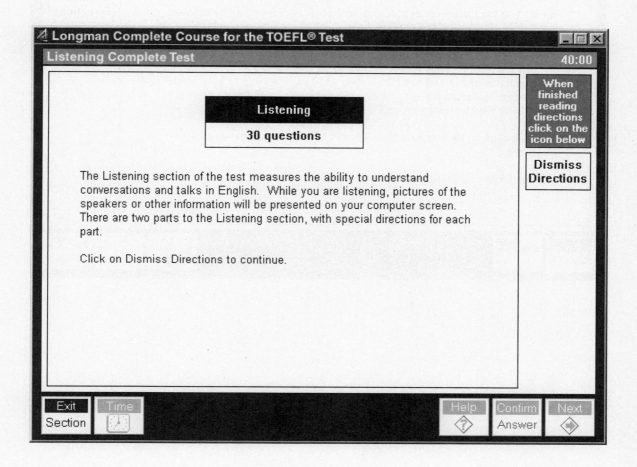
LISTENING

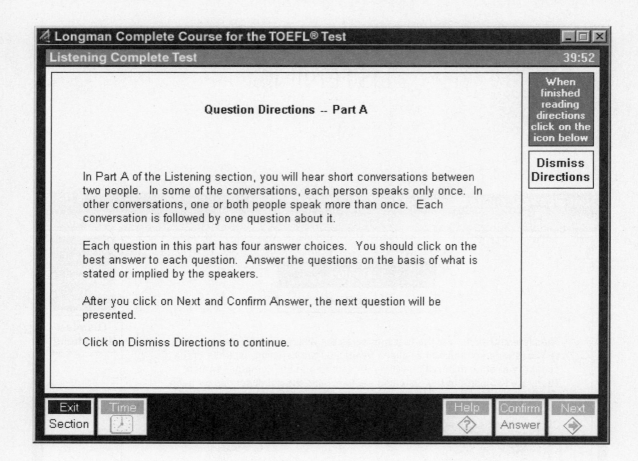

1. What does the woman mean?
   - ○ She could not comprehend the chemistry lecture.
   - ○ She has not had time to look at the assignment.
   - ○ It was possible for her to complete the problem.
   - ○ She could not understand the problem.

2. What does the woman mean?
   - ○ She will lend it to the man.
   - ○ She never lent the book to Jim.
   - ○ Jim wants to borrow the book.
   - ○ Jim has the book.

3. Who is Dr. Barton most likely to be?
   - ○ A physician
   - ○ An astronomer
   - ○ A philosopher
   - ○ An engineer

4. What does the woman suggest?
   - ○ Starting on their exam preparation
   - ○ Leaving for the exam
   - ○ Going home to study
   - ○ Going to her job

5. What does the woman say about the performance?
   - ○ It met her expectations.
   - ○ It was what she had hoped to see.
   - ○ It was rather mediocre.
   - ○ It was the last performance.

6. What does the man mean?
   ◯ He's already talked to the professor about the assignment.
   ◯ There is no assignment for tomorrow.
   ◯ He's not sure what the professor will talk about.
   ◯ The professor discussed the assignment only briefly.

7. What does the man mean?
   ◯ He doesn't know how far away the exhibit is.
   ◯ He's uncertain about the fee.
   ◯ The exhibit is not very far away.
   ◯ He's sure the exhibit is free.

8. What does the man mean?
   ◯ He thinks the lecture was really interesting.
   ◯ He's not sure if the ideas are workable.
   ◯ He understood nothing about the lecture.
   ◯ He's not sure what the woman would like to know.

9. What does the woman say to the man?
   ◯ He missed an opportunity.
   ◯ He was late for his trip.
   ◯ He should take the next boat.
   ◯ He should send in his application.

10. What had the woman expected?
    ◯ That John would pick them up for the concert
    ◯ That the concert would start earlier
    ◯ That John would not be going to the concert
    ◯ That they would be late to the concert

11. What does the man mean?
- ⬭ He enjoyed the trip immensely.
- ⬭ The boat trip was really rough.
- ⬭ He couldn't have enjoyed the trip more.
- ⬭ The water was not very rough.

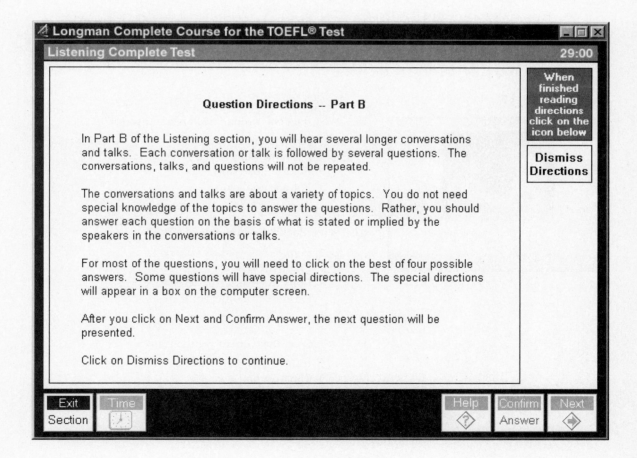

Longman Complete Course for the TOEFL® Test

Listening Complete Test   29:00

Question Directions -- Part B

In Part B of the Listening section, you will hear several longer conversations and talks. Each conversation or talk is followed by several questions. The conversations, talks, and questions will not be repeated.

The conversations and talks are about a variety of topics. You do not need special knowledge of the topics to answer the questions. Rather, you should answer each question on the basis of what is stated or implied by the speakers in the conversations or talks.

For most of the questions, you will need to click on the best of four possible answers. Some questions will have special directions. The special directions will appear in a box on the computer screen.

After you click on Next and Confirm Answer, the next question will be presented.

Click on Dismiss Directions to continue.

When finished reading directions click on the icon below

Dismiss Directions

Exit Section | Time | Help | Confirm Answer | Next

Questions 12–14

12. What does the man want to do?
    - ○ Cook dinner
    - ○ Visit his friend
    - ○ Surprise the woman
    - ○ Go out to eat

13. What does the woman not like about Clark's?
    - ○ The quality of the food
    - ○ The location of the restaurant
    - ○ The type of service
    - ○ The size of the portions

14. What do they finally decide to do?
    - ○ Share a meal
    - ○ Complain to the manager
    - ○ Go somewhere else
    - ○ Stay home for dinner

Questions 15–17

15. Why does the woman need her transcript?
    - ○ For a job interview
    - ○ For a meeting with the registrar
    - ○ For a scholarship
    - ○ For a school club

16. What does the woman need to do?
    - ○ Phone the registrar's office
    - ○ Complete a form
    - ○ Copy the transcript herself
    - ○ Request five different forms

17. When can the woman get the transcript?
    - ○ Immediately
    - ○ The next day
    - ○ In a few days
    - ○ In five weeks

Questions 18–21

Listen to a lecture in a government class. The professor is talking about Washington, D.C.

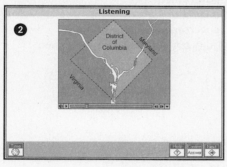

18. Which name has NOT been used for the city discussed in the lecture?

○ Columbia
○ Washington
○ District of Columbia
○ Washington, D.C.

19. The city of Washington, D.C. belongs to which state?

○ Virginia
○ Maryland
○ Washington
○ none of the above

20. Identify the part of the map that used to belong to Washington, D.C. but no longer does.

Click on the correct letter.

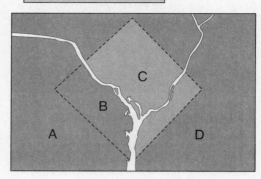

21. What is stated in the lecture about the government of Washington, D.C.?

Click on 2 answers.

☐ In the beginning, it did not elect its own government.
☐ In the beginning, it did elect its own government.
☐ Today it does not elect its own government.
☐ Today it elects its own government.

Questions 22–25

Listen to a discussion about a geography lecture. The discussion is on weather fronts.

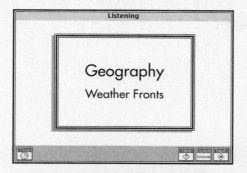

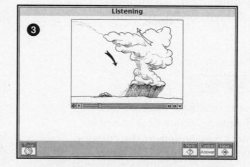

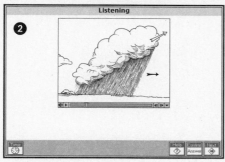

22. What is a weather front?
   - ◯ An entire mass of air
   - ◯ A kind of tropical storm
   - ◯ The leading edge of an air mass
   - ◯ A specific type of cloudy weather

23. Where do fronts originate?

   Click on 2 answers.

   - ☐ Cold fronts originate near the poles.
   - ☐ Warm fronts originate near the poles.
   - ☐ Cold fronts originate near the equator.
   - ☐ Warm fronts originate near the equator.

24. What is stated about a warm front?

   Click on 2 answers.

   - ☐ A warm front moves north in the northern hemisphere.
   - ☐ At a warm front, warm air moves under cold air.
   - ☐ There is slow and steady rain or snow at a warm front.
   - ☐ There is violent weather at a warm front.

25. What is stated about a cold front?
   - ◯ A cold front moves north in the northern hemisphere.
   - ◯ At a cold front, warm air moves under cold air.
   - ◯ There is slow and steady rain or snow at a cold front.
   - ◯ There is violent weather at a cold front.

Questions 26–30

Listen to a lecture in a gemology class. The professor is talking about the history of gem-cutting.

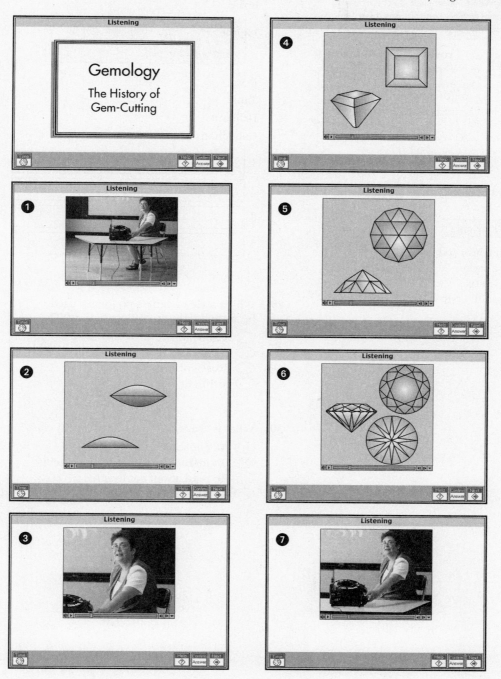

26. What are the characteristics of each of these gemstones?

Click on a word. Then click on the empty box in the correct column. Use each word only once.

brilliant	rose	cabochon
Unfaceted	Faceted only on the top	Faceted on the top and bottom

27. Which styles of stones were polished and not cut?

Click on 2 answers.

- ☐ The cabochon style
- ☐ The rose style
- ☐ The table style
- ☐ The brilliant style

28. The professor explains the order that each of these styles of gems appeared in history. Put the styles of gems in their historical order.

Click on a word. Then click on the space where it belongs. Use each word one time only.

Rose

Table

Brilliant

Cabochon

1
2
3
4

29. Which style of gem is no longer used because it does not reflect light well?

- ◯ Cabochon
- ◯ Table cut
- ◯ Rose cut
- ◯ Brilliant cut

30. What is the assignment for the next class?

- ◯ To cut some gems
- ◯ To identify the style of some gems
- ◯ To read about some gems
- ◯ To polish some gems

STRUCTURE (Computer)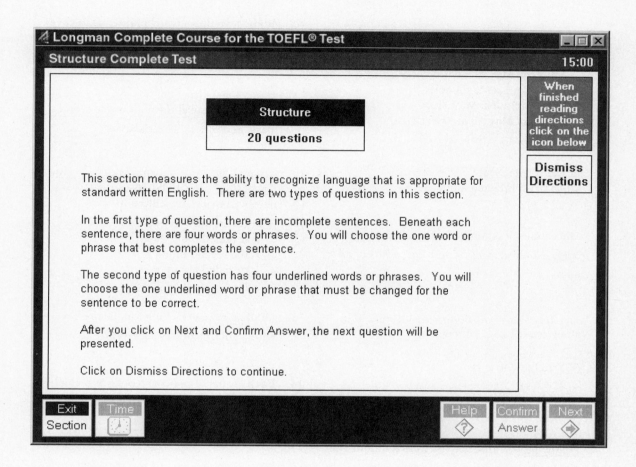

Longman Complete Course for the TOEFL® Test   ▭ ▭ ✕

Structure Complete Test   15:00

When finished reading directions click on the icon below

Dismiss Directions

> **Structure**
>
> **20 questions**

This section measures the ability to recognize language that is appropriate for standard written English. There are two types of questions in this section.

In the first type of question, there are incomplete sentences. Beneath each sentence, there are four words or phrases. You will choose the one word or phrase that best completes the sentence.

The second type of question has four underlined words or phrases. You will choose the one underlined word or phrase that must be changed for the sentence to be correct.

After you click on Next and Confirm Answer, the next question will be presented.

Click on Dismiss Directions to continue.

Exit Section   Time   Help   Confirm Answer   Next

1. Orchids <u>come</u> in a <u>wide variety</u> of <u>colorful</u>, shapes, and <u>scents</u>.

2. Before European <u>settlers</u> arrived and began <u>to exterminate</u> grizzlies, 50,000 to 100,000 of <u>the bears</u> may have <u>exist</u> south of Canada.

3. _____, the author of *Little Women,* began writing stories before she was 10 years old.
   - ⬭ Louisa May Alcott
   - ⬭ For Louisa May Alcott
   - ⬭ When Louisa May Alcott
   - ⬭ Louisa May Alcott was the

4. <u>Rabies</u> is a <u>serious</u> disease <u>carried</u> in the saliva of <u>an infected</u> animals.

5. The caliber of a gun is the diameter of <u>his</u> bore, usually <u>expressed</u> in <u>hundredths</u> of <u>an</u> inch.

6. The *Mayflower* was bound for Virginia, but a hurricane _____ off course.
   - ⬭ blew it
   - ⬭ to blow it
   - ⬭ it blew
   - ⬭ blowing it

7. <u>Following</u> volcanic activity in Martinique in 1902, a <u>huge</u> number of six-foot fer-de-lance <u>snake</u> left the mountains and <u>slithered</u> into the city of Pierre.

8. <u>To make</u> a lithograph, an artist <u>used</u> a flat stone of <u>a kind</u> that will <u>soak up</u> oil and water.

9. William Henry Harrison, _____ of pneumonia shortly after being inaugurated, served only 31 days as president of the United States.
   - ⬭ died
   - ⬭ he dies
   - ⬭ who died
   - ⬭ the death

10. Acidic lava flows <u>ready</u> and tends to cover <u>much larger</u> areas, while <u>basic</u> lava is more <u>viscous</u>.

11. Sounds <u>can travel</u> <u>through</u> water, <u>wood</u>, glass, and <u>others</u> materials.

12. Seismic reflection profiling has _____ the ocean floor is underlain by a thin layer of nearly transparent sediments.
    - ⬭ reveal that
    - ⬭ revealed that
    - ⬭ the revelation of
    - ⬭ revealed about

13. All of <u>an</u> anteater's long tongue <u>are</u> covered with a <u>sticky</u> salivary <u>secretion</u>.

14. <u>Each</u> kernel of popcorn contains a small <u>amount</u> of water, which <u>turned</u> to steam when the kernel is <u>heated</u>.

15. All fossil fuels, whether _____, liquid, or gas, are the result of organic material being covered by successive layers of sediment over the course of millions of years.
    - ⬭ solid
    - ⬭ are solid
    - ⬭ they are solidly
    - ⬭ solids are

16. <u>Acoustical</u> <u>engineer</u> is concerned with <u>the</u> <u>technical</u> control of sound.

17. _____, the faster its molecules move.
    ○ A liquid gets hotter
    ○ To get a liquid hotter
    ○ For a liquid to get hotter
    ○ The hotter a liquid gets

18. <u>Navigational</u> <u>position</u> is <u>frequently</u> expressed <u>on</u> latitude and longitude.

19. In the 1450s, German <u>craftsman</u> Johannes Gutenberg <u>introduced</u> the <u>printed</u> press <u>into</u> Europe.

20. People who were born at very high altitudes often have larger chests and lungs _____ who live at sea level.
    ○ those do
    ○ than do
    ○ do those
    ○ than do those

READING (Computer)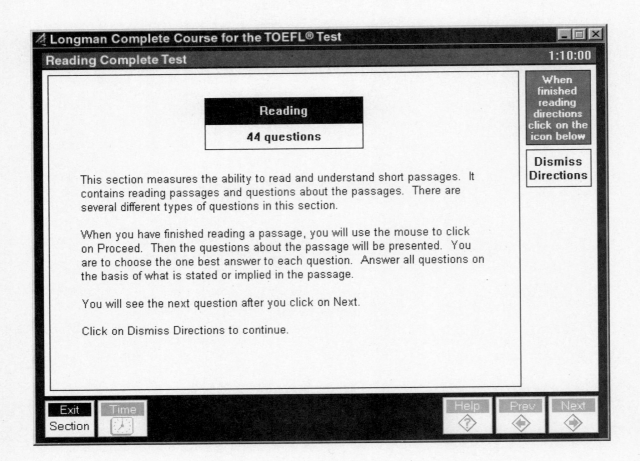

Reading

44 questions

This section measures the ability to read and understand short passages. It contains reading passages and questions about the passages. There are several different types of questions in this section.

When you have finished reading a passage, you will use the mouse to click on Proceed. Then the questions about the passage will be presented. You are to choose the one best answer to each question. Answer all questions on the basis of what is stated or implied in the passage.

You will see the next question after you click on Next.

Click on Dismiss Directions to continue.

PASSAGE ONE (Questions 1–11)

Narcolepsy is a disease characterized by malfunctioning sleep mechanics. It can consist of a sudden and uncontrollable bout of sleep during daylight hours and disturbed sleep during nighttime hours. It occurs more often in men than in women, and it commonly makes its appearance during adolescence or young adulthood. At least a half million Americans are believed to be affected by narcolepsy.

Narcolepsy can take a number of forms during daylight hours. **9A** One common symptom of the disease during daytime hours is a sudden attack of REM (rapid-eye movement) sleep during normal waking hours. **9B** This occurs in some people hundreds of times in a single day, while others only have rare occurrences. **9C** During a sleep attack, narcoleptics may experience automatic behavior; even though asleep, they may continue automatically performing the activity they were involved in prior to falling asleep. **9D** Others experience cataplexy during daytime hours; cataplexy involves a sudden loss of muscle tone that may cause the head to droop or the knees to wobble in minor attacks or a total collapse in more serious attacks. **9E** Cataplexy seems to occur most often in conjunction with intense emotion or excitement.

During sleep hours, narcolepsy can also manifest itself in a variety of ways. During the transitional phase that precedes the onset of sleep, it is common for hallucinations to occur. These hallucinations, known as hypnagogic phenomena, consist of realistic perceptions of sights and sounds during the semi-conscious state between wakefulness and sleep. Narcoleptics may also suffer from night wakening during sleep, resulting in extremely fragmented and restless sleep. Then, upon waking, a narcoleptic may experience sleep paralysis, the inability to move, perhaps for several minutes, immediately after waking.

1. Which of the following would be the most appropriate title for the passage?
   - ◯ A Good Night's Sleep
   - ◯ A Cure for Narcolepsy
   - ◯ An Unusual Sleep Disturbance
   - ◯ Hallucinations during Sleep

2. Look at the word malfunctioning in paragraph 1. This word is closest in meaning to
   - ◯ improperly working
   - ◯ regularly waking
   - ◯ incorrectly classifying
   - ◯ harshly interpreting

3. At which of the following ages would a person be most likely to develop narcolepsy?
   - ◯ 10
   - ◯ 20
   - ◯ 30
   - ◯ 40

4. Click on the sentence in paragraph 1 that indicates that approximate number of narcoleptics in the United States.

5. Look at the word bout in paragraph 1. Click on the word in paragraph 2 that is closest in meaning to bout.

6. Which of the following would be most likely to occur during daily activities?
   - ◯ Automatic behavior
   - ◯ Hallucinations
   - ◯ Night wakening
   - ◯ Sleep paralysis

7. Which of the following involves a complete collapse?
   - ◯ Automatic behavior
   - ◯ Cataplexy
   - ◯ Hallucinations
   - ◯ REM sleep

8. Click on the sentence in paragraph 2 that describes what seems to precipitate cataplexy.

9. The following sentence could be added to paragraph 2.

They may, for example, continue walking, or driving, or stirring a pot until the activity is interrupted by external forces.

Where would it best fit in the paragraph? Click on the square (■) to add the sentence to the paragraph.

10. When would hypnagogic phenomena most likely occur?

○ Just after going to bed
○ In the middle of the night
○ Soon after waking
○ After getting up

11. Click on the paragraph that describes how a narcoleptic's sleep is disturbed during the night.

PASSAGE TWO (Questions 12-21)

What is commonly called pepper in reality comes from two very different families of plants. Black and white pepper both come from the fruit of the *Piper nigrum*, a vine with fruits called peppercorns. The peppercorns turn from green to red as they ripen and finally blacken as they dry out. The dried-out peppercorns are ground to obtain black pepper. White pepper, which has a more subtle flavor than black pepper, comes from the same peppercorns as black pepper; to obtain white pepper, the outer hull of the peppercorn, the pericarp, is removed before the peppercorn is ground.

17A Red and green peppers, on the other hand, come from a completely different family from black and white pepper. 17B Red and green peppers are from the genus *Capsicum*. 17C Plants of this type generally have tiny white flowers and fruit which can be any one of a number of colors, shapes, and sizes. 17D These peppers range in flavor from very mild and sweet to the most incredibly burning taste imaginable. 17E

Christopher Columbus is responsible for the present-day confusion over what a pepper is. The *Piper nigrum* variety of pepper was highly valued for centuries, and high demand for pepper by Europeans was a major cause of the fifteenth-century push to locate ocean routes to the spice-growing regions of Asia. When Columbus arrived in the New World in 1492, he was particularly interested in finding black pepper because of the high price that it would command in Europe. Columbus came across plants from the *Capsicum* family in use among the people of the New World, and he incorrectly identified them as relatives of black pepper. Columbus introduced the spicy *Capsicum* chili peppers to Europeans on his return from the 1492 voyage, and traders later spread them to Asia and Africa. These *Capsicum* peppers have continued to be called peppers in spite of the fact that they are not related to the black and white pepper of the *Piper nigrum* family.

12. The purpose of this passage is to
    ◯ explain why there is confusion today over peppers
    ◯ provide the scientific classification of various types of peppers
    ◯ demonstrate that it was Columbus who brought peppers to Europe
    ◯ classify the variety of sizes, shapes, and colors of peppers

13. Look at the word turn in paragraph 1. This word could best be replaced by
    ◯ revert
    ◯ exchange
    ◯ veer
    ◯ change

14. According to the passage, both black and white peppers
    ◯ come from different plants
    ◯ change colors after they are ground
    ◯ are ground from dried out peppercorns
    ◯ have the same flavor

15. What part of the *Piper nigrum* is the pericarp?
    ◯ The seed inside the fruit
    ◯ The outer covering of the fruit
    ◯ The pulp inside the vine
    ◯ The outer covering of the vine

16. What usually does NOT vary in a *Capsicum* plant?
    ◯ The color of the flower
    ◯ The size of the fruit
    ◯ The shape of the fruit
    ◯ The color of the fruit

17. The following sentence could be added to paragraph 2.

    Bell peppers are the most mild, while habaneros are the most burning.

    Where would it best fit into the paragraph? Click on the square (■) to add the sentence to the paragraph.

18. Look at the word push in paragraph 3.
    This word could best be replaced by
    ○ shove
    ○ strength
    ○ drive
    ○ hit

19. Look at the word them in paragraph 3.
    Click on the word or phrase in paragraph 3
    that them refers to.

20. It can be inferred from the passage that
    chili peppers originally came from
    ○ Europe
    ○ Asia
    ○ America
    ○ Africa

21. Click on the sentence in paragraph 3 that
    explains the mistake that Columbus made.

PASSAGE THREE (Questions 22-32)

There is a common expression in the English language referring to a blue moon. When people say that something happens "only once in a blue moon," they mean that it happens only very rarely, once in a great while. This expression has been around for at least a century and a half; there are references to this expression that date from the second half of the nineteenth century.

The expression "a blue moon" has come to refer to the second full moon occurring in any given calendar month. A second full moon is not called a blue moon because it is particularly blue or is any different in hue from the first full moon of the month. Instead, it is called a blue moon because it is so rare. The moon needs a little more than 29 days to complete the cycle from full moon to full moon. Because every month except February has more than 29 days, every month will have at least one full moon (except February, which will have a full moon unless there is a full moon at the very end of January and another full moon at the very beginning of March). It is on the occasion when a given calendar month has a second full moon that a blue moon occurs. This does not happen very often, only three or four times in a decade.

The blue moons of today are called blue moons because of their rarity and not because of their color; however, the expression "blue moon" may have come into existence in reference to unusual circumstances in which the moon actually appeared blue. **32A** Certain natural phenomena of gigantic proportions can actually change the appearance of the moon from Earth. **32B** The eruption of the Krakatao volcano in 1883 left dust particles in the atmosphere, which clouded the sun and gave the moon a bluish tint. **32C** This particular occurrence of the blue moon may have given rise to the expression that we use today. **32D** When Mount Pinatubo erupted in the Philippines in 1991, the moon again took on a blue tint. **32E**

22. This passage is about
    ○ an idiomatic expression
    ○ an unusual color
    ○ a month on the calendar
    ○ a phase of the moon

23. Look at the word rarely in paragraph 1. This word is closest in meaning to
    ○ hardly
    ○ barely
    ○ seldom
    ○ scarcely

24. How long has the expression "once in a blue moon" been around?
    ○ For around 50 years
    ○ For less than 100 years
    ○ For more than 100 years
    ○ For 200 years

25. Click on the drawing of the moon that could be a "blue moon."

26. Which of the following might be the date of a "blue moon?"
    ○ January 1
    ○ February 28
    ○ April 15
    ○ December 31

27. How many blue moons would there most likely be in a century?
    ○ 4
    ○ 35
    ○ 70
    ○ 100

28. Click on the word in paragraph 2 that is closest in meaning to "color."

29. Click on the sentence in paragraph 2 that describes the duration of a lunar cycle.

30. According to the passage, the moon actually looked blue

   ⬭ after large volcanic eruptions
   ⬭ when it occurred late in the month
   ⬭ several times a year
   ⬭ during the month of February

31. Look at the expression given rise to in paragraph 3. This expression could best be replaced by

   ⬭ created a need for
   ⬭ elevated the level of
   ⬭ spurred the creation of
   ⬭ brightened the color of

32. The following sentence could be added to paragraph 3.

Another example occurred more than a century later.

Where would it best fit into the paragraph? Click on the square (■) to add the sentence to the paragraph.

PASSAGE FOUR (Questions 33-44)

Though Edmund Halley was most famous because of his achievements as an astronomer, he was a scientist of diverse interests and great skill. In addition to studying the skies, Halley was also deeply interested in exploring the unknown depths of the oceans. One of his lesser-known accomplishments that was quite remarkable was his design for a diving bell that facilitated exploration of the watery depths.

The diving bell that Halley designed had a major advantage over the diving bells that were in use prior to his. Earlier diving bells could only make use of the air contained within the bell itself, so divers had to surface when the air inside the bell ran low. Halley's bell was an improvement in that its design allowed for an additional supply of fresh air that enabled a crew of divers to remain underwater for several hours.

The diving contraption that Halley designed was in the shape of a bell that measured three feet across the top and five feet across the bottom and could hold several divers comfortably; it was open at the bottom so that divers could swim in and out at will. The bell was built of wood, which was first heavily tarred to make it water repellent and was then covered with a half-ton sheet of lead to make the bell heavy enough to sink in water. The bell shape held air inside for the divers to breathe as the bell sank to the bottom.

The air inside the bell was not the only source of air for the divers to breathe, and it was this improvement that made Halley's bell superior to its predecessors. In addition to the air already in the bell, air was also supplied to the divers from a lead barrel that was lowered to the ocean floor close to the bell itself. Air flowed through a leather pipe from the lead barrel on the ocean floor to the bell. The diver could breath the air from a position inside the bell, or he could move around outside the bell wearing a diving suit that consisted of a lead bell-shaped helmet with a glass viewing window and a leather body suit, with a leather pipe carrying fresh air from the diving bell to the helmet.

33. The subject of the preceding passage was most likely Halley's
   - childhood
   - work as an astronomer
   - many different interests
   - invention of the diving bell

34. Which of the following best expresses the subject of this passage?
   - Halley's work as an astronomer
   - Halley's many different interests
   - Halley's invention of a contraption for diving
   - Halley's experiences as a diver

35. Halley's bell was better than its predecessors because it
   - was bigger
   - provided more air
   - weighed less
   - could rise more quickly

36. Look at the expression ran low in paragraph 2. This expression is closest in meaning to
   - moved slowly
   - had been replenished
   - sank to the bottom
   - was almost exhausted

37. How long could divers stay underwater in Halley's bell?
   - Just a few seconds
   - Only a few minutes
   - For hours at a time
   - For days on end

38. It is NOT stated in the passage that Halley's bell
   - was wider at the top than at the bottom
   - was made of tarred wood
   - was completely enclosed
   - could hold more than one diver

39. Look at the expression at will in paragraph 3. This expression could best be replaced by

  ⬭ in the future
  ⬭ as they wanted
  ⬭ with great speed
  ⬭ upside down

40. It can be inferred from the passage that, were Halley's bell not covered with lead, it would

  ⬭ float
  ⬭ get wet
  ⬭ trap the divers
  ⬭ suffocate the divers

41. Click on the drawing that shows what Halley's underwater breathing apparatus looked like.

42. Click on the sentence in paragraph 4 that indicates how air traveled from the barrel to the bell.

43. Click on the paragraph that describes diving bells that preceded Halley's.

44. This passage would most likely be assigned reading in a course on

  ⬭ astronomy
  ⬭ recreation
  ⬭ oceanography
  ⬭ physiology

WRITING COMPLETE TEST
(Computer)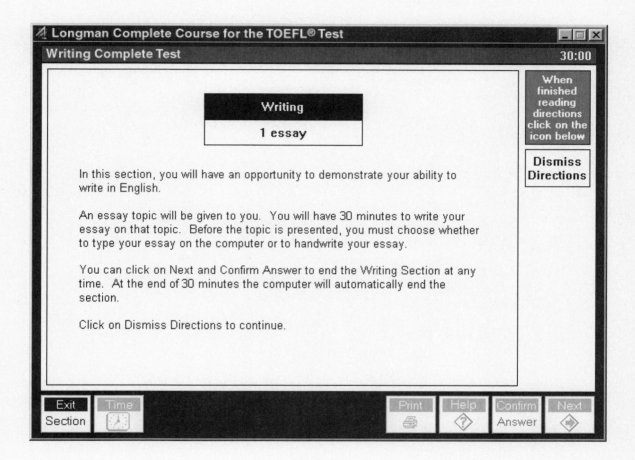

Longman Complete Course for the TOEFL® Test

Writing Complete Test   30:00

> **Writing**
>
> **1 essay**

When finished reading directions click on the icon below

Dismiss Directions

In this section, you will have an opportunity to demonstrate your ability to write in English.

An essay topic will be given to you. You will have 30 minutes to write your essay on that topic. Before the topic is presented, you must choose whether to type your essay on the computer or to handwrite your essay.

You can click on Next and Confirm Answer to end the Writing Section at any time. At the end of 30 minutes the computer will automatically end the section.

Click on Dismiss Directions to continue.

Exit Section | Time | Print | Help | Confirm Answer | Next

What change from the twentieth century will have the most effect on life in the twenty-first century? Give reasons and details to support your answer.

APPENDIX A: **Similar Sounds**

DIRECTIONS: In each exercise first read the group of words aloud with the correct pronunciation. Then listen to the statements, each of which contains one of the words. Finally, choose the letter of the word you have heard.

   NOW BEGIN THE RECORDING AT EXERCISE A1.

EXERCISE A1

A. pit	C. pat	E. pout
B. pet	D. put	F. pot

EXERCISE A2

A. heat	C. hut	E. height
B. hit	D. hot	F. hate

EXERCISE A3

A. cat	C. cot	E. kite
B. cut	D. caught	F. coat

EXERCISE A4

A. bill	C. bull	E. bale
B. bell	D. ball	F. bowl

EXERCISE A5

A. cap	C. cup	E. cop
B. cape	D. keep	F. cope

EXERCISE A6

A. bead	C. bed	E. bud
B. bid	D. bad	F. bowed

EXERCISE A7

A. neat	C. net	E. knot
B. night	D. nut	F. note

EXERCISE A8

A. seek	C. sack	E. sock
B. sick	D. soak	F. sake

EXERCISE A9

A. seed	C. sad	E. side
B. said	D. sawed	F. sighed

EXERCISE A10

A. heal	D. hail	G. howl
B. hill	E. hole	H. whole
C. haul	F. hall	I. hull

EXERCISE A11

A. beat	D. bat	G. bait
B. bit	E. but	H. bite
C. bet	F. bought	I. boat

APPENDIX B: **Two- and Three-Part Verbs**

DIRECTIONS: Each of the following sentences contains a two- or three-part verb in italics. Read the sentence and try to understand the italicized expression. Then, find the meaning of the expression in the list that follows the exercise, and write the letter of the answer on the line.

EXERCISE B1

_____   1.   He's been smoking too much. He really needs to *cut down.*

_____   2.   The company had to *cut off* the electricity because the bill was unpaid.

_____   3.   He kept teasing me, so finally I told him to *cut it out.*

_____   4.   He is working hard because he really wants to *get ahead* in his career.

_____   5.   She is such a nice person that she is easily able to *get along* with everyone.

_____   6.   Could you explain a little more clearly? I really don't understand what you are trying to *get at.*

_____   7.   When he stole some money from her, she really wanted to do something to *get back at* him.

_____   8.   We have enough money to *get by* for a few months; we won't have a lot of extras, but we will survive.

_____   9.   She was sick for several weeks, but now she has started to *get over* it.

_____   10.   There are too many clothes in my closet. I need to *get rid of* some of them.

DEFINITIONS—Exercise B1	
A. stop it	**F.** manage
B. get revenge against	**G.** advance
C. recover from	**H.** throw away
D. decrease it	**I.** stop the supply of
E. be friendly	**J.** imply

EXERCISE B2

_____   1.   He read the untrue stories about himself in the newspaper, but he tried not to react. He just tried to *brush it off*.

_____   2.   I haven't played Scrabble in quite some time. I'll have to *brush up on* the rules before we play.

_____   3.   While we were walking in the mountains, we were lucky enough to *come across* a waterfall. It was quite a surprise to find such a beautiful thing.

_____   4.   She is not feeling well; she thinks she is about to *come down with* the flu.

_____   5.   While I'm on my trip, do you think you could *look after* my cats?

_____   6.   The police detective was not sure how the crime was committed. She decided to *look into* it further.

_____   7. Here is my application. Could you take a few moments to *look it over?*

_____   8. The brother always used to *pick on* his younger sister. His favorite tricks were to pull her hair, tease her, or scare her.

_____   9. You have tried on three dresses, but you can't afford all of them. You'll have to *pick out* just one.

_____   10. Could you *pick* me *up* after school today? I'll wait for you out in front of the school.

DEFINITIONS—Exercise B2	
A. take care of	**F.** bother
B. review; relearn	**G.** not let it have an effect
C. choose	**H.** unexpectedly find
D. get sick with	**I.** come and get
E. look at it briefly	**J.** investigate

EXERCISE B3

_____   1. We have some new neighbors. I think I'll *call on* them later this afternoon.

_____   2. The principal had to *call off* the class on Tuesday because the teacher was sick.

_____   3. The politician should *call for* a decrease in taxes.

_____   4. Why don't you *call* me *up* about 9:00? I'll be waiting by the phone.

_____   5. I don't need this bicycle any more. It's not worth too much money, so I think I'll just *give* it *away.*

_____   6. Here's the book I borrowed from you, and now I think I should *give* it *back.*

_____   7. I've done all I can. I just can't do anything more. I *give up.*

_____   8. The teacher has to *put off* the exam until next week because the students are not prepared.

_____   9. She has to *put on* her coat before she goes out into the cold winter weather.

_____   10. He's such a mean man that it's difficult to *put up with* him.

DEFINITIONS—Exercise B3	
A. donate	**F.** cancel
B. visit	**G.** delay
C. tolerate	**H.** telephone
D. request; suggest	**I.** dress in
E. return	**J.** surrender

EXERCISE B4

_____   1.   I was scared last night because someone tried to **break into** my house.

_____   2.   He and she have been friends for more than two years, but now they've decided to **break off** their relationship.

_____   3.   I'm really excited to be selected as master of ceremonies. I've never done this before, but I'm really going to try to **carry it off**.

_____   4.   After her husband was killed in an accident, she tried hard to **carry on** with her life.

_____   5.   I'm going to **hold off** taking my vacation. I was scheduled to take my vacation this week, but I'll take it next month instead.

_____   6.   My boss told me that my work had been very good recently and that she wanted me to **keep it up**.

_____   7.   Many of the employees of the company are worried; they've heard a rumor that the company is going to **lay off** a number of employees.

_____   8.   While I was at the market, I was surprised to **run into** a friend I hadn't seen in months.

_____   9.   If I didn't buy milk at the store, we would **run out of** it at breakfast in the morning.

_____   10. That boy has been playing baseball all day. I know he's going to **wear out** soon.

DEFINITIONS—Exercise B4	
A. postpone	**F.** completely use the supply of
B. succeed	**G.** end
C. fire	**H.** unexpectedly meet
D. tire	**I.** continue
E. unlawfully enter	**J.** continue

EXERCISE B5

_____ 1. The newspapers tend to **play up** sensational stories if they want to improve their circulation.

_____ 2. He knew that it would be difficult to win the tournament, but he worked hard to **pull it off**.

_____ 3. She tends to **show off** a lot. She's very beautiful, and she wants everyone to notice her.

_____ 4. He was supposed to come at 9:00, but he didn't **show up** until 10:00.

_____ 5. Do you know when the wedding will **take place?** I heard that it would be next June.

_____ 6. Neither my roommate nor I like to do the dishes, so we **take turns.**

_____ 7. I don't know how to play golf, but it's a sport that I would like to **take up**.

_____ 8. He applied for the job, but the manager decided to **turn down** his application because he was not really qualified.

_____ 9. The students must **turn in** their papers on Thursday. The teacher has said that the papers can't be even one day late.

_____ 10. Because I swim so many hours every day, I sometimes feel that I'm going to **turn into** a fish.

DEFINITIONS—Exercise B5	
A. try to attract attention	**F.** refuse
B. submit	**G.** succeed
C. happen	**H.** begin (a hobby)
D. increase the significance of	**I.** become
E. arrive	**J.** alternate

APPENDIX C: **Idioms**

DIRECTIONS: Each of the following sentences contains an idiom in italics. Read the sentence and try to understand the idiom. Then find the meaning of the idiom in the list that follows, and write the letter of the answer on the line.

EXERCISE C1

_____ 1. He's holding down two jobs and attending school. He's really *burning the candle at both ends.*

_____ 2. She's buying a lot of new furniture before she even has a job. She's *putting the cart before the horse.*

_____ 3. Every time he opens his mouth, he immediately regrets what he said. He's always *putting his foot in his mouth.*

_____ 4. He's not telling me exactly what happened. He's *beating around the bush.*

_____ 5. She wanted to get that man's phone number, but she wasn't sure of his last name or where he lived. It was like *looking for a needle in a haystack.*

_____ 6. He's always too fast and out of control on his motorcycle. He's *playing with fire.*

_____ 7. She keeps asking if I was the one who was spreading rumors about her, but I wasn't. She's *barking up the wrong tree.*

_____ 8. He took the best portions for himself and didn't leave enough for the others. He's just *looking out for number one.*

_____ 9. She's been working on that assignment for over two months, and I don't think she's ever going to finish it. She's *taking forever and a day.*

_____ 10. She has to go to the bank, and while she's out she'll stop and visit her friend. She's *killing two birds with one stone.*

_____ 11. He was admitted to Harvard, and he would have gone there but he forgot to send in the appropriate form in time. He has really *missed the boat.*

_____ 12. I know that you thought that this part of the program was difficult, but wait until you see the next part. You're *jumping out of the frying pan and into the fire.*

DEFINITIONS—Exercise C1	
A. making a mistake	**G.** missed an opportunity
B. accomplishing two things at once	**H.** saying embarrassing things
C. doing something dangerous	**I.** speaking indirectly
D. doing things in the wrong order	**J.** doing something difficult
E. going from bad to worse	**K.** taking a really long time
F. doing too much	**L.** thinking only about himself

EXERCISE C2

_____ 1. His only two choices are to give up his free time or to pay a lot of money, and he doesn't like either choice. He's *between a rock and a hard place*.

_____ 2. She got 100 percent on the exam and the other students were below 70 percent. She's *head and shoulders above the rest*.

_____ 3. Every day he fixes meals, cleans the apartment, and goes to the market. It's *all in a day's work*.

_____ 4. She's a well-known lawyer, a good skier, a great cook, and a painter. She's a *jack-of-all-trades*.

_____ 5. Every time he puts the toys away, the children just take them out again. Keeping the house clean when the children are there is *like trying to swim upstream*.

_____ 6. Anytime I need help I go to her because I know she'll help me any way she can. She's *one in a million*.

_____ 7. He thought he was going to have to come into the office and work on both Saturday and Sunday, but now he doesn't have to. He's *off the hook*.

_____ 8. She and her classmates all have to read five chapters, write a paper, and prepare for an exam this week. They're *all in the same boat*.

_____ 9. He and his brother have the same hair, the same eyes, the same smile, and the same expressions. They're *like two peas in a pod*.

_____ 10. When I saw him with an older man, I just knew that the man had to be his father. He's *a chip off the old block*.

_____ 11. She's had so much to do to get ready for the trip that she's been running around all day. Now she's *on her last legs*.

_____ 12. I can't think of the answer, but it will come to me in just a minute. It's *on the tip of my tongue*.

DEFINITIONS—Exercise C2	
A. very tired	**G.** in the same situation
B. the best	**H.** nothing out of the ordinary
C. exactly alike	**I.** accomplished at many things
D. really wonderful	**J.** an idea that is not in words
E. really difficult or frustrating	**K.** not responsible any longer
F. just like his father	**L.** without any good options

EXERCISE C3

_____ 1. Do you think you could help me out with the math homework? *Two heads are better than one.*

_____ 2. What was it like when the announcement of the disaster came over the radio? *You could have heard a pin drop.*

_____ 3. We could either go out to dinner tonight or stay home and cook. *Six of one, half dozen of the other.*

_____ 4. I know you like the food at this restaurant, but I just don't care for it. *To each his own.*

_____ 5. I got to the bank just one minute after closing time. *Just my luck.*

_____ 6. My boss has asked me to respond immediately to this fax. *No sooner said than done.*

_____ 7. Don't worry about what the boss just said to you. *His bark is worse than his bite.*

_____ 8. It seems impossible for me to go to graduate school because I just can't afford it. But I'm going to try. *Where there's a will, there's a way!*

_____ 9. Everything seems to be going the way that it should. *So far, so good!*

_____ 10. Just think that because you locked your keys in the car, you got to meet that nice, handsome, young locksmith. *Every cloud has a silver lining!*

_____ 11. I've got to accept the fact that it's going to take more than seven years of school if I want to become a doctor. After all, *Rome wasn't built in a day.*

_____ 12. She loves my wardrobe, but I wish I had her clothes. *The grass is always greener on the other side of the fence.*

DEFINITIONS—Exercise C3	
A. It was really quiet.	**G.** Bad things are accompanied by good.
B. It's good to work together.	**H.** You always want what you don't have.
C. It's been going well up to now.	**I.** Everyone has a different opinion.
D. I'm not so fortunate.	**J.** His words are worse than his actions.
E. It doesn't matter.	**K.** If you want something, you can do it.
F. It will be done immediately.	**L.** Everything takes time.

EXERCISE C4

_____ 1. He finally got a job; he couldn't continue to sit around doing nothing. He had to ***turn over a new leaf.***

_____ 2. When he told his mother that he didn't need to study for the exam because he knew he would get a good grade, his mother responded, ***"Don't count your chickens before they're hatched."***

_____ 3. When I asked my friend to do some of my work for me, she replied that I would have to ***stand on my own two feet.***

_____ 4. You've been offered this job, and the offer may not remain on the table for too long, so you'd better take this one while you have the chance. You need to ***strike while the iron is hot.***

_____ 5. When you guessed that I would get the promotion, you ***hit the nail right on the head.***

_____ 6. Before you accept the position, you should find out everything you can about the company. You should ***look before you leap.***

_____ 7. She was appointed to the environmental protection committee, and she's really excited because this is something she's been interested in for some time. This is something she can ***sink her teeth into.***

_____ 8. If you want to be the one who gets noticed at work, you need to ***dot all the i's and cross all the t's*** on every task that you do.

_____ 9. You need to learn to relax. Every time there's a lot of work to do, you just ***run around like a chicken with its head cut off.***

_____ 10. I really prepared for that exam. It should ***be a piece of cake.***

_____ 11. She thinks she should confess what she did, but no one really seems interested in knowing. Instead, she decides to ***let sleeping dogs lie.***

_____ 12. He never has to work for anything because his parents will give him anything he asks for. He seems to ***have been born with a silver spoon in his mouth.***

DEFINITIONS—Exercise C4	
A. start over again	**G.** were exactly right
B. be extremely easy	**H.** depend on something you don't have
C. do it myself	**I.** be spoiled
D. pay attention to every detail	**J.** get really involved in
E. think before you act	**K.** take advantage of a good opportunity
F. leave something alone	**L.** act overly nervous and excited

APPENDIX D: **Prepositions**

DIRECTIONS: Study the list of prepositions. Then underline the prepositions in each sentence. Circle the prepositional phrases (prepositions + modifiers + objects). The number in parentheses indicates how many prepositions you should find in each group of sentences.

PREPOSITIONS				
about	behind	except	on	under
above	below	for	onto	underneath
across	beneath	from	outside	unlike
after	beside	in	over	until
against	between	inside	past	up
along	beyond	into	since	upon
among	by	like	through	versus
around	despite	near	throughout	with
as	down	of	to	within
at	during	off	toward	without

EXERCISE D1 (21 prepositions)

1. Advocacy of technology as the panacea for our environmental woes is not without its detractors.

2. State Highway 227 runs east of U.S. Highway 101, from San Luis Obispo in the north to Arroyo Grande in the south.

3. All four components of the Milky Way appear to be embedded in a large, dark corona of invisible material.

4. Over the last three decades, we have seen a consistent worldwide decline in membership of private-sector international trade union federations.

5. There is not complete agreement on the correlation of the various cultures and the glacial sequence, but many think that the Villafranchion, characterized by crudely worked pebble tools, roughly spherical in form, belongs in the early phase of the First Glacial period.

EXERCISE D2 (34 prepositions)

1. A combination of factors appear to have led to the decline of the beetle, all of them directly or indirectly due to human influence but none conclusively proven.

2. At ground level, ozone is produced by a photochemical interaction of the Sun with gases such as nitrogen oxides and unburnt hydrocarbons.

3. The Army of the Potomac under General George Meade and the Army of Northern Virginia under General Robert E. Lee had stumbled upon each other four days earlier at the edge of this little Pennsylvania county seat of 2,400 inhabitants.

4. With this sudden and vast wealth, by the turn of the century, Trinity Church was an ecclesiastical empire with 8,500 communicants and nine chapels scattered around New York City besides the main church itself.

5. Through modern film footage, this video production retraces the route followed by Meriwether Lewis and William Clark during their epochal two-year (1804–1806), eight-thousand-mile round-trip journey by keelboat, on horseback, on foot, and by canoe up the Missouri River, across the Continental Divide, and down the Snake and Columbia Rivers to the Pacific Ocean.

EXERCISE D3 (35 prepositions)

1. During the era from the end of the Civil War to about 1890, there was a land settlement boom within the United States.

2. By coincidence, the Finnish results were released at the same time that an American study confirmed the cancer-fighting potential of a chemical in broccoli known as sulforaphane.

3. At windswept Kitty Hawk, along North Carolina's Outer Banks, the Wright Brothers National Memorial pays tribute to the brothers and their historic first flight on December 17, 1903.

4. A wide central hall, running past the Garden Court, from one end of the building to the other, has four large cases of souvenirs from both palaces, including a program printed for President Warren G. Harding's visit.

5. Like historians raiding an archive of ancient texts, two atmospheric scientists are sifting through old satellite data, looking for a means of extending ozone records back in time in order to prove or disprove a hypothesis; on the basis of ground measurements made in Antarctica since the 1950s, researchers believe that the annual Antarctic ozone hole first appeared in a mild form during the late 1970s and then grew worse in the 1980s.

APPENDIX E: **Word Endings**

Word endings in English often tell you how a word is used grammatically in English; therefore, it is very important for you to recognize some common word endings. If you recognize a word ending on a word that you do not know, you can tell how the word should be used grammatically, even if you do not understand the meaning of the word.

EXERCISE E1: *Noun (Thing) Endings*

The following *noun (thing)* endings are very common in English. It is important for you to study them and become familiar with them.

NOUN (THING) ENDINGS			
-ism	socialism	*-ment*	government
-nce	excellence	*-ty*	beauty
-ness	sadness	*-age*	marriage
-ion	information	*-ship*	friendship

Using one of the endings above, change each of the following words into a *noun (thing)*:

1.	member	_____	9. alcohol	_____
2.	kind	_____	10. permanent	_____
3.	real	_____	11. mile	_____
4.	move	_____	12. confuse	_____
5.	human	_____	13. leader	_____
6.	elect	_____	14. sudden	_____
7.	break	_____	15. improve	_____
8.	intelligent	_____	16. equal	_____

EXERCISE E2: *Noun (Person) Endings*

The following *noun (person)* endings are very common in English. It is important for you to study them and become familiar with them.

NOUN (PERSON) ENDINGS			
-er	employer	**-ist**	tourist
-or	actor	**-cian**	musician

Using one of the endings above, change each of the following words into a *noun (person):*

1.	teach	_____	9.	perfection	_____
2.	type	_____	10.	program	_____
3.	beauty	_____	11.	electricity	_____
4.	ideal	_____	12.	invest	_____
5.	invent	_____	13.	build	_____
6.	clinic	_____	14.	natural	_____
7.	special	_____	15.	advice	_____
8.	ranch	_____	16.	mathematics	_____

EXERCISE E3: *Adjective Endings*

The following *adjective* endings are very common in English. It is important for you to study them and become familiar with them.

ADJECTIVE ENDINGS			
-ent	excellent	**-ive**	expensive
-ant	important	**-ous**	dangerous
-ful	careful	**-al**	natural
-ic	economic	**-able**	capable
-less	careless	**-ible**	possible

Using one of the endings above, change each of the following words into an *adjective:*

1.	heart	_____	9.	courage	_____
2.	nature	_____	10.	use	_____
3.	athlete	_____	11.	enthusiasm	_____
4.	mystery	_____	12.	motion	_____
5.	help	_____	13.	tradition	_____
6.	impress	_____	14.	change	_____
7.	intelligence	_____	15.	permanence	_____
8.	comfort	_____	16.	attract	_____

EXERCISE E4: *Verb Endings*

The following verb endings are very common in English. It is important for you to study them and become familiar with them.

VERB ENDINGS			
-en	softe*n*	*-ize*	memor*ize*
-ate	popul*ate*	*-ify*	not*ify*

Using one of the endings above, change each of the following words into a *verb:*

1.	dark	_____	9.	different	_____
2.	final	_____	10.	identity	_____
3.	just	_____	11.	light	_____
4.	separation	_____	12.	glamour	_____
5.	short	_____	13.	person	_____
6.	intense	_____	14.	sweet	_____
7.	investigation	_____	15.	liberal	_____
8.	industrial	_____	16.	demonstration	_____

EXERCISE E5: *Adverb Ending*

The following *adverb* ending is very common in English. It is important for you to become familiar with it.

ADVERB ENDING	
-ly	real*ly*

Using the ending above, change each of the following words into an *adverb:*

1.	final	_____	9.	great	_____
2.	careful	_____	10.	complete	_____
3.	obvious	_____	11.	eager	_____
4.	recent	_____	12.	absolute	_____
5.	strong	_____	13.	correct	_____
6.	perfect	_____	14.	sudden	_____
7.	fearful	_____	15.	doubtful	_____
8.	quick	_____	16.	regular	_____

EXERCISE E6: *All Endings Together*

Identify each of the following words as a *noun-thing* (NT), a *noun-person* (NP), an *adjective* (ADJ), an *adverb* (ADV), or a *verb* (V).

_____ 1. heighten

_____ 2. forgetful

_____ 3. imperialism

_____ 4. effusively

_____ 5. cashier

_____ 6. columnist

_____ 7. aggravate

_____ 8. glamorous

_____ 9. vintage

_____ 10. statistician

_____ 11. desertification

_____ 12. submissive

_____ 13. nocturnal

_____ 14. establishment

_____ 15. impertinent

_____ 16. impertinently

_____ 17. togetherness

_____ 18. pharmacist

_____ 19. craftsmanship

_____ 20. manageable

_____ 21. speechless

_____ 22. tremendously

_____ 23. liability

_____ 24. counselor

_____ 25. civic

_____ 26. sensitize

_____ 27. ambiance

_____ 28. justification

_____ 29. interpretive

_____ 30. personify

EXERCISE E7: *All Endings Together*

Circle the letter of the word that correctly completes each sentence.

1. The _____ of the news could not be stressed enough.
   (A) important   (B) importance   (C) importantly

2. The detective _____ that the maid committed the robbery.
   (A) theorized   (B) theoretician   (C) theoretic

3. It is _____ that they live so close to the school.
   (A) convenience   (B) convenient   (C) conveniently

4. The patient responded _____ to the medication.
   (A) weaken   (B) weakness   (C) weakly

5. The psychologist explained his ideas on _____ interaction.
   (A) social   (B) society   (C) socialize

6. Not everyone wants a job as a _____.
   (A) mortal   (B) mortally   (C) mortician

7. You should not _____ the problem.
   (A) minimal   (B) minimize   (C) minimally

8. Because of a traffic _____, he had to appear in court.
   (A) violate   (B) violator   (C) violation

9. The children ran _____ toward the entrance of the park.
   (A) excitedly   (B) excited   (C) excitement

10. The company was unable to _____ enough profit to stay in business.
    (A) generator   (B) generate   (C) generation

11. She picked up a piece of _____ rock.

    (A) volcano   (B) vulcanize   (C) volcanic

12. He responded _____ to the rude question.

    (A) explosively   (B) explosion   (C) explosive

13. Because your medical problem is serious, you need to see a _____.

    (A) specialize   (B) special   (C) specialist

14. The coach was able to _____ the athletes to perform better.

    (A) motivate   (B) motivator   (C) motivation

15. He was not concerned about the _____ of his actions.

    (A) careless   (B) carelessness   (C) carelessly

16. This portion of the report should be completed _____ of the other part.

    (A) independence (B) independent   (C) independently

17. The view of the mountains was _____.

    (A) magnify   (B) magnificent   (C) magnification

18. It was necessary for the speaker to _____ her message.

    (A) clarify   (B) clarity   (C) clarification

19. The _____ of the village was the soldiers' primary goal.

    (A) liberate   (B) liberation   (C) liberal

20. He gave an _____ incorrect answer to the question.

    (A) obvious   (B) obviously   (C) obviate

EXERCISE E8: *All Endings Together*

The following sentences contain a number of underlined words. Each of the underlined words *may* or *may not* be correct. Circle the underlined words that are incorrect, and make them correct.

1. The police <u>inspect</u> <u>organized</u> an <u>intensively</u> search for the robber.

2. The newspaper <u>reporter</u> did not <u>exact</u> <u>appreciate</u> the <u>negation</u> comments about her article.

3. He became <u>penniless</u> and <u>homeless</u> when a <u>seriousness</u> ill made him <u>unable</u> to work.

4. On the old college campus, the ivy-covered walls of the <u>colonial</u> buildings <u>create</u> an aura of <u>gentility</u> and <u>tradition</u>.

5. Maya Angelou is a <u>poem</u>, <u>composition</u>, and <u>author</u> of two <u>autobiographically</u> works, *I Know Why the Caged Bird Sings* and *My Name*.

6. The process of <u>Americanization</u> <u>encouragement</u> immigrants to <u>assimilation</u> American attitudes, <u>cultural</u>, and <u>citizenship</u>.

7. During the previously war, the national defense establish found itself in greatness need of linguists.

8. The escalate of hostilities between the two nations has proven far more seriousness than analyze had previously expected.

9. Social is becoming increasingly dependence on complex computers for the arrange of its affairs.

10. If someone has an educator in the humanities, he or she is prepared to deal with abstractions or complex and to feel comfortably with subtleties of thought.

11. It is possibly to demonstrate that the mathematical odds for success of the program increase dramatically with the additional of increased financial backing.

12. It would be fatally for the administration to underestimate the determine of the protesters to have the new law overturned.

APPENDIX F: **Irregular Verb Forms**

DIRECTIONS: Fill in the boxes with the correct forms of the verb.

EXERCISE F1

	VERB	PAST	PARTICIPLE		VERB	PAST	PARTICIPLE
1.		beat	beaten	25.		fought	fought
2.	become		become	26.	find		found
3.		began	begun	27.		fit	fit
4.	bet		bet	28.	fly	flew	
5.	bite	bit		29.	forget		forgotten
6.	blow	blew		30.	forgive	forgave	
7.	break		broken	31.		froze	frozen
8.	bring		brought	32.	get		gotten
9.		built	built	33.	give	gave	
10.	buy	bought		34.	go	went	
11.	catch		caught	35.		grew	grown
12.		chose	chosen	36.		had	had
13.	come		come	37.	hear		heard
14.	cost	cost		38.	hide	hid	
15.		cut	cut	39.		hit	hit
16.	dig		dug	40.	hold	held	
17.	do	did		41.	hurt	hurt	
18.	draw	drew		42.	keep		kept
19.		drank	drunk	43.		knew	known
20.	drive	drove		44.		led	led
21.	eat		eaten	45.	leave	left	
22.	fall	fell		46.		lent	lent
23.		fed	fed	47.	let		let
24.	feel	felt		48.		lost	lost

	VERB	PAST	PARTICIPLE		VERB	PAST	PARTICIPLE
49.	make	made		68.		sang	sung
50.		meant	meant	69.	sink		sunk
51.	meet	met		70.	sit	sat	
52.	pay		paid	71.		slept	slept
53.	prove		proven	72.	speak	spoke	
54.		put	put	73.	spend		spent
55.	quit		quit	74.		stood	stood
56.		read	read	75.		stole	stolen
57.	ride	rode		76.	swim	swam	
58.	ring	rang		77.	take		taken
59.		rose	risen	78.	teach	taught	
60.	run	ran		79.	tear		torn
61.	say	said		80.		told	told
62.		saw	seen	81.	think	thought	
63.		sold	sold	82.		threw	thrown
64.	send		sent	83.		understood	understood
65.		shot	shot	84.	wear		worn
66.	show		shown	85.		won	won
67.		shut	shut	86.	write	wrote	

APPENDIX G: **Formation of the Passive**

DIRECTIONS: In the following exercises, sentences are shown in both *active* and *passive*. Fill in the blanks in the sentences with whatever is needed to complete the sentences.

EXERCISE G1

ACTIVE	PASSIVE
1. He *writes* many letters.	Many letters _____ by him.
2. He *wrote* many letters.	Many letters _____ by him.
3. He *has written* many letters.	Many letters _____ by him.
4. He *had written* many letters.	Many letters _____ by him.
5. He *would write* many letters.	Many letters _____ by him.
6. He *would have written* many letters.	Many letters _____ by him.
7. He *is writing* many letters.	Many letters _____ by him.
8. He *was writing* many letters.	Many letters _____ by him.
9. He *will write* many letters.	Many letters _____ by him.
10. He *will have written* many letters.	Many letters _____ by him.
11. He *is going to write* many letters.	Many letters _____ by him.
12. He *should write* many letters.	Many letters _____ by him.

EXERCISE G2

ACTIVE	PASSIVE
1. Soon the armies _____ the battle.	The battle will be fought by the armies soon.
2. The company is going to buy the equipment.	_____ by the company.
3. Someone _____ in the yard.	A hole was being dug in the yard.
4. The referee had already blown the whistle.	The whistle had _____.
5. Parents _____ good values.	Children should be taught good values by parents.
6. She keeps her valuable jewelry in the safe.	_____ in the safe.
7. The enemy's torpedoes _____	The ship was sunk by the enemy's torpedoes.
8. What you said hurt me.	I _____ hurt by _____.
9. Someone _____ now.	The children are being fed now.
10. You should not have said it so strongly.	_____ so strongly.

EXERCISE G3

ACTIVE	PASSIVE
1. _____ elections _____.	Elections will be held next month by the club.
2. The team won the game in the final seconds.	_____ in the final seconds.
3. Someone is taking photographs of the wedding.	Photographs _____ _____.
4. Someone _____.	The passport had already been stolen.
5. She reads the incoming mail daily.	The incoming mail _____ daily.
6. _____ should not _____ the electricity.	The electricity should not have been shut off.
7. People had bet a lot of money on the game.	A lot _____ on the game.
8. No one _____ in several weeks.	The car has not been driven in several weeks.
9. She would spend many hours on the project.	_____ on the project.
10. They _____ at a large profit.	The house could have been sold at a large profit.

EXERCISE G4

ACTIVE	PASSIVE
1. The guards were bringing the prisoner into court.	The prisoner _____ into court.
2. The agent _____.	The tourists are going to be met by the agent.
3. She _____ several times.	That dress had already been worn several times.
4. Someone tore his clothing during the fight.	_____ during the fight.
5. We are doing everything we can think of.	Everything _____.
6. No one _____.	The money will not ever be found.
7. He would have told me what happened.	I _____ what happened.
8. Someone _____ so much.	The horse should not have been ridden so much.
9 A fisherman caught a shark close to shore.	A shark _____ close to shore.
10. No one _____ really did.	What he really did is not known.

APPENDIX H: **Irregular Plurals**

DIRECTIONS: Study the irregular plurals in the chart in Skill 41. Then indicate whether each of the following is correct (C) or incorrect (I).

EXERCISE H1

_____	1. one men		_____	9. several naughty children
_____	2. lots of data		_____	10. an in-depth analyses
_____	3. a surprising hypothesis		_____	11. one hundred alumni
_____	4. one fast-growing fungi		_____	12. lots of bright tooth
_____	5. various criterion		_____	13. various exotic cacti
_____	6. a few mice		_____	14. two required thesis
_____	7. each syllabi for the class		_____	15. the earth's axis
_____	8. a young deer		_____	16. lots of woolly sheep

EXERCISE H2

_____	1. both types of fungus		_____	9. a pair of strong ox
_____	2. a new curricula		_____	10. the X and Y axes
_____	3. two large foot		_____	11. two different theses
_____	4. a new bacteria		_____	12. each beautiful women
_____	5. one terrible crisis		_____	13. a recent alumnus
_____	6. a big, fat salmon		_____	14. two delicious fish
_____	7. many kinds of stimuli		_____	15. the only radius
_____	8. one tiny mouse		_____	16. a scientific syntheses

EXERCISE H3

_____	1. both lengthy syllabus		_____	9. an unexpected diagnoses
_____	2. some strict criteria		_____	10. an aching teeth
_____	3. a fat goose		_____	11. each nuclei of the atom
_____	4. some new hypotheses		_____	12. several fresh trout
_____	5. both young child		_____	13. a thorny cactus
_____	6. a green-colored bacilli		_____	14. each filthy feet
_____	7. many natural phenomenon		_____	15. surrounded by parenthesis
_____	8. each fish in the aquarium		_____	16. some fast-moving deer

APPENDIX I: **Word Parts**

Word parts in English can often give you a clue about the meaning of a word; therefore, it is very important for you to recognize some common word parts. If you recognize one of the word parts in a word that you do not know, you can often get a pretty good idea about the meaning of a word.

EXERCISE I1: *What You Do*

The following word parts describe things you *do*. Study these word parts because they appear in numerous words in English.

WHAT YOU DO					
PART	MEANING	EXAMPLE	PART	MEANING	EXAMPLE
cede/ceed	(go)	pro*ceed*	**rupt**	(break)	e*rupt*
cred	(believe)	*cred*it	**scrib/scrip**	(write)	de*scrib*e
graph	(write)	auto*graph*	**sect**	(cut)	bi*sect*
ject	(throw)	e*ject*	**ven**	(come)	inter*ven*e
mit/miss	(send)	e*mit*	**ver**	(turn)	di*ver*t
mute	(change)	com*mute*	**viv**	(live)	sur*viv*e
port	(carry)	de*port*			

Using the word parts above to help you, match the definitions on the right with the words on the left.

_____ 1. *emissary*

_____ 2. *rupture*

_____ 3. *intersection*

_____ 4. *porter*

_____ 5. *permutation*

_____ 6. *convention*

_____ 7. *vivacious*

_____ 8. *avert*

_____ 9. *exceed*

_____ 10. *credo*

_____ 11. *scribble*

_____ 12. *graphology*

_____ 13. *projectile*

A. ideology or *belief*

B. cause to *turn*

C. the result of a *change*

D. *write* hastily and messily

E. *break* in accustomed friendly relations

F. study of hand*writing*

G. meeting where many people *come* together

H. something that is *thrown*

I. keenly *alive* and brisk

J. person who is *sent* to deliver a message

K. person who *carries* baggage

L. where one road *cuts* through another

M. *go* beyond expectations

EXERCISE I2: *Where and When*

The following word parts describe *where* or *when* things happen. Study these word parts because they appear in numerous words in English.

WHERE			WHEN		
PART	MEANING	EXAMPLE	PART	MEANING	EXAMPLE
cir	(around)	*circulate*	**ante**	(before)	*anterior*
ex	(out)	*exit*	**fore**	(before)	*foretell*
in	(in)	*include*	**fin**	(end)	*finish*
re	(back)	*return*	**pre**	(before)	*previous*
sub	(under)	*subway*	**post**	(after)	*postpone*
tele	(far)	*telephone*			
trans	(across)	*transatlantic*			

Using the word parts above to help you, match the definitions on the right with the words on the left.

_____ 1. *refund*

_____ 2. *subordinate*

_____ 3. *forefather*

_____ 4. *transgress*

_____ 5. *postern*

_____ 6. *incision*

_____ 7. *premature*

_____ 8. *expel*

_____ 9. *antechamber*

_____ 10. *telegraph*

_____ 11. *finale*

_____ 12. *circuit*

A. cut *into* something

B. occurring *before* the expected time

C. room that serves as an *entrance* to a larger room

D. give money *back*

E. apparatus for sending a message over a *distance*

F. *conclusion* of a program

G. *go across* a limit or boundary

H. circular course *around* an area

I. occupying a *lower* class, rank, or status

J. relative who came *before* you

K. force someone to go *out* of a place

L. *back* door to a church

EXERCISE I3: *Parts of the Universe and Parts of the Body*

The following word parts describe parts of the *universe* or parts of the *body*. Study these word parts because they appear in numerous words in English.

UNIVERSE			BODY		
PART	MEANING	EXAMPLE	PART	MEANING	EXAMPLE
geo	(earth)	geology	**corp**	(body)	corporation
terr	(earth)	territory	**card**	(heart)	cardiology
hydr	(water)	hydroplane	**derm**	(skin)	dermatologist
aqua	(water)	aquatic	**man**	(hand)	manual
astr	(star)	astronaut	**dent**	(teeth)	dentist
pyr	(fire)	pyrotechnics	**ped/pod**	(feet)	pedestrian
			cap	(head)	captain

Using the word parts above to help you, match the definitions on the right with the words on the left.

_____ 1. *geocentric*

_____ 2. *dentures*

_____ 3. *podiatry*

_____ 4. *capstone*

_____ 5. *dermatitis*

_____ 6. *corpulent*

_____ 7. *aquanaut*

_____ 8. *hydraulic*

_____ 9. *cardiovascular*

_____ 10. *terrace*

_____ 11. *pyrometer*

_____ 12. *manacles*

_____ 13. *asterisk*

A. an under*seas* explorer

B. a series of raised levels of *earth*

C. relating to the *heart* and blood vessels

D. figure of a *star* (*) used as a reference mark

E. having the *earth* as the center

F. *hand*cuffs

G. treatment of *foot* problems

H. having a fleshy *body*

I. *top* or final rock used to complete a structure

J. apparatus for measuring *high temperatures*

K. inflammation of the *skin*

L. operated by *water* under pressure or in motion

M. false *teeth*

EXERCISE I4: *Human States*

The following word parts describe *human states*. Study these word parts because they appear in numerous words in English.

HUMAN STATES					
PART	MEANING	EXAMPLE	PART	MEANING	EXAMPLE
am	(love)	amiable	**path**	(feeling)	sympathy
phil	(love)	Philadelphia	**mania**	(crazy)	maniac
bene	(good)	benefit	**phobia**	(fear)	claustrophobia
eu	(good)	euphemism	**psycho**	(mind)	psychology
mal	(bad)	malcontent	**bio**	(life)	biology
dys	(bad)	dysfunction	**mor**	(death)	mortal

Using the word parts above to help you, match the definitions on the right with the words on the left.

_____ 1. *euphoric*

_____ 2. *moribund*

_____ 3. *pathetic*

_____ 4. *malign*

_____ 5. *enamored*

_____ 6. *acrophobia*

_____ 7. *benevolent*

_____ 8. *biosphere*

_____ 9. *kleptomania*

_____ 10. *dyslexia*

_____ 11. *bibliophile*

_____ 12. *psychosis*

A. *fear* of high places

B. part of the earth's crust where *living* beings exist

C. stealing as a result of an *emotional disturbance*

D. any severe form of *mental* disorder

E. reduced ability or *lack of* ability to read

F. *lover* of books

G. in a *dying* state

H. speak *negatively* and harmfully about

I. feeling especially *happy*

J. evoking pity or *compassion*

K. in *love*

L. wanting to do *good* to others

EXERCISE I5: *People and Their Senses*

The following word parts describe *people* or their *senses*. Study these word parts because they appear in numerous words in English.

PEOPLE			SENSES		
PART	MEANING	EXAMPLE	PART	MEANING	EXAMPLE
pater	(father)	*patriarch*	**spec**	(see)	*spectator*
mater	(mother)	*maternity*	**vis/vid**	(see)	*visit/video*
frater	(brother)	*fraternal*	**scope**	(see)	*telescope*
domin	(master)	*domination*	**phon**	(hear)	*telephone*
jud	(judge)	*judgment*	**aud**	(hear)	*audience*
anthro	(people)	*anthropology*	**dic**	(say)	*dictate*
demo	(people)	*democracy*	**loc/loq**	(speak)	*eloquent*

Using the word parts above to help you, match the definitions on the right with the words on the left.

———— 1. *cacophony*

———— 2. *judiciary*

———— 3. *fraternize*

———— 4. *spectacle*

———— 5. *audiology*

———— 6. *patrimony*

———— 7. *periscope*

———— 8. *dominant*

———— 9. *anthropoid*

———— 10. *loquacious*

———— 11. *visualize*

———— 12. *valedictory*

———— 13. *matriarchal*

———— 14. *endemic*

A.   exerting *authority* or influence

B.   *see* in your mind

C.   being ruled or headed by a *woman*

D.   discordant *sound*

E.   exceedingly *talkative*

F.   system of *courts* in a country

G.   pertaining to a particular *people* or locality

H.   instrument to *view* obstructed objects

I.   farewell *speech* at a graduation ceremony

J.   science of *hearing*

K.   estate inherited from a *father* or ancestors

L.   associate in a friendly or *brotherly* way

M.   impressive *sight* or *view*

N.   resembling a *human being*

EXERCISE I6: *Size and Amount*

The following word parts describe *sizes* or *amounts*. Study these word parts because they appear in numerous words in English.

SIZE			AMOUNT		
PART	MEANING	EXAMPLE	PART	MEANING	EXAMPLE
min	(small)	minimum	*ambi*	(both)	ambivalent
micro	(small)	microphone	*multi*	(many)	multiple
macro	(large)	macroeconomics	*poly*	(many)	polygon
mega	(large)	megaphone	*omni*	(all)	omnipotent
magn	(large)	magnify	*auto*	(self)	automatic

Using the word parts above to help you, match the definitions on the right with the words on the left.

_____	1.	*autonomous*	A.	*tiny* plant or animal
_____	2.	*magnum*	B.	*great number* of persons or things
_____	3.	*minuscule*	C.	able to eat *all* types of food
_____	4.	*microorganism*	D.	universe as a *whole*
_____	5.	*polyglot*	E.	*very small*
_____	6.	*ambidextrous*	F.	*self*-governing
_____	7.	*omnivorous*	G.	able to speak or write *many* languages
_____	8.	*macrocosm*	H.	*giant* stone
_____	9.	*multitude*	I.	*large* bottle, for wine or champagne
_____	10.	*megalith*	J.	able to use *both* hands

EXERCISE I7: *Number*

The following word parts describe *numbers*. Study these word parts because they appear in numerous words in English.

NUMBER					
PART	MEANING	EXAMPLE	PART	MEANING	EXAMPLE
sol	(one)	*solo*	**quad**	(four)	*quad*ruplets
uni	(one)	*unique*	**oct**	(eight)	*oct*opus
mono	(one)	*monologue*	**dec**	(ten)	*dec*ade
bi	(two)	*bicycle*	**cent**	(hundred)	*century*
du	(two)	*duet*	**mil**	(thousand)	*millimeter*
tri	(three)	*triple*	**semi**	(half)	*semifinal*

Using the word parts above to help you, match the definitions on the right with the words on the left.

_____ 1. *bifocals*

_____ 2. *quadrennial*

_____ 3. *millennium*

_____ 4. *solitaire*

_____ 5. *tripartite*

_____ 6. *duplex*

_____ 7. *decathlon*

_____ 8. *unicorn*

_____ 9. *octogenarian*

_____ 10. *centennial*

_____ 11. *monorail*

_____ 12. *semiprivate*

A. mythical horselike animal with *one* horn

B. card game played by *one* person

C. *eighty*-year-old person

D. *partly* alone and *partly* shared

E. *hundredth* anniversary

F. train on *one* track

G. eyeglass lenses with *two* parts

H. occurring every *four* years

I. athletic contest involving *ten* events

J. period of a *thousand* years

K. building divided into *two* houses

L. divided into *three* sections

EXERCISE I8: *Opposites*

The following word parts describe *opposites*. Study these word parts because they appear in numerous words in English.

OPPOSITES					
PART	MEANING	EXAMPLE	PART	MEANING	EXAMPLE
anti	(against)	*anti*war	**im**	(not)	*im*perfect
contra	(against)	*contra*st	**il**	(not)	*il*legal
mis	(error)	*mis*spell	**in**	(not)	*in*correct
un	(not)	*un*true	**ir**	(not)	*ir*regular
dis	(not)	*dis*like			

Using the word parts above to help you, match the definitions on the right with the words on the left.

_____	1.	*illiterate*	A.	immoral act
_____	2.	*inedible*	B.	separate from
_____	3.	*contradict*	C.	medicine to counteract the effects of poison
_____	4.	*dissociate*		
_____	5.	*immature*	D.	childish
_____	6.	*misdeed*	E.	unable to be cured or solved
_____	7.	*irremediable*	F.	unable to read or write
_____	8.	*unarmed*	G.	deny or say the opposite
_____	9.	*antidote*	H.	unable to be eaten
			I.	without weapons

EXERCISE I9: *All Word Parts Together*

Study the word list at the top of each box. Then read each sentence and place the letter of an appropriate word in the sentence. You should use each word one time only, without changing the form.

A. WHO ARE THESE CHARACTERS?		
A. *autobiographer*	E. *introvert*	I. *polygamist*
B. *benefactor*	F. *manicurist*	J. *psychopath*
C. *corpse*	G. *misanthrope*	K. *spectator*
D. *expatriate*	H. *mortician*	L. *triathlete*

1. Someone who lives *outside* of his or her own country is a(n) _____.
2. Someone who works beautifying the *hands* and nails of others is a(n) _____.
3. Someone who *hates other people* is a(n) _____.
4. Someone who works preparing *dead* people for burial is a(n) _____.
5. Someone who is a dead *body* is a(n) _____.
6. Someone who is *writing* the story of his or her *own life* is a(n) _____.
7. Someone who is married to *more than one* person is a(n) _____.
8. Someone who competes in *three* related sports is a(n) _____.
9. Someone who *watches* while others perform is a(n) _____.
10. Someone who does *good* deeds for others is a(n) _____.
11. Someone who, because of *mental illness*, acts without morals is a(n) _____.
12. Someone who *turns* all his or her feelings *inward* is a(n) _____.

B. WHAT IS IT USED FOR?		
A. *aqueduct*	E. *microdot*	I. *terrarium*
B. *hydrant*	F. *missile*	J. *telescope*
C. *kaleidoscope*	G. *monocle*	K. *tripod*
D. *megaphone*	H. *submarine*	L. *unicycle*

1. A(n) _____ is useful when you want to travel *underwater.*
2. A(n) _____ can be used if you want to *see* something from *far* away.
3. A(n) _____ is a little difficult to ride because it has only *one* wheel.
4. A(n) _____ contains *water* that can be used to fight fires.
5. A(n) _____ is used to *send* some explosives to the enemy.
6. A(n) _____ can be used when you want to *grow plants* indoors.
7. A(n) _____ is a *tiny* spot that contains lots of information; spies have been known to use this.
8. A(n) _____ helps you see well out of *one* eye.
9. A(n) _____ is useful if you want to make *a big sound.*
10. A(n) _____ was constructed in olden times to *carry water* from place to place.
11. A(n) _____ lets a child look and *see* a variety of shapes and colors.
12. A(n) _____ is a *three-footed* stand that can be used to support a camera.

C.   WHAT ARE THESE THINGS REALLY LIKE?

A. *antebellum*   E. *illegible*   I. *minute*
B. *audiovisual*   F. *infinite*   J. *misfired*
C. *euphonious*   G. *invisible*   K. *portable*
D. *extraterrestrial* H. *irreversible*   L. *subterranean*

1. A(n) _____ television is one that can be *carried.*
2. Ink that is _____ can*not* be *seen* without a special lamp.
3. A(n) _____ decision is one that can*not* be *changed* back to what it was.
4. Handwriting that is _____ is *difficult to read.*
5. A(n) _____ source of water is one that is located *underground.*
6. A(n) _____ weapon is one that was shot in the *wrong way.*
7. A(n) _____ house is one that was built *before* the war.
8. Films or other _____ teaching materials can be both *seen* and *heard.*
9. Details that are _____ are really, really *small* and *unimportant.*
10. Music that is _____ is really *pleasant sounding.*
11. A(n) _____ supply of money is one that is *never-ending.*
12. A(n) _____ rock is one that came to earth *from outer space.*

D.   WHAT ON EARTH ARE YOU DOING?

A. *circumvent*   E. *dissect*   I. *premeditate*
B. *decapitate*   F. *exhale*   J. *prevent*
C. *dehydrate*   G. *interject*   K. *reverse*
D. *disinter*   H. *minimize*   L. *transmit*

1. If you _____ something, you take the *water* out of it.
2. If you _____ something, you *move around* it to avoid it.
3. If you _____ a murder, you think about it *before* you do it.
4. If you _____ something, you *turn* it in the *opposite* direction.
5. If you _____ someone, you cut his or her *head* off.
6. If you _____ something, you try to make it seem *smaller* and *less important.*
7. If you _____ when you are smoking, you breathe *out.*
8. If you _____ a few ideas into a conversation, you *throw* them *in* quickly.
9. If you _____ a body, you take it *out of the ground.*
10. If you _____ something, you *cut it in two.*
11. If you _____ something, you take action *beforehand* to stop it from occurring.
12. If you _____ a message, you *send it from one place to another.*

E.   DO YOU KNOW PEOPLE LIKE THIS?

A. *ambivalent*	E. *incredulous*	I. *maternal*
B. *amorous*	F. *indomitable*	J. *omnipotent*
C. *antiquated*	G. *introspective*	K. *subtle*
D. *bilingual*	H. *magnanimous*	L. *unselfish*

1. Someone who is _____ has power and control over *everything*.
2. Someone who is _____ can*not believe* what is happening.
3. Someone who is _____ is always *looking inside* for answers.
4. Someone who is _____ acts in a *motherly* fashion.
5. Someone who is _____ is always falling *in love*.
6. Someone who is _____ can*not* be *subjugated*.
7. Someone who is _____ acts in an *under*stated way.
8. Someone who is _____ does what is best *for others*.
9. Someone who is _____ speaks *two* languages.
10. Someone who is _____ comes from an *earlier* time.
11. Someone who is _____ does *not* take *either* side in a discussion.
12. Someone who is _____ would generously give *everything he or she has* to others.

F.   HOW'S YOUR HEALTH?

A. *antibiotic*	E. *epidemic*	I. *revive*
B. *biopsy*	F. *epidermis*	J. *postmortem*
C. *cardiogram*	G. *euthanasia*	K. *psychosomatic*
D. *dentifrice*	H. *malignant*	L. *semiconscious*

1. If you are only *half* awake or aware, you are _____.
2. When *all the people* in an area get a disease, it is a(n) _____.
3. When someone is almost dead and is brought *back to life*, the doctor has been able to _____ him or her.
4. A(n) _____ is done when *living* tissue is cut out of a body in order to study it.
5. A(n) _____ tumor is one that is found to be cancerous, or *bad*.
6. You should use a _____ on your *teeth* to keep them healthy.
7. A doctor will use a _____ to test the health of a patient's *heart*.
8. A substance that is used *against* harmful *living* organisms is an _____.
9. A(n) _____ illness occurs when someone *thinks* he or she is sick but really is not.
10. The outer layer of a patient's *skin* is called the _____.
11. If a person is really suffering from an incurable disease, sometimes a loved one might use _____ to put him or her to death for his or her own *good*.
12. *After* someone has *died*, a(n) _____ is conducted.

G.   HOW DO YOU DO THIS?

A. *circumnavigate*	E. *intercede*	I. *reject*
B. *contravene*	F. *postdate*	J. *remit*
C. *inscribe*	G. *preview*	K. *subvert*
D. *inspect*	H. *recede*	L. *transplant*

1. To _____ a book, you *look* at it *ahead of time.*
2. To _____ a tree, you take it out of the ground and *move* it *to another place.*
3. To _____ a machine, you *look into* it very carefully and check for problems.
4. To _____ a check, you write a date that is *after* today's date.
5. To _____ a payment, you *send* it in.
6. To _____ someone, you *under*mine the support that he or she has.
7. To _____ in a problem, you *go* right *into* the middle of it.
8. To _____ a fish that you catch, you *throw* it *back.*
9. To _____ a book, you *write* a message *in* it.
10. To cause something to _____, you make it *go back.*
11. To _____ in a bad situation, you act *against* it or do the *opposite* of what is happening.
12. To _____ an island, you sail all the way *around* it.

H.   WHO NEEDS FRIENDS LIKE THESE?

A. *abrupt*	E. *immutable*	I. *malevolent*
B. *apathetic*	F. *inaudible*	J. *misinformed*
C. *domineering*	G. *injudicious*	K. *monotonous*
D. *immoral*	H. *judgmental*	L. *morbid*

1. A friend who is _____ wants *bad* things to happen to others.
2. A friend who is _____ always makes *judgments* (often negative) about others.
3. A friend who is _____ always insists on *controlling* every solution.
4. A friend who is _____ can*not* be *heard* when he or she speaks.
5. A friend who is _____ does *not feel* strongly about anything.
6. A friend who is _____ is only concerned with *death.*
7. A friend who is _____ can *never* be persuaded to *change.*
8. A friend who is _____ does *not* make wise or well-thought-out *decisions.*
9. A friend who is _____ does *not* do the *correct* or *right* thing.
10. A friend who is _____ *cuts* off others when they try to speak or act.
11. A friend who is _____ *never has* the *correct* facts.
12. A friend who is _____ always speaks in the *same tone* of voice.

I. CAN YOU GUESS WHAT IT IS?

A. *antecedent*	E. *controversy*	I. *mutation*
B. *autograph*	F. *foreword*	J. *octave*
C. *benediction*	G. *manuscript*	K. *postscript*
D. *biography*	H. *misnomer*	L. *soliloquy*

1. If you refer to something that came *before*, it is a(n) _____.
2. If you give a *speech* all *by yourself* in a play, it is a(n) _____.
3. Words *written* at the *end* of a letter make up a(n) _____.
4. If you ask a famous person to *write* his name *himself*, you get his _____.
5. At the beginning of the book, *before* the main part of the text, you may find a(n) _____.
6. If you *write* the story of someone's *life*, you write a(n) _____.
7. A musical interval that is *eight* notes apart is a(n) _____.
8. If you *write* something by *hand*, it is a(n) _____.
9. If two people argue *against* each other, they have a(n) _____.
10. If you *say* a few *good* words to close a ceremony, you give a(n) _____.
11. A sudden *change* in the offspring of a plant or animal is a(n) _____.
12. If you call something by an *incorrect name*, it is a(n) _____.

J. YOU'RE IN BUSINESS?

A. *autocratic*	E. *export*	I. *patron*
B. *bankrupt*	F. *magnate*	J. *semiannual*
C. *bilateral*	G. *monopoly*	K. *subsidiary*
D. *demographics*	H. *multimedia*	L. *visionary*

1. A branch company that comes *under* the control of the parent company is called a(n) _____.
2. When *one* company has control of a particular field of business, it has a(n) _____.
3. A(n) _____ agreement is an equal agreement for *both* sides.
4. Before marketing a product, you must check the _____, the characteristics of the *people* you want to sell to.
5. To send goods *out* of the country is to _____ them.
6. If a company is completely *broke* and has no money or resources left, it is _____.
7. A(n) _____ leader makes all the decisions *alone*.
8. If you have a sale every *six months*, it is a(n) _____ sale.
9. Advertising that is in newspapers, on radio, and on television is _____ advertising.
10. If you believe that "the customer is always right," then you might call a customer a(n) _____.
11. The type of leader who can *see* what is coming in the future and be prepared for it is a(n) _____.
12. A person of *great* influence and importance in a field of business is a(n) _____.

K.   DO YOU SUFFER FROM THIS?

A. *circumlocution*	E. *dyspepsia*	I. *prejudice*
B. *contradiction*	F. *egomania*	J. *pyromania*
C. *disrespect*	G. *irrationality*	K. *solitude*
D. *duplicity*	H. *monomania*	L. *zoophobia*

1. Someone who does *not think* logically suffers from _____.
2. Someone who likes _____ prefers to be *alone*.
3. Someone who is *afraid* of animals suffers from _____.
4. Someone who acts with _____ makes up his or her mind *before* the facts are known.
5. Someone who is able to focus on *only one* thing suffers from _____.
6. Someone who suffers from _____ has a *mental problem* and believes that he or she is the only important person in the world.
7. Someone who has something *wrong* with his or her digestive system suffers from _____.
8. Someone who *speaks indirectly* about something uses _____.
9. Someone who is guilty of *double*-dealing and deception is guilty of _____.
10. Someone who deals with others with _____ does *not* act *politely* with them.
11. Someone who *says* one thing one day and the *opposite* the next day is guilty of a(n) _____.
12. Someone who likes to start *fires* and watch them burn and destroy suffers from _____.

L.   CAN YOU FIGURE THIS OUT?

A. *amity*	E. *credibility*	I. *matricide*
B. *aquaculture*	F. *geopolitics*	J. *paternalism*
C. *astrology*	G. *hydrolysis*	K. *telepathy*
D. *astrophysics*	H. *macrobiotics*	L. *vitality*

1. If you are a good *friend* to people, then you believe in _____.
2. If you divide a compound into other compounds by taking up the elements of *water*, you use _____.
3. If you *kill your mother*, you are guilty of _____.
4. If you grow things in *water*, then you make use of _____.
5. If you lead a business or a country as if you are a *father*, then you believe in _____.
6. If you are *lively* and *active*, then you have _____.
7. If you are interested in the physical properties of the *stars*, then you are interested in _____.
8. If you are *believable*, then you have _____.
9. If you want to *lengthen* your *life* by means of a vegetarian diet, then you believe in _____.
10. If you believe that the *stars* and other heavenly bodies influence your life, you believe in _____.
11. If you use mental _____, you are able to understand what someone is thinking or *feeling* from *far* away.
12. If you are interested in the effect of the layout of the *land* on the power and sovereignty of a country, then you are interested in _____.

SCORING INFORMATION

SCORING YOUR PAPER PRE-TESTS, POST-TESTS, AND COMPLETE PRACTICE TEST

When your paper TOEFL test is scored, you will receive a score between 20 and 68 in each of the three sections (Listening Comprehension, Structure and Written Expression, and Reading Comprehension). You will also receive an overall score between 217 and 677. You can use the following chart to estimate the scores on your paper Pre-Tests, Post-Tests, and Complete Practice Test.

NUMBER CORRECT	CONVERTED SCORE SECTION 1	CONVERTED SCORE SECTION 2	CONVERTED SCORE SECTION 3
50	68	–	67
49	67	–	66
48	66	–	65
47	65	–	63
46	63	–	61
45	62	–	60
44	61	–	59
43	60	–	58
42	59	–	57
41	58	–	56
40	57	68	55
39	57	67	54
38	56	65	54
37	55	63	53
36	54	61	52
35	54	60	52
34	53	58	51
33	52	57	50
32	52	56	49
31	51	55	48
30	51	54	48
29	50	53	47
28	49	52	46
27	49	51	46
26	48	50	45
25	48	49	44
24	47	48	43
23	47	47	43
22	46	46	42
21	45	45	41

NUMBER CORRECT	CONVERTED SCORE SECTION 1	CONVERTED SCORE SECTION 2	CONVERTED SCORE SECTION 3
20	45	44	40
19	44	43	39
18	43	42	38
17	42	41	37
16	41	40	36
15	41	40	35
14	37	38	34
13	38	37	32
12	37	36	31
11	35	35	30
10	33	33	29
9	32	31	28
8	32	29	28
7	31	27	27
6	30	26	26
5	29	25	25
4	28	23	24
3	27	22	23
2	26	21	23
1	25	20	22
0	24	20	21

You should first use the chart to determine your converted score for each section. Suppose that you got 30 correct in the first section, 28 correct in the second section, and 43 correct in the third section. The 30 correct in the first section means a converted score of 51. The 28 correct in the second section means a converted score of 52. The 43 correct in the third section means a converted score of 58. (See the chart below.)

	SECTION 1	SECTION 2	SECTION 3
NUMBER CORRECT	30	28	43
CONVERTED SCORE	51	52	58

Next, you should determine your overall score in the following way:

1. <u>Add the three converted scores together.</u> $51 + 52 + 58 = 161$

2. <u>Divide the sum by 3.</u> $161/3 = 53.7$

3. <u>Then multiply by 10.</u> $53.7 \times 10 = 537$

The overall TOEFL score in this example is 537.

CHARTING YOUR PROGRESS

Each time you take a Pre-Test, Post-Test, or Complete Practice Test, you should record the results in the chart that follows. In this way, you will be able to keep track of the progress you make.

PAPER TOEFL TESTS

Fill in your score on each test section as you take it. Then after you have taken all three sections of a particular test, compute your overall score and add it to the chart.

	LISTENING COMPRE-HENSION	STRUCTURE AND WRITTEN EXPRESSION	READING COMPRE-HENSION	OVERALL SCORE
PRE-TEST				
POST-TEST				
COMPLETE PRACTICE TEST				

COMPUTER TOEFL TESTS

Keep track of the number correct on each test section as you take it.

	LISTENING	STRUCTURE	READING
PRE-TEST			
POST-TEST			
COMPLETE PRACTICE TEST			

RECORDING SCRIPT

LISTENING DIAGNOSTIC PRE-TEST (Paper)

Part A, page 3

1. (woman) Are you enjoying your coffee?
   (man) It tastes extremely bitter this morning!
   (narrator) WHAT DOES THE MAN MEAN?

2. (woman) Can you tell me how often the philosophy class meets?
   (man) It meets twice a week, for an hour and a half each time.
   (narrator) WHAT DOES THE MAN MEAN?

3. (man) I'm tired of just sitting here!
   (woman) Relax. I'm sure that the flight will depart within a few minutes.
   (narrator) WHAT DOES THE WOMAN MEAN?

4. (woman) The science project is due next week.
   (man) I suppose I'll have to start working on it now.
   (narrator) WHAT DOES THE MAN MEAN?

5. (man) I'd like to order a dozen roses. Do you deliver?
   (woman) Yes. We can deliver anywhere in the city by this afternoon.
   (narrator) WHERE DOES THIS CONVERSATION PROBABLY TAKE PLACE?

6. (woman) Did you enjoy the biology lecture?
   (man) The professor droned on and on about cell division.
   (narrator) WHAT DOES THE MAN MEAN?

7. (man) What do I need to cash a check?
   (woman) I have to see a driver's license and a credit card.
   (narrator) WHAT DOES THE WOMAN MEAN?

8. (woman) Have you been able to find an apartment yet?
   (man) It's difficult to find affordable housing in New York.
   (narrator) WHAT DOES THE MAN MEAN?

9. (woman) Why were you so late in getting home from work?
   (man) My boss had me finish all the month-end reports.
   (narrator) WHAT DOES THE MAN MEAN?

10. (man) Ms. Jones did not look too happy as she left her classroom.
    (woman) She was angered by her rowdy students.
    (narrator) WHAT DOES THE WOMAN MEAN?

11. (woman) The prices at this store are really outrageous!
    (man) You can say that again!
    (narrator) WHAT DOES THE MAN MEAN?

12. (woman) I don't like this weather very much.

(man) We haven't see rain like this for many years!
(narrator) WHAT DOES THE MAN MEAN?

13. (man) Professor Martin, what do you think of the composition that I turned in last week?
    (woman) Without question, you need to improve the quality of your writing.
    (narrator) WHAT DOES PROFESSOR MARTIN SAY ABOUT THE STUDENT?

14. (woman) Where should I go next?
    (man) You must stand in this line so that the agent can check your passport.
    (narrator) WHAT DOES THE MAN MEAN?

15. (man) Did Paul get his work done?
    (woman) He couldn't finish the assignment because the library was closed.
    (narrator) WHAT DOES THE WOMAN SAY ABOUT PAUL?

16. (woman) The lawyer spent hours and hours working on that case.
    (man) It's true that he prepared hard for the case, but his work was for nothing.
    (narrator) WHAT DOES THE MAN MEAN?

17. (woman) Do you know when the papers for Professor Jenkins' history class are due?
    (man) They're due next week, aren't they?
    (narrator) WHAT DOES THE MAN MEAN?

18. (woman) Are you happy with the work that the contractor did on your house?
    (man) I'm rather dissatisfied with it.
    (narrator) WHAT DOES THE MAN MEAN?

19. (man) I can't find a typist to finish my term paper by tomorrow morning.
    (woman) Why not do it yourself?
    (narrator) WHAT DOES THE WOMAN SUGGEST?

20. (man) I can't get this television set connected to the cable.
    (woman) Oh, it's as easy as pie.
    (narrator) WHAT DOES THE WOMAN MEAN?

21. (man) Is Bob doing a good job in the office?
    (woman) He never manages to turn in his budget reports on time.
    (narrator) WHAT DOES THE WOMAN SAY ABOUT BOB?

22. (man) Has the auto mechanic told you how much work the car needs?
    (woman) He indicated that the repairs would be quite extensive.
    (narrator) WHAT DOES THE WOMAN MEAN?

23. (woman) Did Betty listen to what her boss said?
    (man) She followed the directions to the letter.
    (narrator) WHAT DOES THE MAN MEAN?

24. (woman) How's Walter doing in his new business?

(man) Well, he hasn't exactly been unsuccessful.

(narrator) WHAT DOES THE MAN MEAN?

25. (woman) Are you going to organize that closet this morning?

(man) I wish I didn't have to.

(narrator) WHAT DOES THE MAN MEAN?

26. (man) Did Sally finish that difficult assignment?

(woman) She gave up before she really got started.

(narrator) WHAT DOES THE WOMAN SAY ABOUT SALLY?

27. (woman) What did Peggy say about the job I did?

(man) She couldn't have said nicer things.

(narrator) WHAT DOES THE MAN SAY ABOUT PEGGY?

28. (man) Your new secretary seems to be doing a great job.

(woman) Rarely do new employees take such initiative.

(narrator) WHAT DOES THE WOMAN MEAN?

29. (woman) Did you enjoy taking care of the children all afternoon?

(man) If you had gotten here any later, I'd have been a wreck.

(narrator) WHAT DOES THE MAN MEAN?

30. (man) I just got back from the market.
(woman) So you did do the shopping!
(narrator) WHAT HAD THE WOMAN ASSUMED ABOUT THE MAN?

Part B, page 7

Questions 31–34

(narrator) Listen to a conversation on a university campus.

(man) You seem to know your way around campus. Have you been here long?

(woman) I'm a senior literature major. I'll be graduating next June.

(man) Your major is literature? Mine is, too. But I'm just beginning my work in my major. I just transferred to this university from a junior college. Perhaps you could tell me about the courses you've got to take for a literature major.

(woman) Well, for a literature major you need to take eight courses, three required courses and five electives. First, you have to take "Survey of World Literature, Parts One and Two." This is really two courses, and it'll take two semesters, and it's required for all literature majors. The other course required for all literature majors is "Introduction to Literary Analysis."

(man) You mean, if I want to specialize in American literature, I still must take two semesters of World literature?

(woman) Yes, because the two semesters are required for all literature majors.

(man) But I only want to study American literature!

(woman) At least you can take all of your five elective courses in the area that you want.

(man) That's what I'll do, then.

31. WHAT IS THE WOMAN'S STATUS AT THE UNIVERSITY?

32. WHAT DOES THE MAN WANT TO LEARN FROM THE WOMAN?

33. HOW MANY TOTAL COURSES MUST A STUDENT TAKE FOR A LITERATURE MAJOR?

34. THE MAN WILL PROBABLY TAKE HIS ELECTIVE COURSES IN WHICH AREA?

Questions 35–38

(narrator) Listen to a conversation between two friends.

(woman) Wasn't that a fascinating lecture on dolphins? I didn't know that dolphins traveled in such large groups, or were able to communicate with other members of their group with those whistle-like sounds.

(man) And they also use clicks as a sort of sonar.

(woman) I really couldn't understand that part of the lecture. You could?

(man) Yes, the dolphins use clicks to identify objects in the water; they can even identify tiny objects more than 100 meters away using these clicks. Scientists believe that a dolphin may even have a sonar-like image in its brain of a distant object so that it can identify the object long before the dolphin can actually see the object.

(woman) So the dolphins use these clicks mostly to identify objects in the water?

(man) I think so, and they have considerably more ability to do this than humans do.

(woman) It is hard to believe that, in addition to these sonar clicks, dolphins are actually learning some human language.

(man) Yes, I believe that the lecturer said that some dolphins had already learned around fifty human commands, and that those dolphins were able to understand not only individual words but words clustered together in sentences!

(woman) Dolphins must certainly be amazing animals to do all of that.

(man) I'm sure they are, and we're only just beginning to find out how intelligent they are.

35. WHERE DID THE WOMAN LEARN ABOUT DOLPHINS?
36. WHY DO DOLPHINS USE CLICKS?
37. APPROXIMATELY HOW MANY HUMAN COMMANDS HAVE SOME DOLPHINS LEARNED?
38. WHAT DOES THE MAN SAY ABOUT DOLPHIN INTELLIGENCE?

Part C, page 8
Questions 39–42

(narrator)   Listen to a welcome address by a member of a club.

(woman)   Welcome to this introductory meeting for new members of the Sierra Club. The Sierra Club is an organization whose goals are centered on the protection of the environment. It was founded in 1892 in San Francisco by naturalist John Muir, who was intent on preserving the natural beauty and harmony of the Sierra Nevadas in eastern California.

Today the Sierra Club boasts almost 200,000 members in all fifty states of the United States. Through activities such as conferences, lectures, exhibits, and films, the organization works to continue the effort begun by John Muir. The Sierra Club also publishes a weekly newsletter, a bimonthly magazine, and various books.

39. WHAT IS THE MAIN OBJECTIVE OF THE SIERRA CLUB?
40. APPROXIMATELY HOW LONG HAS THE SIERRA CLUB BEEN IN EXISTENCE?
41. WHAT AREA WAS JOHN MUIR ESPECIALLY INTERESTED IN SAVING?
42. WHERE DOES THE SIERRA CLUB HAVE MEMBERS?

Questions 43–46

(narrator)   Listen to a talk by a university employee.

(man)   The next stop on our campus tour for new freshmen is the university sports complex. This university has extensive sports facilities and is dedicated to providing maximum student access to these facilities.

On the right you can see the university stadium, which is used for football and soccer as well as track and field. The gymnasium straight ahead contains the arena that is used for basketball and gymnastics. The gymnasium also includes an up-to-date exercise room with a large variety of the latest equipment; the exercise room is open to any student with valid student I.D., not just members of athletic teams. The pool complex is behind the gymnasium, and that is also open for general student use, except when the swim team, the diving team, or the water polo team is practicing.

To the left, you can see the tennis courts and outdoor volleyball courts. It is possible to take instruction classes in these sports, or you are welcome to sign up for court time at the Athletic Department office if you just want to play with some of your friends.

These are just some of the sports facilities that are available to you here, but I think you can see that this university makes an effort to provide the best opportunity for its students to take part in sports. Now, let's continue on to the Art Center.

43. WHO IS PROBABLY LISTENING TO THIS TALK?
44. WHAT IS NEEDED TO GET INTO THE EXERCISE ROOM?
45. WHERE SHOULD A STUDENT GO TO RESERVE A TENNIS COURT?
46. WHAT WILL THE STUDENTS PROBABLY DO NEXT?

Questions 47–50

(narrator)   Listen to a talk given by a professor.

(woman)   Today's lecture is on the difference between the two literary styles of realism and naturalism. These two styles have in common a faithfulness to actual experience and a mistrust of idealism.

Although they do have several similarities, realism and naturalism should be clearly differentiated. The realist objectively reports on events, with the accuracy of the description as the prime motive. The naturalist, on the other hand, has more of a philosophic bent; naturalist writings express the writer's philosophy that human actions are determined by natural laws such as heredity and environment.

47. THIS TALK WOULD PROBABLY BE GIVEN IN WHICH OF THE FOLLOWING COURSES?
48. WHAT POINT IS THE SPEAKER TRYING TO MAKE ABOUT REALISM AND NATURALISM?
49. WHICH OF THE FOLLOWING BEST DESCRIBES REALISM?
50. WHICH OF THE FOLLOWING DOES NOT INFLUENCE HUMAN ACTIONS, ACCORDING TO NATURALIST IDEAS?

LISTENING DIAGNOSTIC PRE-TEST
(Computer)

Part A, page 11

1. **(man)** How would you like to go skiing this weekend?
   (woman) I was kind of scared the last time I tried it, but I'd like another chance to try it again.
   (narrator) WHAT DOES THE WOMAN MEAN?

2. **(woman)** You couldn't get into your apartment? Why not?
   (man) The key they gave me wouldn't fit into the lock.
   (narrator) WHAT DOES THE MAN MEAN?

3. **(man)** Is Professor Nash a good lecturer?
   (woman) He doesn't speak very loudly, but otherwise he's great.
   (narrator) WHAT DOES THE WOMAN SAY ABOUT PROFESSOR NASH?

4. **(woman)** You got a ticket? How did that happen?
   (man) The car was parked in a no-parking zone.
   (narrator) WHAT DOES THE MAN MEAN?

5. **(woman)** Did you see Sally's presentation?
   (man) I sure did.
   (woman) Was she prepared for her presentation? I'm not sure she spent much time working on it.
   (man) Trust me. She couldn't have been more prepared.
   (narrator) WHAT DOES THE MAN SAY ABOUT SALLY?

6. **(man)** Can you believe that tuition has gone up for next year?
   (woman) I can believe it. The fee increase wasn't exactly unexpected.
   (narrator) WHAT DOES THE WOMAN MEAN?

7. **(woman)** I can't believe how fast the professor spoke during the lecture on physiology.
   (man) You can say that again!
   (narrator) WHAT DOES THE MAN MEAN?

8. **(man)** So you have a part-time job on the newspaper?
   (woman) Well, I do for now. But I've heard that some of the employees are getting laid off. I hope I still have a job after that.
   (narrator) WHAT DOES THE WOMAN SAY ABOUT THE EMPLOYEES?

9. **(woman)** Could I borrow your notes from yesterday's lecture?
   (man) Sorry, I'd let you borrow my notes if I had them, but I don't.
   (woman) Then you <u>weren't</u> in class yesterday either.
   (narrator) WHAT DID THE WOMAN BELIEVE?

10. **(woman)** The conference last weekend was really great!
    (man) I heard that it was. I really wish I had been able to go.
    (narrator) WHAT DOES THE MAN MEAN?

Part B, page 14
Questions 11–12
(man) Did you see Carl?
(woman) Yes, I did. His leg was in a cast, and he was on crutches.
(man) Do you know what happened to him?
(woman) I heard that he tripped and fell down the stadium steps at the football game last Saturday evening.
(man) That's how he broke his leg? He tripped and fell down in the stadium?
(woman) That's just what happened.

11. WHAT HAPPENED TO CARL?
12. HOW DID CARL BREAK HIS LEG?

Questions 13–15
(woman) This is an interesting assignment we have for psychology class.
(man) Interesting? It's going to be a lot of work.
(woman) What's so hard about it? We just have to make up a survey questionnaire related to theories from the class.
(man) Making up a survey questionnaire isn't so hard. But we have to find 50 people to fill out the questionnaire and then write up a report analyzing the data.
(woman) It'll be easy to find 50 people to fill out the questionnaire. We can do that in one afternoon at the Student Union. That actually sounds like fun to me.
(man) That's good. I don't mind preparing the questionnaire and analyzing the data, but getting 50 people to answer the questionnaire does <u>not</u> seem like fun to me.

13. WHAT DO THE STUDENTS HAVE TO PREPARE?
14. HOW MANY PEOPLE MUST RESPOND TO THE QUESTIONNAIRE?
15. WHAT DOES THE MAN NOT WANT TO DO?

Questions 16–20
(narrator) Listen to a discussion about a history course. The discussion is on the Outer Banks.

(woman 1) We certainly have a lot of questions to review for our history exam.
(man) Yes, we do, but we're almost finished. We only have two questions to go.
(woman 2) Only two more questions? That's great. Let's get going on them, and we'll be finished preparing for this exam soon… Now, what's the next question on the study list?

(woman 1)	The next question on the study list asks about famous historical places on the Outer Banks.
(woman 2)	The Outer Banks? Where are the Outer Banks?
(man)	Look at the map in the book. The Outer Banks are a series of islands stretching along the coast of North Carolina.
(woman 1)	Now, the question asks about famous historical places on the Outer Banks. Can you come up with any?
(man)	Let's see. There's the Lost Colony on Roanoke.
(woman 1)	Can you see Roanoke Island on the map? That was where the Lost Colony was located.
(woman 2)	Wait a minute. The Lost Colony? What was the Lost Colony?
(man)	The Lost Colony was the group of settlers from England that landed on Roanoke Island in 1587. When a supply ship returned there three years later, the colonists had disappeared. To this day, no one knows what happened to them.
(woman 1)	Okay, I think Roanoke Island is one good answer to a question about famous historical places on the Outer Banks. Now, what about Ocracoke Island? Isn't Ocracoke Island famous for something?
(woman 2)	All I know about Ocracoke Island is that it's where Blackbeard had his hideout.
(man)	Blackbeard, the pirate?
(woman 2)	Yes. Blackbeard had his hideout on Ocracoke Island, early in the eighteenth century. He used to move up and down the coast from his hideout on Ocracoke and attack ships and steal their goods.
(woman 1)	Okay, so we've got historical places on Roanoake Island and Ocracoke Island for answers to the question. Can you come up with any other historical places on the Outer Banks?
(man)	What about the Wright brothers? Didn't they make their flights on the Outer Banks?
(woman 2)	Yes, it was at Kill Devil Hill, outside of Kitty Hawk, that the Wright brothers made their flights.
(man)	On December 7, 1903, they managed to get a power-driven plane in the air, for just a short time. But the plane was flying.
(woman 2)	Their first flight was only 12 seconds long. They tried four flights on the same day, and by the end of the day, they got the plane to stay up for fifty-nine seconds, almost a full minute.
(woman 1)	Okay. I think we have enough information to answer that question. We've got historical places on Roanoke

	Island, Ocracoke Island, and Kitty Hawk.
(man)	I agree. Why don't we leave the question on the Outer Banks and move on to another question?
(woman 2)	That's great! There's only one more question on our study list. After we finish that question, we'll be done with the list.

16. WHAT ARE THE STUDENTS DOING?
17. WITH WHAT PLACE ARE THESE PEOPLE ASSOCIATED?
18. WHEN DID THESE PEOPLE LIVE?
19. WHAT IS STATED ABOUT THE INHABITANTS OF THE LOST COLONY?
20. HOW LONG WAS THE LONGEST FLIGHT THAT THE WRIGHT BROTHERS TOOK ON DECEMBER 3, 1903?

Questions 21–25

(narrator)	Listen to a lecture in a zoology class. The professor is talking about hibernation.
(professor)	When it begins getting cold in the north as winter approaches, different types of animals deal with the approach of the cold weather in different ways. Some animals move south to warmer weather, some animals increase their activity to stay warm, and other animals hibernate during the cold weather. Today, we'll be discussing this third category of animals, the animals that hibernate. These are the animals like groundhogs and bears that go into a state of unconsciousness during the cold winter months.

The first animal we'll look at is the groundhog. The groundhog is one of the best-known hibernators. It goes into its burrow four or five feet underground sometime in the fall, and it doesn't come out until spring. A groundhog stays in its underground burrow for the entire winter, without coming out. Because the groundhog hibernates so completely, it's the groundhog that has achieved prominence in our folklore as the animal that is responsible for determining whether or not winter is over and it's safe to come out of hibernation.

According to folklore, the groundhog will come out of the burrow where it's hibernating on Groundhog Day in February. If winter is over, the groundhog will remain out of its burrow, but if winter is going to last for a while longer, the groundhog will see its shadow and scurry back into its burrow.

We've discussed the groundhog, which hibernates throughout the cold weather. Other animals that hibernate in a similar fashion are bats and squirrels. Now we'll look at the bear, which hibernates in a different manner.

Bears do not hibernate as completely as groundhogs, bats, or squirrels. In the southern half of the United States, bears do not hibernate at all because the weather doesn't get cold enough for them to hibernate. In the northern half of the United States, bears may not stay in hibernation for the entire winter. They may come out of their hibernation during the winter and wander about before returning to hibernation.

A very important point that I'd like you to understand is that hibernation is different from sleep, and these differences between sleep and hibernation are seen in body temperature and heart rate. The main characteristics of hibernation, which are very different from sleep, are that body temperature and heart rate decrease significantly.

When an animal comes out of hibernation, the heart rate and body temperature increase to the levels normal during waking hours. During the period when a large animal such as a bear is coming out of hibernation, the animal's entire body does not warm at once.

The area around the heart warms up first. As the heart warms up, it begins beating at its normal rate, and it is then able to pump blood around the rest of the body and heat up the rest of the body.

These are the main points that we need to cover about hibernation. Now, we'll take a short break before moving on to the next subject.

21. WHAT IS NOT MENTIONED BY THE PROFESSOR AS A WAY THAT VARIOUS TYPES OF ANIMALS PREPARE FOR THE COLD WEATHER?
22. WHAT IS NOT STATED IN THE LECTURE ABOUT GROUNDHOG DAY?
23. WHICH OF THE FOLLOWING IS NOT A GOOD HIBERNATOR?
24. WHAT HAPPENS TO BODY TEMPERATURE AND HEART RATE DURING HIBERNATION?
25. WHAT PART OF THE BEAR WAKES UP FIRST FROM HIBERNATION?

Questions 26–30

(narrator)   Listen to a lecture in a science class. The professor is talking about Three-Mile Island.

(professor)   Today, I'll be talking about an accident at a nuclear power plant. The accident I'll be discussing is the one that occurred at Three-Mile Island in 1979. By the end of the lecture, you should understand what factors contributed to the accident there.

You can see Three-Mile Island in this photograph. The nuclear reactor at Three-Mile Island is in the middle of a river in the state of Pennsylvania. This nuclear reactor has two PWRs, which means that it has two pressurized water reactors. The problem that occurred in 1979 was in the Number Two pressurized water reactor.

Now we're going to discuss what happened in the Number Two reactor at Three-Mile Island.

The important thing to understand about the accident was that there was a series of problems rather than a single problem.

The series of problems occurred in the water-cooling system. The initial problem was that a cooling system valve stuck open and cooling water ran out.

Unfortunately, the problem did not end when the cooling valve stuck open because operators misinterpreted the instrument readings. They knew there was a problem. They thought the cooling system had too much water rather than too little water. Because they thought that there was too much water, they shut off the emergency cooling water. As a result, there was no water to cool the nuclear reactor.

There wasn't a complete nuclear meltdown when the emergency cooling water was turned off, but there was a partial nuclear meltdown. A nuclear meltdown would exist if the uranium in the fuel core melted completely. In this situation, heat built up in the fuel core until the uranium began to melt, but it didn't melt down completely.

I hope you can understand the series of events that led to the problem at Three-Mile Island. It all started with the stuck valve in the cooling system and was exacerbated by the misinterpreted readings and the improper shutdown of the emergency cooling system.

Fortunately, the meltdown that did occur was only partial and not complete.

26. WHAT DO THE INITIALS PWR STAND FOR?
27. HOW MANY PWRS ARE THERE ON THREE-MILE ISLAND?
28. WHAT DOES THE LECTURER SAY ABOUT THE PWRS DURING THE ACCIDENT?
29. WHAT ERRORS DID THE OPERATORS MAKE?
30. THE PROFESSOR EXPLAINS A SERIES OF EVENTS. PUT THE EVENTS IN THE ORDER IN WHICH THEY OCCURRED.

SHORT DIALOGUES (Paper and Computer)

TOEFL EXERCISE 1, page 30

1. *(woman)*   How soon will you be leaving?
   (man)   I'm on my way now.
   (narrator)   WHAT DOES THE MAN MEAN?

2. *(man)*   Was Steve able to get into the house?
   (woman)   I left the door unlocked for him.
   (narrator)   WHAT DOES THE WOMAN ASSUME STEVE DID?

3. *(man)*   The dinner special is roast turkey with mashed potatoes and gravy, and apple pie for dessert.
   (woman)   That doesn't sound good to me.
   (narrator)   WHAT DOES THE WOMAN MEAN?

4. *(woman)*   Could you help me with my physics homework tonight? I'm really having trouble with it.
   (man)   Sorry, I'm busy tonight.
   (narrator)   WHAT DOES THE MAN IMPLY?

5. *(man)*   What did you think of Professor Martin's lecture on the migratory habits of whales?
   (woman)   I couldn't keep my eyes open.
   (narrator)   WHAT DOES THE WOMAN MEAN?

6. *(woman)*   Have this month's bills been paid, or is that something we need to take care of now?
   (man)   I paid the phone and electricity, but not the credit cards.
   (narrator)   WHAT DOES THE MAN MEAN?

7. *(man)*   Will you be able to get back from running all your errands by four o'clock?
   (woman)   I'll be back as quickly as I can.
   (narrator)   WHAT DOES THE WOMAN SAY THAT SHE'LL DO?

8. *(man)*   Have you seen Tim? I really need to talk with him about the phone bill.
   (woman)   Well,... he was here just a minute ago.
   (narrator)   WHAT DOES THE WOMAN SAY ABOUT TIM?

9. *(man)*   There's a car parked in my spot even though the sign says that this space is reserved.
   (woman)   I guess we'll have to park somewhere else.
   (narrator)   WHAT DOES THE WOMAN MEAN?

10. *(woman)*   Do we have enough food for all the guests who are attending the reception this evening?
    (man)   The refrigerator's about to burst.
    (narrator)   WHAT DOES THE MAN MEAN?

TOEFL EXERCISE 2, page 32

1. *(woman)*   What did you think of the final exam in algebra?
   (man)   It was too easy!
   (narrator)   WHAT DOES THE MAN MEAN?

2. *(woman)*   How are you feeling today?
   (man)   I'm really feeling rather sick.
   (narrator)   HOW IS THE MAN FEELING?

3. *(man)*   Has your family been in business for quite some time?
   (woman)   No, the family business was just established last year.
   (narrator)   WHAT DOES THE WOMAN SAY ABOUT THE FAMILY BUSINESS?

4. *(woman)*   Did you have to wait at the airport for a long time?
   (man)   No, the plane landed right on schedule.
   (narrator)   WHAT DOES THE MAN MEAN?

5. *(man)*   Do you want to join me in the pool?
   (woman)   Oh, I'll just run and put my suit on.
   (narrator)   WHAT DOES THE WOMAN IMPLY?

6. *(man)*   Last night's fire burned the entire hillside.
   (woman)   At least the homes were saved.
   (narrator)   WHAT DOES THE WOMAN MEAN?

7. *(man)*   Should I add more salt and pepper to the soup?
   (woman)   No, I think there's enough.
   (narrator)   WHAT DOES THE WOMAN MEAN?

8. *(woman)*   How are you able to pay your college fees?
   (man)   I was fortunate to get a scholarship.
   (narrator)   WHAT DOES THE MAN MEAN?

9. *(man)*   How successful was the corporation last year?
   (woman)   It made quite a big profit.
   (narrator)   WHAT DOES THE WOMAN SAY ABOUT THE CORPORATION?

10. *(woman)*   Chuck is on his way to the bank now, isn't he?
    (man)   Yes, he is. He thinks his bank account is overdrawn.
    (narrator)   WHAT DOES THE MAN MEAN?

TOEFL EXERCISE 3, page 34

1. *(man)*   How long until you'll be ready to leave?
   (woman)   First, I need to water the grass.
   (narrator)   WHAT DOES THE WOMAN MEAN?

2. *(man)*   Do you think I should buy this sweater?
   (woman)   But it doesn't really seem to fit right.
   (narrator)   WHAT DOES THE WOMAN MEAN?

3. *(woman)*   Is Walter's job near here?

(man) Walter's been commuting to Boston on a regular basis.

(narrator) WHAT DOES THE MAN SAY ABOUT WALTER?

4. (woman) Did Bob memorize every detail in the chapter?

(man) He wasn't able to master the lesson.

(narrator) WHAT DOES THE MAN SAY ABOUT BOB?

5. (man) It's so sad what happened to the animals.

(woman) Yes, it is. Whenever there's a forest fire, many animals die.

(narrator) WHAT DOES THE WOMAN MEAN?

6. (woman) Do you want to take a look in this store?

(man) You bet. The shoes are on sale for twenty dollars a pair!

(narrator) WHAT DOES THE MAN MEAN?

7. (woman) Why didn't Tom come with us this afternoon?

(man) He was attending a required biology lab.

(narrator) WHAT DOES THE MAN MEAN?

8. (woman) Why are you waiting here by the front door?

(man) The mail should arrive at noon, and I'm expecting something important.

(narrator) WHY IS THE MAN WAITING?

9. (woman) Do you think it'll rain today?

(man) I heard on the news that a bad storm is heading in.

(narrator) WHAT DOES THE MAN MEAN?

10. (woman) Is there any way I could help you with dinner?

(man) Would you mind chopping vegetables for salad?

(narrator) WHAT DOES THE MAN ASK THE WOMAN?

TOEFL EXERCISE (Skills 1–3), page 35

1. (woman) Let's stop and get something to drink.

(man) Some coffee would be nice.

(narrator) WHAT DOES THE MAN MEAN?

2. (man) Let's go for a walk in the park.

(woman) No, not today. It's too cloudy and cold.

(narrator) WHAT DOES THE WOMAN MEAN?

3. (man) I have trouble sleeping at night.

(woman) You could try counting sheep.

(narrator) WHAT DOES THE WOMAN SUGGEST TO THE MAN?

4. (woman) Have you heard that the department is changing the graduation requirements for our major?

(man) Yes, and I just can't believe it!

(narrator) WHAT DOES THE MAN MEAN?

5. (man) I think we're going to be here for a while.

(woman) But we've been standing in line for almost an hour!

(narrator) WHAT DOES THE WOMAN MEAN?

6. (woman) The conductor is coming down the aisle.

(man) Yes, he is collecting the train fare from the passengers.

(narrator) WHAT IS HAPPENING?

7. (woman) Have you heard about the new management training program?

(man) It will start later this week.

(narrator) WHAT DOES THE MAN MEAN?

8. (man) Does anyone know where the fire got started?

(woman) It must have started in the attic.

(narrator) WHAT DOES THE WOMAN MEAN?

9. (woman) Aren't you going to tell me exactly what happened?

(man) I assumed that you already knew the truth.

(narrator) WHAT DOES THE MAN MEAN?

10. (man) Have you seen any of the sketches Dave did for his art professor?

(woman) I've seen some of them, and they were fantastic!

(narrator) WHAT DOES THE WOMAN SAY ABOUT DAVE?

TOEFL EXERCISE 4, page 38

1. (woman) I didn't bring my laboratory manual today.

(man) You can share mine. Today we're conducting the experiment on photosynthesis, and we can work together.

(narrator) WHERE DOES THIS CONVERSATION PROBABLY TAKE PLACE?

2. (man) This is flight 707 requesting permission to land.

(woman) Flight 707, you are cleared for landing.

(narrator) WHO IS THE MAN?

3. (woman) Do you want to do the dishes now or later?

(man) I'd rather put them off as long as possible.

(narrator) WHAT WILL THE MAN PROBABLY DO?

4. (man) How much of a tip should I leave?

(woman) Oh, a dollar's plenty. The service wasn't very good.

(narrator) WHERE DOES THIS CONVERSATION PROBABLY TAKE PLACE?

5. (woman) Can I pick up my shoes on Tuesday? I need them for a party that night.

(man) They should be fixed by then.

(narrator) WHO IS THE MAN?

6. (woman) Did you get pictures of the lions?

(man) Yes, and now let's go to the other side of the park. I want to see the exotic birds.

(narrator) WHERE DOES THIS CONVERSA-TION PROBABLY TAKE PLACE?

7. (man) Could you put the letters in the pending file now?

(woman) Yes. Then I can answer them tomorrow.

(narrator) WHAT WILL THE WOMAN PROBABLY DO TOMORROW?

8. (man) The lights are flashing, and everyone's going in.

(woman) We should take our seats now before the second act starts.

(narrator) WHERE DOES THIS CONVERSA-TION PROBABLY TAKE PLACE?

9. (woman) Have you responded to Bob's dinner invitation yet?

(man) I'll take care of it right away.

(narrator) WHAT WILL THE MAN PROBABLY DO NEXT?

10. (man) Can you fill this prescription for me?

(woman) If you leave the prescription, I can have it filled in about ten minutes.

(narrator) WHO IS THE WOMAN?

TOEFL EXERCISE 5, page 40

1. (man) Would you like to go to the new restaurant on the corner?

(woman) Is that the one that serves vegetarian food?

(narrator) WHAT DOES THE WOMAN WANT TO KNOW?

2. (man) Has Harry heard from the law school yet?

(woman) Yes, he was admitted by the law school for the fall semester.

(narrator) WHAT HAPPENED TO HARRY?

3. (man) Mark said that you were a lot of help.

(woman) Well, I took care of his plants while he was out of town.

(narrator) WHAT DOES THE WOMAN MEAN?

4. (woman) Do you know what happened during the lightning storm?

(man) Yes, several trees were destroyed.

(narrator) WHAT DOES THE MAN MEAN?

5. (man) Did you see Sally? Her leg's in a cast.

(woman) Yes, I know. She told me that she broke her leg skiing in the mountains.

(narrator) WHAT HAPPENED TO SALLY?

6. (woman) The horses are not in very good shape now.

(man) They were ridden too long and too hard.

(narrator) WHAT DOES THE MAN MEAN?

7. (woman) Why didn't you order coffee?

(man) I thought it had already been ordered.

(narrator) WHAT DOES THE MAN MEAN?

8. (man) How are your friends going to get home from the airport after their trip?

(woman) Their car was left in the airport lot.

(narrator) WHAT DOES THE WOMAN MEAN?

9. (man) Has the class chosen a representative?

(woman) The other students appointed Mac class representative.

(narrator) WHAT DOES THE WOMAN MEAN?

10. (woman) Wasn't the building damaged in the earthquake?

(man) Yes, it was. And when this happened, the inhabitants were paid by the insurance company.

(narrator) WHAT DOES THE MAN MEAN?

TOEFL EXERCISE 6, page 42

1. (man) The passenger arrived in a taxi.

(woman) Yes, and then she had the taxi driver wait at the corner.

(narrator) WHAT DOES THE WOMAN MEAN?

2. (man) Did you go to the concert last night?

(woman) Yes, it was great, and I got to hear Jane play the harp.

(narrator) WHAT DOES THE WOMAN MEAN?

3. (woman) Did the children like the new baby-sitter?

(man) Not really, because she made them go to bed early.

(narrator) WHAT DOES THE MAN MEAN?

4. (man) Why is that man throwing the ball so carefully?

(woman) He is tossing the ball to his young son.

(narrator) WHAT DOES THE WOMAN SAY ABOUT THE FATHER AND SON?

5. (man) Did the professor tell her students about the lecture this evening?

(woman) Yes, she directed her students to attend it.

(narrator) WHAT DOES THE WOMAN MEAN?

6. (woman) I cannot find the clerk.

(man) The floor manager sent him back to the supply room.

(narrator) WHAT HAPPENED, ACCORDING TO THE MAN?

7. (woman) Will the students be able to get hold of the books that they need?

(man) The librarian had them reserve the books for two days.

(narrator) WHAT DOES THE MAN MEAN?

8. (man) Were elections held last night, as scheduled?

(woman) Yes, and the board elected Tony chairman for another year.

(narrator) WHAT DOES THE WOMAN MEAN?

9. (woman) At the trial the defendant was found guilty.

(man) Yes, the judge called the defendant a murderer.

(narrator) WHAT DOES THE MAN MEAN?

10. (woman) Have the names of the new committee members been announced?

(man)	Congratulations! You've been appointed to serve on the committee.
(narrator)	WHAT DOES THE MAN MEAN?

TOEFL EXERCISE (Skills 4–6), page 43

1.	(woman)	Can I help you?
	(man)	I need two stamps and a padded mailing envelope, please.
	(narrator)	WHERE DOES THIS CONVERSATION PROBABLY TAKE PLACE?
2.	(man)	Why were the students coming to the teacher's office?
	(woman)	They had to hand in their papers.
	(narrator)	WHAT DOES THE WOMAN MEAN?
3.	(man)	Did Mark stop at the service station?
	(woman)	Yes, he had the attendant check the oil in his car.
	(narrator)	WHAT DOES THE WOMAN MEAN?
4.	(woman)	I'd like a burger and fries, please.
	(man)	To stay, or to go?
	(narrator)	WHO IS THE MAN?
5.	(woman)	Maybe we should make some more copies now, just in case.
	(man)	Additional copies can be printed as needed.
	(narrator)	WHAT DOES THE MAN MEAN?
6.	(man)	What did the professor ask the students to do?
	(woman)	He required them to buy two books.
	(narrator)	WHAT DOES THE WOMAN MEAN?
7.	(woman)	Did Jim see a doctor this morning?
	(man)	Yes, and the doctor told him to return to the office to see him next week.
	(narrator)	WHAT DOES THE MAN MEAN?
8.	(man)	Have you sent the tissue samples to the laboratory?
	(woman)	Not yet, but I'll get it done in the next half hour.
	(narrator)	WHAT WILL THE WOMAN PROBABLY DO NEXT?
9.	(man)	Has there been a change in senior class president?
	(woman)	Yes, Mary replaced Sue in that position.
	(narrator)	WHAT DOES THE WOMAN MEAN?
10.	(man)	Did you find that television program interesting?
	(woman)	I certainly did. The current political situation was analyzed effectively by the panel.
	(narrator)	WHAT DOES THE WOMAN MEAN?

TOEFL REVIEW EXERCISE (Skills 1–6), page 44

1.	(man)	Why do you think Peter said that?
	(woman)	I think he was really angry.
	(narrator)	WHAT DOES THE WOMAN SAY ABOUT PETER?
2.	(man)	Why is Hannah so happy?
	(woman)	Her parents have allowed her to stay up late.

(narrator)	WHAT DOES THE WOMAN MEAN?
3. (woman)	I'd like some unleaded gas, please.
(man)	Would you like me to fill it up?
(narrator)	WHERE DOES THE MAN PROBABLY WORK?
4. (man)	What do you suggest for breakfast?
(woman)	Well, you could have cereal or eggs, or both.
(narrator)	WHAT DOES THE WOMAN MEAN?
5. (woman)	Did Ellen help you a lot with your training?
(man)	She really urged me to do my best.
(narrator)	WHAT DOES THE MAN MEAN?
6. (man)	Did you hear what happened to Rob's car last night?
(woman)	Yeah, I heard that it was stolen.
(narrator)	WHAT DOES THE WOMAN MEAN?
7. (woman)	We need to get some milk for tomorrow morning. What about this carton?
(man)	Maybe we should get the large one instead of the small one.
(narrator)	WHAT DOES THE MAN SUGGEST?
8. (man)	What happened when the businesspeople arrived in the office?
(woman)	Well, first they were greeted by the receptionist.
(narrator)	WHAT DOES THE WOMAN MEAN?
9. (woman)	Did you see that? The police officer was talking to the tourist.
(man)	Yes, and then he made the tourist come to the station.
(narrator)	WHAT DOES THE MAN MEAN?
10. (woman)	Do you want to go up to Carmel for the weekend?
(man)	That seems like a terrific idea to me!
(narrator)	WHAT DOES THE MAN MEAN?

TOEFL EXERCISE 7, page 46

1. (man)	Are you going to take out the trash?
(woman)	I have no time to do it.
(narrator)	WHAT DOES THE WOMAN MEAN?
2. (woman)	Are you worried about the interview?
(man)	It's unimportant to me.
(narrator)	WHAT DOES THE MAN MEAN?
3. (woman)	Do you have all the notes for Psychology 101?
(man)	I didn't miss a single lecture.
(narrator)	WHAT DOES THE MAN MEAN?
4. (woman)	Do you know the library's summer hours? I need to go there this evening.
(man)	It's never open past six o'clock in the summer.
(narrator)	WHAT DOES THE MAN MEAN?
5. (woman)	How often should I water the plants while you're gone?
(man)	No more than once a week.
(narrator)	WHAT SHOULD THE WOMAN DO?

6. (man)   Did you enjoy your meal? That restaurant is very famous.

(woman)   The food was good, but I was dissatisfied with the service.

(narrator)   WHAT DOES THE WOMAN MEAN?

7. (woman)   Do you think that Bob really wanted me to go home?

(man)   He wasn't kidding when he told you to leave.

(narrator)   WHAT DOES THE MAN SAY ABOUT BOB?

8. (woman)   Can we finish this project before closing time?

(man)   If we work on nothing else.

(narrator)   WHAT DOES THE MAN MEAN?

9. (man)   Would you mind staying an hour more?

(woman)   I'd rather not.

(narrator)   WHAT DOES THE WOMAN SAY ABOUT STAYING?

10. (woman)   Would you recommend the hotel where you stayed in New York?

(man)   The hotel provided service that was unequaled!

(narrator)   WHAT DOES THE MAN SAY ABOUT THE HOTEL?

TOEFL EXERCISE 8, page 48

1. (man)   Do you think Ron Rogers will be elected?

(woman)   Well, it's not completely impossible.

(narrator)   WHAT DOES THE WOMAN IMPLY ABOUT RON?

2. (woman)   How was your tennis match today?

(man)   I didn't serve well, and I didn't volley well either.

(narrator)   WHAT DOES THE MAN SAY ABOUT HIS TENNIS GAME?

3. (man)   Was Gary prepared for the debate?

(woman)   It is no surprise that he was unprepared.

(narrator)   WHAT DOES THE WOMAN SAY ABOUT GARY?

4. (man)   Did you go out dancing with everyone else last night?

(woman)   I was not feeling well, so I didn't go out.

(narrator)   WHAT DOES THE WOMAN MEAN?

5. (woman)   Do you think Paula understands what she's done?

(man)   She isn't unaware of the trouble she's caused.

(narrator)   WHAT DOES THE MAN SAY ABOUT PAULA?

6. (man)   Did your friends finish the term paper for history class?

(woman)   Steve wasn't able to finish it, and Paul wasn't either.

(narrator)   WHAT DOES THE WOMAN MEAN?

7. (man)   Can you believe that George walked out of the restaurant without paying for his share of the meal?

(woman)   It was irresponsible of him not to pay the bill.

(narrator)   WHAT DOES THE WOMAN MEAN?

8. (man)   What happened when Harry applied to Milhouse University?

(woman)   It was unfortunate that he wasn't admitted to the university.

(narrator)   WHAT DOES THE WOMAN SAY ABOUT HARRY?

9. (woman)   What did you think of the essay that I wrote?

(man)   The first draft of the essay wasn't well written, and the second wasn't much better.

(narrator)   WHAT DOES THE MAN MEAN?

10. (man)   Has Roger been disturbed by all of the recent problems?

(woman)   He hasn't been unaffected.

(narrator)   WHAT DOES THE WOMAN MEAN?

TOEFL EXERCISE 9, page 50

1. (woman)   Do you expect a lot of rain this month?

(man)   It hardly ever rains in July.

(narrator)   WHAT DOES THE MAN MEAN?

2. (man)   Were all three students accepted to the university?

(woman)   Only John was accepted.

(narrator)   WHAT DOES THE WOMAN MEAN?

3. (man)   Did Mark do well in Professor Franks's class?

(woman)   Mark barely passed the history exam that Professor Franks gave.

(narrator)   WHAT DOES THE WOMAN MEAN?

4. (woman)   I can't believe how long we've been here.

(man)   Dr. Roberts almost never keeps his patients waiting long.

(narrator)   WHAT DOES THE MAN MEAN?

5. (man)   I can't believe Betty is not at work this week!

(woman)   Only rarely does Betty take a vacation in winter.

(narrator)   WHAT DOES THE WOMAN MEAN?

6. (man)   Does Steve study very much?

(woman)   He hardly ever opens a book.

(narrator)   WHAT DOES THE WOMAN SAY ABOUT STEVE?

7. (woman)   Was the philosophy exam very long?

(man)   I scarcely had time to finish it.

(narrator)   WHAT DOES THE MAN MEAN?

8. (man)   I was so bored at the staff meeting!

(woman)   Seldom have staff meetings lasted this long.

(narrator)   WHAT DOES THE WOMAN MEAN?

9. (woman)   Are you enjoying the barbecue?

| (man) | Only rarely have I tasted such delicious meat. |
| (narrator) | WHAT DOES THE MAN MEAN? |

10. (woman) Does your broken arm hurt very much?
(man) Only if I try to move.
(narrator) WHAT DOES THE MAN MEAN?

TOEFL EXERCISE 10, page 52

1. (man) Are you pleased with the exam results?
(woman) I couldn't be happier.
(narrator) WHAT DOES THE WOMAN MEAN?

2. (woman) Is Paula lazy, as usual, this semester?
(man) She's never tried harder.
(narrator) WHAT DOES THE MAN MEAN?

3. (man) Was it a good sale? Did you buy a lot?
(woman) Prices couldn't have been any lower.
(narrator) WHAT DOES THE WOMAN SAY ABOUT THE SALE?

4. (woman) What do you think of Betsy?
(man) I don't know a more intelligent woman.
(narrator) WHAT DOES THE MAN SAY ABOUT BETSY?

5. (woman) Did the patient really need the surgery?
(man) It couldn't have been more unnecessary.
(narrator) WHAT DOES THE MAN MEAN?

6. (man) Did any of you get hurt in the accident?
(woman) We couldn't have been luckier.
(narrator) WHAT DOES THE WOMAN IMPLY?

7. (woman) How do you think you did on the final exam in biology?
(man) Nothing could have been more difficult than that exam!
(narrator) WHAT DOES THE MAN MEAN?

8. (man) Are you ready to accept the new position?
(woman) Nobody wants that job more than I do.
(narrator) WHAT DOES THE WOMAN MEAN?

9. (man) How did you do in the race?
(woman) Only one person was faster.
(narrator) WHAT DOES THE WOMAN MEAN?

10. (woman) Do you think that the math project this semester was easy?
(man) Seldom has a math project been more complicated.
(narrator) WHAT DOES THE MAN MEAN?

TOEFL EXERCISE (Skills 7–10), page 53

1. (man) Do you think you could try a little harder?
(woman) It's impossible for me to do more.
(narrator) WHAT DOES THE WOMAN MEAN?

2. (man) What are you so upset about?

| (woman) | Not once on this trip has the bus left on time. |
| (narrator) | WHAT DOES THE WOMAN MEAN? |

3. (man) Was there enough soup to go around?
(woman) There was barely enough soup for everyone at the table.
(narrator) WHAT DOES THE WOMAN MEAN?

4. (man) Do you really want to move to Florida?
(woman) I couldn't want anything more!
(narrator) WHAT DOES THE WOMAN MEAN?

5. (man) Did you turn in your research paper for history class?
(woman) I couldn't turn it in because it was incomplete.
(narrator) WHAT DOES THE WOMAN MEAN?

6. (woman) Do you think that your friends enjoyed their trip to the Museum of Modern Art?
(man) Sylvia doesn't care for modern art, and neither does Tim.
(narrator) WHAT DOES THE MAN MEAN?

7. (woman) Can your friends go with us this afternoon, or do you think they will be too busy?
(man) They hardly ever work in the afternoon.
(narrator) WHAT DOES THE MAN SAY ABOUT HIS FRIENDS?

8. (woman) Do you think we could turn the air-conditioner on? I'm really uncomfortable?
(man) The air-conditioner never works when it gets warm.
(narrator) WHAT DOES THE MAN IMPLY?

9. (woman) I heard that your exam results were not too bad.
(man) Actually, I've never done worse.
(narrator) WHAT DOES THE MAN MEAN?

10. (man) Did the committee come to a decision about the parking problem?
(woman) The committee shouldn't have decided the issue when so many members weren't present.
(narrator) WHAT DOES THE WOMAN MEAN?

TOEFL REVIEW EXERCISE (Skills 1–10), page 54

1. (man) What should I do to get over this?
(woman) You should drink plenty of fluids, take this medicine once every eight hours, and return here to my office next week.
(narrator) WHERE DOES THIS CONVERSATION PROBABLY TAKE PLACE?

2. (man) Did you find anything at the store?
(woman) I just bought a great shirt!
(narrator) WHAT DOES THE WOMAN MEAN?

3. (man) Did you enjoy the hotel where you stayed in Hawaii?
(woman) The view of the ocean couldn't have been better.

(narrator)	WHAT DOES THE WOMAN MEAN?	

4. (woman) You look like you're not feeling too well.
(man) Actually, I'm just kind of tired. All I need is a bit of rest.
(narrator) WHAT WILL THE MAN PROBABLY DO NEXT?

5. (woman) Do you think that Mary will forgive me for what I did?
(man) She isn't exactly an unforgiving person.
(narrator) WHAT DOES THE MAN SAY ABOUT MARY?

6. (man) Has Martha already gone on vacation?
(woman) She can't take her vacation until next week.
(narrator) WHAT DOES THE WOMAN SAY ABOUT MARTHA?

7. (man) I'm looking for some people who just came into the restaurant.
(woman) The waitress seated them at a table in the back.
(narrator) WHAT DOES THE WOMAN MEAN?

8. (man) Let's go to the market and get some fresh fruit.
(woman) I was there this morning, and the market scarcely had any.
(narrator) WHAT DOES THE WOMAN SAY ABOUT THE MARKET?

9. (man) I'm thinking about taking a few classes at the local adult school.
(woman) It's never too late to go back to school.
(narrator) WHAT DOES THE WOMAN MEAN?

10. (man) I don't think I can make it all the way to the top of the mountain.
(woman) I dare you to try!
(narrator) WHAT DOES THE WOMAN MEAN?

TOEFL EXERCISE 11, page 56

1. (man) I'd like to take a trip down the coast this weekend.
(woman) Me, too.
(narrator) WHAT DOES THE WOMAN MEAN?

2. (woman) I would like to see Matt elected to the town council next month.
(man) So would I.
(narrator) WHAT DOES THE MAN MEAN?

3. (man) I'm not sure if I should take beginning or intermediate French next semester.
(woman) Neither am I.
(narrator) WHAT DOES THE WOMAN MEAN?

4. (man) The food in the cafeteria is not exactly the best food I have ever tasted.
(woman) You can say that again!
(narrator) WHAT DOES THE WOMAN MEAN?

5. (woman) This party certainly has been fun!
(man) I'll say!

(narrator) WHAT DOES THE MAN MEAN?

6. (man) I'm not about to condone what she did!
(woman) I'm not either.
(narrator) WHAT DOES THE WOMAN MEAN?

7. (woman) Those people upstairs always have such loud parties.
(man) Don't they!
(narrator) WHAT DOES THE MAN MEAN?

8. (man) This meal is really delicious!
(woman) Isn't it!
(narrator) WHAT DOES THE WOMAN MEAN?

9. (man) I can't imagine what he was thinking about when he bought that car.
(woman) Neither can I!
(narrator) WHAT DOES THE WOMAN MEAN?

10. (woman) This should be a two-semester course. One semester is just not enough time to learn all the material.
(man) You can say that again!
(narrator) WHAT DOES THE MAN MEAN?

TOEFL EXERCISE 12, page 59

1. (woman) Are we supposed to read all ten chapters before the exam?
(man) As far as I can tell, we are.
(narrator) WHAT DOES THE MAN MEAN?

2. (man) You're out of apple pie!
(woman) Sorry. Why not try the cherry pie?
(narrator) WHAT DOES THE WOMAN SUGGEST?

3. (woman) Do you know when the movie starts?
(man) It starts at 8:00, doesn't it?
(narrator) WHAT DOES THE MAN MEAN?

4. (woman) We can't leave now. We have to do the dishes.
(man) Let's leave the dishes until later.
(narrator) WHAT DOES THE MAN SUGGEST?

5. (man) Do you think Matt has enough talent for the role?
(woman) As far as I can tell.
(narrator) WHAT DOES THE WOMAN MEAN?

6. (woman) Did you hear that Mary's in the hospital with a broken leg?
(man) Let's go visit her.
(narrator) WHAT DOES THE MAN SUGGEST?

7. (man) Where are the children?
(woman) They've gone to the park to play ball, haven't they?
(narrator) WHAT DOES THE WOMAN MEAN?

8. (man) I need some graph paper for my math assignment.
(woman) I'm all out. Why don't you check with Tom next door?
(narrator) WHAT DOES THE WOMAN SUGGEST?

9. (woman) Is the utilities bill due on the first or the fifteenth?
(man) On the fifteenth, as far as I know.

(narrator)   WHAT DOES THE MAN MEAN?

10. (man)   We need to decide whether or not we are going to buy that house.
    (woman)   It's such a big decision. Let's sleep on it before we decide.
    (narrator)   WHAT DOES THE WOMAN SUGGEST?

TOEFL EXERCISE 13, page 61

1. (man)   Greg should be here any moment.
   (woman)   Then, he is coming to the party!
   (narrator)   WHAT HAD THE WOMAN ASSUMED?

2. (woman)   My motorcycle is over there. That's how I got to school today.
   (man)   So you can ride a motorcycle.
   (narrator)   WHAT HAD THE MAN ASSUMED?

3. (man)   I'm having a few friends over for dinner tonight. Would you like to come?
   (woman)   So you do know how to cook!
   (narrator)   WHAT HAD THE WOMAN ASSUMED?

4. (woman)   I'm so tired from all that exercise.
   (man)   Then, you did run three miles this morning.
   (narrator)   WHAT HAD THE MAN ASSUMED?

5. (man)   I just spent five hours working on my research project.
   (woman)   Bob, you were in the library.
   (narrator)   WHAT HAD THE WOMAN ASSUMED ABOUT BOB?

6. (man)   I just finished carrying the last piece of furniture.
   (woman)   Then, you have moved into a new apartment!
   (narrator)   WHAT HAD THE WOMAN ASSUMED ABOUT THE MAN?

7. (woman)   Would you like to share some of this piece of chocolate cake?
   (man)   So you do eat sweets.
   (narrator)   WHAT HAD THE MAN ASSUMED?

8. (man)   I'm studying now for my driver's license test.
   (woman)   Then, you will take the test this afternoon.
   (narrator)   WHAT HAD THE WOMAN ASSUMED?

9. (woman)   I'm heading off to physics class now.
   (man)   Then you did register for that course!
   (narrator)   WHAT HAD THE MAN ASSUMED ABOUT THE WOMAN?

10. (woman)   The plumber just left.
    (man)   Then the pipes have been cleared.
    (narrator)   WHAT HAD THE MAN ASSUMED?

TOEFL EXERCISE (Skills 11–13), page 62

1. (man)   The phone bill is certainly high this month!
   (woman)   I'll say!
   (narrator)   WHAT DOES THE WOMAN MEAN?

2. (woman)   I saw Bill in calculus class this morning.
   (man)   Then he's not sick anymore.
   (narrator)   WHAT HAD THE MAN ASSUMED?

3. (man)   I don't know how I'm going to get this paper done by Monday.
   (woman)   Why not stay home tonight instead of going out?
   (narrator)   WHAT DOES THE WOMAN SUGGEST?

4. (woman)   The cafeteria is closed in the mornings.
   (man)   So, the cafeteria doesn't serve breakfast!
   (narrator)   WHAT HAD THE MAN ASSUMED?

5. (woman)   Do you think we can park in that lot without getting a ticket?
   (man)   As far as I know.
   (narrator)   WHAT DOES THE MAN MEAN?

6. (woman)   I'm so glad to be finished with that class!
   (man)   You can say that again!
   (narrator)   WHAT DOES THE MAN MEAN?

7. (woman)   I couldn't finish any of the math problems that Professor Allen assigned for today.
   (man)   Neither could I.
   (narrator)   WHAT DOES THE MAN MEAN?

8. (man)   I just got back from the post office.
   (woman)   Then, you did remember to mail the package!
   (narrator)   WHAT HAD THE WOMAN ASSUMED?

9. (woman)   I'm afraid there won't be enough space in my car.
   (man)   Let's take my car instead; it's bigger than yours.
   (narrator)   WHAT DOES THE MAN SUGGEST?

10. (woman)   These muffins taste really great.
    (man)   They were freshly made this morning, weren't they?
    (narrator)   WHAT DOES THE MAN MEAN?

TOEFL REVIEW EXERCISE (Skills 1–13), page 63

1. (man)   Here are all your phone messages.
   (woman)   I need to respond to these right away.
   (narrator)   WHAT WILL THE WOMAN PROBABLY DO NEXT?

2. (man)   Can we meet next Tuesday at 3:00?
   (woman)   I'll have to check my calendar.
   (narrator)   WHAT DOES THE WOMAN MEAN?

3. (woman)   Did you have enough to pay for the bicycle?
   (man)   Only barely.
   (narrator)   WHAT DOES THE MAN MEAN?

4. (man)   Did the television get fixed?
   (woman)   I had Bob look at it, and now it works.
   (narrator)   WHAT DOES THE WOMAN MEAN?

5. (man) Did your new assistant do a good job today?
   (woman) I couldn't say that he was helpful.
   (narrator) WHAT DOES THE WOMAN SAY ABOUT THE ASSISTANT?

6. (man) Walk-through registration took me three hours to complete.
   (woman) Why not try registering by mail next semester?
   (narrator) WHAT DOES THE WOMAN SUGGEST?

7. (woman) Were you able to get in touch with Paula?
   (man) I wasn't able to give her a call because her number was unlisted.
   (narrator) WHAT DOES THE MAN MEAN?

8. (man) Did you have a problem when you arrived at the train station?
   (woman) There was nowhere to store my luggage.
   (narrator) WHAT DOES THE WOMAN MEAN?

9. (woman) I just sent in my forms to the psychology department.
   (man) So you are going to major in psychology!
   (narrator) WHAT HAD THE MAN ASSUMED?

10. (man) That exam couldn't have been more difficult!
    (woman) I'll say!
    (narrator) WHAT DOES THE WOMAN MEAN?

TOEFL EXERCISE 14, page 65

1. (man) Do you think we'll be able to get tickets for the concert?
   (woman) I wish there weren't so many people in line in front of us.
   (narrator) WHAT DOES THE WOMAN MEAN?

2. (woman) I'm sorry I didn't tell you about the parking ticket.
   (man) I wish you had told me about it.
   (narrator) WHAT DOES THE MAN MEAN?

3. (man) Did you see the work schedule for next week?
   (woman) I wish I didn't have to work so many hours then.
   (narrator) WHAT DOES THE WOMAN IMPLY?

4. (man) Are you happy with the changes in the requirements for graduation?
   (woman) I wish the department had not made the changes.
   (narrator) WHAT DOES THE WOMAN MEAN?

5. (woman) Are you going to the theater with us this weekend?
   (man) I wish I had enough money to go.
   (narrator) WHAT DOES THE MAN IMPLY.

6. (woman) Did you hear how Harry did on the astronomy exam?
   (man) I bet he wishes he had studied harder.
   (narrator) WHAT DOES THE MAN MEAN?

7. (man) Do you have a good schedule of classes this semester?
   (woman) I wish I didn't need to take this algebra course. I'm not very good at math.
   (narrator) WHAT DOES THE WOMAN IMPLY?

8. (woman) Your apartment is in a really great location!
   (man) But I wish I had been able to find something cheaper.
   (narrator) WHAT DOES THE MAN MEAN?

9. (woman) Why are you sitting all the way in the back of the auditorium?
   (man) I wish I hadn't arrived so late. Then I could have gotten a better seat.
   (narrator) WHAT DOES THE MAN IMPLY?

10. (woman) Are you going to the football game this weekend?
    (man) I wish I could, but I have to work on my sociology paper.
    (narrator) WHAT DOES THE MAN MEAN?

TOEFL EXERCISE 15, page 67

1. (woman) I'm glad I called and told you about the meeting.
   (man) If you had not called me, I would not have known.
   (narrator) WHAT DOES THE MAN MEAN?

2. (man) I always seem to get stopped by the police.
   (woman) If you drove more slowly, the police would not stop you so often.
   (narrator) WHAT DOES THE WOMAN MEAN?

3. (man) Do you know that some offices are closed next Friday?
   (woman) Wouldn't it be nice if we didn't have to work on Friday?
   (narrator) WHAT DOES THE WOMAN MEAN?

4. (woman) I don't think that the letter that I mailed last week arrived.
   (man) If you had put enough postage on it, the letter would have arrived.
   (narrator) WHAT DOES THE MAN MEAN?

5. (woman) Do you have a pet dog?
   (man) I would like to have one, if it didn't require so much attention.
   (narrator) WHAT DOES THE MAN MEAN?

6. (man) Did the other students know we were having a psychology exam today?
   (woman) Had they known about the exam, they would've prepared for it.
   (narrator) WHAT DOES THE WOMAN SAY ABOUT THE OTHER STUDENTS?

7. (woman) We're all going out to a great restaurant tonight. Do you want to come with us?
   (man) If it didn't cost so much, I would.
   (narrator) WHAT DOES THE MAN MEAN?

8. (woman) Do you think Joe saw the car coming around the corner so fast?

(man)	Had he seen the car coming, he would've been able to get out of the way.
(narrator)	WHAT DOES THE MAN MEAN?
9. (woman)	I really don't want to be here now.
(man)	If you didn't want to be here, then why are you here?
(narrator)	WHAT DID THE MAN ASSUME?
10. (man)	Kathy couldn't have known that the first prize in the contest was a trip to Hawaii.
(woman)	She would've worked harder on her art project if she had known what first prize was.
(narrator)	WHAT DOES THE WOMAN MEAN?

TOEFL EXERCISE (Skills 14–15), page 68

1. (man)	Did you enjoy the film?
(woman)	I wish it had not been so violent.
(narrator)	WHAT DOES THE WOMAN MEAN?
2. (woman)	Did you remember to close the windows before we left?
(man)	If I had left the windows open, the rain would have gotten in.
(narrator)	WHAT DOES THE MAN MEAN?
3. (man)	Are your parents able to come to the graduation ceremonies?
(woman)	I wish they were able to come.
(narrator)	WHAT DOES THE WOMAN MEAN?
4. (woman)	Are you going on vacation next week?
(man)	I would miss the conference if I took my vacation next week.
(narrator)	WHAT DOES THE MAN MEAN?
5. (woman)	You have chemistry lab this afternoon, don't you?
(man)	Yes, and I really wish I didn't have to go there.
(narrator)	WHAT DOES THE MAN MEAN?
6. (man)	How could they have run out of gas?
(woman)	Had they filled up the tank at the last service station, they wouldn't have run out of gas.
(narrator)	WHAT DOES THE WOMAN MEAN?
7. (woman)	You have such a heavy schedule this semester.
(man)	I really wish I had not registered for so many courses.
(narrator)	WHAT DOES THE MAN MEAN?
8. (man)	Do you take the bus to work every day?
(woman)	If I didn't take the bus, I don't know how I would get there.
(narrator)	WHAT DOES THE WOMAN MEAN?
9. (man)	Do you have any eggs that I could borrow? I need them for a dish I'm preparing.
(woman)	I wish I had bought some when I was at the store.
(narrator)	WHAT DOES THE WOMAN MEAN?
10. (woman)	How is Teresa feeling?

| (man) | If she had taken the medicine that the doctor prescribed, she might be feeling a lot better. |
| (narrator) | WHAT DOES THE MAN MEAN? |

TOEFL REVIEW EXERCISE (Skills 1–15), page 69

1. (man)	This tea is awfully hot.
(woman)	Why not wait a few minutes?
(narrator)	WHAT DOES THE WOMAN SUGGEST?
2. (woman)	I'd like two tickets to the six o'clock show, please.
(man)	That will be ten dollars.
(narrator)	WHERE DOES THIS CONVERSATION PROBABLY TAKE PLACE?
3. (woman)	Are you glad that the semester's about over?
(man)	I'm not exactly sad that it's ending.
(narrator)	WHAT DOES THE MAN MEAN?
4. (woman)	How much damage did the storm do?
(man)	The trees behind the house were knocked down.
(narrator)	WHAT DOES THE MAN MEAN?
5. (woman)	I hear the football team lost again.
(man)	As usual.
(narrator)	WHAT DOES THE MAN MEAN?
6. (man)	I have to be at the office at 8:00 every morning.
(woman)	Then, you did get a job!
(narrator)	WHAT HAD THE WOMAN ASSUMED ABOUT THE MAN?
7. (woman)	How was your vacation in the islands?
(man)	If I had not lost my passport, I would have enjoyed it a lot more.
(narrator)	WHAT DOES THE MAN MEAN?
8. (woman)	Can you tell me which bus I should take to get to Riverdale?
(man)	The number 8 bus, I think.
(narrator)	WHAT DOES THE MAN INDICATE?
9. (man)	Did the laboratory assistant get a lot done?
(woman)	He couldn't finish more than one experiment.
(narrator)	WHAT DOES THE WOMAN MEAN?
10. (man)	I really wish the semester would end soon!
(woman)	You can say that again!
(narrator)	WHAT DOES THE WOMAN MEAN?

TOEFL EXERCISE 16, page 71

1. (man)	The new neighbors have just moved in.
(woman)	Maybe we should call on them.
(narrator)	ACCORDING TO THE WOMAN, WHAT SHOULD THEY DO?
2. (woman)	You know, I'm really enjoying this class now.
(man)	I am, too. At first it was kind of boring, but now it's turning into something fascinating.

	(narrator)	WHAT DOES THE MAN MEAN?
3.	*(man)*	I heard you had a bad headache this morning.
	(woman)	Yes, but I think I'm getting over it now.
	(narrator)	WHAT DOES THE WOMAN MEAN?
4.	*(man)*	I'd like to stop smoking, but it's really hard for me.
	(woman)	Well, at least you should try to cut down.
	(narrator)	WHAT DOES THE WOMAN MEAN?
5.	*(man)*	Why was the client unhappy?
	(woman)	The lawyer turned down his case.
	(narrator)	WHAT DOES THE WOMAN MEAN?
6.	*(woman)*	I really like Marsha.
	(man)	Me, too. She is just so friendly with everyone.
	(narrator)	WHAT DOES THE MAN SAY ABOUT MARSHA?
7.	*(woman)*	Are you going out or staying here tonight?
	(man)	I can't go out. I have to look after the children.
	(narrator)	WHAT DOES THE MAN MEAN?
8.	*(woman)*	Did you see in the paper this morning that one section of the factory is closing down today?
	(man)	Yes, and some of the workers will be laid off.
	(narrator)	WHAT DOES THE MAN SAY ABOUT THE WORKERS?
9.	*(woman)*	I heard that you're trying out for the football team. Won't that be difficult?
	(man)	Yes, but I'm really going to try to pull it off.
	(narrator)	WHAT DOES THE MAN MEAN?
10.	*(man)*	I locked the keys in the car again.
	(woman)	Oh, I don't know why I put up with you.
	(narrator)	WHAT DOES THE WOMAN MEAN?

TOEFL EXERCISE 17, page 73

1.	*(man)*	I was fifteen minutes late for class today.
	(woman)	Better late than never.
	(narrator)	WHAT DOES THE WOMAN MEAN?
2.	*(woman)*	Do you want to work on the biology experiment together?
	(man)	Two heads are better than one.
	(narrator)	WHAT DOES THE MAN MEAN?
3.	*(man)*	I really don't want to work on the report now.
	(woman)	There's no time like the present.
	(narrator)	WHAT DOES THE WOMAN MEAN?
4.	*(man)*	I just sold the last copy of that book this morning. You'll have to try again next week.
	(woman)	Just my luck.
	(narrator)	WHAT DOES THE WOMAN MEAN?

5.	*(man)*	I know you like this restaurant, but I just don't like the food here.
	(woman)	To each his own.
	(narrator)	WHAT DOES THE WOMAN MEAN?
6.	*(man)*	Would it be possible for you to drop these letters in the mailbox for me?
	(woman)	No sooner said than done.
	(narrator)	WHAT DOES THE WOMAN MEAN?
7.	*(woman)*	Did you hear that Abbie won the art scholarship?
	(man)	You could have knocked me down with a feather.
	(narrator)	WHAT DOES THE MAN MEAN?
8.	*(man)*	I have to read all six chapters this weekend.
	(woman)	We're all in the same boat.
	(narrator)	WHAT DOES THE WOMAN MEAN?
9.	*(woman)*	Anne's project for the science fair was incredible.
	(man)	She's really head and shoulders above the rest.
	(narrator)	WHAT DOES THE MAN SAY ABOUT ANNE?
10.	*(man)*	I can't believe how many forms I have to fill out to apply for the scholarship.
	(woman)	Yes, and you should be sure to dot all the i's and cross all the t's.
	(narrator)	WHAT DOES THE WOMAN MEAN?

TOEFL EXERCISE (Skills 16–17), page 74

1.	*(man)*	Do you do the cooking every night?
	(woman)	No, my roommate and I take turns.
	(narrator)	WHAT DOES THE WOMAN MEAN?
2.	*(man)*	Did you meet Hank's father at the game last night?
	(woman)	Yes, I did. You know, Hank's really a chip off the old block.
	(narrator)	WHAT DOES THE WOMAN SAY ABOUT HANK?
3.	*(man)*	Do you want to go to the football game with us tonight?
	(woman)	No, thanks. I think I'm coming down with something.
	(narrator)	WHAT DOES THE WOMAN MEAN?
4.	*(woman)*	I can't believe what Hal said to the teacher!
	(man)	Yeah, he really put his foot in his mouth.
	(narrator)	WHAT DOES THE MAN SAY ABOUT HAL?
5.	*(man)*	I'm going to the market now.
	(woman)	Could you hold off going for a few minutes? I'd like to go with you.
	(narrator)	WHAT DOES THE WOMAN MEAN?
6.	*(man)*	I got a parking ticket, but I don't think I want to pay it.
	(woman)	You know, you're really playing with fire.
	(narrator)	WHAT DOES THE WOMAN MEAN?

7. (man) The noise from those machines is really bothering me.
(woman) Yeah, I wish we could just ask them to cut it out.
(narrator) WHAT DOES THE WOMAN MEAN?

8. (man) Did Fred tell you his theory about who took the money?
(woman) Yes, and I really think he's barking up the wrong tree.
(narrator) WHAT DOES THE WOMAN MEAN?

9. (man) This course is too hard for me. I think I'll just drop it.
(woman) Even though it's hard, you should keep at it as long as you can.
(narrator) WHAT DOES THE WOMAN TELL THE MAN?

10. (man) How's the chemistry homework coming?
(woman) It's like trying to swim upstream.
(narrator) WHAT DOES THE WOMAN MEAN?

TOEFL REVIEW EXERCISE (Skills 1–17), page 74

1. (woman) Could you put some more wood in the fireplace?
(man) I'll have to bring some in from outside.
(narrator) WHAT DOES THE MAN IMPLY?

2. (man) Alice, I thought you were working late tonight.
(woman) I was supposed to, but my conference was called off.
(narrator) WHAT HAPPENED TO ALICE?

3. (woman) Why are you getting out of the water?
(man) The lifeguard motioned that we should move in that direction.
(narrator) WHERE DOES THE CONVERSATION PROBABLY TAKE PLACE?

4. (woman) Did you enjoy the evening at the nightclub?
(man) I wish there had been a little more room on the dance floor.
(narrator) WHAT DOES THE MAN MEAN?

5. (man) I just sent off the letter that you wrote.
(woman) Then, you did figure out how to use the fax machine.
(narrator) WHAT HAD THE WOMAN ASSUMED ABOUT THE MAN?

6. (woman) I guessed that you would buy that new car.
(man) And you hit the nail on the head.
(narrator) WHAT DOES THE MAN MEAN?

7. (woman) Is that your research paper for English Lit.?
(man) Yes, and it's almost finished. Do you think you could look it over for me?
(narrator) WHAT DOES THE MAN WANT?

8. (man) Has everyone been informed?
(woman) No one is unaware of the situation.
(narrator) WHAT DOES THE WOMAN MEAN?

9. (woman) Did you sleep well last night?
(man) If the alarm were not so loud, I would never have woken up.

(narrator) WHAT DOES THE MAN MEAN?

10. (woman) I could not believe the story in the news about the problem with the airplane.
(man) Yeah, I saw it, too! The pilot was forced to land the plane in a field.
(narrator) WHAT DOES THE MAN MEAN?

LONG CONVERSATIONS (Paper)

EXERCISE 20, page 82

1. (narrator) The first part of Conversation 1 is:
(man) I'm looking for a part-time job on campus.
(narrator) WHAT IS THE TOPIC OF CONVERSATION 1?

2. (narrator) The first part of Conversation 2 is:
(woman) Hi, Jack. It's good to see you again. Are you ready to get down to business again after spring break?
(man) Not really, but I guess I don't really have too much choice, do I? And it's going to be particularly hard to get back to work since I just had the most fantastic vacation ever.
(woman) Really? What did you do?
(man) I went kayaking on the Klamath River.
(narrator) WHAT IS THE TOPIC OF CONVERSATION 2?

3. (narrator) The first part of Conversation 3 is:
(man) Did you read the article that the professor assigned for tomorrow's class? It was really interesting.
(woman) No, not yet. What was it about?
(man) It was about pollution, specifically one kind of pollution called acid rain.
(narrator) WHAT IS THE TOPIC OF CONVERSATION 3?

EXERCISE 21, page 83

Conversation 1

(narrator) Listen to the beginning of Conversation 1, and try to imagine the situation.
(man) I'm looking for a part-time job on campus.
(woman) Then you've come to the right place. The campus employment office is here just to help students like you find jobs on campus.
(man) I'm glad to hear that, because I really need to start earning some money.

1. WHO IS PROBABLY TALKING?
2. WHERE DOES THE CONVERSATION TAKE PLACE?

Conversation 2

(narrator) Listen to the beginning of Conversation 2, and try to imagine the situation.

(woman)	Hi, Jack. It's good to see you again. Are you ready to get down to business again after spring break?
(man)	Not really, but I guess I don't really have too much choice, do I? And it's going to be particularly hard to get back to work since I just had the most fantastic vacation ever.
(woman)	Really? What did you do?
(man)	I went kayaking on the Klamath River.

1. WHO IS PROBABLY TALKING?
2. WHEN DOES THE CONVERSATION TAKE PLACE?
3. WHAT IS THE SOURCE OF THE MAN'S INFORMATION?

Conversation 3

(narrator)	Listen to the beginning of Conversation 3, and try to imagine the situation.
(man)	Did you read the article that the professor assigned for tomorrow's class? It was really interesting.
(woman)	No, not yet. What was it about?
(man)	It was about pollution, specifically one kind of pollution called acid rain.

1. WHO IS PROBABLY TALKING?
2. WHEN DOES THE CONVERSATION TAKE PLACE?
3. WHAT IS THE SOURCE OF THE INFORMATION?

TOEFL EXERCISE 22, page 85

Questions 1–5

(narrator)	Listen to the following conversation about a part-time job.
(man)	I'm looking for a part-time job on campus.
(woman)	Then you've come to the right place. The campus employment office is here just to help students like you find jobs on campus.
(man)	I'm glad to hear that, because I really need to start earning some money.
(woman)	Let me ask you some questions to help determine what kind of job would be best. First of all, how many hours a week do you want to work?
(man)	I need to work at least ten hours a week, and I don't think I can handle more than twenty hours with all the courses I'm taking.
(woman)	And when are you free to work?
(man)	All of my classes are in the morning, so I can work every weekday from noon on. And of course I wouldn't mind working on the weekends.
(woman)	I'll try to match you up with one of our on-campus student jobs. Please fill out this form with some additional information about your skills, and leave the form with me today. Then

	you can call me back tomorrow, and maybe I'll have some news for you.
(man)	Thanks for your help.

1. WHAT DOES THE MAN WANT TO DO?
2. WHERE DOES THE CONVERSATION PROBABLY TAKE PLACE?
3. HOW MANY HOURS OF WORK DOES THE MAN WANT PER WEEK?
4. WHEN CAN THE MAN WORK?
5. WHAT DOES THE WOMAN TELL THE MAN TO DO TOMORROW?

Questions 6–10

(narrator)	Listen to a conversation between two friends.
(woman)	Hi, Jack. It's good to see you again. Are you ready to get down to business again after spring break?
(man)	Not really, but I guess I don't really have too much choice, do I? And it's going to be particularly hard to get back to work since I just had the most fantastic vacation ever.
(woman)	Really? What did you do?
(man)	I went kayaking on the Klamath River.
(woman)	Kayaking?
(man)	Yes, you know what a kayak is, don't you? It's a long, narrow boat, the kind first used by the Eskimos. It's quite popular now on white-water rivers.
(woman)	Oh, I know what a kayak is. I was just surprised that you would take a trip like that. Weren't you scared?
(man)	At first, I was. But after I learned some techniques for maneuvering the kayak, it wasn't so bad. We didn't start out on the river. We had three whole days of instruction in a shallow pool first. Then, when we finally got out on the river, I felt ready for it.
(woman)	Did you spend the nights camping outside on the ground? That alone would make the trip unappealing to me.
(man)	Oh, no. The accommodations were fantastic. Each person on the trip had a private cabin, and the facilities included a hot tub, a lodge where you could have a drink and relax, and a top-notch cafeteria with great food.
(woman)	Now, that part of the trip does sound good to me. But I don't think I'd like the part that involves riding through rough water in a small kayak.
(man)	Oh, you should try it; I know you'd like it. I'm going to do it again myself, as soon as I can afford to spend the time and the money.
(woman)	Well, better you than me.

6. WHEN DOES THE CONVERSATION PROBABLY TAKE PLACE?
7. WHAT ARE THE MAN AND WOMAN DISCUSSING?

8. HOW MUCH INSTRUCTION DID THE MAN HAVE BEFORE GOING OUT ON THE RIVER?

9. WHICH OF THE FOLLOWING IS NOT PART OF THE KAYAKING TRIP?

10. HOW DOES THE WOMAN FEEL ABOUT TAKING A KAYAKING TRIP?

Questions 11–15

(narrator)	Listen to a conversation between two classsmates.
(man)	Did you read the article that the professor assigned for tomorrow's class? It was really interesting.
(woman)	No, not yet. What was it about?
(man)	It was about pollution, specifically one kind of pollution called acid rain.
(woman)	Why is it called acid rain?
(man)	It's called acid rain because the rain or some other kind of precipitation has been polluted with acid.
(woman)	Where does the acid come from?
(man)	From cars or factories, anything that burns coal or oil. These are made up mostly of sulfur dioxide and nitrogen oxides, which react with water vapor to form sulfuric acid or nitric acid.
(woman)	You mean that when coal or oil is burned, acid gets formed. And when it rains or snows, the acids fall back on earth.
(man)	Exactly. That's why it's so dangerous. Acid rain has been falling over areas of northern America and northern Europe, and if this isn't checked, the effect on the water supply and plant and animal life could be disastrous.
(woman)	This is something important. I really need to read that article.

11. WHAT IS THE TOPIC OF THIS CONVERSATION?

12. WHAT ENERGY SOURCES CAUSE ACID RAIN?

13. HOW IS SULFURIC ACID FORMED?

14. ACCORDING TO THE MAN, WHERE IS ACID RAIN A PROBLEM?

15. WHAT ACTION DOES THE WOMAN THINK SHE SHOULD TAKE NEXT?

TOEFL REVIEW EXERCISE (Skills 18–22), page 86

Questions 1–4

(narrator)	Listen to a man asking a woman for directions.
(man)	Can you tell me how to get to the Music Building from here? I have a lecture to attend there.
(woman)	Oh, are you new to campus?
(man)	Yes, I just got here last night.
(woman)	Well, to get to the Music Building, you have two choices. If you want to go right now you can walk straight down this street until you're past the Commons, and then turn right. The Music Building will be straight ahead.
(man)	How long will it take to get there?
(woman)	About twenty minutes.
(man)	What's my other choice?
(woman)	If you don't mind waiting around for a while, you can take the shuttle bus. The bus only takes about five minutes to get there.
(man)	But I have to wait for the bus?
(woman)	That's right.
(man)	Well, I guess I might as well walk.

1. WHERE DOES THE MAN WANT TO GO?

2. HOW MANY DIFFERENT ROUTES TO THE MUSIC BUILDING DOES THE WOMAN SUGGEST?

3. WHAT IS THE PROBLEM WITH TAKING THE SHUTTLE BUS?

4. WHAT DOES THE MAN FINALLY DECIDE TO DO?

Questions 5–9

(narrator)	Listen to a woman talk to a friend about her vacation.
(man)	How was your trip to Wyoming last summer?
(woman)	It was fantastic. Some of the most beautiful scenery in the country is in Wyoming.
(man)	Where did you go in Wyoming?
(woman)	We drove by Devil's Tower National Monument, and we spent a few days in Laramie. But we spent most of our vacation in Yellowstone National Park.
(man)	You went to Yellowstone? I wish I could've gone! I've heard that Yellowstone is just magnificent.
(woman)	It's the oldest and largest national park in the United States. And it's got spectacular waterfalls, hot springs, and geysers.
(man)	Did you see Old Faithful?
(woman)	Of course we saw Old Faithful. It's the best known of the geysers there. We couldn't visit Yellowstone without seeing Old Faithful.
(man)	Do you think you'll be taking another vacation in Yellowstone again? If you do, I'd like to go next time.

5. HOW DOES THE WOMAN DESCRIBE HER WYOMING VACATION?

6. HOW DID THE WOMAN PROBABLY TRAVEL ON VACATION?

7. WHICH OF THE FOLLOWING DID THE WOMAN DO ON VACATION?

8. WHICH OF THE FOLLOWING IS A WELL-KNOWN SIGHT IN YELLOWSTONE?

9. WHAT WOULD THE MAN LIKE TO DO?

Questions 10–13

(narrator)	Listen to a conversation between two friends.
(man)	How are you going to spend this year's Thanksgiving vacation?

(woman)	I'm going to spend it with my family. We celebrate very traditionally. We go to my grandparents' house and have a big Thanksgiving dinner. It's really the only time in the year that my whole family gets together.	
(man)	In my family we just have a big feast, too. We don't really stop and think about how Thanksgiving Day developed, how new colonists in Massachusetts had a three-day feast to give thanks for surviving the first terrible winter and for gathering their first corn harvest the following year.	
(woman)	Did you know that the original Thanksgiving Day was celebrated in July?	
(man)	No, I thought Thanksgiving had always been in November.	
(woman)	The first Thanksgiving was celebrated on July 30, 1623. After that, Thanksgiving was celebrated at many different times. It wasn't until 1863 that Abraham Lincoln declared the last Thursday in November as a day of thanksgiving, and this holiday has been celebrated in November ever since.	

10. WHAT IS THE SUBJECT OF THIS CONVERSATION?
11. HOW WILL THE WOMAN SPEND THANKSGIVING?
12. WHAT WERE THE MASSACHUSETTS COLONISTS THANKFUL FOR?
13. ACCORDING TO THE SPEAKER, WHEN IS THANKSGIVING CELEBRATED TODAY?

LONG TALKS (Paper)

EXERCISE 25, page 93

1.	*(narrator)*	The first part of Talk 1 is:
	(woman)	Welcome to Biology 101. I'm Professor Martin, and this is your laboratory assistant, Peter Smith.
1.	*(narrator)*	WHAT IS THE TOPIC OF TALK 1?
2.	*(narrator)*	The first part of Talk 2 is:
	(man)	In yesterday's class, we discussed the volcanoes located in the area known as the Ring of Fire, an area which basically encircles the Pacific and includes the United States's Mount St. Helens as well as Japan's Mt. Fuji and Argentina's Aconcagua, the highest mountain in the Western Hemisphere. Most of the world's approximately 500 active volcanoes are located along the Ring of Fire, and the eruptions that take place there are among the most violent in the world.

		Today, we are going to discuss the volcanoes of Hawaii, which are quite different from the volcanoes in the Ring of Fire.
2.	*(narrator)*	WHAT IS THE TOPIC OF TALK 2?
3.	*(narrator)*	The first part of Talk 3 is:
	(woman)	I hope you've enjoyed your visit so far in Washington, D.C. Today, we're going on a tour of the Smithsonian.
3.	*(narrator)*	WHAT IS THE TOPIC OF TALK 3?

EXERCISE 26, page 94

Talk 1

(narrator)	Listen to the beginning of Talk 1, and try to imagine the situation.	
(woman)	Welcome to Biology 101. I'm Professor Martin, and this is your laboratory assistant, Peter Smith. This course meets twice a week for lecture and once a week for laboratory assignments.	

1. WHO IS PROBABLY TALKING?
2. WHERE DOES THE TALK PROBABLY TAKE PLACE?
3. WHEN DOES THE TALK PROBABLY TAKE PLACE?
4. WHAT COURSE IS BEING DISCUSSED?

Talk 2

(narrator)	Listen to the beginning of Talk 2, and try to imagine the situation.	
(man)	In yesterday's class, we discussed the volcanoes located in the area known as the Ring of Fire, an area which basically encircles the Pacific and includes the United States's Mount St. Helens as well as Japan's Mt. Fuji and Argentina's Aconcagua, the highest mountain in the Western Hemisphere. Most of the world's approximately 500 active volcanoes are located along the Ring of Fire, and the eruptions that take place there are among the most violent in the world.	
	Today, we are going to discuss the volcanoes of Hawaii, which are quite different from the volcanoes in the Ring of Fire.	

1. WHO IS PROBABLY TALKING?
2. WHERE DOES THE TALK PROBABLY TAKE PLACE?
3. WHEN DOES THE TALK PROBABLY TAKE PLACE?
4. WHAT COURSE IS BEING DISCUSSED?

Talk 3

(narrator)	Listen to the beginning of Talk 3, and try to imagine the situation.	

(woman)   I hope you've enjoyed your visit so far in Washington, D.C. Today, we're going on a tour of the Smithsonian.

1. WHO IS PROBABLY TALKING?
2. WHERE DOES THE TALK TAKE PLACE?
3. WHEN DOES THE TALK TAKE PLACE?

TOEFL EXERCISE 27, page 96

Questions 1–5

(narrator)   Listen to a talk given by a professor.

(woman)   Welcome to Biology 101. I'm Professor Martin, and this is your laboratory assistant, Peter Smith. This course meets twice a week for lecture and once a week for laboratory assignments.

The text for this course is *Introduction to Biological Sciences,* by Abramson. You should get the text and read the first chapter before the next class. You will also need to get the laboratory manual that accompanies the text.

I've passed out a copy of the course syllabus. This syllabus lists the reading assignments and exam dates. Note that we will cover one chapter a week for each of the next fifteen weeks in the semester, and there will be three exams throughout the course.

Grades in this course are based on your exam grades and your grades on the laboratory assignments. Are there any questions?

1. WHEN DOES THIS TALK PROBABLY TAKE PLACE?
2. HOW OFTEN WILL PROFESSOR MARTIN GIVE LECTURES?
3. WHAT IS THE ASSIGNMENT FOR THE NEXT CLASS?
4. WHAT INFORMATION IS GIVEN IN THE SYLLABUS?
5. WHAT WILL THE PROFESSOR USE TO DETERMINE THE FINAL COURSE GRADES?

Questions 6–10

(narrator)   Listen to a lecture given by a professor.

(man)   In yesterday's class, we discussed the volcanoes located in the area known as the Ring of Fire, an area which basically encircles the Pacific and includes the United States's Mount St. Helens as well as Japan's Mt. Fuji and Argentina's Aconcagua, the highest mountain in the Western Hemisphere. Most of the world's approximately 500 active volcanoes are located along the Ring of Fire, and the eruptions that take place there are among the most violent in the world.

Today, we are going to discuss the volcanoes of Hawaii, which are quite different from the volcanoes in the Ring of Fire. Hawaiian volcanoes are not located along the Ring of Fire and are therefore not caused by the movement of the Earth's plates against each other. Instead, Hawaii is located in the middle of the Ring of Fire, above a massive plate rather than where two plates meet. The result is that Hawaiian volcanoes are much gentler than those in the Ring of Fire: Hawaiian volcanoes have much less gas in them, which causes less explosive eruptions, and the lava in Hawaiian volcanoes is thinner, which results in mounds that are long and low rather than high and steep because the lava flows farther and builds mounds gradually with long, low slopes. Mauna Loa, the name of one of Hawaii's most famous volcanoes, actually means "long mountain."

6. WHAT WAS THE TOPIC OF YESTERDAY'S LECTURE?
7. WHAT IS THE TOPIC OF TODAY'S LECTURE?
8. WHERE ARE MOST OF THE WORLD'S ACTIVE VOLCANOES LOCATED?
9. WHAT IS CHARACTERISTIC OF HAWAII'S VOLCANOES?
10. WHAT IS MAUNA LOA?

Questions 11–15

(narrator)   Listen to a talk about the Smithsonian.

(woman)   I hope you've enjoyed your visit so far in Washington, D.C. Today, we're going on a tour of the Smithsonian, The Smithsonian is actually several museums, each with a different focus, situated together on a mall. These museums in total have more than sixty million items on exhibit. The first Smithsonian museum we'll visit is the Museum of Natural History, which has various types of stuffed animals, and exhibits showing the lifestyles of early American Indians and Eskimos. From the Museum of Natural History, we'll go on to the National Air and Space Museum, where we'll see displays that show the development of flight. In this museum you can see the airplane that Orville Wright used to make his first flight and the airplane that Charles Lindbergh used to cross the Atlantic. After we visit those two museums as a group, you'll have free time to visit some of the other Smithsonian museums: the Museum of American History, the Smithsonian Arts and Industries Building, and the various art museums located on the

Smithsonian Mall. After our trip to the Smithsonian today, we'll go on to the White House and Capitol Building tomorrow.

11. WHO IS PROBABLY GIVING THIS TALK?
12. HOW MANY ITEMS ARE ON EXHIBIT IN THE SMITHSONIAN MUSEUMS?
13. ACCORDING TO THE TALK, WHICH MUSEUM HAS EXHIBITS OF EARLY ESKIMOS?
14. WHICH MUSEUM WILL THEY VISIT AS A GROUP?
15. WHERE WILL THEY GO TOMORROW?

TOEFL REVIEW EXERCISE (Skills 23–27), page 97

Questions 1–4

(narrator)   Listen to a talk by a librarian.

(woman)   Hello and welcome to the library. I'm Ms. Martin, the assistant librarian, and this is the library orientation tour for new graduate students in the business department. If you are not a newly admitted graduate student or your major is not business, then you are in the wrong place.

Now let's get started. I'm sure you understand that, as graduate students, you will be required to do a tremendous amount of research. Here at the library, we try to make this process as easy as possible for you. The library is open for extensive hours, from 7:00 a.m. until midnight seven days a week, so that you will have access to library research facilities almost any time that you want. During final exam week, the library is open twenty-four hours a day, and there are library staff members available to help you whenever the library is open.

During this tour, we will be concentrating on two areas of the library. The first area is the computerized search facilities, which are located on the second floor of the library. On the computer systems located in this area, you can conduct computer searches for books as well as articles in magazines, newspapers, and journals. On the floor above the computer area are reference materials devoted specifically to business. In this area, you can find references for books and periodicals related to business and annual reports on major corporations.

Now that we have completed this little introduction, we are ready to start the tour. Please follow me.

1. WHO IS MS. MARTIN TALKING TO?
2. WHAT ARE THE LIBRARY'S HOURS DURING FINAL EXAM WEEK?

3. WHAT TWO AREAS WILL THE TOUR CONCENTRATE ON?
4. WHAT ARE THE STUDENTS PROBABLY GOING TO DO NEXT?

Questions 5–8

(narrator)   Listen to a talk in a lecture series.

(man)   This is the fourth lecture in a series of Personal Health Care lectures presented by Student Health Services. I'm Dr. Hall, a dermatologist, and tonight I will be speaking about the effects of stress on the skin.

The relationship between skin problems and stress is rather complicated: skin problems often accompany stress, but it is not the stress itself that directly causes the skin problems. Instead, it is the side effects of stress, such as the use of alcohol, tobacco, and caffeine, that are often to blame.

Alcohol consumed in large quantities can cause problems with the skin by increasing the flow of blood to the skin; this makes the skin feel warmer and can really worsen the itching that accompanies conditions such as hives or rosacea. Nicotine and caffeine, on the other hand, cause problems by reducing the supply of blood to the skin; this in turn keeps the skin from being properly nourished.

Thank you very much for your attention, and I hope that you will return next week for the next lecture in the series.

5. WHO IS THE SPEAKER?
6. WHAT IS THE TOPIC OF THE TALK?
7. WHICH OF THE FOLLOWING CAN WORSEN ITCHING?
8. HOW DOES CAFFEINE IRRITATE THE SKIN?

Questions 9–12

(narrator)   Listen to a lecture given by a professor.

(woman)   In today's class, we will be discussing the nineteenth century crash of the gold market. When the U.S. gold market crashed on September 24, 1869, the day became known as Black Friday. What set the stage for the crash was the excessive amount of paper currency issued by the government to finance the Civil War. At the end of the war, speculators in New York tried to capitalize on the inflated price of gold in relationship to paper currency by cornering the gold market. Their effort to corner the market was based on what turned out to be false assurances from the president's brother-in-law that the United States government

would not sell off any of its gold
reserves. When the U.S. Treasury
announced $4 million in gold sales,
the bottom fell out of the gold market
and the price of gold crashed.

9. WHEN WAS THE DAY KNOWN AS BLACK FRI-
DAY?
10. WHAT HAPPENED ON THE DAY KNOWN AS
BLACK FRIDAY?
11. WHO SUPPLIED THE GOLD SPECULATORS
WITH FALSE INFORMATION?
12. WHAT DID THE GOLD SPECULATORS WANT
THE U.S. GOVERNMENT TO DO?

CASUAL CONVERSATIONS
(Computer)

TOEFL EXERCISE 28, page 100

Questions 1–3

(woman)	Where are you heading now? You seem to be in a bit of a hurry.
(man)	I'm on my way to the Music Building. I have a rehearsal in about fifteen minutes.
(woman)	A rehearsal? For what?
(man)	I play in the university orchestra, and there are orchestra rehearsals three times a week.
(woman)	You play in the orchestra? What instrument do you play?
(man)	I actually play two instruments. I play the violin in the orchestra, and I also play the piano.
(woman)	I can't believe you can play two instruments. I can't even play one.

1. WHERE IS THE MAN GOING?
2. HOW OFTEN DOES THE ORCHESTRA MEET
FOR PRACTICE?
3. HOW MANY MUSICAL INSTRUMENTS DOES
THE WOMAN PLAY?

Questions 4–5

(woman)	Do you know how many papers we're going to have to write in this course? I'm a little confused about this.
(man)	The professor said in class that there would be two papers.
(woman)	That's what he said in class, but the syllabus says that there are three papers.
(man)	Oh, that's right. I did see that on the syllabus. I can understand why you're confused. I am, too.
(woman)	I think we had better ask the professor about this at the next class. It's important.
(man)	Yes, it is. We do need to know for sure how many papers we have to write.

4. WHAT IS THE WOMAN CONFUSED ABOUT?
5. WHAT DO THEY DECIDE TO DO?

Questions 6–8

(man)	Can you tell me about parking on campus? I don't have a car yet, but I've decided to get one.
(woman)	Parking is kind of difficult on campus because there just aren't enough spaces for all the people who want to park. You do know that if you're going to park on campus, you'll need a parking sticker?
(man)	A parking sticker? What kind of parking sticker?
(woman)	Well, if you're only going to park on campus once in a while, you can get a daily sticker each day that you park. But if you're going to be parking on campus often, then you really should get a permanent sticker.
(man)	Well, I guess I need a permanent sticker then.

6. WHAT IS TRUE ABOUT THE MAN?
7. WHAT DOES THE WOMAN SAY ABOUT PARK-
ING ON CAMPUS?
8. WHAT DOES THE MAN SAY THAT HE NEEDS?

Questions 9–11

(man)	What a hard exam that was!
(woman)	It wasn't just hard—it was long. I couldn't believe that we had fifty true-false questions plus two essay answers to write, all in only an hour.
(man)	I didn't mind the true-false questions. In fact, I kind of enjoyed them. But I don't like writing essay answers, so I really didn't like an exam with two essays to write.
(woman)	Well, I did mind the true-false questions. I spent too much time on them, and then I didn't have enough time to write the essays. I knew the answers to the essays, but I wrote the information so quickly that I'm not sure if my answers made any sense.
(man)	I guess we'll just have to wait and see how we did when we get the exams back. After all, everyone in the class had the same time limit we did.

9. WHAT WAS TRUE ABOUT THE EXAM?
10. HOW DID THE MAN FEEL ABOUT THE TRUE-
FALSE QUESTIONS?
11. HOW DID THE WOMAN DO ON THE ESSAY
QUESTIONS?

ACADEMIC DISCUSSIONS
(Computer)

EXERCISE 29, page 114
TOEFL EXERCISE 29, page 115

Questions 1–2

(narrator) Listen to a discussion by a group of students taking a meteorology class. The discussion is on the formation of hail.

(woman 1) Okay, I think we understand how snow and rain are formed. Now, we need to discuss the formation of hail.

(man) What is hail exactly? How does it differ from snow and rain?

(woman 2) Hail is really frozen drops of rain.

(man) And how do the drops of rain get frozen?

(woman 1) They get frozen when they are pushed up into higher elevations where it is colder.

(man) And how does that happen?

(woman 2) Hailstones develop in cumulonimbus clouds that have grown very tall. They can actually be as tall as six miles.

(man) That's right. The cumulonimbus clouds are so tall that they are much warmer at the bottom than at the top.

(woman 1) And sometimes air currents blow drops of water in a cloud up higher into the cloud.

(man) Where it's colder, so the drops freeze into ice…. Do the drops fall to the earth then?

(woman 2) Usually not just after one trip up. Usually the drops are not heavy enough then to fall to the earth.

(man) So the drops rise and fall a number of times within the cloud.

(woman 1) And each time a drop rises and falls, it adds another layer of ice.

(man) So a hailstone actually has a number of layers of ice on it? One layer for each time that it is pushed up and freezes again.

(woman 2) Yes, and after it builds up enough layers, it gets too heavy.

(man) And that's when it falls to earth.

(woman 2) Exactly.

1. IN THE DISCUSSION, THE STUDENTS EXPLAIN THE INITIAL STAGES IN THE FORMATION OF A HAILSTONE FROM A DROP OF WATER. SUMMARIZE THE PROCESS BY PUTTING THE STEPS IN ORDER.

2. IN THE DISCUSSION, THE STUDENTS EXPLAIN HOW A HAILSTONE HITS THE EARTH. SUMMARIZE THE PROCESS BY PUTTING THE STEPS IN ORDER.

Questions 3–5

(narrator) Listen to a discussion in a physiology class. The discussion is on types of fractures.

(instructor) Now, we're going to review the information on various types of fractures, or broken bones. Yesterday, we talked about three types of fractures. Do you remember what they were? Clair?

(Clair) They were simple, compound, and greenstick fractures.

(instructor) Yes, exactly. Now can you tell me how a simple fracture and a compound fracture differ? Are they different because of the number of fractures? Dave?

(Dave) No, the difference between a simple and a compound fracture refers to how much damage there is to the tissue around the broken bone rather than the number of breaks in the bone. In a simple fracture, the bone is broken, but there is little damage to the tissue around the bone. In a compound fracture, the bone is broken and there's a lot of damage to the tissue around the broken bone.

(instructor) How much tissue damage is there in a compound fracture? Gail?

(Gail) In a compound fracture, the broken bone comes through the skin.

(instructor) So, when we talk about the difference between a simple and a compound fracture, this doesn't refer to the number of breaks in a bone; instead, it refers to the amount of tissue damage. How do we refer to the number of breaks in a bone? Clair?

(Clair) To talk about the number of breaks in a bone, we talk about a single, a double, or a multiple break. A single fracture means one break, a double fracture means two breaks, and a multiple fracture means more than two breaks.

(instructor) Okay, I hope this distinction is clear, that we talk about single and double fractures to refer to the number of fractures and simple and complex fractures refer to how much tissue damage there is around the break. Now, we have just one more type of fracture to discuss, and that's the greenstick fracture. Dave, can you tell me who generally suffers from greenstick fractures?

(Dave) Greenstick fractures are usually found in children.

(instructor) That's true. And what is a greenstick fracture? Gail?

(Gail) A greenstick fracture means that the bone bends and maybe it breaks part of the way, but it doesn't break all the way through. The name "greenstick" refers to a young green plant that might bend instead of breaking.

(instructor) So, is a greenstick fracture a very serious fracture? Clair?

(Clair)   No, a greenstick fracture is usually the least serious type of fracture because the bone is not broken all the way through. The compound fracture, where the broken bone comes through the skin, is the most serious type of fracture.

3. HOW MANY BREAKS IN THE BONE ARE THERE IN EACH OF THESE FRACTURES?
4. HOW ARE EACH OF THESE FRACTURES DESCRIBED?
5. HOW SERIOUS IS EACH OF THESE FRACTURES?

Questions 6–7

(narrator)   Listen to a discussion by a group of students taking a law class. The students are discussing Clarence Darrow.

(man 1)   We need to know about Clarence Darrow and some of his more famous cases. Why don't we go over this now?

(woman)   Okay, I know that Clarence Darrow was a famous lawyer. What were some of his most famous cases?

(man 2)   He was famous for the Eugene Debs case, and the Loeb-Leopold case, and the Scopes trial.

(woman)   He was also famous for his part in resolving a coal strike.

(man 1)   Okay, let's go over each of these cases and make sure we understand them. The first one was the Eugene Debs case in 1895. Darrow defended Debs, who was the president of the railroad workers union, after the railroad workers went on strike.

(man 2)   Wasn't the strike by the railroad workers called the Pullman strike?

(man 1)   Yes, it was; it was named after the Pullman, which was a type of railroad car.

(woman)   The next situation was the Pennsylvania coal strike in 1902. Clarence Darrow was asked by the president of the United States to arbitrate the coal strike.

(man 1)   So this wasn't actually a trial; it was an arbitration.

(woman)   That's true. Now, there are two other trials we need to know about: the Loeb-Leopold trial and the Scopes trial.

(man 2)   The Loeb-Leopold trial was in 1924. This was a very famous murder trial.

(woman)   And Clarence Darrow was the defense attorney in this trial?

(man 2)   Exactly.

(woman)   Now, the last case we need to be familiar with is the Scopes trial, but I don't know much about that.

(man 1)   The Scopes trial in 1925—also known as the Scopes Monkey trial—was about evolution, about whether mankind evolved from monkeys.

(woman)   And who was Scopes?

(man 1)   Scopes was a high school biology teacher who was charged with breaking the law because he taught evolution in school.

(woman)   And Clarence Darrow was the defense attorney in this trial?

(man 1)   Yes, he was.

(man 2)   I think we have covered the information we need to know about Darrow. We know about three of the trials in which he served as defense attorney.

(woman)   And we also know about the strike he helped to arbitrate.

6. WITH WHAT EVENT WAS EACH OF THE DEFENDANTS ASSOCIATED?
7. A HISTORICAL SERIES OF EVENTS IN THE LIFE OF CLARENCE DARROW IS PRESENTED IN THE DISCUSSION. PUT THE EVENTS IN THE CORRECT CHRONOLOGICAL ORDER.

EXERCISE 30, page 119
TOEFL EXERCISE 30, page 120

Questions 1–5

(narrator)   Listen to a discussion by some students who are taking a drama class. They are discussing their class project on the play *Our Town*.

(Bill)   We need to get going on our class project for drama class. We have to present a scene from one of the plays we're studying in class, in costume and with props. Our performance is in only three weeks, and that's not very much time for all we have to do.

(Tina)   Let's see. We've already decided on a scene. We're going to do one of the scenes from Thornton Wilder's play *Our Town*.

(Chuck)   And we know who's going to play each part. Bill, you're going to be the Stage Manager—that's a big part in this play. Tina, you're going to play Emily, and I'm going to play George. We're going to do a scene from the part of the play that takes place before George and Emily's wedding. I've already started learning my lines. What about you two?

(Bill)   I've already started working on my lines.

(Tina)   And I'm familiar with mine, too. I think we're ready to read through the scene together.

(Chuck)   Why don't we discuss what we're going to do about costumes and props first, and then we can run through the scene together.

(Tina)   That sounds like a good idea.

(Bill)   I think so, too.

1. WHEN IS THE STUDENTS' PERFORMANCE?
2. WHICH OF THESE IS NOT A CHARACTER IN THE SCENE?

3. IT IS MOST LIKELY THAT THE STUDENTS ARE HOW FAMILIAR WITH THEIR LINES?
4. WHAT IS STATED ABOUT THE SCENE?
5. WHAT ARE THE STUDENTS PROBABLY GOING TO DISCUSS NEXT?

Questions 6–12

(narrator)   Listen to a discussion about a geology class. The students are discussing iron pyrite.

(woman 1)   The next type of mineral we need to talk about is iron pyrite.

(man)   Iron pyrite? Isn't that what's also called fool's gold?

(woman 1)   Yes, it is.

(woman 2)   Why is iron pyrite called fool's gold?

(man)   It's called fool's gold because it can look something like gold, and some people who found iron pyrite thought they had found gold.

(woman 1)   So iron pyrite sort of looks like gold? What exactly does it look like?

(man)   It can be shiny golden in color, but its crystals have a different shape from gold crystals. Iron pyrite crystals are cubical in shape, while crystals of gold are not.

(woman 2)   How does iron pyrite get its shiny golden color if it's not made of gold?

(woman 1)   I know the answer to that. Iron pyrite gets its shiny golden color from the mix of elements in it.

(man)   Iron pyrite is made from a mix of elements?

(woman 1)   Yes, iron pyrite is a compound of iron and sulfur, so it's very different from gold because it's made of this compound.

(woman 2)   And it's also quite different from gold in how it reacts to heat. Iron pyrite has a strong reaction to heat.

(man)   Why? What happens when iron pyrite is heated?

(woman 2)   When iron pyrite is heated, it smokes and develops a strong odor.

(man)   And gold doesn't have that kind of reaction to heat?

(woman 1)   No, it doesn't.

(woman 1)   Do you know where the name *pyrite* came from?

(man)   I think I know that. It came from the Greek word for fire, didn't it?

(woman 1)   Yes, it did. If you strike iron pyrite with metal, then it produces sparks. Some ancient cultures used to use iron pyrite to start fires. They couldn't use gold that way.

(man)   So iron pyrite did have some use, even if it really wasn't gold.

6. IN WHAT WAY IS IRON PYRITE SIMILAR TO GOLD?
7. IT IS IMPLIED IN THE DISCUSSION THAT WHAT TYPE OF PEOPLE THOUGHT IRON PYRITE WAS GOLD?

8. WHAT IS IRON PYRITE COMPOSED OF?
9. HOW DOES IRON PYRITE REACT TO HEAT?
10. HOW DOES GOLD MOST LIKELY REACT TO HEAT?
11. WHERE DID THE WORD *PYRITE* COME FROM?
12. WHAT CAN BE INFERRED FROM THE DISCUSSION ABOUT GOLD IN ANCIENT CULTURES?

Questions 13–18

(narrator)   Listen to a discussion in a history class. The discussion is on the history behind the name *California*.

(instructor)   Today, we'll be talking about California and where California got its name. First of all, who was it who actually gave California its name? Lynn?

(Lynn)   California was given its name by a Spanish explorer.

(instructor)   And which Spanish explorer gave California its name? Rick?

(Rick)   It was Spanish explorer Hernan Cortes who gave California its name. Cortes visited the lower part of California in the first half of the sixteenth century and named the area California.

(instructor)   How did Cortes decide on the name *California*? Did he just make the name up, or did he take it from another source? Pam?

(Pam)   He got the name *California* from a series of stories that were popular in Spain at the time.

(instructor)   And what kind of series contained a place called California? Lynn?

(Lynn)   The series was a fantasy serial that was a best-seller at the time. It was about a knight and his son who traveled the world looking for new lands and new adventures. One of the places that came across in the story was an unusual place called California.

(instructor)   And what was California like in the best-selling stories?

(Rick)   In the stories, California was an island that was populated by Amazons.

(Pam)   The Amazons were all women.

(Lynn)   And they were tall and powerful warriors.

(Rick)   And the only metal on the island was gold.

(Pam)   So all the utensils and ornaments were made out of gold.

(Lynn)   And the female warriors wore armor made of gold and carried weapons made of gold.

(instructor)   So Cortes named the place that he visited California because he thought it was like the fictional place from the fantasy series, even though he didn't see any inhabitants resembling those of the fictional California. He incorrectly assumed that it was an island, like the fictional place, and I think he hoped that it was also full of gold, like the fictional California.

13. WHO GAVE THE AREA OF NORTH AMERICA KNOWN AS CALIFORNIA ITS NAME?
14. IN WHICH OF THESE YEARS WAS THE AREA OF NORTH AMERICA KNOWN AS CALIFORNIA MOST LIKELY GIVEN ITS NAME?
15. HOW WAS THE NAME *CALIFORNIA* FIRST USED?
16. WHAT WAS THE FICTIONAL CALIFORNIA LIKE?
17. WHAT IS NOT STATED IN THE DISCUSSION ABOUT THE INHABITANTS OF THE FICTIONAL CALIFORNIA?
18. WHAT CAN BE INFERRED ABOUT THE CALIFORNIA THAT CORTES VISITED?

EXERCISE 31, page 124
TOEFL EXERCISE 31, page 125
Questions 1–3

(narrator) Listen to a discussion by a group of students in a meteorology class. The discussion is on theories about the behavior of storms.

(instructor) We have just one more topic to cover before we finish for today. I'd like to look at some early theories about how storms develop. The two men I'd like to discuss are William Redfield and James Espy. Redfield and Espy were two American meteorologists from the nineteenth century, and they had differing theories on how storms behave. Espy argues that centripetal force was at work in storms. Can anyone explain what direction these winds would be moving if centripetal force were involved? Anne?

(Anne) Centripetal force would cause winds to be moving inward from all directions toward the center of the storm. But that's not what really happens, is it?

(instructor) No, Espy's theory was that centripetal force pushed the winds of a storm inward toward the center from all directions. Espy's theory has not proven to be very accurate. Now, who was involved in a debate with Espy in the nineteenth century? Lee?

(Lee) Redfield was the other meteorologist. Did he agree or disagree with Espy?

(instructor) Redfield disagreed with Espy. Redfield argued that the winds in a storm rotated around the center of the storm in a counterclockwise direction. Can you explain Redfield's ideas to me? Chris?

(Chris) Redfield believed that the winds in a storm rotated around the center of the storm, so the winds would be moving in a circular path. And he believed that the winds move in a

counterclockwise direction, which means that they move in the opposite direction from the direction that a clock moves.

(instructor) That's a good description of Redfield's ideas about how the winds in a storm behave. Now, for the most important question. We've already said that Espy's theory on how the winds in a storm behave wasn't very accurate. What about Redfield's theory? Was his theory accurate or inaccurate? Anne?

(Anne) I think that Redfield's description was quite close to what actually happens in a storm.

(instructor) Exactly.

1. HOW DID REDFIELD BELIEVE THAT THE WINDS IN STORMS BEHAVE?
2. HOW DID ESPY BELIEVE THAT THE WINDS IN STORMS BEHAVE?
3. WHICH OF THESE DIAGRAMS MOST CLOSELY REPRESENTS WHAT WINDS ACTUALLY DO DURING A STORM?

Questions 4–6

(narrator) Listen to a group of students discussing information from a zoology class. The discussion is on the opossum.

(man 1) The next animal we need to discuss is the opossum. The opossum is another kind of marsupial.

(woman) A marsupial? What's a marsupial?

(man 2) A marsupial is an animal that carries its young in a pouch.

(woman) Oh, like a kangaroo.

(man 2) Exactly.

(woman) And how long do young opossums stay in their mother's pouch?

(man 1) For about two months. Then, when the babies are about two months old, they come out of their mother's pouch, but they don't go very far. For the next few months, they go everywhere with their mother

(man 2) They just ride along on their mother's back.

(woman) So young opossums spend the first two months in their mother's pouch and the next two months hanging on her back?

(man 1) That's right. Now, aren't opossums animals that play dead?

(man 2) Yes, they are.

(woman) And that's why we talk about playing 'possum if we're talking about pretending that we're asleep or dead.

(man 2) Exactly.

(man 1) So when an opossum is frightened by an attacker, it doesn't run away?

(man 2) That's right. It just rolls over on its back, kind of curls up, and pretends that it's dead.

(woman) I guess it's just hoping that the attacker will think it's dead and will go away and leave it alone.

4. WHERE WOULD A ONE-MONTH-OLD BABY OPOSSUM MOST LIKELY BE FOUND?
5. WHERE WOULD A THREE-MONTH-OLD OPOSSUM MOST LIKELY BE WHILE ITS MOTHER IS WALKING AROUND?
6. WHAT DOES AN OPOSSUM DO WHEN IT IS THREATENED?

Questions 7–9

(narrator) Listen to a discussion from an American history class. The discussion is on Chimney Rock.

(instructor) What I want to discuss next is Chimney Rock. What can you tell me about Chimney Rock?

(woman 1) Chimney Rock was one of the major landmarks for pioneers traveling west in the nineteenth century.

(man) It was on the Oregon Trail. Pioneers on the Oregon Trail would stop at Chimney Rock because it was close to the Platte River. It was a good place to stop because of the water supply.

(instructor) And what does Chimney Rock look like?

(woman 2) Chimney Rock is a giant spire of sandstone on top of a large mound.

(woman 1) It kind of looks like a large candle on top of a birthday cake.

(man) A very large candle; it's 500 feet high.

(instructor) And where is Chimney Rock located?

(woman 2) As we said before, it's on the Oregon Trail close to the Platte River; it's just south of the Platte River, actually.

(woman 1) And it's on the Great Plains, so the area around it is flat. That's one reason why it is so noticeable.

(man) But it's not in the middle of the Great Plains. It's close to where the Great Plains run into the Rocky Mountains.

(instructor) And what did it mean to the pioneers when they saw Chimney Rock?

(woman 2) When the pioneers saw Chimney Rock, it meant that they had almost finished the long trip across the prairie.

(woman 1) It also meant that they were almost at the next stage of their trip, the Rocky Mountains.

7. WHICH OF THESE MOST CLOSELY RESEMBLES CHIMNEY ROCK?
8. WHERE IS CHIMNEY ROCK LOCATED IN RELATION TO THE PLATTE RIVER?
9. WHERE IS CHIMNEY ROCK LOCATED IN RELATION TO THE GREAT PLAINS AND THE ROCKY MOUNTAINS?

TOEFL REVIEW EXERCISE (Skills 29–31), page 128

Questions 1–5

(narrator) Listen to a discussion in an American history class. The discussion is about an early American coin.

(instructor) Today we're going to talk about a coin from early in the history of the United States. It was the first coin issued by the United States government, and it was issued in 1787. This coin was known by two names: it was known as both the Fugio coin and the Franklin coin. First of all, can you tell me why it was called the Fugio coin? Laura?

(Laura) It was called the Fugio coin because it had the word *fugio* on the front of the coin. Fugio is a Latin word which means "I fly."

(instructor) And this coin was also called the Franklin coin. Why was it called the Franklin coin? Was Benjamin Franklin on it?

(Doug) No, it was called the Franklin coin because Franklin was given credit for the wording on the coin.

(instructor) Now, let's look at the front of the coin. Can you describe the front of it for me? Sarah?

(Sarah) The front of the coin has a sundial in the middle with a sun shining down on the sundial.

(instructor) Yes, both a sun and a sundial are there. And what else? Laura?

(Laura) There's a date along one side and the word *fugio* along the other side. And then there's some wording at the bottom.

(instructor) And what words are along the bottom?

(Doug) The wording along the bottom is *Mind your business*. The coin is called the Franklin coin because Franklin is given credit for this wording.

(instructor) Now let me describe the back of the coin for you because we don't have a photograph of the back of the coin. On the back of the coin, there's a large circle made up of thirteen linked circles, and in the middle of the circle are the words *We are one*.

(Sarah) So there are thirteen circles linked into one circle on the back?

(instructor) Yes, and do you understand the symbolism of the thirteen circles linked on the back of the coin?

(Laura) I think so, particularly with the words *We are one*. This design on the back of the coin symbolizes the thirteen original colonies linked into one country.

(Doug) That's a very appropriate idea for the first coin issued by the United States after the country won its independence.

1. BY WHAT TWO NAMES IS THIS COIN KNOWN?
2. WHEN WAS THIS COIN FIRST ISSUED?
3. FOR WHICH PART OF THE COIN WAS FRANKLIN GIVEN CREDIT?
4. WHAT DO THE CIRCLES ON THE BACK OF THE COIN LOOK LIKE?
5. WHAT WORDS ARE ON THE BACK OF THE COIN?

Questions 6–10

(narrator)   Listen to a group of students discussing a presentation for a business class. The discussion is on the marketing of Kleenex.

(man 1)   Our presentation for marketing class is in a few days. Let's see what information we have come up with.

(woman)   Okay. Our topic for the presentation is the marketing of Kleenex early in its history. We're supposed to show how the early marketing of Kleenex helped to turn it into such a successful product.

(man 2)   There seem to be three clear phases in the early history of Kleenex. First, its use during World War I, second its use as a substitute for facecloths during the 1920s, and third, its use as a substitute for handkerchiefs during the 1930s. For the presentation, how about if I talk about the first phase, the use of Kleenex during World War I.

(man 1)   And I'll talk about the second phase, its use as a substitute for facecloths.

(woman)   And that leaves me with the third phase, the use of Kleenex as a substitute for handkerchiefs.

(man 2)   Now, don't forget that we're supposed to focus on the <u>marketing</u> of the product during each of the phases, not just the history.

(man 1)   Okay, why don't we review the key points for each of these phases now, with an emphasis on the marketing of the product during each phase.

(woman)   Sounds like a good idea to me.

(man 2)   So, I'll go first. The first phase of the product was its use during World War I. Cotton was in short supply during the war, so the Kimberley-Clark company developed Kleenex for use in bandages and gas masks. During this first phase, the company did not need to worry about marketing the product. Because it was during a war, there was very high demand for the product.

(man 1)   Now, for the second phase. After the war, the company had a huge surplus of Kleenex, and it had to market the product. During the 1920s, Kimberly-Clark decided to market Kleenex as a high-end and glamorous substitute for facecloths. It used famous actresses in its marketing, and women who wanted to be glamorous like the celebrities used Kleenex in place of facecloths.

(woman)   Now, on to the third phase. While Kimberly-Clark was marketing Kleenex only for use as a facecloth, a number of people began writing in to the company saying that there was another use for Kleenex besides its use as a facecloth: Kleenex was even more useful as a replacement for handkerchiefs. In 1930, the company's marketing department decided to conduct consumer testing to determine if the product should be presented as a facecloth or as a handkerchief. The results of the consumer testing showed that a large majority thought Kleenex was more useful as a handkerchief than as a facecloth.

6. WHAT ARE THE STUDENTS DOING?
7. MATCH THE USE OF THE PRODUCT TO THE PERIOD OF TIME WHEN THAT USE PREDOMINATED.
8. WHAT WAS THE SITUATION AT KIMBERLY-CLARK AT THE END OF WORLD WAR I?
9. HOW DID KIMBERLY-CLARK LEARN THAT ITS PRODUCT HAD A USE AS A HANDKERCHIEF?
10. MATCH THE USE OF THE PRODUCT TO THE MARKETING STRATEGY ASSOCIATED WITH THAT USE.

Questions 11–15

(narrator)   Listen to a discussion by a group of students in an oceanography class. The discussion is on atolls.

(instructor)   In this course, we have discussed a number of the ocean's unusual features. Today, we're going to discuss atolls and how they're formed. First, can you tell me what an atoll is? Beth?

(Beth)   An atoll is a ring-shaped mass of coral and algae.

(instructor)   That's right. An atoll is made of coral and algae. And where are atolls found? Jim?

(Jim)   Atolls are found in tropical and subtropical areas of the ocean, where the water temperature is fairly warm. The coral and reef-building algae grow best in fairly warm water.

(instructor)   Now, let's look at how atolls are formed. We'll look at a series of three diagrams and discuss what is happening in each. This diagram shows the first step in the process. What does the diagram show? Linda?

(Linda)   This diagram shows a new volcanic island that has formed.

(instructor)   And what's growing around the volcanic island?

(Linda)	A coral reef is growing around this new volcanic island.
(instructor)	Now let's look at the second diagram. Beth, can you describe what's happening in this diagram?
(Beth)	The second diagram shows that the volcanic island has started to erode—it's worn down.
(instructor)	And what's happened with the coral reef while the volcanic island has eroded?
(Beth)	The coral reef has continued to grow.
(instructor)	Now let's look at the third diagram in the series. What's happening in this diagram? Jim?
(Jim)	In this diagram, you can see that the volcanic island has worn down so far that it's below the level of the ocean. The coral has built up even further, so the coral is above the water, and the remains of the volcano are under water.
(instructor)	Yes, and it's at this stage when the ring of coral is called an atoll. The volcano has sunk, and there's a pool of water inside the atoll. Now, what do we call the pool of water that remains inside an atoll? Linda?
(Linda)	The pool of water inside the atoll is called a lagoon.
(instructor)	That's correct. The body of water inside an atoll is called a lagoon. You seem to understand quite clearly how atolls result when coral reefs around volcanic islands continue to grow as the volcanic islands themselves diminish. That's all for today. I'll see you next class.

11. WHAT IS AN ATOLL MADE OF?
12. WHICH OF THESE IS AN ATOLL?
13. WHERE DO ATOLLS TEND TO GROW?
14. IN THE DISCUSSION, THE PROCESS OF THE FORMATION OF ATOLLS IS DISCUSSED. SUMMARIZE THE PROCESS BY PUTTING THE STEPS IN ORDER.
15. WHERE IS THE LAGOON?

ACADEMIC LECTURES (Computer)

EXERCISE 32, page 143
TOEFL EXERCISE 32, page 144

Questions 1–2

(narrator)	Listen to a lecture in a geography class. The professor is talking about lakes.
(professor)	Today, we're going to look at three of the world's largest lakes, the Caspian Sea, Lake Superior, and Lake Baikal. Each of these lakes was formed in a different way, and these three lakes clearly demonstrate the three major ways that a lake can form.

The first lake I'm going to discuss is the Caspian Sea, which is the largest inland body of water in the world. The Caspian Sea is a saltwater lake between Europe and Asia. It's believed that this lake was originally connected to the world's oceans, which would account for its saltwater content. As the earth's plates moved, this arm of the ocean was cut off.

The next lake I'm going to discuss is Lake Superior, which is one of the Great Lakes in North America and is the largest freshwater lake in the world. Lake Superior, along with the other Great Lakes, was formed by glaciers. Glaciers covered the northern part of North America until 10,000 years ago and were responsible for carving out the Great Lakes, including Lake Superior.

The third lake I'm going to discuss is Lake Baikal, which is in Russia. Lake Baikal formed when the earth's crust broke apart at a fault. Because Lake Baikal formed over a split in the earth's crust, it is a very deep lake, the deepest lake in the world. Lake Baikal is so deep that, even though its surface area is much smaller than the surface area of Lake Superior, it could hold the water of all the Great Lakes combined.

1. HOW ARE EACH OF THESE LAKES DESCRIBED IN THE LECTURE?
2. HOW WAS EACH OF THESE LAKES FORMED?

Questions 3–5

(narrator)	Listen to a lecture in an archeology class. The professor is talking about the formation of fossils.
(professor)	Fossils are generally considered to be the remains of plants and animals that have turned to stone. There are a number of processes by which a living organism can be converted to a fossil, but each of the known processes generally have a number of characteristics in common.

After an animal dies, its soft tissues break down. After the soft tissues have decomposed, only the hard parts of the body, such as the bones and teeth, remain.

Over a long period of time, the hard tissue becomes buried under layers of sediment. As more layers of sediment cover the hard tissue, it becomes buried more and more deeply.

When the bones are buried deep in the earth, they come into contact with ground water, and a change begins to occur. Minerals from the ground water seep into the bones and, over long periods of time, the minerals eventually replace the bones. This is the actual step when fossilization occurs, when minerals from the ground water have replaced the actual hard tissue from the original body.

The buried fossilized remains, which are buried deep within the earth, may then make their way back to the surface. As the earth moves, the remains are pushed around. If they get closer to the surface, they may either actually reach the surface, where they can been seen, or get near enough to the surface, where they can be dug out.

3. IN THE LECTURE, THE PROFESSOR DESCRIBES HOW THE PROCESS OF FOSSILIZATION GETS STARTED. SUMMARIZE THE PROCESS BY PUTTING THE STEPS IN ORDER.
4. IN THE LECTURE, THE PROFESSOR EXPLAINS WHAT HAPPENS TO THE BURIED BONES. SUMMARIZE THE PROCESS BY PUTTING THE STEPS IN ORDER.
5. IN THE LECTURE, THE PROFESSOR EXPLAINS WHAT HAPPENS AFTER THE HARD TISSUE HAS FOSSILIZED UNDERGROUND. SUMMARIZE THE PROCESS BY PUTTING THE STEPS IN ORDER.

Questions 6–8

(narrator) Listen to a lecture in a nutrition class. The professor is talking about olive oil.

(professor) Today, I'll be talking about various types of olive oil and the processes by which they are produced. Olive oil can be produced by a cold process or by a heated process; the highest quality oils are produced by the cold-press process.

Let me explain the cold-press process. Olive oil can be made without heat by pressing very ripe olives. Because no heat is used in this process, the color and taste of the olive oil is not affected. What results from this first pressing of the olives is called virgin olive oil. You may also have heard of extra virgin olive oil. Like virgin olive oil, extra virgin olive oil is from the first cold pressing. Extra virgin olive oil is made from special olives with a low acid content. Thus, extra virgin olive oil has a lower acid level than virgin oil, but they both come from the first cold pressing of the olives.

After the olives have been pressed once, they are pressed again, numerous times. Olive oil that comes from a later pressing is called cold-pressed olive oil; it is not called virgin olive oil

because it comes from a later pressing.

Now, we'll talk about pure olive oil. Some olive oil is called pure olive oil rather than virgin oil or cold-pressed olive oil. If an olive oil is called pure olive oil, this means that it contains only olive oil, but it was not obtained through a cold-press process. A product called pure olive oil has often been obtained from a heat process, which has an effect on the color and taste of the oil.

The final type of olive oil I'd like to mention briefly is light olive oil. When the label of a bottle of olive oil says that it is light olive oil, this probably means that the oil in the bottle is not pure olive oil. Some other type of oil has been added to the olive oil to lighten the taste.

6. IN THE LECTURE, THE PROFESSOR DESCRIBES THE COLD-PRESS PROCESS. SUMMARIZE THE PROCESS BY PUTTING THE STEPS IN ORDER.
7. WHAT ARE THE DIFFERENT GRADES OF OLIVE OIL?
8. WHAT ARE THE DIFFERENT TYPES OF OIL PRODUCED BY THE COLD-PRESS PROCESS?

EXERCISE 33, page 149
TOEFL EXERCISE 33, page 150

Questions 1–8

(narrator) Listen to a lecture in a botany class. The professor is talking about conifers.

(professor) Today, I'll be talking about conifers, which are the type of trees, such as pines, that have cones instead of colorful flowers. About a third of the world's trees are conifers, and the vast majority of conifers are found in the great conifer forests of North America and Siberia.

Both the oldest and the biggest trees in the world belong to the conifer family. The oldest known living tree is a four-thousand-year-old bristlecone pine, which is located in California. The giant redwoods, which are also found in California, are the largest trees; they can be several hundred feet tall and weigh as much as 2,000 tons. An interesting note about the giant redwoods is that, even though the trees are so large, they have relatively small cones.

What is true of most, but not all, conifers is that they are evergreens with needle-like leaves. The needle-like shape to tree leaves evolved as a reaction to drought. When compared with a flat leaf, a needle presents a much smaller surface area, which decreases the amount of water lost through the leaves. Because most conifers are evergreens, they lose and replace their needles throughout the year, rather than shedding all their leaves in one season, as deciduous trees do.

1. WHAT IS TRUE ABOUT ALL CONIFERS?
2. WHAT PERCENT OF THE WORLD'S TREES ARE CONIFERS?
3. IT IS IMPLIED IN THE LECTURE THAT MOST CONIFERS ARE FOUND IN WHICH HEMISPHERE?
4. WHAT IS TRUE ABOUT THE BIGGEST AND OLDEST TREES?
5. WHICH OF THE FOLLOWING IS MOST LIKELY A GIANT REDWOOD?
6. WHAT CAN BE INFERRED FROM THE LECTURE?
7. WHY DID NEEDLE-SHAPED LEAVES EVOLVE?
8. WHAT CAN BE DETERMINED FROM THE LECTURE ABOUT DIFFERENT TYPES OF TREES?

Questions 9–14

(narrator)   Listen to a lecture in an education class. The professor is talking about early teachers.

(professor)   All of you are enrolled in this introductory education course because you want to become teachers. I'd like to introduce this course with a little information about the life of a teacher a century ago. I hope you'll appreciate how much the life of a teacher has changed over the past century.

Early in the twentieth century, the life of a teacher was quite different from what it is now. There were very strict rules that governed every aspect of the teacher's life. The rules were not just about how a teacher could conduct herself in the classroom and on the school grounds. There were also numerous rules that governed just about everything a teacher did.

Here are some of the rules. Teachers had to follow strict rules about their appearance; they were sometimes told not to wear colorful clothing, not to dye their hair or wear it loose, and not to wear their skirts above the ankle. Teachers' whereabouts during after-school hours were also strictly regulated; there were rules forbidding teachers to go to bars and to ice cream parlors, there were rules requiring teachers to be at home after 8:00 in the evening, and there were rules forbidding them to leave town without permission. Just about any action a teacher wanted to take could be regulated. Teachers could be forbidden to smoke or to drink; they were also sometimes forbidden to spend time with men or to marry if they wanted to remain teachers.

9. WHO IS LISTENING TO THIS LECTURE?
10. THE RULES DISCUSSED IN THIS LECTURE RELATE TO WHAT PERIOD OF TIME?
11. IT IS IMPLIED IN THE LECTURE THAT THE TEACHERS DISCUSSED IN THE LECTURE HAD WHAT KIND OF LIFESTYLE?
12. WHAT RULES ABOUT CLOTHING ARE DISCUSSED IN THE LECTURE?
13. WHERE WOULD A TEACHER FROM THE ERA DISCUSSED IN THE LECTURE MOST LIKELY BE AT 9:00 IN THE EVENING?
14. WHERE WERE THE TEACHERS IN THE LECTURE FORBIDDEN TO GO?

Questions 15–22

(narrator)   Listen to a lecture in an astronomy class. The professor is talking about Venus.

(professor)   Today, we'll be discussing the planet Venus, which is the second planet in our solar system and is almost the same size as our Earth, which is the fifth largest planet in the solar system.

The planet Venus is easily visible in the sky from Earth, although not always as a complete globe. It goes through phases, just like the Moon. Sometimes it's fully visible, like a full moon, sometimes it's half visible, and sometimes it is only a small crescent. It's actually at its brightest when it's a crescent.

Venus is a very hot planet. The temperature there can reach almost to 500 degrees centigrade, or 900 degrees Fahrenheit. It's so hot on Venus for two primary reasons: first, it's hot because of its closeness to the Sun, and second, it's hot because of its atmosphere. Its atmosphere is almost entirely carbon dioxide, which holds in the heat from the Sun extremely well.

Venus is also well-known for the clouds that cover it. As you know, Venus is visible to us on Earth, but it's not actually the planet that we see; it's the clouds. The surface of Venus can't be seen, even with a telescope, because of the clouds that surround the planet. The clouds on Venus are very different from the clouds on Earth. Earth's clouds are made of water vapor, but on Venus there is no water. The clouds on Venus are actually made of sulfuric acid. These clouds help to contribute to the brightness of Venus in our sky. When Venus appears to shine so brightly, it's because the light of the sun is reflecting off of Venus's clouds of sulfuric acid.

15. IT CAN BE INFERRED FROM THE LECTURE THAT VENUS IS HOW LARGE IN RELATION TO THE OTHER PLANETS IN OUR SOLAR SYSTEM?
16. HOW DOES VENUS COMPARE WITH THE MOON?
17. WHAT CAN BE INFERRED ABOUT VENUS WHEN IT IS IN A FULL PHASE?
18. WHAT ARE THE HIGHEST TEMPERATURES ON VENUS?
19. WHY IS IT HOT ON VENUS?
20. WHAT IS IMPLIED IN THE LECTURE ABOUT THE CLOUDS THAT SURROUND VENUS?
21. WHICH OF THE FOLLOWING ARE TRUE, ACCORDING TO THE LECTURE?
22. WHY IS VENUS SO BRIGHT?

EXERCISE 34, 155
TOEFL EXERCISE 34, page 156

Questions 1–3

(narrator)   Listen to a lecture in a course on Native American studies. The lecture is on Iroquois houses.

(professor)   Iroquois houses were very sophisticated buildings known as long houses. These houses were long, single-story houses with U-shaped roofs. They were windowless, but they did have some vents in the roof.

There was a doorway at the end of a longhouse, and above the doorway was a carving of an animal. This carved animal just above the doorway indicated the clan, or family, that the group living inside belonged to. The insignia above the doorway might be a turtle if the inhabitants were part of the clan of the turtle, or it might be a bear if the inhabitants were a part of the clan of the bear.

An Iroquois village consisted of a number of these longhouses. Around an Iroquois village, there was usually a stockade, which is a defensive wall or barrier made of wooden posts. The stockade around an Iroquois village was typically hexagonal in shape, which means that it was six-sided. It had vertical wood posts around the outside of the stockade, and these posts had sharpened ends pointing upward for further protection.

1. HOW DOES THE PROFESSOR DESCRIBE AN IROQUOIS HOUSE?
2. WHAT PART OF THE HOUSE INDICATES WHAT CLAN THE INHABITANTS BELONG TO?

3. HOW DOES THE PROFESSOR DESCRIBE THE STOCKADE SURROUNDING AN IROQUOIS VILLAGE?

Questions 4–6

(narrator)   Listen to a lecture in a biology class. The lecture is on tropism in plants.

(professor)   Today, I'll be talking about the concept of tropism as it relates to plants. Tropism, for those of you who don't know, refers to a bending of a plant or a part of a plant, in response to an outside stimulus.

There are three important kinds of tropism. They are phototropism, geotropism, and hydrotropism. In each of these kinds of tropism, a plant, or a part of the plant, bends in response to a different kind of outside stimulus.

First, we'll discuss phototropism. The outside stimulus in phototropism is light. When a plant is affected by phototropism, it grows in the direction of a light source such as the Sun.

The second kind of tropism is geotropism. In geotropism, the outside stimulus is gravity. In a plant affected by geotropism, the affected part of the plant grows directly downward because of the pull of gravity. When a plant is affected by geotropism, it's often the root structure that's affected.

The final kind of tropism that I'll discuss today is hydrotropism. When hydrotropism affects a plant, this means that the plant is drawn toward water. A plant under the effect of hydrotropism will grow in the direction of its water source.

4. WHICH OF THESE PLANTS IS EXHIBITING PHOTOTROPISM?
5. WHICH OF THESE ROOT SYSTEMS IS EXHIBITING GEOTROPISM?
6. WHAT IS THE STIMULUS FOR HYDROTROPISM?

Questions 7–10

(narrator)   Listen to a lecture in an archeology class. The lecture is on some archeological finds at Little Salt Spring.

(professor)   Little Salt Spring in Florida has provided some very important archeological finds. Little Salt Spring was once believed to be just a shallow lake, but then a deep sinkhole with almost vertical sides was discovered beneath the lake. Twelve thousand years ago, the water level was much lower, down to the level of the sinkhole, and the sinkhole provided drinking water for humans and animals. In the sinkhole, archeologists have discovered a number of items that give clues to the lifestyle of the inhabitants around the sinkhole 12,000 years ago.

I'd like to talk about two of the important archeological discoveries from the sinkhole. One was a weapon, and the other was an animal trap. These discoveries provide insight into the type of hunter society that lived around the sinkhole.

The weapon that was found was a boomerang, which is a very ancient type of weapon. The boomerang was found deep in the sinkhole. It was on a ledge in the vertical side of the sinkhole. The boomerang that was found in Little Salt Spring is the world's oldest known boomerang.

The second discovery was an animal trap that consisted of wooden stakes dug into the earth at the edge of the sinkhole. This animal trap was at the top of the sinkhole, where the sinkhole meets the lake. In ancient times, when the water level was down at the level of the sinkhole, animals would come to the sinkhole to drink. The inhabitants of the area had built a trap at the top of the sinkhole to trap animals that came there to drink.

7. WHAT TYPE OF WEAPON WAS FOUND AT THE SINKHOLE?
8. WHERE WAS THE WEAPON FOUND?
9. WHERE WAS THE WATER LEVEL 12,000 YEARS AGO?
10. WHERE WAS THE TRAP FOUND?

TOEFL REVIEW EXERCISE (Skills 32–34), page 159

Questions 1–5

(narrator)   Listen to a lecture in an American history class. The lecture is on the St. Louis Arch.

(professor)   Today, we'll be looking at a structure that is popularly called the St. Louis Arch. We'll be looking at how it was constructed and, more importantly, why it was constructed and what it commemorates.

In this photo you can see the 630-foot high stainless steel arch. It's remarkable for its engineering; it has no inner form; instead it is dependent on its two hollow legs for support. There are trams inside the legs to take visitors to an observatory at the top of the arch.

Most people call it the St. Louis Arch because it is in St. Louis, but its real name is the Jefferson National Expan-

sion Memorial. It's a memorial because it was built in memory of the expansion of the nation beyond St. Louis. It's named after Jefferson because it was under the presidency of Thomas Jefferson that the greatest expansion of the country took place.

In 1804, several years after the start of Jefferson's presidency, Lewis and Clark set out from St. Louis to explore new territories to the west. Their expedition was a 4,000-mile trip from St. Louis to the Pacific Northwest and back that lasted a little more than two years. In the years following the expedition of Lewis and Clark, thousands of pioneers set off from St. Louis and headed west.

In was to honor this period of expansion that the arch was constructed. The arch itself was designed to represent a gateway, or a doorway, to the west. At the base of the arch there's a subterranean museum. This museum is named the Museum of Westward Expansion because it honors all the pioneers who headed west from St. Louis. In the middle of the museum is a statue of the president who was responsible for much of this expansion, Thomas Jefferson.

1. WHAT DOES THE PROFESSOR SAY ABOUT THE ARCH?
2. WHERE ARE EACH OF THESE FEATURES OF THE ARCH LOCATED?
3. WHY IS THE ARCH NAMED AFTER JEFFERSON?
4. IT IS IMPLIED IN THE LECTURE THAT IT IS APPROXIMATELY WHAT DISTANCE BETWEEN ST. LOUIS AND THE PACIFIC NORTHWEST?
5. THE PROFESSOR EXPLAINS A HISTORICAL SERIES OF EVENTS. PUT THE EVENTS IN ORDER.

Questions 6–10

(narrator)   Listen to a lecture in a geology class. The lecture is on the structure of the earth.

(professor)   Today, I'm going to give you a brief overview of the structure of the earth. The earth is made up of a number of layers. From the outside to the inside, the main layers are the crust, the mantle, and the core.

Let's look at a diagram of the earth's main layers. The crust is the thin outer layer, then there is the mantle, and finally there's the core, which is divided into the outer core and the inner core.

First, let's talk about the crust. The crust is a thin, hard layer of rock. As you can see in the diagram, the crust is quite thin. The crust is about 20 miles thick under land masses. Under the oceans, the crust is even thinner. The crust is only about 4 miles thick under the oceans.

Now, let's talk about the mantle. The mantle makes up the greatest part of the earth. The mantle is about 1,800 miles deep. It's made of stony materials that were created from silicate minerals. The mantle is a huge mass of stony material.

Now, we'll look at the core, which actually has two distinct parts, the outer core and the inner core. Neither the outer core nor the inner core is as wide as the mantle; the outer core is less than 1,400 miles wide, and the inner core has a radius of 800 miles. The outer core is a layer of liquid metal; it definitely has liquid nickel and iron, and it may have other substances. The outer core is the only liquid layer. The inner core is composed of nickel and iron, as the outer core is, but the inner core is not a liquid layer like the outer core. It is extremely hot at the inner core, but there's also an extreme amount of pressure on the minerals in the inner core that keeps them firm rather than liquid.

That is all for our overview of the various layers that make up the earth. We'll be having a quiz on the material next class, so be prepared.

6. HOW THICK IS THE CRUST?
7. WHAT ARE EACH OF THE LAYERS COMPOSED OF?
8. WHICH LAYER IS 1,800 MILES WIDE?
9. WHAT MINERALS ARE IN THE CORE?
10. APPROXIMATELY HOW FAR IS IT FROM THE SURFACE OF THE EARTH TO ITS CENTER?

Questions 11–16

(narrator)   Listen to a lecture in a linguistics class. The professor is talking about the history of the letter *c*.

(professor) The letter *c* in today's English has two very different pronunciations. It can be pronounced like a *k*, as in the words *car, can,* or *coal.* It can also be pronounced like an *s*, as in the words *cent, circle,* or *cease.* Let's look at the history and development of the letter *c* to understand how these two very different pronunciations for one letter came to be.

Precursors of the letter *c* existed as the third letter of a number of early alphabets. Look at the letters from these early alphabets, from early Semitic, from Phoenician, and from early Greek. These letters were the predecessors of the letter *c.* They were each the third letter in their respective alphabets, and they were all formed with a shorter and a longer line meeting at a sharp angle. In each of these languages, the letter was pronounced with a hard *g* sound, as in *go* or *get.* This letter did not have an *s* or *k* sound.

As languages developed, this early *c* was used for both the *g* sound as in *go* and *get* and the *k* sound as in *kite* or *kid.* The angular letter seen here from early Latin had two sounds, a *k* sound and a *g* sound. By the classical Latin period, these two sounds were differentiated. The early Latin angular letter was rounded to create the letter *c* of today; this letter was pronounced with a *k* sound. A new letter was created by adding a line to the *c.* This new letter had a *g* sound. Thus, in classical Latin, the letter *c* was pronounced only with a *k* sound.

The final change was the addition of the *s* sound to the letter *c.* This happened because of the French influence on English. There was a major influence of French on the English language with the victory of the Normans over the Saxons in Britain in 1066. Because of this French influence, the letter *c* took on the *s* sound in addition to the *k* sound that it already had.

Let's look at this chart of the pronunciation of the letter *c.* At this point in the English language, the letter *c* has a *k* sound when it precedes the vowels *a, o, u,* or a consonant such as *l.* The letter *c* generally has an *s* sound in front of the vowels *e, i,* and *y.*

To summarize, there were four stages in the development of the pronunciation of the third letter of the alphabet. In the beginning, the third letter of the alphabet was pronounced with a *g* sound. Then, in early Latin, the third letter had two sounds, *g* and *k.* In later Latin, a new letter was created for the *g* sound, and the letter *c* had only a *k* sound. Finally, because of the French influence on English, the letter *c* also took on an *s* sound.

11. WHICH OF THE FOLLOWING LETTERS WAS NOT A PREDECESSOR OF THE LETTER *C*?
12. HOW WAS THE THIRD LETTER OF THE ALPHABET PRONOUNCED IN PHOENICIAN AND EARLY GREEK?

13. IN WHICH LANGUAGE WAS THE LETTER *G* CREATED?

14. THE LETTER *C* TOOK ON AN *S* SOUND BECAUSE OF AN INFLUENCE FROM WHICH LANGUAGE?

15. WHICH OF THE FOLLOWING ENGLISH WORDS BEGIN WITH AN *S* SOUND?

16. THE PROFESSOR DISCUSSES STAGES IN THE HISTORY OF THE THIRD LETTER OF THE ALPHABET. PUT THE FOLLOWING HISTORICAL STAGES IN ORDER.

LISTENING POST-TEST (Paper)

Part A, page 165

1. *(woman)* Are the exams corrected yet?
   (man) No, but they'll be corrected by noon.
   (narrator) WHAT DOES THE MAN MEAN?

2. *(woman)* Has Martha's visa arrived yet?
   (man) I think it arrived last month.
   (narrator) WHAT DOES THE MAN MEAN?

3. *(man)* What did the professor do in the first class? I missed it because I was late.
   (woman) She outlined the course requirements.
   (narrator) WHAT DOES THE WOMAN MEAN?

4. *(woman)* How did Chuck look when you visited him in the hospital?
   (man) He's looked better.
   (narrator) WHAT DOES THE MAN MEAN?

5. *(man)* How much was tuition increased for next month?
   (woman) More than I can afford.
   (narrator) WHAT DOES THE WOMAN MEAN?

6. *(woman)* How were the grades on the history exam.
   (man) No one got above a C.
   (narrator) WHAT DOES THE MAN MEAN?

7. *(woman)* You know, this is the second time this week that you've been late to class!
   (man) It was impossible to find a place to park before the ten o'clock class!
   (narrator) WHAT DOES THE MAN MEAN?

8. *(man)* Can I help you find something?
   (woman) Yes, thank you. I need to get a new rug.
   (narrator) WHAT DOES THE WOMAN MEAN?

9. *(woman)* I'd like to open an account.
   (man) Would you like a savings account or an interest-bearing checking account?
   (narrator) WHERE DOES THIS CONVERSATION PROBABLY TAKE PLACE?

10. *(woman)* Why does Jane spend so much time in San Francisco?
    (man) She has a cousin there, so she likes to visit, especially during the holidays.
    (narrator) WHAT DOES THE MAN MEAN?

11. *(woman)* Are you really hungry?
    (man) I feel like I haven't eaten in weeks.
    (narrator) WHAT DOES THE MAN MEAN?

12. *(man)* The traffic outside is really loud!
    (woman) I'll say!
    (narrator) WHAT DOES THE WOMAN MEAN?

13. *(man)* Have you seen the headlines yet today?
    (woman) I haven't had a chance to read a word.
    (narrator) WHAT ARE THEY PROBABLY DISCUSSING?

14. *(man)* I'm not ready yet, and it's going to take me a while longer.
    (woman) You'd better hurry. Take five minutes too long, and you'll miss the bus.
    (narrator) WHAT DOES THE WOMAN MEAN?

15. *(woman)* I think it's impossible for me to pass this class.
    (man) You should never say "impossible."
    (narrator) WHAT DOES THE MAN MEAN?

16. *(man)* Why were you thanking Tom?
    (woman) He lent me enough money to pay the rent.
    (narrator) WHAT DOES THE WOMAN MEAN?

17. *(woman)* Are you enjoying the dessert?
    (man) Never have I tasted such delicious cake!
    (narrator) WHAT DOES THE MAN SAY ABOUT THE CAKE?

18. *(man)* Why are you so late getting here?
    (woman) Oh, I ran into my cousin Carl, and we stayed and talked for a while.
    (narrator) WHAT DOES THE WOMAN MEAN?

19. *(woman)* Do you know where Debbie is?
    (man) Her purse is still here, so she must still be in the apartment.
    (narrator) WHAT DOES THE MAN SAY ABOUT DEBBIE?

20. *(man)* Do you know when rent is due?
    (woman) The landlord collects it on the first of the month, without fail.
    (narrator) WHAT DOES THE WOMAN MEAN?

21. *(woman)* My car is making some funny noises.
    (man) Why not take it to a mechanic?
    (narrator) WHAT DOES THE MAN SUGGEST TO THE WOMAN?

22. *(man)* Martha's holding down two jobs at the same time.
    (woman) She'd better take it easy.
    (narrator) WHAT DOES THE WOMAN MEAN?

23. *(woman)* Did you get to the airport in plenty of time?
    (man) There was scarcely enough time to get there.
    (narrator) WHAT DOES THE MAN IMPLY?

24. *(woman)* You should put some money in the parking meter.
    (man) Parking fees aren't necessary on the weekend, are they?
    (narrator) WHAT DOES THE MAN MEAN?

25. (man) How is your boss feeling about his retirement?

(woman) Oh, he isn't too unhappy to be retiring.

(narrator) WHAT DOES THE WOMAN IMPLY ABOUT HER BOSS?

26. (woman) Oh, I see you have a new car.

(man) I wish I had been able to buy the car I really wanted.

(narrator) WHAT DOES THE MAN MEAN?

27. (woman) Did you hear the president's announcement this morning?

(man) Yes, the president appointed Mr. Drew head of the newly formed commission.

(narrator) WHAT DOES THE MAN MEAN?

28. (man) Were you upset by what Richard said to you?

(woman) I couldn't have been more infuriated!

(narrator) WHAT DOES THE WOMAN MEAN?

29. (man) Let me just get these last plates put away. Then, I'll be ready to go.

(woman) So you did do the dishes.

(narrator) WHAT HAD THE WOMAN ASSUMED?

30. (woman) Why did you get that kind of fruit?

(man) I wouldn't have bought these cherries had I known that grapes were so cheap.

(narrator) WHAT DOES THE MAN MEAN?

Part B, page 168

Questions 31–34

(narrator) Listen to a conversation between two friends who are making plans.

(woman) Do you have any plans this weekend?

(man) There's so much to choose from on campus that I'm not sure what I'm going to do.

(woman) The football game's on Saturday night, and I'm going with a group of friends. Do you want to go with us?

(man) Of course I'd like to go to the football game: it's the biggest game of the season. And it sounds like fun to go with a large group of people.

(woman) Good. We'll be meeting at the cafeteria for dinner at six o'clock on Saturday night, and then we'll go on to the game together.

(man) That takes care of my plans for Saturday night. But now I need to make a decision about Sunday afternoon. The music department is sponsoring a concert then, and I'd really like to hear that concert. But there's also a play being presented by the drama department that I really wanted to see. It's too bad those two events are at the same time.

(woman) You know, if you go to the game on Saturday night and a concert or play

on Sunday, that doesn't leave much time for studying.

(man) Oh, well. Maybe I can do that the weekend after this one.

31. WHAT IS THE WOMAN PLANNING TO DO SATURDAY?

32. WHY DOES THE MAN WANT TO GO TO THE FOOTBALL GAME?

33. WHAT IS AT THE SAME TIME AS THE MUSIC DEPARTMENT'S CONCERT?

34. WHEN DOES THE MAN PLAN TO STUDY?

Questions 35–38

(narrator) Listen to a conversation between a man and a woman.

(woman) Have you ever thought about all the tons of garbage that's out in space circling the Earth?

(man) Tons of garbage circling the Earth? What do you mean?

(woman) I saw a television program about it last night, and according to the program, there's about 3,000 tons of metal out there in space, traveling at speeds around 17,000 miles per hour.

(man) Where did all this garbage come from?

(woman) Well, it comes from all those space missions that have gone up since 1957. Every time a rocket ship goes up into space, it leaves a lot behind, and this stuff goes into orbit around the Earth: booster rockets, solar panels, remnants of satellites, and even nuclear reactors.

(man) Isn't it dangerous to have all this stuff out there?

(woman) Some space scientists are worried about possible collisions between this orbiting junk and spaceships, particularly manned spacecrafts; however, so far there haven't been any such accidents.

(man) Well, I hope that they're going to do something about this, both for the sake of safety and for the sake of the environment.

(woman) Me, too. I know that right now the problem is being studied by numerous scientists; hopefully, they'll be able to find solutions before the problem gets too much worse.

35. WHAT ARE THE MAN AND WOMAN DISCUSSING?

36. WHERE DID THE WOMAN LEARN ABOUT THIS PROBLEM?

37. APPROXIMATELY HOW MUCH METAL IS IN ORBIT IN SPACE?

38. WHAT DOES THE WOMAN HOPE WILL HAPPEN?

Part C, page 169

Questions 39–42

(narrator)   Listen to a sociology professor talk to her class.

(woman)   Before I start today's sociology lecture, I'd like to talk with you about the papers that you should be working on. As you know, the topic for the paper is the relationship between gun control and violence. The paper itself is due in two weeks, but I would like to see your outlines by Friday of this week so that I can be sure that you are on the right track with the assignment.

You need to do some research for this paper, so you should be spending some time in the library. I would like you to have at least three books and at least three recent journal articles as sources.

The paper should be five pages long; in addition to the five pages of composition, you should have a title page and a one-page reference list of the sources that you used in preparing the paper.

39. WHEN DOES THIS TALK PROBABLY TAKE PLACE?
40. WHEN IS THE PAPER DUE?
41. WHAT TYPES OF REFERENCES SHOULD BE USED IN WRITING THE PAPER?
42. HOW MANY TOTAL PAGES SHOULD BE IN THE PAPER, INCLUDING THE TITLE PAGE AND THE REFERENCE LIST?

Questions 43–46

(narrator)   Listen to a talk about Hawaii.

(man)   For those of you taking part in the trip to Hawaii next week, I'd like to give you a little information about the weather that you can expect there.

You can expect the average daily temperature there to be about 80 degrees Fahrenheit or 26 degrees Celsius. This is the average daily temperature in the springtime, when we will be there; it is interesting to note that it only gets a few degrees warmer in the summer and a few degrees cooler in the winter.

One important factor that keeps the temperature so constant and moderate in Hawaii is the trade winds. These are winds that blow in on the northeast, or windward, side of the islands on an almost daily basis; the trade winds blow through the islands an average of slightly more than 300 days per year, and they are the strongest during the heat of the afternoon and turn into a cooling breeze in the evening. The trade winds also keep the humidity down, which makes the weather even more pleasant.

I hope this information will help you to understand the weather conditions that you're going to encounter next week on your trip; it should also help you decide what types of clothes you should be packing for your trip.

43. IN WHAT SEASON OF THE YEAR WILL THE TRIP TAKE PLACE?
44. WHAT IS THE WEATHER LIKE IN HAWAII?
45. WHAT IS TRUE ABOUT THE TRADE WINDS?
46. WHAT WILL THE PEOPLE LISTENING TO THE TALK PROBABLY BE DOING SOON?

Questions 47–50

(narrator)   Listen to an instructor talk to her class about Walt Whitman.

(woman)   The topic of today's lecture is Walt Whitman, an American poet and author of the renowned collection of poems *Leaves of Grass*. This volume of poems is a celebration of America, full of pride in the United States and reverence for the goals of American democracy.

Whitman began writing *Leaves of Grass* in the middle of the nineteenth century, and the first edition appeared in 1855 with only twelve poems. Several other editions of *Leaves of Grass* appeared throughout Whitman's lifetime with additional poems; *Leaves of Grass* grew and matured right along with Whitman.

The longest and best-known poem in *Leaves of Grass* is "Song of Myself," which appeared in the first edition. The poem "When Lilacs Last in the Dooryard Bloomed" was added to a later edition. This poem was written at the time of Abraham Lincoln's death in 1865 and contained Whitman's reflections on that event. Lincoln's death occurred in April, in the spring, in a season of new life. This poem reflects that spring can be at the same time a period of death and a period of rebirth.

47. THIS LECTURE WOULD PROBABLY BE A PART OF WHICH COURSE?
48. WHAT IS THE MOST COMMON THEME IN *LEAVES OF GRASS*?
49. WHAT BEST DESCRIBES *LEAVES OF GRASS*?
50. WHICH IS THE LONGEST AND BEST-KNOWN POEM BY WHITMAN?

LISTENING POST-TEST (Computer)

Part A, page 172

1. (man) Are you ready to work on the history paper?
   (woman) I will be, in a couple of minutes. I have to finish the math problems before I start on history.
   (narrator) WHAT DOES THE MAN MEAN?

2. (man) Do you know what time it is?
   (woman) I just heard the clock strike noon.
   (narrator) WHAT DOES THE WOMAN MEAN?

3. (woman) Why did the class move to a different room?
   (man) We couldn't get into our regular classroom. Someone lost the key to it.
   (narrator) WHAT DOES THE MAN MEAN?

4. (man) Should we leave for class now?
   (woman) But it's not time for class yet.
   (narrator) WHAT DOES THE WOMAN MEAN?

5. (woman) I hope we don't have a quiz today. I'm not really very prepared on the material for today.
   (man) I don't think we will. This professor rarely, if ever, gives quizzes.
   (narrator) WHAT DOES THE MAN MEAN?

6. (man) Is the rent check due on the first of the month?
   (woman) It is, as far as I know.
   (narrator) WHAT DOES THE WOMAN MEAN?

7. (woman) Did your nieces and nephews like the gifts you got for them?
   (man) They couldn't have been more excited when they saw what I got.
   (narrator) WHAT DOES THE MAN SAY ABOUT HIS NIECES AND NEPHEWS?

8. (man) Have you been studying for long?
   (woman) For hours, and I'm all worn out.
   (narrator) WHAT DOES THE WOMAN MEAN?

9. (woman) Did you go to the party last night?
   (man) If I had known about it, I would have.
   (narrator) WHAT DOES THE MAN SAY ABOUT THE PARTY?

10. (man) What are you doing during break next week?
    (woman) I'll be staying at the beach with my family.
    (man) So you did decide to take the trip after all.
    (narrator) WHAT DID THE MAN BELIEVE ABOUT THE WOMAN?

Part B, page 175

Questions 11–12

(man) I have a problem, and I hope you can help me out.
(woman) What's your problem?
(man) I need to be absent from class on next Friday because I have a doctor's appointment, and I'll need to borrow someone's notes.
(woman) Well, you can certainly borrow mine, if you don't mind my messy handwriting.
(man) Thanks very much. Notes in messy handwriting are much better than no notes at all.

11. WHAT PROBLEM DOES THE MAN HAVE?
12. WHAT PROBLEM DOES THE WOMAN HAVE?

Questions 13–15

(woman) Do you enjoy playing chess?
(man) Yes, I really do.
(woman) Well, you might think about joining the chess club. I belong to it, and it's a lot of fun.
(man) What does the chess club do?
(woman) The members get together once a week for friendly competitions. Then each semester, the three best players from the club compete in a tournament with players from other schools.
(man) The meetings once a week sound like a lot of fun, but I don't think I'm ready to take part in a tournament against other schools.
(woman) Well, why don't you come with me this Wednesday and try out one of the weekly meetings? You can come to the meetings for a while and then see if you're ready to compete in a tournament in a few months.

13. HOW OFTEN DOES THE CHESS CLUB MEET?
14. HOW OFTEN ARE TOURNAMENTS HELD?
15. WHO COMPETES IN THE TOURNAMENTS?

Questions 16–20

(narrator) Listen to a lecture in a botany class. The professor is talking about leaf arrangements.

(professor) Today we're going to talk about phyllotaxy. Phyllotaxy is a scientific term that refers to the arrangement of leaves on the stem of a plant. On most plants, leaves are arranged in a definite pattern. It is very unusual for a plant to have randomly placed leaves. One of the main reasons leaves on a plant stem are arranged in an orderly way is to ensure that each leaf is exposed to the maximum amount of light with a minimum amount of interference from other leaves.

The first type of leaf arrangement is the alternate arrangement. You can see this type of leaf arrangement in the diagram. In this type of leaf arrangement, there is only one leaf at each node, which is the spot where the leaf is attached to the stem.

The next type of leaf arrangement is the opposite arrangement, which you can see in the diagram. In this type of leaf arrangement, there are two leaves at each node, and these two leaves are opposite each other on the stem. This type of leaf arrangement is not as common as the alternate arrangement, with one leaf at each node.

The last type of leaf arrangement that we're going to look at is called the whorled leaf arrangement. This type of leaf arrangement is the least common of all. It is not as common as either the opposite or the alternate arrangement. In this type of arrangement, three or more leaves are attached to the stalk of the plant at the same node. In the diagram, you can see three leaves at the same node; it's also possible for there to be more than three leaves at the same node, and the leaf arrangement would still be considered a whorled arrangement.

Now that we have looked at these three different types of leaf arrangements, I have an assignment for you. Your assignment is to visit the university's botanical garden. Were you aware that this university has quite an extensive botanical garden? In the botanical garden, there are examples of many different kinds of plants, and each plant is labeled with the name of the plant as well as other information about the plant. For your assignment, you're to find three examples of each of these different types of leaf structures, write down the names of the plants that have these leaf structures, and turn in your lists on Friday. It will be quite easy for you to find examples of the alternate leaf structure because, as I said before, this is the most common type of leaf structure. It will be a bit more difficult to find examples of the opposite structure, but by far the most difficult leaf arrangement for you to find will be the whorled structure because this leaf arrangement is so rare. You'll have to spend some time finding examples of the whorled leaf arrangement in our botanical garden. See you on Friday with your lists.

16. THE PROFESSOR DISCUSSES FOUR TYPES OF LEAF ARRANGEMENTS. MATCH THE TYPE OF LEAF ARRANGEMENT TO ITS DESCRIPTION.
17. IDENTIFY THE NODE.
18. THE PROFESSOR DESCRIBES HOW COMMON THESE LEAF ARRANGEMENTS ARE. MATCH THE LEAF ARRANGEMENT TO ITS DESCRIPTION.

19. WHAT DOES THE PROFESSOR SAY ABOUT THE BOTANICAL GARDEN?
20. HOW MANY EXAMPLES DO THE STUDENTS HAVE TO FIND FOR THEIR ASSIGNMENT?

Questions 21–25

(narrator)	Listen to a discussion from a geography class. The discussion is about the Great Salt Lake.
(instructor)	Today we're going to talk about two lakes, the Great Salt Lake and Lake Bonneville. Most people are quite familiar with the Great Salt Lake, but not everyone is quite as familiar with Lake Bonneville.
	First of all, let's look at a map that shows both the Great Salt Lake and Lake Bonneville. Now, Gwen, what can you tell me about the Great Salt Lake and Lake Bonneville?
(Gwen)	Lake Bonneville was a lake during prehistoric times. The Great Salt Lake is the largest surviving remnant of the prehistoric Lake Bonneville.
(instructor)	Yes, and how old is Lake Bonneville?
(Gwen)	Lake Bonneville came into existence a million years ago.
(instructor)	And how big was it?
(Gwen)	It was an enormous lake that covered about 20,000 square miles.
(instructor)	Gwen has explained that the Great Salt Lake is a small remnant of Lake Bonneville and that Lake Bonneville was 20,000 square miles in size. Now, Nick, just how big is the Great Salt Lake?
(Nick)	The present Great Salt Lake is much smaller than Lake Bonneville was. The Great Salt Lake covers about 1,700 square miles. This seems like a rather large lake today, but it is much smaller than the lake that preceded it.
(instructor)	Exactly. The Great Salt Lake is much smaller than Lake Bonneville, less than 10% of the size of Lake Bonneville, in fact. And there is another big difference between the two lakes, besides the size. It has to do with the water. Can you tell me how the water in the Great Salt Lake differs from the water in Lake Bonneville? Pat?
(Pat)	A big difference between Lake Bonneville and the Great Salt Lake is that Lake Bonneville was a freshwater lake, while the Great Salt Lake (as you can tell from is name) is a saltwater lake.
(instructor)	Exactly. Now let's look at the reasons why this lake has become a saltwater lake and, in fact, has water much saltier than ocean water. And what is it that makes the Great Salt Lake so salty, Gwen?
(Gwen)	What makes the Great Salt Lake so salty is that it has no outlet. Three

rivers feed into it, the Bear River, the Weber River, and the Jordan River. These rivers carry a million tons of minerals and salts into the Great Salt Lake each year.

(instructor) And what about these three rivers, the Bear River, the Weber River, and the Jordan River? Nick?

(Nick) These rivers feed into the Great Salt Lake. They don't provide any outlet from the lake.

(instructor) And how does this make the lake so salty? Pat?

(Pat) There's no way for these minerals and salts to exit from the lake because the lake has no outlet. The water that flows into the lake from these three rivers evaporates and leaves the salts.

(instructor) And how much salt is there in the lake today?

(Pat) Over the lifetime of the lake, six billion tons of salts have built up. That is why the Great Salt Lake has a much higher salt content than the oceans.

(instructor) Excellent. You seem to understand the important points about the Great Salt Lake and Lake Bonneville. Now let's move on to another topic.

21. WHEN DID LAKE BONNEVILLE COME INTO EXISTENCE?
22. HOW DOES THE GREAT SALT LAKE COMPARE IN SIZE TO LAKE BONNEVILLE?
23. WHAT IS STATED IN THE LECTURE ABOUT THE WATER IN THE TWO LAKES?
24. IN WHICH DIRECTION DOES THE WATER IN THE RIVERS FLOW?
25. HOW MUCH SALT HAS BUILT UP IN THE GREAT SALT LAKE?

Questions 26–30

(narrator) Listen to a lecture in an American history class. The professor is talking about Hawaii.

(professor) Today we're going to talk about the last monarch to rule in the land that today makes up the United States. This last monarch was a queen; she was Queen Liliuokalani of Hawaii. To understand Queen Liliuokalani's situation, I'm going to give you some background about the history of Hawaii before I discuss Queen Liliuokalani. The two people I'd like to discuss to help you to understand Queen Liliuokalani's situation are Captain James Cook and King Kamehameha.

Captain James Cook arrived in the Hawaiian Islands in 1778 and gave the islands the name Sandwich Islands in honor of a British nobleman, the Earl of Sandwich. When Captain Cook arrived in the islands near the end of the eighteenth century, various islands in the chain were under the control of different native kings.

The next person we're going to look at is King Kamehameha. Kamehameha spent almost thirty years uniting the Hawaiian Islands under one ruler, and by 1810, a few decades after Captain Cook's arrival, all of the islands were united under one king, King Kamehameha. King Kamehameha was the first ruler to reign over all of the islands together. He ruled over all the islands until 1819. A number of other kings of the Hawaiian Islands followed Kamehameha during the nineteenth century.

Now we'll discuss Queen Liliuokalani, the last monarch of Hawaii. Liliuokalani became queen after her brother, King Kalakaua, died in 1891. Liliuokalani was the first and only female monarch to rule the Hawaiian Islands, and she was the final monarch of Hawaii. Liliuokalani became queen during a period when a large percentage of the population believed that it was better to have a democratic government than a monarchy. Liliuokalani refused to consider ending the monarchy and also refused to consider limiting the power of the monarchy and initiating a democratic government. In 1893, two years after she became queen, she developed a constitution granting complete power to the monarch. At that point, she was removed from the monarchy. Over the next few years, there were a number of plots to try to reinstitute the monarchy. By 1898, Liliuokalani had renounced her claim to the royal throne of Hawaii. She received a pension from the government and returned to her royal estates, where she lived out her life for the next 20 years with the title of queen but without the authority as the last monarch of the Hawaiian Islands.

I know that the Hawaiian names are a bit difficult to remember, but I hope you understand the important main points, that it was King Kamehameha who unified the Hawaiian Islands under one monarch and it was Queen Liliuokalani who was the final monarch of the Hawaiian Islands. That's all for today.

26. WHEN DID EACH PERSON LIVE?
27. WHAT DOES THE PROFESSOR SAY ABOUT JAMES COOK?
28. THE PROFESSOR EXPLAINS A SERIES OF EVENTS. PUT THE EVENTS IN ORDER.

29. WHAT DID LILIUOKALANI BELIEVE, ACCORDING TO THE PROFESSOR?
30. WHICH OF THE FOLLOWING DID NOT HAPPEN TO LILLUOKALANI?

LISTENING COMPLETE TEST (Paper)

Part A, page 515

1. (woman) Carla said that you were rather rude.
   (man) It's unfair of her to say that about me.
   (narrator) WHAT DOES THE MAN MEAN?

2. (man) I don't think this painting is very good.
   (woman) It's better than the first one, isn't it?
   (narrator) WHAT DOES THE WOMAN SAY ABOUT THE PAINTING?

3. (woman) Your graduation ceremony is this afternoon.
   (man) I can't believe it. I've graduated at last!
   (narrator) WHAT DOES THE MAN MEAN?

4. (woman) I got this dress for only five dollars!
   (man) Five dollars! How did you get it so cheap?
   (narrator) WHAT DOES THE MAN MEAN?

5. (man) I just got my third parking ticket this week.
   (woman) Why don't you try putting more money in the parking meter when you park your car?
   (narrator) WHAT DOES THE WOMAN SUGGEST THAT THE MAN DO?

6. (woman) Were you able to get hold of the book that you wanted?
   (man) I couldn't. At the bookstore, they told me that it wasn't available yet.
   (narrator) WHAT DOES THE MAN MEAN?

7. (woman) Professor Mitchell's lecture certainly went on and on for quite some time.
   (man) I thought he was never going to finish.
   (narrator) WHAT DOES THE MAN IMPLY ABOUT THE LECTURE?

8. (man) You don't have the notes from yesterday's physics class?
   (woman) No, I don't. Do you think I could borrow yours?
   (narrator) WHAT DOES THE WOMAN MEAN?

9. (man) You said that you wanted to go shopping this afternoon. What do you want to get?
   (woman) I think I'd like to get my dad a new wallet for his birthday.
   (narrator) WHAT DOES THE WOMAN MEAN?

10. (woman) You didn't go into the pool, even for a quick dip?
    (man) I put my big toe in and decided that the water was too cold for me.
    (narrator) WHAT DOES THE MAN MEAN?

11. (man) Do you know where your sweater is?
    (woman) I think I left it at my sister's house, but I'm not sure.
    (narrator) WHAT DOES THE WOMAN MEAN?

12. (man) I need for you to work on these new accounting reports.
    (woman) But I scarcely have time to finish the ones I already have.
    (narrator) WHAT DOES THE WOMAN IMPLY?

13. (woman) How much longer do you think you're going to stay on that exercise machine?
    (man) I give up!
    (narrator) WHAT DOES THE MAN MEAN?

14. (woman) Look at those waves coming in. They're as huge as I've ever seen them.
    (man) You can say that again!
    (narrator) WHAT DOES THE MAN MEAN?

15. (man) Are you ready for the political science exam today? I stayed up all night studying for it.
    (woman) Didn't you know that the professor put it off until next week?
    (narrator) WHAT DOES THE WOMAN MEAN?

16. (woman) I haven't turned in my schedule change form yet. Do you think that's a problem?
    (man) You haven't turned it in yet? It's absolutely essential that you turn the form in immediately.
    (narrator) WHAT DOES THE MAN MEAN?

17. (woman) I'd like to try on some rings, please.
    (man) Do you prefer rings in gold or silver?
    (narrator) WHERE DOES THIS CONVERSATION PROBABLY TAKE PLACE?

18. (man) Look at this. You made an awful lot of long distance calls last month.
    (woman) I called my family even more than usual. That's why the bill's so much higher than usual.
    (narrator) WHAT ARE THE MAN AND WOMAN PROBABLY DISCUSSING?

19. (man) What do you think of your new boss?
    (woman) I couldn't be more impressed with him.
    (narrator) WHAT DOES THE WOMAN MEAN?

20. (woman) Mike, do you know when the recital starts?
    (man) It starts at three o'clock, doesn't it?
    (narrator) WHAT DOES MIKE MEAN?

21. (woman) If your tooth is hurting you so much, perhaps you should see your dentist right away.
    (man) I don't really want to, but I guess I don't have much choice.
    (narrator) WHAT WILL THE MAN PROBABLY DO NEXT?

22. (man) I need to buy some stamps.

(woman)	Then you'd better get to the post office quickly, because it closes at five o'clock.
(narrator)	WHAT CAN BE INFERRED FROM THE CONVERSATION?

23.
(woman)	Do you know how I can find the journal article that we're supposed to read for class tomorrow?
(man)	The professor copied it and put it on reserve in the library.
(narrator)	WHAT DOES THE MAN MEAN?

24.
(woman)	I really think you should try to be a little calmer.
(man)	If I were any calmer, I'd be asleep.
(narrator)	WHAT DOES THE MAN MEAN?

25.
(man)	I don't think that news report can possibly be true.
(woman)	Neither do I!
(narrator)	WHAT DOES THE WOMAN MEAN?

26.
(woman)	Has management decided on a new policy for pay raises?
(man)	It's still up in the air. I think it will be discussed again at the meeting next Friday.
(narrator)	WHAT DOES THE MAN MEAN?

27.
(woman)	I can't believe it's snowing today.
(man)	It wasn't exactly unexpected.
(narrator)	WHAT DOES THE MAN MEAN?

28.
(man)	How do you think you did on the literature exam that you had this morning?
(woman)	I really wish I could take it over again.
(narrator)	WHAT DOES THE WOMAN IMPLY?

29.
(woman)	You didn't have to wait outside. You could've just opened the door and walked right in.
(man)	So the door was not locked!
(narrator)	WHAT HAD THE MAN ASSUMED?

30.
(man)	My guess is that you're leaving the office now and heading straight home.
(woman)	You've hit the nail on the head!
(narrator)	WHAT DOES THE WOMAN SAY ABOUT THE MAN?

Part B, page 518

Questions 31–34

(narrator)	Listen as a man and woman discuss a haircut.
(woman)	Hi, Bob. Your hair looks nice. It's a bit shorter than usual, isn't it?
(man)	A bit shorter? I don't think so. It's a lot shorter. When I look in the mirror, I don't even know who is looking back at me.
(woman)	So you got your hair cut, but you didn't get the haircut that you wanted?
(man)	This is not even close to the haircut that I wanted. I asked to have hair trimmed just a little bit, and the hairstylist really went to town. When I

	looked down at the floor, there were piles of hair, my hair, on the floor. I couldn't believe it!
(woman)	Well, what did you say to the hairstylist?
(man)	What could I say? The hair was already cut off. I couldn't exactly say, "Please put it back on," although that's exactly what I did want to say.
(woman)	Well, at least your hair'll grow back soon.
(man)	That's what everyone is saying to me, "It'll grow back, it'll grow back. But it won't grow fast enough to make me happy.
(woman)	Maybe after you get used to it, you'll like it a bit more.

31. WHAT SEEMS TO BE TRUE ABOUT BOB'S HAIRCUT?
32. HOW DOES BOB SEEM TO FEEL ABOUT HIS HAIRCUT?
33. WHAT DID BOB SEE ON THE FLOOR?
34. WHAT DO PEOPLE KEEP SAYING TO BOB?

Questions 35–38

(narrator)	Listen to a conversation about a man's great-grandmother.
(man)	I talked to my great-grandmother on the phone this morning.
(woman)	Your great-grandmother? Do you talk with her often?
(man)	I try to call her at least once a week. She's a really wonderful woman, and she's over eighty-five years old. I enjoy talking to her, because she's so understanding and because she gives me good advice.
(woman)	What advice did she have for you today?
(man)	(laughs) She told me to be careful because a big storm is coming.
(woman)	She said that a big storm is coming? Is she a weather forecaster?
(man)	Not exactly. She says that she can feel it in her bones when a storm is coming. I know it sounds funny, but when she feels it in her bones that a storm is coming, she's usually right.
(woman)	That's not actually so funny. When people get older, the tissue around their joints can become stiff and swollen. Just before a storm, the air pressure often drops, and this drop in air pressure can cause additional pressure and pain in swollen joints. So when your great-grandmother tells you she thinks a storm is coming, she probably has some aching in her joints from the decreasing air pressure.
(man)	Then, I had better pay more attention to my great-grandmother's weather forecasts!

35. HOW OFTEN DOES THE MAN USUALLY TALK TO HIS GREAT- GRANDMOTHER?

36. WHAT DID THE MAN'S GREAT-GRAND-MOTHER TELL HIM ON THE PHONE THIS MORNING?

37. WHERE DOES THE MAN'S GREAT-GRAND-MOTHER SAY THAT SHE FEELS A STORM COMING?

38. WHAT WILL THE MAN PROBABLY DO IN THE FUTURE?

Part C, page 519
Questions 39–42

(narrator)   Listen to a talk by a tour guide in the Everglades National Park.

(man)   Today we're going to be taking a tram tour through part of the Everglades National Park. Quite probably we'll be seeing a number of crocodiles sunning themselves by the side of the water or poking their heads up through the water. Needless to say, we will not be getting off the tram at any time until we leave the area because of the danger posed by the crocodiles.

By the way, you've probably heard of the expression "crying crocodile tears." It is common to say that someone is crying crocodile tears when he or she is pretending to be sad or full of regret. Crocodiles always appear to have tears in their eyes, but they are not crying because of sadness, or even pretended sadness. Instead, a crocodile uses its tear ducts to get rid of extra salt from its body. A crocodile does not sweat the same way that humans do and must get rid of extra salt through tears. So if you see a crying crocodile, do not think that it's feeling sad; it is basically sweating through its eyes.

Look! Over there on the right. There are two large crocodiles on the water's edge, right next to the fallen trees. You can get out your cameras and take pictures from here on the tram, but no, you cannot get off the tram to get any closer.

39. WHERE DOES THIS TALK TAKE PLACE?

40. WHAT DOES THE EXPRESSION "CRYING CROCODILE TEARS" MEAN WHEN IT IS USED TO DESCRIBE HUMANS?

41. WHY DO CROCODILES HAVE TEARS IN THEIR EYES?

42. WHAT DOES THE TOUR GUIDE RECOMMEND?

Questions 43–46

(narrator)   Listen to the following lecture by a university professor.

(woman)   Please take your seats now because I would like to begin today's lecture.

Today, we will be discussing one of the more elegant and distinct forms of nineteenth-century transportation—the clipper ship.

Clipper ships of the nineteenth century were the graceful, multisailed, oceangoing vessels that were designed for maximum speed. They were given the name "clipper" ship in reference to the fact that they "clipped along" at such a fast rate of speed.

Clipper ships were constructed with a large number of sails in order to maximize their speed. They often had six to eight sails on each of the masts, and ships commonly had three and perhaps four masts. The speeds that they achieved were unbelievably fast for the era; clipper ships could, for example, accomplish the amazing feat of traveling from New York to San Francisco in less than a hundred days.

Clipper ships first came into use in the United States in the 1840s. They were originally intended to make the trip from New York, around the tip of South America, and on to China in order to transport tea to the United States. Once gold was discovered in California in 1848, clipper ships were immediately put into use to carry large numbers of gold prospectors and large amounts of mining supplies from the East Coast to California. With the success of the American clipper ships, the British began their own fleet of clipper ships to transport goods from the far reaches of the British Empire.

That's all for today's class. Don't forget that there's a written assignment due on Friday.

43. IN WHICH COURSE WOULD THIS LECTURE MOST PROBABLY BE GIVEN?

44. WHAT IS THE MOST LIKELY MEANING OF THE EXPRESSION "TO CLIP ALONG"?

45. WHAT WERE CLIPPER SHIPS FIRST USED FOR IN THE UNITED STATES?

46. WHAT DOES THE PROFESSOR REMIND THE STUDENTS ABOUT?

Questions 47–50

(narrator)   Listen to the following talk by a drama coach to a group of actors.

(man)   I know that some of you are feeling more than a little nervous about tonight's performance, and I want you to understand that this is quite a natural feeling. You are going to be on a stage in front of a lot of people tonight, and it's normal to be experiencing some nerves. I would like to help you to understand these feelings and not to let them interfere with your performance.

What you are experiencing is called stage fright. Stage fright is the fear that develops before you give a performance in front of an audience. Stage fright is not just experienced by actors and actresses; it can also be experienced by musicians, athletes, teachers—anyone who performs in front of a group of people. It occurs before a performance when a performer is concerned about looking foolish in front of others. Just before tonight's performance, if you are feeling a bit tense, if your knees are shaking, if your stomach has butterflies in it, and if you are thinking about how bad your performance could be, then you have a major case of stage fright.

To control stage fright, you can work to control both the physical reactions and the negative thoughts. To combat the physical reactions, you can try techniques such as deep breathing, muscle relaxation, or even just laughing to relieve some of the pressure. To combat the negative thoughts, you should force yourself to focus on what you have to do rather than on what other people are going to think.

That's all I have to say for now. I'll see you back here at six o'clock because the performance starts at eight o'clock. Just remember that if you begin to feel at all nervous, try some deep breathing to relax and focus your thoughts on the performance that you are about to give. See you this evening.

47. WHO WOULD PROBABLY NOT EXPERIENCE STAGE FRIGHT IN THEIR WORK?
48. WHAT PHYSICAL REACTION MIGHT SOMEONE WHO IS EXPERIENCING STAGE FRIGHT COMMONLY HAVE?
49. HOW CAN SOMEONE COMBAT THE NEGATIVE THOUGHTS ASSOCIATED WITH STAGE FRIGHT?
50. WHEN SHOULD THE ACTORS ARRIVE AT THE THEATER?

LISTENING COMPLETE TEST (Computer)

Part A, page 540

1. (woman) Have you looked at the chemistry problem?
   (man) No, I haven't, have you?
   (woman) Yes, and it was impossible to comprehend it.
   (narrator) WHAT DOES THE WOMAN MEAN?

2. (man) Do you have the book that you borrowed from Jim? I need to use it.
   (woman) No, sorry. I don't. I already returned it to Jim.
   (narrator) WHAT DOES THE WOMAN MEAN?

3. (man) Where are you going now?
   (woman) I'm heading to a talk by Dr. Barton.
   (man) Oh, what's the talk on?
   (woman) There's going to be a solar eclipse later this month. Dr. Barton's giving a talk on what to expect during the eclipse.
   (narrator) WHO IS DR. BARTON MOST LIKELY TO BE?

4. (woman) That exam's going to be really difficult.
   (man) It is. We have a lot of work to prepare for it.
   (woman) Let's get going on it now.
   (narrator) WHAT DOES THE WOMAN SUGGEST?

5. (man) Did you enjoy the theater performance last night?
   (woman) It wasn't all I had hoped for.
   (narrator) WHAT DOES THE WOMAN SAY ABOUT THE PERFORMANCE?

6. (woman) Do you understand what we're supposed to do for tomorrow?
   (man) Not really. The professor barely talked about the assignment.
   (narrator) WHAT DOES THE MAN MEAN?

7. (man) There's a great new exhibit at the museum. Do you want to go?
   (woman) Do you know if we have to pay a fee to see the exhibit?
   (man) Not as far as I know.
   (narrator) WHAT DOES THE MAN MEAN?

8. (woman) That lecture on the realities of entrepreneurship in the twenty-first century was really fascinating, wasn't it?
   (man) I'm not sure if it was or not. I didn't understand a word.
   (narrator) WHAT DOES THE MAN MEAN?

9. (man) I forgot to send the scholarship application in on time.
   (woman) You really missed the boat!
   (narrator) WHAT DOES THE WOMAN SAY TO THE MAN?

10. (man) John will pick us up at 7:30 for the concert. That should give us plenty of time to get there.
    (woman) So John is going after all!
    (narrator) WHAT HAD THE WOMAN EXPECTED?

11. (woman) Did you enjoy the trip?
    (man) Not really. If the water hadn't been so rough and the boat hadn't rolled around so much, I would've enjoyed it more.
    (narrator) WHAT DOES THE MAN MEAN?

Part B, page 543

Questions 12–14

(man)	Do you want to go out to Clark's Restaurant tonight?
(woman)	I'd like to go out, but maybe not to Clark's.
(man)	Why not Clark's? The food's great there.
(woman)	Well, I really like the food at Clark's, but the meals are just too big for me.
(man)	How about if we share a meal since they're so big?
(woman)	That sounds like a good idea. Half of a dinner from Clark's is just the right amount for me.

12. WHAT DOES THE MAN WANT TO DO?
13. WHAT DOES THE WOMAN NOT LIKE ABOUT CLARK'S?
14. WHAT DO THEY FINALLY DECIDE TO DO?

Questions 15–17

(woman)	Do you know how I can get a copy of my transcript? I need one for a scholarship I'm applying for.
(man)	Yes, I do. You can get a copy of your transcript from the registrar's office.
(woman)	I just go to the registrar's office and ask for a copy of my transcript and I'll get one?
(man)	Well, it's not quite that easy. You need to go to the registrar's office and fill out a form, a transcript request form. Then you turn in the form with a five dollar fee.
(woman)	So I have to fill out a form and pay a fee. Then will I get the transcript?
(man)	You turn in the form and pay a fee, and then you have to wait several days for the transcript to be processed before you can get it.

15. WHY DOES THE WOMAN NEED HER TRANSCRIPT?
16. WHAT DOES THE WOMAN NEED TO DO?
17. WHEN CAN THE WOMAN GET THE TRANSCRIPT?

Questions 18–21

(narrator)	Listen to a lecture in a government class. The professor is talking about Washington, D.C.
(professor)	Today we'll be talking about the city of Washington, D.C. First of all, let me give you a little background about its name. The original name of the city was Washington City; it was, of course, named after the first president of the United States, George Washington. In later years, the name was changed to the District of Columbia, and today it is most commonly called Washington, D.C., where D.C. is the abbreviated form of District of Columbia.

There are two points that I would like to make about Washington, D.C. First of all, this city is unusual in the United States because it is the only U.S. city that is not part of any state. Second of all, this city was the only U.S. city which, for quite some time, was not self-governing.

Now, let's look at a map of Washington, D.C. as we discuss the first point. In the early years of the country, the founding fathers believed that the capital of the United States should not be part of any state. When a location was chosen for the capital city, two states were asked to give up land for a capital city. You can see on the map that the District of Columbia was originally a square, with the Potomac River cutting through the square. The area to the northeast of the Potomac originally belonged to the state of Maryland, and the area to the southwest of the Potomac originally belonged to the state of Virginia. In the middle of the nineteenth century, the portion of the square that had previously belonged to Virgina, the portion to the southwest of the Potomac, was returned to the state of Virginia. Today the District of Columbia is no longer a square. Instead, the District of Columbia is the portion of the square to the northeast of the Potomac.

The second unusual point that I would like to make about Washington D.C. is that, for most of its history, it was not a self-governing city. When the city was established, it was decided that its government would be appointed by the president of the United States; the citizens of Washington, D.C, would not elect their own city government. In addition, the citizens of Washington, D.C. for quite some time had no representation in Congress, and they were ineligible to vote for the president of the United States. The citizens of Washington, D.C. were given the right to vote for their government only relatively recently. Citizens of Washington, D.C. were first eligible to vote for the president of the United States in the 1964 election; they did not have a representative in Congress until 1970, and they did not elect their own city officials until 1974.

Please read the chapter on Washington, D.C. in your textbook and answer the questions at the end of the chapter before next class. I'll see you then.

18. WHICH NAME HAS NOT BEEN USED FOR THE CITY DISCUSSED IN THE LECTURE?
19. THE CITY OF WASHINGTON, D.C. BELONGS TO WHICH STATE?
20. IDENTIFY THE PART OF THE MAP THAT USED TO BELONG TO WASHINGTON, D.C. BUT NO LONGER DOES.
21. WHAT IS STATED IN THE LECTURE ABOUT THE GOVERNMENT OF WASHINGTON, D.C.?

Questions 22–25

(narrator)   Listen to a discussion about a geography lecture. The discussion is on weather fronts.

(man 1)   We need to discuss the information from our geography class about weather fronts. First of all, what is a weather front?

(woman 1)   A weather front is a leading or front end of a mass of air. This mass of air could be cold or warm.

(man 2)   If the mass is cold air, then it's called a cold front.

(woman 2)   And if the mass of air is warm air, then it's called a warm front.

(man 1)   And where do the different types of air masses come from?

(woman 1)   Cold air masses come from polar air.

(man 2)   This means that cold air fronts come from the north in the northern hemisphere and from the south in the southern hemisphere.

(woman 2)   Warm air masses come from the tropics. They move north from the equator in the northern hemisphere and south from the equator in the southern hemisphere.

(man 1)   Now, let's look at the diagram of a warm front. What happens at a warm front?

(woman 1)   At a warm front, warm air moves slowly over cooler air.

(man 2)   When this happens, there's a layer of low grey clouds, and it rains or snows steadily.

(woman 2)   And the cloud and wet weather at a warm front can last for days at a time.

(man 1)   Let's look now at a cold front. There's a diagram of a cold front here.

(woman 1)   At a cold front, fast-moving cold air cuts under the warm air.

(man 2)   The warm air is pushed up rapidly, and this sudden movement causes violent weather.

(woman 2)   Exactly. At a cold front, there can be strong winds and thunderstorms. The storms caused by a cold front arrive quickly and leave quickly.

(man 1)   Finally, let's summarize what we need to understand about weather fronts. There are two types of fronts, cold fronts and warm fronts.

(woman 1)   In both of these types of fronts, the cold air is under the warm air.

(man 2)   In a warm front, the warm air moves slowly over the cold front, and there is ongoing rain or snow.

(woman 2)   An in a cold front, the cold air moves suddenly under the warm air, and there is violent weather that moves rapidly into and out of an area.

(man 1)   That sounds like all we need to know about weather fronts. See you in class.

22. WHAT IS A WEATHER FRONT?
23. WHERE DO FRONTS ORIGINATE?
24.. WHAT IS STATED ABOUT A WARM FRONT?
25. WHAT IS STATED ABOUT A COLD FRONT?

Questions 26–30

(narrator)   Listen to a lecture in a gemology class. The professor is talking about the history of gem-cutting.

(professor)   Today I'll be talking about different styles of gem-cutting, particularly about how these different styles developed historically. The various styles of gems that I'll be talking about are the cabochon, the table cut, the rose cut, and the brilliant cut.

The first style of gem-cutting, which you can see in this drawing, is the cabochon. The cabochon is a rounded shape, without facets. The cabochon style is quite old. It was the earliest style used to finish gems. The cabochons in these drawings are shown from the side. A cabochon could be a simple cabochon, with a rounded top and a flat bottom, or it could be a double cabochon, which is rounded on both the top and the bottom. It was discovered early on that powders of harder materials such as diamonds could be used to polish gemstones, and many ancient cultures used this method to finish gems.

The cabochon cut was not a faceted cut. A facet, for those of you who do not know, is a flat surface cut into a gem. It's not clear when faceting of stones first developed. Stones were faceted as early as the fifteenth century in Europe, and they may have been faceted earlier than that in other cultures.

Now, we'll look at one of the earliest styles of faceted gems, the table cut. You can see a table cut stone, from the top and from the side, in these drawings. Early stones faceted in this way were probably not actually cut but were polished to this shape, using powders of harder stones such as diamonds. Some stones, including diamonds, occur naturally in an eight-sided double pyramid. To create a table cut from an eight-sided double pyramid, it's necessary only to polish a flat surface on the top of one side of the naturally occurring eight-sided shapes.

The next stage in the development of gem-cutting is the rose cut. In a rose cut, a stone is actually cut rather than polished. This was one of the earliest methods of faceting the entire surface of a diamond, or other gem. The rose cut involved cutting up to 32 triangular facets on the top of a diamond and a flat surface on the bottom. This type of cut was beneficial because it maintained much of the original stone. However, it does not reflect light in a way that maximizes the stone's shine and brilliance. Because it does not reflect light as well as other cuts, the rose cut is no longer used much today.

The last type of cut we'll look at is the brilliant cut. The brilliant cut came into use after the other styles. You can see a brilliant cut from the top and the side. The brilliant cut is faceted on the side and top and also on the bottom. A stone with a brilliant cut in the correct proportions reflects the maximum amount of light out through the top of the stone and creates a stone that, as its name indicates, shines the most brilliantly. This style of stone is used quite often today because it's so reflective.

We have seen four different styles of gems today, in the order that they were developed historically. Two of them, the cabochon and the table cut, are polished rather than cut to create the style, while the other two are actually cut. Before next class, please look over the photos of gems at the end of the chapter and identify the style of each stone.

26. WHAT ARE THE CHARACTERISTICS OF EACH OF THESE GEMSTONES?
27. WHICH STYLES OF STONES WERE POLISHED AND NOT CUT?
28. THE PROFESSOR EXPLAINS THE ORDER THAT EACH OF THESE STYLES OF GEMS APPEARED IN HISTORY. PUT THE STYLES OF GEMS IN THEIR HISTORICAL ORDER.
29. WHICH STYLE OF GEM IS NO LONGER USED BECAUSE IT DOES NOT REFLECT LIGHT WELL?
30. WHAT IS THE ASSIGNMENT FOR THE NEXT CLASS?

APPENDIX

APPENDIX EXERCISE A1

1. He **put** his head on the pillow.
2. His **pet** rat got out of the cage.
3. The soup was cooking in a **pot** on the stove.
4. When the child didn't get what he wanted, he began to **pout**.
5. When you wash your face, you should **pat** it gently to dry it.
6. When he bit into a cherry, his tooth struck a **pit**.

APPENDIX EXERCISE A2

1. The water was too **hot** to enjoy.
2. He was impressed by the **height** of the building.
3. He **hit** the ball as hard as he could.
4. They lived in a grass **hut** near the beach.
5. The **heat** was too much for him.
6. He was filled with **hate** because of what happened.

APPENDIX EXERCISE A3

1. The children were trying to fly their **kite**.
2. He went to sleep on a **cot**.
3. There is a **cat** stuck up in a tree.
4. Because of the cold, she decided to wear her **coat**.
5. He **cut** the sandwich in half.
6. I **caught** a cold last week.

APPENDIX EXERCISE A4

1. She had a **bowl** of cereal for breakfast.
2. The **bill** needs to be paid immediately.
3. The **bell** announces the start of classes.
4. The farmer gave the horses a **bale** of hay.
5. The **bull** ws standing in the field.
6. I had a **ball** at the party.

APPENDIX EXERCISE A5

.1 A **cop** stopped at the scene of the accident.
2. She pulled on her **cape** before going out in the snow.
3. I am afraid that I just can't **cope** with all these problems.
4. He pulled the **cap** down over his eyes.
5. A **cup** of broth would taste good now.
6. He needs to **keep** on trying.

APPENDIX EXERCISE A6

1. It's too **bad** the weather isn't better.
2. The rose **bud** was a soft pink color.
3. She's been in **bed** for over twelve hours.
4. One large **bead** came off of her dress.
5. He made a **bid** on the property.
6. The musician **bowed** after the performance.

APPENDIX EXERCISE A7

1. The weather is much cooler at **night**.
2. They need a new **net** to play badminton.
3. The **note** just arrived in the mail today.
4. He tied the two strings together in a tight **knot**.
5. She keeps her room extremely **neat**.
6. Her specialty in the kitchen is a **nut** pie.

APPENDIX EXERCISE A8

1. All she wants is to **soak** in the tub.
2. The sandwich is in a paper **sack**.
3. The parents are staying together for the **sake** of the children.
4. The politician will **seek** another term in office.
5. She's relaxing because she feels rather **sick** today.
6. He put his right **sock** on his foot.

APPENDIX EXERCISE A9

1. She parts her hair on the right **side**.
2. He **sawed** the large log into smaller pieces.
3. What happened last night was too **sad**.
4. She **sighed** when she heard the news.
5. The **seed** that she planted has begun to sprout.
6. I can't believe what was **said**.

APPENDIX EXERCISE A10

1. The office is down the **hall**.
2. The rabbit jumped into a **hole** in the ground.
3. She climbed up to the top of the **hill**.
4. He ate the **whole** piece of cake.
5. She tried to **haul** the heavy suitcases up the steps.
6. Suddenly a wolf began to **howl**.
7. The **hull** of the ship needs to be repaired.
8. The rain was accompanied by some **hail**.
9. The wound has not yet begun to **heal**.

APPENDIX EXERCISE A11

1. The **boat** was docked in the harbor.
2. The strongest hitter picked up a **bat**.
3. Before the game the woman made a **bet**.
4. He needs some **bait** to go fishing.
5. Her heart skipped a **beat**.
6. No one **but** Tom has shown up yet.
7. At the store she **bought** some vegetables.
8. he took a large **bite** of the apple.
9. It does not matter one single **bit**.

NOTES

NOTES

NOTES

NOTES

ANSWER KEY

LISTENING

LISTENING DIAGNOSTIC PRE-TEST (Paper)

1. C	11. D	21. B	31. A	41. C
2. B	12. A	22. B	32. C	42. B
3. D	13. B	23. D	33. C	43. B
4. A	14. C	24. C	34. C	44. C
5. B	15. D	25. C	35. D	45. D
6. B	16. A	26. A	36. B	46. A
7. B	17. B	27. C	37. C	47. C
8. A	18. A	28. B	38. D	48. B
9. C	19. D	29. D	39. B	49. A
10. A	20. C	30. A	40. C	50. C

LISTENING DIAGNOSTIC PRE-TEST (Computer)

1. 2	5. 4	9. 1	13. 1
2. 1	6. 2	10. 3	14. 3
3. 3	7. 3	11. 4	15. 2
4. 2	8. 2	12. 3	16. 2

17. *Roanoke Island: Lost Colonists*
    Ocracoke Island: Blackbeard
    Kitty Hawk: Wright Brothers
18. *16th century: Lost Colonists*
    18th century: Blackbeard
    20th century: Wright Brothers

19. 1, 3	22. 2	25. B	28. 2
20. 2	23. B	26. 4	29. 1
21. 4	24. 2, 4	27. 2	

30. *The cooling valve stuck open.*
    Instruments were misread.
    The cooling water was shut off.
    A partial meltdown occurred.

EXERCISE 1

1. D	2. B	3. C

TOEFL EXERCISE 1

1. A	3. D	5. C	7. D	9. D
2. C	4. B	6. A	8. C	10. A

EXERCISE 2

1. D	2. B	3. C

TOEFL EXERCISE 2

1. D	3. A	5. C	7. B	9. B
2. A	4. C	6. D	8. A	10. D

EXERCISE 3

1. C	2. D	3. B

TOEFL EXERCISE 3

1. C	3. D	5. B	7. C	9. A
2. A	4. B	6. C	8. D	10. C

TOEFL REVIEW EXERCISE (Skills 1–3)

1. C	3. D	5. A	7. B	9. C
2. A	4. D	6. D	8. C	10. B

EXERCISE 4

1. B	2. C	3. D

TOEFL EXERCISE 4

1. B	3. D	5. B	7. A	9. C
2. A	4. B	6. C	8. C	10. A

EXERCISE 5

1. C	2. C	3. A

TOEFL EXERCISE 5

1. D	3. A	5. C	7. C	9. D
2. B	4. B	6. C	8. B	10. D

EXERCISE 6

1. D	2. C	3. A

TOEFL EXERCISE 6

1. C	3. B	5. A	7. D	9. C
2. B	4. B	6. C	8. D	10. D

TOEFL EXERCISE (Skills 4–6)

1. C	3. A	5. B	7. D	9. A
2. B	4. C	6. B	8. C	10. B

TOEFL REVIEW EXERCISE (Skills 1–6)

1. D	3. B	5. C	7. A	9. B
2. D	4. D	6. B	8. A	10. D

EXERCISE 7

1. C	2. A	3. C

TOEFL EXERCISE 7

1. A	3. B	5. D	7. B	9. D
2. D	4. C	6. C	8. A	10. B

EXERCISE 8

1. A	2. D	3. B

TOEFL EXERCISE 8

1. D	3. B	5. C	7. C	9. D
2. A	4. D	6. B	8. D	10. A

EXERCISE 9

1. D	2. B	3. D

TOEFL EXERCISE 9

1. A	3. A	5. D	7. C	9. C
2. D	4. C	6. A	8. A	10. D

EXERCISE 10

1. A	2. C	3. C

TOEFL EXERCISE 10

1. D	3. A	5. A	7. B	9. A
2. C	4. D	6. B	8. A	10. A

TOEFL EXERCISE (Skills 7–10)

1. C	3. C	5. D	7. B	9. A
2. B	4. B	6. D	8. C	10. B

TOEFL REVIEW EXERCISE (Skills 1–10)

1. A	3. B	5. C	7. C	9. B
2. B	4. A	6. C	8. D	10. D

EXERCISE 11

1. D	2. B	3. A

TOEFL EXERCISE 11

1. D	3. A	5. D	7. C	9. A
2. B	4. D	6. C	8. B	10. C

EXERCISE 12

1. A	2. D	3. D

TOEFL EXERCISE 12

1. B	3. B	5. D	7. D	9. A
2. B	4. A	6. A	8. A	10. A

EXERCISE 13

1. A	2. C	3. B

TOEFL EXERCISE 13

1. C	3. A	5. A	7. A	9. D
2. D	4. D	6. C	8. C	10. A

TOEFL EXERCISE (Skills 11–13)

1. D	3. C	5. A	7. D	9. D
2. B	4. A	6. D	8. B	10. B

TOEFL REVIEW EXERCISE (Skills 1–13)

1. B	3. D	5. C	7. A	9. A
2. A	4. B	6. C	8. D	10. C

EXERCISE 14

1. C	2. D	3. D

TOEFL EXERCISE 14

1. C	3. C	5. B	7. A	9. C
2. D	4. D	6. A	8. B	10. C

EXERCISE 15

1. A	2. D	3. C

TOEFL EXERCISE 15

1. B	3. D	5. C	7. A	9. B
2. A	4. A	6. B	8. D	10. A

TOEFL EXERCISE (Skills 14–15)

1. C	3. A	5. D	7. C	9. B
2. B	4. C	6. D	8. B	10. C

TOEFL REVIEW EXERCISE (Skills 1–15)

1. C	3. B	5. A	7. A	9. A
2. D	4. C	6. B	8. B	10. D

EXERCISE 16

1. D	2. C	3. D

TOEFL EXERCISE 16

1. D	3. C	5. B	7. C	9. B
2. A	4. B	6. A	8. C	10. A

EXERCISE 17

1. D	2. B	3. B

TOEFL EXERCISE 17

1. D	3. C	5. D	7. C	9. D
2. C	4. B	6. A	8. C	10. D

TOEFL EXERCISE (Skills 16–17)

1. B	3. D	5. A	7. C	9. C
2. A	4. C	6. C	8. D	10. B

TOEFL REVIEW EXERCISE (Skills 1–17)

1. A	3. C	5. A	7. C	9. D
2. B	4. C	6. C	8. C	10. A

EXERCISE 18 (answers may vary)

Questions 1 through 5: *looking for a job on campus*
Questions 6 through 10: *a trip taken during a school vacation*
Questions 11 through 15: *one type of pollution, acid rain*

EXERCISE 19

1. *What…to do?*
2. *Where does the conversation probably take place?*
3. *How many…?*
4. *How often…?*
5. *What…to do?*
6. *When does the conversation probably take place?*
7. *What kind of trip is it?*
8. *How long?*
9. *What were they doing during the trip?*
10. *How does she feel about…?*
11. *What is the topic of the conversation?*
12. *What energy source?*
13. *How is…formed?*
14. *Where…?*
15. *What should she do?*

EXERCISE 20

Conversation 1: *looking for a part-time job on campus*
Conversation 2: *a kayaking trip that the man took on the Klamath River*
Conversation 3: *one kind of pollution called acid rain*

EXERCISE 21 (Answers may vary)

Conversation 1
  1. *a student and an employment office worker*
  2. *in the campus employment office*

Conversation 2
  1. *two students*
  2. *during the spring semester, right after spring break*
  3. *a trip that he just took*

Conversation 3
  1. *two students*
  2. *sometime during the semester*
  3. *an article that the man read*

TOEFL EXERCISE 22

1. A	4. B	7. C	10. D	13. B
2. C	5. D	8. B	11. D	14. C
3. C	6. D	9. A	12. C	15. D

TOEFL EXERCISE (Skills 18–22)

1. C	4. A	7. D	10. A	13. D
2. B	5. B	8. C	11. C	
3. D	6. A	9. B	12. B	

EXERCISE 23 (Answers may vary)

Questions 1 through 5: *the requirements of a biology class*
Questions 6 through 10: *the volcanoes in the Ring of Fire or Hawaii*
Questions 11 through 15: *a tour of the Smithsonian*

EXERCISE 24

1. *When* does the talk probably take place?
2. *How often...?*
3. *What* are the students told?
4. *What...?*
5. *What...?*
6. *What is the topic* of the talk?
7. *What is the topic* of the talk?
8. *Where...?*
9. *What is true* about volcanoes?
10. *What is...?*
11. *Who is the speaker?*
12. *How many?*
13. *Which* museum?
14. *Which* museum?
15. *Where* are they going next?

EXERCISE 25 (Answers may vary)

Talk 1: the first day of class in Biology 101
Talk 2: the volcanoes of Hawaii
Talk 3: a tour of the Smithsonian

EXERCISE 26 (Answers may vary)

Talk 1
1. *Professor Martin*
2. *in biology class*
3. *on the first day of class*
4. *Biology 101*

Talk 2
1. *a professor*
2. *in a university class*
3. *sometime during the semester*
4. *maybe geology (because the topic is volcanoes)*

Talk 3
1. *a tour guide*
2. *in Washington, D.C.*
3. *in the middle of a tour*

TOEFL EXERCISE 27

1. C	4. C	7. C	10. C	13. B
2. B	5. D	8. C	11. B	14. D
3. D	6. B	9. A	12. D	15. A

TOEFL REVIEW EXERCISE (Skills 23–27)

1. D	4. D	7. A	10. C
2. D	5. C	8. C	11. C
3. A	6. B	9. B	12. D

TOEFL EXERCISE 28

1. 4	4. 2	7. 2	10. 3
2. 3	5. 1	8. 3	11. 1
3. 1	6. 4	9. 2	

EXERCISE 29 (Answers may vary)

1. a. ordering (process)
   b. process of the formation of hail
      • A drop of water rises and falls repeatedly within a cloud.
      • Each time it rises and falls, it adds a new layer of ice.
      • After it builds up enough layers, it becomes too heavy.
      • Then, it falls to the earth.

2. a. classification
   b. classification by number of fractures:
      • single fracture (one fracture)
      • double fracture (two fractures)
      • multiple fracture (numerous fractures)

      classification by types of fractures:
      • simple fracture (complete fracture, not through the skin)
      • compound fracture (complete fracture, through the skin)
      • greenstick fracture (partial fracture, with bending)

      classification by degree of seriousness
      • greenstick fracture (less serious)
      • simple fracture (serious)
      • compound fracture (more serious)

3. a. both classification and ordering (chronology)
   b. classification of types of trials:
      • Eugene Debs (trial of a union leader)
      • Loeb and Leopold (murder trial)
      • John Scopes (evolution trial)

      chronological ordering of events:
      • 1895: trial of Eugene Debs, president of the railroad workers union (Pullman Strike)
      • 1902: arbitration of the Pennsylvania Coal strike
      • 1924: trial of Loeb and Leopold for the murder of a teenager
      • 1925: trial of John Scopes for teaching evolution (Monkey Trial)

TOEFL EXERCISE 29

1. *It rises within a cloud.*
   It freezes for the first time.
   It falls within the cloud.
   It picks up water.

2. *It rises and falls repeatedly in the cloud.*
   It adds new layers of ice.
   It becomes too heavy.
   It falls to the ground.

3. *One break: single fracture*
   Two breaks: double fracture
   Numerous breaks: multiple fracture

4. *Complete fracture with no broken skin: simple fracture*
   Partial fracture: greenstick fracture
   Complete fracture with broken skin: compound fracture

5. *Less serious: greenstick fracture*
   Serious: simple fracture
   More serious: compound fracture

6. *Pullman Strike: Eugene Debs*
   Evolution in the classroom: John Scopes
   Murder trial: Loeb and Leopold

7. *He defended the railway union president.*
   He arbitrated a coal strike.
   He defended the murderers of a teenager.
   He took part in the Monkey Trial.

EXERCISE 30 (Answers may vary)

1. a. *in three weeks*
   b. *the Stage Manager, George, Emily*
   c. *before George and Emily's wedding*
   d. *slightly familiar (just started learning lines)*
   e. *discuss costumes and props and then run through the scene (one suggests this, and the other two agree)*

2. a. *looks like gold, with a shiny golden color*
   b. *a compound of iron and sulfur*
   c. *it smokes and develops a strong odor*
   d. *from the Greek word for 'fire'*
   e. *they were fools (from fool's gold)*

f. *it does not smoke or develop a strong odor (iron pyrite smokes and smells, and gold does not have the same kind of reaction)*

g. *it does not start fires easily (iron pyrite was used to start fires, and gold could not be used that way)*

3. a. *a Spanish explorer*
   b. *in a best-selling Spanish fantasy series*
   c. *an island full of gold*
   d. *Amazons, who were powerful female warriors*
   e. *sometime between 1500 and 1550 (in the first half of the sixteenth century)*
   f. *no Amazons and not an island (no inhabitants like those in the fictional work, and an incorrect assumption that California was an island)*

TOEFL EXERCISE 30

1. 3	5. 2, 4	9. 1, 2	13. 1	17. 4
2. 3	6. 1	10. 3	14. 2	18. 1, 3
3. 2	7. 2	11. 4	15. 1	
4. 1,3	8. 2, 4	12. 2	16. 2, 4	

EXERCISE 31

(Various answers are possible.)

TOEFL EXERCISE 31

1. D	3. D	5. B	7. A	9. C
2. A	4. C	6. A	8. C	

TOEFL REVIEW EXERCISE (Skills 29–31)

1. 2, 4
2. 3
3. D
4. A
5. 4
6. 2
7. *Before 1920: gas mask*
   In the 1920s: facecloth
   In the 1930s: handkerchief
8. 1, 4
9. 1
10. *Famous actresses: facecloths*
    No marketing: bandages
    Consumer testing: handkerchiefs
11. 1
12. D
13. 1, 3
14. *A volcanic island forms.*
    Coral begins to grow.
    The volcano erodes.
    The volcano disappears underwater.
15. C

EXERCISE 32 (Answers may vary)

1. a. classification
   b. classification by outstanding characteristic:
      • *Caspian Sea (largest lake)*
      • *Lake Baikal (deepest lake)*
      • *Lake Superior (largest freshwater lake)*

      classification by type of formation:
      • *Caspian Sea (cut off from oceans)*
      • *Lake Superior (carved out by glaciers)*
      • *Lake Baikal (created over a fault)*

2. a. ordering (process)
   b. process of the formation of fossils:
      • *An animal dies.*
      • *Soft tissues decompose.*
      • *Hard tissues remain.*
      • *Hard tissues become buried.*

      • *Layers of sediment cover the bones.*
      • *The bones sink to the level of the ground water.*
      • *Minerals from the ground water enter the bones.*
      • *Minerals eventually replace the bones.*

3. a. both classification and ordering (process)
   b. classification by types of olive oil:
      • *extra virgin olive oil (cold-pressed from the first pressing, lower acid)*
      • *virgin olive oil (cold-pressed from the first pressing, higher acid)*
      • *cold-pressed olive oil (cold-pressed from a later pressing)*
      • *pure olive oil (heat processed)*
      • *light olive oil (a mix of olive oil and some other type of oil)*

      process for making cold-pressed olive oil:
      • *The olives are pressed for the first time.*
      • *Virgin olive oil results.*
      • *The crushed olives are repressed.*
      • *Cold-pressed olive oil results.*

TOEFL EXERCISE 32

1. *Largest lake: Caspian Sea*
   Deepest Lake: Lake Baikal
   Largest freshwater lake: Lake Superior

2. *Cut off from the oceans: Caspian Sea*
   Carved out by glaciers: Lake Superior
   Created over a fault in the crust: Lake Baikal

3. *An animal dies.*
   Soft tissues decompose.
   Hard tissues remain.
   Hard tissues become buried.

4. *Layers of sediment cover the bones.*
   The bones sink to the level of the ground water.
   Minerals from the ground water enter the bones.
   Minerals eventually replace the bones.

5. *The fossilized remains are buried.*
   The earth moves the buried remains.
   The remains may be pushed close to the surface.
   Humans may discover the remains.

6. *The olives are pressed for the first time.*
   Virgin olive oil results.
   The crushed olives are repressed.
   Cold-pressed olive oil results.

7. *Olive oil of the highest quality: virgin olive oil*
   Olive oil affected by heating: pure olive oil
   Olive oil mixed with other oils: light olive oil

8. *From the first pressing, with lower acid: extra virgin olive oil*
   From the first pressing, with higher acid: virgin olive oil
   From a later pressing: cold-pressed olive oil

EXERCISE 33 (Answers may vary)

1. a. *trees with cones instead of flowers*
   b. *one-third*
   c. *a conifer, a 4,000-year-old bristlecone pine in California*
   d. *conifers, giant redwoods in California several hundred feet tall and weighing 2,000 tons*
   e. *evolved as a reaction to drought*
   f. *Conifers lose and replace their needles throughout the year, deciduous trees shed their leaves in one season.*
   g. *in the northern hemisphere (in North America and Siberia)*
   h. *very big (several hundred feet tall and weighing 2,000 tons)*

2. a. *students in an introductory education course*
   b. *early twentieth century*
   c. *no colorful clothing, no skirts above the ankle*
   d. *no bars, no ice cream parlors*

e. *very strict (had to follow lots of rules)*
f. *at home (had to be at home by 8:00)*

3. a. *both visible from Earth*
   b. *500 degrees Centigrade, or 900 degrees Fahrenheit*
   c. *its closeness to the Sun and its atmosphere*
   d. *made of carbon dioxide*
   e. *made of sulfuric acid*
   f. *the Sun reflecting off the clouds*
   g. *the 6th largest (almost the same size as the earth, the 5th largest)*
   h. *not at its brightest when full (at its brightest when a crescent)*
   i. *must be thick (the clouds hide the surface of Venus)*

TOEFL EXERCISE 33

1. 4	6. 2, 4	11. 2	16. 3	21. 1, 4
2. 2	7. 1	12. 2, 3	17. 2	22. 4
3. 1	8. 2, 3	13. 1	18. 1, 4	
4. 1, 3	9. 4	14. 2, 4	19. 2, 4	
5. 2	10. 3	15. 4	20. 1	

EXERCISE 34 (Various answers are possible.)

TOEFL EXERCISE 34

1. C	3. D	5. A	7. D	9. C
2. B	4. B	6. A	8. B	10. C

TOEFL REVIEW EXERCISE (Skills 32–34)

1. 1, 2
2. *At the top: observatory*
   In the legs: trams
   Under the ground: museum
3. 3
4. 2
5. *Jefferson became president.*
   Lewis and Clark set out to explore the west.
   Thousands of settlers set out from St. Louis.
   The arch was built.
6. 1, 4
7. *Compressed minerals: inner core*
   Stony silicates: mantle
   Liquid minerals: outer core
8. C
9. 1, 4
10. 2
11. B
12. 2
13. 4
14. 3
15. 2, 4
16. *It had only a **g** sound.*
    *It had both a **k** and a **g** sound.*
    *It had only a **k** sound.*
    *It had both a **k** and an **s** sound.*

LISTENING POST-TEST (Paper)

1. D	11. A	21. D	31. B	41. D
2. D	12. C	22. D	32. C	42. D
3. A	13. D	23. A	33. A	43. B
4. D	14. C	24. D	34. D	44. B
5. C	15. C	25. A	35. A	45. B
6. D	16. B	26. C	36. D	46. A
7. A	17. A	27. C	37. B	47. D
8. C	18. C	28. D	38. C	48. B
9. B	19. B	29. D	39. B	49. D
10. A	20. B	30. B	40. C	50. B

LISTENING POST-TEST (Computer)

1. 1	4. 1	7. 4	10. 1	13. 1
2. 4	5. 3	8. 2	11. 4	14. 4
3. 2	6. 3	9. 4	12. 1	15. 2

16. *One leaf per node: alternate*
    Two leaves per node: opposite
    Three leaves per node: whorled
17. B
18. *Least common: whorled*
    Neither most nor least common: opposite
    Most common: alternate
19. 1, 4
20. 3
21. 3
22. 4
23. 1, 4
24. D
25. 4
26. *End of the eighteenth century: James Cook*
    Beginning of the nineteenth century: Kamehameha
    End of the nineteenth century: Liliuokalani
27. 4
28. *The islands had different monarchs.*
    Kamehameha became king.
    Liliuokalani became queen.
    The monarchy disappeared.
29. 4
30. 2

STRUCTURE

STRUCTURE DIAGNOSTIC PRE-TEST (Paper)

1. D	4. B	7. A	10. C	13. D
2. D	5. C	8. A	11. A	14. B
3. D	6. C	9. B	12. A	15. A

16. B	*are*	29. C	*and*
17. C	*became*	30. B	*was designed by*
18. B	*was declared*	31. B	*short courses*
19. A	*the brightest star*	32. D	*moved*
20. C	*rest*	33. A	*actor*
21. C	*materials*	34. C	*live*
22. B	*previously*	35. C	*result of*
23. C	*used*	36. B	*the project*
24. D	*their*	37. B	*profitable*
25. A	*imported*	38. D	*been mined*
26. C	*the*	39. C	*other*
27. C	*their*	40. B	*making*
28. D	*amount*		

STRUCTURE DIAGNOSTIC PRE-TEST (Computer)

1. 3	*recorded*	11. 3	
2. 2	*was*	12. 2	*number*
3. 4		13. 2	*officially opened*
4. 3	*them*	14. 4	
5. 3		15. 1	*A typical*
6. 2	*but*	16. 2	*made*
7. 2	*larger than*	17. 2	
8. 4		18. 2	*relies on*
9. 4	*died*	19. 3	*expensive*
10. 3	*razed*	20. 1	

EXERCISE 1

1. I   missing subject   (could be *he went*)
2. C
3. I   missing verb   (could be *is available*)
4. I   double verb   (*has* and *provides*)
5. C

6. I   double subject   (*text* and *it*)
7. C
8. I   missing verb   (could be *departure is sched-uled*)
9. I   missing subject   (could be *I found*)
10. I   double verb   (*is* and *processes*)

EXERCISE 2

1. C
2. I   missing subject   (could be *he took*)
3. C
4. C
5. I   missing subject   (could be *the doctor has been practicing*)
6. C
7. I   double subject   (*shopping* and *it*)
8. C
9. I   missing subject   (could be *she took*)
10. C

EXERCISE 3

1. C
2. I   missing subject   (could be *Bob, a friend*)
3. C
4. I   missing subject   (could be *Mr. Smith, the chief executive officer*)
5. C
6. C
7. I   missing subject   (could be *the electric heater, a wall heating unit*)
8. C
9. I   missing comma   (*computer, the most powerful*)
10. C

EXERCISE 4

1. C
2. I   double verb   (*are completing* and *should report*)
3. C
4. I   double verb   (*are giving* and *attract*)
5. C
6. I   double verb   (*was trying* and *was often interrupted*)
7. C
8. C
9. I   double verb   (*were announcing* and *received*)
10. C

EXERCISE 5

1. I   double verb   (*was offered* and *was not accepted*)
2. C
3. I   double verb   (*were taught* and *will be*)
4. C
5. I   double verb   (*were reached* and *were*)
6. C
7. I   double verb   (*is served* and *is*)
8. I   double verb   (*are listed* and *have*)
9. C
10. C

EXERCISE (Skills 1–5)

1. C
2. I   missing subject   (could be *she went*)
3. I   double verb   (*were grown* and *were harvested*)
4. C
5. C

6. I   missing verb   (could be *is in the shopping mall*)
7. C
8. I   missing subject   (could be *he threw*)
9. I   double subject   (*construction* and *it*)
10. C

TOEFL EXERCISE (Skills 1–5)

1. B   3. A   5. C   7. A   9. D
2. A   4. D   6. C   8. B   10. A

EXERCISE 6

1. C
2. I   missing subject   (could be *no rain has fallen*)
3. I   missing connector   (could be *and it has been*)
4. I   misplaced connector   (should be *The quality…so I changed*)
5. C
6. I   missing subject   (could be *yet it is*)
7. C
8. C
9. I   misplaced connector   (should be *You can drive…, or you can get*)
10. I   missing connector   (could be *so he flew*)

EXERCISE 7

1. C
2. I   missing subject   (could be *before they are admitted*)
3. C
4. I   missing connector   (could be *After the ground had been prepared*)
5. C
6. I   missing verb   (could be *The building is*)
7. I   missing subject   (could be *it can be sent*)
8. C
9. C
10. I   missing comma   (*counted, the outcome*)

EXERCISE 8

1. C
2. I   missing connector   (could be *Though the commandant left*)
3. I   missing verb   (could be *unless he or she meets*)
4. C
5. I   missing subject   (could be *wherever you need*)
6. C
7. I   missing verb   (could be *your application is*)
8. I   missing comma   (*explained, all visitors*)
9. C
10. C

EXERCISE (Skills 6–8)

1. C
2. I   unnecessary connector   (omit *Or*)
3. I   missing verb   (could be *a problem occurred*)
4. I   incorrect connector   (should be *as soon as*)
5. C
6. I   missing connector   (could be *so the king has not returned*)
7. C
8. C
9. I   missing subject   (could be *while it is*)
10. C

TOEFL EXERCISE (Skills 6–8)

1. D	3. C	5. D	7. C	9. B
2. D	4. B	6. B	8. D	10. D

TOEFL REVIEW EXERCISE (Skills 1–8)

1. C	3. C	5. A	7. C	9. D
2. B	4. C	6. D	8. B	10. A

EXERCISE 9

1. C
2. I   missing verb   (could be *manual describes*)
3. C
4. I   missing connector   (could be *Why he refused*)
5. I   missing subject   (could be *We talked*)
6. I   extra subject   (omit *it*)
7. C
8. I   missing verb   (could be *when the paper is due is certain*)
9. I   missing connector   (could be *When the contract will be awarded*)
10. C

EXERCISE 10

1. C
2. I   missing verb   (could be *which is*)
3. C
4. I   missing verb   (*signing* could be *must sign*)
5. I   extra subject   (omit *he*)
6. C
7. C
8. I   missing verb   (could be *whatever is*)
9. C
10. I   missing verb   (could be *whoever is*)

EXERCISE 11

1. C
2. I   missing verb   (could be *is for sale*)
3. I   incorrect connector   (*whom* could be *which*)
4. C
5. I   extra subject   (omit *it*)
6. C
7. C
8. I   missing verb   (could be *was funny*)
9. I   missing subject   (could be *we were having*)
10. C

EXERCISE 12

1. C
2. I   missing connector/ subject   (could be *which are trying*)
3. I   missing verb   (could be *who is*)
4. I   incorrect connector/ subject (*which* should be *who*)
5. I   extra subject   (omit *it*)
6. C
7. I   missing connector/ subject   (could be *which is*)
8. I   extra subject   (omit *they*)
9. C
10. I   missing verb   (could be *that was on sale are also on sale*)

EXERCISE (Skills 9–12)

1. I   missing subject   (could be *he was coming*)
2. C
3. I   extra subject   (omit *she*)
4. C
5. I   missing subject   (could be *we want*)
6. I   incorrect connector   (*whom* could be *which*)
7. I   incorrect connector   (*that* should be *what*)
8. I   missing connector   (could be *That he was*)
9. I   extra subject   (omit *it*)
10. C

TOEFL EXERCISE (Skills 9–12)

1. A	3. B	5. C	7. A	9. B
2. D	4. D	6. C	8. B	10. C

TOEFL REVIEW EXERCISE (Skills 1–12)

1. A	3. B	5. B	7. C	9. D
2. C	4. A	6. B	8. C	10. B

EXERCISE 13

1. C
2. I   (*sat* should be *sitting*)
3. C
4. I   (*purchasing* should be *purchased*)
5. I   (omit *who*)
6. I   (omit *were*)
7. I   (*placing* should be *placed*)
8. C
9. I   (*heard* should be *hearing*)
10. I   (illogical reduction)

EXERCISE 14

1. C
2. I   (*left* should be *leaving*)
3. C
4. C
5. I   (*selecting* should be *selected*)
6. I   (illogical reduction)
7. C
8. I   (*buy* should be *buying*)
9. C
10. C

EXERCISE (Skills 13–14)

1. I   (*was*)
2. C
3. C
4. I   (*needed* should be *needing*)
5. C
6. I   (omit *was*)
7. C
8. I   (*decided* should be *deciding*)
9. C
10. C

TOEFL EXERCISE (Skills 13–14)

1. A	3. B	5. D	7. B	9. B
2. A	4. B	6. D	8. D	10. B

TOEFL REVIEW EXERCISE (Skills 1–14)

1. D	3. D	5. D	7. C	9. A
2. A	4. B	6. B	8. D	10. D

EXERCISE 15

1. I   (should be *the new directories will*)
2. C
3. I   (should be *can new students*)
4. C
5. I   (should be *the plane can*)
6. C
7. C
8. I   (should be *has it*)
9. C
10. C

EXERCISE 16

1. C
2. I   (should be *is a big house*)
3. C
4. I   (should be *is the stream*)
5. C
6. I   (should be *the food was*)
7. I   (should be *can farmers*)
8. I   (should be *are the two trees*)
9. C
10. I   (should be *were a man and a woman*)

EXERCISE 17

1. I   (should be *did the boy write*)
2. C
3. C
4. I   (should be *have I gone*)
5. I   (should be *He went*)
6. I   (should be *has their secretary*)
7. C
8. I   (should be *did she leave*)
9. C
10. C

EXERCISE 18

1. C
2. I   (could be *you should*)
3. I   (should be *If he has*)
4. C
5. I   (should be *if you could*)
6. I   (should be *had he not*)
7. C
8. C
9. C
10. C

EXERCISE 19

1. C
2. I   (should be *were the other members*)
3. C
4. C
5. I   (should be *that the condition of these tires is*)
6. C
7. C
8. C
9. C
10. I   (*does he need* should be *he needs*)

EXERCISE (Skills 15–19)

1. I   (should be *land developers have*)
2. I   (should be *did I believe*)
3. C
4. C
5. I   (should be *are the offices*)
6. C
7. I   (should be *does it snow*)
8. C
9. C
10. I   (should be *Should he*)

TOEFL EXERCISE (Skills 15–19)

| 1. D | 3. A | 5. D | 7. C | 9. C |
| 2. A | 4. C | 6. B | 8. A | 10. B |

TOEFL REVIEW EXERCISE (Skills 1–19)

| 1. B | 3. A | 5. D | 7. C | 9. D |
| 2. D | 4. A | 6. C | 8. B | 10. B |

EXERCISE 20

1. C
2. I   (*have* should be *has*)
3. I   (*is* should be *are*)
4. C
5. C
6. I   (*have* should be *has*)
7. I   (*have* should be *has*)
8. C
9. I   (*are* should be *is*)
10. C

EXERCISE 21

1. C
2. I   (*was* should be *were*)
3. I   (*is* should be *are*)
4. I   (*are* should be *is*)
5. C
6. C
7. I   (*was* should be *were*)
8. I   (*was not changed* should be *were not changed*)
9. C
10. C

EXERCISE 22

1. C
2. I   (*is* should be *are*)
3. I   (*is* should be *are*)
4. C
5. I   (*do* should be *does*)
6. I   (*was so many* should be *were so many*)
7. I   (*has* should be *have*)
8. I   (*have* should be *has*)
9. C
10. I   (*was* should be *were*)

EXERCISE 23

1. I   (*admire* should be *admires*)
2. C
3. I   (*were* should be *was*)
4. I   (*are* should be *is*)
5. C
6. I   (*take* should be *takes*)
7. C
8. I   (*are* should be *is*)
9. C
10. I   (*have* should be *has*)

EXERCISE (Skills 20–23)

1. I   (*has* should be *have*)
2. I   (*was* should be *were*)
3. I   (*have* should be *has*)
4. C
5. I   (*was* should be *were*)
6. I   (*have* should be *has*)
7. C
8. I   (*have* should be *has*)
9. I   (*does* should be *do*)
10. I   (*have* should be *has*)

TOEFL EXERCISE (Skills 20–23)

1. B		6. C *have*
2. D		7. D *involves*
3. B *is*		8. A *were*
4. A *are trying*		9. B *is*
5. C *is*		10. B *are*

TOEFL REVIEW EXERCISE (Skills 1-23)

1. A
2. C
3. C
4. C
5. B
6. C *qualify*
7. B *was*
8. A *which*
9. A *a flag is*
10. B *documents*

EXERCISE 24

1. I (*in a restaurant* should be *a server*)
2. C
3. C
4. I (*finishing* should be *finished*)
5. C
6. C
7. I (*that we go by train* should be *taking the train*)
8. C
9. I (*those letters should be answered* should be *letters to answer*)
10. C

EXERCISE 25

1. I (*you can take* should be *take*)
2. C
3. I (*or* should be *nor*)
4. C
5. I (should be *but also to*)
6. I (*you wrote* should be *what you wrote*)
7. I (*or* should be *and*)
8. C
9. I (omit the second *you can graduate*)
10. I (omit *was it*)

EXERCISE 26

1. C
2. I (*to eat* should be *eating*)
3. C
4. I (should be *what you did yesterday*)
5. I (should be *the one we had before*)
6. C
7. C
8. I (should be *music in my country*)
9. I (should be *the one in the high school*)
10. I (*How to buy* should be *Buying*)

EXERCISE (Skills 24–26)

1. I (*dine* should be *dining*)
2. C
3. I (should be *what had come before*)
4. I (*or* should be *nor*)
5. I (*mediocrity* should be *mediocre*)
6. I (should be *but also in the afternoon*)
7. C
8. I (*helps you* should be *helpful*)
9. C
10. C

TOEFL EXERCISE (Skills 24–26)

1. D
2. C
3. D
4. B
5. D *water*
6. D *and*
7. D *the prison population in any other state*
8. D *philosophical*
9. B *to preserve*
10. D *or*

TOEFL REVIEW EXERCISE (Skills 1–26)

1. B
2. A
3. B
4. A
5. B
6. A
7. C *endowed*
8. B *is*
9. D *bone*
10. C *there are*

EXERCISE 27

1. I (*abundanter* should be *more abundant*)
2. C
3. I (*importantest* should be *important*)
4. C
5. I (*more long* should be *longer*)
6. I (*than* should be *of*)
7. C
8. I (omit *more*)
9. C
10. C

EXERCISE 28

1. C
2. I (*more* should be *the most*)
3. C
4. I (should be *more difficult than the second*)
5. I (*more* should be *most*)
6. C
7. I (*the best of* should be *better than the food in*)
8. C
9. C
10. I (*the longest of* should be *longer than*)

EXERCISE 29

1. I (should be *the harder*)
2. C
3. I (*the worst* should be *the worse*)
4. C
5. I (should be *the less the noise comes through*)
6. I (should be *The faster you run*)
7. C
8. C
9. I (*The earliest* should be *The earlier*)
10. I (should be *the better time you'll have*)

EXERCISE (Skills 27–29)

1. I (omit *more*)
2. I (should be *taller than the other tree*)
3. C
4. I (*the closest* should be *the closer*)
5. I (*bigger* should be *the biggest*)
6. I (*most hot* should be *hottest*)
7. C
8. C
9. C
10. C

TOEFL EXERCISE (Skills 27–29)

1. B
2. D
3. D
4. D *than*
5. D *the most*
6. C *in*
7. C *most controversial*
8. B *more*
9. B *milder*
10. A *The most widely*

TOEFL REVIEW EXERCISE (Skills 1–29)

1. A
2. D
3. D
4. D *than*
5. C *was*
6. A *are cactus plants*
7. A *who*
8. B *the largest*
9. B *is*
10. A *earlier*

EXERCISE 30

1. I   (*drunk* should be *drank*)
2. C
3. C
4. I   (*broke* should be *broken*)
5. I   (*completes* should be *completed*)
6. C
7. I   (*rode* should be *ridden*)
8. I   (*saw* should be *seen*)
9. C
10. I   (*respond* should be *responded*)

EXERCISE 31

1. I   (*eat* should be *eating*)
2. C
3. I   (*took* should be *taken*)
4. C
5. I   (*build* should be *building*)
6. C
7. I   (*submit* should be *submitted*)
8. I   (*merge* should be *merging*)
9. C
10. I   (*duplicates* should be *duplicated*)

EXERCISE 32

1. C
2. I   (*finishes* should be *finish*)
3. C
4. C
5. I   (*clicks* should be *click*)
6. C
7. C
8. I   (*liked* should be *like*)
9. C
10. I   (*has* should be *have*)

EXERCISE (Skills 30–32)

1. I   (*gave* should be *given*)
2. C
3. C
4. I   (*drunk* should be *drank*)
5. I   (*has* should be *have*)
6. C
7. C
8. I   (*has* should be *have*)
9. I   (*be* should be *been*)
10. I   (*rose* should be *risen*)

TOEFL EXERCISE (Skills 30–32)

1. C   *been*
2. C   *established*
3. C   *would have*
4. D   *coming*
5. B   *won*
6. D   *hold*
7. D   *been*
8. B   *made*
9. C   *have*
10. D   *tried*

TOEFL REVIEW EXERCISE (Skills 1–32)

1. A
2. D
3. C
4. B
5. D
6. B   *lowest*
7. A   *are*
8. B   *was ordered*
9. C   *nor*
10. C   *are*

EXERCISE 33

1. I   (*tell* should be *told*)
2. C
3. I   (*goes* should be *went*)
4. I   (*reads* should be *read*)
5. I   (*went* should be *goes*)
6. I   (*is* should be *was*)
7. C
8. I   (*goes* should be *went*)
9. I   (*intended* should be *intends*)
10. C

EXERCISE 34

1. C
2. I   (*had* should be *has*)
3. I   (*have* should be *had*)
4. C
5. I   (*finish* should be *had finished*)
6. C
7. C
8. I   (*were* should be *had been*, *had been* should be *was*)
9. I   (*have worked* should be *worked*)
10. C

EXERCISE 35

1. C
2. I   (*have* should be *had*)
3. I   (*have arrived* should be *arrived*)
4. C
5. C
6. I   (*have been* should be *were*)
7. I   (*are* should be *have been*)
8. I   (*votes* should be *voted*)
9. C
10. I   (*had* should be *have*)

EXERCISE 36

1. I   (*will* should be *would*)
2. C
3. I   (*will* should be *would*)
4. I   (*would* should be *will*)
5. C
6. I   (*has* should be *had*)
7. C
8. I   (*will* should be *would*)
9. I   (*would* should be *will*)
10. C

EXERCISE (Skills 33–36)

1. I   (*receives* should be *received*)
2. C
3. I   (*was* should be *is*)
4. I   (*have left* should be *left*)
5. I   (*would* should be *will*)
6. I   (*has* should be *had*)
7. C
8. C
9. I   (*will* should be *would*)
10. C

TOEFL EXERCISE (Skills 33–36)

1. C   *spent*
2. A   *became*
3. C   *would*
4. B   *served*
5. A   *has*
6. C   *will*
7. C   *lost*
8. D   *became*
9. D   *will potentially raise*
10. D   *is*

TOEFL REVIEW EXERCISE (Skills 1–36)

1. B
2. D
3. C
4. D
5. D   *measured*
6. C   *is*
7. B   *have been working*
8. A   *country is in*
9. B   *planted*
10. A   *Inasmuch as*

EXERCISE 37

1. I (*be* should be *been*)
2. C
3. I (*lending* should be *lent*)
4. I (*chose* should be *chosen*)
5. C
6. I (*playing* should be *played*)
7. C
8. C
9. I (*clean* should be *cleaned*)
10. C

EXERCISE 38

1. I (*parked* should be *was parked*)
2. C
3. I (*done* should be *been done*)
4. C
5. I (*sent* should be *been sent*)
6. I (*will plan* should be *will be planned*)
7. I (*left* should be *was left*)
8. I (*won* should be *was won*)
9. I (*made* should be *were made*)
10. I (*do not drive* should be *are not driven*)

EXERCISE (Skills 37–38)

1. I (*be* should be *been*)
2. I (*struck* should be *was struck*)
3. I (*feeds* should be *fed*)
4. C
5. I (*been leased* should be *leased*)
6. I (*placed* should be *been placed*)
7. I (*finishing* should be *finished*)
8. I (*pay* should be *are paid*)
9. I (*rode* should be *ridden*)
10. C

TOEFL EXERCISE (Skills 37–38)

1. C
2. D
3. B
4. D *covered*
5. C *be picked*
6. D *replaced*
7. B *added*
8. D *was lost*
9. A *have been*
10. D *had been protected*

TOEFL REVIEW EXERCISE (Skills 1–38)

1. A
2. B
3. B
4. B (omit *have*)
5. B *are sound waves*
6. D *but also*
7. C *more*
8. B *spent*
9. B *as*
10. C *should*

EXERCISE 39

1. I (*part* should be *parts*)
2. C
3. I (*way* should be *ways*)
4. I (*piece* should be *pieces*)
5. I (*days* should be *day*)
6. I (*days* should be *day*)
7. C
8. I (*dress* should be *dresses*)
9. I (*bills* should be *bill*)
10. C

EXERCISE 40

1. C
2. I (*amount* should be *number*)
3. C
4. C
5. I (*much* should be *many*)
6. C
7. I (*much* should be *many*)
8. I (*less pages* should be *fewer pages*)
9. C
10. I (*less* should be *fewer*)

EXERCISE 41

1. I (*is* should be *are*)
2. C
3. I (*is* should be *are*)
4. I (*were* should be *was*)
5. C
6. C
7. I (*were* should be *was*)
8. I (*teeth* should be *tooth*)
9. I (*fungi* should be *fungus*)
10. C

EXERCISE 42

1. I (*poets* should be *poems*)
2. C
3. I (*sculpture* should be *sculptor*)
4. I (*engineer* should be *engineering*)
5. C
6. C
7. I (*critics* should be *criticisms*)
8. C
9. I (*statistic* should be *statistician*)
10. I (*acting* should be *actor*)

EXERCISE (Skills 39–42)

1. I (*exam* should be *exams*)
2. I (*analyses* should be *analysis*)
3. I (*musical* should be *musician*)
4. C
5. I (*nurse* should be *nursing*)
6. C
7. C
8. C
9. I (*producer* should be *production*)
10. I (*excursion* should be *excursions*)

TOEFL EXERCISE (Skills 39–42)

1. D *respects*
2. D *year*
3. A *many*
4. D *phenomenon*
5. B *hero*
6. C *planet*
7. C *number*
8. A *investigations*
9. C *is used*
10. C *applicant*

TOEFL REVIEW EXERCISE (Skills 1–42)

1. B
2. D
3. C
4. C
5. D
6. A *is indicated*
7. A *Much*
8. C (omit *has*)
9. C *projects*
10. C *diseases*

EXERCISE 43

1. C
2. I (*I* should be *me*)
3. I (*they* should be *them*)
4. C
5. I (*her* should be *she*)
6. C
7. C
8. I (*them* should be *they*)
9. C
10. I (*her* should be *she*)

EXERCISE 44

1. I (*her* should be *hers*)
2. C
3. I (*theirs* should be *their*)
4. C
5. I (*theirs* should be *their*)
6. C
7. C
8. I (*our* should be *ours*)
9. C
10. I (*yours* should be *your*)

EXERCISE 45

1. I (*they* should be *he or she*)
2. C
3. I (*them* should be *it*)
4. I (*them* should be *it*)
5. C
6. C
7. I (*its* should be *their*)
8. I (*them* should be *it*)
9. C
10. I (*them* should be *him or her*)

EXERCISE (Skills 43–45)

1. I (*its* should be *their*)
2. I (*his* should be *he*)
3. C
4. I (*they cost* should be *it costs*)
5. C
6. C
7. I (*I* should be *me*)
8. I (*theirs* should be *their*)
9. C
10. I (*their* should be *his or her*)

TOEFL EXERCISE (Skills 43–45)

1. B *his*
2. C *they*
3. C *their*
4. C *he*
5. A *they cause*
6. B *he*
7. C *it*
8. C *their*
9. C *it*
10. D *them*

TOEFL REVIEW EXERCISE (Skills 1–45)

1. B
2. C
3. A
4. C *his (or her)*
5. C *number*
6. C *was praised*
7. D *a hydrogen bomb explodes*
8. B *forms*
9. D *becomes*
10. A *line*

EXERCISE 46

1. I (*pleasant* should be *pleasantly*)
2. C
3. I (*expensively* should be *expensive*)
4. C
5. C
6. I (*complete* should be *completely*)
7. I (*truly* should be *true*)
8. I (*incorrect* should be *incorrectly*)
9. I (*completely* should be *complete, terribly* should be *terrible*)
10. C

EXERCISE 47

1. I (*angrily* should be *angry*)
2. C
3. I (*sweetly* should be *sweet*)
4. C
5. C
6. C
7. I (*unhappily* should be *unhappy*)
8. I (*quick* should be *quickly*)
9. C
10. I (*difficultly* should be *difficult*)

EXERCISE 48

1. I (should be *a fantastic sale*)
2. C
3. C
4. I (should be *has carefully selected*)
5. C
6. I (should be *an expensive restaurant*)
7. C
8. I (should be *has subsequently altered them*)
9. I (should be *the intensive program*)
10. C

EXERCISE (Skills 46–48)

1. I (should be *the dim lights*)
2. I (*exhaustedly* should be *exhausted*)
3. I (*remarkable* should be *remarkably*)
4. I (*careful* should be *carefully*)
5. C
6. I (should be *had regularly attended*)
7. C
8. C
9. I (*certainly* should be *certain*)
10. I (should be *immediately put out*)

TOEFL EXERCISE (Skills 46–48)

1. D *unusual*
2. B *already adopted*
3. B *fatal*
4. D *heavily*
5. B *industrial*
6. C *lengthy*
7. C *reliably*
8. B *rapidly destroying*
9. D *district banks*
10. C *successfully*

TOEFL REVIEW EXERCISE (Skills 1–48)

1. C
2. D
3. B *its*
4. C *fewer*
5. B (omit *has*)
6. D *and*
7. C *recently*
8. D *are*
9. A *was given back*
10. D *equally exciting*

EXERCISE 49

1. C
2. I (*seasonally* should be *seasonal*)
3. I (*lately* should be *late*)
4. I (*terribly* should be *terrible*)
5. C
6. I (*negatively* should be *negative*)
7. C
8. I (*solitarily* should be *solitary*)
9. I (*regularly* should be *regular*)
10. I (*unhealthily* should be *unhealthy*)

EXERCISE 50

1. C
2. I (*alive* should be *live*)
3. I (*lone* should be *alone*)
4. I (*afraid* should be *frightened*)
5. C
6. C
7. C
8. I (*asleep* should be *sleeping*)
9. C
10. I (*an alone* should be *a lone*)

EXERCISE 51

1. I (*completing* should be *completed*)
2. C
3. I (*satisfied* should be *satisfying*)
4. I (*filling* should be *filled*)
5. C
6. C
7. I (*reducing* should be *reduced*)
8. I (*worked* should be *working*)
9. C
10. I (*unpaying* should be *unpaid*)

EXERCISE (Skills 49–51)

1. I (*appreciating* should be *appreciated*)
2. I (*damaging* should be *damaged*)
3. I (*alike* should be *like*)
4. I (*interested* should be *interesting*)
5. C
6. C
7. I (*asleep* should be *sleeping*)
8. C
9. C
10. I (*frightened* should be *frightening*)

TOEFL EXERCISE (Skills 49–51)

1. C *westerly*
2. A *annual*
3. C *great*
4. D *lone*
5. A *viewed*
6. B *sleep*
7. B *disputed*
8. C *nightly*
9. A *Signed*
10. D *lively*

TOEFL REVIEW EXERCISE (Skills 1–51)

1. A
2. C
3. B
4. A
5. D *involved*
6. B *evolved*
7. B *alike*
8. D *correct completion*
9. A *Using*
10. C *which was held*

EXERCISE 52

1. I (should be *a trip*)
2. C
3. I (should be *a memo*)
4. I (should be *a car*)
5. C
6. C
7. C
8. C
9. I (should be *A teacher*)
10. C

EXERCISE 53

1. I (should be *an hour*)
2. C
3. I (should be *an umbrella*)
4. C
5. I (should be *an unacceptable idea*)
6. C
7. I (should be *a uniform*)
8. C
9. I (should be *an honest mistake*)
10. I (should be *an account*)

EXERCISE 54

1. C
2. I (*pills* should be *pill*)
3. C
4. I (*members* should be *member*)
5. C
6. C
7. I (*subjects* should be *subject*)
8. C
9. I (*lessons* should be *lesson*)
10. I (*reasons* should be *reason*)

EXERCISE 55

1. I (should be *the Snake River*)
2. C
3. I (should be *the head*)
4. I (should be *the best grade*)
5. c
6. I (should be *the most beautiful girl*)
7. C
8. C
9. I (should be *the center*)
10. I (should be *the Lincoln Memorial*)

EXERCISE (Skills 52–55)

1. I (should be *took money*, should be *a sweater*)
2. C
3. C
4. I (should be *the room*, should be *plant*)
5. I (should be *a law*)
6. I (should be *the laboratory manual*, should be *the next class*)
7. I (*mistake* should be *mistakes*, should be *an honest effort*)
8. I (*indications* should be *indication*)
9. C
10. I (should be *a group tour*, should be *a fee*, should be *the first of the month*)

TOEFL EXERCISE (Skills 52–55)

1. D (omit *a*)
2. C *a plant*
3. B *the heart*
4. D *a*
5. C *the*
6. A *Radar*
7. D *the federal government*
8. A *A*
9. C *other*
10. D *the Army*

TOEFL REVIEW EXERCISE (Skills 1–55)

1. D
2. B
3. A
4. D *tragedies*
5. B *used*
6. C *number*
7. A *their*
8. C *made*
9. D *layer*
10. D *graduates*

EXERCISE 56

1. C
2. I (should be *rely on*)
3. C
4. I (should be *bring up*)
5. I (should be *consult with*)
6. C
7. I (should be *approve of*)
8. C
9. I (should be *result in*)
10. C

EXERCISE 57

1. I (should be *deal with*)
2. C
3. I (should be *sided with*)
4. I (should be *turned down*)
5. I (should be *depend on*)
6. I (should be *looked after*)
7. C
8. I (should be *beware of*)
9. C
10. I (should be *blamed his brother for*)

EXERCISE (Skills 56–57)

1. C
2. I (should be *forgive you for*)
3. I (should be *excels in*)
4. C
5. I (should be *reminds me of*)
6. C
7. C
8. I (should be *interfere with*)
9. I (should be *waited for*)
10. I (should be *laughs at*, should be *looks at*)

TOEFL EXERCISE (Skills 56–57)

1. C *in*
2. A *occurrence of edema*
3. C *of*
4. A *According to legend*
5. B *to*
6. D *as*
7. B *means of strings*
8. D *close to Fort Sumner*
9. D *according to*
10. D *with*

TOEFL REVIEW EXERCISE (Skills 1–57)

1. C
2. A
3. B
4. B *on*
5. D *bulletin*
6. C *became*
7. C *and*
8. A *will Antarctic icebergs*
9. A *the largest*
10. D *effect of water*

EXERCISE 58

1. I (*did* should be *made*)
2. C
3. I (*makes* should be *does*)
4. I (*did* should be *made*)
5. C
6. C
7. C
8. I (*do* should be *make*)
9. I (*makes* should be *does*)
10. C

EXERCISE 59

1. I (*like* should be *alike*)
2. C
3. I (*Alike* should be *Like*)
4. C
5. I (*alike* should be *like*)
6. C
7. C
8. I (*alike* should be *like*)
9. C
10. C

EXERCISE 60

1. C
2. I (*the another* should be *another*)
3. C
4. I (*others* should be *other*)
5. C
6. C
7. C
8. I (*a other* should be *another*)
9. C
10. I (*cartridges* should be *cartridge*)

EXERCISE (Skills 58–60)

1. C
2. I (*does* should be *makes*)
3. C
4. I (*routes* should be *route*)
5. I (*like* should be *alike*)
6. C

7. C
8. I (*doing* should be *making*)
9. I (*did* should be *made*)
10. I (*others* should be *other*)

TOEFL EXERCISE (Skills 58–60)

1. B *alike*
2. A *Another*
3. D *make*
4. A *Unlike*
5. C *other*
6. A *Like*
7. B *done*
8. D *alternative*
9. C *like*
10. A *Another*

TOEFL REVIEW EXERCISE (Skills 1–60)

1. A
2. A
3. D *other*
4. C *known*
5. C *taken*
6. B *piece*
7. A *like*
8. B *fans*
9. C *romance*
10. D *of*

STRUCTURE POST-TEST (Paper)

1. A
2. D
3. A
4. D
5. C
6. C
7. C
8. B
9. B
10. D
11. B
12. D
13. C
14. A
15. C
16. B *travel*
17. B *has*
18. C *types*
19. C *to verify*
20. A *were*
21. D *recorded*
22. A *unlike*
23. D (omit *a*)
24. A *Many*
25. C *it was*
26. B *other*
27. C *than*
28. B *recently*
29. D (omit *it was built*)
30. B *have there*
31. A *the mobility*
32. B *as*
33. D *battle fatigue*
34. C *a damaged*
35. C *gravitational*
36. D *are not determined*
37. B *the revolution*
38. B *such as*
39. D *electricity*
40. B *made*

STRUCTURE POST-TEST (Computer)

1. 1 *than*
2. 3 *became*
3. 1
4. 2 *rode*
5. 3 *their*
6. 3
7. 3 *include*
8. 1 *A*
9. 1 *Like*
10. 2
11. 3 *were*
12. 4 *the cells of smaller*
13. 3
14. 4 *the*
15. 3 *were issued*
16. 2
17. 1 *alone*
18. 4
19. 3 *suitable*
20. 2 *nucleus*

READING

READING DIAGNOSTIC PRE-TEST (Paper)

1. C
2. B
3. A
4. C
5. A
6. B
7. D
8. A
9. B
10. B
11. B
12. A
13. D
14. C
15. A
16. D
17. B
18. C
19. D
20. D
21. C
22. B
23. A
24. C
25. D
26. D
27. B
28. B
29. A
30. C
31. C
32. D
33. A
34. B
35. A
36. D
37. B
38. A
39. D
40. C
41. B
42. C
43. B
44. A
45. B
46. A
47. A
48. B
49. D
50. D

DIAGNOSTIC PRE-TEST (Computer)

1. 4	16. *unattached*	31. C
2. *battle*	17. 3	32. P2
3. 1	18. *UV radiation*	33. 4
4. 1	19. 1	34. 1
5. 3	20. A	35. 2
6. P2, S3	21. P3, S6	36. 4
7. 2	22. 2	37. 1
8. *fought*	23. 1	38. 3
9. 4	24. *uncomplicated*	39. *publications*
10. C	25. 3	40. 2
11. P4	26. 4	41. E
12. 2	27. P4, S3	42. P4, S4
13. 4	28. 2	43. *numerous*
14. 3	29. 4	44. P4
15. C	30. 4	

TOEFL EXERCISE 1

1. B	3. B	5. D	7. C	9. C
2. C	4. A	6. B	8. A	

TOEFL EXERCISE 2

1. B	3. B	5. A
2. P3	4. P3	6. P2

TOEFL EXERCISE (Skills 1–2)

1. C	3. C	5. P2	7. D	9. P1
2. B	4. B	6. P3	8. A	10. P3

TOEFL EXERCISE 3

1. C	4. C	7. C	10. B
2. B	5. D	8. B	11. D
3. D	6. A	9. B	

TOEFL EXERCISE 4

1. A	3. B	5. D
2. D	4. D	6. A

TOEFL EXERCISE 5

1. C	3. A	5. B
2. *farmers*	4. *tourists*	6. *industrial average*

TOEFL EXERCISE (Skills 3–5)

1. B	6. D	12. B
2. *George Washington*	7. D	13. *Camp David*
3. D	8. B	14. C
4. B	9. *tar*	15. B
5. C	10. C	16. C
	11. D	17. C

TOEFL REVIEW EXERCISE (Skills 1–5)

1. C	8. D	15. *continents*
2. D	9. A	16. D
3. B	10. A	17. D
4. A	11. A	18. D
5. *his speech*	12. P2	19. P2
6. B	13. C	
7. C	14. B	

TOEFL EXERCISE 6

1. A	3. D	5. B	7. A
2. C	4. D	6. D	8. B

TOEFL EXERCISE 7

1. A	3. C	5. C
2. C	4. B	6. A

TOEFL EXERCISE (Skills 6–7)

1. A	4. A	7. A	10. C
2. D	5. B	8. C	11. B
3. A	6. B	9. C	12. A

TOEFL REVIEW EXERCISE (Skills 1–7)

1. D	13. *mood elevation*
2. *Mason-Dixon Line*	14. C
3. A	15. A
4. B	16. B
5. C	17. *medium (of television)*
6. A	18. B
7. P2	19. D
8. B	20. D
9. B	21. A
10. D	22. A
11. A	23. P2
12. B	

TOEFL EXERCISE 8

1. D	3. *set free*	5. D	7. C
2. D	4. C	6. C	8. *phenomenon*

TOEFL EXERCISE 9

1. C	4. B	7. A	10. B
2. D	5. *turned*	8. C	
3. A	6. C	9. D	

TOEFL EXERCISE 10

1. D	3. B	5. *discern*	7. C
2. *globular*	4. *mortal*	6. A	8. D

TOEFL EXERCISE 11

1. C	3. B	5. C	7. *line*
2. D	4. A	6. B	

TOEFL EXERCISE (Skills 8–11)

1. *solely*	7. D	13. *line*	19. *work*
2. D	8. C	14. D	20. *keep*
3. C	9. D	15. C	21. A
4. B	10. *teeth*	16. C	
5. *seeped*	11. C	17. *clear*	
6. *die*	12. A	18. B	

TOEFL REVIEW EXERCISE (Skills 1–11)

1. D	14. A
2. A	15. C
3. C	16. B
4. D	17. B
5. B	18. D
6. *manner of walking*	19. D
7. C	20. C
8. B	21. B
9. P3	22. D
10. C	23. *Congress*
11. D	24. C
12. C	25. B
13. *deal*	

TOEFL EXERCISE 12

1. B	4. D	7. P2, S3	10. P2, S2
2. P1, S3	5. A	8. A	
3. P1, S5	6. P2, S2	9. C	

TOEFL EXERCISE 13

1. A	3. C	5. D	7. C	9. B
2. D	4. D	6. A	8. A	

TOEFL EXERCISE 14

1. B	3. B	5. D	7. C
2. D	4. D	6. D	

TOEFL EXERCISE (Skills 12–14)

1. D	6. P3, S3	11. D	16. D
2. A	7. D	12. B	17. D
3. C	8. D	13. B	18. B
4. A	9. B	14. B	
5. E	10. B	15. P1, S2	

TOEFL REVIEW EXERCISE (Skills 1–14)

1. B	16. C
2. A	17. B
3. C	18. C
4. B	19. B
5. Copland	20. C
6. D	21. P1
7. gamut	22. B
8. P1, S2	23. B
9. P1, S4	24. C
10. D	25. funding
11. C	26. canal commission
12. A	27. C
13. D	28. C
14. somewhat	29. P3
15. C	30. B

READING POST-TEST (Paper)

1. D	11. B	21. D	31. C	41. C
2. C	12. D	22. A	32. A	42. D
3. B	13. C	23. C	33. B	43. C
4. B	14. A	24. A	34. C	44. A
5. B	15. B	25. C	35. B	45. D
6. A	16. D	26. B	36. B	46. B
7. C	17. B	27. D	37. A	47. A
8. D	18. C	28. B	38. B	48. C
9. B	19. A	29. A	39. D	49. D
10. D	20. D	30. B	40. A	50. B

READING POST-TEST (Computer)

1. 2	16. newspapers	30. P3, S3
2. 3	and magazines	31. 3
3. 1	17. 3	32. C
4. 4	18. information	33. P2
5. 3	19. 1	34. 2
6. mixed breed	20. P4, S3	35. 3
7. 2	21. P3	36. 2
8. Experts	22. 4	37. diamond
9. 4	23. 1	38. P2, S5
10. P3, S9	24. 3	39. 3
11. 4	25. 2	40. 4
12. 3	26. B	41. 1
13. 3	27. 1	42. 2
14. 1	28. packages	43. 4
15. B	29. 4	44. P3

WRITING

EXERCISE 4

1. (A) employee	[L2]	[L9]		
(B) worker	[L3]			
2. (A) priorities	[L4]	[L6]	[L8]	
(B) them	[L7]			
3. (A) manner	[L10]			
style	[L9]			
(B) It	[L12]			

4. (A) First of all	[L2]	
(B) S5	[L7–10]	
5. (A) for example	[L4]	
(B) for instance	[L10]	
(C) i.e.	[L13]	

EXERCISE 7A

1. I	*meaning*	missing verb
2. I	When you *found*	extra subordinate clause connector
3. C	*reaction was*	
4. I	*leaves*	missing subject
5. I	*indication*	missing verb
6. C	*no one has collected*	
7. I	Why *committee met*	extra subordinate clause connector
8. I	*cannot submit*	missing subject
9. I	*refusal*	missing verb
10. C	*idea shocked*	
11. I	Since *each was*	extra subordinate clause connector
12. I		missing subject and verb
13. C	*discussion has been scheduled*	
14. I	*situation*	missing verb
15. I	that *books were*	extra subordinate clause connector
16. C	*dean decided*	
17. I		missing subject and verb
18. I	If *outcome had been*	extra subordinate clause connector
19. C	*results have been posted*	
20. I	What *students were*	extra subordinate clause connector

EXERCISE 7B

1. I	*researcher completed* , *results were*
2. C	*meeting did not take place* , so *it will have*
3. I	*I expected* , however *it was*
4. C	*sales were* ; as a result, *manager has been given*
5. I	*We finished* and then *we submitted*
6. C	*employees come* , but *this does not seem*
7. C	*team won* . Next, *it will compete*
8. I	*lightbulb has burned out* ☐ *I need*
9. I	*manager is hiring* , then *we will not have*
10. C	*chapter was* , yet *I finished*
11. I	*You must turn in* , otherwise *grade will be lowered*
12. C	*decision has not yet been made* . Therefore, *we must wait*
13. I	Afterwards *construction was completed* , *traffic moved*
14. C	*course requires* ; in contrast, *course required*
15. I	*flight is scheduled* , *we must head*
16. C	*building has* ; *tower is*
17. C	*We have* , or *we will have*
18. C	*I have worked* ; finally, *I will be*
19. I	*bookstore is* ☐ *we should go*
20. I	*It has been raining* , consequently, *streets are*

EXERCISE 7C

1. I *tickets (that I ordered) they will be delivered*
2. C *(How I will be able to get all this work done) is*
3. C *excuse (that you gave me) was*
4. I *(What the lecturer said) it was*
5. I *place (where we agreed to meet) it was*
6. C *person (whose friendship I cherish most) is*
7. I *(Who is responsible for the accident) it is*
8. I *(That the story is on the front page of the paper) it is*
9. I *contractor (who painted the house) he did*
10. C *(Why she was the one) (who got the job) is*
11. I *(What happened just before our arrival) it is*
12. C *clothes (that we purchased at the sale) were*
13. C *room (in which the seminar will be held) is*
14. I *(What will happen to her next) it is (what concerns me the most)*
15. C *receptionist (who regularly answers the phone) is*
16. I *(What the manager wrote in the report) it was*
17. I *classmate (who presented the report) he did*
18. C *(How such a thing could happen) is*
19. C *situation (in which I found myself) was (in which all of the facts are not known)*
20. I *(Why he has done) (what I told him not to do with the money) (that I gave him) it is*

EXERCISE 7 (A-C)

1. What you need to do before going on a **vacation** (7C) **is** to decide where you will go on your vacation. You may decide to go to a quiet place with a quiet and natural **setting**; (7B) **instead** you may decide to go to a big city with a fast-paced life. Each of these types of vacation (7A) **has something** to offer. (3 errors)

2. The reasons that it can be a good idea to go to a quiet and natural location for a **vacation** (7C) **are** numerous. First of all, a vacation in a natural setting **allows** (7A) you to relax and slow down the pace of your life for a while. Instead of hurrying from place to place as you are used to **doing** (7A), **you** can spend your time doing nothing more than enjoying the beauty of the location. Then, **after** (7A) **you are** thoroughly relaxed, what you **can do** (7C) **is** to take part in outdoor activities such as hiking or swimming. All of this will leave you completely relaxed and free of stress by the end of your vacation. (5 errors)

3. It can be nice to go to a quiet and natural spot for a **vacation**; (7B) **however,** it can also be quite an adventure to go to a big and fast-paced city for a vacation. The main reason that it can be a good idea to take a vacation in a big **city** (7C) **is** to take part in so many activities that are unavailable in your hometown. On a big city vacation, numerous cultural events that might not be available in your hometown, such as theatrical performances, concerts, and art and museum **exhibits,** (7C) **are** available. On a big city vacation, (7A) **you will also have** access to some of the world's finest restaurants and shopping. After your big city vacation has **ended** (7A), **you** will have a whole range of new experiences that are not part of your daily life. (5 errors)

4. For me, the type of vacation that I decide to **take** (7C) **depends** on my life prior to the vacation. I work as a legal assistant in a law **office**; (7B) **this** job is often repetitious and dull but is sometimes quite frantic just prior to a major case. After a slow and boring period of **work** (7A), **all** I want is to head to a fast-paced vacation in a big city. However, if my **job** (7A) **has been** frantic and busy prior to my vacation, **then** (7A) **I want** to head to a quiet and beautiful place where I can relax. Thus, I enjoy different types of **vacations;** (7B) **the type** of vacation depends on the pace of my life before the vacation. (6 errors)

EXERCISE 8A

1. Something very important for students to decide as they near the end of their studies **is** (23) whether **they should** (15) work for another company or to go into business for themselves. As a university student, this decision about my future **is** (20) one that I face soon myself. To me, each of these positions **has** (23) clear advantages, in particular depending on the stage of your career. (4 errors)

2. There **are** (22) numerous advantages to working for another company, particularly early in your career. One of the advantages **is** (21) that working in someone else's company **provides** (20) a situation with the security of a regular paycheck and less responsibility than you would have **were you** (18) to be the owner of the company. Also, not until you start your own business **do you need** (17) to come up with the finances to back the company. Thus, all of this **indicates** (21) that it is better to work for other people early in your career while you are gaining the knowledge and experience you need to start your own company. (6 errors)

3. Then, later in your career, it may be advantageous for you to go into business for yourself. The main reason for going into business for yourself **is** (20) that in your own company you are able to decide on what direction **you want** (15) your company to go. However, only when you have gained enough knowledge and experience **is it** (22) a good idea to go into business for yourself. This is when **you will** (15) be ready to deal with the responsibility, pressure, and financial needs of owning a company. (4 errors)

4. Nothing **is** (23) more important to me than having my own company one day. However, what seems very clear to me now is that beginning my career working in someone else's company **is** (20) best. In this situation, not only **can I** (17) work with more security and less pressure, but I can also build up my financial resources and learn from others. Then, **should I** (18) manage to gain enough experience, knowledge, and confidence and build up my financial resources, I hope eventually to open my own company, where **I can** (15) determine exactly how **I would** (15) like the company to operate. (6 errors)

EXERCISE 8B

1. I am a university student, and I am studying in the university for a number of reasons. Of course, one of my reasons for going to school, studying hard, and **obtaining** (24) a university degree is to succeed financially; the more money I make, **the better it will be** (29) for me. However, financial success is not my **most important** (27) reason for going to the university. Instead, I am going to the university for a much **broader** (27) reason than that: I believe that a university education will give me a much **richer** (24) and better life, not just in a financial way. (5 errors)

2. One way that a university education makes your life **more enjoyable** (27) is to give you the opportunity to have a career that you really desire and **appreciate** (24). Having a career that you like is much better than **having a job** (26) that just pays the bills. I, for exam-

ple, am studying to be a marine biologist. I will have the **best** (28) career for me; I will be rewarded not only in terms of money **but also** (25) in terms of enjoyment of my career. (5 errors)

3. Another way that a university education can enrich your life is to provide a **broader** (27) knowledge, **understanding** (24), and appreciation of the world around you than you already have. It provides you with an understanding of both the history of your own culture and **the influence of** (25) history on the present. It also provides you with an understanding of other cultures and shows you that other cultures are neither exactly the same as nor **are they** (25) completely different from your own culture. Finally, it provides you with an understanding of the universe around you and **shows** (24) you how the universe functions. (5 errors)

4. Thus, in getting a university education, I can say that financial success is certainly one goal that I have. However, the goal of financial success is not as important as **another goal that I have** (26). My primary goal in getting a university education is the goal of achieving a **fuller** (27) life, certainly one with financial security but more importantly one that is rewarding both in terms of professional opportunities **and** (25) in terms of awareness and understanding of life around me. The closer I get to achieving this goal, **the happier I will be** (29). (4 errors)

EXERCISE 8C

1. When something unexpected happens, different people **react** (33) in a variety of ways. I wish I could **react** (32) calmly to unexpected situations. However, unfortunately, I usually react with panic. The following example shows my usual reaction to situations when I have **been** (30) completely unprepared for them. (3 errors)

2. This example of the way that I react to unexpected situations **occurred** (35) in history class last week. The professor had told us that we **would** (36) be covering the material in Chapters 10 through 12 in class on Thursday. By the time I arrived in class, I **had** (34) read all of the assigned material, and I understood most of what I had **studied** (30). While I was **relaxing** (31) in my chair at the beginning of class, the professor **announced** (36) that there would be a pop quiz on the material in the assigned chapters. I was **prepared** (38) on the material because I **had** (34) studied all of it thoroughly before class. (8 errors)

3. However, I was **faced** (31) with an unexpected situation, and I do not react well to unexpected situations. Instead of feeling relaxed at the announcement of the unexpected quiz because I was so prepared, I was completely **filled** (37) with anxiety by the situation. As the professor was **writing** (31) the questions on the board, I **became** (33) more and more nervous. I was unable to think clearly, and I knew that I would **do** (32) a bad job on the quiz because this **is** (33) what always happens to me when I feel panic. As I stared at the questions on the board, I **was** (34) unable to think of the correct answers. It was as if I had not **prepared** (30) at all for class. Then, the professor collected the papers from the class, including my basically blank piece of paper. Just after the papers had been **collected** (38), the answers to all the questions came to me. (9 errors)

4. You can **see** (32) from this example that my usual reaction to something unexpected is to panic. In the future, I **hope** (36) that I will learn to react more calmly, but up to now I **have** (34) not learned to react this way. On the basis of my past behavior, however, it

seems that I currently **have** (33) a stronger tendency to react with panic than with calm. (4 errors)

EXERCISE 8D

1. I was not a very good **athlete** (42) in high school, but I wanted with all of **my** (44) heart to be on the football team. My desire to be on the team had little to do with athletics and was perhaps not for the best of reasons; the strong **stimulus** (41) for **me** (43) to make the team was that team members were well-known in the school and **they** (45) became very popular. This desire to be on the football team in high school, and the fact that through hard **work** (42) I managed to accomplish something that I wanted so much, even if **it** (43) was something petty, turned out to be the single most valuable **experience** (39) of my years in high school. (8 errors)

2. I had to work very hard to make the football team in high school, and for some time this seemed like an impossible **goal** (39). A large **number** (40) of students in my school, more than a hundred and fifty of them, spent many of **their** (44) afternoons trying out for a team with **fewer** (40) than forty positions. After a lot of hard work on my part, and after I had demonstrated to the coaches that **they** (45) could count on me to keep going long after everyone was exhausted, I managed to make the team as a secondary **player** (42). Even with so **much** (40) effort, I was never going to be a sports **phenomenon** (41) or even a member of the first team, but I did accomplish my goal of making the team. (8 errors)

3. The valuable lesson that I learned through this experience was not the joy of **competition** (42) or the **many** (40) benefits of teamwork, several **lessons** (39) very commonly associated with participation in team sports. Instead, the valuable lesson that I learned was that hard work and determination could be very important in helping **me** (43) accomplish each **goal** (39) that I want to reach. Even if others have more talent, I can work harder than **they do** (45) and still perhaps find **success** (42) where **the** (43) do not. (8 errors)

EXERCISE 8E

1. I understand that it seems **important** (47) for (54) **students** to prepare **their assignments early** (48) rather than procrastinate in getting assignments done. However, although I understand this **clearly** (46), I always seem to wait until the **final** (46) minute to get **assigned** (51) projects done. There are two reasons why I **regularly** (46) procrastinate on my **academic assignments** (48) in spite of the fact that this is not **the** (55) best way to get my work done. (9 errors)

2. One reason that I tend to be **an** (53) eternal procrastinator is that I work much more **efficiently** (46) under pressure than I do when I am not under pressure. For example, I can accomplish so much more in a two-hour period when I have a **definite** (46) deadline in two hours than I can during **a like** (50) period without the pressure of a **strict deadline** (48). Without a deadline, the two-hour period seems to fly by with **minimal** (46) accomplishment, but with **a** (53) **rapidly** (46) **approaching** (51) deadline I seem quite **capable** (47) of making every minute of the two-hour period count. (10 errors)

3. Another reason that I tend to procrastinate is that if I start preparing early, it **generally takes** (48) more of my time. If, for example, I have **a paper** (52) due in six weeks, I can start working on the paper now and work on it on a **daily** (49) basis, and that paper will

take up a lot of my time and energy during the **following** (51) six weeks. However, if I wait to begin work on the paper until **the week** (52) before it is due, I have to go off some place where I can be **alone** (50) and spend all of my time and energy that week on the paper, but it will only take one week of my **valuable time** (48) and not six weeks. (7 errors)

4.   In summary, it seems that I always wait until the last minute to complete (54) **assignments** because I am afraid that I will waste too much time by starting early. It would be **a good idea** (52), however, for me to make **an** (53) effort to get work done **efficiently** (46) and early so that I do not always have to feel **tense** (47) about getting work done at **the** (55) last minute. (6 errors)

EXERCISE 8F

1.   Some people **do** (58) their best to avoid confrontations, while **other** (60) people often seem to get **involved in** (57) confrontations. There can be problems with either type of behavior; thus, I always try to be **like** (59) people at either extreme and remain moderate in my approach **to** (56) confrontation. (5 errors)

2.   To some people, confrontation should be avoided **at** (56) all costs. These people will **do** (58) nothing even after something terribly wrong has happened to them. They, for example, stay silent when they are pushed around or when they are **blamed for** (57) something they did not do. Unfortunately, it is quite probable that others will take advantage **of** (56) people **like** (59) this. Thus, people who avoid confrontations will find that they do not get as much **out of** (57) **life** as they deserve because **others** (60) always take advantage of them. (7 errors)

3.   **Like** (59) people who avoid confrontations, **other** (60) individuals go to the opposite extreme; they take part **in** (56) confrontations too easily. When something small happens accidentally, they become enraged and **make** (58) a big deal of it as if they had been terribly wronged. Perhaps, for example, someone accidentally bumps **into** (56) them or mistakenly says something offensive; in this type of situation, they create a serious confrontation. While it is true that other people will try hard not to provoke this type of person, it is also true that **others** (60) will **make** (58) an effort to avoid spending much time in the company of such a person. Thus, people who get involved in confrontations easily will find it hard to develop close friendships and relationships with **others** (60). (8 errors)

4.   I try to **do** (58) the right thing by avoiding either extreme type of behavior. I always try to behave in a **like** (59) manner, without overreacting or underreacting. If someone offends me **by** (56) chance, I try to **brush it off** (57) and **keep on** (56) going as if nothing had **happened to** (57) me. If someone intentionally succeeds **in** (56) bothering me, however, I try to react without anger but with a reaction that shows that behavior **like** (59) this is unacceptable. In this way, I do not **make** (58) the mistake of wasting time on unimportant situations, but I prevent **other** (60) instances of bad behavior toward me **from** (56) recurring. (11 errors)

LISTENING COMPLETE TEST (Paper)

1. B	11. C	21. C	31. A	41. C
2. A	12. A	22. A	32. C	42. A
3. D	13. A	23. A	33. D	43. C
4. B	14. D	24. D	34. C	44. B
5. C	15. A	25. D	35. B	45. A
6. C	16. C	26. B	36. B	46. D
7. D	17. B	27. B	37. A	47. A
8. A	18. B	28. D	38. D	48. D
9. B	19. B	29. C	39. C	49. D
10. D	20. D	30. D	40. D	50. C

STRUCTURE COMPLETE TEST (Paper)

1. C	9. D	17. C	25. D	33. A
2. D	10. B	18. A	26. C	34. B
3. B	11. C	19. C	27. D	35. C
4. A	12. A	20. C	28. C	36. C
5. B	13. D	21. D	29. A	37. A
6. C	14. C	22. D	30. D	38. A
7. A	15. B	23. A	31. B	39. C
8. A	16. A	24. B	32. C	40. C

READING COMPLETE TEST (Paper)

1. C	11. B	21. C	31. B	41. B
2. D	12. B	22. D	32. A	42. B
3. A	13. D	23. A	33. C	43. C
4. A	14. A	24. A	34. D	44. A
5. B	15. C	25. B	35. A	45. D
6. C	16. C	26. D	36. D	46. B
7. D	17. A	27. A	37. C	47. D
8. B	18. B	28. D	38. B	48. C
9. A	19. D	29. A	39. D	49. A
10. D	20. B	30. D	40. D	50. C

LISTENING COMPLETE TEST (Computer)

1. 4	8. 3	15. 3	22. 3
2. 4	9. 1	16. 2	23. 1, 4
3. 2	10. 3	17. 3	24. 1, 3
4. 1	11. 2	18. 1	25. 4
5. 3	12. 4	19. 4	
6. 4	13. 4	20. B	
7. 2	14. 1	21. 1, 4	

26. *Unfaceted: cabochon*
Faceted only on the top: rose
Faceted on the top and bottom:brilliant
27. 1, 3
28. *Cabochon*
Table
Rose
Brilliant
29. 3
30. 2

STRUCTURE COMPLETE TEST (Computer)

1. 3	*colors*	11. 4	*other*
2. 4	*existed*	12. 2	
3. 1		13. 2	*is*
4. 4	*infected*	14. 3	*turns*
5. 1	*its*	15. 1	
6. 1		16. 2	*engineering*
7. 3	*snakes*	17. 4	
8. 2	*uses*	18. 4	*in*
9. 3		19. 3	*printing*
10. 1	*readily*	20. 4	

READING COMPLETE TEST (Computer)

1. 3	16. 1	31. 3
2. 1	17. E	32. D
3. 2	18. 3	33. 2
4. P1, S4	19. *plants*	34. 3
5. *attack*	20. 3	35. 2
6. 2	21. P3, S4	36. 4
7. 2	22. 1	37. 3
8. P2, S6	23. 3	38. 3
9. D	24. 3	39. 2
10. 1	25. D	40. 1
11. P3	26. 4	41. A
12. 1	27. 2	42. P4, S3
13. 4	28. hue	43. P2
14. 3	29. P2, S4	44. 3
15. 2	30. 1	

APPENDIXES

EXERCISE A1

1. D	3. F	5. C
2. B	4. E	6. A

EXERCISE A2

1. D	3. B	5. A
2. E	4. C	6. F

EXERCISE A3

1. E	3. A	5. B
2. C	4. F	6. D

EXERCISE A4

1. F	3. B	5. C
2. A	4. E	6. D

EXERCISE A5

1. E	3. F	5. C
2. B	4. A	6. D

EXERCISE A6

1. D	3. C	5. B
2. E	4. A	6. F

EXERCISE A7

1. B	3. F	5. A
2. C	4. E	6. D

EXERCISE A8

1. D	3. F	5. B
2. C	4. A	6. E

EXERCISE A9

1. E	3. C	5. A
2. D	4. F	6. B

EXERCISE A10

1. F	3. B	5. C	7. I	9. A
2. E	4. H	6. G	8. D	

EXERCISE B1

1. D	3. A	5. E	7. B	9. C
2. I	4. G	6. J	8. F	10. H

EXERCISE B2

1. G	3. H	5. A	7. E	9. C
2. B	4. D	6. J	8. F	10. I

EXERCISE B3

1. B	3. D	5. A	7. J	9. I
2. F	4. H	6. E	8. G	10. C

EXERCISE B4

1. E	3. B	5. A	7. C	9. F
2. G	4. I	6. J	8. H	10. D

EXERCISE B5

1. D	3. A	5. C	7. H	9. B
2. G	4. E	6. J	8. F	10. I

EXERCISE C1

1. F	4. I	7. A	10. B
2. D	5. J	8. L	11. G
3. H	6. C	9. K	12. E

EXERCISE C2

1. L	4. I	7. K	10. F
2. B	5. E	8. G	11. A
3. H	6. D	9. C	12. J

EXERCISE C3

1. B	4. I	7. J	10. G
2. A	5. D	8. K	11. L
3. E	6. F	9. C	12. H

EXERCISE C4

1. A	4. K	7. J	10. B
2. H	5. G	8. D	11. F
3. C	6. E	9. L	12. I

EXERCISE D1

1. of; as; for; without
2. of; from; in; to; in
3. of; in; of
4. over; in; of
5. on; of; by; in; in; of

EXERCISE D2

1. of; to; of; of; due to
2. at; by; of; with; such as
3. of; under; of; under; upon; at; of; of
4. with; by; of; with; around; besides
5. through; by; during; by; on; on; by; up; across; down; to

EXERCISE D3

1. during; from; of; to; within
2. by; at; of; in; as
3. at; along; to; on
4. past; from; of; to; of; from; for
5. like; of; through; for; of; in; in; on; of; in; since; in; during; in

EXERCISE E1

(There may be more than one possible answer.)

1. membership
2. kindness
3. reality
4. movement
5. humanity
6. election
7. breakage
8. intelligence
9. alcoholism
10. permanence
11. mileage
12. confusion
13. leadership
14. suddenness
15. improvement
16. equality

EXERCISE E2

1. teacher
2. typist
3. beautician
4. idealist
5. inventor
6. clinician
7. specialist
8. rancher
9. perfectionist
10. programmer
11. electrician
12. investor
13. builder
14. naturalist
15. advisor
16. mathematician

EXERCISE E3

(There may be more than one possible answer.)

1. heartless
2. natural
3. athletic
4. mysterious
5. helpful/less
6. impressive
7. intelligent
8. courageous
9. useful/less
10. enthusiastic
11. motionless
12. traditional
13. changeable
14. permanent
15. attractive

EXERCISE E4

(There may be more than one possible answer.)

1. darken
2. finalize
3. justify
4. separate
5. shorten
6. intensify
7. investigate
8. industrialize
9. differentiate
10. identify
11. lighten
12. glamourize
13. personify
14. sweeten
15. liberalize
16. demonstrate

EXERCISE E5

1. finally
2. carefully
3. obviously
4. recently
5. strongly
6. perfectly
7. fearfully
8. quickly
9. greatly
10. completely
11. eagerly
12. absolutely
13. correctly
14. suddenly
15. doubtfully
16. regularly

EXERCISE E6

1. V	9. NT	17. NT	25. ADJ	
2. ADJ	10. NP	18. NP	26. V	
3. NT	11. NT	19. NT	27. NT	
4. ADV	12. ADJ	20. ADJ	28. NT	
5. NP	13. ADJ	21. ADJ	29. ADJ	
6. NP	14. NT	22. ADV	30. V	
7. V	15. ADJ	23. NT		
8. ADJ	16. ADV	24. NP		

EXERCISE E7

1. B	5. A	9. A	13. C	17. B
2. A	6. C	10. B	14. A	18. A
3. B	7. B	11. C	15. B	19. B
4. C	8. C	12. A	16. C	20. B

EXERCISE E8

1. inspector; intensive
2. exactly; negative
3. serious; illness
4. (no errors)
5. poet; composer; autobiographical
6. encourages; assimilate; culture
7. previous; establishment; great
8. escalation; serious; analysts
9. society; dependent; arrangement
10. education; complexities; comfortable
11. possible; addition
12. fatal; determination

EXERCISE F1

1. beat	30. forgiven	59. rise
2. became	31. freeze	60. run
3. begin	32. got	61. said
4. bet	33. given	62. see
5. bitten	34. gone	63. sell
6. blown	35. grow	64. sent
7. broke	36. have	65. shoot
8. brought	37. heard	66. showed
9. build	38. hidden	67. shut
10. bought	39. hit	68. sing
11. caught	40. held	69. sank
12. choose	41. hurt	70. sat
13. came	42. kept	71. sleep
14. cost	43. know	72. spoken
15. cut	44. lead	73. spent
16. dug	45. left	74. stand
17. done	46. lend	75. steal
18. drawn	47. let	76. swum
19. drink	48. lose	77. took
20. driven	49. made	78. taught
21. ate	50. mean	79. tore
22. fallen	51. met	80. tell
23. feed	52. paid	81. thought
24. felt	53. proved	82. throw
25. fight	54. put	83. understand
26. found	55. quit	84. wore
27. fit	56. read	85. win
28. flown	57. ridden	86. written
29. forgot	58. rung	

EXERCISE G1

1. are written
2. were written
3. have been written
4. had been written
5. would be written
6. would have been written
7. are being written
8. were being written
9. will be written
10. will have been written
11. are going to be written
12. should be written

EXERCISE G2

1. will fight
2. The equipment is going to be bought
3. was digging a hole
4. already been blown
5. should teach their children
6. Her valuable jewelry is kept
7. sank the ship
8. was...what you said
9. is feeding the children
10. It should not have been said

EXERCISE G3

1. The club will hold...next month
2. The game was won by the team
3. are being taken of the wedding
4. had already stolen the passport
5. is read by her
6. (Someone)...have shut off
7. of money had been bet

8. has driven the car
9. Many hours would be spent (by her)
10. could have sold the house

EXERCISE G4

1. was being brought (by the guards)
2. is going to meet the tourists
3. had already worn that dress
4. His clothing was torn
5. we can think of is being done
6. will ever find the money
7. would have been told (by him)
8. should not have ridden the horse
9. was caught by a fisherman
10. knows what he

EXERCISE H1

1. I	5. I	9. C	13. C
2. C	6. C	10. I	14. I
3. C	7. I	11. C	15. C
4. I	8. C	12. I	16. C

EXERCISE H2

1. I	5. C	9. I	13. C
2. I	6. C	10. C	14. C
3. I	7. C	11. C	15. C
4. I	8. C	12. I	16. I

EXERCISE H3

1. I	5. I	9. I	13. C
2. C	6. I	10. I	14. I
3. C	7. I	11. I	15. I
4. C	8. C	12. C	16. C

EXERCISE I1

1. J	4. K	7. I	10. A	13. H
2. E	5. C	8. B	11. D	
3. L	6. G	9. M	12. F	

EXERCISE I2

1. D	4. G	7. B	10. E
2. I	5. L	8. K	11. F
3. J	6. A	9. C	12. H

EXERCISE I3

1. E	4. I	7. A	10. B	13. D
2. M	5. K	8. L	11. J	
3. G	6. H	9. C	12. F	

EXERCISE I4

1. I	4. H	7. L	10. E
2. G	5. K	8. B	11. F
3. J	6. A	9. C	12. D

EXERCISE I5

1. D	4. M	7. H	10. E	13. C
2. F	5. J	8. A	11. B	14. G
3. L	6. K	9. N	12. I	

EXERCISE I6

1. F	3. E	5. G	7. C	9. B
2. I	4. A	6. J	8. D	10. H

EXERCISE I7

1. G	4. B	7. I	10. E
2. H	5. L	8. A	11. F
3. J	6. K	9. C	12. D

EXERCISE I8

1. F	3. G	5. D	7. E	9. C
2. H	4. B	6. A	8. I	

EXERCISE I9A

1. D	4. H	7. I	10. B
2. F	5. C	8. L	11. J
3. G	6. A	9. K	12. E

EXERCISE I9B

1. H	4. B	7. E	10. A
2. J	5. F	8. G	11. C
3. L	6. I	9. D	12. K

EXERCISE I9C

1. K	4. E	7. A	10. C
2. G	5. L	8. B	11. F
3. H	6. J	9. I	12. D

EXERCISE I9D

1. C	4. K	7. F	10. E
2. A	5. B	8. G	11. J
3. I	6. H	9. D	12. L

EXERCISE I9E

1. J	4. I	7. K	10. C
2. E	5. B	8. L	11. A
3. G	6. F	9. D	12. H

EXERCISE I9F

1. L	4. B	7. C	10. F
2. E	5. H	8. A	11. G
3. I	6. D	9. K	12. J

EXERCISE I9G

1. G	4. F	7. E	10. H
2. L	5. J	8. I	11. B
3. D	6. K	9. C	12. A

EXERCISE I9H

1. I	4. F	7. E	10. A
2. H	5. B	8. G	11. J
3. C	6. L	9. D	12. K

EXERCISE I9I

1. A	4. B	7. J	10. C
2. L	5. F	8. G	11. I
3. K	6. D	9. E	12. H

EXERCISE I9J

1. K	4. D	7. A	10. I
2. G	5. E	8. J	11. L
3. C	6. B	9. H	12. F

EXERCISE I9K

1. G	4. I	7. E	10. C
2. K	5. H	8. A	11. B
3. L	6. F	9. D	12. J

EXERCISE I9L

1. A	4. B	7. D	10. C
2. G	5. J	8. E	11. K
3. I	6. L	9. H	12. F

Single User License Agreement:

IMPORTANT: READ CAREFULLY

WARNING: BY OPENING THE PACKAGE YOU AGREE TO BE BOUND BY THE TERMS OF THE LICENSE AGREEMENT BELOW

This is a legally binding agreement between You (the user or purchaser) and Addison Wesley Longman, Inc., a Pearson Education company (the Publisher). By retaining this license, any software media or accompanying written materials or carrying out any of the permitted activities, You agree to be bound by the terms of the license agreement below. If You do not agree to these terms, then promptly return the entire publication (this license and all software, written materials, packaging and any other components received with it) with Your sales receipt to Your supplier for a full refund.

SINGLE USER LICENSE AGREEMENT

❏ YOU ARE PERMITTED TO:

✓ Use (load into temporary memory or permanent storage) a single copy of the software on only one computer at a time. If this computer is linked to a network, then the software may only be installed in a manner such that it is not accessible to other machines on the network.

✓ Use the software with a class provided it is only installed on one computer

✓ Transfer the software from one computer to another provided that you only use it on one computer at a time

✓ Print out individual screen extracts from the disk for (a) private study or (b) to include in Your essays or classwork with students

✓ Photocopy individual screen extracts for Your schoolwork or classwork with students

❏ YOU MAY NOT:

✗ Rent or lease the software or any part of the publication

✗ Copy any part of the documentation, except where specifically indicated otherwise

✗ Make copies of the software, even for backup purposes

✗ Reverse engineer, decompile or disassemble the software or create a derivative product from the contents of the databases or any software included in them

✗ Use the software on more than one computer at a time

✗ Install the software on any networked computer or server in a way that could allow access to it from more than one machine on the network

✗ Include any material or software from the disk in any other product or software materials except as allowed under "You are permitted to"

✗ Use the software in any way not specified above without prior written consent of the Publisher

✗ Print out more than one page at a time

ONE COPY ONLY

This license is for a single user copy of the software. THE PUBLISHER RESERVES THE RIGHT TO TERMINATE THIS LICENSE BY WRITTEN NOTICE AND TO TAKE ACTION TO RECOVER ANY DAMAGES SUFFERED BY THE PUBLISHER IF YOU BREACH ANY PROVISION OF THIS AGREEMENT.

The Publisher owns the software. You only own the disk on which the software is supplied.

LIMITED WARRANTY

The Publisher warrants that the disk or CD-ROM on which the software is supplied is free from defects in materials and workmanship under normal use for ninety (90) days from the date You received them. This warranty is limited to You and is not transferable. The Publisher does not warrant that the functions of the software meet Your requirements or that the media is compatible with any computer system on which it is used or that the operation of the software will be unlimited or error free.

You assume responsibility for selecting the software to achieve Your intended results and for the installation of, the use of, and the results obtained from the software. The entire liability of the Publisher and Your only remedy shall be replacement free of charge of the components that do not meet this warranty.

This limited warranty is void if any damage has resulted from accident, abuse, misapplication, service or modification by someone other than the Publisher. In no event shall the Publisher or its suppliers be liable for any damages whatsoever arising out of installation of the software, even if advised of the possibility of such damages. The Publisher will not be liable for any loss or damage of any nature suffered by any part as a result of reliance upon or reproduction of any errors in the content of the publication.

The Publisher does not limit its liability for death or personal injury caused by its negligence. This license agreement shall be governed by and interpreted and construed in accordance with New York State law.

For technical assistance, you may call (877) 546-5408 or e-mail epsupport@pearsoned.com.